Lexical Priming

KU-483-619

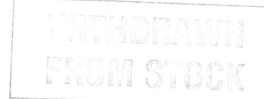

Lexical Priming proposes a radical new theory of the lexicon, which amounts to a completely new theory of language based on how words are used in the real world. Here they are not confined to the definitions given to them in dictionaries but instead interact with other words in common patterns of use.

Classical theory holds that grammar is generated first and words are then dropped into the opportunities thus created; Hoey's theory reverses the roles of lexis and grammar, arguing that lexis is complexly and systematically structured and that grammar is an outcome of this lexical structure. He shows that the phenomenon of 'collocation', the property of language whereby two or more words seem to appear frequently in each other's company (e.g., 'inevitable' and 'consequence'), offers a clue to the way language is really organised. Using concrete statistical evidence from a corpus of newspaper English, but also referring to travel writing and literary texts, the author argues that words are 'primed' for use through our experience with them, so that everything we know about a word is a product of our encounters with it. This knowledge explains how speakers of a language succeed in being fluent, creative and natural.

Provocative and compelling, *Lexical Priming* presents an original new theory, offering a rigorous but accessible framework for the study of language. It is a must for anyone involved in corpus linguistics or with an interest in what shapes the way we use and understand words.

Michael Hoey is a leading figure in English Language and Applied Linguistics and a highly respected researcher and author. His *Patterns of Lexis of Text* (OUP) won the Duke of Edinburgh English Speaking Union prize in 1991. He is currently Baines Professor of English Language at the University of Liverpool.

Lexical Priming

A new theory of words and language

Michael Hoey

Routledge
Taylor & Francis Group

LONDON AND NEW YORK

A · H · R · B

arts and humanities research board

First published 2005
by Routledge
2 Park Square, Milton Park, Abingdon, Oxon OX14 4RN

Simultaneously published in the USA and Canada
by Routledge
270 Madison Ave, New York, NY 10016

Routledge is an imprint of the Taylor & Francis Group

© 2005 Michael Hoey

Typeset in Perpetua by Graphicraft Limited, Hong Kong
Printed and bound in Great Britain by Cromwell Press,
Trowbridge, Wiltshire

All rights reserved. No part of this book may be reprinted or
reproduced or utilised in any form or by any electronic,
mechanical, or other means, now known or hereafter
invented, including photocopying and recording, or in any
information storage or retrieval system, without permission in
writing from the publishers.

British Library Cataloguing in Publication Data
A catalogue record for this book is available from the British Library

Library of Congress Cataloging in Publication Data
Hoey, Michael.
    Lexical priming : a new theory of words and language /
Michael Hoey.
        p. cm.
Includes bibliographical references.
    1. Lexicology.   2. Grammar, Comparative and general.
3. Discourse analysis.   4. Creativity (Linguistics)   I. Title.

    P326.H58 2005
    413.028–dc22   2004018252

ISBN 0–415–32862–4 (hbk)
ISBN 0–415–32863–2 (pbk)

To Randolph Quirk and John Sinclair, and in memory of Eugene Winter.

They showed me that the study of grammar, lexis and text could be fascinating and taught me independence of mind.

Contents

List of tables and figures   viii
Important note   xi
Acknowledgements   xii

1 Collocation and lexical priming   1

2 Lexical priming and meaning   16

3 Lexical priming and grammar   38

4 Lexical priming and lexical relations   63

5 Lexical priming and polysemy   81

6 Lexical priming and text: two claims   114

7 Lexical priming and text: a third claim   129

8 Lexical priming and grammatical creativity   152

9 Lexical priming and other kinds of creativity   169

10 Some theoretical and practical issues   178

Bibliography   189
Index   197

Tables and figures

Tables

2.1	The parallelism of constant/variable in a matching clause relationship	20
2.2	The parallelism of constant/variable in a sample of concordance data for *hour*	21
2.3	Distribution of temporal expressions of *winter* across propositions of different generality	33
2.4	The collocates of *consequence* identified by *WordSmith* as occurring immediately prior to the node word	34
2.5	The collocates of *consequences* identified by *WordSmith* as occurring immediately prior to the node word	35
3.1	Distribution of tense (and other) choices in clauses containing *winter* prepositional phrases	39
3.2	Percentage of each word sequence occurring with each tense (or other verbal) choice	39
3.3	Percentage of each tense (or other verbal) choice occurring with each word sequence	39
3.4	Distribution of temporal expressions with *winter* across Material and Relational processes	40
3.5	The distribution of the *winter* word sequences across clauses organised round Material, Relational and other processes	41
3.6	The distribution of Material and Relational processes across clauses containing the *winter* word sequences	41
3.7	A comparison of the grammatical distribution of *consequence* in the clause with that of four other nouns	46
3.8	A comparison of the grammatical distribution of *consequence* in the nominal group with that of four other nouns	49
3.9	The proportions of initial Themes in sentence-initial and non-sentence-initial clauses	51

3.10 Grammatical distribution of first noun in the sentences of three
Guardian features   52

3.11 The distribution of markers of definiteness and indefiniteness for
consequence and four other abstract nouns   56

3.12 A comparison of *consequence* and *use* in respect of indefiniteness
markers   56

3.13 A comparison of *consequence* and four other nouns in respect of
definiteness markers   57

3.14 The distribution across Subject, Object and Complement of
reason + postmodification in clauses that affirm or deny
(knowledge of) the reason   61

4.1 The colligations of the co-hyponyms *accountant, actor,*
actress, architect and *carpenter* (adapted from Hoey 2000)   66

4.2 The distribution of metaphorical uses across the co-hyponyms
accountant, actor, actress, architect and *carpenter* (adapted from
Hoey 2000)   67

4.3 The distribution of markers of (in)definiteness for *consequence*
and *result*   71

4.4 The distribution of markers of indefiniteness across *consequence*
and *result*   72

4.5 The distribution of markers of definiteness across *consequence*
and *result*   73

4.6 Frequency of potential collocates for *round the world* and *around*
the world   75

4.7 Distribution of markers of (in)definiteness between *round the world*
and *around the world*   78

5.1 Items functioning as non-specific deictics (adapted from Halliday
1994: 182)   84

5.2 The contrasting collocations, semantic associations, pragmatic
associations, colligations and textual colligations of the two uses
of *consequence*   87

5.3 Occurrences of prepositions preceding nominal groups with
reason (= cause) as head   91

5.4 A count of the instances of *reason* (= cause) occurring with the
different specific deictics (classification adapted from Halliday
1994: 181)   92

5.5 A count of the instances of *reason* (= rationality, logic) occurring
with the different specific deictics (classification adapted from
Halliday 1994: 181)   93

5.6 Patterns of coordination and listing associated with *reason*
(= rationality, logic)   95

5.7 A count of the instances of *reason* (= cause) occurring with
unspecific deictics (classification adapted from Halliday 1994: 182)   96

5.8   A count of the instances of *reason* (= rationality, logic) occurring
       with unspecific deictics (classification adapted from Halliday
       1994: 182)   96
5.9   A comparison of *reason* (= rationality, logic) with the nouns with
       which it is coupled in terms of their ability to appear in the
       plural or with an unspecific deictic   97
5.10   The distribution of possessive pronoun + *reason* across the
       sentence   100
5.11   A comparison of the frequency of co-occurrence of possessives
       with *reason* and *reasons*   101
5.12   A comparison of the collocates of the two senses of *immunity*   106
5.13   A comparison of the semantic associations of the two senses of
       immunity   106
5.14   A comparison of the colligations of the two senses of *immunity*   107
7.1   A matrix analysis of the Grant/Lee passage   136
7.2   The distribution of the students' paragraph break choices   137
7.3   A match of the paragraphing decision of the students with the
       organisational and lexical factors that might have led to those
       decisions   144
7.4   A comparison of the paragraphing decisions of the two sets of
       informants on the original and modified passage   147

Figures

3.1   A map of the priming of verb choice of *consequence* as head of
       a nominal group functioning as Subject   57
3.2   A map of the key colligational primings of *consequence* as head
       of a nominal group functioning as Subject   58
4.1   The semantic associations of *consequence* and *knock-on*   69
5.1   Clause patterns associated with *reason* (= cause) as head of a
       nominal group in Subject function   89
5.2   Some key primings of *reason* (= cause) functioning as Complement   91
7.1   A partial representation of the organisation of the passage   137
8.1   A map of the interlocking of linguistic levels (taken from
       Hoey 1991a: 213)   164
8.2   An alternative mapping of linguistic levels   165
8.3   The priming prosodies that bind the colligations etc. of Bill
       Bryson's first clause   167

Important note

The corpus I make use of in this book (except where I note otherwise) is made up of just over 95 million words of *Guardian* news and features text, supplemented by slightly more than 3 million words from the British National Corpus (written text) and 230,000 words of spoken data. It can be inferred from the nature of my corpora that most of the claims I make are to be seen in the first place as restricted to newspaper writing. It will be for others to determine whether they can be extended to other genres or domains or to the language as a whole. I see it as an asset, not a limitation, to be working with a corpus largely emanating from a single source. It means that claims, though necessarily limited, are securely grounded.

In investigating these corpora I made extensive use of *WordSmith* (Scott 1999), a sophisticated suite of software that allows one (among many other things) to concordance any item, to sequence and sort concordance lines and, most crucially for my purpose as will become apparent in later chapters, to consult the original texts from which the lines were drawn. It also plots the distribution of a word over the corpus, thereby ensuring that one can take account of the potential distorting effects of the word's occurring with much greater frequency in any one text. It also provides wordlists for any text or texts and calculates the collocations and key word sequences for any particular word. Without *WordSmith*, much of what I report in this book would either have been impossible or painfully difficult for me to have investigated (there was labour enough even so).

Acknowledgements

Corpus-based work is slow and often painful, though I am perhaps masochist enough to sometimes get pleasure in the midst of the pain. It can sometimes take half a day to complete an analysis that will produce a single sentence or indeed a single cell in a table. Without time to do the job properly, a book like this would be hard to contemplate, let alone complete. I am therefore very grateful to David Mills, my former Head of Department, for granting me study leave 'out of turn' and to Phil Davis, my latter Head of Department, who was prepared not only to endorse the decision but to give me extra time if my application to the Arts and Humanities Research Board (AHRB) was unsuccessful. This greatly boosted my morale at an important time and I am very grateful to both of them. My morale was further boosted by the generosity of the AHRB who agreed to match the time given me by the university (project title: *Lexical Priming – a lexically driven theory of language*, AHRB reference RL/AN 2268/APN 18024). The generosity of both the AHRB and the university has enabled me to make the book in your hands a great deal more coherent and consistent than it would otherwise have been. (Once you have read it, you may of course wish they had given me even more time – or none at all!)

My university's generosity has been matched by my colleagues in English Language, who have necessarily had to cover my teaching in my absence. That this has been without a hint of disgruntlement has been much appreciated and is entirely typical of them.

I am grateful too to Louisa Semlyen at Routledge both for commissioning the book and for treating me throughout with understanding, patience and good humour. The same gratitude goes to Christabel Kirkpatrick, Elizabeth Walker, Julene Knox and Sue Hadden. Their combination of friendliness and professionalism has been most welcome. Julian Edge, Ramesh Krishnamurty, David Deterding, Linda Bawcom, Britt Erman and Dave Willis all gave me valuable advice and support on draft material.

Although this book was written from scratch and does not incorporate any previously published articles, many of the ideas it contains, and quite a lot of the examples, have been presented at a number of conferences and in a number of articles published out of those conferences. These opportunities to work out my thinking and the feedback I have received have been of the utmost importance. In particular there were five conferences in 2002 which I used quite deliberately to present different aspects of the descriptive approach I was developing and I am extremely grateful to Karin Aijmer, Bengt Altenberg, Geoff Thompson, Susan Hunston, Guy Aston, Alan Partington, John Morley and Tony McEnery for the opportunity that their conferences (and proceedings) in Göteborg, Liverpool, Bertinoro, Camerino and Lancaster gave me to do this. Again, during 2003 and 2004 I used conferences in Zaragoza and Beirut organised by Maria José Luzón Marco, Nola Bacha and Rima Bahous to work out ideas in Chapters 5 and 6. I am also, even more importantly, grateful for all these people's friendship and support.

Books happen in real time and in real places, and those places and that time are filled with people who keep you sane. It is tempting here to thank by name all the friends I am grateful to, but my fear of missing in the rush of the moment someone important in the end outweighs my wish to express gratitude. But a few people must be named. My daughter, son and son-in-law, Alice, Richard and Ste, have offered me love and bought me beers (occasionally), and made sure I kept my work in proportion. Most important of all, Sue, my wife, has been an unfailing and loving support as always. She has even managed to look interested when I go on yet again about some abstruse facet of lexical priming that has caught my attention. No one could ask for more.

Permission has been granted by the *Guardian* for the use of a number of short extracts that appear as numbered examples in this book. The author and publisher wish to acknowledge that the following examples are © Guardian Newspapers Limited 1991: Chapter 2, pp. 24–6, examples 11, 14, 17, 20, 21 and 22; Chapter 3, p. 48, example 7, p. 51, example 16, and p. 60, example 40; Chapter 4, p. 76, examples 19 and 20; Chapter 5, p. 92, examples 16 and 20, p. 94, example 22, p. 102, examples 48, 50 and 51, and p. 108, example 73.

1 Collocation and lexical priming

Introduction

In this book I want to argue for a new theory of the lexicon, which amounts to a new theory of language. The theory reverses the roles of lexis and grammar, arguing that lexis is complexly and systematically structured and that grammar is an outcome of this lexical structure. The theory grew out of an increasing awareness that traditional views of the vocabulary of English were out of kilter with the facts about lexical items that are routinely being thrown up by corpus investigations of text. What began as an attempt to account for collocation turned into an exploration of grammatical, semantic, sociolinguistic and text-linguistic phenomena. This book is the story of my intellectual journey. Accordingly it begins with my journey's starting point – the pervasiveness of collocation.

The traditional view of the lexicon and grammar

The classical theory of the word is well reflected in those two central compendia of linguistic scholarship of the eighteenth and nineteenth centuries – the dictionary and the thesaurus. According to such texts, words have pronunciation, grammar(s), meaning(s), etymology and relationships with words of closely related meanings (synonyms, superordinates, co-hyponyms, antonyms). According to the theory underpinning these texts, lexis interacts with phonology through pronunciation, with syntax through the grammatical categories that lexical items belong to, with semantics through the meanings that the lexical items have and with diachronic linguistics through their etymology. In the most extreme versions of the theory, the connection between the word and the other systems has been so weak that it has been possible to argue that grammar is generated first and the words dropped into the grammatical opportunities thereby created (e.g. Chomsky 1957, 1965) or that the semantics is generated first and the lexis merely actualises the semantics (e.g. Pinker 1994).

Theories of lexis that can claim to be more sophisticated, such as systemic-functional linguistics, likewise sometimes represent the relationship between grammar and lexis as if the precise lexical choice was the last choice to be made. Even if one starts from the assumption that lexis is chosen first, or at least earlier, it is easy to assume that it passes through what might be regarded as a grammatical filter which organises and disciplines it. Tagmemics treats lexis as having as much theoretical importance as grammar (Pike and Pike 1982), in that this theory posits three hierarchies – the grammatical hierarchy, the phonological hierarchy and the referential or lexical hierarchy, but such a tripartite division only underlines how separate the levels of lexis and grammar are conceived to be.

The picture I have just sketched is in some respects lacking in light and shade. Construction grammar, for example, does not separate syntax and the lexicon in the manner I have been describing (Fillmore *et al.* 1988; Goldberg 1995). Even so, its theory still talks of lexical constructions and syntactic constructions, and a key tenet of the grammar is that grammatical patterns have precise meanings that are distinct from those of the lexical items used in the patterns. Chomsky (1995) assigns inter-language variation to the lexicon. Hudson's *Word Grammar* (1984), as its name implies, starts from the assumption of a connection between lexical and syntactic description. Likewise Hunston and Francis (2000) identify and describe the close relationships found between lists of specific lexical items and the availability of particular grammatical patterns, and in so doing arrive at much more interesting accounts of grammar than are normal in descriptive grammars (as illustrated in Francis *et al.* 1996, 1998). A precursor of this work was the *Cobuild English Grammar* (Sinclair 1990). Nevertheless they continue with a separation of lexis and grammar; indeed, their approach depends upon it. I shall return to these grammars in Chapter 8, along with a discussion of the work of Sinclair, who goes furthest in dissolving the distinction between lexical study and grammatical study and whose work was in several important respects the starting point for the positions presented here.

Collocation and naturalness

The problem with all but the last two theories is that they account only for what is possible in a language and not for what is natural. This book is concerned, in part, with how naturalness is achieved and how an explanation of what is natural might impinge on explanations of what is possible. A key factor in naturalness, much discussed in recent years, is collocation, and this is therefore an appropriate place to start such an explanation. Collocation is, crudely, the property of language whereby two or more words seem to appear frequently in each other's company (e.g. *inevitable* + *consequence*). (I shall provide a more careful characterisation below.) Collocations – recurrent combinations of words – are both pervasive and subversive. Their pervasiveness is widely recognised in corpus linguistics; probably all lexical items have collocations (Sinclair 1991; Stubbs 1996). The notion is usually attributed to Firth ([1951]1957), and certainly his discussion of the concept underpins all that has followed on the subject. Interestingly, though, Doyle (2003) draws attention to the fact that the word *collocation* was being used in linguistic discourse prior to Firth; in this connection he draws attention to a citation from 1940 in the *Oxford English Dictionary* (1995). This observation is confirmed by inspection of the 1928 edition of *Webster's New International Dictionary*, which has the following entry for *collocation*:

> **collocation** . . . Act of placing, esp. with something else; state of being placed with something else; disposition in place; arrangement.
>
> The choice and *collocation* of words. *Sir W Jones.*
>
> . . . COLLOCATION denotes an arrangement or ordering of objects (esp. words) with reference to each other.

It is improbable that the eighteenth-century amateur linguist Sir William Jones, who is traditionally credited with having set in motion the nineteenth-century's exploration of language change and language families, can also be credited with the late twentieth-century's exploration of lexical relations, though I have not sought out the original from which the quotation is taken to verify that assumption. But the *OEDs* and *Webster's* definitions do suggest that collocation has been slowly maturing as a notion.

As befits a notion that has been developing slowly and whose study has been transformed with the onset of large corpora and sophisticated software, collocation is a word with a number of definitions. Partington (1998) groups these neatly into textual, statistical and psychological definitions. The textual definition is closest to the use of the word exemplified in the Webster definition quoted above: 'the occurrence of two or more words within a short space of each other in a text' (Sinclair 1991: 170). This definition (which I should add does not reflect Sinclair's own use of the term) is not useful and can result in a woolly confusion of single instances of co-occurrence with repeated patterns of co-occurrence. I shall not be using collocation in this way. Whenever I need to refer to the occurrence of two or more words within a short space of each other, I shall talk of 'lexical co-occurrence'.

Hoey's opinion

The statistical definition of collocation is that it is 'the relationship a lexical item has with items that appear with greater than random probability in its (textual) context' (Hoey 1991a: 6–7). This definition, though better, confuses method with goal. It is true that to discover collocations one needs to examine the statistical distribution of words and that those that occur in each other's company more often than can be accounted for by the mechanisms of random distribution can be said to collocate. But the definition says nothing interesting about the phenomenon; it gives no clues as to why collocation should exist in the first place. For this we need to turn to Partington's third type of definition – the 'psychological' or 'associative' definition.

There are two well-known 'psychological' definitions, and neither is successful for our purposes, though they are both insightful. The first is that provided by Halliday and Hasan (1976: 287) in their pioneering work on cohesion in English. They refer to collocation as a cohesive device and describe it as 'a cover term for the kind of cohesion that results from the co-occurrence of lexical items that are in some way or other typically associated with one another, because they tend to occur in similar environments'. Their discussion of collocation as a cohesive device, and the exemplification they provide, makes it clear that they are not talking about the regular co-occurrence of words in close proximity to each other. The association they refer to must therefore be a psychological one, in which words are regularly associated in the mind because of the way they are regularly encountered in similar textual contexts. As a definition, it is hard to operationalise and indeed Hasan (1984) abandons the concept, replacing it with more specific semantic relations (hyponymy, meronymy etc.). It does however place collocation where it belongs – as a property of the mental lexicon. (We shall revisit Halliday and Hasan's notion in Chapter 6, where it will be found to have a proper place in an account of text after all.)

The second definition comes from Leech (1974: 20), who talks of 'collocative meaning' which, he says, 'consists of the associations a word acquires on account of the meanings of words which tend to occur in its environment'. As couched, this is too general to cover the word in its most common current usage. It also implies that the word acquires connotations as a result of the words that surround it, a position that was formulated by Louw (1993) and taken up by Stubbs (1995, 1996). This position is discussed in Chapter 2 and is not uncontroversial (see Whitsitt 2003). Leech's definition does however pick up both the statistical reality and the psychological reality and, most valuably, posits a causal connection between the two. Partington (1998: 16), commenting on his definition, notes that 'it is part of a native speaker's communicative competence . . . to know what are normal and what are unusual collocations in given circumstances'. I would quarrel with the wording here in that Partington allows for 'unusual collocations' but the point he is making is important.

We now have to consider what counts as being in the environment of another word and, more fundamentally still, whether the word or the lemma is the appropriate analytical category in this context. Jones and Sinclair (1974) provided the first influential computational analysis of collocation. Their corpus was only 147,000 words – computers at that time struggled to deal with even that much data – but it was sufficient to allow them to determine that the optimum span for identifying collocation is up to four words on either side of the node word (the node word being the word under investigation and typically shown at the centre of the concordance lines). This finding has not been seriously disputed, though collocational software will often permit a wider span (e.g. ±5).

Collocational analysis can be done on lemmas or words. Renouf (1986), Sinclair (1991), Stubbs (1996) and Tognini-Bonelli (2001) have all argued against conflating items sharing a common lemma (e.g. *political*, *politics*; *break*, *broke*; *onion*, *onions*) on the grounds that each word has its own special collocational behaviour. In Hoey (1991a, 1991b) I found it useful to work with lemmas, but for present purposes I concur with these linguists that conflation often disguises collocational patterns. Williams (1998) notes that in the context of molecular biology research papers the collocates of the word *gene* and those of the word *genes* are quite distinct, both prior and subsequent to the node word. Doyle (2003) likewise shows that there are few shared collocates between grammatically related forms of lemmas in scientific textbooks; he looks, for example, at *amplifier*, *amplifiers* (only three shared collocates), *circuit*, *circuits* (only two shared collocates), *frequency*, *frequencies* (only one shared collocate) and *shift*, *shifts* where he finds no shared collocates at all. When various forms of a lemma do share collocates (e.g. *training* and *trained* share collocation with *as a teacher*), they can of course be discussed together, but common collocates should never be assumed.

So our definition of collocation is that it is a psychological association between words (rather than lemmas) up to four words apart and is evidenced by their occurrence together in corpora more often than is explicable in terms of random distribution. This definition is intended to pick up on the fact that collocation is a psycholinguistic phenomenon, the evidence for which can be found statistically in computer corpora. It does not pick up on the causal relationship identified by Leech, but only because that will be attended to separately.

The pervasiveness of collocation

The importance of collocation for a theory of the lexicon lies in the fact that at least some sentences (and this puts it cautiously) are made up of interlocking collocations such that they could be said to reproduce, albeit with important variations, stretches of earlier sentences (Hoey 2002). It could be argued that such sentences owe their existence to the collocations they manifest. As evidence of these claims, consider the following two sentences:

> In winter Hammerfest is a thirty-hour ride by bus from Oslo, though why anyone would want to go there in winter is a question worth considering.

> Through winter, rides between Oslo and Hammerfest use thirty hours up in a bus, though why travellers would select to ride there then might be pondered.

One of these sentences is drawn from Bill Bryson's travel book *Neither Here Nor There* (1991) about his trips around Europe and is indeed, in some respects, the first sentence of the book (if we discount a quotation from Bertrand Russell and introductory material). The other is best seen as a translation from Bill Bryson's English into my altogether less fluent English. I have attempted to maintain the meaning of the original and the sentences share a number of words and lemmas in common – *winter*, *Hammerfest*, *thirty*, *hour(s)*, *ride(s)*, *bus*, *Oslo*, *though*, *why*, *would*, *to*, *there*. Yet I assume few readers would hesitate in assigning the first sentence to Bill Bryson and the second to me. The first is natural; the second is clumsy. However, according to the theories of the lexicon that have dominated linguistic thought for the past 200 years there is no reason to regard the naturalness or clumsiness of the sentences as being of any importance. Both sentences are, after all, grammatical. Both use words in reasonably acceptable ways; though the second sentence contains an unfamiliar image of 'using up' hours, it draws upon a familiar enough metaphor (Lakoff and Johnson 1980), namely that time is money. Both sentences are textually appropriate as well; there is no apparent reason why either should not begin a text. Both are meaningful. I want however to argue that what distinguishes Bryson's sentence from my version is that his is made up of normal collocations and mine is made up of what Partington referred to as 'unusual collocations'.

The naturalness of the first sentence and the clumsiness of the second are not immaterial. They are properties of those sentences and are as much in need of explanation as any other feature of language. There is no reason why linguistic theory should not be as much concerned with naturalness as with creativity, as has been recognised for some years (e.g. McCarthy 1988). Indeed, as I shall argue in Chapters 8 and 9, accounts of creativity in language need to take account of naturalness if they are properly to explain creativity. One of the obvious ways in which the two sentences differ, I am claiming, is in respect of their collocations. In my corpus, the words *in* and *winter* occur together 507 times; this means that 1 in 15 instances of *winter* occurs in the word sequence *in winter* in my data. And 1 in 6 instances of *hour* occurs with a number, and there are 35 cases of *thirty* or *30* occurring with *hour(s)*. The words *bus* and *ride* occur in the same environment 53 times (though usually as *bus ride*), the words *ride* and *hour* occur together 12 times and *ride* and *from* occur together 121 times. The combination *by bus* occurs 116 times and the three-word combination *by bus from* occurs 7 times.

The collocations just listed interlock. So *hour* collocates with *thirty* but it also collocates with *ride*. Likewise *ride*, in addition to collocating with *hour*, collocates with *by* and *bus*. *Bus* also collocates with *by*. Both *ride* and *bus* collocate with *from*.

The same kinds of point can be made about the second clause of Bryson's sentence. The combination *though why* occurs 24 times, *why anyone would* occurs

28 times, *why anyone would/should want to* occurs 23 times, *want to go* occurs 355 times and *want to go there* occurs 15 times.

Diagrammatically the interlocking produces the following:

thirty — hour — ride — by — bus — from
though — why — anyone — would — want — to — go — there

Compare this with the picture for my contrived rewritten version. The combination of *through* and *winter* occurs 7 times (as opposed to 507 instances of *in winter*), *rides between* occurs once, *in a bus* occurs 15 times (as opposed to 116 instances of *by bus*) and *use x hours up* (where x stands for any number) is not attested at all. The same is true of the second half of the sentence. The combination *travellers would* occurs 13 times (as opposed to 122 instances of *anyone would*) and *would select* occurs 21 times (as opposed to 573 instances of *would want*). (The latter frequencies are of course affected by the comparative rarity of *travellers* and *select*, as opposed to *anyone* and *select*, but this does not alter the point and in any case is not true of the earlier combinations.)

It is worth noting that even my rewritten version still makes use of existing collocations; it is hard to construct a meaningful sentence without calling upon them. My version has fewer of them, though, and those it does have are weaker and do not interconnect.

Priming as an explanation of collocation

I imagine many readers will not have needed convincing of the pervasiveness of collocation; it has been much noted in the literature and Sinclair (1991), in particular, has teased out some of its less obvious and more interesting properties. The subversiveness of collocation has however rarely been given much attention. The reason that it is subversive of existing descriptions of the lexicon is that the pervasiveness requires explanation and many current theories cannot do this. Butler (2004) argues for a greater awareness in corpus linguistics of the need for a more powerful and cognitively valid theory, while showing that existing theories have an even greater obligation to test and modify their claims against corpus data. A good starting point for a cognitively valid theory would seem to be the pervasiveness of collocation.

As we have seen, any explanation of the pervasiveness of collocation is required to be psychological because, as we have seen, collocation is fundamentally a psychological concept. What has to be accounted for is the recurrent co-occurrence of words. If they were stored in our minds separately or in sets, the kinds of collocational naturalness displayed in the Bryson sentence would be inexplicable. The most appropriate psychological concept would seem to be that of **priming**, albeit tweaked slightly. As discussed in the psycholinguistic literature (e.g. Neely 1977, 1991; Anderson 1983), the notion of semantic priming is used to discuss the way a 'priming' word may provoke a particular 'target' word. For example, a listener, previously given the word *body*, will recognise the word *heart* more quickly than if they had previously been given an unrelated word such as *trick*; in this sense, *body* primes the listener for *heart*. This has an obvious connection with word association games. The word *body* sets up a word association with *heart*, which the word *trick* does not (at least for me). The focus in psycholinguistic discussion is on the relationship between the prime and the target, rather than on the priming item *per se*. In the discussion that follows, however, priming is seen as a property of the word and what is primed to occur is seen as shedding light upon the priming item rather than the other way round.

We can only account for collocation if we assume that every word is mentally **primed** for collocational use. As a word is acquired through encounters with it in speech and writing, it becomes cumulatively loaded with the contexts and co-texts in which it is encountered, and our knowledge of it includes the fact that it co-occurs with certain other words in certain kinds of context. The same applies to word sequences built out of these words; these too become loaded with the contexts and co-texts in which they occur. I refer to this property as **nesting**, where the product of a priming becomes itself primed in ways that do not apply to the individual words making up the combination. Nesting simplifies the memory's task (Krishnamurty, personal communication; see also Krishnamurty 2003). Necessarily the priming of word sequences is normally a second phase in the priming; occasionally, of course, a child acquires the primings of a combination first and the primings of the individual words later (e.g. *all gone*). There is no difference in principle between acquiring the word (or word sequence) and acquiring the knowledge of its collocations, though presumably recognition of the word must notionally precede recognition of recurrent features, in that the word has to have occurred twice (at least) for the latter process to begin. Chomsky (1986) distinguishes the study of linguistic data, which he terms 'E-Language' (externalised language), from 'I-Language' (internalised language), the language found in the brains of speakers. Lexical priming is intended as a bridge between the two perspectives.

The notion of priming is entirely compatible with Giddens' (1979) discussion of the relationship between human agency and social structure, where each individual action reproduces the structure and the structure shapes the individual action; indeed, Giddens applies his theory to language. Priming in the fullest form, as described in this book, might be seen as the explication of Giddens' claims. Stubbs (1996: 56) notes, preparatory to a discussion of Giddens' work: 'Speakers are free, but only within constraints. Individual speakers intend to communicate with one another in the process of moment to moment interaction. The reproduction of the system is the unintended product of their routine behaviour'. The crucial phrase here is 'only within constraints'. The notion of priming completes the circle begun here by Stubbs. Priming leads to a speaker unintentionally reproducing some aspect of the language, and that aspect, thereby reproduced, in turn primes the hearer. It is not necessary to assume, though, that what is reproduced is a system as usually understood. Indeed, as we shall see in subsequent chapters, priming can be seen as reversing the traditional relationship between grammar as systematic and lexis as loosely organised, amounting to an argument for lexis as systematic and grammar as more loosely organised. This position is similar to that of Hanks (1996, 2004). My argument here also follows a similar line to that of Hopper (1988, 1998), who argues that grammar is the output of what he calls 'routines', collocational groupings, the repeated use of which results in the creation of a grammar for each individual. He terms this process 'emergent grammar' and importantly every speaker's grammar is different because every speaker's experience and knowledge of routines is different; Hopper also makes use of the notion of priming, though as a less central notion.

Some of the properties of priming

In this section some of the characteristics of priming are considered. Necessarily, since we have so far only considered collocation, these characteristics are formulated in terms of their application to collocation, but, importantly, the claims here are made for **all** types of priming as discussed in the remainder of the book.

Priming need not be a permanent feature of the word or word sequence; in principle, indeed, it never is. Every time we use a word, and every time we encounter it anew, the experience either reinforces the priming by confirming an existing association between the word and its co-texts and contexts, or it weakens the priming, if the encounter introduces the word in an unfamiliar context or co-text or if we have chosen in our own use of it to override its current priming. It follows that the priming of a word or word sequence is liable to shift in the course of an individual's lifetime, and if it does so, and to the extent that it does so, the word or word sequence shifts slightly in meaning and/or function for that individual. This may be referred to as **a drift in the priming**. Drifts in the priming of a word, occurring for a number of members of a particular community at the same time, provide a mechanism for temporary or permanent language change. Again, Stubbs (1996: 45), drawing on Halliday's (1991, 1992) analogy between linguistic systems and weather systems, puts it well: 'Each day's weather affects the climate, however infinitesimally, either maintaining the status quo or helping to tip the balance towards climatic change'.

It will be observed that I have referred to contexts as well as co-texts. This is because it is demonstrable that collocations are limited in principle to particular domains and genres, and even these are fluid. Baker (forthcoming) warns:

approaches that focus on different discourses need to acknowledge that the concept of discourses as discrete and separate entities is problematic. Discourses are constantly changing, interacting, merging, reproducing and splitting off from each other. Therefore a corpus-based analysis of any discourse must be aware that it can only provide static snap-shots that give the appearance of stability but are bound to the context of the data set.

An example of contextual limitation is the collocation of *recent* and *research*, which is largely limited to academic writing and news reports of research. Re-expressed in terms of priming, *research* is primed in the minds of academic language users to occur with *recent* in such contexts and no others. The words are not primed to occur in recipes, legal documentation or casual conversation, for example. In short, collocational priming is sensitive to the contexts (textual, generic, social) in which the lexical item is encountered, and it is part of our knowledge of a lexical item that it is used in certain combinations in certain kinds of text.

This is not a new idea, though it may be expressed here in unfamiliar terms. Firth referred in 1951 to 'more restricted technical or personal collocations'. The only difference between his 'restricted technical collocations' and domain-specific primings (apart from the psycholinguistic focus of the latter) is that I would argue that the latter are the norm, rather than the exception. Firth's notion of 'personal collocations' is still closer to that of priming, in that it is an inherent quality of lexical priming that it is personal in the first place and can be modified by the language user's own chosen behaviour in the second place. Firth comments on personal collocations that:

> The study of the usual collocations of a particular literary form or genre or of a particular author makes possible a clearly defined and precisely stated contribution to what I have termed the spectrum of descriptive linguistics, which handles and states the meaning by dispersing it in a range of techniques working at a series of levels.
>
> (Firth [1951]1957: 195)

The position I am advocating here is also related to that of reading theorists such as Smith (1985), who talks of the importance to the learner-reader of their having experience of a word in a variety of contexts – intertextual, extratextual, intratextual. These contexts are important in that without them the word will not be appropriately primed. This said, it does not follow that priming may **only** occur in specific domains and/or genres. It does however follow that we should be wary of over-generalising claims about primings. I shall return to this point on several occasions.

Primings nest and combine. For example, *winter* collocates with *in*, producing the phrase *in winter*. But this phrase has its own collocations, which are separate from those of its components. So *in winter* collocates with a number of forms of the word *BE* (i.e. *is, was, are, were,* etc.), which as far as I am aware neither *in* nor *winter* do. This then is an instance of a nesting that might be represented as follows:

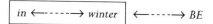

Or to take a more complex example, the word *word* collocates with *say, say a word* in turn collocates with *against,* and *say a word against* collocates with *won't.* (We shall return to this example in subsequent chapters.) In this way, lexical items (Sinclair 1999, 2004) and bundles (Biber *et al.* 1999) are created.

Primings may crack, and one of the causes of cracking is education. If, for example, a word is primed for someone as collocating with a particular other word and a teacher tells that person that it is incorrectly primed (e.g. *you* and *was*) the result is a potential crack in the priming. Cracks can be mended either by rejecting the original priming or by rejecting the attack on the priming. Better still, they can be healed by assigning the original priming to one context (e.g. family) and the later priming to another context (e.g. the classroom, science, public speaking). Not all cracks get healed and the result can be uncertainty about the priming, a codification of the crack, leading to long-term linguistic insecurity. We will return to this issue in Chapter 10.

As the possibility of cracking suggests, one of the implications of lexical priming is that each individual's experiences of language, and the primings that arise out of these experiences, are unique. Since our experience of language suggests that communication takes place, there must be harmonising principles at work to ensure that each individual's primings do not differ too greatly from those of others. Education is one of these, but there are others as important, including the property of self-reflexivity. The harmonising principles are discussed in the final chapter after we have reviewed the full range of semantic and grammatical facets of priming.

The notion of priming as here outlined assumes that the mind has a mental concordance of every word it has encountered, a concordance that has been richly glossed for social, physical, discoursal, generic and interpersonal context. This mental concordance is accessible and can be processed in much the same way that a computer concordance is, so that all kinds of patterns, including collocational patterns, are available for use. It simultaneously serves as a part, at least, of our knowledge base.

Primings can be receptive or productive. **Productive primings** occur when a word or word sequence is repeatedly encountered in discourses and genres in which we are ourselves expected (or aspire) to participate and when the speakers or writers are those whom we like or wish to emulate. **Receptive primings** occur when a word or word sequence is encountered in contexts in which there is no probability, or even possibility, of our ever being an active participant – party political broadcasts, interviews with film stars, eighteenth-century novels – or where the speaker or writer is someone we dislike or have no empathy with – drunken football supporters, racists, but also sometimes stern teachers and people of a different age group.

Although productive primings are more interesting, receptive primings have their importance too. It is as a result of these that we recognise allusion, quotation and pastiche, and indeed just as collocation requires priming as an explanation, so do these recognised literary properties. Our ability (sometimes) to recognise plagiarism may possibly arise from the same mental concordance. A person's encounter with lexical items in the plagiarised text, I would hypothesise, sometimes results in the new instances of the items being stored near to the items from the original and a consequent recognition of the similarity/ identity of the two texts (though other factors come into play as well, such as incongruities of style).

The existence of allusion in the above list may also suggest that our mental concordance is tagged for the importance of the text in which a word or word sequence is encountered. Thus the claimed greatness of a literary work or the centrality of a religious text may ensure that an encounter with a word in such writings has a bigger impact on the priming than a similar encounter with the word in a less valued work. The same may be true of words encountered in conversation; words spoken by a close friend are likely to affect our primings more directly than those spoken by someone to whom we are indifferent.

Primings can be transitory or (semi-)permanent. Speakers or writers may combine certain words repeatedly in a discourse and this repeated combination may become part of the cohesion of the text. The listener or reader will grow to expect these words together in the text in question, but unless subsequent texts reinforce the combination it will not become part of the permanent priming of either of the words. Emmott (1997) discusses priming in these terms where a reader is primed to construct a frame which permits them to process more effectively the text they are reading.

Priming as an explanation of other linguistic features

In the above discussion, I have talked as if words and word sequences are primed for collocation only and all the examples I have so far given have played along with this assumption. However, once we accept that collocation can only be accounted for in terms of priming, the possibility opens up that priming will explain other features of the language. Indeed it is the argument of this book that priming is the driving force behind language use, language structure and language change. I shall therefore conclude this chapter with a statement of the hypotheses that the remainder of the book will be concerned with exploring.

Priming hypotheses

Every word is primed for use in discourse as a result of the cumulative effects of an individual's encounters with the word. If one of the effects of the initial priming is that regular word sequences are constructed, these are also in turn primed. More specifically:

1 Every word is primed to occur with particular other words; these are its collocates.
2 Every word is primed to occur with particular semantic sets; these are its semantic associations.
3 Every word is primed to occur in association with particular pragmatic functions; these are its pragmatic associations.
4 Every word is primed to occur in (or avoid) certain grammatical positions, and to occur in (or avoid) certain grammatical functions; these are its colligations.
5 Co-hyponyms and synonyms differ with respect to their collocations, semantic associations and colligations.
6 When a word is polysemous, the collocations, semantic associations and colligations of one sense of the word differ from those of its other senses.
7 Every word is primed for use in one or more grammatical roles; these are its grammatical categories.
8 Every word is primed to participate in, or avoid, particular types of cohesive relation in a discourse; these are its textual collocations.
9 Every word is primed to occur in particular semantic relations in the discourse; these are its textual semantic associations.
10 Every word is primed to occur in, or avoid, certain positions within the discourse; these are its textual colligations.

Very importantly, all these claims are in the first place constrained by domain and/or genre. They are claims about the way language is acquired and used in specific situations. This is because we prime words or word sequences, as already remarked, in a range of social contexts and the priming, I argue, takes account of who is speaking or writing, what is spoken or written about and what genre is being participated in, though the last of these constraints is probably later in developing than the other two. One reason why some of the features described in this book have been given only limited attention is that traditionally descriptions of language have treated the language as monolithic. Even corpus linguists have characteristically worked with general corpora. But certain kinds of feature only become apparent when one looks at more specialised data.

Returning to the list of claims, the first has already been argued for and will not be further discussed in this book. Claims 2 and 3 are explored in Chapter 2, claim 2 in some detail. Claims 4, 5 and 6 are discussed in Chapters 3, 4 and 5 respectively, with claim 7 being given briefer attention in Chapter 8. The textual claims (8, 9, 10) are explained in Chapters 6 and 7, with preliminary supportive evidence. Chapters 8 and 9 consider the implications of lexical priming for discussions of creativity, and the final chapter considers some of its implications for L1 and L2 learning.

Primings can be studied from two perspectives. We can study their operation from the perspective of the primed word or word sequence. Thus we might, for instance, look at all the primings associated with the word *consequence*. Alternatively, we can observe their operation in combination. So we might look at all the primings that contribute to the production of a sentence such as the one cited earlier from Bill Bryson's *Neither Here Nor There*. In each of the following chapters I shall do both (and indeed the word *consequence* and the Bill Bryson sentence will both be examined), though the weighting will differ as the chapters progress. Thus, initially most of the attention will be on the individual word, but in later chapters, where the focus is on textual priming, we will be more concerned with the ways primings combine.

The status of the corpus as evidence of priming

I have talked of the language user as having a mental concordance and of the possibility that they process this concordance in ways not unrelated (though much superior) to those used in corpus linguistic work. However, it does not automatically follow that exploration of the nature of priming can be achieved through the study of computer corpora. A corpus, whether general – like the British National Corpus or the Bank of English – or specialised – such as the *Guardian* corpus used in this work – represents no one's experience of the language. Not even the editor of the *Guardian* reads all the *Guardian*, I suppose, and certainly only God (and corpus linguists) could eavesdrop on all the many different conversations included in the British National Corpus. On the other hand, the personal 'corpus' that provides a language user with their lexical primings is by definition irretrievable, unstudiable and unique. We have therefore a problem: we have a posited feature of language acquisition and use, one of whose characteristics is that it is differently actualised for every language user.

If my analogy between the mental concordance and the computer concordance is correct, the computer corpus cannot tell us what primings are present for any language user, but it can indicate the kinds of data a language user might encounter in the course of being primed. It can suggest the ways in which priming might occur and the kinds of feature for which words or word sequences might be primed. In other words, it can serve as a kind of laboratory in which we can test for the validity of claims made about priming. If in subsequent chapters I sometimes write as if words or word sequences have priming independently of individual speakers, this should be regarded as no more than a convenient shorthand. Words are never primed *per se*; they are only primed for someone (and, as we shall see in Chapter 8, it is not only, or even primarily, the word that is primed). All that a corpus can do is indicate that certain primings are likely to be shared by a large number of speakers, and only in that sense is priming independent of the individual. As already noted, in the final chapter I shall return to the issue of how it comes to be that primings are shared.

2   Lexical priming and meaning

What collocation will not account for: semantic association

If lexical priming only operated with regard to collocations, it would be an anomalous but not especially interesting characteristic of language. It would have nothing to say about linguistic creativity and be of little or no theoretical importance. However, a glance at the Bill Bryson sentence shows that there is more to say about the way it has been constructed than can be accounted for in terms of collocation alone. Take the word *hour* in the word sequence *thirty-hour ride*. For most speakers it is likely to be primed to collocate with *ride*, but there is no evidence in my corpus of its being likely to collocate with *thirty*. On the basis of my corpus evidence, *hour* is likely to be primed for many speakers of English to collocate with *half an, one, two, three, four* and *twenty four*, but *thirty* only occurs once in my data. It is not to the point to argue that a larger corpus might show it to reach the threshold of collocability, both because it will always be possible to find a number that has not yet been shown to collocate and because it is nonsense to suppose that any user of the language would feel they were breaking new linguistic ground if they used a number with *hour* that they had never heard anyone else use. More subtly, the same goes for the collocation of *hour* with *ride* in that it also collocates with *drive, flight* and *journey*. Listing such collocates is theoretically trivial and unrevealing about the possibilities of its occurring with other 'journeying' words such as *meander, slog* or *odyssey*, for example. If however we assume that the priming is operating at a more abstract level, we can say that for most speakers of English the word *hour* is likely to be primed for semantic association with NUMBER and JOURNEY. Thus *thirty-hour ride* belongs to a pattern that (in my corpus) also includes:

> *half*-hour *drive*
> *four*-hour *flight*
> *two*-hour *trip*
> *three*-hour *journey*

two-hour *hop*
three-hour *slog*

The relative banality of this observation supports the argument that this is the way the word *hour* is typically primed for native speakers; the claim is that when we formulate what we want to say, primings like the above shape the wording we use. But whereas collocation can only account, by definition, for the routine, the notion of semantic association can account for some aspects of creativity. There is no instance of *a 27-hour meander* in my corpus but if it ever occurred the semantic associations just described would account for it without in any way detracting from its novelty. If the distances between planets or stars were being discussed, other time units would be used — *week*, *light year* — and in principle expressions such as *27-week flight* or *150 light-year odyssey* could be created, still on the basis of the same semantic associations.

As noted in Chapter 1, primings nest. Here, as a first step, we note that the NUMBER-hour-JOURNEY (or NUMBER-TIME-JOURNEY) combination collocates with *a*. The resultant word sequence may in turn form an association with VEHICLE:

a three-hour *car* ride
a 12-hour *bus* ride
a five-hour *coach* ride
a two-hour *ferry* ride
a half-hour *train* ride
a two-hour ride *by four-wheel drive vehicle*

Note that the word sequence *a 27-hour meander by sledge* is as readily explained by this combination of primings as are the attested examples listed above. Note, too, that such a word sequence (were it ever to occur) would be impossible to explain by collocation alone. We would have to assume that although *hour* was primed to occur with *two* and *bus*, a totally unconnected range of factors led to its occurrence with *27* or *sledge*. It is more elegant to assume that words and word sequences are also primed for semantic association. Of course, for particular speakers, because of particular communicational needs or because of particular linguistic experiences, a particular word may be primed to occur with another without there being corpus evidence to support the priming. Nevertheless, despite the unpredictability of priming and the uncertain status of corpus evidence with regard to its presence or absence, there will always be co-occurrences that cannot be accounted for in terms of collocation. Semantic association is a necessary generalisation and appears to reflect a regular kind of lexical priming. It is probable, but not theoretically necessary, that collocations are primed first and that the semantic commonality between collocates produces the more abstract priming, whether as a result of self-reflection or because of encounters with co-occurrences that share the semantic feature(s) of the already recognised collocates. The primings move outwards from specific words to the semantic set, and in so doing permit creative choices to be made that in themselves reinforce the more general priming. (However, the possibility must be allowed for that the semantic associations of a word are primed first, with the collocates arising from a person repeatedly making the same selection from the semantic set.)

If the claim that primings move out from collocations to semantic associations is correct, it does not follow that a corpus will necessarily reflect the collocations that led to the semantic association, since these may differ from person to person. Names are the obvious instance of this. In my childhood, the word *nanny* collocated with *Hoey* as in *Nanny Hoey* and the word *nan* with *Robinson* (as in *Nan Robinson*). As a consequence of this, I am now primed to recognise *Nanny* or *Nan* as titles primed to occur with surnames when reference is being made to a grandmother. No corpus will ever reflect my personal primings, though, and every other adult who uses the titles, or understands them, will have been differently primed (apart from minor points of overlap, where children's literature makes use of these words). An instance in the Bryson sentence of the way names get primed is in the following semantic association:

SMALL PLACE is a NUMBER-TIME-JOURNEY — (by VEHICLE) — from LARGER PLACE.

My corpus includes the sentences:

1   Ntobeye is a two-hour ride by four-wheel drive vehicle from the vast refugee camp at Ngara.
2   The village is a four-hour drive from London.
3   Pamuzindo is an hour's drive from Harare.

Substitute *Hammerfest* for *Ntobeye* in sentence 1, *thirty* for *two*, *bus* for *four-wheel drive vehicle* and *Oslo* for *the vast refugee camp at Ngara* and the first half of Bryson's sentence appears.

Though a large corpus will attest a fair number of sentences containing mentions of *Oslo*, it would be a corpus of enormous magnitude that would contain more than a handful of references to *Hammerfest*. Clearly only northern Norwegians are likely to have the word primed for any collocations, and these will presumably be with Norwegian words as a rule. Although it is possible, even probable, that Bill Bryson researched his journey to this small town, we do not have to assume that his sentence was the product of collocational primings arrived at as a result of his researches. It would be sufficient that as a child he heard parents and fellow town-people talk of how far Des Moines, the small town where he lived, was from the nearest big city, when, for example, they were asked where exactly it was that they lived. The point here is that while there may indeed be semantic associations that on the basis of corpus evidence do not have corresponding collocations, these general semantic associations (i.e. associations primed for many speakers of the language) may be based on local collocations (i.e. collocations primed for only a few speakers) of the kind that the average corpus is unlikely to detect.

Good examples of the operation of semantic association, which also illustrate the way primings nest, are provided by Baker (forthcoming) and Bastow (2003), though they do not use the terms outlined here. Baker notes that when *daylight* collocates with *broad*, it is usually in the context of *in*. The word sequence *in broad daylight* is then further primed to occur with 'something bad happening, usually connected to crime or violence'. Examples from his data include:

> . . . having been abducted and then stabbed in broad daylight . . .
> . . . was snatched off a bus in broad daylight . . .
> . . . a 'Mirista' who was captured in broad daylight . . .

Reporting on a study of US defence speeches, Bastow notes firstly that *men* and *women* collocate with each other in this domain. The resulting binomial word sequence *men and women* then collocates with *young*, or, to put it in the terms of this book, in the domain of US defence the typical speech writer is primed to collocate *men and women* with *young*. (I hope, however, that I may be permitted the shorter and more convenient formulation hereafter without compromising my original claim.) The word sequence *young men and women* then has a semantic association with COMPLIMENTS:

> bright young men and women
> very capable young men and women
> dedicated young men and women
> finest young men and women
> high-quality young men and women
> the finest of young men and women
> outstanding young men and women
> special-gifted, serious-minded young men and women
> superb young men and women
> talented young men and women
> But as impressive as those young men and women are
> fit, well-adjusted young men and women

(data from Bastow 2003)

Bastow's data also provide support for the point made in the previous chapter that priming occurs, in principle, within specific domains and/or genres. As he himself notes, the behaviour of the word sequence *men and women* in a general corpus is rather different, having, for example, a collocation with *between*, which does not manifest itself in his US defence corpus.

Constant/variable patterns in semantic association

Although familiarity with concordances may blunt awareness of the fact, it can hardly be missed that there is a great measure of parallelism in data such as that provided above. Such parallelism is not, though, only a property of concordances; it is also a property of spoken and written discourse. Winter (1974, 1979) noted that one of the basic relations in text was that of the matching relation, where two clauses in a text are matched for similarity or difference. Examples of matching relations are contrast relations, for example:

4   Seven or eight were arrested, but I was the only one charged

and compatibility relations, for example:

5   My husband was furious, so was I.

Matching relations are, according to Winter, characteristically established by the repetition of key clausal elements and the replacement of others, which can be talked of in terms of patterns of constant and variable (Hoey 1983). An example is the sentence you read four sentences ago, namely *Such parallelism is not, though, only a property of concordances; it is also a property of spoken and written discourse*. This can be represented in tabular fashion as shown in Table 2.1. Tables of this kind can however be used to represent corpus data with equal facility, as shown in Table 2.2.

It is not an accident that clause relations and concordance output can be represented in similar ways. Semantic association, when it occurs in a precisely repeated textual context, functions as a kind of intertextual matching. The speaker/writer, primed to associate a word or word sequence with a particular semantic context, recognises the similarities between what they want to say at a particular point and what they have heard or read at other times, and (re)produces

Table 2.1 The parallelism of constant/variable in a matching clause relationship

Such parallelism	is	not only	a property of	concordances
it	is	also	a property of	spoken and written discourse
Constant: such parallelism	is		a property of	**multiple utterances/ sentences**
Variable: —		— [correlative] —		**whether or not coherent**

Table 2.2 The parallelism of constant/variable in a sample of concordance data for *hour*

	half-	hour	drive
	four-	hour	flight
	two-	hour	trip
	three-	hour	journey
	two-	hour	hop
Constant:	**number**	*hour*	**(type of) journey**
Variable:	**which**	—	**which type**

the priming. Thus the person responsible for writing a US defence speech (in Bastow's data), recognising that what they want to say about US troops is much the same as what others have previously said, comes up with an utterance that is (partly) in a relation of matching compatibility with those earlier utterances (Hoey 1983).

In the same way that data illustrating semantic association can be regarded as forming textual relations, so text can be regarded as generating data for semantic associations. We can interpret matching relations of compatibility or contrast in text either as textual exploitations of existing semantic associations or as creations of 'nonce' primings for a brief textual moment. In the former case, the writer/speaker makes use of the priming of a word or word sequence by drawing on that priming twice in quick succession and thereby making it visible and available for interpretation (e.g. as contrast). In the latter case, the juxtaposition is not licensed by the primings available for the writer/speaker (or, more accurately, not by the primings for semantic association – it is likely that other primings are conformed to), but the presentation of the juxtaposition creates for the reader/listener a temporary priming such that the matching is interpreted in terms of that priming.

Darnton (2001) notes that the repetition of single words in writing for children is of limited efficacy in encouraging the development of reading skills, but that the use of repetition as part of matching relations is of an altogether greater value. New words are more readily understood by children because of the repeated context in which they occur. We can interpret this as indicating that successful stories for children encourage them to make use of their priming experience, to take a step in abstraction from collocational priming to semantic associational priming or to rediscover semantic associations in writing that have previously only been encountered in speech. Many of the 'nonce' primings created by the matching relations become permanent for the child (and subsequent adult), despite their original temporary status. For children brought up in English or American homes and exposed to traditional folk tales, 'I'll huff and I'll puff' and 'What big teeth you've got!' represent permanent primings for *huff*, *puff* and *teeth*.

Semantic prosody, semantic preference and semantic association

The concept of semantic association is not my own, although the label is. It grows out of two different concepts, sometimes confused with each other (including by me, e.g. Hoey 1997b). It was early noticed that the collocations of a word or word sequence often group in interesting ways. Sinclair (1991: 112) notes that 'many uses of words and phrases show a tendency to occur in a certain semantic environment. For example, the verb *happen* is associated with unpleasant things – accidents and the like'. So when John Travolta's character in *Pulp Fiction* utters the words 'Shit happens', he is summing up an important characteristic of *happens*, that it often occurs with bad things, especially when the subject is fleshed out. For example:

6   . . . until food runs out or **some other disaster** *happens*

7   . . . and as a result of his action **something unpleasant** *happens* to him.

This phenomenon was labelled **semantic prosody** (Louw 1993), by analogy with Firth's view of the sound system as prosodically organised. Firth (1957) argued that when we pronounce a word such as /ʃɪp/ our mouth is already shaping the [ɪ] sound even as it makes the [ʃ] sound. There is a sense then in which the [ɪ] sound has spread over its neighbours, a fact which conventional phonetic script representations of the sound system disguise. He therefore favoured a phonetic description that did not treat each sound as a discrete element to be combined with other discrete elements but recognised that certain features are spread over the conventionally recognised units. In the same way, according to Louw, certain features of a word's meaning are to be found already present in its surrounds. Its influence is spread around so that it affects and limits the choices available to the user, a fact which conventional representations in thesauri and dictionaries disguise and which most grammars ignore. Stubbs (1995) illustrates semantic prosody with the item *cause*, which, to an even greater extent than *happen*, carries bad news around with it; cancers are 'caused' much more frequently than cures. It is worth quoting his discussion in a little detail since his example is insightful. He states the prosody, gives sample collocates supporting the prosodic statement and then provides sentence illustrations:

1 CAUSE: A *cause* is something that makes something happen. To *cause* something means to make it happen.

1a Most frequently, >90%, the circumstances are *unpleasant*. Typically, what is caused is: an accident, cancer, concern, damage, death, disease, pain, a problem, problems, trouble.

1b The circumstances can include a wide range of *unpleasant* things, mostly expressed as *abstract nouns*, such as: alarm, anger, anxiety, chaos, commotion, confusion, crisis, delay, difficulty, distress, embarrassment, errors, explosion, harm, loss, inconvenience, nuisance, suspicion, uneasiness.

1c Frequently, the unpleasant collocates are *medical*: Aids, blood, cancer, death, deaths, disease, heart, illness, injury, pain, suffering, symptoms, stress, virus . . .

1g . . . typical examples are:

— the rush hour causes problems for London's transport
— dryness can cause trouble if plants are neglected
— considerable damage has been done to buildings
— I didn't see anything to cause immediate concern
— some clumsy movement might have caused the accident

(Stubbs 1995: 247)

The term **semantic prosody**, however, is inappropriate as a way of describing the processes operating in the Bryson example and in Baker's and Bastow's data on a number of counts. In the first place, Louw and Stubbs both seem to limit it to positive and negative effects. Thus *happens* and *cause* have in these terms negative prosody. But while Bastow's example of *young men and women*'s association with what I have labelled COMPLIMENT is easily interpreted as positive prosody, the examples of NUMBER and JOURNEY do not admit of such interpretation. In several papers, I sought to extend the term to cover such cases (e.g. Hoey 1997a, 1997b, 1998), but I now recognise that this was unhelpful and would ask readers of those papers to interpret my references to semantic prosody as references to **semantic association**.

In the second place, the prosodic claim has come under attack. Although he is comfortable with the notions of collocation and colligation (see Chapter 3), Whitsitt (2003) challenges the claim made for semantic prosody that words are coloured by their characteristic surroundings, arguing that this position is flawed both philosophically and in terms of its ability to cope with readily available counter-evidence, particularly where language functions metaphorically. His arguments are convincing, though perhaps the difference is not as great as Whitsitt thinks between saying that *cause* (for example) is negative because its collocates are characteristically negative (a position which Whitsitt correctly identifies as unsustainable) and saying that because the co-texts of *cause* are characteristically negative we may interpret negatively those co-texts that are on the face of it neutral. O'Halloran and Coffin (2004), for example, present evidence that a succession of negative co-texts for a word encountered in a particular newspaper text permits a negative reading of an otherwise apparently neutral co-text.

The third reason for not persisting with the term is one of clarity; quite simply, the term has another, rather different sense. Louw (1993) ascribes his use of the term to personal communication from Sinclair, but Sinclair himself (1999) uses the term to refer to the meaningful outcome of the complex of collocational and other choices made across a stretch of language. For the phenomenon I am talking about in this chapter he uses the term **semantic preference**.

The terms semantic preference and semantic association may be seen as interchangeable. My reason for not using Sinclair's term is that one of the central features of priming is that it leads to a psychological preference on the part of the language user; to talk of both the user and the word having preferences would on occasion lead to confusion. Accordingly, the term that is used here, as will already be apparent, is the bland but transparent one of **semantic association**. The change of term does not represent a difference of position between Sinclair and myself.

The definition of **semantic association** that we have arrived at is that it exists when a word or word sequence is associated in the mind of a language user with a semantic set or class, some members of which are also collocates for that user.

The semantic associations of *consequence*

At the end of Chapter 1, I noted that one can look at linguistic phenomena either as they apply in a particular piece of text or as they apply in the use of a particular word. I want now to consider in a little detail the operation of semantic associations in connection with a particular word. Stubbs (1995) looked, as we have seen, at the verb *cause*; to complement this, let us look at what is caused, i.e. at the noun *consequence*, in its meaning of 'result' (as opposed to 'significance'). From a concordance of 1,817 lines drawn substantially from the *Guardian* corpus but supplemented by data from the Bank of English, I found 456 instances of *consequence* premodified by an adjective and sought to classify the adjectives according to their semantic similarities.

The first and largest of the semantic associations of *consequence* identified in my corpus was a class of adjectives that alluded to the underlying logic of the process that *consequence* was describing; this semantic association comprised 59 per cent of all premodifying adjectives. Examples are:

8 Whatever his decision, it will be seen as a **logical** *consequence* of a steady decline in influence.

9 . . . it is the **ineluctable** *consequence* of having been in power for ever . . .

10 Mr Haughey's support for liberal reform is a **direct** *consequence* of the election of President Mary Robinson last November.

11 What is certain is that the results of Milosevic's experiment will be under intense scrutiny in Moscow with the **probable** *consequence* that a

suitable scion of the Romanov family is crowned Tsar by the Patriarch of All the Russians.

12 . . . disability is not a **natural** and **inevitable** *consequence* of old age.

Unsurprisingly, perhaps, given the size of the group, the 'logic' adjectives can, with a little ingenuity, be further divided into three sub-classes (rather as *cause* has a semantic association of 'disease' which is a sub-class of the association of 'bad things' noted by Stubbs). The distinction between the sub-classes is not watertight but has, I hope, value all the same. The first sub-class refers to necessity (*unavoidable, inevitable, inexorable, inescapable*, and so on); instances 8 and 9 illustrate this sub-class. The second sub-class refers to the directness or the stages of the logical process (*direct, ultimate, long-term, immediate, knock-on* and so on); instance 10 exemplifies this. The third sub-class is concerned with the naturalness or expectedness of the process (*likely, predictable, possible, probable, natural* and the like); this use is illustrated in instance 11. A coupling of members of two of these sub-classes can be seen in instance 12.

The 'logical' association accounts for a clear majority of the adjectives premodifying *consequence* in my sample. The next largest semantic association exemplifies the insight originally expressed by Louw in that it is made up of adjectives that evaluate negatively the consequence to which they are attached. This association accounts for 15 per cent of the cases examined and includes such items as *awful, dire, appalling, sad* and *regrettable*. (One 'logic' adjective, *inexorable*, was also included in the count because its connotations are so negative.) Examples are:

13 The **doleful** *consequence* is that modern British society has been intensely politicised.

14 Yet another **disastrous** *consequence*, Smallweed assumed, of having the Tories in power for so long.

15 The Mecca tragedy was the **grisly** *consequence* of a deep antagonism.

16 . . . the affair was the latest **ludicrous** *consequence* of the 1983 pro-life amendment.

The third semantic association suggested by the data is that *consequence* associates with adjectives expressing a view as to the seriousness of the consequence. This category accounted for 11 per cent of the adjectives examined and included items such as *serious, important, significant* and *modest*. Examples are:

17 One **important** *consequence* of this obsessive militarism has been a silent and undiscussed brain drain.

18 The most **serious** *consequence* of this crime has been the effect on the children.

19   . . . not every **significant** *consequence* of an action which is known to an individual will be equally important to the morality of the action.

20   The most **prominent** *consequence* of this is that Americans shoot each other in industrial quantities.

Adjectives referring to the seriousness of a consequence overwhelmingly outweigh those (like *modest*) claiming that the consequence was of no great importance.

The final association observed in the data concerned adjectives that referred to the UNEXPECTEDNESS of the consequence; these account for 6 per cent of the instances considered. Examples are *unintended*, *odd* and *strange*. This association complements the third sub-category of the first group, in that consequences that conform to the logic of the situation are expected ones. Interestingly, though, adjectives referring to the unexpectedness outnumber those referring to the expectedness in a ratio of 2:1. Typical occurrences are the following:

21   But this ascent from gut hatred to a plateau of sweet reason has had an **unforeseen** *consequence*.

22   But that vastness, and the sheer sparseness of matter, has another **curious** *consequence*: extraterrestials are rare.

23   Yet that very process brought its own **surprising** *consequence*.

24   String theory – the idea that all the bits that add up to matter are just different modes of vibrations of infinitesimal bits of string – has an **odd** *consequence*.

When all the semantic associations of *consequence* are grouped together, they account for 90 per cent of all adjectives that premodify the word. What this means is that if the corpus reflects an individual's experience of reading the *Guardian* (or perhaps other) newspaper, then the word *consequence* will be primed for the reader in such a way that they will expect it to occur with such associations. It may also mean that writers for the *Guardian* are productively primed to use *consequence* with these associations.

Pragmatic association

Just as a word or word sequence may be primed for semantic associations, so it may be primed pragmatically as well. **Pragmatic association** occurs when a word or word sequence is associated with a set of features that all serve the same or similar pragmatic functions (e.g. indicating vagueness, uncertainty). The boundaries between pragmatic association and semantic association are not going to be clear cut, because priming occurs without reference to theoretical distinctions of this sort. An example, though, of the operation of pragmatic association is that the word *sixty*, in addition to being typically primed for semantic association with UNITS OF TIME, UNITS OF DISTANCE and AGE, is typically associated with expressions of VAGUENESS. Thus I attest in my data:

about	*sixty*
over	*sixty*
around	*sixty*
more than	*sixty*
an average of	*sixty*
some	*sixty*
almost	*sixty*
nearly	*sixty*
fifty to	*sixty*
between fifty and	*sixty*
fifty or	*sixty*
up to	*sixty*
maybe	*sixty*
getting on for	*sixty*
a good	*sixty*
	sixty or more
	sixty-odd
	sixty-some
	sixty plus
	sixty or so

In writing, the pragmatic association just illustrated only applies to the literal form of *sixty*, not to the numeral form 60. They are therefore differently primed, despite being apparently no more than alternative orthographic versions of the same word. In speech, the distinction of course does not operate; my spoken corpus is too small to allow me to make confident claims about the operation of the above pragmatic association in conversation, but I would predict that most speakers are primed to use *sixty* with VAGUENESS in a range of types of spoken discourse (but not perhaps courtroom discourse or parliamentary debates). Where exactness is needed, I predict that it would often be made explicit, i.e. *exactly sixty*, but that this would not be true of, say, *sixty-four*. My spoken data, meagre as they are, partly support these predictions, in that I have four instances of *sixty-four*, *sixty-nine* etc., none of which are marked for VAGUENESS, and four instances of *sixty*, two of which are definitely marked for VAGUENESS:

25 It's fifty, sixty or more.
26 There are maybe fifty, sixty, I've lost count of the number.

A third is arguably marked for VAGUENESS:

> 27 Sent out more than fifty. I did sixty and Caroline copied even more.

The word *reason* provides us with another instance of priming for pragmatic association. The relation of affirmation-denial has been shown (Winter 1979; Williames 1985; Hoey 1983, 2001) to be a pivotal feature of writer/reader and speaker/listener relationships, and *reason* is typically primed to associate with acts of DENIAL — denial either that something is a reason, or that the reason is known, or that the reason matters. Just as LOGIC could be divided into three sub-categories of semantic association for *consequence*, so DENIAL can probably be sub-divided along the lines just mentioned. However, here I group them together. Examples include:

28	Mahathir sees no	*reason* to tinker with success
29	Unless you have any	*reason* to suspect a murder, I'd . . .
30	But there was no	*reason* on God's earth why I . . .
31	There is no	*reason* to suppose that our stay here . . .
32	Really I see no	*reason* why I should be obliged to . . .
33	They'd have no	*reason* to come to the surface
34	That's not the	*reason* why . . .
35	There's no medical	*reason* why a baby needs to change

as well as a number of idiomatic word sequences such as:

for some *reason*
for no obvious *reason*
for some unknown *reason*
for some *reason* or other
whatever the *reason*

Statistical support for this pragmatic association comes in the form of an analysis I undertook of 7238 instances of *reason* with postmodification. Of these, 4747 were found to affirm the reason and 2491 either denied the reason or denied knowing what it was. It has been shown (Halliday 1993; Halliday and James 1993) that the ratio of positive to negative clauses in general English is 9:1. Here however we have a ratio of close to 2:1. What this means is that when speakers or writers use *reason*, they are typically primed to use it as part of a pre-emptive move in their dealings with their audience. The listener/reader may, in the particular textual context, have an expectation that the speaker/writer will answer the question 'Why?' (see e.g. Hoey 1983, 2001). Using a construction with *reason* of the kind considered above, the speaker/writer can override such an expectation.

The issues raised by these data for *sixty* and *reason* are similar to those we have already considered. We have the same posited relationship between collocation and association and, to some extent, the same possibility of intertextual matching, though there are grounds for seeing this as a potential point of contrast with semantic association. Pragmatic association can be studied from two directions. On the one hand we can look at the operation of pragmatic factors on data of particular kinds, as do Partington and Morley (2002), Partington (2003, 2004), Garcia and Drescher (2003) and Pinna (2003). This work is throwing up valuable evidence for the discourse considerations under which pragmatic associations operate. On the other hand, pragmatic markers can be looked at as items in their own right with their own priming; see for example the work of Marín-Arrese (2003) and her colleagues in Spain. It is quite possible that this will prove a readier route to the study of pragmatic associations, since it is not yet clear how often pragmatic associations are attached to individual words as opposed to word sequences and clauses that may themselves be the product of various collocational, semantic associational and (as we shall see) colligational primings. In Chapter 1, I showed how the expression *won't say a word against* is built out of collocational nesting. That discussion necessarily simplified the picture somewhat. Firstly, *say* belongs to the semantic set COMMUNICATIVE INTERCHANGE, other members of which include *hear* and *spoke*. Secondly, and more pertinently in this context, the nested combination COMMUNICATIVE INTERCHANGE *a word against* is characteristically primed to have pragmatic association with both denial and hypotheticality – for example:

36   And I would never say a word against him.
37   . . . it is difficult to find anyone prepared to say a word against him.
38   They looked rough, but Esther would not hear a word against them.

Preliminary evidence suggests that this is the norm and that nested combinations of words are more likely to be primed for pragmatic association than individual words.

The role of intuition in identifying semantic and pragmatic association

I have been arguing that for *Guardian* readers and writers, *consequence* is primed to participate in a number of semantic associations and that *sixty* is primed to participate in a particular pragmatic association, in the same way that both words participate in a number of collocations. But it may be objected that I have relied unduly on intuition with regard to what is included or excluded in the lists. There is no avoiding the fact that I have used intuition and that my intuition, like everybody else's, has no privileged status. Another analyst might have *consequence* point to semantic association often operating under tight constraints. But should we limit the description of semantic associations to particular grammatical positions? Although most of the cases of semantic association operating in the Bill Bryson sentence do pivot about single words or specified word combinations and are dependent on grammatical positioning, there are a couple of cases where the associations seems less dependent on a fixed word ordering and do not manifest the kinds of parallelism apparent in the examples given in the opening section of this chapter.

As examples of semantic association not being dependent on a particular grammatical ordering, consider the following data. The word sequence *by bus* occurs 110 times in my corpus. Of these 65 (59 per cent) are associated with location, but the location is not always provided in the same structural form:

39   We were taken by bus **to another camp**
40   One of my staff was going **home** by bus
41   Railway passengers were ferried by bus **between Radlett and St Albans**
42   A traveller who had reached **the border town of Myawadi** by bus **from Rangoon** yesterday . . .
43   While crossing **Quito, Ecuador**, by bus, I noted the following message . . .

Ten (9 per cent) are associated with measurement of time, again with some variation in the wording of the measurement dominating:

44   Once she had got to Bassi, **four hours away** by bus . . .
45   This is unlikely to help **the half hour** she has to spend each morning getting to work by bus
46   . . . the Czech Republic, who set off by bus from Prague **on Sunday afternoon with the intention of arriving in time for last night**'s opening ceremony

Both these associations are of course reflected in Bill Bryson's sentence. Perhaps unexpectedly, only one instance of *by bus* occurs with a measurement of distance (except in so far as time is used indirectly to measure distance) and, again, there is no measurement of distance in the Bryson sentence.

Sticking with the same sentence, *in winter* seems to have a semantic association with 'timeless truths' as opposed to reports of specific events. It is instructive as a way of demonstrating this to compare the distribution of *in winter* in my corpus with that of similar wordings such as *in the winter*, *during the winter* and *that winter* (see Table 2.3). Percentages refer to the proportion of instances of the word

Table 2.3 Distribution of temporal expressions of *winter* across propositions of different generality

	in winter (226)	in the winter (331)	during the winter (203)	that winter (26)
specific event	29 (13%)	179 (54%)	130 (64%)	26 (100%)
timeless truth	197 (87%)	152 (46%)	73 (36%)	—

sequence in question. I have emboldened those percentages that seem to indicate likely strong semantic associations.

At first sight, one might seek to attribute this distribution to the absence of a marker of definiteness in the word sequence *in winter* and its presence in the other three temporal expressions in the table. However, that would be to misread the table. In the first place, the distribution shows that the word sequence *in winter* can be used in the reporting of a specific event. In the second place, it shows that two of the other temporal expressions are regularly used in timeless truths. Indeed, *in the winter*, which only differs from *in winter* in its inclusion of the definite article, occurs with timeless truths nearly half the time. Markers of definiteness correlate with the reporting of specific events; they do not provide grounds for denying that *in winter* is primed for *Guardian* readers and writers to occur with 'TIMELESS' TRUTH.

In the instances just discussed the evidence appears to suggest that semantic associations are not grammatically restricted when they are primed. We should not, however, be in too much of a rush to assume grammatical freedom for semantic associations. If the case for the relationship between collocation and semantic association has been correctly made, we would expect to find that the properties of collocation are reflected in semantic association. Closer inspection of the data for representation of location and measurement of time in association with *by bus* shows in fact that though there is variation in the representation of this semantic association, certain structures dominate. For location it is the *to* PLACE and *from* PLACE structures; for measurement of time it is the NUMBER *hours (away) from* structure.

With regard to grammatical restriction, we find that though there are indeed some collocates that appear to be primed so that they have a degree of positional freedom, many are tied to one position and one grammatical relationship. Consider, for example, the following data generated by *WordSmith* (Scott 1999), given in Tables 2.4 and 2.5, which list the top 20 collocates of *consequence* and of *consequences* occurring immediately prior to the node word in order of decreasing

Table 2.4 The collocates of *consequence* identified by *WordSmith* as occurring immediately prior to the node word

	Total	Left	Right	L5	L4	L3	L2	L1
THE	1,408	661	747	104	81	52	152	272
INEVITABLE	85	85	0	1	2	0	0	82
ONE	115	10	14	4	3	7	19	68
DIRECT	52	48	4	0	1	0	0	47
LITTLE	42	39	3	0	6	0	10	23
ANOTHER	32	30	2	0	1	1	7	21
ANY	29	22	7	1	1	0	1	19
NATURAL	21	19	2	0	0	1	1	17
LOGICAL	15	15	0	0	0	0	0	15
IMMEDIATE	11	11	0	0	0	0	0	11
ITS	49	27	22	7	4	4	3	9
ONLY	50	29	21	5	4	5	7	8
SERIOUS	13	10	3	1	0	1	0	8
POSSIBLE	11	9	2	1	0	0	0	8
LIKELY	18	12	6	2	1	1	1	7
NECESSARY	9	8	1	0	0	2	0	6
IMPORTANT	13	8	5	0	1	0	1	6
POLITICAL	17	11	6	2	2	1	0	6
SOME	32	14	18	3	2	2	1	6
GREAT	15	6	9	0	1	0	0	5

frequency. The analyses were derived from 1,764 instances of *consequence* and 3,611 instances of *consequences*. *WordSmith* does not identify collocates of one or two letters' length; thus *a* and *in* are missing from the first list, for example, although inspection of the concordance shows both words to be very frequent collocates. (Also, not all of the items identified by *WordSmith* as collocates would necessarily be so identified if other measures were used.)

The first column in each table indicates the collocates identified by the program. The second column gives the total number of occurrences of the putative collocate in the environment of ± 5 words prior and subsequent to the node word. The third and fourth columns, fairly obviously, indicate the broad distribution of the collocate on either side of the node word. The remaining columns indicate the exact positions prior to the node word in which the collocate occurs. It will be seen that some of the collocates are highly position-specific. Thus in Table 2.4, *inevitable*, the most common lexical collocation of *consequence*, occurs 85 times in the data, and 82 of these are immediately prior to the node word (conventionally indicated in such tables as being to the left of the node word, that being the spatial position in the concordance from which these data were derived); there are no instances whatsoever of its occurrence subsequent

Table 2.5 The collocates of *consequences* identified by *WordSmith* as occurring immediately prior to the node word

	Total	Left	Right	L5	L4	L3	L2	L1
THE	3,928	2,614	1,314	208	158	156	543	1,549
SERIOUS	156	143	13	0	4	2	15	122
POLITICAL	130	112	18	4	9	12	0	87
ITS	218	167	51	11	18	15	39	84
DISASTROUS	91	85	6	0	0	1	5	79
SOCIAL	98	86	12	1	4	11	0	70
DIRE	87	80	7	0	3	0	7	70
ECONOMIC	123	97	26	4	5	24	0	64
AND	952	611	341	119	130	113	202	47
FINANCIAL	52	49	3	1	1	4	0	43
TERM	51	45	6	1	3	1	3	37
ENVIRONMENTAL	45	39	6	2	0	3	0	34
NEGATIVE	29	29	0	0	0	0	1	28
DEVASTATING	39	33	6	0	3	0	3	27
GRAVE	30	27	3	0	0	0	1	26
THEIR	208	68	140	19	11	5	9	24
HAVE	469	372	97	49	60	83	157	23
PRACTICAL	23	23	0	0	0	0	1	22
POSSIBLE	44	40	4	2	2	3	11	22
TERRIBLE	32	28	4	1	3	0	3	21

to the node word (shown as RIGHT in the table), despite the apparent plausibility of an utterance such as *the consequence was inevitable*. Similarly, 47 out of 52 instances of *direct* and all 11 occurrences of *immediate* occur immediately prior to *consequence*, and 87 out of 115 instances of *one* and 28 out of 32 instances of *another* occur either one or two places prior, with immediately prior position being the heavily preferred option. Most strikingly of all, in the same table, *logical* occurs 15 times with *consequence* and all 15 occurrences are in the same position *vis-à-vis* the node word. The same general pattern will be seen to repeat itself for a number of other items in Table 2.4.

The same goes for *consequences*, as can be seen in Table 2.5. Of 156 instances of *serious*, for example, 143 occur prior to *consequences* and of these 122 occur immediately prior. Similarly, the 130 occurrences of *political* in the environment of *consequences* include 112 before the node, and 87 of these occur as (part of) the word sequence *political consequences*. Again, the pattern repeats itself through Table 2.5. It will be noted, by the way, that these lists confirm the conclusions reached by Renouf, Sinclair, Stubbs and others, discussed in Chapter 1, that the collocational behaviours of grammatically different instances of a lemma may overlap very little; we might therefore expect to see the same lack of overlap in semantic association.

As a way of addressing the possible grammatical restrictions on the primings of semantic association, and given the above data for the collocations of *consequence* (Table 2.4), let us look again at the distribution of key collocates associated with the four main semantic associations of *consequence*, discussed above. For example, *inevitable* is the most common collocate belonging to the semantic set of LOGIC (NECESSITY), with which *consequence* has a semantic association. If *inevitable* is restricted in position as a collocate, is there a similar restriction on the semantic association? And do cognate forms of *inevitable*, *inevitably*, *inevitability* collocate with *consequence*, in which case is there a similar freedom for the semantic association of LOGIC (NECESSITY)? The question then is whether the association is primed to occur in structures as various as:

47   **Inevitably** the *consequence* was that . . .
48   The *consequence* was **inevitable**.
49   The **inevitability** of this *consequence* was . . .

(all fabricated)

Investigation suggests that such fabrications do not have their match in actual performance. I examined 1817 examples of *consequence*, looking for the four associations occurring in grammatical positions other than that of the modifying adjective to *consequence*. In particular I looked for them in the structures represented by the examples given above (47–9). However, despite repeatedly re-sorting the concordance in order to highlight different possibilities and despite the intuitive naturalness of fabricated examples such as 47, the four major semantic associations described above as being formed by *consequence* were virtually never found in structures other than premodifying adjective. For instance, there was only one case of the structure represented by example 47 that contained one of the recognised associations, namely:

50   **Unfortunately** the *consequence* of this is that the stigma stays with me . . .

There were likewise very few examples of the combination of association and grammatical structure represented by fabricated example 48. Indeed the three examples below are all there were in 1817 lines:

51   . . . a hazardous *consequence* is perhaps **unavoidable**.
52   The second *consequence* is more **relevant** to the newspapers themselves.
53   The *consequence* was **evident** in the state of housing, schools, hospitals.

Not one example occurred in my data of the possibility represented by example 49, despite the intuitive naturalness of fabrications such as:

Table 3.1 Distribution of tense (and other) choices in clauses containing *winter* prepositional phrases

	in winter (**226**)	*in the winter* (**331**)	*during the winter* (**203**)	*that winter* (**26**)
Present tense	133	111	61	—
Past tense	40	165	74	26
Present perfect	5	5	19	—
Modal	25	28	24	—
None	23	22	25	—

Table 3.2 Percentage of each word sequence occurring with each tense (or other verbal) choice

	in winter (**226**)	*in the winter* (**331**)	*during the winter* (**203**)	*that winter* (**26**)
Present tense	**59%**	34%	30%	—
Past tense	18%	**50%**	36%	**100%**
Present perfect	2%	2%	9%	—
Modal	11%	8%	12%	—
None	10%	7%	12%	—

Table 3.3 Percentage of each tense (or other verbal) choice occurring with each word sequence

	in winter (**226**)	*in the winter* (**331**)	*during the winter* (**203**)	*that winter* (**26**)
Present tense	**44%**	**36%**	20%	—
Past tense	13%	**54%**	24%	9%
Present perfect	17%	17%	**66%**	—

with the various word sequences. I have emboldened those percentages that seem to deserve comment.

What Table 3.2 seems to confirm is that *in winter* is indeed likely to be primed for *Guardian* readers to occur in clauses with the present tense, with 59 per cent of cases of *in winter* occurring with this tense. The word sequence *in the winter* on the other hand is likely to be primed to occur in clauses with the past tense; expectedly, *that winter* appears to allow of no other possibility, though with different data one might speculate that modal auxiliaries might also occur.

Table 3.3 shows the same data from the perspective of the distribution of the tenses (and other verbal group choices) across the word sequences. It presents the same picture as Table 3.2 but with slightly different emphases. If the present tense is chosen and a *winter* word sequence is to be used, there is an 80 per cent chance of its beginning with *in*, with *in winter* being the most likely option. If the past tense is chosen under the same conditions, *in the winter* is as likely to occur as all the other options put together. If the present perfect is chosen, it is the word sequence *during the winter* that is most likely to occur.

What these data indicate is that one's choice of tense or aspect may be made at the same time as one's choice of temporal expression. The word *winter* is primed to occur with *in*, *in the*, *during* and *that* (as opposed, for example, to *within* or *inside*). The nested combinations *in winter*, *in the winter*, *during the winter* and *that winter* are then primed to occur with the different tense and aspect possibilities. Of course, the priming also works the other way round. So the nesting of *winter* and present tense is typically primed to produce *in winter*, while the nesting of *winter* and *have* + VERB is typically primed to produce *during the winter*.

An analysis of the kind just reported throws up other observations. In the course of my investigation, I noticed that when the *winter* word sequences were in initial position, they occurred with particular types of clause process. Two of these seemed especially to be distributed in a non-random fashion: Material processes and Relational processes. Halliday (1994) says of Material processes that they are 'processes of "doing"'. They express the notion that some entity 'does' something – which may be 'done' to some other entity (p. 102). They have an obligatory actor and an optional goal (the 'directed at' entity in the clause). Of Relational processes he says that they 'are those of being . . . The central meaning of clauses of this type is that something is' (p. 112). They have either an identifier and an identified or a carrier and an attribute.

Analysed with regard to these two kinds of process, the distribution was as shown in Table 3.4. Excluding *that winter* from the picture, because there are too few data, the distribution of each word sequence across the processes and

Table 3.4 Distribution of temporal expressions with *winter* across Material and Relational processes

	in winter (46)	*in the winter* (50)	*during the winter* (35)	*that winter* (10)
Material process (84)	21	34	25	4
Relational process (43)	24	13	5	1
Other processes (12)	1	3	5	3
				+2 as subject

Table 3.5 The distribution of the *winter* word sequences across clauses organised round Material, Relational and other processes

	in winter (**46**)	*in the winter* (**50**)	*during the winter* (**35**)
Material process	46%	**68%**	**71%**
Relational process	**52%**	26%	14%
Other processes	**2%**	6%	**14%**

Table 3.6 The distribution of Material and Relational processes across clauses containing the *winter* word sequences

	in winter (**46**)	*in the winter* (**50**)	*during the winter* (**35**)
Material process	26%	**43%**	31%
Relational process	**57%**	31%	12%

of each process across the word sequences is as in Tables 3.5 and 3.6. As previously I have emboldened the percentages that seem worth commenting on. Table 3.5 shows how the *winter* word sequences are distributed across clauses containing Material, Relational or other processes. Table 3.6 shows how Material and Relational processes are distributed across clauses containing the *winter* word sequences. Because we are looking only at clause-initial instances of the *winter* expressions, the data are fewer and any conclusions drawn must be tentative. However, Tables 3.5 and 3.6 suggest that, for readers of the *Guardian*, *in the winter* and *during the winter* are likely to be quite strongly primed to occur with Material process verbs and that *in winter* will probably be primed to occur with Relational process verbs, though here the priming may be less strong. It will be noticed that in Bill Bryson's opening sentence to *Neither Here Nor There* the thematised word sequence *in winter* occurs in a clause in the present tense that makes use of a Relational process. It is no wonder that it seems so natural; he has instinctively followed his primings.

When I constructed my alternative version of Bill Bryson's sentence in Chapter 1, I did more than avoid the characteristic collocations and semantic associations associated with the vocabulary of the sentence. I also, in several cases, avoided the characteristic grammar associated with that vocabulary. An example of this is my use of *pondered* in the clause 'though why travellers would select to ride there then might be *pondered*'. There are 1,057 uses of the lemma PONDER as a verb in my corpus, and only 8 of these are passive. The word *pondered* is generally comparatively rare, being used 22 times as part of the perfect aspect and 142 times as a past tense verb. The lemma PONDER appears to avoid both the past tense and the passive in my data. While the former may be specific to newspaper English, the latter is hypothesised to be true of many genres and domains. My 'translation' of Bryson's sentence therefore introduced a relatively infrequent word in a highly infrequent grammatical structure (for that word).

Priming for Relational processes might have semantic implications but they are not of the same kind as those we were considering in Chapter 2; the same may be said for tense choice. The preferred avoidance of *is, are, was, were, be, am, being, been, get, got* + *pondered* can hardly be handled as a collocational matter. Collocations are not formulated in terms of combinations that are avoided (though they could be) and such an approach would involve the same inelegance of formulation that we considered in Chapter 2 in connection with semantic association. What we have in each of these cases is a kind of grammatical 'collocation' (though it is a different phenomenon from collocation between a lexical word and a grammatical word). The label that has been given such a relationship is 'colligation', as briefly mentioned in Chapter 1.

A brief history of the term 'colligation'

The notion of colligation has its origin in Firth, who introduced it thus:

> The statement of meaning at the grammatical level is in terms of word and sentence classes or of similar categories and of the inter-relation of those categories in colligation. Grammatical relations should not be regarded as relations between words as such – between 'watched' and 'him' in 'I watched him' – but between a personal pronoun, first person singular nominative, the past tense of a transitive verb and the third person singular in the oblique or objective form.
>
> (Firth [1951]1957: 13)

This formulation makes it hard to distinguish from grammar. However, when Halliday used the notion in his study of the *Secret History of the Mongols*, he used it in an importantly different way:

> The sentence that is set up must be (as a category) larger than the piece, since certain forms which are final to the piece are not final to the sentence. Of the relation between the two we may say so far that: 1, a piece ending in *liau* or *jˇe* will normally be final in the sentence; 2, a piece ending in *sˇi₂*, *ŋa*, *heu* or *san ŋgeu₂* will normally be non-final in a sentence; 3, a piece ending in *lai* or *kiu* may be either final or non-final in a sentence.
>
> (Halliday 1959: 46; cited by Langendoen 1968 as an example of Halliday's use of colligation)

It will be seen that Halliday is here using 'colligation' to mean the relation holding between a word and a grammatical pattern, thus creating a midway relation between grammar and collocation, and this is the sense in which the term will be used in this and subsequent chapters.

The last five years have seen something of a resurgence of interest in colligation (see e.g. Sinclair 1996, 1999, 2004; Hoey 1997a, 1997b; Hunston 2001; Partington 2003). Sinclair's work and mine developed independently but since we were colleagues for many years at the University of Birmingham and we worked closely together on the *Collins COBUILD English Language Dictionary*, it is more than possible that I acquired the concept during discussions with him. Or it may simply be an idea whose time has come.

Having said that, the idea was in fact in play before the resuscitation of Firth's label. Colligation is implicitly illustrated in Sinclair (1991) in a number of places and Francis (1993), with its focus on corpus-driven grammar, also makes use of the concept, if not the word. In Hoey (1993), I show some of the colligational patterns associated with the word *reason*, again without making use of Firth's term.

A definition of colligation

The basic idea of colligation is that just as a lexical item may be primed to co-occur with another lexical item, so also it may be primed to occur in or with a particular grammatical function. Alternatively, it may be primed to avoid appearance in or co-occurrence with a particular grammatical function.

So far we have talked about colligation as the grammatical associations a word or word sequence is primed to favour or avoid, but it is significant that Halliday, in the quotation given above, also formulates the colligational relationship in terms of sentential position. This is an important extension. It means that colligation may be interpreted as going beyond traditional grammatical relations and embracing such phenomena as the positioning of a word or word sequence within the sentence or paragraph and even its positioning within the text as a whole, as I shall argue in Chapter 7.

For current purposes, I suggest that *colligation* can be defined as:

1 the grammatical company a word or word sequence keeps (or avoids keeping) either within its own group or at a higher rank;
2 the grammatical functions preferred or avoided by the group in which the word or word sequence participates;
3 the place in a sequence that a word or word sequence prefers (or avoids).

There are two things to note about this formulation. Firstly, colligational statements can be negative as well as positive. So it is a legitimate colligational statement to say of a particular lexical verb that it does not occur with the primary auxiliaries or that it avoids sentence-final position. We have already noted that *PONDER* is typically primed to avoid the passive voice. We might add that *in winter* appears, on the basis admittedly of scant data, to be primed to avoid processes other than Material and Relational (see Table 3.6).

In the remainder of this chapter I shall seek to show how a colligational description might proceed and the kind of insights into the nature of lexical priming that might be gained from this kind of description. With this in mind I turn once again to the long-suffering word *consequence* whose living conditions will once again be submitted to detailed inspection.

A colligational description of *consequence*

In pursuit of the potential colligations of *consequence* I examined 1,809 instances of *consequence* in total, drawn from the *Guardian*-dominated corpus used in the previous chapter. As before, we have to be careful about assuming that patterns represented in my corpus (or any corpus, come to that) are indicative of primings that any individual may have. I reiterate that the corpus can only indirectly show us the kinds of ways that it is likely that a reader of the *Guardian* may be primed to use or recognise the word.

Consequence has two meanings, one of which, 'logical outcome', we were considering in the previous chapter. The other meaning, 'importance', is much rarer, only occurring 169 times in 1,808 lines. The relationship between the two uses of the word will be discussed in Chapter 5. In this chapter it is again the more common use to which I wish to give attention.

Consequence in its more usual sense is undeniably a common word in the language (at least in its written form); we would expect it to appear in every grammatical position and so it does. The question is whether *consequence* with this meaning is characteristically primed to occur in certain positions rather than others or to avoid certain grammatical contexts in favour of others.

A noun will always be part of some group or other word sequence and that group or word sequence will normally perform some function in a clause. One can therefore look at the distribution of any noun in terms of its occurrence within clause or group. In the next two sections we will examine the distribution of *consequence* in both clause and group, comparing its distribution with that of other nouns.

The colligations of *consequence* in the clause

The question I choose to address first is whether *consequence* may be typically primed to have a preference for (or an aversion to) certain grammatical functions within the clause or whether its use in all grammatical positions is exactly that which we would expect of any noun. To this end 1,619 instances of this use of the word were analysed to see whether they occurred as part of the Subject, as part of the Object, as part of the Complement or as part of a prepositional phrase functioning as Adjunct.

Obviously the raw figures or percentages of occurrence in each grammatical position will by themselves tell us little about the colligational preferences of *consequence*. We need to compare the grammatical distribution of this noun with that of other apparently similar nouns. In the first sentence of this section there are six singular nouns – *question, preference, aversion, clause, use* and *noun*. For purposes of comparison then I have taken four of these (*noun* and *clause* are excluded to avoid using linguistic terms, which might be taken to operate at a different degree of abstractness to the other words in the comparison) and examined their grammatical distribution. Three hundred instances were considered of each of the comparison words (except for *aversion* for which only 203 instances could be found), though the full 1,615 instances of *consequence* were analysed. Senses that were clearly separable and idiomatic uses that did not retain the word's primary function were not included in the sample of 300; thus, for example, instances of *the X in question* and references to *preference shares* were excluded from the analysis.

My use of the terms Subject, Object, Complement and Adjunct is in line with normal use, except that, unlike Halliday (1994) for example, I distinguish Object from Complement (as do Sinclair 1972; Quirk *et al.* 1972, 1985; and Biber *et al.* 1999, 2002). Following these linguists, I define Object as having a different referent from Subject (unless it is filled by one of the self-reflexive pronouns such as *himself*) and as characteristically following transitive verbs, for example:

> 1 I urge you to commute *the death sentences that have been passed on them* [Object].

Complement on the other hand is defined as having the same referent as Subject (again excepting cases of the self-reflexive pronouns) and typically follows the verb BE and other equative verbs such as BECOME and SEEM, for example:

> 2 Both are *guilty of the vilest crimes* [Complement].

My analysis treated it as immaterial at this stage whether *consequence* appears as head of the nominal group or as part of the pre- or postmodification. So both 3 and 4 were picked up as examples of *consequence* functioning as Subject:

> 3 *A consequence of writing biography, even of the interim sort that I have just produced,* [Subject] is preoccupation with the topic.

Table 3.7 A comparison of the grammatical distribution of *consequence* in the clause with that of four other nouns

	Part of Subject	Part of Object	Part of Complement	Part of Adjunct	Other
consequence	24% (383)	**4% (62)**	**24% (395)**	**43% (701)**	5% (74)
question	26% (79)	27% (82)	20% (60)	22% (66)	4% (13)
preference	21% (63)	38% (113)	7% (21)	30% (90)	4% (13)
aversion	23% (47)	38% (77)	8% (16)	22% (45)	8% (17)
use	22% (67)	34% (103)	6% (17)	36% (107)	2% (6)

4   . . . *the danger of impregnation as a consequence of a split condom* [Subject] was vastly less than the chance of picking up a sexually transmitted disease . . .

Instances of *consequence* occurring within a subordinate clause were treated as belonging to the Subject, Object, Complement or Adjunct of that clause unless the clause was itself postmodifying. Anything that did not fit the four basic grammatical categories was simply analysed as other (though the exclusions in fact mask another important colligation of *consequence* as we shall later see). Given these definitions, you might like to speculate how you might expect the word *consequence* to be distributed across the different grammatical functions.

As anyone who attempts the grammatical analysis of authentic data knows, one encounters rather more cases where a correct analysis is problematic than one might anticipate on the basis of conveniently simple, made-up examples. It is not always possible to distinguish postmodification, particularly of an adjective, from a prepositional phrase functioning as Adjunct; Adjuncts and postmodifying prepositional phrases are not quite as neatly separable as one might imagine. Particles following a verb are another area where existing criteria do not always let one arrive at an intuitively satisfying analysis.

Nevertheless, the analyses of the six words were largely unproblematic and the results are to be found in Table 3.7. As previously, I have emboldened those results worthy of attention. You will see that *consequence* is quite strikingly different from the other words in the table in its distribution among the grammatical functions. Only in the case of Subject is the distribution of *consequence* the same as that for the other nouns in our sample. For all the other clausal functions, there are positive or negative colligations for which the word is likely to be primed, and these deserve attention.

1   There is a clear negative colligation between *consequence* and the grammatical function of Object. The other nouns occur as part of Object between a sixth and a third of the time. *Consequence* on the other hand occurs within Object in less than 1 in 20 cases.

2   To compensate, there is a positive colligation between *consequence* and the Complement function. Only one of the other nouns – *question* – comes close to the frequency found for *consequence*. The others occur within Complement four times less often than *consequence*.

3   There is also a positive colligation between *consequence* and the function of Adjunct, *consequence* occurring here nearly half the time. The other nouns in our sample occur between around a quarter and a third of the time.

Whether or not these colligational findings were in line with your expectations, they are amenable in part to explanation in terms of communicative need. We are inclined as speakers and writers to characterise states of affairs as having been caused by something else. It is obvious, then, that we would have regular need of using *consequence* in the Complement, since that is one of the normal ways available to us for expressing a characterisation. The colligational preference for the Adjunct function is explained by the prevalence of the two phrases *as a consequence* and *in consequence*. Nevertheless, these are explanations after the event; after all, for example, one might have imagined that there would have been sufficient instances of *have a/the consequence* to undermine the negative colligation of *consequence* as regards Object.

There are complex issues here concerning the status of the grammatical categories I am using here and elsewhere. I am of course claiming that they do not exist independently of the primings that give rise to them. And yet any colligational statement of the kind I have been making both depends upon and appears to affirm the validity of pre-existing grammatical categories. In fact, though, the functions of Object and Complement are dependent on the verb choices that are made. Each verb is separately primed to be followed by certain, often fairly specific, nominal groups. We saw in Chapter 2 how language users might generalise out of the specifics of the primed collocates to a more general and in some respects more abstract category, which in turn would permit them to make creative choices that were still compatible with the general priming. In the same way, the language user may generalise out of the primed words and word combinations to create a 'grammatical' category that will permit them to make unexpected choices while conforming to the generalised priming. The grouping of primings leads to a degree of patterning and to linguistic creativity.

Crucially, though, the extent to which this happens and the ways in which it happens may vary from language user to language user. There is not, I claim, a single grammar to the language (indeed there is not a single language), but a multiplicity of overlapping grammars that are the product of the attempt to generalise out of primed collocations. However, those primed collocations are the result of others' utterances, and the source utterances will have been tempered by the grammars that the speakers or writers had created for themselves; furthermore, few priming utterances will be entirely unaffected by the harmonising effects of education, social pressure and the media, and many will be hugely affected. So the degree of overlap between users' grammars is normally substantial. The categories used here and throughout this book are assumed to have some priming reality for most (but not necessarily all) users of the language, though relatively few of them would recognise the terminology used (often unsatisfactorily and incompletely) to label their primed categories. We will return to this issue later in the chapter.

Characteristic colligational primings of consequence within the nominal group

We have seen that *consequence* is colligationally quite distinct from (at least some) other nouns, both in terms of its grammatical preferences and its grammatical aversions at the level of the clause. How about at the rank of the group or phrase? There are in principle three grammatical possibilities here: *consequence* could occur as head of the nominal group in which it appears, as premodifier or as part of the postmodification, for example:

5   He says **a** *consequence* **of the fires** is that pressure throughout the field will fall [*consequence* as head].

6   . . . and *consequence* **modelling** and risk estimates and risk contours can be produced [*consequence* as premodifier].

7   If **the talk of bad blood** *as a consequence of* **the B&H quarter final washout fiasco** is true [*consequence* as part of the postmodification] . . .

Again, you are invited to speculate whether *consequence* occurs with higher or lower frequency than normal in any of these three positions. To answer this question, I undertook an analysis of all the nominal groups within which the word appeared in the 1,615 citations out of my corpus. As before, its syntactic behaviour was compared with that of the four nouns *question, preference, aversion* and *use* (300 of each, except for *aversion*, of which, as already noted, there were only 203). It would have been interesting to see whether the patterns that emerged were likely to be affected by the grammatical function of the noun within the clause, but the samples of the words used for comparison would have become unrepresentative at the level of the individual functions.

Table 3.8 shows that, as before, *consequence* is clearly different in its distribution from the other nouns in our sample, though just as *question* was the only noun to come close to *consequence* in its colligational preference for the Complement function, so also here *question* differs less from *consequence* than do the other nouns. In the first place, it will be noted that while all the nouns occur most frequently as heads of their own nominal groups, in the case of *consequence* the tendency is so overwhelming as to effectively rule out any other grammatical

Table 3.8 A comparison of the grammatical distribution of *consequence* in the nominal group with that of four other nouns

	Head of nominal group	*Part of the postmodification of the nominal group*	*Premodifier of nominal group*
consequence	**98% (1,588)**	**2% (26)**	**0.06% (1)**
question	92% (275)	8% (25)	—
preference	84% (253)	13% (39)	3% (8)
aversion	82% (167)	12% (24)	6% (12)
use	75% (226)	24 % (72)	1% (2)

position in the group. Even *question* occurs proportionally four times as often as *consequence* in postmodification and the other nouns all occur in postmodification much more frequently – between an eighth and a third of the time. What this tells us is that consequences are never used to narrow down other noun-heads – they are always the centre of attention. Secondly, all the nouns except *question* show a small tendency to occur as premodification. *Consequence* shows no such tendency at all. (My intuition is that your intuitions were more reliable on this matter than on clause functions, but then, perhaps, my intuition is untrustworthy.)

Since all the nouns occur more often in head function than as (part of the) pre- or postmodification, it is probably better not to formulate the colligational association for *consequence* in positive terms but in negative terms. Thus the posited typical primings are as follows:

1   *consequence* is typically primed to colligate negatively with premodification;
2   *consequence* is typically primed to colligate negatively with postmodification.

The characteristic primings of **consequence** *with respect to Theme*

Examination of our 1,615 examples of *consequence* reveals that 43 per cent of these (698, to be exact) were found to be part of the Theme of the clauses in which they appeared and 518 of them were sentence-initial as well. Theme is defined by Halliday (1994: 37) as 'the element which serves as the point of departure of the message; it is that with which the clause is concerned' and here it is operationalised as any textual material in a clause up to and including the Subject, where the Subject precedes the main verb of the clause. In those cases where the Subject follows the main verb, Theme is taken to be any textual material preceding the main verb. In this I broadly follow Davies (1988) and Berry (1989).

Characteristic examples of *consequence* being used as part of Theme are the following:

Table 3.10 Grammatical distribution of first noun in the sentences of three *Guardian* features

	Subject	Adjunct	Other clausal functions	No clausal function or no noun in Theme
1st noun in Theme of sentence (240)	50% (121)	19% (45)	3% (7)	28% (67)
1st noun in Theme of sentence excluding 3rd and 4th categories	72%	28%	–	–

The persistent noun-ness of *consequence* means that the figures in Table 3.9 are only partially relevant. Accordingly I also considered the first noun of each sentence within the Theme and categorised it according to whether it was found within Subject or Adjunct (or elsewhere). I did not look at non-sentence-initial clauses. Pronouns and existential *there* were not counted, which explains the high proportion of sentences with no noun in Theme. The results are presented in Table 3.10 in two forms, firstly with the figures included for other clausal functions (and for no grammatical function, in instances where one does not have a complete clause), and then without. It will be seen that the results are comparable to those in Table 3.9.

By either of the measures used, on a normal distribution we could have expected Adjuncts to have comprised between a quarter and a third of instances of *consequence* in Theme. So the near 50:50 division of instances of thematised *consequence* into Subjects and Adjuncts suggests that *consequence* is typically primed to occur as part of a thematised Adjunct. As we shall see in Chapter 7, the colligation of *consequence* with Theme is the tip of an iceberg of textual positioning that a word may be primed for. In anticipation of the discussion in Chapter 7, I will label the thematic colligation of *consequence* a **textual colligation**.

I have laboured the analytical processes in this section because I want to make it clear that the kind of corpus investigation necessary to establish plausible primings needs to be cautious and thorough. Elsewhere in this book, because of the desire to produce an accessible text and because of the exigencies of space, I have not always shown the background analyses in such detail; their absence from the text should not be taken as evidence of their non-existence.

In the next two sections we will look more closely at the two dominant Adjunct forms involved in the colligation we have just established.

Typical colligational primings *of* in consequence

The first thing to note about *in consequence* is that it has positive priming for use in Theme rather than Rheme ('Rheme' being here defined as anything occurring

Table 3.13 A comparison of *consequence* and four other nouns in respect of definiteness markers

	the	*Possessive*	*this, that*
consequence	247 (99%)	2 (1%)	—
question	67 (96%)	3 (4%)	—
preference	10 (25%)	28 (70%)	2 (5%)
aversion	7 (27%)	19 (73%)	—
use	21 (64%)	12 (36%)	—

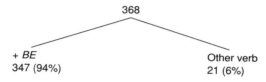

Consequence as head of nominal group functioning as Subject

368

+ BE
347 (94%)

Other verb
21 (6%)

Figure 3.1 A map of the priming of verb choice of *consequence* as head of a nominal group functioning as Subject

colligational preferences of the comparator nouns.) *Consequence* occurs with a possessive construction less than any of the other nouns. Put more precisely, *consequence* is likely to be primed negatively for occurrence with possessive constructions (see Table 3.13).

When *consequence* appears as head of the nominal group functioning as Subject, the clause it is part of follows quite predictable lines. This can perhaps be best indicated in a series of diagrams. Figure 3.1 shows the verb choices associated with *consequence* as Subject. In the calculations, only lexical *BE* has been counted, not auxiliary *BE* in progressive and perfect constructions. As can be seen, *consequence* is strongly primed for collocation with BE. The resulting structures are quite predictable as Figure 3.2 shows: 79 per cent of all instances of *consequence* as Subject conform to one of two structures: *consequence* + *BE* + *that* clause and *consequence* + *BE* + nominal group, with the latter frequently being a nominalisation of a clause. The figures for nominalisations here are very much on the cautious side, with only clear-cut cases being included, usually with residual clausal elements attached. Thus 27 was counted but 28 was not:

27 But the *consequence* could be the retention of large numbers of alternative syllabuses in the subject.
28 The *consequence* has been an austerity drive.

Even where the priming is apparently weaker, with the *consequence* + *BE* + *to* clause, there is further priming to be identified in that this structure

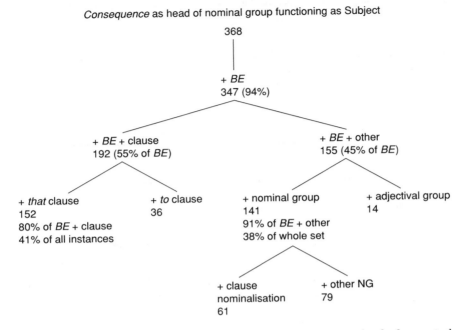

Figure 3.2 A map of the key colligational primings of *consequence* as head of a nominal group functioning as Subject

favours postmodification of *consequence* (29 out of 36 instances, i.e. 81 per cent). If the more common *consequence* + *BE* + *that* clause is chosen, the proportion of instances of postmodified *consequence* drops to 77 out of 191 (i.e. 40 per cent).

Colligational nesting

I have commented in a number of places on the phenomenon of nesting whereby a combination of words will have priming separate from (though built up from) the primings of the individual words. It will be apparent from our consideration of *consequence* that nesting does not only take the form of the building of word sequences and lexical items. It can also be the case that when a word or word sequence combines with a particular colligational priming (positive or negative), this nesting in turn has further primings, which may be of any kind – collocational, semantic associational or colligational. So Figure 3.2 shows that the nesting of *consequence* with Subject is primed to collocate with the lemma *BE* and then this nesting is further primed to colligate with *that* clauses. (The objection that *consequence* was not found to be primed to occur as Subject either positively or negatively will be addressed in Chapter 8.)

The property of the nesting of primings is an important one in that it allows us to go some way beyond certain kinds of grammatical description. In particular it helps us to explain the existence of grammatical structures in apparent free variation. To illustrate this, let us return to the word *reason*, which was discussed in Chapter 2 in connection with pragmatic association. In my corpus and for most speakers *reason* is positively primed to colligate with postmodification, and this colligational priming takes five unequally favoured forms. These are:

> *reason* + clause (without connector) (1,006 instances in my data)
>> 29 **One** *reason* **events have moved so fast** is that there is a powerful new player on the international scene.
> *reason* + *that* clause (129 instances in my data)
>> 30 **The only** *reason* **that there has not been a serious accident** is the provision of hustle alarms on the trains . . .
> *reason* + *why* clause (1,531 instances in my data)
>> 31 But **the** *reason* **why they are limiting the number of children** remains a matter of dispute.
> *reason* + *for* + non-finite clause or nominal group (often a nominalisation) (2,608 instances in my data)
>> 32 **Her** *reason* **for opposing it** relies on the fact that women of every ethnic group are mainly at risk from men of their own ethnic group.
> *reason* + *to* + non-finite clause (2,005 instances in my data)
>> 33 But **the main** *reason* **to doubt Mr Yeltsin's summit strategy** is domestic, rather than foreign.

On the face of it, there would appear to be considerable freedom of choice among these structures. Sentence 33 is capable of being rewritten as sentences 34, 35, 36 and 37 without obvious violation of naturalness:

> 34 But the main *reason* one might doubt Mr Yeltsin's summit strategy is domestic, rather than foreign.
> 35 But the main *reason* that one might doubt Mr Yeltsin's summit strategy is domestic, rather than foreign.
> 36 But the main *reason* why one might doubt Mr Yeltsin's summit strategy is domestic, rather than foreign.
> 37 But the main *reason* for doubting Mr Yeltsin's summit strategy is domestic, rather than foreign.

The question then is: is each of the five nested primings illustrated above itself primed for a different textual purpose? Note the specificity of the question. I am not exploring whether different kinds of postmodifying clause have different functions in general; I am investigating whether different kinds of postmodifying clause (or nominal group) are primed for different purposes in the specific circumstance of their occurring with *reason*.

Given that we have seen that *consequence* has variable distribution across the functions of Subject, Object and Complement and that there are colligational choices that are dependent on which function is chosen, it makes sense to investigate whether the different nestings behave differently as regards clause function. We also noted in Chapter 2 that *reason* has a pragmatic association with DENIAL and I referred there to the 2:1 ratio between affirmations and denials of *reason*, in contrast with the general ratio of 9:1 of positive and negative sentences, which we would expect to map closely onto affirmations and denials (though the map is not exact). It would seem worthwhile to check whether the nestings connect with this priming. With this in mind all instances of *reason* + postmodification were examined for clausal function (a small number that occurred in non-clausal contexts were excluded both from the count of instances and from the analysis.) The clauses in which they appeared were then examined to see whether they were affirming a reason or denying (or denying knowledge of) a reason. Examples 29, 30, 32 and 33 above are all affirming; 31 on the other hand denies knowledge of a reason.

Other instances of denial (in clauses that respectively use *reason for* + nominal group, *reason to* + non-finite clause and *reason why* + clause in Complement function) are:

38   . . . there's no *reason* for the anxiety.

39   There was no *reason* not to inform me beforehand.

40   There must have been a good *reason*, somewhere at the screenplay level, why people like Jeff Bridges, Tommy Lee Jones, Suzy Amis (so memorable in *The Ballad of Little Jo*) and Forest Whitaker decided to appear in *Blown Away*. But . . .

It will be noticed from the last that denial of (knowledge of) reason need not involve the use of the recognised negative markers.

The results of the analysis are shown in Table 3.14. Here, the ratio of affirmation/denial is markedly skewed from 9:1, so we can assume that we are looking at evidence of priming of the nested combination; such cases have been highlighted. In some cases it was not clear whether what was being denied was the reason or something else in the clauses. The figure in brackets represents the total of instances that would result from including such doubtful cases; a few instances of other problems of allocation are included here as well. It is perhaps of interest that all doubtful cases occur when *reason* + postmodification occurs as Subject. These figures are not included in subsequent calculations.

Inspected closely, the table shows that when *reason* is used as (part of) Subject, it is primed for affirmation (1,895:66, an affirmation-denial ratio of 29:1), with

Table 3.14 The distribution across Subject, Object and Complement of *reason* + postmodification in clauses that affirm or deny (knowledge of) the reason

	Subject *reason affirmed*	Subject *reason denied*	Complement *reason affirmed*	Complement *reason denied*	Object *reason affirmed*	Object *reason denied*
reason + clause	**698**	17 (38)	210	42	14	4
reason + *that* clause	77	–	40	9	–	3
reason + *for* x	**1,091**	36 (49)	610	**392**	305	**161**
reason + *why* clause	7	10 (17)	594	**629**	61	**223**
reason + *to* V	22	3	286	**536**	732	**426**

affirmation over three times as common as might be predicted on the basis of the positive-negative clause ratio. When *reason* is used as (part of) Complement on the other hand, it is primed for denial (1,740:1,608, not far off a 50:50 ratio). (With Object, *reason* is more weakly primed for denial.) From the pragmatic perspective, the choice of affirming a reason would seem to invite the simultaneous choice of Subject. The choice of rejecting a reason (or saying that it is unknown or is unimportant) invites use of the Complement (or Object).

The nesting of *reason* and Subject function and of *reason* and Complement (or Object) function may permit the priming just described, but it offers us no clues as to why particular kinds of postmodification might have been chosen. Indeed I have no evidence that the nesting of *reason* and Subject or Complement would not operate equally well without the presence of postmodification. However, if we look at the rows of Table 3.14, rather than at the columns as above, we find that the different postmodifying structures with which *reason* appears also distribute themselves differently between affirmation and denial. The nesting of *reason* + clause without connector is apparently primed for affirmation (in an affirmation-denial ratio of 15:1). No other nesting approaches this ratio; the relatively infrequent *reason* + *that* clause is the closest, with an affirmation-denial ratio of 10:1, which is too close to the norm of 9:1 to be of any interest. On the other hand, the nesting of the *reason* + *why* clause seems to be primed for denial, irrespective of the grammatical function to which it is being put. Indeed, the priming of the *reason* + *why* clause for denial appears to override the priming of *reason* + Subject. It will be noted, though, that the conflict is resolved by simple avoidance of Subject function when a *reason* + *why* clause is being used.

Conclusion

In this chapter we have witnessed (in what has probably seemed exhausting detail) the way a word's patterns of use are characteristically controlled by its colligations and the way these patterns of use, through nesting, are in turn primed for particular purposes. Not every one of these colligations will occur in every domain and genre and not every speaker/writer will be primed for these colligations in newspaper text, but every domain and genre will have its own characteristic colligations (which may well overlap with the ones found for newspaper text) and every speaker/writer will be primed in some way for the domains and genres with which they are familiar. In Chapter 8 I shall argue that colligation, with appropriate modification to take account of morphology and phonology, can be used to construct grammars rather different from those we are accustomed to considering. The fundamental claim made in the first three chapters of this book has been that the semantic and grammatical relationships a word or word sequence participates in are particular to that word or word sequence and do not derive from prior self-standing semantic and grammatical systems, though they do contribute to the posterior creation of those systems.

4 Lexical priming and lexical relations

Introduction

I have been arguing that words can be primed for collocation, semantic association and colligation and that the notions of priming and nesting permit, in
principle, the formulation of quite complex representations of naturalness
without jeopardising our ability to account for creativity in language. We have
seen, however, that it may sometimes not be the word or word sequence that is
being primed but the semantic set, created by the operation of abstraction from
a variety of individual primings. For example, in Chapter 2, I implicitly assumed
that semantic sets might themselves participate in lexical primings, when we
considered the combination SMALL PLACE is a NUMBER-TIME-JOURNEY-(by VEHICLE)-
from LARGER PLACE. This gives rise to the possibility that our focus on the way
that words or word sequences form semantic associations may be insufficiently
generalised and that instead of formulating semantic association as 'item x has
a semantic association with semantic set Y, represented by items a, b and c' we
should formulate the association thus: 'semantic set X, represented by items p,
q and r, has a semantic association with semantic set Y, represented by items a,
b and c'. Such a reformulation would imply that the SMALL PLACE is a NUMBER-
TIME-JOURNEY-(by VEHICLE)-from LARGER PLACE combination was the norm and
that therefore the starting point for much priming description should be the
semantic set. This would be in line with (though still different from) work
congruent with the position proposed in this book, such as *Pattern Grammar*
(Hunston and Francis 2000), the schema-based approach of Michael Barlow (e.g.
Barlow 2000) and construction grammar (Goldberg 1995). It would mean that
priming as so far presented was only the tip of the iceberg and indeed insufficiently generalised.

If, however, priming description were to centre on the semantic set, it would
need to be the case that members of a semantic set should share the great
majority of primings. Although some of the instances of semantic association we
have considered have involved sets with uncertain memberships (e.g. LOGIC

(NECESSITY))), others, like JOURNEY and NAMED PLACE, have drawn their memberships from the hyponyms of a particular superordinate. (The hyponym-superordinate relation is the relationship of instance to general, illustrated in the relationship of *spaniel, poodle, Alsatian* [co-hyponyms] to *dog* [superordinate]). Since co-hyponyms are usually readily identifiable, it seems sensible to start by exploring whether they share the great majority of primings. If they do share their primings, then we will need to reformulate our claims about semantic association along the lines suggested above.

Co-hyponymy

A suitable example of semantic association, for our purposes, is that formed by the lemma *train*, analysed in considerable detail by Campanelli and Channell (1994) (cited by Stubbs 1996). *Train* is primed to collocate with *as a* in newspaper data and the nested combination *train* as a* (where *train** stands for *train, trains, trained* and *training*) is typically primed to associate with SKILLED ROLE OR OCCUPATION. My corpus has 292 instances of *train* as a*, and of these 262 are followed by an occupation or related role. Examples from corpus are:

TRAIN* as a teacher (25)
TRAIN* as a doctor (12)
TRAIN* as a nurse (11)
TRAIN* as a lawyer (11)
TRAIN* as a painter (8)
TRAIN* as a dancer (7)
TRAIN* as a barrister (5)
TRAIN* as a chef (5)

All the above are clear collocates, but my data also include such words or word sequences as *cobbler, concentration camp guard* and *Braille shorthand typist*. For most users of the language, *Braille shorthand typist* will not be primed as a collocation of TRAIN *as a* (though for someone who is blind or someone who works for the Royal Society of the Blind it may indeed be so primed), but it is likely to be explicable in terms of their priming of TRAIN *as a* as having a semantic association with SKILLED ROLE OR OCCUPATION. Put the other way round, the semantic set SKILLED ROLE OR OCCUPATION can be said to be primed to have a collocation with the word sequence TRAIN *as a*. The question then is: do the members of this set share other primings?

For the purposes of answering this question, I took, as my sample of hyponyms of SKILLED ROLE OR OCCUPATION, the words *accountant, actor, actress, architect* and *carpenter*. The words *actor* and *actress* were chosen to see whether hyponyms differing only in terms of gender would differ in any other way. (My data are not new enough to reflect the recent change in the use of *actor* from male-specific to gender-neutral; this is an interesting case of priming drift, presumably given a conscious push at the beginning.) I looked at 1,045 instances of *accountant*, 3,194 instances of *actor*, 1,710 instances of *actress*, 2,020 instances of *architect* and 245 instances of *carpenter*.

One might reasonably have predicted that SKILLED ROLE OR OCCUPATION words like *architect* and *accountant* would share many collocates; *employ(ed)*, *work(ed)* and *good* seem reasonable candidates, for example. Yet *WordSmith's* (Scott 1999) collocation calculation facility throws up very few shared collocates. The words *actor* and *actress* both collocate with *director*, *best*, *film*, *singer* and *former* (the last a telling reminder of the transitory nature of the acting profession for many). Otherwise there is little that is shared. *Architect* shares the collocate *Sir* with *actor*, perhaps reflecting the relative frequency with which architects and actors are honoured in the UK as opposed to accountants or carpenters (or researchers in English language). The other major lexical collocates of *architect* are *designed*, *new* and *chief*, none of which it shares with the others in the list. The main collocates of *architect* are *chartered*, *year*, *pounds* and *said*, the last of which it shares with *carpenter*. It shares with *actor* and *actress* the collocate *former*. The major collocates of *carpenter* are *aged*, *father* and *son*, which do not relate to the job in the way that those of its fellow hyponyms do.

All of this suggests that the various hyponyms of SKILLED ROLE OR OCCUPATION are typically primed quite differently from each other, at least as far as collocation is concerned. However, we cannot draw any large conclusions from this. After all, *walk* collocates with *minute* and *minutes*, which *flight* does not, and *ride* collocates with *taxi*, which *walk* does not. Both *ride* and *walk* collocate with *bus*, but with *ride*, *bus* usually precedes it or, as in the Bill Bryson example, appears in the word sequence *by bus*. With *walk*, on the other hand, *bus* almost always follows *walk* and *walk* is never connected to the word sequence *by bus*. Yet, as we saw in Chapter 2, all these JOURNEY words are usually primed to participate in the patterns NUMBER-TIME-VEHICLE-JOURNEY and NUMBER-TIME-JOURNEY-by-VEHICLE: the real test of whether co-hyponyms behave the same way will be with respect to primings for colligation and semantic association.

There are a number of basic colligations we would expect our chosen set of co-hyponyms to share. As countable concrete nouns sharing a common superordinate, we might expect them all to take definite and indefinite articles (e.g. *the architect*, *a local architect*). We might expect them all to take classifiers (e.g. *the ornamentarian architect*) and possessives (*not just another developer's architect*). We might expect them also to be themselves possessors, either as possessive determiner or as a postmodifying *of*-phrase (*the architect's brief*; *the skills of an architect*). We might expect them to occur in parentheses (*Sir Robert Smirke, the architect of the British Museum*) and apposition (*the Viennese architect Adolf Loos*). Despite the obviousness of these expectations, investigation of the colligations of

Table 4.1 The colligations of the co-hyponyms *accountant, actor, actress, architect* and *carpenter* (adapted from Hoey 2000)

Grammatical construction	accountant (1,045 instances)	actor (3,194 instances)	actress (1,710 instances)	architect (1,961 instances)	carpenter (245 instances)
Indefinite article	26%	22%	18%	16%	**42%**
Classifier	**26%**	12%	10%	8%	<u>4%</u>
'Possessor' construction i.e. 's & *of* noun phrase (NP)	6%	8%	**17%**	8%	**16%**
'Possessed' construction	**10%**	<u>1%</u>	<u>0%</u>	5%	<u>2%</u>
Apposition	14%	21%	**31%**	18%	<u>2%</u>
Parenthesis	17%	<u>8%</u>	12%	13%	**26%**

accountant, actor, actress, architect and *carpenter* shows that they differ grammatically among themselves. In other words, despite their being co-hyponyms they are each primed in their own way. Table 4.1 picks up each of the constructions just mentioned and shows how distinctively these features are distributed across the five co-hyponyms. Figures in bold suggest a positive priming; underlined figures suggest a negative priming.

To begin with the word with least absolute frequency, *carpenter*, is apparently quite strongly primed to occur with an indefinite article or in a parenthesis; both constructions are illustrated in this sentence:

1   Her father, a *carpenter*, became a permanent invalid when she was three . . .

Given that parenthesis is a relatively rare construction even in the parenthesis-rich waters of newspaper English, the fact that one in four instances of *carpenter* participates in such a structure is striking. It also appears to be primed to occur in possessive constructions, for example,

2   The *carpenter*'s benches were well-lit by rooflights.

A possible explanation for this is that carpenters have distinctive tools and equipment that they use in their work, unlike, say, accountants or actors.

On the other hand, *accountant* is strongly primed to occur with a classifier and less strongly to occur with a possessive construction. One in four instances of *accountant* occur with a classifier in my data and one in ten architects are possessed! Although not in itself a high percentage, 10 per cent is twice as frequent proportionally as the co-hyponym next most likely to occur with a possessive, *architect*. Both uses are illustrated in 3:

3   Perhaps the chef had put his back out, or had been called to task by his
     turf *accountant*.

For the writers of newspaper text, it would appear that *actress* is primed to
occur in apposition (*the Czech actress Anny Ondra*). This is one priming that is
unlikely to move from receptive to productive for the majority of *Guardian*
readers and is a particularly clear instance of the way primings are constrained
by the social/generic context. Like *carpenter*, *actress* is primed to occur in possessive constructions about a sixth of the time. However, the table disguises a
difference between the two co-hyponyms. Whereas *carpenter* appears on a roughly
50–50 basis in *'s* constructions and *of* constructions, *actress* avoids the *'s* construction, appearing almost exclusively in the postmodifying *of* construction.
Both the positive primings of *actress* are illustrated in 4:

4   Digs were notoriously bad in London and in desperation the mother of
     the *actress* Fay Compton founded a hostel called The Theatre Girls'
     Home in Greek Street, Soho.

The only hyponym not to be strongly primed to favour or avoid one of the
grammatical patterns mentioned is *architect* though, as I shall argue in Chapter 8,
this is not to say that it is not primed at all colligationally. However, the word is
distinguished from its fellow co-hyponyms all the same in that, as Table 4.2
shows, it is alone in being frequently used as a metaphor (*He was the main
architect of the peace plan*), with *actor* the only other word with any record
of metaphorical use. We will return to the metaphorical use of *architect* briefly
and in passing in Chapter 8, where the more general issue of creativity is
handled.

Cumulatively, the evidence seems to suggest that co-hyponyms do not in fact
share a good proportion of their primings, and this in turn suggests that it would
be mistaken to expect the majority of semantic association statements to be
formulated in terms of one semantic set having a semantic association with
another set. The particularity of our account of priming appears to be justified.
The collocational and colligational behaviour of the co-hyponyms we considered

Table 4.2 The distribution of metaphorical uses across the co-hyponyms *accountant,*
actor, actress, architect and *carpenter* (adapted from Hoey 2000)

Grammatical construction	*accountant* *(1,045 instances)*	*actor* *(3,194 instances)*	*actress* *(1,710 instances)*	*architect* *(1,961 instances)*	*carpenter* *(245 instances)*
Metaphor	0%	5%	0%	**23%**	1%

are too variable in their characteristic priming for them to routinely allow generalisation in terms of the priming of a whole semantic set. This does not, however, mean that co-hyponyms never so group. Apart from the NAMED PLACE BE x *hours* JOURNEY *from* BIGGER NAMED PLACE example that triggered this investigation, we have also seen that 'occupation' co-hyponyms group for the purposes of collocating with *TRAIN as a*. Normally, though, the evidence suggests that we should continue to articulate such statements in terms of the more specific nested combination's priming with the semantic set rather than the other way round.

Synonymy

In any semantic set, there may be members, often co-hyponyms, so close in meaning that we label them 'synonyms' (or 'similonyms': Bawcom 2003). They seem to have a psychological reality (Cruse 1986) and in continuous text they have long been noted as a cohesive device (Halliday and Hasan 1976; Hoey 1983), sometimes defended or criticised under the label 'elegant variation'. In particular genres and domains, such as the traditional liturgy of the Anglican Church, synonyms are coupled together in a regular way and therefore of course share the same context, for example, *trouble and adversity*; *the anguish and the grief*; *dear and precious* (all examples taken from *The Treasury of Devotion*: Carter [1869]1957). It cannot therefore be assumed that because non-synonymous co-hyponyms do not share all their collocations, colligations and semantic associations, synonyms such as *beneath/under*, *distribute/hand round* and *consequence/ result* will also typically not share such primings. Indeed the attractive prospect arises that perhaps the existence of characteristically shared primings will provide the conditions for a trustworthy definition of synonyms.

The question then is: do synonyms share all their primings for most users? If they do, we would need to argue that because of their similarity of use synonyms get primed the same way and that the primings then transfer from the individual items to the small semantic set which contains them, presumably with some tidying up of discrepant primings in the process.

To explore this, I shall return to the description of *consequence* again, because so many of the semantic associations and colligations have already been described.

There is an example from the 'logic' association of *consequence* that provides tentative support for the view that synonyms may share primings for users. Among the one-off items that occurred with *consequence* in the 'logic' association was the item *knock-on*. This item only occurs once with *consequence*:

5   . . . with the **knock-on** *consequence* of lower benefit upratings and public expenditure savings.

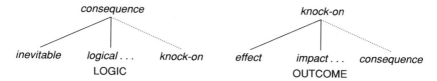

Figure 4.1 The semantic associations of *consequence* and *knock-on*

This of course further illustrates the fact that not all manifestations of semantic association are also common collocates of the word with which they occur. The important feature of this word, however, is that it is primed for many users to occur with other items with a similar meaning to *consequence*. In particular, it occurs with *effect* and *effects* very frequently. Out of 280 examples of *knock-on* in its non-sporting sense, 251 accompany one of these words; a further 9 accompany items like *benefits* (i.e. positive consequences) and *impact* ('an effect or influence' – *Macmillan Essential Dictionary* 2003).

What this means is that *knock-on* is strongly primed for semantic association with 'logical outcome', which its combination with *consequence* illustrates, though not prototypically. In other words, we have a situation that can be represented diagrammatically as shown in Figure 4.1, where unbroken lines represent instances of the association that also qualify as collocations and broken lines represent instances of the association that do not.

Such an interweaving of two semantic associations does not however involve an extension of the notion of semantic association. We have as yet no evidence that the semantic sets 'logic' and 'outcome' are in a direct prosodic relation with each other, only that two of the associations around *consequence* and *knock-on* intersect. To examine whether semantic sets interact, we must consider another item with broadly the same meaning as *consequence* (candidate items include *result, outcome* and *effect*). If it can be shown that such an item shares the associations of *consequence*, then we can say that we have evidence of the situation described earlier, viz: 'semantic category X, represented by items *p, q* and *r*, has a semantic association with semantic category Y, represented by items *a, b* and *c*'. The item I chose to investigate for this purpose was *result. Result* is a near synonym of *consequence* and for most language users they share a number of collocations (e.g. *direct, inevitable, likely, one* and *as a*). They also, for most language users, share the colligational primings:

> *The result/consequence was that*
> *This was a result/consequence of*

In a concordance of 15,952 lines (*result* is greatly more common than *consequence*) there were 14,307 nominal uses of the word, of which 1,758 were immediately preceded by an adjective. As in Chapter 2, I sought to group the adjectives according to semantic similarity, using the categories established for *consequence* as a starting-point. I found that there were points of similarity but also of difference in the associations of the two words. Of the four associations associated with *consequence*, only two appeared to operate for *result*. The first of these was the LOGIC association: 37 per cent of the adjectives associated with *result* commented on the logic of the process, for example:

6   It was as a **direct** *result* of Britten hearing Vishnevskaya that he conceived the idea of having a soprano soloist singing with the choir in the Latin settings of the liturgies.
7   The **end** *result* was world domination.
8   The **immediate** *result* of their collaboration was the hit single Jumping Jack Flash.

We can say therefore that *result* and *consequence* share the association of LOGIC, though it is a less dominant association for the former item (37 per cent as against 59 per cent).

The second association to be shared by both items was the minor association of UNEXPECTEDNESS, although, for *result*, it is more minor still, accounting for only 4 per cent of the adjectives accompanying the noun. Still, UNEXPECTEDNESS is slightly over twice as likely to be encoded as EXPECTEDNESS, a situation similar to that pertaining to *consequence*.

That exhausts the common associations of *result* and *consequence*, despite their obvious similarity of meaning and apparent similarity of contexts of use (and as we shall see below, there are differences between the two items even in the shared association of LOGIC). The other associations identified for *consequence* are missing. To begin with, while we found that 15 per cent of adjectives accompanying *consequence* were negative in tone, for *result* the proportion has halved (8 per cent). More significantly, the proportion of positive adjectives has risen from a stingy 3 per cent accompanying *consequence* to 22 per cent accompanying *result*. Put another way, the ratio of negative to positive adjectives for *consequence* is 5:1; for *result* it is 2:5. So *result* has a positive association, not a negative one. The picture is the same for the other association linked with *consequence*. SERIOUSNESS accounts for 11 per cent of instances of premodified *consequence* but for only 2 per cent of such cases of *result*. In their place, *result* has other minor associations: ACCURACY (4 per cent, as opposed to 0.7 per cent for *consequence*) and SAMENESS/DIFFERENCE (5 per cent, as opposed to no occurrences for *consequence*).

Even the area of closest similarity hides difference. While both *result* and *consequence* have strong associations with LOGIC, they differ considerably with regard to which sub-categories they favour. For *consequence* much the most common of these is INEVITABILITY, accounting for almost half of the LOGIC association, a fact also reflected in the fact that the most common adjectival premodifying collocate of *consequence* is *inevitable*. In the order of INEVITABILITY, (IN)DIRECTNESS and (UN)EXPECTEDNESS, the three sub-categories occur with *consequence* in the proportions 5:3:2. The proportions for *result* are quite different. By far and away the most common sub-category of the LOGIC association is the one reporting on the directness of the logical process being described or the stages involved in it; again this is reflected in the fact that the two most common adjectival collocates of *result* are *direct* and *end*. The (IN)DIRECTNESS sub-category accounts for 78 per cent of all LOGIC adjectives occurring with *result*. The proportions of the three sub-categories for *result*, in the same order as before, are 1:8:1. Thus even where there is a shared association, at a greater delicacy it is found to be only partly shared.

It would seem then that extension of the notion of semantic association to cover synonymous relations should proceed cautiously. The evidence thus far is that synonyms are primed differently.

The same pattern reveals itself with colligation. As well as sharing some colligations, *consequence* and *result* differ in important respects in their use in the *Guardian* (and, therefore, presumably for many language users). We saw in Chapter 3 that *consequence* favours indefiniteness compared with other abstract nouns. If we now compare *consequence* with *result*, we see that *result* colligates strongly with definiteness (see Table 4.3).

It would seem that if a language user wants to talk of an outcome that is both positive and definite, they will typically be primed to choose *result*. If on the other hand they want to talk of a negative, indefinite outcome, *consequence* is likely to feel the more natural choice.

It is important, however, not to overstate the position with regard to the typical primings of *consequence* for indefiniteness and *result* for definiteness. It is true that, proportionally, *result* is far more likely to be definite. In terms of absolute numbers, though, because of the much greater frequency of *result* in newspaper writing (and, one suspects, in speech and many other types of writing), there are as many instances of indefinite *result* in my corpus as there are of indefinite *consequence*. Secondly, though *consequence* is proportionally far more likely to co-occur with indefinite markers than is the case for the other abstract nouns examined, it is still in absolute terms more likely to occur with the definite article (or other markers of indefiniteness) than with indefinite markers.

Table 4.3 The distribution of markers of (in)definiteness for *consequence* and *result*

	Definite	*Indefinite*
consequence	249 (67%)	125 (33%)
result	3,508 (94%)	214 (6%)

Table 4.4 The distribution of markers of indefiniteness across *consequence* and *result*

	a	*another*	*one*	*every*	*any*
consequence	28 (22%)	20 (16%)	76 (61%)	1	—
result	76 (37%)	12 (6%)	105 (51%)	1	11 (5%)

There is no contradiction in the above points. Colligations, collocations and semantic associations may be weak or strong, and their strength is measured against the frequency of the choice in the language as a whole. (I am aware of statistical problems with this formulation, which arise both from the fact that an underlying assumption of lexical priming is that there is no single, monolithic 'language' and from the fact that the multiplicity of factors that affect the possibility of the choice include the varying colligational and semantic association factors that I am here trying to describe and distinguish, but the point can at least be made validly with regard to near-synonyms and perhaps co-hyponyms.) The explanation therefore for the raw figures lies in the fact that indefiniteness is rarer in text than definiteness. The colligations of *result* reflect that rareness; those for *consequence* to some extent challenge it.

Because of the overall greater frequency of *result* in my data, there are sufficient instances of its use with indefinite markers to permit a further comparison between the two synonyms, with respect to the markers of indefiniteness that the two words occur with. As before, we are only concerned with *consequence* and *result* in Subject function. Obviously the numbers for *any* and *every* would shoot up with *reason* in Complement and Object functions and for *a* with *consequence* in Adjunct function (see Table 4.4).

At first sight, the synonyms do not differ greatly in their priming for indefinite markers, when used as Subject. They are alike in favouring *one* as the most common marker of indefiniteness, then *a*, followed by *another*, with *any* and *every* as the least common. But this disguises several interesting differences. Firstly, *one* is almost three times as likely to occur with *consequence* as the next most frequent option, *a*. Compare this with the frequencies for *result*, where *one* is barely more than a third more likely to occur than *a*. Secondly, *another* is nearly as frequent as *a* with *consequence*, but only occurs one sixth as often with *result*. Finally, *any* does not occur with *consequence* in its outcome sense, a point we shall return to in the next chapter when we consider polysemy. Figures here, however, are not large and any conclusions drawn can only be tentative pointers to possible patterns of difference. And of course it must once again be reiterated that a corpus cannot determine what the primings of any individual will be; it can only suggest the kinds of primings that might occur (and, in the case of a text-type-specific corpus such as mine, indicate the receptive primings that a

Table 4.5 The distribution of markers of definiteness across *consequence* and *result*

	the	*Possessive*	*this/that*	*None*
consequence	247 (99%)	2 (1%)	–	–
result	3,278 (93%)	97 (3%)	118 (3%)	13

regular user of such texts might receive). A corpus can only tell us what the primings of an individual would be if that corpus was their exact and only linguistic experience.

It was noted above that *consequence* in absolute terms occurred with a marker of definiteness two thirds of the time. This means that there is sufficient data to permit a comparison of the two near-synonyms in respect of their co-occurrence with the definite article, possessive constructions and the determiners *this* and *that* when they are serving as (part of the) Subject. As can be seen from Table 4.5, there are no examples in my data of *this consequence* or *that consequence* as Subject, whereas *this result* and *that result* do occur in Subject function, albeit relatively rarely. We can therefore postulate that *consequence* is also colligationally primed to avoid the demonstratives. What this means is that we appear to be primed never to choose to characterise an earlier statement as being a consequence, whereas we are comfortable about characterising a previous statement as a result. The reasons for this are not immediately apparent, but I would suggest that consequences may be unintended or unexpected and therefore unpredictable, whereas results may be expected and planned for (scientific results, football results, election results). It is easier to recognise a planned-for outcome and it may be more natural to want to discuss such outcomes, whereas if an outcome is unexpected, it will not be recognised by a reader or listener as being an outcome until this is pointed out to them. If this explanation holds water, it is evidence for an interlocking of textual decision and lexical decision, such that the combination has a direct but subtle effect on the grammatical patterns in which it can appropriately (as opposed to acceptably) appear.

Cumulatively, with all caveats and cautions in place, the evidence suggests that synonyms are typically not identically primed. There are indeed shared primings, and in so far as there are, they reflect the close similarity of sense. But they also differ in important ways, the differences marking variations in use and context and providing a reason for the existence of the synonyms in the first place. We are arriving at a position where even small semantic sets comprising words with near identical meanings do not behave as sets often enough to warrant starting a description of priming with such sets. Words are individually primed – this is a central premise of priming theory – and it would seem that they remain individually primed.

Synonymous expressions sharing a word

We are left with one last possibility to explore. Sometimes we have expressions with the same meaning that share lexis but differ in their construction. An example of such a pair of synonymous expressions is *round the world* and *around the world*. Since they share the words *the world* and the morpheme *round*, the issue is no longer one of whether we should abstract from particular primings to semantic sets. Instead the issue is whether the primings of the nested combination of *round the world* and the primings of the nesting of *round* with *a-* in prior position and *the world* in subsequent position are the same or different. If they are alike, we will have found the limiting case for distinguishing primings. If they are not alike, we will be looking at priming differences arising from a single sound/single letter morpheme (*a-*). (The possibility of morphological priming is discussed in Chapter 8.)

On the face of it, we would expect *around the world* and *round the world* to be in free distribution. Intuition suggests they mean the same thing and it is easy to find examples which are closely parallel:

9 . . . getting communities in Britain and *round the world* to really participate in their own development.

10 . . . as long as the green Heineken logo continues to appear on bars in Britain and *around the world*.

11 Towns and cities *around the world* notched up record-breaking temper-
atures last week.

12 Cities *round the world* try to market themselves by presenting their best features while glossing over the worst.

13 She seems to have spent a long time travelling *round the world*, . . .

14 And there is certainly nothing new about people travelling *around the world*, then returning to Britain.

It will be noticed that in each of these pairs the word sequences are not just being used in very similar ways; they actually co-occur with the same lexis. The existence of such parallel expressions suggests that they are primed for some users in similar ways. Of course, it could be that for such co-occurrences one speaker has *round the world* (and not *around the world*) primed while a second speaker is primed to use *around the world* (and not *round the world*). A corpus, after all, merges the primings of many different writers. However, I have no evidence to suggest that this is the case in this instance and shall operate on the assumption that the corpus is giving us a reasonable approximation of the way these word sequences are typically primed for most language users.

The synonymous expressions *round the world* and *around the world* may be similarly primed, but they differ in frequency in my data. There are 448 of the

Table 4.6 Frequency of potential collocates for *round the world* and *around the world*

	round the world (448)	around the world (1,798)	Ratio
all a/round the world	22	46	1:2
from a/round the world	5	199	1:20
halfway a/round the world	28	6	9:2
markets a/round the world	5	30	1:6
people a/round the world	3	34	1:11
race around the world	2	14	1:7
SAIL a/round the world	28	14	2:1
TRAVEL a/round the world	10	12	5:6
a/round the world for	4	24	1:6
a/round the world in	26	59	4:9
a/round the world in 80	18	9	2:1
a/round the world in x days	17	9	2:1

former and 1,798 of the latter, making *around the world* almost exactly four times as frequent as *round the world*. Furthermore, the figure for *round the world* is heavily distorted by the presence of 112 instances of the name *Whitbread Round The World Race*. All but one of these was removed, leaving the figures for the two expressions as 336 and 1,798 respectively with *around the world* being slightly more than five times as common in my data as *round the world*. (Four other instances with Whitbread were retained because they differed in what followed *world* – namely *fleet* (2) and *yacht race* (2).)

Table 4.6 supports the initial impression that the synonymous expressions may be similarly primed for most users, showing as it does that they share a number of collocations. With the exceptions of *people* and *race* immediately prior to *round* and of *for* immediately after *world*, all the items listed in the table reach the threshold of recognition as collocates in *WordSmith* for both word sequences; in the case of these three potential collocates, the spread across the two expressions mirrors their overall relative frequency. Thus far, they behave as we originally predicted synonyms might. However, a glance at the table reveals a whole series of differences in terms of relative frequency. Cases where the distribution differs markedly have been emboldened. (The counts for SAIL and TRAVEL are for the lemma, rather than for the individual word forms.)

The table suggests that there are differences in the strength of priming of the two expressions as regards their collocates. So *around the world* is strongly primed in the *Guardian* to occur with *from* and *people*, while *round the world* is primed to occur with *halfway* and the lemma SAIL. The raw figures of occurrence for the lemma TRAVEL are more or less the same, but proportionally the collocation is much stronger for *round the world*. Curiously, given that the English title of Jules Verne's book (and of the subsequent films) is *Around the World in Eighty Days*, it is *80* rather than *eighty* that is the primed collocate for both word sequences and when *80 days* are being talked about, it is *round the world* that is the more common expression. Indeed it occurs twice as often as *around the world* with *80 days*, despite being five times **less** likely to occur in general. (Was the original inappropriately translated, I wonder?)

Further inspection of the data shows that the expected semantic associations for our synonymous word sequences follow the same lines as the collocations. So both word sequences have a semantic association with *in* + NUMBER, but *round* picks up five cases and *around* four. Examples are:

> 15   . . . in their quest to sail *round the world* in 77 days.
> 16   . . . Enza New Zealand's record attempt to sail *around the world* in under 79 days.

Around the world has a semantic association with *in* + MEASUREMENT OF TIME, with four instances of units other than days; there is no evidence of such an association for *round the world*. An example with both NUMBER and MEASUREMENT OF TIME associations in operation is the following:

> 17   . . . a satellite link to take visitors '*around the world* in 8 minutes'.

A second association that the word sequences share is that of JOURNEY, as might have been predicted from the collocations we considered above. Examples are 15 and 16 above and 18–20 below, which have been chosen to illustrate non-collocational instances of JOURNEY:

> 18   He **trudged around the world** in his subject's footsteps.
> 19   The idea is deceptively simple: **bum round the world**, go to football matches . . .
> 20   . . . is it really necessary to **slog halfway round the world** to watch seabirds killing one another?

In my data there are 142 instances of JOURNEY + *around the world* (and *around the world* + JOURNEY) and 139 instances of JOURNEY + *round the world* (and *round the world* + JOURNEY). This suggests that once again the two expressions share the same priming but differ in the strength of that priming. Of the two, *round the world* is much more strongly primed, with 41 per cent of all instances of *round the world* conforming to this semantic association as opposed to a lowly 8 per cent of instances of *around the world*. (The proportion of *round the world* would have been still higher, had I not disallowed the 111 instances of *Whitbread Round The World Race*.) The difference between the synonymous expressions suggests an explanation as to why *round the world* occurs with *80 days* twice as often as does *around the world*, despite the title of Jules Verne's book in English. Nevertheless, in raw figures there are still slightly more instances with *around the world*.

A minor semantic association that appears to belong only to *round the world* is that of MEASUREMENT, as in:

> 21 Removing and disposing of the tape later was itself a problem, incidentally, since it is calculated that the Israelis bought enough to go seven times *round the world*.

This occurs six times (as opposed to once with *around the world*). Not important in itself, perhaps, but in conjunction with the previous semantic association and the collocations of SAIL and TRAVEL it points to a significant tendency that separates the otherwise synonymous expressions. *Round the world* is more literal with 171 occurrences (51 per cent) referring to the act of circling the globe, as opposed to 187 uses (10 per cent) of *around the world*.

What we are really looking at with these data is a partial limitation on the uses of *round the world*. The expressions are synonymous as regards circling the globe and occur with almost exactly the same frequency. But *around the world* is clearly being used extensively in other ways. The most obvious of these is contexts where *around the world* means something like 'all over the world', there being no suggestion of direction, ordering or movement. Examples are:

> 22 Inside their house is filled with curios from *around the world*.
> 23 Fuji Garuji had caused the building of 20 pagodas *around the world*, often located in places of great historical significance and beauty.

There are 1,611 instances of *around the world* with this looser sense, compared with 165 instances of *round the world*. So *around the world* is ten times more likely than *round the world* to be chosen to express the scale, scope or spread of a phenomenon. Crudely, if you are being literal, you are likely to be primed to go for *round*; if you're being vague, your priming is probably to go for *around*. But – and this needs underlining – we are talking about biases, we are **not** talking about either expression monopolising a sense.

The pattern, perhaps predictably in the light of our other comparisons in this chapter, is the same for the characteristic colligations of the two prepositional phrases. In this context a number of features were examined. In the first place I looked at the behaviour of both word sequences as postmodification of a noun head. Where it was unclear whether the word sequence was postmodifying or not, I erred on the side of caution and included the case in my count whenever the postmodification alternative made sense, even if it seemed the less likely interpretation. (Of course, the existence of such an endemic ambiguity, which

Table 4.7 Distribution of markers of (in)definiteness between *round the world* and *around the world*

	round the world (336 instances)	around the world (1,798 instances)
Definiteness (excl. possessives)	7	51
Possessives	9	59

seems never to trouble writers and readers, suggests that the problem lies in the grammar we are using.) On the other hand, all cases of the common construction *there is/are x a/round the world* were treated as not postmodifying; they will be discussed separately below.

Looking then at the use of *round the world* and *around the world* as postmodification, we immediately find that there is a big difference between the two word sequences in terms of their likelihood of occurring as postmodification. Close to half (49 per cent) of all instances of *around the world* are postmodifying as opposed to just over a fifth (21 per cent) of all instances of *round the world*. It is *around the world*, in other words, that is primed to occur as a postmodifier.

Whichever word sequence is chosen, it is likely to occur with a plural noun head. Put the other way round, both word sequences seem to be primed to avoid singular noun heads, though the priming is again slightly stronger for *around the world*. Only 13 per cent are singular with *around the world*, as opposed to 21 per cent with *round the world*. The same pattern occurs with indefiniteness. Both word sequences typically occur in indefinite nominal groups. Again putting the point negatively, they seem both to be primed to avoid the definite article (see Table 4.7). On the basis of its crude frequency in the language, we might have expected *the* to have predominated but it is in fact much the rarer option for both word sequences; indeed possessives occur in each case as often as the definite article and demonstratives.

So far the evidence for seeing *around the world* and *round the world* as free variants or, alternatively, as clearly distinct like *consequence* and *result* is ambivalent. There are shared collocations, semantic associations and colligations, on the one hand; on the other, there are differences of weighting of priming and there is a cluster of collocations and an association that are effectively only associated with one of the expressions. The question, then, is: are there any colligations that clearly belong to one of the expressions and not to the other? The answer is that there is one such case.

The colligation that distinguishes the two expressions is the clearest evidence we have that they are not in free variation. The word sequence *round the world* occurs 29 times as a premodifier, as in:

24   . . . make you feel so guilty that you sign up as sponsor for a charity *round the world* sack race.

25   Students' *round the world* scam costs BT dear [headline]

26   . . . Ffyona Campbell, 27-year-old *round the world* walker who completed her 11-year, 19,586 mile trek on Saturday and now plans to raise a family.

Around the world occurs only once in such a grammatical role.

In conclusion, it would seem as if the synonymous word sequences we have been considering are primed similarly but distribute themselves differently across the lexical, semantic and grammatical terrain. Thus both expressions collocate with *halfway* and *markets*, but one of them is far more strongly primed than the other for such collocates. Both expressions can be used vaguely or to describe the circumference of the earth, but one is favoured for the first use and the other (proportionally) for the second. Both expressions can occur as postmodification or as premodification, but one occurs much more often as postmodification and the other is used almost exclusively when premodification is needed. The situation is similar therefore to the one we considered for *consequence* and *result*. The shared meaning means that there is overlap in the primings, but ultimately it is the difference in (the weighting of) the primings that justifies the existence of the alternatives. The morpheme *a-*, which is all that distinguishes the word sequences, is as significant a difference as any other that we have considered.

All the evidence in this chapter supports the view that primings are distinctive to the word. Tucker (1996) holds a similar position with respect to antonyms. He shows how antonymous items such as *like* and *dislike* share some structures (e.g. *I like/dislike dressing for dinner*) but, crucially, differ in others (e.g. *I like/ *dislike to dress for dinner*). Likewise, Krishnamurty (2002) shows that antonyms have quite distinct collocational profiles. The assumption in this book has of course been that what is primed is the word, not the meaning of the word, and while semantic sets may, through abstraction from parallel primings, be themselves primed, the discovery that semantic sets, whether or not they make use of synonymy, co-hyponymy or antonymy, share only a limited range of collocations, semantic associations and colligations is simply confirmatory of that original assumption.

In the light of the above discussion, we may hypothesise that synonyms differ in respect of the way they are primed for collocations, colligations, semantic associations and pragmatic associations and the differences in these primings represent differences in the uses to which we put our synonyms.

But if we accept that it is the word (or word sequence or syllable) that is primed, not the sense, a new question comes into view. All my discussion and examples have glossed over the fact that, for example, *consequence* can mean 'importance' as well as 'result' or that *reason* can mean 'logical faculty' as well as 'explanation'. We need to ask what happens with polysemous (or, more rarely, homonymous) items. Do the same primings apply, irrespective of the use to which a word is being put? And if they do not, how are they kept apart? That will be the subject of the next chapter.

5 Lexical priming and polysemy

Polysemy and definition

Sinclair (1987), commenting on the development of the *Collins COBUILD English Language Dictionary*, notes that each meaning of a word can be associated with a specific collocation or pattern. Much subsequent lexicographical practice has indeed been informed by this observation.

Sinclair's observation is positively formulated. The point he is making is that a distinctive colligational or collocational pattern indicates a separate use of the word. As formulated, though, it would be possible in principle for two polysemous uses of a word each to have their own distinctive patterns for, say, 30 per cent of the time. Such a distribution would be clear-cut grounds for a lexicographer to make allowance for the polysemy thereby demonstrated. It would also reflect itself in the characteristic priming of the language user, with each polysemous use being primed for the patterns in question with which it was associated. It would still, however, leave undescribed the 40 per cent of cases which fell into neither set of characteristic patterns. For these 40 per cent of cases, presumably ambiguity would be an ever-present possibility.

Experience suggests (and Sinclair's work elsewhere supports the view) that ambiguity in language in use (as opposed to decontextualised and fabricated examples) is a rarity. This suggests that Sinclair's claim can be couched contrastively, such that the patterns of one use of a polysemous word always distinguish it from those of the other uses of the word. We are, I want to suggest, primed to recognise these contrastive patterns and to reproduce them. More precisely, I shall argue in this chapter that the collocations, semantic associations and colligations a word is primed for will systematically differentiate its polysemous senses and that ambiguity (or humour) will always result from our use of a word in ways not in accordance with these primings. If this position convinces, the meanings of a word will have to be interpreted as the outcome of its primings, not the object of the primings.

The drinking problem hypotheses

In the film *Airplane*, we are told of a pilot who is no longer permitted to fly because he has a 'drinking problem'. The next shot shows him spilling a non-alcoholic drink all over himself; his problem is in fact that he misses his mouth when he tries to drink. The joke depends on the order of the words. If we had been told he had a 'problem drinking' it would have been sad rather than funny; on the other hand, if he had been described as having 'a problem with drinking' the joke would be back in place again. In other words, although the collocation between *drinking* and *problem* is the same in each case, there is only one grammatical combination that can mean that someone has a problem getting liquid into their mouth or throat. It is not, I hypothesise, an accident that on the one hand we often need to talk about alcoholism and have a number of ways of doing so and on the other rarely need to talk about the physiological disorder and have only one way of doing so. The more common meaning of alcoholism in effect drives the rarer meaning into a grammatical corner. This observation leads to the following hypotheses, which I somewhat whimsically have termed the 'drinking problem' hypotheses (Hoey 1997b, 2004b):

1 Where it can be shown that a common sense of a polysemous word is primed to favour certain collocations, semantic associations and/or colligations, the rarer sense of that word will be primed to avoid those collocations, semantic associations and colligations. The more common use of the word will make use of the collocations, semantic associations and colligations of the rarer word but, proportionally, less frequently.

2 Where two senses of a word are approximately as common as each other, they will both avoid each other's collocations, semantic associations and/or colligations.

3 Where either (1) or (2) do not apply, the effect will be humour, ambiguity (momentary or permanent), or a new meaning combining the two senses.

Drinking problem hypothesis 1 – the effect of the primings of a common sense on a rare sense: *consequence*

We begin by looking at hypothesis 1, and for this purpose I have taken two words that are polysemous but have one use that is far more common than the other(s). The first of these is that of *consequence* (discussed here for the last time, you will no doubt be relieved to learn) and the second is that of *reason*. The more common use of *consequence* occurs 91 per cent of the time in my data, meaning that the two uses of this polysemous word occur in a 10:1 ratio. The situation with *reason* is still more extreme, with the more common use accounting for 96 per cent of all occurrences of the word. The ratio of common to less common use of this particular word is therefore 24:1. This means that both words are appropriate for testing the first drinking problem hypothesis, which of course predicts that the sense of these polysemous words that respectively occurs only 9 or 4 per cent of the time will be primed to avoid the collocations, semantic associations and colligations associated with the much commoner sense.

Consequence *(= result) versus* consequence *(= importance)*

Consequence has two senses – 'result' and 'importance', as noted at the end of Chapter 4. To explore these, I examined 1,809 instances of *consequence* in total, drawn from the *Guardian*-dominated corpus used in the previous chapter. The 'importance' meaning is much the rarer, only occurring with certainty 169 times in 1,809 lines. (One line was ambiguous between the two senses and one was counted as an instance of the 'importance' sense, though it was possible to read it the other way.) Furthermore, the 'importance' sense occurs in only one regular grammatical structure of consequence (though a number of other structures occur on single occasions) and that is the one I have contrived to use in the first clause of this sentence. We will give the 'importance' use a little attention first.

The first colligational statement to make about *consequence* in its 'importance' sense is a negative one: there are next to no examples of it functioning as the noun head of a nominal group anywhere other than in a prepositional phrase. Only five examples occur in a non-prepositional phrase position, and three of these follow the verb HAVE, for example:

1   Booth's predicament would have little *consequence* had it not added a
     further molehill to the mountain of trouble and doubt established before.

All five instances of non-prepositional *consequence* (= importance) occur in Object function, which we saw in Chapter 3 was the function that *consequence* (= result) avoided. There are therefore, self-evidently, no instances of *consequence* (= importance) functioning as noun head in a nominal group serving as Subject in a clause. What this actually means is that we never formulate our clauses with *consequence* (= importance) as their topic. This is a fact about the word, not about the word's sense. The word's closest synonym, *importance,* occurs quite naturally as topic. In the first 100 instances of the word *importance* extracted from my corpus, 15 occur as head of a nominal group functioning as Subject in the clause.

A second colligational fact about *consequence* (= importance) is that it seems never to occur with a specific deictic. I can only attest one instance in my data and that is the ambiguous case already mentioned. This occurs in an article about a legal dispute over pensions with the European Union and quotes the word sequence 'the consequence thereof for other benefits' from a Treaty of Rome directive. Without access to the original it is impossible to determine whether

Table 5.1 Items functioning as non-specific deictics (adapted from Halliday 1994: 182)

		Singular		*Unmarked*
Total	Positive	*each every*		
	Negative		*neither (not either)*	**no (not any)**
Partial	Selective	*one another*	*either*	**some any**
	Non-selective	*a(n)*		

'effect' or 'importance' is meant – neither fits entirely comfortably. I will return to this example at the end of my discussion of *consequence*.

Consequence (= importance) does occur with non-specific deictics, but only with a restricted subset of them. In the language taken as a whole the full range of choices available to the user are as shown in Table 5.1.

Out of this range of possibilities, *consequence* (= importance) occurs quite frequently with all the unmarked non-specific deictics (i.e. the final column, emboldened in the table) and, apart from just two examples of co-occurrence with *a*, with none of the others. We saw in Chapter 3 that *consequence* (= result), by contrast, avoids *any*; it also avoids *some* and *no*. This is an example of the drinking problem hypotheses in operation, since, as we saw, *consequence* avoids combination with *any* despite its colligational preference for indefiniteness. The reason for this, we can now see, would appear to be that the other sense of *consequence*, where it means 'importance', has a collocational preference for occurring with *any*. This turns out to be part of a systematic pattern of distinguishing preferences and avoidance for the two senses of *consequence*.

It is worth stepping aside from our argument for a moment to make two points. Firstly, the possibility of making a colligational statement of the kind we have just been observing also serves to provide cautious authentication of the grammatical categories/classification used in its formulation. Thus in this instance Halliday's apparently complex grammatical classification tidies up the contrast between the two senses of *consequence* and will be seen to do the same for *reason* below. It does not however demonstrate that such categories have a prior or independent status from the colligations that they enable us to report. Indeed it will be argued in the next chapter that all grammatical systems bring together, and generalise out of, a multitude of colligational likelihoods, in the same way that colligational statements bring together and abstract from collocational ones.

The second aside I want to make at this juncture is a point made already in Chapter 3 but worthy of reiteration – namely that that colligational primings are not grammatical rules, whatever importance they may be proved to have in the formulation and validation of such rules. This means that there is no such thing as a counterexample to a colligational statement. It is quite possible to encounter a sentence that is an exception to one or more colligational primings. For example, we saw above that *consequence* (= importance) rarely occurs other than as part of a prepositional group (five cases out of 169 examples) and that when it does it occurs with HAVE on three out of five occasions. We also noted that it virtually never occurs with any deictic other than unmarked ones (two cases out of 169 examples). Yet here is a sentence, not conspicuously unnatural, that manages to use *consequence* (= importance) as head of a nominal group, with a singular deictic and following a verb other than HAVE, in other words running contrary to all but one of my colligational claims:

2   They long to do something, to run a town, to enjoy a decent small *consequence*.

Importantly, though, it still conforms to one colligational priming – the one that says that if it occurs outside a prepositional phrase it will occur as Object.

Turning now to a pragmatic association of *consequence* (= importance), we find that if it is used with *of* to postmodify another noun, which happens 55 per cent of the time (93 instances), it may be used to affirm or deny the importance of the event or entity referred to in the clause, but it is much more likely to be denying it:

3   Some were people of **no great** *consequence*.
4   Shareholders have a right to expect that **nothing** of *consequence* is missing from the prospectus.
5   This means there will be **only one** league match of *consequence* this weekend.

Denial of importance is, in fact, three times as common as affirmation. The most common way in which importance is denied is through the inclusion of a negative unmarked deictic (as in 3 above) or a negative noun head (as in 4). Negativity is also sometimes attached to the verb:

6   Joseph B. Vasquez's Hangin' With The Homeboys (Cannons, Haymarket etc., 15) **hardly** takes itself seriously enough to be considered a black movie of great *consequence*.

A more indirect expression of denial takes the form of the use of the deictic *any*, for example:

7   . . . one of the few remaining corners of **any** *consequence* to be found on the race tracks of the world.

Here the implication is that almost all other corners are of no importance.

This denial is even more pronounced when *of consequence* is used as an Adjunct, which it is in 64 cases in my data. Only 9 of these affirm importance. Almost all of the rest deny it within the prepositional phrase, for example:

8   The minister's cut off date, it adds, is of **little** *consequence*.
9   The money she paid was of **no great** *consequence*.
10   But my foibles are of **no** *consequence*.

What all this means is that *consequence* (= importance) is primed pragmatically for denial, this occurring in the data examined 79 per cent of the time. There are however no instances in my data of *consequence* (= result) being denied. It is perhaps worth adding that there is no obvious reason why this should be so. After all, the related word *reason*, for example, is, as we have seen, frequently denied: *That's not the reason why . . .* And *result*, which we have discussed as a near-synonym of *consequence*, can be denied (though it is admittedly not a common option):

11   This Japanese achievement is not the *result* of working longer hours.

This pragmatic association links up interestingly with two of the colligational primings of *consequence* (= importance). The first of these is that *consequence* (= importance) is primed never to occur as Subject (and therefore of course it never occurs as Theme). The second is that, when used as Adjunct (i.e. not as postmodification to some other noun), the phrase *of consequence* is likewise primed to avoid Theme position, at least in newspaper English. There are in fact only five instances of this use of the phrase in Theme position in the whole of my data (and one of these is genuinely ambiguous between the two uses of *consequence*, as I shall show at the end of this section). The explanation for both colligational phenomena may lie in the fact that, as an implication of the pragmatic association with denial, *consequence* (= importance) is much more likely to be used to describe the unimportance of something than its importance.

When *of consequence* is used as postmodification, the incidence of occurrence in Theme increases but is still fairly low, only occurring there a quarter of the time. In Hoey (1996), on the basis of a much smaller set of data, randomly selected from the Bank of English, I hypothesised that the reason why *of consequence* did not occur in Theme as Adjunct was that we rarely need to thematise the unimportance of something (whereas the importance of something is frequently thematised). It is therefore interesting to note that, of the ten positive Adjuncts found in the larger data set, half are thematised, for example:

12   Of more *consequence* may be two proposals aimed at giving spectators a full ration.

13   Of even greater *consequence*, the participation of adolescents in society
was of special interest in the latter part of the war.

Given that none of the 55 negative cases are thematised, the results suggest that
this explanation holds water. But of course the other explanation, and the one
in focus here, is that this is an instance of the operation of drinking problem
hypothesis 2 (see p. 82). According to this hypothesis the reason *consequence*
(= importance) avoids thematised position may be to avoid potential confusion
with *consequence* (= result), which we have seen occurs frequently in Theme.

A summary of the priming differences between consequence (= importance) and consequence (= result)

Table 5.2 couples what we have learnt about *consequence* (= importance) with
what we learnt in previous chapters about *consequence* (= result), and shows that
on a whole range of characteristic primings, the two uses of *consequence* systematically differ, thereby supporting the first drinking problem hypothesis. On the
basis of the evidence summarised in Table 5.2 it would be safe to argue that
Guardian readers are likely to be receptively primed in such a way as to distinguish
the two senses along the lines suggested. They may of course not distinguish the
two senses productively this way. For many users of the language the productive
priming of *consequence* (= importance) will simply be that it collocates in prepositional phrases with *of*; the other features may not occur in their primings. Indeed
for some users there may be no contrast in primings at all, for the simple reason
that either *consequence* (= importance) does not occur in their speech, being
reserved only for the reception of the writing of others, or it is not included in
their vocabulary, either productively or receptively. This will not however prevent them from avoiding the collocations, semantic associations and colligations
of *consequence* (= importance) when using *consequence* (= result), because all the

Table 5.2 The contrasting collocations, semantic associations, pragmatic associations,
colligations and textual colligations of the two uses of *consequence*

	consequence (= result)	*consequence* (= importance)
Collocation with *any*	−	+
Collocation with *of*	−	+
Colligation with subject and complement	Positive	Negative
Semantic association with LOGIC	+	−
Semantic association with NEGATIVE EVALUATION	+	−
Pragmatic association with DENIAL	−	+
Textual colligation with theme	Positive	Negative

instances they will have read (or heard) of *consequence* (= result) will have themselves avoided such features.

Drinking problem hypothesis 1 – the effect of the primings of a common sense on rare senses: *reason*

It may be felt that I chose myself an easy option with *consequence*. After all, it is overwhelmingly used only with *of* and it is quite possible that for many users of the language this is its one and only priming. I therefore now turn to another polysemous item – *reason*. This word has a number of senses. The first and much the most common sense is the one considered in the last chapter when we looked at the different postmodifying options available for *reason* and the primings that each nested combination had. The other senses are various but two dominate – 'logic' and 'rationality' – illustrated by the following two sentences (both authentic, though they look fabricated!):

14 When they're older, you can use *reason*.
15 His ego has finally taken over his *reason*.

Between them, *reason* (= logic), *reason* (= rationality) and an assortment of idiomatic uses account for 703 occurrences of *reason* in my data, just over 5 per cent of the 13,556 instances of *reason* I examined. All the remainder, needless to say, apart from 48 instances of reason as a verb, were cases of *reason* (= cause). According to the first drinking problem hypothesis, the rarer senses of *reason* should avoid the primings of the common sense. Since all the rarer senses have to avoid the same collocations, colligations, and semantic and pragmatic associations, I have for the time being treated these senses together.

Some key primings of reason (= cause)

In this section, we will look at some of the characteristic primings of *reason* (= cause). From these we will generate a series of possible primings that we would expect *reason* (= rationality, logic) to avoid.

   The first set of such primings to be considered relate to the use of *reason* (= cause) as head noun in a nominal group functioning as Subject. The choice of Subject in itself is about average for nouns. This therefore is not a priming special to *reason* (= cause), though it is still a priming, for reasons that will be discussed in Chapter 8. Once the Subject has been selected, however, a number of strong primings come into operation. These are found in Figure 5.1 which provides a great deal of information about the way that primings shape and, to some extent, restrict the choices we make when we use *reason* (= cause). However, my intention here is to focus on the effects that these primings have on *reason* (= rationality,

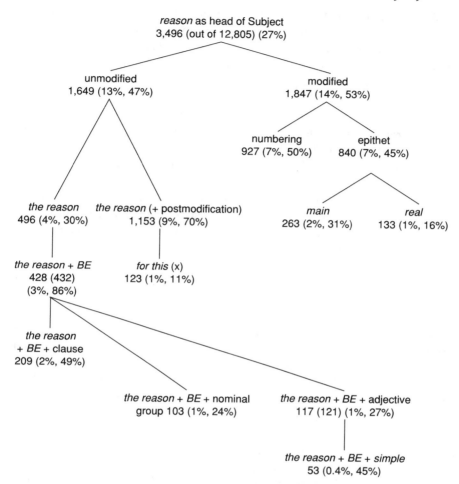

Figure 5.1 Clause patterns associated with *reason* (= cause) as head of a nominal group in Subject function

logic). A number of key primings of *reason* (= cause) are apparent from our analysis. In the first place, we note that *the* triggers a range of further primings. Our first point of comparison must therefore be with regard to the deictics:

(a) On the basis of the drinking problem hypothesis, it is predicted that *reason* (= rational faculty, logic) will avoid *the* in any circumstance where the further primings of *reason* (= cause) might be expected.

Secondly I note that *reason* is often thematised. In addition to the 3,496 cases in the figure, a further 994 prepositional phrase constructions are thematised, making *reason* Theme 35 per cent of the time. Although this is not an exceptional proportion, it indicates that *reason* (= cause) has no aversion to Theme and may indeed be weakly primed for occurrence in Theme. Given the absolute frequency of *reason* (= cause) in my newspaper data, this means that it occurs with this textual function a great number of times.

> (b) On the basis of the drinking problem hypothesis it is predicted that *reason* (= rationality, logic) will have an aversion to Theme or occur in Theme under distinctly different conditions, i.e. not with *the* or with any of the prepositions associated with *reason* (= cause).

Thirdly, I draw attention to the priming of *reason* (= cause) for combinations with BE. As already noted, the diagram understates the frequency of these, but even as it stands, it is clear that we need to look at the way *reason* (= rationality, logic) combines with BE (or otherwise).

> (c) On the basis of the drinking problem hypothesis it is predicted that *reason* (= rationality, logic) will avoid Subject with BE.

We need now to look at the patterns that are associated with the use of *reason* (= cause) as Complement. In my data there are 2,114 instances of *reason* (= cause) as the head of a nominal group functioning as Object but there are 3,620 cases of its occurring as head of a nominal group in Complement function. While these figures do not suggest any aversion to Object, they certainly support the view that, in the *Guardian*, *reason* is strongly primed for Complement function, and the vast majority of these occur with BE. As with the Subject, once the function of Complement has been selected, further primings come into view (see Figure 5.2). The figures for *which* as Subject do not discriminate between relative clause and question use. The figures for *that* as Subject, interestingly, include only five instances of the relative clause use.

It would appear that *reason* (= cause) in Complement function strongly favours *there* and pronouns (apart from the personal pronouns *she, he, I, you* and *they*, of which there are only 38 in my data):

> (d) On the basis of the drinking problem hypothesis, it is predicted that *reason* (= rationality, logic) will avoid the PRONOUN/*there* + BE + *reason* structure. We would expect that the pronouns *this* and *that* would be particularly avoided.

We also note the strong association with denial with *there*, which both contributes to and reflects the association of Complement with denial noted in the previous chapter. The drinking problem hypothesis would accordingly lead us to

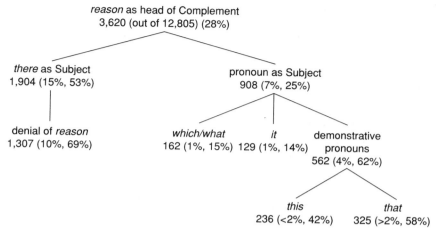

Figure 5.2 Some key primings of *reason* (= cause) functioning as Complement

predict that *reason* (= rationality, logic) will avoid co-occurrence with denial. Two of the most common forms of denial with *there* and *reason* (= cause) take the forms *there is/was no reason* and *there isn't/wasn't any reason*:

(e)   On the basis of the drinking problem hypothesis, it is predicted that *reason* (= rationality, logic) will not co-occur with the unspecific deictics *no* and *any*.

Having examined *reason* (= cause) functioning as (part of) Subject and Complement, we now turn to consider the primings associated with another of its colligations, namely its association with prepositional phrases. Table 5.3 shows the distribution of *reason* (= cause) across the range of prepositions. The figures are for all prepositional phrases in which *reason* is head of the nominal group

Table 5.3 Occurrences of prepositions preceding nominal groups with *reason* (= cause) as head

about	13	*on*	17
as	305	*over*	2
at	6	*than*	3
by	88	*to*	29
for	2,398	*with*	167
into	2	*without*	85
of	54		

preceded by the preposition. No care has been taken to eliminate the effects of verb choice (e.g. the effect of *turned* on *turned it into a reason for* . . .), since such effects are largely overridden by the quantity of data considered.

As can be seen, the prepositions it is particularly primed to occur with are *for* and *as*. Examples of the uses of *reason* (= cause) with *for* and *as* are the following:

16 The first 'political' Chancellor for ages; and hailed by political pundits, on appointment, for precisely that broad brush *reason*.

17 For the same *reason*, all signs to Belgrade have been blotted out.

18 For this *reason*, the backers need to make the first approach.

19 However, broken blood vessels were given as the *reason* for his disappointing performance.

20 But when things go wrong, commentators who have nothing more constructive to offer pick on T-shirts and stubble chins as a *reason*.

These data would lead us therefore to expect *reason* (= rationality, logic) to avoid such prepositions.

(f) On the basis of the drinking problem hypothesis, it is predicted that *reason* (= rationality, logic) will avoid occurring after *for* and *as*.

In subsequent sections we will test each of these hypotheses (though, for reasons of clarity of exposition, I will take prediction (e) out of order).

Prediction (a): reason, the *and the other specific deictics*

We predicted above that *reason* (= rationality, logic) would avoid co-occurrence with *the*. Given, however, that the deictics proved a fruitful source of comparison between the two senses of *consequence*, it makes sense to broaden our comparison of the two senses of *reason* to see how they compare across all the specific deictics. Table 5.4 presents the frequency of occurrences of *reason* (= cause) with the different specific deictics available for combination with it.

Table 5.4 A count of the instances of *reason* (= cause) occurring with the different specific deictics (classification adapted from Halliday 1994: 181)

	Determinative	Interrogative
Demonstrative	*this* 426 *that* 152 *the* 4,503	*which(ever)* 4 *what(ever)* 123
Possessive	*my* 32 *your* 7 *our* 7 *his* 45 *her* 12 *its* 8 *their* 31 *one's* 1 *X's* 21	*whose(ver)* 4

Table 5.5 A count of the instances of *reason* (= rationality, logic) occurring with the different specific deictics (classification adapted from Halliday 1994: 181)

	Determinative	Interrogative
Demonstrative	*this* 0 *that* 0 *the* 4	*which(ever)* 0 *what(ever)* 0
Possessive	*my* 7 *your* 1 *our* 0 *his* 10 *her* 1	*whose(ver)* 1
	its 3 *their* 9 *one's* 1 *X's* 1	

Interpreting these statistics is not as straightforward as it might seem since all the deictics are common words in the language. For the moment we will simply note that *reason* (= cause) appears to be colligationally primed in the *Guardian* with demonstrative determinatives; 39 per cent of all instances of *reason* (= cause) occur with one of them (usually *the*).

If we now compare the distribution of instances of *reason* (= rationality, logic) across the same set of grammatical possibilities, we find almost the mirror opposite of the distribution found for *reason* (= cause) (see Table 5.5). It will be immediately noticed that whereas *reason* (= cause) had an apparent positive priming for demonstrative determinatives, *reason* (= rationality, logic) occurs hardly at all in such a context. Only four instances of *reason* (= rationality, logic), constituting a tiny 0.6 per cent of all such instances, occur with *the* and there are no instances at all with the other two demonstrative determinatives. Prediction (a) has therefore been fully confirmed.

It might be argued that this is because the meaning of *reason* does not permit such choices. However, *imagination*, with which *reason* (= rationality, logic) is often coupled, occurs quite comfortably with *the*. The following example from my data is a prime piece of evidence in support of my position:

21 Natural selection enriches and disciplines the imagination by *the reason-ing faculty*.

Apart from illustrating *imagination* with *the*, it shows a periphrastic expression (*the reasoning faculty*) that seems to have been used with no other purpose than to avoid invading the territory of *reason* (= cause). It also shows that there is sometimes a need to use the definite article with the rarer sense of *reason*.

Broadly speaking, then, we have evidence that where *reason* (= cause) is characteristically positively primed for a colligation with a class of specific deictics, we have avoidance by *reason* (= rationality, logic) of that class. With this in mind, it is productive to look at the four exceptions in Table 5.5, where the priming of *reason* (= rationality, logic) to avoid the definite article was overridden. After all, these represent a challenge to prediction (a), albeit not a powerful one:

22   In the age of the New Man, the New Sense, the New *Reason*, a return to decent values, I was a social leper, a cultural dinosaur, a sex junkie . . .

23   Instead of being equally shared between its two rulers, the *Reason* and the Imagination, it falls alternately under the sole and absolute dominion of each.

24   And by conscripting the unconscious, magnetizers claimed they could restore those parts that the conscious *Reason* or Will wouldn't reach.

25   This name led me to wonder whether the plant which Shakespeare knew by this name ('The insane root which takes the *reason* prisoner') was this common hedgerow native . . .

Let us deal with the quotation from Shakespeare first. Two explanations offer themselves. The first is that there has been a drift in the primings associated with *reason* (= rationality, logic) over the centuries; colligation and collocation can be presumed to be subject to the same possibilities of change as grammar and lexis have traditionally been recognised to be. The other is that that Shakespeare, known to be highly creative with other aspects of the language, is here being so with colligation and collocation. Preliminary discussions with linguists holding medieval corpora suggests that the latter may be the better explanation.

Turning now to the other three instances, one of the first things of note is that they show *reason* (= rationality, logic) with a capital letter. There are 31 instances of *reason* (= rationality, logic) in my data with a capital letter, excluding those cases where it is part of a title or the initial word in a sentence or headline. This means that over 4 per cent of uses of *reason* in its rarer senses are capitalized, a huge proportion compared with most words (other than names). This in turn means that it is primed among *Guardian* writers for capitalisation and this priming allows it to override the need to avoid *the*. There is no equivalent tendency for *reason* (= cause) to be capitalised. If we discard a handful of cases where the first couple of words of an article have been capitalised, titles and a handful of sentence-initial cases, there are only nine instances of *reason* (= cause) that are capitalised in my corpus – less than 0.1 per cent of cases. This is incidentally a good example of a priming that cannot be assumed to belong to all users of the language, and of course it is only possible in written genres.

The other characteristic that the first three instances share is that they all involve coordination or listing. This turns out to be a highly characteristic feature of *reason* (= rationality, logic). Re-examination of the full set of data for *reason* (= logic, logical faculty) shows this to be an important priming in my data. Table 5.6 shows the various patterns of coupling with other nouns that were found featuring *reason* (= rationality, logic), together with their absolute frequency in my data and the percentage of instances of *reason* (= rationality, logic) that occur in each pattern. It shows that over a third of instances of *reason*

Table 5.6 Patterns of coordination and listing associated with *reason* (= rationality, logic)

h and h	e.g. *I always put my faith in* **reason and kindness**	155	22%
h (n)or h	e.g. *He does not believe in freedom of will, the effectiveness of his literary works, in* **reason or revolution**	35	5%
h over h	e.g. *The Association of Metropolitan Authorities said the new inspection system was a 'triumph of* **political dogma over reason***'*	12	<2%
h (rather) than h	e.g. *This sound account of his preferences — for the original textures of a church, for poetry that succeeded when he responded to* **instinct rather than reason**, *for endlessly alive chintzes, and for proto-Socialism — has been updated*	10	>1%
h, h, h	e.g. **Clarity, elegance, reason, perfectionism**: *these, as John Willett has reminded us, were the guiding principles of Brecht's theatre*	9	>1%
hq and hq	e.g. *Here was a subject in which all her obsessions met:* **the nature of faith and the mechanics of reason**, *the darkness of enlightenment, the old debate of nature—nurture given flesh, the cruelty of certainty*	6	<1%
Other patterns	e.g. *She uses* **reason as well as power** *to achieve her objectives*	19	3%
		241	**35%**

(= rationality, logic) occur in some kind of coupling or listing structure. The table shows that *reason* (= rationality, logic) is primed in the *Guardian* and elsewhere to be coupled with other abstract nouns. (Indeed, as four of the examples indicate, the coupling may occur inside larger lists.) This is not reflected in the data for *reason* (= cause). Indeed I could find no instances of its occurring at all (though with 12,805 instances it is not possible to be categorical, even after a slow and careful inspection). We will see below that this is not the only case where usage of the more common sense appears to be affected by the characteristic primings of the rarer sense.

Prediction (e): reason, no, any *and the other unspecific deictics*

Encouraged by the results reported in the previous section, I am choosing to go out of order in terms of our earlier predictions and we therefore turn immediately to the distribution of unspecific deictics across the senses of *reason*, two of

Table 5.7 A count of the instances of *reason* (= cause) occurring with unspecific deictics (classification adapted from Halliday 1994: 182)

		Singular		*Unmarked*
Total	Positive	each 1 *every* 281		
	Negative		*neither* 1 *not either* 0	*no* 2,311 *not any* 159
Partial	Selective	one 1,059	*either* 0	*some* 553 *any* 68
		another 277		
	Non-selective	*a(n)* 1,002		

Table 5.8 A count of the instances of *reason* (= rationality, logic) occurring with unspecific deictics (classification adapted from Halliday 1994: 182)

		Singular		*Unmarked*
Total	Positive	each 0 *every* 0		
	Negative		*neither* 3 *not either* 0 *nor* 1	*no* 4 *not any* 0
Partial	Selective	one 0 *another* 0	*either* 0	*some* 0 *any* 3
	Non-selective	*a(n)* 0		

which – *no* and *any* – were predicted to differentiate the common sense from the rarer sense(s). Table 5.7 shows the frequency of occurrence of *reason* (= cause) with the range of possibilities identified by Halliday (1994). The table shows strong priming for unmarked and partial unspecific deictics (with the exception of the *either* set) and much weaker priming for total positive unspecific deictics. In addition to our earlier prediction, we might expect, on the basis of our consideration of the specific deictics, that *reason* (= rationality, logic) will avoid the primed areas but possibly occur with *either* or *neither*. Halliday does not include *or* and *nor* in his table, presumably because they are coordinators. In the counts that follow, it is therefore assumed that an instance of *reason* preceded by either of these items partakes of the deixis attached to the noun with which it is coordinated. (As it happens, one of the occurrences uses *nor* in place of *neither* – see example 33, p. 98 – so this instance is included in my count.)

As Table 5.8 shows, *reason* (= rationality, logic) avoids all but a tiny handful of the unspecific deictics. Once again, then, *reason* (= rationality, logic) is seen to avoid the primings of its bigger neighbour. There are just four occurrences with *no*, three with *neither,* one with *nor* and three with *any*.

It might seem that the explanation this time lies simply in the fact that *reason* (= rationality, logic) is an uncountable noun and therefore has no need to occur with unspecific deictics such as *a* and *one*, but that is to look down the telescope

Table 5.9 A comparison of *reason* (= rationality, logic) with the nouns with which it is coupled in terms of their ability to appear in the plural or with an unspecific deictic

Reason and kindness	. . . one still hears stories of kindnesses to students	. . . it would be a kindness to draw a veil over them
Reason or revolution	. . . there were no other socialist revolutions	There will be a revolution by the big clubs
Dogma over reason	Gone are the old certitudes and dogmas of class	PRP is nothing more than a dogma . . .
Instinct rather than reason	These instincts don't die immediately with the child . . .	'There may be an instinct which says "I want to go hunter-gathering over the hills"' he said
Clarity, elegance, reason, perfectionism	Such clarities appear noticeably absent in 1991	Geography seems to lend it a clarity and objectivity it does not possess
	He was suddenly a warrior, entitled to bear the weapons of history and to display their deadly elegances	She has an elegance, a simplicity, a purity of character
		A perfectionism never before evident in your life now afflicts you
The nature of faith and the mechanics of reason	Must these faiths inevitably be in conflict with one another?	The enemy that matters is consumerism, a faith in itself, the green equivalent of Lucifer
Reason as well as power	Just as bad is an uncontrolled judiciary with unlimited powers	Central Office will disband the association, a power some regard as legally questionable

the wrong way. It is, I would argue, an uncountable noun **because** it has to avoid the primings of *reason* (= cause). Consider for a moment the list of examples given in Table 5.6 (all drawn, of course, from my data). If we examine the nouns with which *reason* is coupled on each occasion, we find that they can almost all occur in the plural or with an indefinite article. To demonstrate this, I repeat the examples in Table 5.9 in the first column and in the second and third columns I provide an example of the noun with which it is coupled being used in the plural and with *a(n)* respectively. I have tried as far as feasible to illustrate the plural or indefinite use with an instance close in meaning to that used in coordination with *reason*.

A glance at the table shows that the only word coupled with *reason* that is not attested in my data as having both plural and indefinite article uses is *perfectionism*. While intuition suggests that it is more than probable that a much larger corpus would still have thrown up no plural uses, it is perhaps worth saying that the word only occurs 38 times in the 100 million words of my data and occurs with the indefinite article even so. All the other nouns have both plural and indefinite uses. Our word *reason* is the exception therefore in having neither, and it is my argument that this is a direct consequence of the need to keep its colligations apart from those of *reason* (= cause).

The general picture, then, is that *reason* (= rationality, logic) avoids unspecific deictics and *reason* (= cause) favours them (apart from those associated with alternatives), and the non-count nature of the former is argued to be a consequence of this situation and not the explanation. But, as before, there are a handful of exceptions – four occurrences of *reason* (= rationality, logic) with *no,* four with *neither/nor* and three with *any.* Let us look at these challenges to the drinking problem hypothesis.

We can quickly dismiss the instances with *no* (and, as it happens, *neither*); these are listed below, along with the solitary example with *nor*:

26 There is *no* rhyme or *reason* here.
27 There was *no* rhyme or *reason* to it.
28 Waiting lists vary greatly, with *no* apparent rhyme or *reason* . . .
29 Sadly there is *no* rhyme nor *reason* in simple boxing terms to the diatribe.
30 . . . there is *neither* rhyme nor *reason* about the numbering.
31 It is just that they seem to be doled out with *neither* rhyme nor *reason.*
32 *Neither* rhyme nor *reason* in contemporary poetry [the title to an article].
33 '*nor* wit nor *reason* can my passion hide'.

All of them, including, perhaps disappointingly, the instances of *neither*, are versions of a familiar idiom, and *reason*, though it retains some of its meaning of 'logic', is not functioning in any way independently of the other elements of the wording. Since the idiom also accounts for the instances with *neither*, we do not need to adduce the drinking problem hypothesis to account for the occurrences of *reason* (= rationality, logic) with *neither* when *reason* (= cause) avoids it. Sinclair (1996, 2004) uses such examples to argue for working with lexical items (which may be many words long), rather than with words, a position we shall return to in Chapter 8.

We are left once again with a quotation from Shakespeare (from *Twelfth Night*). This time, his use needs no special pleading in that it of course complies with the rarer *reason*'s priming for coupling (as, in fossilised form, does *rhyme or reason*).

The three occurrences with *any* are more interesting:

34 If there is *any* intelligence or *reason*, Red Star will play in Zagreb . . .
35 And along with their arrogance, their fees swelled beyond *any reason.*
36 There is also considerable speculation as to whether the Iraqi leader shows *any reason* at all.

Example 34 illustrates yet again the coupling tendency of *reason* (= rationality, logic), though a residual ambiguity persists for this reader. Examples 35 and 36, however, are genuinely ambiguous and therefore support the third drinking problem hypothesis.

Example 35 is, I think, irresolvably ambiguous in that it can mean in context two equally justifiable things. The ambiguity of example 36 can be resolved , but it is only when it is set in its fuller context that it becomes unambiguous:

> 37   For George Bush to put the problems down to 'the misguided actions
> of one man' ignores both the facts and the roots of wider feelings.
> However, the focus on Saddam does not stop at substituting his per-
> sonal reasoning for the collective experience of Arab peoples. There is
> also considerable speculation as to whether the Iraqi leader shows *any*
> *reason* at all. From the time Kuwait was invaded the sanity of Saddam
> began to be questioned. At first it was unclear whether the invective
> was meant metaphorically or literally . . .
>
>   (© Guardian Newspapers Limited 1991)

I will examine these cases in the final section of this chapter when I look at all the ambiguous cases together that have been thrown up by the analysis.

Prediction (b): reason, *possessive deictics and Theme*

The best place to start an exploration of prediction (b), which was that *reason* (= rationality, logic) would avoid serving as Theme except under conditions that were clearly distinct from those of *reason* (= cause), would seem to be with regard to an area where the rarer sense(s) would seem to be uninhibited by the behaviour of the commoner sense. Tables 5.3 and 5.4 showed one such area where *reason* (= rationality, logic) holds its own against its powerful neighbour, and that is in respect of its combination with the possessives. Just under 5 per cent of instances occur with a possessive, which, as a proportion of the total number of instances, is a higher proportion than that achieved by *reason* (= cause) (just over 1 per cent). Even here, though, closer inspection shows that *reason* (= cause) has the whip hand, and Theme is, as predicted, the place where this is demon-strated. It is instructive to look at the distribution of possessives for the different senses of *reason* (see Table 5.10). (For the purposes of calculation, identification of first position takes no account of subordinators or coordinators nor of auxilia-ries in interrogatives.)

As can be seen, *reason* (= rationality, logic) is typically primed to avoid combining with a possessive determinative in sentence-initial position, i.e. as part of Theme. Not one case of POSSESSIVE DETERMINATIVE + *reason* (= rationality, logic) occurs in such a position. On the other hand, in this combination *reason* (= cause) appears to have no aversion to being sentence Theme.

Table 5.10 The distribution of possessive pronoun + *reason* across the sentence

	reason (= cause) 1st position in sentence	*reason* (= rationality, logic) 1st position in sentence	*reason* (= cause) Other positions	*reason* (= rationality, logic) Other positions
my	24	0	8	7
your	3	0	4	1
our	5	0	2	0
its	2	0	6	3
his	14	0	31	10
her	7	0	5	1
their	2	0	29	9

If one inspects the possessive combinations with respect to their grammatical function, one finds that POSSESSIVE DETERMINATIVE + *reason* (= cause) occurs frequently as Subject. Of the 57 thematised cases, 44 have this function. Furthermore, of the instances in non-sentence-initial position, 21 are also head of a nominal group functioning as Subject, where they serve as clausal Theme. This means that 46 per cent of instances of POSSESSIVE DETERMINATIVE + *reason* (= cause) are part of either sentence or clause Theme. By contrast only four (13 per cent) of the non-initial instances of *reason* (= rationality, logic) are (part of) Subject, and one of these is not the head of the nominal group in which it appears and is therefore immediately distinguished from *reason* (= cause). What, then, we have is evidence of the rare sense (or senses) of the word *reason* struggling to avoid encroaching on the Theme primings of the word's most common sense.

As with previous exceptions, it is instructive to examine the three remaining instances of *reason* (= rationality, logic) that defy the general pattern and occur as Theme for their clauses. They are:

38   I am distraught with you and my thoughts and *reason* are confused.
39   I do not want to be a dictator but my *reason* and conscience told me I had to submit the proposals.
40   Men, her *reason* told her, would be shocked.

Example 40 is an instance of *reason* (= rationality, logic) invading the colligational primings of *reason* (= cause). The presence of *told,* however, with which *reason* (= rationality, logic) collocates and with which *reason* (= cause) never occurs, counterbalances the effect of this. The other two make use again of the characteristic priming of the rarer sense for coupling with another abstract noun, and one of them also utilises the collocation with *told* just mentioned.

Table 5.11 A comparison of the frequency of co-occurrence of possessives with *reason* and *reasons*

Possessives with *reason* (= cause) (out of 12,805 instances)	*my* 32 *your* 7 *our* 7 *his* 45 *her* 12 *its* 8 *their* 31 *one's* 1 X's 21
Possessives with *reasons* (= causes) (out of 8,259 instances)	*my* 19 *your* 17 *our* 8 *his* 103 *her* 31 *its* 33 *their* 101 *one's* 0 X's 44

In other words, what we are seeing is that when *reason* (= rationality, logic) is used in an area where *reason* (= cause) is also used, the way that other primings of the former are used mark its occurrences out clearly, thereby eliminating any possibility of ambiguity. Furthermore, the commoner sense does not make as much use of deictics from that area as might be predicted on the basis of the frequency of the words in the language and the behaviour of the plural. As we have seen, the proportion of instances of *reason* (= cause) making use of the possessive is just over 1 per cent. That this is significantly lower than might have been expected is suggested by a comparison with the plural *reasons*. The word *reasons* is only used to mean 'causes', there appearing to be no instance of *reason* (= rationality, logic) in my data, and this means that there are no pressures on it with regard to the possessives. Table 5.11 shows the raw frequencies of possessives occurring with the singular *reason* and the plural *reasons*.

In total there are 356 instances of possessives occurring with *reasons* (amounting to a little over 4 per cent of cases) as opposed to 164 instances with *reason* (= cause). In other words, once *reason* (= rationality, logic) is removed from the equation, the frequency increases fourfold proportionally and falls in line with the proportion of instances occurring with the rarer sense(s), as we saw above. This further supports the claim made in the first drinking problem hypothesis that we make use of the common sense of the word in such a way as to avoid unnecessary conflict with the primings we have for the rare sense of the word.

Prediction (c): **reason** *and Subject with* BE

We have just seen that POSSESSIVE DETERMINATIVE + *reason* (= rationality, logic) avoids Subject function. Prediction (c) was that, given that *reason* (= cause) is primed to colligate as Subject with BE and the other equatives (SEEM, BECOME, GROW), there would be no instances of *reason* (= rationality, logic) + BE etc. where *reason* was the head of its own nominal group.

Investigation of my data revealed that out of the 703 instances of *reason* (= rationality, logic), just 10 challenge this prediction. We can therefore broadly confirm that the rarer sense of *reason* does indeed avoid combination with BE. The ten cases, however, represent a challenge, albeit not a large one, to the prediction and therefore need to be examined more closely, as we have done for previous sets of exceptions. One of these we have already seen in our consideration of prediction 2 – example 37 – and that needs no further discussion. The remaining nine instances are as follows:

41   Human *reason* is a fallible guide, they murmur . . .
42   But what comes across is the idea that *reason* is always dangerous . . .
43   If sweet *reason* and turning a blind eye are not enough and you feel you have to use some form of punishment, do so without excessive anger or physical force.
44   . . . Shaffer comprehends the revenge motive while suggesting that *reason* is valueless unless informed by feeling.
45   . . . nobody has ever suggested that *reason* is what gets things done in the Middle East.
46   '*Reason* is a political entity, and never more so than when its claim is to have transcended politics' [quotation from Stanley Fish].
47   Sadly, balance and *reason* have been rare on both sides.
48   Lust and *reason* are enemies.
49   'Beware of popular revolts when *reason* becomes helpless,' he said . . .

Three of these illustrate the coupling priming – 43, 47 and 48 – though 43 is untypical in having a coupling with a non-finite clause. This leaves six challenges to account for. Of these, two manifest characteristic collocations of *reason* (= rationality, logic). *Human* is a collocate of *reason* (= rationality, logic), the combination occurring in my data nine times (1 per cent of all occurrences), and *sweet* is a strong collocate, occurring 24 times with the rarer sense (3 per cent of all occurrences). Neither epithet occurs with *reason* (= cause) on any occasion.

We can eliminate one more of the challenges by reference to semantic association. The rarer sense(s) of *reason* can be shown to have a semantic association with EMOTION with 46 occurrences of the association occurring in my data. (This is incidentally an instance of a semantic association that is not syntactically tied.) Other examples are:

50   John Monie comes from that cerebral, calculating school of Australian coaching whose motto might be '*Reason* before Emotion'.
51   And it is true that the cult-minded people I've known as an adult mistrust their *reason* with a passion I find terrifying.
52   Jill Barton, of the Surrey Wildlife Trust, spends much of her life trying to reinstate *reason* into a county gone mad for roads.

This semantic association can be seen in example 44 (*feeling* of course being the EMOTION component), and, like the coupling and the collocates *told*, *human* and *sweet*, has the effect of counterbalancing the intrusion of *reason* (= rationality, logic) into the territory of *reason* (= cause).

We are finally left with three challenges to the prediction – examples 42, 46 and 49. Two of these are in quotation marks, which to some extent separates them from their immediate textual surroundings. Also, all three have of course no determiner, so they are in that respect in conformity with the characteristic priming for *reason* (= rationality, logic). Neither factor is sufficient to fully counterbalance the effects of choosing the *reason* (= rationality, logic) + BE etc. combination. (After all, *with good reason* and *by reason of* also lack a determiner and *reason* (= cause) can begin a quotation.) However, given the frequency of BE in the language, I would argue that three instances (0.1 per cent of the data) do not constitute a refutation of prediction (c).

Prediction (d): there/PRONOUN + BE + reason

The fourth prediction, made on the basis of the common primings of *reason* (= cause) in Complement function, was that the rarer sense(s) of *reason* would avoid the PRONOUN/*there* + BE + *reason* structure. This proves to be uncomplicatedly confirmed. There are only seven challenges to the prediction, and these are quickly distinguished from the uses associated with *reason* (= cause). Five have already been given as examples 21, 22, 24, 25 and 30 in our consideration of the occurrences of *reason* (= rationality, logic) with the deictics, and need no further discussion here. The remaining two challenges are:

53 Just two doors away, in Committee Room 9, there was more clarity and *reason* . . .
54 Fourth, they are anti-*reason*.

One is a coupling; the other a nonce word using *reason* as one of its components. The fourth prediction is accordingly confirmed.

Prediction (f): reason with for and as

Prediction (e) was of course handled out of sequence in order to treat the deictics together. We are therefore left with our sixth and final prediction that *reason* (= rationality, logic) will avoid being preceded by *for* and *as*. As far as *as* is concerned, the data for *reason* (= rationality, logic) are clear-cut – *reason* (= rationality, logic) does not occur with preceding *as*, not even with sentence subordinator *as*. Examination of the data with regard to *for*, however, reveals seven challenges to the prediction. Two of these are straightforwardly instances of coupling:

55 'It should also raise its voice for *reason* and dialogue in the face of the mounting intolerance and racism in our republic,' he said.

56 . . . he will have struck early for decisiveness and *reason* in policy making.

A further two are also instances of coupling, but in one case the coordination is with a word sequence rather than a single word and in the other the coupling takes one of the minority forms. In the latter case the presence of *for* is accounted for by the fact that the verb *substituting* is typically primed to collocate with *for*.

57 Applauded for his *reason* and willingness to compromise, Meyer was modernising ossified union structures . . .

58 The writer seeks to draw attention away from his lack of cogent argument by substituting ridicule for *reason*.

The remaining three, like 58, are explicable in terms of a competing collocational priming for *for* by a variety of words:

59 Dr Kohl took a tough line on trade union wage demands and called for *reason* among striking workers. [Collocation of *called* with *for*]

60 His image is of a character who stands for reason . . . [collocation of *stands* with *for*]

61 They can only hope that the doctors will eventually be grateful for cerebral sweet reason . . . [collocation of *grateful* with *for*]

The last of the above examples, of course, also features the characteristic collocation of *reason* (= rationality, logic) with *sweet*. We can therefore safely conclude that once again a prediction generated by the first drinking problem hypothesis has been confirmed.

More generally, we have found that all the predictions generated by drinking problem hypothesis 1 have been confirmed. It would seem to be the case that when polysemous words are primed in our minds, the rarer senses get primed in such a way as to ensure that their primings do not overlap with those of the most common sense.

Drinking problem hypothesis 2

We saw above that even where one sense of a word is overwhelmingly the most common, it still prefers proportionally to avoid the primings associated with the rarer senses; examples of this were the relative avoidance by *reason*

(= cause) of possessive pronouns and capitalisation. For this reason (to use a by now all too familiar expression), I do not intend to linger long on drinking problem hypothesis 2. Much of the detail of the argument would be of the same kind as already presented. I shall simply look, without consideration of exceptions or detailed statistics, at a word with two senses that are clearly distinct and approximately as common as each other in my data. The word I have chosen is *immunity*, defined in *Macmillan English Dictionary for Advanced Learners* as follows:

> **immunity 1.** [C/U] a situation in which someone is not affected by something such as a law because they have a special job or position: + **from** *immunity from prosecution* ◆ **grant sb immunity** *They would be granted immunity if they gave evidence in court.* →DIPLOMATIC IMMUNITY **2** [singular/U] the protection that someone's body gives them against a particular disease + **to** *It is possible to develop an immunity to many illnesses.*

The virtue of this polysemous word is that its separate senses are quite distinct (though not unconnected). There are therefore no problems in deciding which sense is intended in any instance. As we shall see in the next section, this is by no means always the case with polysemous senses.

There are 574 instances of 'legal' *immunity* and 102 of 'medical' *immunity* in my corpus, which is a better ratio than obtained for either *consequence* or *reason* but still leaves the 'legal' sense six times as common as the 'medical' sense. However, the figures mask the existence of a number of multi-word lexical items which do not require analysis. These are *public interest immunity certificate,* which occurs exactly 100 times, with *public immunity certificate* and *interest immunity certificate* accounting for another 62 cases between them. With these word sequences removed, the 'legal sense' drops to 412, leaving us with a ratio of very close to 4:1 in my data. Add to this the fact that the proportions are certainly distorted by the media's predilection for stories about political intrigue and we can feel comfortable that the spread permits investigation of the second drinking problem hypothesis.

Analysis of these data produces the set of contrasts shown in Tables 5.12, 5.13 and 5.14, which show the collocations, semantic associations and colligations of each sense compared with their (non-)occurrence in connection with the other sense.

Table 5.12 shows the collocations of the two senses. Lemmata are capitalized. As can be immediately seen, the collocations associated with the one sense are avoided by the other.

The semantic associations for both senses of *immunity* are given in Table 5.13. Examples of the semantic association of 'legal' *immunity* with GIVE, TAKE AWAY and SEEK are the following:

Table 5.12 A comparison of the collocates of the two senses of *immunity*

'Legal' immunity	'Medical' immunity
collocates with *certificate* (12 instances) (122 if omitted multi-word items are included)	no instances
collocates with *prosecution/prosecutor* (67 instances)	no instances
collocates with *parliamentary* (55 instances)	no instances
collocates with LIFT (27 instances)	no instances
collocates with *legal* (15 instances)	no instances
collocates with CHARGE (15 instances)	no instances
collocates with *committee* (11 instances)	no instances
collocates with CLAIM (10 instances)	no instances
collocates with *diplomatic* (10 instances)	no instances
collocates with *sovereign* (7 instances)	no instances
collocates with *Crown* (6 instances)	no instances
no instances	collocates with NATURAL (11 instances)
no instances	collocates with *infection* (8 instances)
1 instance	collocates with ACQUIRE (5 instances)

Table 5.13 A comparison of the semantic associations of the two senses of *immunity*

'Legal' immunity	'Medical' immunity
has semantic association with GIVE	
71 instances	6 instances
has a semantic association with TAKE AWAY	
115 instances	5 instances
has semantic association with SEEK	
38 instances	2 instances
has semantic association with CRIME	
13 instances	no instances
	has semantic association with GET
2 instances	16 instances
	has semantic association with INCREASE
no instances	8 instances

GIVE

62   . . . his lawyer tells me his client has been **granted** *immunity* from prison because of his age.

63   Yesterday they **offered** virtual *immunity* from prosecution to those involved in minor acts during the riots if they came forward to give evidence.

TAKE AWAY

64 They will be **stripped of** their *immunity* when they give up their seats.

65 . . . there will be a third attempt to **cancel** my MP's *immunity* from prosecution.

66 . . . investigators cannot call him in unless his parliamentary *immunity* is **lifted**.

SEEK

67 . . . a sovereign borrower can **claim** legal *immunity* or ignore a foreign court's judgement by pleading 'force majeure' (superior power).

68 As Bill Clinton **seeks** *immunity* from the latest charges against him . . .

Examples of 'medical' *immunity*'s semantic association with GET and INCREASE are:

GET

69 You get an infection, you **develop** *immunity*, and you either get well or you die.

70 This type of *immunity* can be naturally **acquired** in two ways . . .

INCREASE

71 . . . most flu sufferers **build up** an *immunity* as they recover.

72 . . . a booster within six to 12 months **increases** *immunity* for up to 10 years.

The colligations for both senses of *immunity* are given in Table 5.14.

It will be seen that the two senses of *immunity* do indeed avoid each other's primings (in the *Guardian*, at least). While this is not surprising in the case of the collocations, it being difficult to imagine contexts in which the 'medical' immunity could be *parliamentary* or the 'legal' immunity *natural*, it is not obvious in

Table 5.14 A comparison of the colligations of the two senses of *immunity*

'Legal' immunity	'Medical' immunity
colligates with *from* + NG	
124 instances	2 instances
colligates with possessive	
112 instances	12 instances
colligates with classifiers	
116 instances	16 instances
colligates as noun modifier to a noun head	
34 instances	2 instances
	colligates with *to* + NG
6 instances	25 instances

the case of the semantic associations and colligations. There is no self-evident reason why 'medical' *immunity* might not be given, for example by means of a course of treatment, nor any reason why such *immunity* might not be possessed, for example by a lucky patient. Similarly there is no reason why 'legal' *immunity* should not be 'created'. Most strikingly, the very presence of the occasional *from* and *to* following the 'medical' and 'legal' senses, respectively, is evidence enough that there is no reason for believing that there are grammatical obstacles occurring in such a position with these senses. And yet the two senses for the most part do not stray into each other's colligations.

Furthermore, the collocations, colligations and semantic associations listed account for a significant proportion of the data for each sense. So the colligations listed in Table 5.14, for example, account for almost two-thirds (271) of instances of 'legal' *immunity*. In total, 377 of the instances of 'legal' *immunity* in my data have one or more of the primings listed for it. In other words, 92 per cent of occurrences of 'legal' *immunity* are immediately distinguished from the other sense of *immunity*. Even 'medical' *immunity*, for which far fewer primings have been identified because of the relative sparsity of data, has 52 per cent of its instances covered by at least one of its primings. Drinking problem hypothesis 2 is therefore affirmed.

Polysemy versus vagueness

I could be accused of having made my life easier in the previous section by choosing a word that has two distinct senses and for which ambiguity is a rarity. What happens, though, when a word has two senses that are closer than the legal and medical senses of *immunity*? Does the second drinking problem hypothesis still operate? The answer is yes and no. My analysis has depended upon my having been able to allocate every example to one or other sense. In fact, though, senses may blur. The word *tea* has two (or three) distinct senses – the drink, the leaves from which the drink is made and the meal at which light refreshment is taken. The first two can for some purposes be treated as a single sense, though there are clear differences in their use. The third, though, is on the face of it quite different and it is possible to partake of the meal *tea* and not drink any.

Nevertheless, in a range of contexts it is impossible to be sure whether what is being described is the meal *tea* or the sharing of a pot of tea. An example is the following:

> 73   . . . the cost of an hour gossiping over tea can never approach the
>   expense of a visit to a restaurant or wine bar.

A restaurant is somewhere where you would go for a meal, like the meal *tea*; on the other hand a wine bar is somewhere where you would go for a drink, like the drink *tea*.

Rather than allocate such instances to one or other sense, it seems better to say that such usages draw on both senses. This is not a contradiction of the drinking problem hypotheses, but a recognition that vagueness is sometimes sought after rather than avoided in language.

As a fuller instance of this, let us look at a word we have already considered in some detail that has two senses that are distinct but are much closer than *immunity*, namely *reason*. When I began my examination of the differences in the typical primings of *reason* (= cause) and *reason* (= rationality, logic), I noted that I was conflating in the rarer 'sense' two closely related but largely distinct senses – *reason* (= rationality) and *reason* (= logic). It is time to separate these senses and see what happens.

Rationality is part of the apparatus of the human being, the human's ability to reason. Logic, on the other hand, is abstract, belonging to no one in particular. There are 455 instances of *reason* (= logic) in my data and 175 instances of *reason* (= rationality).

If we look at the characteristic primings of the two senses, we find that *reason* (= rationality) has the following typical primings, at least as regards newspaper data:

- it colligates with possessives (17 per cent);
- it has a semantic association with LOSS (12 per cent), with the collocation *lost*, which occurs 8 times, accounting for 40 per cent of the occurrences of the semantic association;
- it collocates with *sweet* (24 occurrences), *human* (7 occurrences), *voices of* (8 occurrences), *voice of* (34 occurrences), *sleep of* (8 occurrences) and *told* (6 occurrences); in total these collocations, which with one exception occur singly, account for 51 per cent of instances of *reason* (= rationality).

Reason (= logic), on the other hand, never occurs with either possessives or LOSS. It also never collocates with *sweet*, *human voice(s)*, *sleep* or *told*, though it does occur with *says*. I therefore infer that *reason* (= logic) avoids the primings of *reason* (= rationality).

The primings of *reason* (= logic) are the following:

- it has a colligational preference for coordination (or other coupling) with abstract nouns or word sequences, occurring in such combinations 217 times (48 per cent of all occurrences of the logic sense);
- it has a colligational aversion to any deictic – if we discount instances of *rhyme (n)or reason*, which might justifiably have been treated separately along with *within reason* and *stands to reason*, there is only one instance of a deictic and that is from the quotation from Shakespeare already discussed (example 33).

It is not as clear as it was the other way round that *reason* (= rationality) avoids the primings of *reason* (= logic). I have already noted that *reason* (= rationality) has a positive colligation for the possessive deictics and it mops up all the other deictics associated with *reason* (= rationality, logic). However, as we have seen, there are relatively few of these. We cannot therefore argue that *reason* (= rationality) is avoiding the territory occupied by *reason* (= logic). Likewise, *reason* (= rationality) couples with another noun (abstract or otherwise) moderately rarely; there are 24 instances of such combinations (14 per cent of all occurrences of the rationality sense). This cannot however be seen as avoidance, though it certainly indicates a typical difference of priming for the two senses.

The truth is that *reason* (= logic) is recognisable as such when, and only when, one of its regular primings is apparent. Still more so, *reason* (= rationality) is only recognisable as such when one of its primings is present. The fact is that I recognise the 'rationality' meaning in these instances exactly **because** they are accompanied by possessives. If the primings are absent, the distinction between *reason* (= logic) and *reason* (= rationality) disappears. An instance of a merged sense might be:

74   *Galileo* remains a seminal masterwork about the eternal struggle of *reason* against superstition and self-betrayal.

As with the *tea* example, nothing is gained by a spurious attempt to resolve the vagueness. It simply does not matter whether a reader interprets *reason* here as rationality or logic. The distinction has been erased.

Drinking problem hypothesis 3 – ambiguity

Another example of the blurring of senses is the word sequence *without good reason,* which I have treated in my analyses above as an instance of *reason* (= cause), partly because there is an equivalent expression, *without good cause.* However, the use of *reason* here, with no deictic, can be thought to draw a little on the 'logic' sense of the word. The equivalent expression *without good cause* might be thought, similarly, to draw upon the sense of *cause* as a set of positions which one strongly supports (as in *fights for the cause*). The point, predictably enough, is that we are all primed slightly differently and may to different degrees draw on our primings to arrive at likely interpretations of what we hear.

There is a fundamental difference between vagueness and ambiguity. Vagueness occurs when it is unclear what precise meaning can be assigned. Ambiguity, on the other hand, occurs when there are two or more entirely precise meanings assignable to a sentence, and they are different meanings. The third drinking problem hypothesis refers to this sense of ambiguity when it proposes that, whenever one sense of a word invades the primings of another, the effect will be humour, ambiguity (momentary or permanent) or a new meaning combining the two senses.

It will be remembered that there was a genuine, albeit momentary, ambiguity in the sentence included in example 37, repeated here for convenience as 75:

75 For George Bush to put the problems down to 'the misguided actions of one man' ignores both the facts and the roots of wider feelings. However, the focus on Saddam does not stop at substituting his personal reasoning for the collective experience of Arab peoples. *There is also considerable speculation as to whether the Iraqi leader shows any reason at all.* From the time Kuwait was invaded the sanity of Saddam began to be questioned. At first it was unclear whether the invective was meant metaphorically or literally . . .

(© Guardian Newspapers Limited 1991)

The problem here is simple. In the first place, *show* collocates with *reason* (= cause), though the same vagueness that applied to *without good reason* applies here equally. Secondly, *reason* (= cause) is primed to occur with *any*, as we have seen. On the other hand, *reason* (= rationality) has, as we have seen, a preference for the Object function. The cohesive ties between *reasoning* and *reason* and between *reason* and *sanity* appear to resolve the ambiguity in favour of *reason* (= rationality), but, without these textual factors, we would presumably feel unable to resolve the ambiguity.

The textual dimension turns out to be important in the following two ambiguous cases of *consequence*:

76 But Article 7.1(a) of this directive which allows members to retain equality in state pensions also refers to 'the *consequence* thereof for other benefits'.

77 His reading of Voltaire's Philosophical Dictionary made him briefly an atheist (Boyer beat religion back into him, to lifelong effect), but of more lasting *consequence* was his discovery of twenty-one sonnets by a Wiltshire clergyman called William Lisle Bowles (1762–1850). The sonnets struck Coleridge with the force of revelation . . .

The ambiguity of the first arises in part from the fact that it has been recontextualised and we have no access to the source text. In other words, the absence of information on cohesion and other textual influences means that we are denied crucial, potentially disambiguating, information. The ambiguity also arises from the fact that priming is posited to be genre and domain specific. The quotation is from legal language and it is more than possible that a corpus of such language would reveal a law-specific priming of *consequence* (= result) for collocation with *thereof*; my newspaper-dominated corpus, however, attests only the single instance. Out of context, the only priming that the example displays is the presence of *the*, which strongly points to the meaning being that of 'result'. Otherwise the grammatical pattern in which it appears is characteristic of neither sense of *consequence*. The use of *for* is a weak priming of *consequence* (= importance), with 4 per cent of instances of this sense occurring with *for*. This priming is reinforced slightly by the presence of a parallel weak priming for *consequence*'s synonym *importance*. On the other hand, less than 1 per cent of instances of *consequence* (= result) are postmodified by *for*. Both senses make sense in the context. In the end, though, the presence of *the*, the guessed-at collocation of *thereof* and the simple improbability of a legal document needing to refer to the importance of anything make this reader resolve the ambiguity in favour of 'result'.

The second instance is perhaps the more interesting and the more genuinely ambiguous. The presence of *of* before *consequence* points apparently unambiguously to the 'importance' sense. The fact that it is thematised, however, runs counter to the typical priming of *consequence* (= importance), this being associated typically with *consequence* (= result), though we saw earlier that thematisation of *consequence* (= importance) is associated with affirmation of importance rather than denial, and this instance is being affirmed. Out of context, then, there is no ambiguity. However, the sentences before and afterwards are full of the language of cause-effect. Here is the example again in the full paragraph in which it appears:

> 78   The destruction of the Bastille in 1789 **drew from** Coleridge impassioned verse in praise of freedom and 'glad Liberty', and the fevered excitement inspired throughout Europe by the early days of the French Revolution **provided** the intellectual climate in which his radical conscience began to form. His reading of Voltaire's Philosophical Dictionary **made** him briefly an atheist (Boyer beat religion back into him, to lifelong **effect**), but of more lasting *consequence* was his discovery of twenty-one sonnets by a Wiltshire clergyman called William Lisle Bowles (1762–1850). The sonnets struck Coleridge with the force of revelation, seeming to him, in their natural use of language and heartfelt expression of personal feeling, unlike anything he had ever read. He made over 40 transcriptions of the sonnets 'as the best presents I could offer to those who had in any way won my regard', and in his own poetic experiments of the next few years **found an** important **model in** the work of the now-forgotten Wiltshire poet.

As can be seen, the whole paragraph (which incidentally comes not from the 96 million word *Guardian* chunk of the corpus but from the British National Corpus supplement) is concerned with different effects on Coleridge, with all the words and word sequences marked in bold signalling a different effect or affect. The textual dimension appears to forcibly support the interpretation of *consequence* here as 'result'. But then again the description of the model in the last sentence as *important* counters this somewhat, since it could be interpreted as cohesive with *consequence*, both arguably referring to the importance of the discovery of Bowles' work to the development of Coleridge as a poet.

The truth is that this use, unlike example 75 above, is permanently ambiguous, and whereas the textual dimension resolved the ambiguity in the *reason* example, here it creates the ambiguity. In short, the ambiguity in this instance arises out of a conflict between a local priming and a textual pattern. Does this mean that we have reached the limits of what priming can account for? Do we need to posit two pressures on the language user – the pressure of the lexical priming and the pressure of the textual imperative? In preparation for that question, the next two chapters concern the textual dimension to lexical priming.

6 Lexical priming and text: two claims

Some claims about textual priming

Lexical priming has so far been talked about in terms of sentence-internal features, though references to priming for Theme have referred to textual colligation and have thereby hinted at a textual dimension. The discussion of ambiguity at the end of the previous chapter, however, showed that a theory of lexical priming needs to address the issue of how text organisation might be affected (or created) by lexical priming, and how conversely it might affect it. Ideally, text should refer here to both speech and writing, but what follows is limited for reasons of space and corpus construction to written text only. I shall argue in Chapter 8 that there are textual and pragmatic matters that stand separate from lexical priming, but we should not be in a rush to dismiss discourse issues as independent of and unconnected with the matters we have been considering in this book. In this chapter I shall argue that lexis is in fact intimately bound up with decisions of discourse organisation.

As a way of arguing this position, I ask the reader to consider once again the clause that begins Bill Bryson's *Neither Here Nor There*:

1   In winter Hammerfest is a thirty-hour ride by bus from Oslo . . .

If all you knew was that this was the first clause of a text, I think you would have certain, fairly clear expectations about the way it might develop. You would expect there to be further discussion of Hammerfest but you would not expect the text to be about Oslo or winter, though you would be unsurprised if the ride was discussed. You might expect some explanation as to where Hammerfest is and why it takes so long to get there. These expectations would become near certainties if you were told (as you already have been) that the clause in question in fact begins a travel book.

The first kind of expectation is associated with the cohesion of the text, the second with its semantic organisation, and they would normally be discussed as text-linguistic features. I have myself discussed both features in such terms; Hoey (1991a), for example, deals with the properties of cohesion and in Hoey (1983, 2001) I consider some of the features of text organisation. Here, however, I want to suggest that your expectations are part of your priming of the vocabulary of the clause. Your experience of the word sequence *in winter* has led you not to expect cohesive chains of lexical items referring to *winter* and still less to anticipate that a text beginning with this word sequence will be about winter. Your experience of place names in Subject function in travel writing however has strongly predisposed you to expect a chain of lexical references to the place, with the place as topic. Likewise your experience of place names has probably been such as to expect mention of location and transport. (Or maybe not – as I have repeatedly emphasised, priming is personal and varies from language user to language user.), In short, the lexis in Bill Bryson's sentence – in all sentences – is textually primed. Just as many features of our personality are apparently latent in our genes from the moment of our birth, so also many of the features of a text – its organization, its cohesion, its chunking – are latent in the lexical items we select. (The analogy is of course inexact, in that no one, I assume, ever composes, still less utters, a text, knowing in advance what the whole text will look like, but then one cannot predict from a child's genes how he or she will turn out.) At the end of this and the next chapter, we will look at how, and to what extent, Bill Bryson conforms to our expectations.

I want to argue that words may be textually primed in three ways:

- Words (or nested combinations) may be primed positively or negatively to participate in cohesive chains of different and distinctive types (**textual collocation**).
- Words (or nested combinations) may be primed to occur (or to avoid occurring) in specific types of semantic relation, e.g. contrast, time sequence, exemplification (**textual semantic association**).
- Words (or nested combinations) may be primed to occur (or to avoid occurring) at the beginning or end of independently recognised discourse units, e.g. the sentence, the paragraph, the speech turn (**textual colligation**). (We have considered positioning within the sentence in earlier chapters and here greater attention is given to the supra-sentential aspects of textual colligation.)

Throughout this book I have been at pains to stress that priming is genre and domain specific in the first instance, though there are many primings that apply across generic and domain boundaries. Predictably, the specificity of the priming is at its greatest when the priming relates to discourse properties, since these have been shown to vary greatly according to genre and text purpose (e.g. Swales 1990; Bhatia 1993).

The claims are formulated in such a way as to permit of the possibility of a lexical item having not only a positive or negative priming but also neutral priming with regard to each of the named features. This distinguishes these potential primings from those so far mentioned. I would hypothesise that all words are primed for one or more collocations, semantic associations and colligations, even if these are on the face of it unremarkable; the ubiquity of colligation in particular is discussed in Chapter 8. I do not however hypothesise that the three kinds of textual priming listed above are properties of all words (or their nested combinations). Of course, if an overwhelming majority of words in English were to prove to be not primed in any of the ways mentioned, we would have to regard it as refutation of the claims I am making, or at the very least as limiting their applicability and interest value.

Claim 1: words (or nested combinations) may be primed positively or negatively to participate in cohesive chains (textual collocation)

As was noted in Chapter 1, collocation is usually regarded in corpus linguistics as a local phenomenon characteristically operating within a short distance of the word in focus (usually three words before and after) and yet the term has also been used in text linguistics (by Halliday and Hasan 1976) to describe the relationship between lexical items in a text that helps to create cohesion in the text – relationships such as *bee – honey*, *door – window*, *candle – flame* and *mountaineering – peaks* (all examples drawn from Halliday and Hasan 1976: 286–7). I want to suggest that the two apparently contradictory uses of the term can be reconciled if we see the cohesive links a word forms in a spoken or written text as its 'textual collocations'. Scott (1999), in his help file, distinguishes 'coherence collocates' from 'neighbourhood collocates', a distinction that seems to make a similar point.

If Halliday and Hasan's examples seem plausible (as they do to me at least), it is because the lexical items they cite are primed to co-occur not in a span of three or four words on either side but in the larger textual environment. So just as *ride* is primed to collocate with *bus*, so it is also primed to occur with *travel* and, importantly, with other occurrences of *ride* across sentences/utterances in a discourse – and, interestingly and by happy chance, *ride* is one of the words considered by Halliday and Hasan (1976: 287), and the examples just given of textual collocation are drawn from their discussion. In a particular text, if the writer goes along with their textual collocational priming, the result will be a text that contains cohesive ties between *ride* and other instances of *ride*, *travel* and *bus*. Textual collocation is therefore what lexis is primed for and the effect of the activation of this priming is textual cohesion. The textual collocation of a word with itself, which results in cohesion by repetition, and the textual collocation of a word with its proform, which results in cohesion by reference, are simply special (albeit numerically extremely common) cases of the more general phenomenon.

Cohesion can be seen as either an integral factor in the creation of coherence in a text (e.g. Halliday and Hasan 1976) or as an epiphenomenon of that coherence (e.g. Morgan and Sellner 1980), and both positions have some merit. It is not, however, necessary to decide between the two perspectives from the point of view of lexical priming. It is sufficient to note that cohesion is a recognisable phenomenon in a text and has been shown to correlate in interesting ways with coherence (e.g. Hasan 1984; Hoey 1991a, 1991b; Parsons 1995), and to recognise that part of our knowledge of a word is a knowledge of the ways in which it is capable of forming cohesive relations.

There are two claims here. The first is that one of the things we know about the words we use is that we expect them to participate in cohesion, or not. Put more formally, words (or nested combinations) may be primed to participate in cohesive chains or links, or to avoid them. The second claim is that we know what kind of cohesion to expect. Words are primed to participate in cohesive chains or links in quite predictable ways. A chain is here defined as three or more items linked by textual collocation, as here defined, including repetition. A link occurs when just two items are so connected.

A cohesive chain may be made up of simple repetition (i.e. repetition with no variation other than that allowed for by grammatical regularity); an example is that of the word *claim* in the previous paragraph. (Though that is not to say that *claim* cannot form other kinds of cohesive links.) Alternatively, it may be made up of simple repetition, co-referential expressions and pro-forms. Consider the following paragraphs:

2   With a spare hour on my hands before lunch in Lebanon this week, I revisited the joys of my childhood, crunched my way across the old Beirut marshalling yards and climbed aboard a wonderful 19th-century rack-and-pinion railway locomotive. Although scarred by bullets, the green paint on the wonderful old Swiss loco still reflects the glories of steam and the Ottoman empire.

For it was the Ottomans who decided to adorn their jewel of Beirut with the latest state-of-the-art locomotive, a train which one carried the German Kaiser up the mountains above the city where, at a small station called Sofar, the Christian community begged for his protection from the Muslims. 'We are a minority,' they cried, to which the Kaiser bellowed: 'Then become Muslims!'

(The first two paragraphs of 'The irresistible romance of a steam train scarred with the bullet holes of battle' by Robert Fisk, *The Independent*, Saturday 12 February 2005, p. 37)

A chain is begun with *a wonderful 19th-century rack-and-pinion railway locomotive* that continues with *the wonderful old Swiss loco, the latest state-of-the-art locomotive* and *train.* The longer a chain is, the more it appears to be related to the topic (though it needs to interrelate with other chains as well) (Hasan 1984).

A cohesive link is the same except that there are only two members in the chain. An example from the passage is *the Ottoman Empire* and *the Ottomans,* where the cohesion takes the form of simple repetition (Hoey 1991a). (There are no further mentions of the Ottomans in Robert Fisk's text.) Cohesive links tend to be less closely associated with the topic of the text. Examples of words that form neither cohesive links nor chains in the passage (or in the remainder of the text) are *hour* and *crunched.*

Positive priming for cohesion

As noted above, the priming I am positing operates at two levels. At the first level, a word is primed to participate in cohesive chains or to avoid them. At the second, the type of textual collocation that the word is primed for is specified. Starting with the first level, all the following items are examples of words typically primed to participate in cohesive chains (or in cohesive ties) in newspaper writing under specifiable conditions: *army, Blair, gay, planet, political, year.*

The list is intended to indicate the range of words that are primed for cohesion. So we have common nouns, names and descriptive adjectives. As will be apparent, the words listed are, in their major senses, non-evaluative and with clear denotations. Though it may be the case that few words that are evaluative or have weak denotations (e.g. *ridiculous, make, action*) are primed for cohesion except in special domains and genres, it certainly is not the case that non-evaluative and readily-defined words are always so primed. Words such as *thirty* and *hour* are not primed for cohesion in travel writing; the semantic set PLACE NAMES, on the other hand, in this particular kind of writing is so primed, but only strongly so when it is in Subject function – an instance of cohesive priming operating on a nested combination of PLACE NAME + SUBJECT. I have noted elsewhere in this book that such priming always starts for each of us as the priming of an individual name, say *Hemel Hempstead* or *Cromer.* From individual instances it is hypothesised that the priming is transferred to the set.

To show the way that cohesive priming works and the limitations of its operation, let us look more closely at the first of the instances in the list given above. The word *army* is typically primed for participation in cohesion. A sample of 65 different texts was examined which contained the word *army.* Only instances with a lower case 'a' were considered, since it could not be assumed that the behaviour of *Army* would be the same. Titles were also not considered, and the statistics that follow for this and other words do not include cohesion between title and the body of the text. For reasons that will be explained below, the combination *army of* was excluded, too. Although concordances were used for the basis of the selection, great care was taken to ensure that each instance taken was drawn from a different text. (Otherwise the statistics would of course have been grossly distorted; a single text with 13 instances of *army* would for example have contained a fifth of the data.)

Of the 65 texts examined, 23 used the instance of *army* within a cohesive chain (which often of course contained further instances of the same word) and 15 used it in a cohesive link, which means that 58 per cent of the texts that contained the word *army* used it cohesively. This suggests that a reader used to reading the *Guardian* might become primed to expect it to participate in cohesive relations.

The observation just made started from the point of view of the text. If we focus on the word, the picture is still clearer. The proportion of instances of *army* that are cohesive is as already noted very much higher than the proportion of texts containing the word – a text using *army* cohesively will usually contain two or more instances of the word, whereas with only a few exceptions a text that does not utilise *army* cohesively will only contain one instance of the word. Looked at from the point of view of the word, 81 per cent of all instances of *army* examined were found to be being used cohesively.

The first thing to note is that, here as previously, priming operates differently depending on the nesting. Instances of non-cohesive *army* are almost one and a half times more likely to make use of the colligational priming *army* + NOUN than are instances of cohesive *army*. Perhaps more important, and certainly statistically more secure, is the fact that when *army* makes use of the collocation *army* + *of*, its tendency to be cohesive drops dramatically, and, as already noted, all instances of *army of* were excluded from the analysis described above. The reason is that this collocation is itself primed for metaphor: 63 out of 108 in my data are metaphorically employed (*the battered army of home-owners, an army of general practitioners, Britain's huge army of investment salesmen*). Of the remaining 45 non-metaphorical instances, 15 are the word sequence *army of occupation* and 10 utilise the semantic association *army of* NUMBER. Interestingly, these particular combinations conform to the original generalisation about the positive priming of *army* for cohesion. So what we have is (for most users, in the context of newspaper writing) a positive priming of *army* for cohesion, except where *army* is followed by *of*, in which case there is a negative priming for cohesion, unless what follows *of* is *occupation* or NUMBER in which case once again we have a positive priming for cohesion. Such complexity is expected to be routinely the case with priming (and not only in connection with textual priming).

Negative priming for cohesion

In our consideration of *army*, our starting point has been that it is positively primed, unless otherwise affected. Some words are on the other hand negatively primed (e.g. *asinine, blink, crossroads, elusive, particularly, wobble*).

All the lexical items in this list appear to be primed to avoid occurring in cohesive chains, though they are no less frequent in my corpus than the items in the previous list. Indeed it is worth dwelling on that fact. One might have predicted that a word's infrequency in the language would make it less available for participation in cohesive chains, but frequency does not seem to be an important factor. As I noted in Hoey (2004a), however, it is much harder to establish that something does not occur and it is a painfully slow process to move from each concordance line into the original text to check for possible cohesion. The items in the above list must therefore be regarded only as provisional.

As before, the list is indicative of the range of the words primed to avoid cohesion and again I present the evidence for the first only. There were 32 instances of *asinine* in my corpus and of the texts in which they occurred, all but one used it in neither a cohesive chain nor a cohesive link. The solitary exception makes use of near-synonyms (the chain being *stupid, asinine, inanities, stupidity, imbecilities, inanity*) but not of repetitions. It is perhaps worth adding that this negative priming for cohesion is not entirely explicable in terms of its being an evaluative adjective; so, after all, is *racist* and that is positively primed for cohesion.

As we saw in Chapter 2, in our discussion of *sixty* and *60*, when it comes to priming, orthography cannot be ignored. The word *crossroads* does not appear to favour appearing in cohesive chains and so is included in list 2; the word *Crossroads*, on the other hand, is the title of a former British soap opera, and, given the British love of soap opera, chains freely.

Priming for cohesive links or short chains

Some words do not participate in cohesive chains but occur quite frequently in cohesive links. This points to the fact that there are words which are primed to form only brief chains or to participate in cohesive links without chaining. Instances are the following: *ago, option, reason, sixty*.

With these words, the pattern is for them not to be part of long cohesive chains. However, they are primed to occur in cohesive links or in short cohesive chains (*one option . . . another option . . . a third option; sixty . . . 35 . . . five*). These chains characteristically are localised within the larger text.

Once again I will illustrate the claim with the first item on the list. I examined a sample of 40 texts containing one or more instances of *ago* with respect to whether *ago* formed cohesive chains. I found that only 2 texts out of the 40 (5 per cent) contained chains of *ago*, though a much higher proportion used *ago* for a single link – 16 (40 per cent) contained such a link. The remaining 22 texts (55 per cent) only had non-cohesive instances of the word. From the lexical perspective, examination of 50 instances of *ago* revealed that only 6 of them occurred in cohesive chains. The rest divided evenly between forming a single link and forming no cohesive relations whatsoever. Although examination of 40 texts is a time-consuming business, the data cannot be considered sufficient for confident generalisation, but the evidence we have allows us to claim tentatively that *ago* is negatively primed for cohesive chains but positively for cohesive links.

Priming for **type** of cohesion

I mentioned earlier that the nature of the cohesive chains for each lexical item varies, and we have just seen an example of this. Whereas *option* is almost always repeated without variation, *sixty* is normally part of a chain containing co-hyponyms (i.e. other numbers). This is normal and a part of our priming with regard to cohesion. Each word that is primed positively for cohesion is also primed, I want to argue, for a particular **type** of cohesion. Thus in a particular genre or domain a word may not be primed to appear in chains made up of simple repetition but it may on the other hand be primed to occur in cohesive chains made up of its hyponyms.

The word *gay* will serve as a useful example. Fifty texts were examined that contained one or more instances of the word *gay* (in its sexual sense) and 36 of these (72 per cent) participated in cohesive chains or links (25 chains, 11 links). From the perspective of the word, there were 131 instances of *gay* in the 50 texts, and 116 of these were cohesive, meaning that 89 per cent of instances of *gay* in my newspaper data were cohesive. (In passing it is worth noting that the situation was strikingly different with the non-sexual sense of *gay*, of which there were no cohesive instances. Textual priming, therefore, like other kinds of priming, contributes to the distinction between polysemous uses of a word.)

The point here, though, is not that *gay* (in the sexual sense) is primed for cohesion. That point, after all, has already been made with *army*. The point here is that *gay* overwhelmingly tends to occur in chains made up of simple repetition; i.e. *gay* is repeated as *gay*, which is then repeated as *gay* and so forth. Of the 25 chains, 20 are either exclusively or predominantly made up of reiterations of the word *gay*. The synonym *homosexual* (or the noun *homosexuality*) occurs in 18 of the chains, but in only 5 do its occurrences outnumber those of *gay*. Other synonyms virtually never occur. These results are in line with those of Baker (2005) who shows how *gay* and *homosexual* belong to separate discourses.

Ago, which we saw was primed for links and very short chains, is another instance of a word that is primed only for simple repetition, the only exceptions being arguable links with *yesterday* (= a day ago) and *last year* (? = a year ago).

On the other hand, the word *planet* functions rather differently. Like *army* and *gay*, *planet* favours cohesive chains. As with *army*, the picture is complicated by the non-participation in cohesive chains of specific combinations such as *on the planet* (which almost always references the all-embracing nature of a generalisation) and *this planet* (which usually refers to Earth). Even with these included in the statistics, however, *planet* forms cohesive chains in 47 per cent of texts in which it appears. Crucially, though, although it does sometimes form chains of simple repetition, it appears just as frequently in chains with its hyponyms (e.g. *planet – Uranus – Saturn – planets – Pluto*). So *planet* is primed, for *Guardian* readers at least, for hyponymy (and meronymy).

More briefly, other words are primed to occur in chains where pronouns are common. *Blair* is an instance of this (e.g. *Mr Blair – his – Mr Blair's – Tony Blair – Mr Blair's – his*). *Blair*, like *Hammerfest*, is an instance of a claim that applies to a semantic set PERSONAL NAME.

I hope that these points are obvious. There is no hyponym to *Blair* and everyone knows he is male and that therefore the masculine pronoun will apply. Likewise, if the domain is the solar system, everybody knows that *planet* is bound to occur in a cohesive chain with hyponyms. But that very obviousness is evidence of the correctness of the claim that the cohesive properties of the word are built into the word itself. This is why Emmott (1989, 1997) and Sinclair (1993, 2004) can argue that cohesion is prospective. Sinclair overstates the position in claiming that the whole of the previous text is encapsulated in the sentence currently being read and Emmott's position is closer to my own (and indeed has been influential upon it) in that she finds a psychological explanation for the operation of cohesion, but the fundamental insight of both is sound when they claim that we do not constantly refer back to the previous text, as the literature on cohesion would have us believe. The reason why we do not refer back, I would argue, is that we are primed to expect cohesion of particular types for particular words and therefore anticipate its occurrence in advance of its appearance.

Claim 2: every lexical item (or combination of lexical items) may have a positive or negative preference for occurring as part of a specific type of semantic relation

Claim 1 looked strange but it was in fact merely an extension of the notion of collocation to take account of a word's long recognised ability to collocate across sentences, though collocation here, however, was importantly extended to include collocation with itself; in other words, lexical repetition. The second claim is similarly strange on first sight but is in fact simply an extension of the notion of semantic association. Indeed, as we shall see, in some of its manifestations it is indistinguishable from the kinds of semantic association we were looking at in Chapter 2. The claim is that every lexical item (or combination of lexical items) may be positively or negatively primed for occurring as part of a specific type of semantic or pragmatic relation or in a specific textual pattern (e.g. contrast, comparison, time sequence, cause-effect, exemplification, problem-solution). Such semantic relations or discourse patterns may be textual, i.e. the relations between clauses or parts of clauses or between larger chunks of text, or they may reflect and incorporate relations between a speaker and a listener of the kind described in conversational analysis (e.g. Schegloff 1972; Schegloff and Sacks 1973) or in discourse analysis (Sinclair and Coulthard 1975), where the relation between a speaker or writer's utterance is in focus. (They may also reflect the interaction between writer and reader.)

I start with *sixty*, whose cohesive priming was briefly referred to on page 120, and which we have looked at in previous chapters. Examination of the textual contexts of 100 instances of the word in my corpus revealed that 41 occurred in a contrast relation, 16 participated in a non-contrastive comparison relation and 37 occurred within the problem component of a problem-solution pattern (Winter 1974; Hoey 1979, 1983, 1993, 2001; Jordan 1980, 1984). This left only 21 instances not accounted for. (The figures fail to add to 100 because a clause can be in more than one textual relation.) So the evidence supports the claim that in newspaper writing *sixty* is strongly primed for use in contrast relations and as the problem component of problem-solution patterns and weakly primed for use in non-contrastive comparison relations.

We find a very similar situation with *ago*, the cohesive properties of which were also considered above. Inspection of 100 instances of thematised *ago* showed that it was strongly primed for occurrence in contrast when it is part of Theme, with 55 appearing as part of a contrast relation and a further 16 appearing in some kind of comparison relation. (The proportions rise still further if instances of *not long ago* and *as long ago as* are discounted.)

As with other kinds of priming, it may be nested combinations that are primed, rather than individual words. So, for example, the combination of *The* + ADJECTIVE + *side* in sentence-initial position has primings that appear to be more distinct than those found for uses without the adjective or the initial positioning. I examined 137 instances of this combination (excluding all national, county and continental adjectives, which were suspected to have primings of their own). Eleven were in titles, and these were discounted, since titles have a different relationship to the rest of the text from that of normal clauses. This left 126 instances available for analysis. Of these, 58 (46 per cent) were part of a contrast relation and 19 (15 per cent) were part of a close parallelism. (Nine of these were in both relations.)

I am perhaps alone in making the claim that lexis is systematically primed for textual semantic association (Hoey 2004a) but I am certainly not the first to make the claim for individual lexical items. McCarthy (1998), for example, notes that *got* is associated with problem (an important element of problem-solution patterns). Hunston (2001) likewise gives several valuable examples of textual semantic association (though of course she does not use the term). She notes, for example, that the combination *may not be* is associated with contrast between ideal and more achievable. Similarly, she notes that *feted as* is associated with contrast.

A return to the Bill Bryson sentence

As this book has developed, I have sought to relate, wherever possible, the different aspects of priming to the sentence of Bill Bryson's with which this book began (more or less). With this in mind we turn now once again to his sentence to see how the claims made in this chapter might apply to it. So far we have only looked at the Bill Bryson sentence in splendid isolation; indeed one of the reasons for choosing the first sentence of a book to illustrate our claims was that it could stand on its own. However, we clearly cannot say much about its textual primings without quoting something of what follows. Space and copyright considerations prevent quotation of great swathes of Bill Bryson's text, but it may be helpful to quote the first two paragraphs of the book and the first sentence of the third. I have numbered the sentences for convenience of reference:

(1) In winter Hammerfest is a thirty-hour ride by bus from Oslo, though why anyone would want to go there in winter is a question worth considering. (2) It is on the edge of the world, the northernmost town in Europe, as far from London as London is from Tunis, a place of dark and brutal winters, where the sun sinks into the Arctic Ocean in November and does not rise again for ten weeks.

(3) I wanted to see the Northern Lights. (4) Also, I had long harboured a half-formed urge to experience what life was like in such a remote and forbidding place. (5) Sitting at home in England with a glass of whisky and a book of maps, this had seemed a capital idea. (6) But now as I picked my way through the grey, late-December slush of Oslo I was beginning to have my doubts,

(7) Things had not started well. (8) I had overslept at the hotel, missing breakfast, and had to leap into my clothes . . .

In respect of priming, names are no different from any other words, except of course that it is a much more common experience to encounter a new – and therefore unprimed – name that it is to encounter an entirely new lexical item. Once a name is encountered a few times, though, it becomes primed in exactly the same way as any other word in the language. When you first read Bill Bryson's sentence, *Hammerfest* was (I assume) unprimed for you. By now, it is perhaps heavily primed for association with *winter*, *bus* and *Oslo*! It is not therefore odd to start our consideration of textual priming in the Bill Bryson sentence by looking at the place-names. *Hammerfest* and *Oslo* share the same cohesive priming in that they are typically primed to collocate textually in travel writing with repetitions of their name, though the nesting of PLACE and subject greatly strengthens the priming. (Claims about the priming of *Hammerfest* are based on the behaviour of other place names in a corpus of travel writing made up of travel magazines; 500 instances were analysed in their textual contexts.) Repetitions of *Hammerfest* do occur in accordance with this priming but not within the passage quoted. They in fact occur 16 pages later after a number of amusing digressions, and the town gets the next chapter to itself. *Oslo* forms a desultory chain, with four further mentions in Chapter 1, one of them in sentence 6.

As place names, *Hammerfest* and *Oslo* are also primed for repetition by pro-forms *it* and *there*. The pro-form *there* linking with *Hammerfest* occurs in the second half of sentence 1 and *it* occurs in sentence 2. As regards the cohesion of place names in travel writing Bill Bryson therefore conforms to the typical priming. (In newspaper writing, other than travel writing, the propensity of place names to form cohesive chains and links appears, albeit without detailed study, to be much reduced. All primings are in principle genre and domain specific, as has been remarked in several places – this is particularly marked of textual primings.)

The word *winter* in sentence 1 is only weakly primed for cohesion in newspaper text. (My travel corpus did not permit its study in travel writing.) Only 10 per cent of the texts examined (9 out of 90) showed any cohesive tendency and of these only 3 showed *winter* in cohesive chains (3 per cent). Looking at the same data from the lexical perspective, I found that 26 per cent of instances of *winter* were cohesive (exactly 100 were examined), split evenly between cohesive chains and cohesive links. The chains were all short. When *winter* does participate in cohesion in my data it is primed for simple repetition and avoids pronouns. This conforms to Bill Bryson's usage, though the chain he produces in his first chapter is slightly longer than some (but this is likely to be where the priming for travel writing is inclined to differ most from that for newspaper writing).

However, the proportion of cohesive links rises dramatically if antonymous links are taken into account. Of the 90 texts considered, 24 (27 per cent)· contained an antonymous relation between *winter* and *summer*, usually across sentence boundaries, and of these only 3 were already cohesive because of the repetition of *winter*. Bryson's text partly matches this expectation. There are a number of references to *summer* in the first chapter, the last occurring only three sentences before a resumed mention of the Hammerfest trip. Whether they would be read as cohesive – or as antonymous – is however less certain.

The words *bus*, *ride* and *hour* are all negatively primed for cohesion in both travel writing and newspapers; clearly, this would not be the case for texts in the domain of transport where the priming for *bus* and possibly the other items would presumably be positive.

Turning now to the second claim, the word *Hammerfest* is, as a member of the set of place-names, primed in travel writing for two types of textual semantic association, namely location and characterisation. These may not look like textual relations but they represent questions that a reader may ask of (part of) a text. So location answers the question:

Where is X?

and characterisation answers the question:

What is it like?

Neither feature has been much handled in text-linguistic terms, though Sutherland (1985) provides a useful preliminary text-linguistic account.

Both features may occur within the sentence or across sentences. An example of their presence within a single sentence (when of course they become temporarily indistinguishable from ordinary semantic association) is example 3:

3   Lying in one of the most untouched pockets of tropical paradise in the Caribbean, with a coastline composed of a multitude of idyllic coves and harbours, it is no accident that Antigua is one of the world's most popular honeymoon destinations.

The Bill Bryson text, however, illustrates the second option. It will be seen that both location and characterisation is provided in sentence 2. However, the characterisation is not expected to be this brief in the genre of travel writing, given the nesting of place, Theme and text-initial position. A fuller characterisation is needed and the beginning of it arrives at the very end of the chapter:

4   We approached Hammerfest from above, on a winding coast road, and when at last it pivoted into view it looked simply wonderful – a fairyland of golden lights stretching up into the hills and around an expansive bay. I had pictured it in my mind as a village – a few houses around a small harbour, a church perhaps, a general store, a bar if I was lucky – but this was a little city. A golden little city. Things were looking up.

This long distance relation is quite typical of the interaction between writer and reader that contributes to the creation and interpretation of a text; the fulfilment of a reader's expectation may be deferred endlessly. So if the word *murdered* occurs in Chapter 1 of a detective story, it will typically be primed textually such that the reader will expect an answer to the question 'Who did it?' The answer may be – indeed is extremely likely to be – deferred until near the end of the book, but the question arising from the priming of *murdered* will remain in the reader's mind. In this respect, textual semantic association is quite unlike local semantic association of the kind described in Chapter 2.

There is another important respect in which textual primings such as textual semantic association differ from local primings. The primings for collocation, semantic association and colligation previously noted have helped distinguish the version Bill Bryson wrote from the relatively unnatural version that I offered in Chapter 1. When it comes to the textual primings discussed in this chapter, however, the differences between the natural and unnatural versions to some extent disappear. Both can, as first sentences, begin texts that utilise the textual collocations (cohesion) and textual semantic associations with which their shared lexis is primed, and their relative naturalness or unnaturalness is unaffected. So substituting my unnatural version for Bill Bryson's original barely affects the coherence or naturalness of the opening of the book, the only change dictated by the substitution being the replacement of the pronoun at the beginning of sentence 2 with the full name of the town to be visited:

> (1) Through winter, rides between Oslo and Hammerfest use thirty hours up in a bus, though why travellers would select to ride there then might be pondered. (2) Hammerfest is on the edge of the world, the northernmost town in Europe, as far from London as London is from Tunis, a place of dark and brutal winters, where the sun sinks into the Arctic Ocean in November and does not rise again for ten weeks.

On the other hand, overriding of the textual primings of the lexis in the first sentence may produce unnatural-sounding text, despite the naturalness of the sentence used. Consider, for example, the following:

> (1) In winter Hammerfest is a thirty-hour ride by bus from Oslo, though why anyone would want to go there in winter is a question worth considering. (2) Bus rides always raise interesting questions about winter travel.
>
> (3) I wanted to see a bus. (4) Also, I had long harboured a half-formed urge to experience what life was like on a bus ride. (5) Sitting at home in England with a glass of whisky and a book of maps, this had seemed a capital idea. (6) But now as I picked my way through the grey, late-December slush of Oslo I was beginning to have my doubts.
>
> (3) Things had not started well. (4) I had overslept at the hotel, missing breakfast, and had to leap into my clothes . . .

I would not claim that this text is incoherent, but I think it is unnatural in much the same way and for much the same reasons that my version of Bill Bryson's first sentence was unnatural. The textual primings of much of the lexis have been overridden. The priming of the place names *Hammerfest* and *Oslo* for cohesion by repetition and pro-form has not been followed, nor have the negative primings of *bus*, *ride* and *hour* for cohesion. The textual semantic associations of PLACE NAME have likewise been set aside. Consequently, the reader struggles to make sense of the otherwise reasonably natural second, third and fourth sentences. The other sentences, including the first, are unaltered.

The naturalness or unnaturalness of both sentences and texts depends on whether speakers or writers conform to or override the primings of the lexis they use. This has two implications. Firstly, it supports the view that lexical priming underpins linguistic choices from the syllable to the discourse. Secondly, it suggests that textual choices and local clausal choices, though driven by the same kinds of priming, are nevertheless partially independent, in that naturalness in the one set of choices is independent of naturalness in the other. This implication will be returned to in Chapters 8 and 9 when we consider creativity in language and the relationship of text and lexis. First, though, we need to consider a third kind of textual priming, which impacts less on questions of naturalness and more on questions of ordering and organisation.

7 Lexical priming and text: a third claim

Introduction

The notion of textual colligation was first introduced in this book in Chapter 3. Our original definition of colligation included as one of its components 'the place in a sequence that a word or word sequence prefers (or avoids)', and this property of colligation was described in connection with *consequence* both in connection with the thematisation of the phrases *as a consequence* and *in consequence*, and (in Chapter 5) in our consideration of the operation of the drinking problem hypotheses on the polysemous uses of *consequence*. In this chapter, however, in addition to providing further evidence for thinking that priming for Theme or Rheme is common, the notion of textual colligation will be extended to cover not only positioning within the sentence but positioning within the speaking turn, the paragraph, the conversation and the text, though limitations in the corpus I am working with mean that observations on the speaking turn and the conversation are sadly going to be brief and programmatic only.

Textual claim 3

Two textual claims were made in Chapter 6, with reference to textual collocation and textual semantic association. The third and final textual claim is the following, which will be seen to be an extension of the part of the definition of colligation just quoted: **'every lexical item (or combination of lexical items) is capable of being primed (positively or negatively) to occur at the beginning or end of an independently recognised "chunk" of text'**. When we encounter language in speech or writing, we are aware of the contexts and co-texts in which we encounter it – that has been an underlying assumption throughout this book. The claim I want to make at this point is that just as we are aware that words are typically used as part of Subjects or Adjuncts, so we are also aware of their textual position. So, for example, our awareness includes the knowledge that (as we have already seen) certain words tend to come early on in a sentence, while others tend to favour final position.

The examples in Chapters 3 and 5, with regard to the use of *consequence* as Theme, relate to priming for sentence-initial position, but a word may equally be primed for other positions in the sentence. As an example of the latter, it is interesting to note that *reason* (= rationality, logic) has a positive priming for end of sentence position. A massive 24 per cent of cases (154 instances) occur as the very last word of the sentences in which they appear. By contrast, only 817 instances of *reason* (= cause) are sentence-final, representing a more normal 6 per cent of cases. This also shows that the drinking problem hypotheses apply to textual primings as much as to other kinds of priming.

Another example of a word sequence primed for Rheme is provided by Bastow (2003), who notes that the writers of US defence speeches are primed to place the nominal group *our men and women in uniform* at the end of clauses (though of course he does not express the insight in the terms I am using). It is worth remarking that Bastow's claim is actually more precise than saying that *our men and women in uniform* appears in Rheme; he is specifying a quite specific position for the word sequence – final position. My investigation of this aspect of textual colligation suggests Rheme is too big and crude a category (everything after the Theme) to permit interesting textual colligational claims, and that Bastow's observation is more characteristic of the precision with which words and word sequences are primed.

This kind of textual colligation is a textual priming, rather than a grammatical priming. After all, the choice of Theme is in part affected by the textual surround. Although Halliday (1994) places Theme-Rheme analysis within his grammatical system, it belongs to his textual metafunction and is better seen in my view as a textual perspective and constraint upon sentence construction. As I shall attempt to show, Theme-Rheme is the tip of an iceberg in respect of our awareness of the textual environment in which we encounter the words we use. Just as a word may be primed to occur (or to avoid occurring) in first or last position in a sentence, so it may also be primed to occur (or avoid occurring) in first or last position in a paragraph, a section or a text. So, for example, *consequence* is not only primed to favour Theme, it is also primed to avoid paragraph-initial and text-initial position. The plural *consequences*, on the other hand, which is less strongly primed to occur as Theme, is positively primed to be paragraph-initial, though it shares the aversion of *consequence* for being text-initial.

With luck, your reaction to these claims will be that what I am saying is self-evident. Obviously writers will sometimes start paragraphs by noting a multiplicity of consequences and then use the next few sentences to spell out what they are. Equally obviously, a single consequence will be linked closely to its cause. If you do react this way, it is, I would argue, because you are primed to use these words in the textual ways I have described. You may then object that *consequence* and *consequences* have long been recognised to have special text organising functions (e.g. Winter 1977; Francis 1986, 1994) and therefore do not count as evidence for textual priming, but I hope what follows will convince you that they behave no differently from other words in respect of their priming for textual position.

One problem, though, must be faced from the outset and that is the difficulty of accessing sufficient data, as I mentioned at the beginning of this chapter. In a written corpus of nearly 100 million words, the number of paragraph boundaries and, of course, the number of texts are far fewer. The evidence for the claims I make in this chapter should be seen as suggestive rather than conclusive.

sixty (again)

Of 307 instances of *sixty* in my data, 208 are thematised, of which an exact 200 are the first word of the sentence. This means that *sixty* is strongly primed for occurrence as part of Theme.

The priming of *sixty* for sentence-initial position is not of course a surprise – indeed, given that many object to starting a sentence with a numeral, it is very much as expected. What however might be surprising is the fact that 14 per cent of all the sentence-initial instances of *sixty* in the newspaper data (9 per cent of all instances) are the first word in the text in which they appear, the first word being defined as either the first word of the title, subtitle or first full sentence. Slightly over a third of these (10) are in combination with *years*.

It might be objected that this finding is the product of the number of instances of *sixty* in sentence-initial position in my data and of the shortness of the texts in my newspaper corpus. If after all a word is put into sentence-initial position often enough in a corpus of short texts, it might well follow that it will appear frequently in text-initial position. If the texts in which sentence-initial *sixty* appears were on average ten sentences long, then there would be a one in ten chance of its being text-initial, without there being any need for an explanation in terms of priming. To check whether this was so, I therefore counted all the sentences in every text where *sixty* was the first word, and found that these texts averaged 20 sentences in length. There is therefore a one in twenty chance of sentence-initial *sixty* occurring at the beginning of a text on the basis of random distribution. Given, though, that the actual proportion of instances of sentence-initial *sixty* that are also text-initial is one in seven, *sixty* is occurring at the beginning of texts three times as often as it should do on the basis of random distribution.

We saw with *army* that textual priming for cohesion varies according to the operation or otherwise of other primings. The same is true for textual colligation. One of the common of collocations of *sixty* is with *per cent*. If this collocation is adopted, the textual priming for text-initial position is overridden. Out of

91 instances of *Sixty per cent* in sentence-initial position, only three are also text-initial. If these are taken out of the equation, we are left with 26 text-initial instances of *sixty* occurring within a data bank of 117 sentence-initial instances. This means that nearly a quarter of all sentence-initial instances are text-initial and that *sixty* occurs text-initially about five times more often than random distribution would predict.

The reasons why *sixty* begins newspaper texts are all related to the goal of newspaper production. Newspapers are more aware of their place in time than any other kind of discourse; a number of articles begin *Sixty years ago . . .* , a fact we shall return to below. An example is:

1   *Sixty years ago*, a dying Elgar went to France to make peace with Delius and hear his music interpreted by a prodigy.

Furthermore, they have a need for particularity; Bell (1991) describes how precise statistics are a characteristic of newspaper writing. If an event affects *sixty* people, it may be a significant event, for example:

2   *Sixty* schools were closed this week in southern Bulgaria as tension mounted between nationalists and ethnic Turks demanding language teaching for their children.

The fact that the choice of *sixty* is the product of external factors does not constitute a challenge to the notion of textual priming. In the first place, the text-initial priming of *sixty* does not extend to *60* (nor do many of its other primings – there is no association of *60* with vagueness, for example). So the choice of *sixty* over *60* is made simultaneously with one of the discoursal choices described above. Secondly, a *Guardian* writer is not obliged to place *sixty* in sentence-initial position. They could just as easily have written:

3   A dying Elgar went to France *sixty years ago* to make peace with Delius and hear his music interpreted by a prodigy.
4   Tension has mounted in southern Bulgaria between nationalists and ethnic Turks demanding language teaching for their children and *sixty* schools have been closed this week.

If these sound less likely as the beginnings of texts, it is only because they no longer contain the appropriate primings for text-initial position.

Thirdly, and importantly from the point of view of critical discourse analysis and sociolinguistics, the claim is that the priming of *sixty* for journalists (and consequently for their readers) is created in exactly the same way as all other primings. They simply have encountered numerous previous examples of *sixty* in text-initial position and unthinkingly reproduce the priming in their own writing, in so doing (re)creating and satisfying an expectation in the readers. Journalists do not think of writing articles that focus on the events of *fifty-nine* or *sixty-one* years ago, even though decades have no special value as a way of talking about changes in the world and even though the events of 59 or 61 years ago are presumably as interesting as those that happened *sixty* years ago. Likewise, because they have been primed by exposure to the writings of such journalists, readers would be puzzled to encounter articles beginning 'Sixty-one years ago . . .'.

I have reiterated throughout this book that claims about priming have to be domain and genre specific and nowhere is this more true than in the area of textual priming. My suggested explanations for the fact that *sixty* is textually primed are entirely dependent on the nature of newspaper writing and have no application to, say, travel writing or academic texts. We shall see shortly that travel writing has its own primings and the same is likely to be true for academic articles too. Upton and Connor (2004) have shown that the different sections and moves that can be used to describe research papers (e.g. Swales 1990) differ in their expression of stance and Gledhill (2000) has shown how collocations differ in scientific papers, depending on whether the words are found in the abstract, introduction, methodology or conclusion sections. Given these demonstrated differences, it would be unexpected if at least the sections were not marked out in the manner I have described. Intuitively, for example, I would guess that the word *recent* might be positively primed for text-initial position in academic articles. Word sequences such as *recent research*, *recent advances* and *recent developments* seem familiar as text-opening gambits (though if there is one thing a corpus linguist quickly learns it is that their intuitions almost always simplify the picture or tell outright lies – primings affect recognition, but they seem to have little impact upon intuitions).

An experiment with paragraphing

With these results in mind, it seems worth revisiting earlier work on paragraphing. In the 1960s a series of influential papers were published that saw the paragraph as a structural unit, with a topic sentence that was then restricted and illustrated (Becker 1965, 1966; Christensen 1965, 1966). Support for this position was to be found in an important but neglected book by Robert Longacre (1968), which showed that some Philippine languages had special markers for paragraph boundaries and offered a structural description of the paragraph, based on tagmemic theory. Although Longacre's evidence is convincing for the languages he describes, the evidence for paragraph structure in English has always seemed suspect (Rodgers 1966; Stern 1976; Hoey 1985), though years of teaching paragraph structure in freshman English classes will have had a priming effect and the structure may be truer today than it was when it was first proposed.

A key paper in the early description of paragraphing was Young and Becker (1966). Never properly published, presumably because it did not chime in with the theoretical interests of the time, but made available as a progress report, the paper described an experiment with paragraphing whereby a short extract from a monograph on American Civil War history was given to a small group of informants in de-paragraphed form and the informants were required to re-paragraph it. What rightly interested Young and Becker was the fact that there was a considerable measure of agreement among their informants as to where the paragraph breaks should come. At the time they interpreted this as evidence of the existence of paragraph structure; I suspect it was the only reasonable interpretation, given the emphasis on sentence structure in linguistics in the 1960s. Nearly 20 years later, however, I argued that the breaks their informants favoured were not made because they were recognising paragraph structural units but because they were responding to their perceptions of the way the text as a whole was structured (Hoey 1985). Either way, Young and Becker's paper showed that paragraphing was not random.

In the light of evidence that some words are primed for particular paragraph and text positions, it seemed worthwhile to revisit Young and Becker's experiment to see whether the informants were in fact revealing how they had been primed. I therefore re-conducted the experiment with a larger sample of informants in 1996. The informants in question were 67 first-year undergraduate students, who had not been taught about either priming or paragraphing (at least not at the university). I reported my findings in Hoey (1997c) and here reinterpret these findings in the light of the theory of lexis proposed in this book.

The passage Young and Becker used in their experiment, and which therefore I also used in mine, was the following, taken from *Lincoln and His Generals* by T. Harry Williams:

1   Grant was, judged by modern standards, the greatest general
2   of the Civil War. He was head and shoulders above any general on either
3   side as an over-all strategist, as a master of what in later wars
4   would be called global strategy. His Operation Crusher plan, the
5   product of a mind which had received little formal instruction in the
6   higher area of war, would have done credit to the most finished
7   student of a series of modern staff and command schools. He was a
8   brilliant theatre strategist, as evidenced by the Vicksburg campaign,
9   which was a classic field and siege operation. He was a better
10   than average tactician, although, like even the best generals of
11   both sides, he did not appreciate the destruction that the increasing
12   firepower of modern armies could visit on troops advancing across
13   open spaces. Lee is usually ranked as the greatest
14   Civil War general, but this evaluation has been made without

15   placing Lee and Grant in the perspective of military
16   developments since the war. Lee was interested hardly at all
17   in 'global' strategy, and what few suggestions he did make to
18   his government about operations in other theatres than his own
19   indicate that he had little aptitude for grand planning.
20   As a theatre strategist, Lee often demonstrated more brilliance
21   and apparent originality than Grant, but his most audacious plans were
22   as much the product of the Confederacy's inferior military
23   position as of his own fine mind. In war, the weaker side
24   has to improvise brilliantly. It must strike quickly, daringly,
25   and include a dangerous element of risk in its plans. Had Lee
26   been a Northern general with Northern resources behind him he would
27   have improvised less and seemed less bold. Had Grant been
28   a Southern general, he would have fought as Lee did.
29   Fundamentally Grant was superior to Lee because in a modern
30   total war he had a modern mind, and Lee did not. Lee
31   looked to the past in war as the Confederacy did in spirit.
32   The staffs of the two men illustrate their outlooks. It would
33   not be accurate to say that Lee's general staff were
34   glorified clerks, but the statement would not be too wide
35   off the mark . . .

As I have noted in papers on Young and Becker's experiment (Hoey 1985, 1997c), this passage is organised according to two major principles. In the first place it makes use of a matrix (Hoey 1991c, 2001), whereby a set of largely parallel questions are asked of two topics – Grant and Lee. The matrix can be set out as shown in Table 7.1. The sequencing of the text follows the first column down until the penultimate question and then moves to the second column, moving back to the first column for the final question. It would be logical therefore to mark the movement across the columns with a paragraph break. Such a break would occur at line 13. It would also be logical to mark the movement back with a break at line 29.

More subtly, there are two places where the parallelism of the two halves of the passage is not strictly maintained. The first occurs when evidence is provided for Grant's superiority as a global strategist. It would be possible to mark the deviation from the symmetry either by marking a paragraph at line 4 where the 'digression' begins or at line 7 where it ends (but probably not at both). The second occurs when a substantial explanation is embarked on for the apparent greater brilliance of Lee. A break at line 23 would mark this.

Finally, the parallelism is weighted in the direction of Grant with Lee being unfavourably compared with him on several counts. It is therefore surprising that Lee comes off better as a theatre strategist. A paragraph break at line 20

Table 7.1 A matrix analysis of the Grant/Lee passage

	Grant	Lee
Who was the greatest general of the Civil War?	Grant was, judged by modern standards, the greatest . . . (lines 1–2)	Lee is usually ranked as the greatest Civil War general . . . (lines 13–16)
Who was the greatest global strategist?	He was head and shoulders above any general . . . (lines 2–4)	Lee was interested hardly at all in global strategy . . . (lines 16–19)
What evidence have you for saying so? OR Give me an example	His Operation Crusher plan . . . (lines 4–7)	–
Who was the greatest theatre strategist?	He was a brilliant theatre strategist . . . He was a better than average tactician . . . (lines 7–13)	As a theatre strategist, Lee often demonstrated more brilliance and apparent originality (lines 20–23)
Why was this?	[answered within 7–13]	In war, the weaker side has to improvise brilliantly . . . [lines 23–28]
Who was the better and why?	Fundamentally Grant was superior to Lee, because . . . he had a modern mind and Lee did not . . . [line 29–31]	

would both mark out the surprising nature of the information and prepare the reader for the detailed explanation that follows.

The matrix analysis, it should be emphasised, does not imply that any of these paragraph breaks should be mandatory, but it would be strange if a large group of informants, given the passage to paragraph, did not among them take some account of the factors I have just described.

The second organising principle that shapes the passage is one of an argument containing statements of different level of generality. The argument's pattern, somewhat crudely represented, is shown in Figure 7.1. Such a pattern would also justify breaks at lines 29 and 32.

So much for the organisation of the passage and the places where paragraph breaks would be motivated. How did my informants in fact choose to paragraph the passage? They were asked to paragraph the passage above, which was in exactly the format given here with the lines numbered; indeed the format is identical to that used by Young and Becker. The students were only given five minutes to decide where to make breaks but were free to decide for themselves

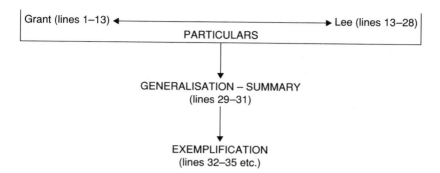

Figure 7.1 A partial representation of the organisation of the passage

Table 7.2 The distribution of the students' paragraph break choices

Line on which sentence starts	Number of informants beginning a paragraph at this point	% of informants making the choice
2	0	—
4	11	17
7	22	33
9	0	—
13	62	94
16	7	11
20	32	49
23	32	49
24	0	—
25	2	3
27	1	2
29	42	64
30	0	—
32 (The . . .)	13	20
32 (It . . .)	5	8

how many breaks were required. Slightly less than half went for three paragraph breaks with the remainder ranging from one to eight; the totality of their decisions of where to break is given in Table 7.2. The total for each paragraph break is given in terms of the lines in which the sentences begin.

As can be seen, the students were not unanimous about the appropriate place to break. No single positive choice enjoyed complete support, though the sentence beginning in line 13 came closest in this respect with 94 per cent favouring this as an appropriate place to break. There were, however, several places where the students were unanimous that a break was not desirable – the sentences beginning on lines 9, 24 and 30 were all roundly rejected as break points. Generally, though, the lack of unanimity casts doubt upon claims for the structural status of the paragraph.

In terms of the organisation of the passage described above, possible explanations for the students' decisions are as follows. The near-unanimity of the break at line 13 marks the place where the passage moves from column 1 to column 2. This move is fundamental to recognition of the parallels that are being created between Grant and Lee in terms of the way they have been evaluated and any decision **not** to break at line 13 would have important implications for the readers in terms of their ability to discern that parallelism.

Other decisions are less likely to affect fundamentally the readers' orientation, but nevertheless may subtly tweak it in a number of ways. The 11 people who broke at line 4 are marking out the place where the parallelism between Grant and Lee breaks down and the 22 people who broke at line 7 are indicating the place where the parallelism returns. The 32 who broke at line 20 are highlighting the place in the text where the answer provided by the writer is unexpected, though strictly there is no deviation from the parallelism, while the 32 who broke at line 23 may have been motivated either by the desire to highlight the move from particulars to supportive generalisation or by the wish to mark a deviation from the parallelism in a manner similar to that posited as an explanation for those who broke at line 4. Those who broke at line 29 – almost two thirds of the students – were presumably indicating the shift to summary and, perhaps, the return to the Grant side of the matrix.

These, then, are the textual explanations for the students' choices. In 1985, when I first considered the Young and Becker experiment, they were the only explanations that I considered necessary. However, there are some problems lurking in the informants' responses. In two places there is real doubt as to where to break, with line 4 and line 7 sharing the burden of indicating deviation from the parallelism of the underlying matrix and lines 20 and 23 evenly divided. Furthermore, seven informants broke at line 16 where there is no justifiable textual reason for breaking and three informants broke at either line 25 or 27, where again there is no obvious structural reason for a break.

One possible explanation for the students' failure to agree on where the most appropriate breaks might come was that they had a conflict to resolve between responding to the structure and communicative purpose of the passage and responding to their priming as reflected in the lexical items that begin the sentences of the passage.

With this in mind, I set about examining whether there was any evidence that the words used at the beginning of each of the students' paragraph breaks were primed to begin (or avoid beginning) a paragraph. My intention in doing so was to identify possible paragraph 'triggers' and see whether there was any correlation between the use of such apparent triggers and the choices made by the students. For this reason, I did not use a large body of data to establish whether words were textually primed in the manner described, simply because the test of their priming would come as much from the students' responses as it would from the corpus. In most cases, the numbers looked at were less than 100 instances, and in a couple of cases, as will be seen, very few indeed. This only matters if we assume that corpora are the only valid evidence for the existence or otherwise of primings. Part of the point of the experiment I am reporting is that priming can be explored in more than one way.

A number of the sentences in the passage have as their first word the names *Grant* and *Lee*, and a number of the more popular paragraph breaks co-occur with their use. It made sense therefore to see whether the semantic set SURNAME was primed for use at the beginnings of paragraphs.

My corpus, as already mentioned, is mainly made up of *Guardian* newspaper text from the years 1991–4, during which period the British prime minister was John Major and the leader of the opposition was Tony Blair. Given that Grant and Lee are in the passage being compared and contrasted, and Major and Blair were in a natural position to be contrasted by virtue of their being electoral opponents, it seemed natural to create two concordances of 100 instances each of the names *Major* and *Blair* and examine them for sentence-initial instances. Surprisingly, given their apparent centrality to British political news, only 5 instances of *Major* and 13 of *Blair* were actually sentence-initial. This strongly suggested that surnames (or at least **these** surnames) are negatively primed for this position. Since my objective was to examine the paragraph priming of surnames, I added a further 22 surnames manually by consulting book reviews and interviews, giving me a total sample of 40 single sentence-initial surnames (i.e. without accompanying first names). This is in itself a tiny sample, but it should be remembered that the corpus analysis in this instance was designed to generate hypotheses about priming that could be checked against the students' paragraphing decisions.

When the 40 surnames that were sentence-initial were examined, it was found that exactly half were also paragraph-initial. So, on admittedly sparse data, it looks as if sentence-initial SURNAME is primed to begin paragraphs. We seem here to be looking at the possibility that when a negative priming (for sentence-initial position) is overridden, a positive priming (for paragraph-initial position) comes into play. As we shall see, this seems to be a quite common kind of nesting in connection with textual colligation, where an overridden negative priming triggers a textual colligational priming.

In the passage that the students paragraphed, a SURNAME begins sentences on lines 1, 13, 16 and 30. Line 1 is automatically the beginning of a paragraph by virtue of beginning the passage (it was also the beginning of a paragraph in the original) and line 13 was the most popular choice made by the students, so the sentences that start on these lines support the view that SURNAME is a trigger for paragraphing. So, in a rather different way, does the sentence that starts on line 16. I remarked above that there appear to be no structural or logical reasons for making a break at this juncture, and yet 11 per cent of the students chose to break there. If SURNAME is primed to begin paragraphs, it may be that these students followed their primings at the expense of their sense of the shape of the passage.

Only the sentence that starts on line 30 provides no support for the hypothesis. This need not worry us. In the first place, it is flanked by sentences which, as we shall see, compete to be a break. Secondly, it is near the end of the extract and there is some evidence to suggest that the students did not in the main choose to make breaks in the last quarter of the text. Thirdly, and most importantly, priming is always a matter of probability rather than requirement.

A very different picture from that found for SURNAME revealed itself when I looked at the word *he*, which, like the surnames *Grant* and *Lee* begins a number of candidate paragraph breaks in the passage (lines 2, 7, 9). Whereas surnames avoided sentence-initial position, the evidence pointed towards *he* being positively primed for this position. Of 100 instances consulted, 30 were in very first position in the sentence. On the other hand, this positive priming for being sentence-initial was not accompanied by a positive priming for paragraph-initial position. In fact *he* occurred in paragraph-initial position in the sample I examined two and a half times less often than would have been occurred as a result of random distribution. So here was a very different hypothesis from that we arrived at for SURNAME – the nesting of *he* with first word in the sentence is negatively primed for beginning a paragraph.

In the passage, there are three places where the pronoun *he* begins a sentence and two of these (on lines 2 and 9) the students unanimously rejected as paragraph boundaries. So, perhaps predictably (but as before I appeal to the predictability as evidence of the psychological truth of textual colligational priming), names are primed to start paragraphs and pronouns are not. The third, however, on line 7, where a third of the students chose to begin a new paragraph, represents a counter example. We shall return to this example shortly, but for now I note that there are good rhetorical grounds for breaking at this juncture in that, as I noted above, it marks the place where the text returns to the (at this stage invisible) parallelism between the two generals. It also returns to the topic of the ways in which Grant is evaluated.

So far we have hypothesised that the negative sentence-initial priming of SURNAME exists alongside a positive paragraph-initial priming and that the positive sentence-initial priming of *he* exists alongside a negative paragraph priming. It would be tempting to assume that this reversal of primings might be regular. However, when I examined 100 instances of the word *his* (which of course begins line 4 of the Civil War passage), I found that, unlike *he*, *his* was negatively primed to begin sentences, but that, like *he*, when it was sentence-initial it was also negatively primed for beginning paragraphs. So *his* is an instance of a word that is negatively primed for both sentence-initial and paragraph-initial position. Seventeen per cent of the students broke at line 4 where the sentence beginning with *his* occurs. This is definitely a minority choice, especially as there are reasonable grounds for breaking here, as we have seen.

Another pronoun that appears at the beginning of a potential paragraph break is *it*, which begins the sentence at line 24. Because of the multitude of uses to which the word *it* is put, no attempt was made to determine whether the pronominal use, like *he*, favoured sentence-initial position. Instead, attention was given to whether it offered a plausible opportunity for a new paragraph. To this end I examined 149 sentence-initial instances of *it* in its anaphoric pronominal use. Only 8 per cent of these (just 12 cases) turned out to be also paragraph-initial position. Given that one in four might have been expected on the basis of random distribution, we can assume that pronominal *it* is negatively primed for beginning paragraphs. This is certainly supported by the students who were again unanimous in not starting a paragraph at line 24.

The instance of *it* at line 24 is not the only case of a sentence in the Civil War passage beginning with *it*. Line 32 also begins with *it*, but here its use is anticipatory rather than anaphoric. In this use, it would appear to be positively primed for paragraph initiation (though this judgement is based on examination of only 65 instances), in that 24 of the 65 instances begin paragraphs. Here, the students do not at first sight provide support. A meagre 8 per cent selected the sentence on line 32 as a paragraph boundary. However, 8 per cent starts to look like a large proportion when one realises that this is the final sentence of the passage and that both the desire to avoid one-sentence stragglers and uncertainty about the way the passage might continue would militate against its selection as the beginning of a new paragraph.

Instances of SURNAME and pronouns account for the initial words of ten of the sentences of the Civil War passage. We are left with a small number of singly occurring phrases. One of these is *as a theatre strategist*, which begins a sentence on line 20 of the passage. Working on the assumption that this was an instance of a local semantic association between *as a* and JOB/WORK ROLE, I looked for instances of this association. Initially I examined 1000 instances of *as a* and found that, excluding the sentence conjuncts *as a consequence*, *as a result* and *as an example* there were only 35 instances of *as a* occurring at the beginning of a sentence. Of these 35 cases, 17 conformed to the semantic association *as a* JOB/WORK ROLE, and eight of these began paragraphs. Such data may not contradict the claim that *as a* JOB/WORK ROLE is primed to begin paragraphs, but they can hardly be used as strong evidence in its support. However, the students' communal judgement is certainly compatible with it; almost exactly half chose to break at line 20.

Another sentence-initial phrase used in the passage is *in war*, which offers the possibility of a paragraph break at line 23. However, it proved very difficult to investigate the primings of this phrase using a corpus. From 215 instances of *in war* as a self-standing prepositional phrase (though including instances of *in war and (in) peace*), there were only 15 examples of the phrase in sentence-initial position – another instance of negative priming for beginning sentences. (There were, however, 56 instances of *in war* in final position in the sentence and a further 33 that were in final position in their clauses, strongly pointing to the phrase having a textual colligation for end position.)

Of the 15 cases of sentence-initial *in war*, few as they were, five were also paragraph-initial. As the average length of the paragraphs which they began was five sentences, this incidence of paragraph-initial cases hints at the phrase being positively primed to begin paragraphs; so, very provisionally, one would hypothesise that *in war* is positively primed to occur sentence-finally and paragraph-initially – but not at the same time! The students' choices certainly support the view that the phrase is positively primed to begin paragraphs when it is sentence-initial. Almost half made a paragraph break at line 23, even though it is really just an extension of the point being made in the previous sentence – another instance, perhaps, where the posited conflict between the priming and the rhetorical shape of the passage was resolved in favour of the priming.

The words *Had X been* do not appear to be primed, one way or the other, for paragraph breaks. Examination of 243 instances of *Had X been* showed that the word sequence's association with paragraph boundaries was dependent on whether SURNAME or PRONOUN filled the spot marked by *X*. Of 25 instances of *Had* SURNAME *been* (all there were in my corpus), 12 are paragraph-initial. On the other hand, out of 158 instances of *Had* PRONOUN *been* (PRONOUN here being limited to the traditional set of *you, he, she, we, they, this, that, these* and *those*) only 29 were paragraph-initial.

These results are entirely in line with those for SURNAME and *he* and *it* given above. However, in so far as there is any evidence about the priming of *Had . . . been* on its own, the evidence points towards the word combination having a different kind of priming for the typical *Guardian* writer (and reader). While it is true that almost half of the instances of *Had* SURNAME *been* are paragraph-initial, the paragraphs are characteristically shorter than is the average for my data as a whole. Calculations of paragraph length in my corpus as a whole suggest that (one-sentence paragraphs as always excluded) the average length is four sentences and that figure has been repeatedly borne out when calculating the average length of particular sets of paragraphs. For *Had* SURNAME *been*, however, the average length of the paragraphs is exactly three sentences and only 2 paragraphs from the 12 considered are above this level.

The same picture occurs with *Had* PRONOUN *been*. At first sight, the average length of the 29 paragraph-initial cases – 3.4 sentences – seems to be only slightly lower than that for paragraph length in the corpus as a whole. But this includes two paragraphs of 10 and 14 sentences length respectively. With these excluded from the calculation, the average comes to under 2.8 sentences per paragraph. A total of 12 of the paragraphs initiated by *Had* PRONOUN *been* are only two sentences in length.

The data are not large, because sentence-initial cases of non-interrogative *Had X been* are not numerous. A further 14 paragraph-initial instances of *Had X been* were however looked at (where the X was either a country's or a company's name, an abstraction or a first name) and these, too, were found to be in short paragraphs, averaging 2.6 sentences. (I have made no calculation of the number of one-sentence paragraphs that occur in typical texts in my corpus as a whole, but my impression while undertaking the analyses was that there were also many more one-sentence paragraphs associated with *Had X been* than I would have expected.) It would therefore seem to be that where *Had X been* is paragraph-initial in newspaper text, we are primed to expect the paragraph that follows to be short. So textual colligational priming is not simply a matter of positioning but of length. Since in newspapers hypothetical statements are unlikely to be the focus of attention, it is not difficult to see how this priming might arise.

It will be remembered that the three people who broke at lines 25 and 27 (*Had Lee been* . . . , *Had Grant been* . . .) had little structural grounds for doing so. Their decision to break in these places is now explicable in terms of the apparent preference of *Had* SURNAME *been* for beginning paragraphs, itself driven by the textual colligational priming of SURNAME. In each case the paragraphs they produced were either one or two sentences in length, as would be predicted on the basis of the data we have been considering.

The word *fundamentally* starts the potential paragraph break at line 29, and instinct (my priming?) would suggest that it is primed positively for beginning paragraphs in this position. Evidence for this, however, is hard to find. Out of 786 instances of *fundamentally*, only 20 were the first word in their sentence, which of course left me with few data to work on: clearly the word does not like to begin sentences. Of the 20 sentence-initial cases, 6 begin paragraphs and 13 do not, with one instance beginning a one-sentence paragraph. The average length of the paragraphs is five sentences, though the mean is four. This means that, subject to the cautions necessary from the paucity of data, we have evidence for believing that *fundamentally* begins paragraphs roughly 50 per cent more often than can be accounted on the basis of random distribution. This putative positive priming is certainly supported by the students, almost two thirds of whom chose to begin a paragraph at line 29.

The word sequence that starts the first sentence on line 32 – *The staffs* – did not permit investigation in my data, there being only one sentence-initial instance in 100 million words. However, *illustrate* was more promising, both because it is considerably more frequent in my corpus and because it is a lexical signal of the generalisation-exemplification relation and might therefore be expected to participate in the chunking of text. A sample of 100 instances of *illustrate* used as a finite verb in main clause constructions with a non-pictorial sense were examined, and it was found that 38 of the instances began paragraphs of more than one sentence. There were in addition 17 single-sentence paragraphs – again, intuitively, a high number. Removing the latter from the calculation, 46 per cent of the instances eligible to begin paragraphs of more than one sentence were indeed paragraph-initial. Since the average length of the paragraphs so begun was 3.7, we can infer that *illustrate* is one and half times more likely to begin a paragraph than random distribution would predict. In accordance with this finding, 20 per cent of the students chose to break at line 32, despite the fact that little of the passage remains beyond this point.

We can represent the match (or mismatch) of the students' choices against the structural grounds for breaking and the textual colligational grounds for breaking, as shown in Table 7.3. I have represented both sets of grounds crudely in terms of **positive** or **negative**. Even allowing for the lack of subtlety in this, there is a considerable matching between students' decisions on where to make a paragraph break and whether there are organisational or colligational grounds

Table 7.3 A match of the paragraphing decision of the students with the organisational and lexical factors that might have led to those decisions

Sentence-initial word or phrase	Line no.	Organisational grounds for breaking	Paragraph-initial colligational priming	% of informants making a paragraph break at this point (67 informants)
Grant	1	Positive	Positive	100 (by default)
He	2	Negative	Negative	0
His	4	Positive	Negative	17
He	7	Positive	Negative	33
He	9	Negative	Negative	0
Lee	13	Positive	Positive	94
Lee	16	Negative	Positive	11
As a JOB/WORK ROLE	20	Positive	Positive	49
In war	23	Positive	Positive	49
It (pronoun)	24	Negative	Negative	0
Had SURNAME been	25	Negative	Positive	3
Had SURNAME been	27	Negative	Positive	3
Fundamentally	29	Positive	Positive	64
Lee	30	Negative	Positive	0
illustrate	32a	Positive	Positive	20
It (anticipatory)	32b	Negative	Positive	8

or not for such a break, the only mismatch coming near the end of the passage when both shortage of time and uncertainty about how the passage might continue will have affected the pattern of decisions.

One point to note with the results presented in Table 7.3 is that textual colligational priming and structural factors only support each other up to a certain point. There is therefore ample reason here why the students should have been undecided as to how to make their paragraph breaks. Pulled one way by structural factors and another by their lexical primings, it is no wonder that there was no unanimity among them. What from a lexical point of view seem unmotivated breaks (at lines 4 and 7) are justifiable in structural terms. More frequently, what from a structural point of view seem anomalous breaks by a minority (at lines 16, 25, 27 and 32) become explicable in terms of lexical priming.

A further experiment

The decisions that were made by the students are open in themselves to further investigation. I have, for example, posited that there is a tension between the structural desire to mark deviation from and return to the parallelism between Grant and Lee on the one hand and the negative priming of *his* and *he* on the other. Why not test whether this is the case by converting one of the pronouns (*his*) to a surname (*Grant's*)? Similarly, I have claimed that the only reason people want to break at line 16 is because the surname is primed for them to begin paragraphs. So why not change *Lee* to a pronoun? If, as I have claimed, the word sequence *as a* JOB/WORK ROLE is primed to begin paragraphs, why not move it later into the sentence? (Of course, this will leave us with *Lee* at the beginning of the sentence, so this will simultaneously have to be converted into a pronoun.) And, if *in war* is apparently primed for beginning paragraphs, what will happen if it is moved to the end of the sentence?

All of these changes do not affect the meaning of the passage and all result in entirely natural sentences (at least to my intuition – I have not undertaken the necessary colligational analysis to prove that they are, though we saw in our analysis above that the latter two changes are in line with the normal use for such nestings). The result is the following adapted passage. As you will see, the line numberings remain the same and the passage still reads normally. I have emboldened the changes.

1 Grant was, judged by modern standards, the greatest general
2 of the Civil War. He was head and shoulders above any general on either
3 side as an over-all strategist, as a master of what in later wars
4 would be called global strategy. **Grant's** Operation Crusher plan, the

5   product of a mind which had received little formal instruction in the
6   higher area of war, would have done credit to the most finished
7   student of a series of modern staff and command schools. He was a
8   brilliant theatre strategist, as evidenced by the Vicksburg campaign,
9   which was a classic field and siege operation. He was a better
10   than average tactician, although, like even the best generals of
11   both sides, he did not appreciate the destruction that the increasing
12   firepower of modern armies could visit on troops advancing across
13   open spaces. Lee is usually ranked as the greatest
14   Civil War general, but this evaluation has been made without
15   placing Lee and Grant in the perspective of military
16   developments since the war. **He** was interested hardly at all
17   in 'global' strategy, and what few suggestions he did make to
18   his government about operations in other theatres than his own
19   indicate that he had little aptitude for grand planning.
20   **He** often demonstrated more brilliance and apparent originality
21   as a theatre strategist than Grant, but his most audacious plans were
22   as much the product of the Confederacy's inferior military
23   position as of his own fine mind. **T**he weaker side
24   has to improvise brilliantly **in war**. It must strike quickly, daringly,
25   and include a dangerous element of risk in its plans. Had Lee
26   been a Northern general with Northern resources behind him he would
27   have improvised less and seemed less bold. Had Grant been
28   a Southern general, he would have fought as Lee did.
29   Fundamentally Grant was superior to Lee because in a modern
30   total war he had a modern mind, and Lee did not. Lee
31   looked to the past in war as the Confederacy did in spirit.
32   The staffs of the two men illustrate their outlooks. It would
33   not be accurate to say that Lee's general staff were
34   glorified clerks, but the statement would not be too wide
35   off the mark . . .

I then gave this modified version (without the emboldening, of course) to 32 native speaker first-year undergraduate students, who had, like the previous group, not been taught about either priming or paragraphing at the university. None of them were party to the previous experiment and the conditions under which they performed the test were the same as with the previous group; the need to ensure no overlap with, or knowledge of, the earlier experiment accounts for the smaller number of informants.

Table 7.4 shows how the second group's choices compare with those of the first group. I have highlighted the lines where the sentences were modified, since it is with these sentences that we are mainly concerned. In the latter part of the

Table 7.4 A comparison of the paragraphing decisions of the two sets of informants on the original and modified passage

Line	Number of second set of informants choosing this point as a paragraph break	% of second set of informants choosing this point as a paragraph break (32 informants)	% of original set of informants choosing this point as a paragraph break (67 informants)
2	0	0	0
4	12	38	17
7	6	19	33
9	1	3	0
13	31	97	94
16	1	3	11
20	7	22	49
23	19	59	49
24	0	0	0
25	5	16	3
27	1	3	3
29	19	59	64
30	2	6	0
32a	5	16	20
32b	1	3	8

passage where no changes were made, the two groups behave in similar fashion. So we again have an isolated decision to break at line 27, presumably driven by the positive priming of *Had* SURNAME *been*. We again have slightly under a third of informants breaking at line 29 and a minority breaking at the first of the sentences on line 32. A couple of informants have chosen this time round to break at line 30, again motivated, one guesses, by the positive priming of SURNAME, and the second sentence on line 32 continues to punch below its lexical priming weight! But generally the pattern of decisions is very similar.

However, earlier in the text, everything has changed. It was hypothesised that changing one of the pronouns on line 4 to a surname would motivate a change of paragraphing practice and so it proves. The proportion of people choosing to paragraph at line 4 has more than doubled, despite its being structurally more natural to break at the point when the parallelism returns. Correspondingly, the latter break has nearly halved in popularity.

It was also hypothesised that removing the surname at the beginning of line 16 would remove the temptation to break there. This proved more or less to be the case; a solitary informant has inexplicably made a break but the proportion has dropped from 11 to 3 per cent.

Perhaps the most radical change in the ways that the two groups of informants have chosen where to break comes at line 20. Moving *as a theatre strategist* later into the sentence and replacing *Lee* by *he* has resulted in a drop from almost half to less than a quarter of informants starting a new paragraph at this juncture despite the continuing good structural reasons for breaking here. Furthermore, the effect of the apparent unavailability of this breakpoint has driven a large proportion of the informants to break at line 23, the proportion rising from 49 to 59 per cent.

The pressure to keep paragraphs to a length of three or four lines, and the apparent unavailability of the sentence that begins on line 24, makes line 23 seem an attractive break. Nevertheless we have to concede that, alone among the hypotheses we were seeking to test, the hypothesis that moving *in war* to the end of the sentence would result in a drop in its popularity as a paragraph break is the one that has not been supported. This deserved further attention. I therefore looked at 137 instances of sentence-initial *The* ADJECTIVE *side* (excluding national, county and continental adjectives). (It will be remembered that this nesting of primings was looked at in connection with textual semantic association, where it was found to be associated with contrast. It hardly needs saying that contrast is built into the accompanying adjective in this instance.)

Eleven of the instances of *The* ADJECTIVE *side* were text-initial, usually in the title, and these were excluded, as were one-sentence paragraphs (of which there were 10). I also excluded any cases at the beginning of quoted speech (9), unless there was also paragraph indentation. Instances elsewhere in speech were regarded as non-paragraph-initial and included in the calculations. Once the exclusions were made, I was left with 106 instances of *The* ADJECTIVE *side*, of which 47 (44 per cent) began paragraphs; the average length of the paragraphs was 3.4 sentences. Random distribution would have accounted for 29 per cent of the cases. We can therefore conclude that all I had done in moving *in war* to the end of the sentence was substitute one paragraph-primed word sequence for another.

A final return to the Bill Bryson passage

The evidence from the corpus investigation and the paragraph experiments points to there being a priming text-initiation and paragraph-initiation, some words being primed positively for these textual positions and others being primed negatively. The Bill Bryson passage quoted on page 124 begins the book *Neither Here Nor There*. It is therefore appropriate we should return a final time to his words to see whether the first sentence contains any likely lexical primings for text-initiation and whether the beginnings of the next two paragraphs are primed for paragraph-initiation.

A clue to one of the textual colligations operative in the Bill Bryson sentence we have so often examined comes in a sentence in my corpus that parallels it quite closely. I have italicized the places where the sentences vary:

5   *Ntobeye* is a *two*-hour ride by *four wheel drive vehicle* from *the vast refugee camp at Ngara*.

The author of this sentence drew on a different PLACE NAME for the subject and a periphrastic phrase is used in place of *Oslo*, the VEHICLE is no longer a *bus* and the time of the journey is shorter, but it is otherwise Bill Bryson's sentence! Hammerfest is much smaller than Oslo and the vastness of the refugee camp couples with my ignorance of Ntobeye to make me assume that Ntobeye is not large. Where two places are named in the same clause, the smaller will have a strong tendency to be thematised and the larger to be at the end of the Rheme; this is a rather specific kind of textual colligation.

Examination of 300 instances of place, drawn from a small specialised corpus of travel writing, revealed a further textual colligation that ties in with this, namely that in travel texts, PLACE NAME is primed colligationally to appear in the structure PLACE NAME + *is* + EVALUATION.

One can either see this as a colligation of PLACE NAME or as a colligation of *is*. From the latter perspective, the word *is* characteristically is primed to occur in the structure subject-verb-complement and, in combination with this structural choice, has as one of its semantic associations in travel writing the double association of PLACE + EVALUATION. The reason I mention this is that this combination in turn is primed to colligate with text-initial position in travel writing. Text-initial examples from my data include the following:

6   Madrid is one of the world's favourite meeting destinations.
7   At the very heart of Europe, Hungary is a magical land bursting with ancient culture . . .

On the face of it, the Bill Bryson sentence does not conform to this pattern, in that the *thirty-hour ride* is presumably factual (though the reader may supply an evaluation of such a long journey in winter). However, there are other textual colligational primings at work in the sentence. Re-examination of the same 300 instances of place names reveals that 133 were paragraph-initial (excluding one-sentence paragraphs). Given that the average length of the paragraphs in the data (as always excluding one-sentence paragraphs) was 3.5 sentences, this means that PLACE NAME is 50 per cent more likely to begin a paragraph than could be explained by random distribution. Furthermore, 31 of the place names are text-initial with another 15 appearing in titles. In other words, 15 per cent of all the place names in my mini-corpus of travel writing begin a text. Given that the texts in my corpus averaged 14 sentences in length, this means that PLACE NAME is twice as likely to begin a travel text as would be predictable on the basis of random distribution. On both counts the Bill Bryson sentence is in conformity with the typical priming of PLACE NAME.

Of the other paragraphs in the extract from *Neither Here Nor There*, one begins *I wanted to* and the other begins *Things*. The latter is an example of a word primed to begin paragraphs. Excluding the usual one-sentence paragraphs, text-initial instances and speech-initiations, I was left in my *Guardian* corpus with 417 sentence-initial instances of *Things*. Over 37 per cent of these (156 cases) were paragraph-initial. So Bill Bryson's usage is in keeping with its priming in newspaper text (though it remains to be investigated whether the priming typically operates in travel writing – my corpus was too small for such an investigation). Incidentally, there were 50 instances in my data of text-initial *Things*. The texts which it begins would have to be no more than nine sentences in length on average for this not to be evidence of its being positively primed for text-initial use. Though of course Bill Bryson does not make use of this priming, his paragraph is the start of a flashback and could be said to start his tale. This hints at more subtle types of priming than those I have discussed, crudely and at inordinate length, in this chapter.

The other paragraph beginning Bryson uses – *I wanted to* – seems to have no special association with paragraph boundaries at all. As I have repeatedly noted, primings are not rules. It is possible to override them. It is of interest that the likely explanation for the boundary is textual – the lack of cohesion between this and the previous paragraph, apart from the complex repetition involving *northern*, indicates a new start. We saw at the end of the previous chapter that the textual and the lexical seem to operate in different ways and here we have further evidence of the fact. I return to this matter in the next chapter.

Some conclusions

The evidence presented in this chapter suggests that we have to connect our systems of description of text organisation with our systems of description of lexis. I have argued for many years that text organisation has a lexical perspective (Hoey 1979, 1983, 1991a) but the implication of this and the previous chapter is that there is a hidden colligational signalling that none of us is pedagogically aware of (though in our own writing we probably show daily awareness in the choices we make and avoid). Writing effectively involves using appropriate text and paragraph beginnings. If there is one conclusion I would want to draw from this and the previous chapters it is that corpora are not just important for the study of the minutiae of language – they are central to a proper understanding of discourses as a whole, and that in turn means that there is no aspect of the teaching and learning of a language that can afford to ignore what corpus investigation can reveal. This is a matter I shall return to in the final chapter.

All of the positional claims I have made in this section are of course formulated in terms of the written word, but there is every reason to suppose that similar claims can be made about the beginning and end of speech turns, conversations and the like. Michael McCarthy (personal communication), who has access to the one of the best spoken corpora in the world (CANCODE), notes that *the* is primed negatively to occur at the beginning of speech turns. Conversely, in 51 examples of *I know* drawn from a small corpus of casual conversation of my own, 26 are either the first words of a turn or within one or two words of the beginning of a turn (e.g. *Yeah I know*, *No no I know*), suggesting that *I know* is typically primed positively for turn beginnings; none are conversation-initial. But work is needed on a much larger body of spoken data.

8 Lexical priming and grammatical creativity

Corpus linguistics versus generative linguistics

Painting in broad-brush strokes, traditional generative grammarians have derived their goals, if not their methods or descriptions, from Chomsky, and for them the distinction of a grammatical sentence from an ungrammatical one has been a central consideration. They have not been interested in probability of occurrence, only in possibility of occurrence. Most of their data have been invented examples and some of these have been hard to envisage in any context. They have, in short, been concerned with the creativity of language. Their models have been designed to account for **any** sentence, however extraordinary or unlikely, as long as informants have been willing to affirm that the sentence in question is an instance of English.

Still painting with a broad brush, corpus linguists in contrast have derived their goals and methods in part from John Sinclair and his associates and in part from what concordancing software currently makes feasible. These linguists have typically seen their goal as the uncovering of recurrent patterns in the language, usually lexical but increasingly grammatical. They have not been much concerned with the single linguistic instance but with probability of occurrence, and their data have been always authentic. They have been concerned with fluency in language rather than creativity, and corpus models have been designed to account for the normal and the naturally occurring.

Like all broad-brush paintings, this lacks light and shade. My account of the generative tradition allows no place for Fillmore, for example, who has been much concerned with matters of fluency and naturalness (Fillmore *et al.* 1988), and my account of current corpus linguistic work ignores the work of Carter (2004), for example, whose encounters with unexpected and inventive usages in spoken corpora has compelled him to place the nature and extent of creativity in language under careful and instructive scrutiny. But I stand by the general picture I have swiftly painted.

In Chapter 1, I argued that Bill Bryson's sentence showed that linguists had to account for naturalness as well as creativity, and in subsequent chapters I have tried to show some of the factors involved in the production/selection of a natural sentence and a natural text. Important as naturalness is, however, no claims about the nature of language can be countenanced that cannot address the issue of how language users are creative in their daily use of language, and in this respect generative grammarians have been perfectly correct in their focus. This and the next chapter accordingly attempt to show how a theory of lexical priming might handle different kinds of creativity.

Types of creativity

There are of course a number of recurrent uses of the term 'creativity' and their relationship is not simple. At one end of an imaginary spectrum, there is the Chomskyan use (Chomsky 1957) – creativity as a fundamental property of language. Chomsky's point, of course, was that we do not recall sentences, we newly create them, and he argued that this ability of any native speaker to newly mint sentences needed to be explained. Although lexical priming has, I hope, been shown to account for much that happens under the guise of newly minting sentences, it would be disingenuous to suggest that creativity in Chomsky's sense is thereby accounted for.

At the other end of the spectrum, there is the literary sense of creativity – original texts that refresh the language and force us to think and see things in new ways. If linguistics cannot say something interesting about literary language, it is an admission that we have not yet got to the heart of our discipline.

The former type of creativity – Chomsky's type – is invisible because it is all around us. All but a trivially small percentage of sentences are creative in his sense of the word. The latter type is on the other hand highly visible and highly valued. All but a trivially small percentage of sentences are uncreative in this second sense of the word.

In between these, there is actually another kind of creativity – sentences that make no claim to be literary but which surprise us in some way, either because they draw attention to themselves by their clever wording or because they are momentarily hard to process or make us aware that they are indeed made of language.

In this chapter I want to address the first of these types of creativity – the Chomskyan type. The concern here is to consider whether lexical priming can account not only for what is natural but also for what is possible. To do this, I will need to consider a number of issues – the nature of grammatical categories, the status of the word, issues of inflection and phonological priming, the movement from lexical to grammatical priming and the relationship between lexical and textual choices.

Grammatical categories

In my discussion of colligation and semantic association in this book, I have talked of grammatical functions and grammatical categories as if they were givens in the system. However, Hunston and Francis (2000) have shown that the grammatical functions can be reformulated in terms of grammatical categories. Although I have used grammatical functions such as Subject and Object as quick and understandable ways of talking about regularity of use in the clause, I believe Hunston and Francis' argument carries weight. So are we left, then, with grammatical categories as the grammatical bedrock without which we cannot have language? Sinclair (1991) seems to argue for this position, but I would like to question the prior existence of even the most basic of grammatical categories such as 'noun' and 'verb'.

The strategy I used in Chapter 3 to establish (some of) the colligations of *consequence* was to compare the word's behaviour with that of other abstract nouns. Likewise in Chapter 4, I compared the colligations of hyponyms and synonyms with each other. Suppose, though, I had compared *consequence* not with *aversion, question* or *use* but with *taught* or *if* or I had compared *architect* not with *actor, actress, accountant* and *carpenter* but with *has* or *on*. What would we have learnt from such comparisons? Fairly obviously, we would have noted that *consequence* and *architect* both collocated with *the, one* and *another* in positions immediately prior to the word. We would also have noted that *consequence* collocated with *a* and *architect* with *an* in this position but that two positions to the left, there was collocation with *a* and *an* for each of the nouns. We would likewise have noted that both words collocated with *of* immediately after the word, though in the case of *architect*, as we have seen, the collocation is predominantly associated with the metaphorical sense of the word. None of these statements would have been true of *taught, if, has* or *on*. We might also have noticed that, when *consequence* occurred with *the* and was given first position, it colligated with a finite verb occurring after it. In short, we would have noted that *consequence* typically operates as a noun.

The statement that *consequence* typically operates as a noun is, as the above list of collocations and colligations indicates, only shorthand for claims of exactly the kind we have been considering throughout this book. The claim that *consequence* is a noun is really a claim about its collocations, colligations and semantic associations. Its nominal status is the product of a cluster of collocations and colligations that only become visible when we stop taking it for granted that it **is** a noun.

The grammatical category we assign to a word, I want to argue, is simply a convenient label we give to the combination of (some of) the word's most characteristic and genre-independent primings. It is in fact the outcome of other factors, not the starting point for a linguistic description. The nested combination of features that we label 'noun' on a particular occasion is, like any other nested combination, capable of being primed for other features, and if the same nested combination occurs for other words, the category 'noun' (or 'verb' or 'adjective') can itself be colligationally primed. Statements of such priming will be, to all intents and purposes, syntactic statements. As shorthand for the nesting I have just described, we can say that the grammatical category a word belongs to is its grammatical priming. So instead of saying that *consequence* is a noun, we could say that *consequence* is strongly primed for use as a noun, 'noun' being here, as I have indicated, a convenient shorthand for a cluster of other primings.

Like all primings, priming for grammatical category is a matter of tendency rather than requirement. So the lexical item *winter*, used in Bryson's (and my) sentence as a noun, can also be used as a verb (*I'll winter in Brussels*), as can *bus*. Consider, too, the following sentence from a recent charity appeal letter from the Intermediate Technology Development Group:

1   If your supporter number ends in 'D', you already Gift Aid your donations.

Although there are interesting things to say about *supporter* and *D*, it is *Gift Aid* that I want to attend to. The capitals are evidence of the word sequence's dominant grammatical priming as nominal group, since we associate capitals with names and not with verbs unless in sentence-initial position, but in this sentence the dominant priming has been overridden. To my knowledge, I have only received one such letter. If, though, subsequent charity appeals were to use *Gift Aid* in a similar way, then I (and other careful readers of charity letters) would become primed receptively to expect its use as (part of) a verbal group in the domain and genre of charity appeals. This would be an example of a drift in the priming, discussed in Chapter 1 (see p. 9).

So far my examples have all been nominal. But the claim applies to other grammatical categories as well. Consider the following sentence, part of a *Guardian* article on Shackleton, originally chosen as an illustration of the 'verb' use of *winter* referred to above:

2   The expedition returns to England, having rescued the men left to *winter* on Elephant Island and picked up the party from McMurdo Sound.

Most of the words in this sentence are attested in my data in a grammatical role different from that used in the above sentence. Without comment, I list the following, all taken from my data; the relevant words are emboldened:

3   Many happy **returns**   (NOUN)
4   When he came **to** . . .   (ADVERB)
5   If you want a share of the prosperity that is there for the **having** (NOUN)

6 One of the **rescued** remarked . . .   (NOUN)
7 the **left** luggage becomes a Pandora's box of horrors and possibilities (ADJECTIVE)
8 In **winter**, Hammerfest is . . .   (of course! NOUN)
9 He went **on** and **on**   (ADVERB)
10 I found it growing there and in more northerly outlets behind a sea wall, heavily **picked** but with little sign of exploitation   (ADJECTIVE)
11 I'm just trying to **up** the ante in home entertainment   (VERB)
12 We are on the **up** and they are on the way down   (NOUN)
13 There's less to **party** about   (VERB)
14 . . . trying to **sound** the depths of voters' feelings   (VERB)

All the above are arguably polysemous uses. Several of the other words have non-dominant grammatical uses, for example:

15 . . . in European rather than purely island terms

where both the parallelism with *European* and the modification by *purely* point to adjectival (as opposed to noun modification) use of *island*, and

16 I am rooting about for the elephant folios, like Prince Alexei Soltikoff's lithos of his Indian travels. Not quite elephant is the 1849 David Roberts Egypt and Namibia . . .

I am not sure what this means but the modification of *elephant* by *not quite* suggests another adjectival use.

If we accept that grammatical categories are labels for combinations of primings, we have also to accept that the primings of some words or word sequences will not permit the application of the conventional grammatical labels (or any labels). Sinclair (1991), for example, argues against the treatment of *of* as a preposition, showing how its collocations and colligations are substantially different from those of other words that we give the label 'preposition' to. A similar argument could be made about other, less ubiquitous, words, such as *ago*, *than* and *far*. What we call grammatical categories are best regarded as post-hoc generalisations from the individual instances of lexical primings. Of course this claim is challenged by inflections, and I shall look at these in a later section after refining and reformulating the general claim I have been making for lexical priming.

Word versus lexical item

The position articulated in the earlier part of the book was built up over a number of years. My inaugural lecture in 1994 and a paper in 1996 presented at

the 23rd International Systemic-Functional Congress in Sydney (neither
for publication) were my first attempts at articulating the notion of coll
and much of the matter in the second half of Chapter 4 was also first pres
in cruder fashion than here, in the latter paper. While all this was going on,
unbeknown to me until later, Sinclair was giving conference papers and publishing articles that explored related ideas, and his work predates mine by at least a
year (Sinclair 1996). As should already be apparent from the first three chapters,
Sinclair and I had arrived independently at similar conclusions. This is not as
surprising as it might seem. Firstly, my own thinking in the mid-90s was heavily
influenced by Stubbs (1995, 1996), who in turn drew heavily on Sinclair's work.
Secondly, as my dedication indicates, I worked alongside Sinclair for 14 years,
including on the *Collins COBUILD English Language Dictionary*; it is almost certain
that I first learnt about colligation in this context. Nevertheless, with full allowance made for these factors, it is interesting that our positions are very similar in
a number of important respects.

Drawing on collocation, colligation, semantic preference (= semantic association in this book) and semantic prosody (which overlaps with the notion of
pragmatic association described in Chapter 2), Sinclair (1996, 2004) shows how
clauses such as *it is not really visible to the naked eye* are made up of 'difficulty'
+ 'visibility' + preposition + *the* + *naked* + *eye*, noting that this combination is in
effect a single choice. He argues that there are very many patterns like this and
that they represent not exceptions in the operation of a grammatical system but
the norm. He terms the patterns 'lexical items' and comments:

> If the model of a lexical item offered . . . turns out to be the only one, and
> the computational search is successful, then a text will be analysed into
> a string of units, each statistically independent of those on either side. The
> major structural categories that have been proposed here – collocation,
> colligation, semantic preference and semantic prosody – and their inter-
> relationships will be elaborated and will assume a central rather than a
> peripheral role in language description.
>
> (Sinclair 2004: 39)

The argument of this book has been that the structural categories Sinclair
lists are indeed central and are categories of the lexicon, constructed for each
language user. We have seen how they interrelate and shall continue to look at
their interrelations in this and subsequent chapters. That there are very many
single choices in English of the kind Sinclair describes is implicit in all our
discussion. For example, we earlier saw that the words *a* + *word* + *against*
collocate with *say* or *hear*, have a semantic association with COMMUNICATIVE
INTERCHANGE, have pragmatic association with 'hypotheticality' and 'denial' and
colligation with modal auxiliaries. All of these features produce what is in

Sinclair's terms a single choice, a single lexical item, illustrated in the embold-ened part of the following example:

17   Thatcher **wouldn't hear a word against** him

However, close as our positions are, they are not identical. In the first place, there is a textual dimension to my approach which will have become apparent in Chapters 6 and 7. In the second place, central to my position is that words have collocations, colligations, etc. **for the individual user** and that corpora can only reflect this indirectly. Thirdly, while accepting the insights tied up in Sinclair's notion of the lexical item, I am less confident that the lexical item can replace the word as an analytical starting point. He is certainly right that there are fewer lexical choices here than words, and this is a challenge to the unthink-ing adoption of the word as the basis of any linguistic description (such as mine), though this chapter will modify my position. There is, though, no obvious boundary to the posited notion of the 'lexical item'. The combination 'hypotheticality' + 'modal auxiliary' + 'denial' + 'production/receipt of com-munication' + *hear/say* + *a word against* in turn has a semantic association/ colligation with 'human subject', a slightly weaker but still strong semantic association/colligation with 'human "prepositional" object', and a textual colliga-tion with sentence-final position. Are these also part of a single lexical item, a single lexical choice? I would argue that the question is not a fruitful one and that it is better not to rush too quickly to close off the upper boundary of the lexical item, particularly in the light of the kind of evidence presented in Chapters 6 and 7. The notion of priming and the operation of nesting can account in a systematic way for the move from the word to the lexical item, and indeed, from the lexical item to the wider text and (as we shall shortly see) from the syllable to the word. My claim is that priming contextualises theoretically and psychologically Sinclair's insights about the lexicon.

Word versus phonological string

But the problem of the 'word' remains. I have formulated priming in terms of words and yet, as Sinclair shows, words are often subsumed within larger entities. Furthermore there are many languages where word boundary is prob-lematic and where the phenomena I have described in this book will operate either at a unit larger than the English word or, more commonly, smaller. The truth is that I have focused on the word as a convenient starting point for the description of priming, rather than for theoretically grounded reasons. Self-evidently for the child or the foreign language learner in an immersion situation, it will always be sounds or stretches of sound that are primed in the first place. The association of a (stretch of) sound with a sense is itself the result of priming, and therefore the priming of words is, strictly, an instance of nesting. For many speakers, *sl* is primed to associate with a slippery quality in *slip* (but also *slimy, slope*), *slip* is primed to have a quasi-collocational preference for *ery* (but also for *way* and *shod*), *slippery* is primed to have a collocational preference for *slope* (but also for *customer*) and *slippery slope* is primed negatively to avoid the Subject function in the clause and positively to end clauses either as prepositional Object or as direct Object. So we move from sound to syntactic position by reference to the same process of priming. All but the first of these involve some nesting.

We should not allow the neat quasi-hierarchical account above to fool us into imagining that the description closely matches the psychological reality, or we will quickly drift back into seeing words as isolates, albeit combining in relatively under-described ways. As mature users of a language our priming presumably moves up and down this hierarchy. We might (at least for the sake of argument) encounter *slippery slope* first and use this as the starting point of our priming for *slippery* and *slip*, which could then be the start of our priming for *sl*. More importantly, what is primed may be a single sound (e.g. [t] or [d], which are primed to colligate with words themselves primed for use as verbs in English) when these sounds appear at the end of a syllable, in the same kind of way that *consequence* is primed to colligate with subject + BE + *that* clause when at the beginning of a clause, or it might be an extended sequence such as [ɪŋ kəlæbəreiʃən wɪð] (*in collaboration with*), where the whole sound sequence is, I suggest, primed for a single sense/function. A phonetic/phonological starting point allows priming to explain wordplay, malapropisms and rhyme.

Priming and grammar

Once we recognise that priming applies in the first place to stretches of sound such as syllables, the natural next step is to recognise that syllables such as *ing*, *to*, and *ful* have their own priming. These too have collocations, colligations and semantic associations. In inflectional languages, an important part of the description of such languages will concern the characteristic primings of key syllables. What we count as grammar is the accumulation and interweaving of the primings of the most common sounds, syllables and words of the language. So grammar is, in such terms, the sum of the collocations, colligations and semantic associations of words like *is*, *was*, *the*, *a* and *of*, syllables like *ing*, *er* and *ly*, and sounds like [t] (at the end of syllables) and [s] and [z] (likewise at the end of syllables). Danks (2003) finds that the processes of word formation are similar in kind to those described in the creation of lexical items; components of words are primed to combine in certain ways, but the priming may be overridden.

From another perspective, what we think of as grammar is the product of the accumulation of all the lexical primings of an individual's lifetime. As we collect and associate collocational primings, we create semantic associations and colligations (and grammatical category primings). These nest and combine and give rise to an incomplete, inconsistent and leaky, but nevertheless workable, grammatical system (or systems). The two perspectives on grammar just described are, in my view, quite compatible, despite their very different foci. The first attends to how a grammarian's object of inquiry relates to lexical priming; it will be seen that I do not see lexical priming as rendering grammatical investigation redundant, though it does indicate that some objectives are more achievable than others in this kind of investigation and alters the way one might interpret grammatical claims and data.

The second perspective attends more to the semantic and grammatical systems a speaker builds up in their lifetime. For some (though not necessarily all) speakers, these systems may in self-reflexive fashion be brought to bear on the lexical primings that gave rise to them and some of the primings may be adjusted to accommodate them to the semantic and grammatical systems that the speaker has built/inferred from others. Alternatively a tension may arise between the data and the system. In such circumstances cracks in the priming may occur as a result of conflict between the original priming and the self-reflexivity of the post-hoc systems. Cracks, briefly mentioned in Chapter 1, are returned to in the final chapter.

The claim then is that language acquisition is a matter of stretches of sound stream becoming primed in such a way that they become imbued, by means of nesting, with a rich and complex web of socially embedded, genre-sensitive collocations, semantic associations, colligations and text colligations (Chapters 1, 2, 3, 6). As a second stage, the language user becomes aware of shared primings between related words (Chapter 5) as well as of distinctive primings for different uses of a word. Out of these they will begin to abstract. Semantic associations and colligations are of course themselves abstractions, but the abstractions that I am positing involve a reflexive priming. To take a concrete example, *blackmail* and *bully* are close co-hyponyms, with a periphrastic superordinate along the lines of 'put someone under pressure to do something they weren't planning to do'. As we saw in Chapter 4, co-hyponyms typically share some (though not all) of their primings. In this case, both *blackmailed* and *bullied* will be primed for many language users to associate semantically with PERSON(s) + BE + (e.g. *He was blackmailed*). The resultant combination is then primed to colligate with + *into* + V-*ing* (e.g. *into working for them*). Examples of sentences reflecting these primings are:

18   He was *blackmailed* into working for them [an authentic example like all the others despite its simplicity].

19   A local man had been *bullied* into guiding them through the treacherous, quaking waste.

For these patterns to be primed in the first place, the language user has of course to have encountered *blackmailed* and *bullied* in these contexts a moderate number of times. This means that they have also encountered the combination PERSON(S) + BE + *blackmailed/bullied* + *into* + V-*ING* a fair number of times. Thus, it is hypothesised, as a second stage (or possibly at the same time), that the language user becomes primed to associate PERSON(S) + BE + . . . NOMINAL GROUP + *into* + V-*ing* with words meaning 'putting someone under pressure to do something they weren't planning to do' and will therefore be prepared both to immediately recognise and perhaps to produce sentences such as:

20 . . . their parents have been *seduced* into believing that antibiotics and other dangerously useless but expensive medicines can save them.

21 . . . yet even this mild-mannered diplomat has been *goaded* into showing exasperation with the United States and Britain.

Once this pattern has been primed in this way, it becomes available both for further primings and for comparison with other patterns. So just as the language user subconsciously had noted that *blackmail* and *bully* share primings, so they also may note that PERSON(S) + *blackmailed/bullied* + PERSON(S) also colligates with + *into* + V-*ing*. They may therefore associate the two patterns and treat them as 'co-hyponyms' of some more abstract pattern meaning the same thing. If they do so, they will have created one of the patterns described by Hunston and Francis (2000) or by Fillmore *et al.* (1988) and Goldberg (1995), and indeed Hunston and Francis categorise the abstract pattern as 'V n *into* n' and list the vocabularies associated with it (p. 117).

I would guess that not all language users make it this far but that the majority do. Certainly the ability to cope orally in the language will demand only that the lexis of the language is appropriately primed for the user. However, the patterns described by the linguists just mentioned are fairly basic and fairly meaningful, and a language user who did not connect up their patterns in such a way would soon stumble in the creation of extended monologues such as are characteristically needed in writing.

The process of abstraction need not stop here. The relationship of PERSON(S) + BE + *blackmailed/bullied* + *into* + and PERSON(S) + BE + *voted/thrown* + *out of* is such as to permit the priming of BE + V-[d], [t], [ɪd] and [n] for co-occurrence with PREPOSITION. At the same time the colligational priming of *blackmailed* and *bullied* for occurrence in both the patterns PERSON(S) (choice 1 from the set) + BE + *blackmailed/bullied* + *into* + and PERSON(S) (choice 2 from the set) + *blackmailed/ bullied* + PERSON(S) (choice 1 from the set) + *into* + (and indeed the colligational priming of *voted* and *kicked* for occurrence in the similar patterns PERSON(S) (choice 1 from the set) + BE + *voted/kicked* + *out of* and PERSON(S) (choice 2 from the set) + *voted/kicked* + PERSON(S) (choice 1 from the set) + *out of*) will permit the colligational priming of PERSON(S) (choice1) + V + PREPOSITION for something that looks like the active/passive distinction. In short, from primings such as these, repeated over many verbs, language users may create for themselves an active/passive distinction and in so doing put themselves on the way to creating a grammar.

Notice that the priming has shifted at each stage. Initially I posited a priming for *blackmailed* and *bullied*, neither of them particularly common words. As a result of these words' shared priming, it is possible for the words BE . . . *into* to become primed. This priming led in my argument to the nested priming of the combination of BE + V + /d/ /t/ and /ɪd/ (and possibly PERSON(S)) to occur with PREPOSITION. At the same time, each of the items in the semantic sets that comprise the verb choices in these patterns was being primed for the pattern PERSON(S) (choice1) + V + PREPOSITION, which in turn was being primed for what are usually referred to as active and passive voice.

This is of course not the only, or even the most likely, way in which the priming of individual words might lead to the creation of grammatical categories or grammatical relationships. My point is not to argue for a particular sequence – that would be futile in any case since it is inherent in the notion of priming that each language user's route to abstraction will be unique to them – but to argue that the principle of priming allows for the creation of grammatical abstractions. Lexical priming does not therefore assume the incorrectness of grammatical work, whether that work is very close to the surface as in the linguists mentioned immediately above, a little more abstract as in systemic linguistics or some way below the surface as in the many generative grammars spawned by the Chomskyan revolution. It does, however, assume that the grammars are never complete, because even the most thorough of grammar-creating language users must constantly encounter non-congruent usages produced by those without a fully integrated grammar (or occasionally, perhaps, without any grammar at all). It also assumes that the grammar cannot have central place in a linguistic description; that privilege belongs to the lexicon.

Priming, discourse and text

There is one area where we have seen on several occasions that lexical priming cannot account for all linguistic choices, and that is in the area of discourse. We have seen in several places in the past few chapters a close relationship between the lexical choice and the textual pattern but also in places a tension between the two. The simple fact cannot be escaped that we do not think of a word and then start uttering, drawing as we progress on all the primings at our disposal. Self-evidently, we instead mostly start with a communicative need, whether that need is an expression of sympathy or a brief apology, an attempt to be vague or pass a turn back to our listener, or an extended act of informing and persuading, such as this book.

There seem to be two fundamental dynamic processes involved in the production of spoken or written interaction. One has been the subject of this book. Every lexical choice starts off a series of options and predilections that result in an amazing fluency in any situation in which the speaker has been primed to perform. The other is the discoursal, and this is the process whereby we decide that we shall speak or write and what we want to say. Sinclair (1996, 2004) refers to semantic prosody as the outcome of all the choices a speaker or writer makes; what I am here envisaging is the obverse of this – the initial impulsion to inform, contradict, praise and so on. If the semantic prosody matches the original intention, presumably the speaker/writer is satisfied.

We have therefore to assume that the discoursal impetus and the lexical priming are interconnected but not coterminous. We also have to assume that primings are stored two-way. If *sorry* is primed in different combinations to occur as part of an expression of sympathy or as an apology, so also feelings of sympathy and apology must be primed to elicit *sorry*. If *and things* is primed to indicate vagueness (Channell 1994) or to indicate willingness to pass a turn (Duncan and Fiske 1977), vagueness and turn-ending must be primed to elicit the words *and things*. If the words *In this book*, with which I began the first chapter of this book, are primed for text-initial position in an academic monograph, then the need to start an academic monograph must be primed to elicit words such as *In this book*. What it is that is primed I have no clear notion of; certainly a human need or discourse context is altogether less precise than a stretch of letters or sounds. But there must be some such two-way priming for all the other primings to be available for activation in communication.

In 1991 I proposed the model of language shown in Figure 8.1 to account for the lexical and textual phenomena I had been describing (Hoey 1991a). The claim I was making was that lexis and text were organised rather than structured and that phonology, syntax and interaction were structural systems needed to act as interfaces between phonic substance and lexis, between lexis and text and between text and the extra-textual context. I want now to modify this position, while retaining much of what was there posited. I would argue that encounters with stretches of phonic substance prime us to accept and produce morphological and syllabic combinations that produce our words. Morphology therefore seems to function as an interface between lexis and phonic substance, though the processes of priming are the same. Phonology on the other hand is perhaps better seen as an abstraction from the primings associated with stretches of phonic substance, of a similar theoretical status to syntax, in that our phonology may have inconsistencies but has a regularising function. Similarly, encounters with words and word sequences result in our being primed to produce acceptable sentences and texts, with grammar being a product of these primings with a regularising function. Thus far my present position differs only slightly from that posited in 1991, though clearly the notion now is of phonology and syntax

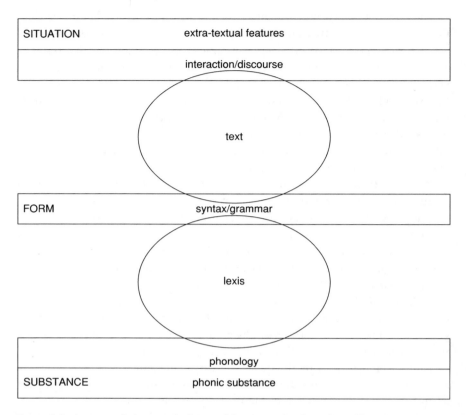

| SITUATION | extra-textual features |
| interaction/discourse |
| text |
| FORM | syntax/grammar |
| lexis |
| phonology |
| SUBSTANCE | phonic substance |

Figure 8.1 A map of the interlocking of linguistic levels (taken from Hoey 1991a: 213)

as products rather than interfaces. However, I would now see text as an interface between lexis and the discoursal need in the extra-textual context, with discourse structure being, again, a product rather than an interface (see Figure 8.2).

However we model the relationship (and I am not wedded to this particular representation), it is clear that we need both the impetus of lexical priming and the representation of discourse need. Wang and McCarthy (2004) note that the principles of reduplication and repetition are amenable to being explained in terms of general probabilistic trends (priming in my terms) (Wang, forthcoming), but that the exceptions are explicable only when the larger organisation of the texts in which they appear are taken into account. I suspect that the motivation for overriding a priming may often be a textual pressure (though, as we have seen, these are themselves subject to description in terms of priming).

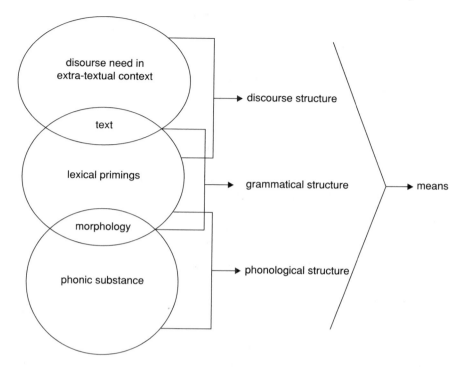

Figure 8.2 An alternative mapping of linguistic levels

Priming prosody

The model presented as Figure 8.2 appears to leave one question glaringly unanswered. If syntax/grammar is not an interface between lexis and text, how do individual primings combine to create text? The answer I shall offer in this section is that of what I term 'priming prosody'.

Throughout this book, I have been arguing two positions, though at times one or other of them has dominated. The first is that every word is characteristically primed for a range of genre, domain and situationally-specific features, which cumulatively account for, and contribute to, what have traditionally been treated as the syntax, semantics, pragmatics and discoursal features of a language. The second is that this priming is individual for each user of the language and therefore the characteristic primings of a word, as reflected in a corpus, need not be any particular user's primings. But the alternative to the characteristic primings is not an absence of priming (except of course when a word is being encountered for the first or second time). Taking into account the broadening of the concept of priming in this chapter, we can assume that every user is primed, more or less specifically, to use every familiar word in every familiar situation in particular ways, and that creativity, in the Chomskyan sense, can be explained in terms of the more general primings, just as naturalness can be explained by the more specific primings. There is, however, one step still to be taken and that is to consider how the primings interact. For that we need the notion of what I term priming prosody (referred to in Hoey 2004b, 2004c, as colligational prosody).

Priming prosody is not the same as semantic prosody (Sinclair 2004) in that Sinclair's concept refers to the meaning outcome of the choices made in an utterance. Priming prosody is concerned with the processes of utterance construction rather than utterance construal, though it is assumed that the two concepts are profoundly related. Priming prosody occurs when the collocations, colligations, semantic associations, textual collocations, textual semantic associations and textual colligations of words chosen for a particular utterance harmonise with each other in such a way as to contribute to the construction and coherence of the utterance. This can be illustrated by reference again to the Bill Bryson sentence we have been examining on and off throughout this book. Figure 8.3 lists in columns (some of) the characteristic collocations, colligations (etc.) of (some of) the component words of the first clause of this sentence. Some of the colligations and other associations listed have not been discussed in any detail, but they are all demonstrable. Between the columns will be found lines of various kinds indicating where words in the clause are likely to share a particular priming, based on corpus evidence. These are claimed to be, for most users, the likely priming prosodies implicated in the construction of this clause.

There are four such prosodies indicated in Figure 8.3. Firstly, we have prosody of collocation with BE, indicated by a straight line. Secondly there is prosody of colligation with relational process, indicated with dotted lines. Thirdly we have prosody of semantic association with PLACE NAME, indicated by a line of dashes. And finally, there is the rather specific prosody of more common/less common PLACE NAME prosody, indicated by a thicker line.

I have indicated that the 'more common place name/less common place name' prosody is more specific than the others. But it is of course possible, as indicated by previous discussion in this chapter, to have more general prosodies. So, for example, as indicated in Figure 8.3, *winter* colligates with PREPOSITION, but of course PREPOSITION also colligates with NOUN and *winter* is primed to occur as NOUN. This therefore is also an instance of priming prosody. The same more general priming prosodies can be shown to operate across the clause (and indeed all clauses). Figure 8.3 therefore represents the priming prosodies that contribute to the naturalness of the clause. A separate figure would be needed to show the full range of prosodies that contribute to its acceptability as a clause of English. Such a figure would be complex but not in principle difficult to create, and it would carry information of the kind handled traditionally by grammars.

Priming prosody is claimed therefore to integrate the kinds of corpus-driven insights discussed in this book and the more abstract descriptions provided

Figure 8.3 The priming prosodies that bind the colligations etc. of Bill Bryson's first clause

elsewhere. To take just one instance, grammarians have disputed whether the head of a noun phrase is (normally) a noun, the standard position adopted (e.g. Halliday 1994; Biber *et al.* 1999), or whether the head is really the determiner (the 'determiner phrase' hypothesis) (Abney 1987 cited by Rappaport 2001). Such a dispute can be resolved, I suggest, by recognising that each of the members of the class of determiners are primed to occur with words that are primed to function as nouns and that such 'noun' words are primed to occur with members of the class of determiners. (The priming prosody thereby created both helps define what counts as a noun and as a determiner in a language.)

With the notion of priming prosody, we leave the Chomskyan concept of creativity and turn to the kinds of creativity that draw attention to themselves – the second and third kind of creativity discussed in the first section of this chapter.

9 Lexical priming and other kinds of creativity

Language that surprises

In the previous chapter, we were concerned with the kinds of creativity that go unnoticed – the natural ability of any language user to produce utterances that are novel. It was argued there that lexical priming provided an adequate account of such creativity. But as we noted, there are other kinds of creativity, where language is used in startlingly novel ways, whether by accident or design. One of these kinds of creativity occurs when someone says or writes something that surprises the recipient, whether because of its incongruity, humour, wordplay or simple oddness. Carter (2004) has shown that linguistic creativity of this kind is deeply embedded in the ordinary language practices of non-literary users of English (if the word 'ordinary' can be used of a facility that is always special, however often it is used). A theory of the lexicon must have something to say about such language.

It also needs to be able to say something about the special – and specially valued – creativity evident in the writing of literary writers. Bill Bryson's creativity can be handled along the lines discussed in previous chapters, but what do we do with the language of writers such as Gerard Manley Hopkins, Dylan Thomas and James Joyce – writers some of whose utterances would not be covered by traditional generative grammars? As I said in Chapter 8, if a linguistic approach cannot say something interesting about literary language, there is something wrong with the approach. Accordingly this chapter concerns itself with surprising language.

Unintended creativity

For a short time, the *Guardian* had as one of its weekly supplements a magazine called *The Editor* and a regular feature of this magazine, known as 'Our readers' reads', was a selection on the back page of cuttings from local newspapers (and elsewhere) submitted by readers who had been surprised and amused by the way language had been used. These were supplemented by comments from the *Guardian* which often highlighted and made more amusing (and visible) the original oddity. One such page included the following:

1   **RABBI BURNS CELEBRATIONS**

     FRIDAY 26th + SATURDAY 27th JANUARY

     An interesting cultural exchange from the *Stevenage Comet*, Jan 11

2   Saturday, 13th January

     FAREWELL NIGHT

     Live Music

     BACKDOOR MEN

     Featuring Jeff Fuller and the Tucker Sisters
        plus Friends
     with Special Guest

     EDDIE MARTIN

     A NIGHT TO BE MISSED

     Free entry – 8 pm start

     Put your diaries away. From the *Post & Weekly News*, Jan 11

3   **POLICE SUBDUED MAN WITH CARVING KNIFE**

     Zero tolerance in Bridlington. From the *Free Press*, Jan 11

All of these are, for different reasons, instances of surprising English or they would not have been included in the column, and all under different circumstances might have been produced deliberately for the purposes of humour or wry comment.

Priming conflict

I want to suggest in this section that just as priming prosody contributes to the apparent naturalness of an utterance, so a lack of prosody may contribute to the apparent unusualness of an utterance. One manifestation of a lack of priming prosody is priming conflict, which occurs when a choice of one priming is overwhelmed by another, more dominant, priming. The result here is either ambiguity or humour.

We saw in Chatper 8 that priming begins with the phonological string. It is also possible (and natural) for orthographic strings to be primed, and it is probable that the two types of priming reinforce each other. In the case of example 1, seen from the former perspective, the phonological string /ræb/ has a range of possible primings + /aɪ/, + /ɪt/ and /iː/, and the wrong one has been chosen. Seen from the latter perspective, *Rabb* has the possible primings *i*, *it* (as in *Peter Rabbit*) and *ie*. Either way, we have priming conflict. In my corpus, the combination *Rabb* + *i* is greatly more common than *Rabb* + *ie* when associating semantically with NAME. There are 323 cases of *Rabbi* + NAME in my data but only seven cases of *Rabbie* + NAME, of which three are *Rabbie* + *Burns*. The dominant priming of *Rabbi* + NAME has therefore been chosen, when the less dominant priming of *Rabbie* + *Burns* needed to be conformed to. Although offered by the *Guardian* as humorous, it is worth noting that if the writer had been James Joyce, the collision would have been applauded.

Note that what is likely to be primed as dominant will vary according to who you are and where you live. For a nationalistic Scot living in Edinburgh, *Rabbie* + NAME is likely to be the dominant priming. The example, however, comes from Stevenage and one might guess that at least some people of non-Scottish descent in the Stevenage area will not have that priming. For them *Rabbi* will be the more likely combination (irrespective of their faith). We have here priming conflict where the dominant priming may have inappropriately shouldered out the less dominant, but in this context more appropriate, priming.

Example 2 also manifests priming conflict. The combination *to be missed* occurs 81 times in my data of which almost 75 per cent are instances of *not to be missed*. The semantic set associated with the latter phrase is 'opportunity' – *opportunity not to be missed*, *chance not to be missed*, *CD not to be missed* etc. However, there are no instances of *a night not to*. Instead, there are 16 instances of *a night to* (excluding references to the film *A Night to Remember*), 13 of which occur, like *not to be missed*, as part of a positive evaluation. The absence of *a night not to* as a priming results in a priming conflict between the desire to reproduce *a night to* and the need to combine *not* with *to be missed*.

The third example is perhaps the most interesting. The semantic association of *man with* + WEAPON is a strong priming for *Guardian* writers, there being 78 instances of the combination in my data. Of these 91 per cent refer to a man holding a weapon, suggesting that the comical reading of example 3 is the natural one. This impression is reinforced by three of the remaining seven instances, which do indeed refer to cases where the man is being attacked with the weapon but have clear disambiguating features. These instances are

> . . . killing a man with his bare hands
> . . . a black man with his truncheon
> . . . a man with the assault rifle

The three examples are all disambiguated by the clash between the marker of definiteness that precedes the weapon and the marker of indefiniteness that precedes *man*. The expectation is that they will either both be definite or both indefinite (or more rarely, definite followed by indefinite).

A fourth instance is disambiguated by the postmodification of *knife*:

> . . . the man with the knife in his throat

which shows the man to be, in a way, holding the knife but not as a weapon.

So how did the sentence come to be produced, given this typical priming of *man with* + WEAPON? The answer lies in a phenomenon we have encountered several times before, where an exception to the dominant priming exists. When we looked at *army* in Chapter 6, we saw it had a particular cohesive priming except where it was in combination with *of* in which case this priming disappeared, unless again it was an instance of *of* + *occupation* or NUMBER, in which case the priming reappeared. It would appear that the same phenomenon is in operation in this instance. The combination HUMAN + *with a . . . carving knife* is not primed the same way as *man with* + WEAPON. In 24 instances in my data, only twice does it refer to the case of a person holding a carving knife. So we have here a clear conflict between two primings, with the dominant priming overwhelming the less frequent one and producing the comic combination. Interestingly, it takes some linguistic skill to avoid the conflict.

So much for the second type of creativity. Clearly I have only scratched the surface of explaining why some sentences surprise us, but I hope I have at least demonstrated that lexical priming has something useful to say about such cases.

Literary creativity

We are left with the third kind of creativity, the kind associated with high literary endeavour. To illustrate the way lexical priming might be used to explain such creativity, I have chosen three types of text: a piece of non-fictional prose by Charles Dickens, part of a poem by Lord Tennyson and the beginning of a poem by Dylan Thomas. The first is immediately recognisable as being by Dickens, despite its being a piece of travel writing, and my aim here is to show how Dickens has created a stylistic effect by overriding a textual collocational priming. The second is an immediately intelligible piece of nineteenth-century verse that regularly crops up in anthologies of English poetry; my aim with this is to show that lexical priming permits an explanation of why one line in it is found by many to be so memorable. The third is a piece of very difficult writing, on the very borders of intelligibility and grammaticality; here my intention is to show how even so the writer makes use of (what are assumed to have been) his lexical primings. The three extracts are intended to cover the gamut of literary creativity from language barely distinguishable from non-literary language to language barely comprehensible.

A passage from Charles Dickens' Pictures from Italy

The passage from Dickens I want to comment on is a very long paragraph taken from one of his travel books (appropriately enough, given the focus elsewhere in this book on travel writing), namely *Pictures from Italy*. The punctuation, which does not conform to twenty-first century practice in places, is Dickens' own:

> One day we walked out, a little party of three, to Albano, fourteen miles distant; possessed by a great desire to go there by the ancient Appian way, long since ruined and overgrown. We started at half-past seven in the morning, and within an hour or so were out upon the open Campagna. For twelve miles we went climbing on, over an unbroken succession of mounds, and heaps, and hills, of ruin. Tombs and temples, overthrown and prostrate; small fragments of columns, friezes, pediments; great blocks of granite and marble; mouldering arches, grass-grown and decayed; ruin enough to build a spacious city from; lay strewn about us. Sometimes, loose walls, built up from these fragments by the shepherds, came across our path; sometimes, a ditch between two mounds of broken stones, obstructed our progress; sometimes, the fragments themselves, rolling from beneath our feet, made it a toilsome matter to advance; but it was always ruin. Now, we tracked a piece of the old road, above the ground; now traced it, underneath a grassy covering, as if that were its grave; but all the way was ruin. In the distance, ruined aqueducts went stalking on their course along the plain; and every breath of wind that swept towards us, stirred early flowers and grasses, springing up, spontaneously, on miles of ruin. The unseen larks above us, who alone disturbed the awful silence, had their nests in ruin; and the fierce herdsmen, clad in sheepskins, who now and then scowled out upon us from their sleeping nooks, were housed in ruin. The aspect of the desolate Campagna in one direction, where it was most level, reminded me of an American prairie; but what is the solitude of a region where men have never dwelt, to that of a Desert, where a mighty race have left their footprints in the earth from which they have vanished; where the resting-places of their Dead, have fallen like their Dead; and the broken hour-glass of Time is but a heap of idle dust! Returning, by the road, at sunset! and looking, from the distance, on the course we had taken in the morning, I almost feel (as I had felt when I first saw it, at that hour) as if the sun would never rise again. But looked its last, that night, upon a ruined world.

It would be very possible to devote a full chapter to exploring the way Dickens exploits and overrides his and our (presumed) primings. But, apart from the obvious pressures of space, one problem presents itself in the analysis of this and the next two texts that makes it undesirable to spend too long on them. I have stressed repeatedly throughout this book that primings are not in principle generalised across all text types, genres and domains, (though no doubt some are, such as primings for grammatical category). Still less can they be trusted to apply across centuries. Dickens wrote *Pictures from Italy* in 1842; his primings and those of his readers can certainly be assumed to be significantly different in respect of travel writing from those of Bill Bryson and his readers and informed by a quite different set of previous reading experiences both of travel writing and of other kinds of text. It will be remembered that the specificity of primings with regard to genre, domain and the like was particularly noted in respect of textual primings. Yet it is the textual priming that Dickens has, I believe, overridden that I want to focus on. Clearly caution is required.

I want to attend to Dickens' use of *ruin*. There are (at least) two uses of *ruin* available to the language user – one is evaluative, where *ruin* is a way of saying that something (a building, an economy, a plan) is in a bad way; the other is descriptive, where *a ruin* may be a tourist attraction and deemed beautiful. The first use is negatively primed with regard to cohesive chains. I examined 40 texts containing this use of *ruin*, and none contained cohesive chains. The second use is also negatively primed for cohesive chains, but they do occasionally occur. I examined 39 texts containing the second sense of *ruin* (I couldn't find a fortieth in my corpus), and there were two chains, both in the context of tourism. Dickens has therefore – according to contemporary primings in a different type of writing – overridden the typical priming for *ruin* and created a substantial chain. More crucially, the chain begins with the descriptive use and quickly turns into a chain of the evaluative sense. The former in my data, as just noted, chains rarely; the latter chains not at all. I repeat the passage with the two senses orthographically marked out, the descriptive being italicised and the evaluative being emboldened. Obviously there is an element of judgement here, but the priming of the two senses informally permits the distinction to be made safely in a number of cases. So, while *a ruin* in my data can be either evaluative or descriptive, *the ruin* has more use in the descriptive sense and *ruin* (without an article) is always evaluative. The word *ruined* is predominantly evaluative, also.

> One day we walked out, a little party of three, to Albano, fourteen miles distant; possessed by a great desire to go there by the ancient Appian way, long since *ruined* and overgrown. We started at half-past seven in the morning, and within an hour or so were out upon the open Campagna. For twelve miles we went climbing on, over an unbroken succession of mounds,

and heaps, and hills, of *ruin*. Tombs and temples, overthrown and prostrate; small fragments of columns, friezes, pediments; great blocks of granite and marble; mouldering arches, grass-grown and decayed; *ruin* enough to build a spacious city from; lay strewn about us. Sometimes, loose walls, built up from these fragments by the shepherds, came across our path; sometimes, a ditch between two mounds of broken stones, obstructed our progress; sometimes, the fragments themselves, rolling from beneath our feet, made it a toilsome matter to advance; but it was always **ruin**. Now, we tracked a piece of the old road, above the ground; now traced it, underneath a grassy covering, as if that were its grave; but all the way was **ruin**. In the distance, *ruined* aqueducts went stalking on their course along the plain; and every breath of wind that swept towards us, stirred early flowers and grasses, springing up, spontaneously, on miles of **ruin**. The unseen larks above us, who alone disturbed the awful silence, had their nests in **ruin**; and the fierce herdsmen, clad in sheepskins, who now and then scowled out upon us from their sleeping nooks, were housed in **ruin**. The aspect of the desolate Campagna in one direction, where it was most level, reminded me of an American prairie; but what is the solitude of a region where men have never dwelt, to that of a Desert, where a mighty race have left their footprints in the earth from which they have vanished; where the resting-places of their Dead, have fallen like their Dead; and the broken hour-glass of Time is but a heap of idle dust! Returning, by the road, at sunset! and looking, from the distance, on the course we had taken in the morning, I almost feel (as I had felt when I first saw it, at that hour) as if the sun would never rise again. But looked its last, that night, upon a **ruined** world.

What Dickens has done here is create a cohesive chain in contradiction of the negative priming of both senses of the word for chaining. Furthermore, a glance at the passage above shows that the evaluative sense dominates; yet this is a travel text and what little chaining does occur with *ruin* occurs in travel writing with the other sense. This points to the fact that he has mingled the senses in a single chain in defiance of normal cohesive practice. Most lexical items are primed cohesively to avoid cohesive links between their polysemous senses. This, like all primings, can be overridden, as Dickens shows.

Dickens' strategy here is typical of creative writing. In the first place, he has maintained the vast majority of the primings associated with *ruin*. Each individual sentence uses *ruin* in a not untypical manner, except perhaps for a couple of cases where one's priming might have predicted *a ruin* in place of *ruin*. The creativity lies in an act of overriding a single, important priming. Secondly, he takes a priming associated with one sense (in this the case the tentative weak priming of *ruin* (= tourist attraction) for cohesive chaining) and uses it with a different sense.

Two lines from Tennyson

The creativity of the novelist usually involves undramatic deviations from the dominant primings (though of course James Joyce shows that this need not be the case). Poetry on the other hand routinely involves more notable deviations. A question that arises here is how memorability is achieved in poetry. It is rare for sentences of prose works to be recalled, though religious texts are an exception. The lines of poems are, however, more frequently remembered. One poem that is often anthologised and is remembered by many older British readers is 'The Charge of the Light Brigade' by Lord Tennyson in which he celebrates the crazy heroism of the Light Brigade who rode to their deaths as a result of a mistaken order.

I want to focus on just two lines from the poem:

> Theirs is not to reason why
> Theirs is but to do and die

So well-known are these lines that when Cecil Woodham-Smith wrote her celebrated book on the military disaster she named it *The Reason Why*.

The first point is that *their* + NOUN, when Subject of its clause, is primed to collocate with BE *to*. The sequence *their* NOUN BE *to*, where the noun is head of its own group functioning as Subject, occurs 87 times in every 10,000 instances of BE *to*. The sequence *their* NOUN BE occurs only 21 times in every 10,000 instances of BE. The same priming is true of *his* + NOUN, *my* + NOUN and so on, leading to the more abstract priming of POSSESSIVE + NOUN for BE *to*. This combination accounts for 5 per cent of all instances of BE *to* (whereas the combination POSSESSIVE + NOUN + BE accounts for 1.4 per cent of instances of BE). There are on the other hand no instances of *theirs* occurring with *is to* (apart from a single quotation from Tennyson's poem). Tennyson has therefore complied with the priming of POSSESSIVE + *is to* but overridden the expectation of a noun.

The second point concerns *to reason why*. It is notable that Cecil Woodham-Smith's book was called *The Reason Why*, not *To Reason Why*. As we saw in Chapter 5, a *why* clause often follows *reason* (= cause). Here however it has been yoked to the verbal use, whose sense is closer to *reason* (= rationality, logic). Once again, then, we have a blend of conformity to a characteristic priming with a notable overriding of a facet of that priming.

A few words from Dylan Thomas

Dylan Thomas wrote slowly and his texts are typically full of sentences that would be excluded from grammars. Here are the first two lines of Thomas' poem '*A grief ago*':

A grief ago,
She who was who I hold, the fats and flower,

You will be disappointed perhaps to learn that I wish to look at the use of just one word in these lines, which however I offer as indicative of how I would approach the rest of the poem. The word is *ago*, which we have already looked at in Chapter 6. The word sequence *a grief ago* has been discussed in the literature in connection with its use of *grief* and I want to place that choice in a larger context. The word *ago* has the following typical primings, offered for each of the types of priming we have considered in this book, presented here without evidence (but see Hoey 2004a):

1 *ago* is primed for collocation with *years*, *weeks* and *days*;
2 it is primed for semantic association with units of time, e.g. *six weeks ago, a minute ago*;
3 it is primed for semantic association with measurement, e.g. *a, six, forty*;
4 it is primed for pragmatic association with statements rather than questions or instructions;
5 it is primed for colligation with Adjunct function;
6 it is negatively primed for cohesion;
7 it is primed to appear in contrast relations;
8 it is primed for paragraph-initial position, when it is sentence-initial;
9 it is primed for text-initial position, when it is sentence-initial.

Dylan Thomas has in fact conformed to six of these primings and has over-ridden only three. He has coupled a marker of measurement (*a*) with *ago*, incorporated it into a statement, used it in an Adjunct, not employed it in any cohesion (it will be remembered that the cohesive link between title and text were systematically excluded from consideration in our exploration of cohesive priming), placed it at the beginning of a verse (which I take to be the nearest equivalent we have to a paragraph) and begun his text with it. The primings he has overridden are the first two (and the semantic association can be seen as a generalisation out of the collocations) and the seventh. In short, even when writers are straining at the limits of what a language is capable of expressing, they make use of more of their primings than they reject. A sentence that overrode all its reader's primings would only be a sentence by virtue of starting with a capital letter and ending with a full stop; it would not correspond to anything recognisable as an instance of language in use.

10 Some theoretical and practical issues

Cracks in the priming

The notion of priming in this book has largely been discussed impersonally, as if it were simply a property of the language. As shorthand, I have in places talked of words being primed, and only the tell-tale words 'typically' and 'characteristically' have hinted at the personal and individual history that lies behind the apparent property of the word. In fact, though, as I hope was made clear in Chapter 1 and sporadically elsewhere, priming is what happens to the individual and is the direct result of a set of unique, personal, unrepeatable and humanly-charged experiences. Words come at us both as children and as adults from a plethora of sources. Parents, caretakers, friends, teachers, enemies, strangers (friendly and scary), broadcasters, newspapers, books, cards, letters, fellow pupils or colleagues — all at different times and to different degrees contribute to our primings.

The contexts in which we encounter lexis contribute to the way it is primed for us and we are in turn and as a result primed to use such lexis in these contexts. But we must not be crude about context. We have enough control of the situation in which we speak to use words as if we were in a particular context, thereby contributing to the creation of such a context (or of a different context that references such a context). Likewise, the kind of context we are in may be felt to drift during the course of our talk and the talk we produce and hear will both have contributed to the drift and be affected by it.

Inevitably, not all of the data we receive from such complex sources will provide a single picture, nor will we feel the same way about the sources of the data. The language of an enemy will prime us differently from the language of a friend, simply because we may not wish to emulate the enemy and may wish to show solidarity with the friend. And two friends, or members of our family, may use a particular word differently, resulting in a conflict in the primings.

Many conflicts are unlikely to create communicative problems; a word may after all have a number of collocates and semantic associations, and it is only if the latter directly contradict each other that a problem is likely to arise for the user. A particular point of conflict (a crack) in the primings, however, would seem to occur as a result of the grammar that each individual is building up out of the primings and which is hypothesised (in Chapter 8) to act self-reflexively on the primings, regularising them and generalising from them.

Cracks, briefly mentioned in Chapter 1, occur when conflicting data about the use of a word or word sequence is received and the language user can find no way of resolving the conflict. The cracks created by the self-reflexive grammar are less overt than those from outside, particularly from education (though the former may be affected by education, which often attempts to model the individual's internalised and personal grammar). As an example of a crack caused by the self-reflexive application of grammar on the primings that gave rise to it, consider the cases of *me and you* and *me and X*. For the great majority of speakers of English *I* is strongly primed to occur in Subject function and *me* is strongly primed to avoid such a function, and, coupled with similar colligational primings for *we*, *she*, *he* and *they*, this leads to a grammatical inference about an aspect of the operation of the pronoun system. But for many of these speakers, *me* will also be primed to collocate with *and* and *you* and to have a semantic association with NAME, as in *me and my friend Alastair*. If therefore there is a need to use one of these expressions in Subject function, there is a conflict between the two primings, which can only be resolved by one overriding the other. If the speaker remains unaware of the conflict, there need be no problem in this, though of course the resolution may make the speaker's inferred grammar of pronouns leak a little more.

In the instance mentioned in the previous paragraph, the crack can be mended in one of two ways or not resolved at all. One way of mending the crack, and certainly the better, is to reserve *me and* NAME or *me and you* for certain social situations and particular types of genre/domain. So in casual conversation with me over a pint of real ale, my son used the word sequence *Me and my friend Alastair* as Subject; it is doubtful whether he would have used the same kind of expression at the press briefings he used to organise as part of his work. For him clearly there is no longer a crack. The other way of mending the crack is simply to treat one of the pairs of primings as receptive only (see Chapter 1 for discussion of receptive and productive primings). This however may result in tension at home or in the classroom.

Sometimes attempts at mending the cracks merely move the problem to another place. So if the *me and you* priming is treated as receptive only and is replaced by *you and I*, there is a risk that the latter will be the result of *I* being primed to collocate with *you + and* and not the result of the self-reflexive functioning of the grammar. If the more specific priming is not overridden by the more general colligational priming of *I* as avoiding all grammatical functions other than Subject, it will give rise to (parts of) utterances such as *between you and I*.

It will be recalled from Chapter 1 that cracks may also occur as a result of conflict between a speaker's primings and someone else's primings; sometimes the conflict is also between the speaker's primings and the other person's post-hoc (but strongly believed in) grammatical system. One of the places where this is particularly likely to happen is, as already mentioned, in the educational system, which introduces another form of self-reflexivity. Explicit input from the teacher, in particular the correction of writing and, sometimes, speech in the classroom, often produces conflict with the primings achieved at home. Indeed the conflict regarding *you and me* described in previous paragraphs is as likely to be provoked by a teacher as by the speakers themselves. Cracks can be resolved either by adjusting the original priming or by rejecting the educational challenge to the priming. Either way, the resolution of such conflicts can be painful. Of course the degree of conflict will vary from person to person. It is not unreasonable to suppose that the child whose home primings least conflict with the school primings will both respond most positively to language in the classroom and will suffer least from the need to resolve the conflict.

Worse than adjusting the original priming or rejecting the new attempt at priming is a permanent uncertainty about the priming, a codification of the crack, leading to long-term linguistic insecurity. Primings are, as was noted in Chapter 1, domain specific. Most cracks can be mended by assigning one set of primings to one domain or social context (e.g. family and friends) and the other set, whether the result of self-reflection or as a result of educational challenge, to a different domain or social context (i.e. education, science, the middle class etc.).

We can combine the notion of cracks in the priming with our recognition in Chapter 8 of the existence of phonological priming to explain how it is that children utter things they have never heard. Take for example the observation that children never hear *goed* but say it all the same. For the vast majority of speakers of English, the sounds [d] and [t] and the syllable [ɪd] are primed to have a semantic association with the very broad set of (different) words used to report actions, but the word *go*, although a member of this set, is not primed to collocate with these sounds. This creates a crack, which is worsened by the fact that, in stories, names and pronouns are typically primed to occur in narratives with a nested combination of action verb and [d][t] or [ɪd]. As a way of mending the crack, the child allows the priming of the more common item [d] to override the negative priming of the less common item (*go*). This is because they will have much more data on [d][t] and [ɪd] than on *go*, and because they are likely to be using GO in a narrative context in conjunction with a name or pronoun (both of which, as just mentioned, are primed in narratives to occur with an action word and [d][t] or [ɪd]).

Harmonising primings

If the view of language put forward in this and the previous two chapters is correct, there are a number of implications, both for linguistics and for sociology.

(We have already alluded briefly to the implications for psychology in Chapter 1.) The first is that grammar is less central to our understanding of the way language works. It is more than likely that many users of a language never construct a complete and coherent grammar out of their primings. Instead they may have bits of grammars, small, self-contained mini-systems that do not connect up but represent partial generalisations from the individual primings (cf. Hopper 1988, 1998).

Secondly, if each person constructs their language out of the primings acquired from a unique set of data, there can be no right or wrong in language (and no absolute distinction between native and non-native speaker, though the latter will have acquired their primings by strikingly different routes). When people claim that something someone else said or wrote is ungrammatical, they are really only claiming that the other person's utterance is different from that predicted by their primings, and of course, hard as it is for anyone to admit, their primings have no special status. (Of course if there were no one whose primings predicted the utterance, that would be of significance, but demonstrating that this was the case would be almost impossible and in any case such utterances are likely to be rare, if we accept the point above about the dissolution of the distinction between native and non-native speakers.)

Built into the above implication is the assumption that everybody's language is unique, because all our lexical items are inevitably primed differently as a result of different encounters, spoken and written. We have different parents and different friends, live in different places, read different books, get into different arguments and have different colleagues, and therefore there is next to nothing that is shared in the data on the basis of which words get primed for us. How is it then that speakers from the same linguistic community (however that is defined) are mutually intelligible?

I have already alluded to one of the mechanisms that ensure that the primings of different speakers harmonise – the makeshift grammars we are constructing (note the present tense and progressive aspect). We never in principle finish our grammar(s), though in old age it may be that new data are no longer processed and ossification of vocabulary and its primings may occur.

Self-reflexive harmonising only goes so far as an explanation of the consistency of primings across speakers. Every culture, I should like to suggest, has external harmonising mechanisms, whether these are oral mechanisms such as songs, proverbs, rituals, drama or folk tales, or written mechanisms such as sacred texts or best-sellers. Labov (1972) describes various harmonising mechanisms at work in New York inner-city black culture, including sounding and competitive narration, that appear to have contributed to the development of hip-hop, a contemporary harmonising mechanism for a generation, at least as regards receptive priming. The most important controlling mechanism, however, in the great majority of industrialised and large-scale cultures (and many non-industrialised and smaller cultures) is that of education. Mastery of a subject is mastery of the collocations, colligations and semantic associations of the vocabulary of the discipline, mastery, in fact, of the domain-specific and genre-specific primings, and the job of teachers is (among other things) to prime the learners' vocabulary appropriately. The examination system in turn is designed (among other things) to verify that the vocabulary of the discipline has been properly utilised – i.e. appropriately primed. Looked at more critically, examinations also seek to ensure that only the examinees whose primings harmonise with those already in positions of influence or power are able to take up positions of influence or power themselves.

A second way in which cultures have sometimes attempted to harmonise their primings is through their shared literary and religious traditions. Where members of a culture share a faith, sacred texts have a harmonising effect. Literary traditions have traditionally been formulated in terms of a literary canon of 'great writers', and feminist complaints against the male-centredness of the canon are justified if we see harmonisation as the exercise of power over the language of others. Whereas we all have different experience of the spoken word, in theory we could all have a shared experience of the written word if we all read the same works. If we all read *Lord of the Flies*, the priming effects on us ought apparently to be similar in that the linguistic data are the same in all cases; actually, however, our previous experience of the lexis encountered will ensure that the priming effects differ in reality, however slightly. In any case, as education has ceased to be designed for an elite in western cultures and as fewer children in many of these cultures are brought up in a faith or at least the same faith, so the harmonising potential of shared traditions has diminished to the point where they have become unimportant. In the English-speaking world it is therefore only in isolated and/or self-contained cultures, and more importantly in sub-cultures within the larger cultures, such as religious denominations or university students of English, that this kind of harmonisation can have any impact.

The third way in which modern cultures harmonise the primings of a linguistic community is through the mass media, which are second only to education in this respect (and possibly have more importance for some speakers). But of course the primings may be different from that promoted by education and they are domain specific. There are also issues here with regard to receptive priming versus productive priming, which apply to the literary canon as well. A newscaster on TV is a member of a linguistic community that the great majority of listeners are unlikely to want to emulate, and the same applies to nineteenth-century novelists (though John Fowles in *The French Lieutenant's Woman* sought to turn his receptive primings into productive ones).

Perhaps the least noticeable type of priming comes in the form of dictionaries and grammars. This is why there is always irritation whenever grammarians and lexicographers argue that their function is to describe, not prescribe. Such a posture is seen by those who instinctively recognise the need for harmonisation as a betrayal. The problem of course is that linguistic scientists find it hard to be linguistic legislators (and vice versa). Every time a new dictionary comes out, I am interviewed about it; and journalists always ask about whether certain new words should have been included. Dictionaries enshrine and enable a degree of harmonisation of priming, but they may contribute to cracks too.

The implications for learners of a second language

This book is offered as a contribution to the development of linguistic thought and as an attempt to ground recent corpus work in a theory sympathetic to the findings coming out of such work. I cannot forget, though, that from 1993 to 2004 I was director of a unit dedicated to the teaching of English as a second or other language. My colleagues and my students would be unforgiving if I did not, however briefly and inadequately, reflect upon the linguistic implications of what I have been saying for the language learner and the language teacher. In any case I have always advocated the bridging of theory and practice. So, if this is the theory, what should be the practice?

The first point to note is that the learning of a second language (L2) is necessarily a very different experience from learning a first one (L1) for a whole raft of reasons, all of which will be very familiar from the literature of second language acquisition. In the first place, when the vocabulary of the first language is primed, it is being primed for the first time. When the second language is learnt, however, the primings are necessarily superimposed on the primings of the first language. So where a bilingual dictionary, a course book or a teacher provides a single word translation of an item designated to be learnt in the second language, the learner will, I claim, immediately activate the primings from the first language. The semantic associations and colligations of the new word will be deemed to be the same as, or at least very similar to, those of the L1 equivalent.

The situation will be more complicated where the distinctions between L1 and L2 are erased. The interconnections between the primings of two languages being acquired alongside each other will need separate study. My discussion in the previous paragraph is not intended as an indirect endorsement of mono-lingual ways of viewing the world but as a representation of the simplest rela-tionship between languages.

The transfer of primings from earlier to later languages is, I suspect, unavoid-able, except where the learner learns through immersion and is never tempted by word-for-word translation (a rare set of circumstances indeed). For some purposes, transference of semantic associations and colligations is likely to be a productive and helpful strategy in the earlier stages of language learning, particularly where the cultural practices associated with the two languages are not overly different. In any case, if the use of semantic associations and colligations transferred from L1 results in the occasional alien utterance, this may be better than the paralysis that would presumably come from the inability to string two words together (to use an old metaphor with a meaning closer to the literal than usual). That said, the language teacher has at some point to decide when or whether to crack these primings. Certainly we can assume that a whole new class of false friends is implied by priming – words that mean exactly the same in the two languages but are primed differently for L1 learners as regards collocations, colligations and semantic associations. Certainly, also, we can assume that the practice of learning words in lists will aggravate this situation, in that a list both strips the words of all their primings and asserts their strict parallelism.

Despite the obvious differences that arise from learning a second or subsequent language as opposed to a first language, the distinction between a native and non-native speaker starts to evaporate when we recognise that we are all learners in some areas of our language and beginners in many others. There is not a set of agreed primings that a learner should acquire; priming is, after all, unique to the individual. Furthermore, as just noted, no L1 speaker is primed to deal with every situation they might encounter. My lexis is not appropriately primed to allow me to produce medical discourse, nor would I use the vocabulary of numismatics (coin collecting) appropriately (and in both areas there will be many lexical items for which I have no priming at all). There are in truth vastly more situations in which I am unprimed than there are in which my fluency will bring me the credit of competence. Even in areas where I can claim expertise, there are sub-areas in which my vocabulary is insufficiently primed to impress. (Phonologists and phoneticians may already have noticed this.) So-called native speakers are non-native in many contexts and all speakers are, according to the position I have been putting forward, in a permanent state of learning. (This is not to deny the existence of a critical period in L1 learning in which the principles and products of priming are laid down for the child and used as the basis of all subsequent priming.)

What distinguishes learners (or more accurately, types of learning) is not therefore whether they are native or non-native but how the primings come into existence. When a speaker is surrounded by evidence – all of it good, in marked contradiction of early claims made by Chomsky (e.g. 1965) – the primings get built up inductively at variable speeds. When however the speaker is not so surrounded, other strategies need to be used.

I am not primed in the lexis of numismatics, but I am primed in some of the lexis involved with philately (stamp collecting). Initially, I had no stamp collecting friends and I primed myself by reading an introductory book on stamp collecting. Each chapter described methods of handling and identifying stamps, with a clear glossary. I then bought a regular stamp magazine (*Gibbons Stamp Monthly*) which contains articles for beginners, again with terms explained. Finally

I forced myself to read some arcane articles on printing methods, watermarking and the like. All the while, I collected stamps and checked them against a catalogue which used the terminology I was acquiring in ways that allowed me to put to the test whether I had understood. If I misunderstood, I might miss something of value or assign a stamp incorrectly, so there were practical consequences to misunderstanding. After a couple of years I then joined a local society and put my primings to the test in the production of conversation. Some of those I spoke with were fully primed in the lexis associated with this context while others, like me, were still in the process of acquiring the necessary lexical primings/knowledge, and in such a context the overlap between acquiring primings and acquiring knowledge is very considerable.

The processes I have just described as a learner in an area of my L1 hitherto unknown to me – you will notice that I hesitate to call it specialism, since one person's specialism may seem bread and butter to another – seem similar to those undergone by many second or subsequent language learners. Such learners seek to acquire the primings associated with those areas of life in which they wish to seem competent and in which the effects of seeming incompetent may be practical as well as social. For each learner, this may vary. If I wish to tour a country, I may want the appropriately primed lexis for food, accommodation and directions, as coursebooks for time immemorial have assumed. I may on the other hand want to read academic texts in the language or engage in conversation about football. Crucially, as any language learner will confirm, the primings we have may serve us in one situation and fail us in another – as indeed is true for the learner of the philatelic lexis. The difference between the two types of learning and learner is one of degree, rather than one of kind.

Apart from the inevitable impact of primings from other languages (usually but not inevitably the first language) and from other contexts, the range of speakers who can prime us when we seek to acquire new primings in another language or another area of a language is radically impoverished compared with the range that will typically be encountered in a situation of immersion. Then, again, the social contexts in which we as learners encounter the language are not only similarly impoverished but are typically experienced in common with other people who have been primed to a similar degree as ourselves and whose own language efforts will, willy-nilly, prime us. Thirdly, the quantity of data from which we will be primed will be markedly less than any immersed learner is likely to encounter.

What are the implications of all this for language learning? It must in this context be recalled that priming is the result of a speaker encountering evidence and generalising from it. For me as a beginner in stamp collecting, the introductory text and beginner sections in the magazines were ways of shortcutting this process. Instead of learning what a perforation gauge was from constant encounters with the word sequence, a definition was provided along with instructions for use. The priming came not from frequent, necessarily unordered encounters but from a single focused and generalising encounter. In the same way, language teaching materials and language teachers can provide essential shortcuts to primings. This can happen in a multitude of ways. Usage notes, drilling exercises, texts or tapes with repeated instances of a word sequence, collocational observations and illustrations or just drawing a class's attention to a feature all may speed up the process, as may judicious use of corpus-based monolingual dictionaries and corpus-based descriptive grammars. Lexicographers and grammarians exposed to concordances are effectively being given an accelerated priming. (Higgins and Johns 1984 and J. Willis 1998 have incidentally shown how such accelerated priming may be directly useful to learners, without the mediation of a dictionary or grammar.) If the lexicographer or grammarian reflects this 'instant' priming in their dictionary or grammatical entry, the entry offers an extremely valuable shortcut to a lexical item's characteristic collocations and colligations.

If shortcuts to priming are provided, and for many learners the classroom and the teaching materials used in the classroom provide the only context for priming, it is essential that the primings are not unhelpful in the area in which they will be used. While it is not possible to say that any set of primings are correct and another incorrect, it certainly is possible to say that someone's primings are not in harmony with those of their likely listeners or readers and that they will accordingly sound unnatural to them. The lexical approach (Lewis 1993) can ensure that primings are harmonious with those of most listeners and readers, and Willis (2003) likewise seeks to integrate grammar and vocabulary teaching in a manner that ought to result in naturalness in the learner. Woolard (2004) seeks to teach the collocations of the most common words in the language, inevitably thereby also integrating the grammatical and lexical. Many of the language teaching materials to which I have been exposed on the other hand have provided me with opportunities to acquire unhelpful primings. Unhelpful primings may result from a textbook's overemphasis on certain features of the language (McEnery 2003), or on its fabricated illustrations of grammatical points. At best, unhelpful primings will result in cracks in the priming when the learner encounters authentic instances of the language away from the teaching context. This may lead to insecurity or distrust of the value of what has been learnt in the classroom. At worst, it may inhibit the development of helpful primings and stunt language growth.

Grammatical notes are a particular kind of shortcut. They may be beneficial if they are rooted in the lexis that gave rise to the grammatical observation but harmful if they are rooted in no characteristic lexis. A grammatical note on the present perfect is likely to be helpful if the pattern is discussed in connection with spoken sequences such as *'ve shown*, *'ve found that* and *'ve learnt that* and written sequences such as *have shown that*, *have found that* and *have learnt that*, but may actively encourage unhelpful priming and result in unnatural output if discussed with no attention to key primings.

Shortcuts may be necessary, but, given the nature of priming for L1 learners, second or subsequent language learners should be exposed to authentic data wherever possible, and the data should both reinforce existing priming (i.e. by overlapping with previously encountered material) and permit new priming to take place. Krashen (1981) must be correct in talking of the need to give learners material at the threshold of their competence; beyond the threshold, priming will not take place – the learner will simply switch off. On the other hand, when the learner is comfortably on this side of the threshold, existing primings will be reinforced but no new ones created.

Authentic data of course come in two forms. If the data are written only, the learner's primings will initially – and perhaps permanently – be of letter sequences. Effectively, learners have to have their lexis primed twice over, both as letter sequences and as sound sequences. I speak from experience here. I read adequately in several languages in which I have low competence as a speaker, mainly, I would argue, because my primings are only for the written word.

These seem to me the main implications for second language learning, though there are others. Several factors, however, seem in need of investigation. The first concerns the conditions under which priming takes place. I have throughout this book talked as if all encounters are equal, but we can assume that this is not so. The devout reader of the Torah, the New Testament or the Koran will presumably be more powerfully primed than the skim-reader of a newspaper found abandoned on a railway seat. Presumably, likewise, if the encounter is accompanied by some important effect or emotion, it will be weighted. We need to investigate the conditions under which priming takes place. It is hard to believe that all activities and all levels of (in)attention have the same effect. There are obvious implications for the possible effectiveness of different kinds of language activity.

A particular area for investigation is the relative effect on priming of production as opposed to reception. To what extent does an utterance produced by a speaker or writer reinforce (or even contribute to creating) that person's primings? This needs to be discovered. If as I suspect the act of production is strongly reinforcing, it might follow that the learner needs to speak or write as often as possible.

On the other hand, if production reinforces a priming, what are the implications for the learner who repeatedly makes a mistake (defined as a word or sound sequence without support from any part of the linguistic communities in which the speaker wishes to mix)? Does the speaker likewise prime themselves with the mistake? Perhaps the 'silent period' sometimes referred to in the literature is one in which the learner waits to be primed by others (though those others may of course themselves be making mistakes).

A brief conclusion

It is not only in the area of language teaching that further investigation is needed. This book has barely alluded to language change. Lexical priming, given its individual nature and its genre and domain specificity, would seem to offer a dynamic mechanism for change worthy at least of exploration. Nor has the book said much about the early stages of a child's acquisition of language, though again the implications are obvious. Intonation, too, needs to be addressed. Are certain words or word sequences primed to occur with certain pitches or tones? Or is intonation entirely independent, in which case it may belong with the discourse impulse in the map of levels I offered in Chapter 8.

Even where I have touched on a topic, my coverage has often been sparse and programmatic. Apart from the obvious point that my data in some cases barely permit more than the most tentative of speculations, I have been brief on how colligations lead to grammar and how creativity operates, and I have only touched upon the phonetic and phonological implications of the position I have been advocating, and that from a position of inadequate knowledge.

But books have to end. I have offered in this one a theory designed to build upon the work of corpus linguists but addressing some of the questions that non-corpus based theoretical and descriptive linguists have found interesting. I have sought to be integrative rather than combative, and I hope that the book may provoke others to develop lexically-driven models.

I referred above to the possibility that priming might contribute to our understanding of language change. When I was a child, I was primed to expect narratives to have the words *The End* in text-final position, in a line of their own and always with initial capitalisation – a textual colligational priming. Along with probably everybody else, I am no longer so primed. But I am going to override both the temporal context within which my former priming operated and the restriction of the priming in that temporal context to narratives only. As I noted in the previous chapter it is possible to override one or more primings for creative purposes, and, after all, whatever its merits or demerits, this is a creative work.

[The End]

Bibliography

Abney, S. P. (1987) The English noun phrase in its sentential aspect, Ph.D. dissertation, MIT.

Adams-Smith, D. (1986) Aspects of register variation in seven popular science articles and the research papers from which they were derived, unpublished MA dissertation, University of Birmingham.

Anderson, J. R. (1983) *The Architecture of Cognition*. Cambridge, MA: Harvard University Press.

Baker, P. (forthcoming) *Public Discourses of Gay Men*. London: Routledge.

Barlow, M. (2000) Usage, blends and grammar, in M. Barlow and S. Kemmer (eds) *Usage Based Models of Language*. Stanford: CSLI Publications.

Bastow, T. (2003) *Friends and allies*: binomials in a corpus of US defence speeches, paper given at ASLA Symposium, Örebro University, 6 November.

Bawcom, L. (2003) Bawcom's blossom. Unpublished presentation given at the Tuscan Word Centre, May.

Becker, A. L. (1965) A tagmemic approach to paragraph analysis, *College Composition and Communication*, 16(4): 237–42.

Becker, A. L. (1966) Symposium on the paragraph, *College Composition and Communication*, 17(2): 67–72.

Bell, A. (1991) *The Language of News Media*. Oxford: Blackwell.

Berry, M. (1989) Thematic options and success in writing, in C. Butler, R. Cardwell and J. Channell (eds) *Language and Literature: Theory and Practice*, pp. 62–80. Nottingham: Nottingham University Press.

Bhatia, V. (1993) *Analysing Genre: Language Use in Professional Settings*. London: Longman.

Biber, D., Johansson, S., Leech, G., Conrad, S. and Finnegan, E. (1999) *Longman Grammar of Spoken and Written English*. Harlow: Longman.

Biber, D. Conrad, S. and Leech, G. (2002) *Longman Student Grammar of Spoken and Written English*. Harlow: Longman.

Bryson, B. (1991) *Neither Here Nor There: Travels in Europe*. London: Secker & Warburg.

Butler, C. (2004) 'Corpus studies and functional linguistic theories' in press.

Campanelli, P. and Channell, J. M. (1994) *Training: An Exploration of the Word and the Concept with an Analysis of the Implications for Survey Design*. London: Employment Department.

Carter, R. (2004) *Language and Creativity: The Art of Common Talk*. London: Routledge.

Carter, Reverend T. T. (ed.) ([1896]1957) *The Treasury of Devotion: A Manual of Prayers*. London: Longman.

Channell, J. (1994) *Vague Language*. Oxford: Oxford University Press.

Chomsky, N. (1957) *Syntactic Structures*. The Hague: Mouton.

Chomsky, N. (1965) *Aspects of the Theory of Syntax*. Cambridge, MA: MIT Press.

Chomsky, N. (1986) *Knowledge of Language*. New York: Praeger Special Studies.

Chomsky, N. (1995) *The Minimalist Program*. Cambridge, MA: MIT Press.

Christensen, F. (1965) A generative rhetoric of the paragraph, *College Composition and Communication*, 16(3): 144–56.

Christensen, F. (1966) Symposium on the paragraph, *College Composition and Communication*, 17(2): 60–6.

Collins COBUILD English Language Dictionary (1987) (Editor-in-chief: J. Sinclair; Editor: P. Hanks). Glasgow: Collins.

Collins Dictionary of the English Language (CDEL) (1979) 1st edn. London: Collins.

Cruse, D. A. (1986) *Lexical Semantics*. Cambridge: Cambridge University Press.

Daneš, F. (1974) Functional sentence perspective and the organization of the text, in F. Daneš (ed.) *Papers on Functional Sentence Perspective*, pp. 105–28. Prague: Academia.

Danks, D. (2003) Separating blends: a formal investigation of the blending process in English and its relationship to associated word formation processes, unpublished Ph.D. thesis, University of Liverpool.

Darnton, A. (2001) Repeat after me: the role of repetition in the life of an emergent reader, in M. Scott and G. Thompson (eds) *Patterns of Text*, pp. 193–212. Amsterdam: John Benjamins.

Davies, F. I. (1988) Reading between the lines: thematic choice as a device for presenting writer viewpoint in academic text, *The ESPecialist*, 9: 173–200.

Doyle, P. G. (2003) Replicating corpus linguistics: a corpus-driven investigation of lexical networks in text, unpublished Ph.D. thesis, University of Lancaster.

Duncan, S. and Fiske, D. W. (1977) *Face-to-face Interaction: Research, Methods and Theory*. Hillsdale, NJ: Lawrence Erlbaum.

Emmott, C. (1989) Reading between the lines: building a comprehensive model of participant reference in real narrative, Ph.D. thesis, University of Birmingham.

Emmott, C. (1997) *Narrative Comprehension: A Discourse Perspective*. Oxford: Clarendon Press.

Fillmore, C. J., Kay, P. and O'Connor, C. (1988) Regularity and idiomaticity in grammatical constructions: the case of *let alone*, *Language*, 64: 501–38.

Firth, J. R. ([1951]1957) A synopsis of linguistic theory, 1930–1955, in F. Palmer (ed.) *Selected Papers of J R Firth 1952–59*, pp. 168–205. London: Longman.

Firth, J. R. (1957) *Papers in Linguistics*. London: Oxford University Press.

Francis, G. (1986) *Anaphoric Nouns* (Discourse Analysis Monographs). Birmingham: ELR, University of Birmingham.

Francis, G. (1993) A corpus-driven approach to grammar – principles, methods and examples, in M. Baker, G. Francis and E. Tognini-Bonelli (eds) *Text and Technology: In Honour of John Sinclair*, pp. 137–56. Amsterdam: John Benjamins.

Francis, G. (1994) Labelling discourse: an aspect of nominal-group lexical cohesion, in M. Coulthard (ed.) *Advances in Written Text Analysis*, pp. 83–101. London: Routledge.

Francis, G., Hunston, S. and Manning, E. (1996) *Collins COBUILD Grammar Patterns 1: Verbs*. London: HarperCollins.

Francis, G., Hunston, S. and Manning, E. (1998) *Collins COBUILD Grammar Patterns 2: Nouns and Adjectives*. London: HarperCollins.

Garcia, P. and Drescher, N. (2003) A corpus-based analysis of pragmatic meaning, paper given at XII Susanne Hübner Seminar 'Corpus Linguistics: Theory and Applications for the Study of English', Universidad de Zaragoza, 19–21 November.

Giddens, A. (1979) *Central Problems in Social Theory*. London: Macmillan.

Gledhill, C. J. (2000) *Collocations in Science Writing*. Tübingen: Gunter Narr Verlag Tübingen.

Goldberg, A. E. (1995) *Constructions: A Construction Grammar Approach to Argument Structure*. Chicago: University of Chicago Press.

Halliday, M. A. K. (1959) *The Language of the Chinese 'Secret History of the Mongols'*. Oxford: Blackwell.

Halliday, M. A. K. (1991) Corpus studies and probabilistic grammar, in K. Aijmer and B. Altenberg (eds) *English Corpus Linguistics*, pp. 30–43. London: Longman.

Halliday, M. A. K. (1992) Language as system and language as instance: the corpus as a theoretical construct, in J. Svartvik (ed.) *Directions in Corpus Linguistics*, pp. 61–77. Berlin: Mouton.

Halliday, M. A. K. (1993) Quantitative studies and probabilities in grammar, in M. Hoey (ed.) *Data, Description, Discourse*, pp. 1–25. London: HarperCollins.

Halliday, M. A. K. (1994) *An Introduction to Functional Grammar*, 2nd edn. London: Arnold.

Halliday, M. A. K. and Hasan, R. (1976) *Cohesion in English*. London: Longman.

Halliday, M. A. K. and James, Z. L. (1993) A quantitative study of polarity and primary tense in the English finite clause, in J. M. Sinclair, M. Hoey and G. Fox (eds) *Techniques of Description: Spoken and Written Discourse*, pp. 32–66. London: Routledge.

Hanks, P. (ed.) (1979) *Collins Dictionary of the English Language*. London: Collins.

Hanks, P. (ed.) (1987) *Collins COBUILD English Dictionary*. London: Collins.

Hanks, P. (1996) Contextual dependency and lexical sets, *International Journal of Corpus Linguistics*, 1(1): 75–88.

Hanks, P. (2004) The syntagmatics of metaphor and idiom, unpublished manuscript.

Hasan, R. (1984) Coherence and cohesive harmony, in J. Flood (ed.) *Understanding Reading Comprehension*, pp. 181–219. Newark, DE: International Reading Association.

Higgins, J. and Johns, T. (1984) *Computers in Language Learning*. London: Collins.

Hoey, M. (1979) *Signalling in Discourse* (Discourse Analysis Monographs No. 6). Birmingham: ELR, University of Birmingham.

Hoey, M. (1983) *On the Surface of Discourse*. London: George Allen & Unwin.

Hoey, M. (1985) The paragraph boundary as a marker of relations between the parts of a discourse, *M.A.L.S. Journal*, 10: 96–107.

Hoey, M. (1991a) *Patterns of Lexis in Text*. Oxford: Oxford University Press.

Hoey, M. (1991b) Another perspective on coherence and cohesive harmony, in E. Ventola (ed.) *Functionao and Systemic Linguistics: Approaches and Uses*, pp. 385–414. Berlin: Mouton de Gruyter.

Hoey, M. (1991c) The matrix organisation of narrative and non-narrative text in English, in *Proceedings of the 5th Symposium on the Description and/or Comparison of English and Greek*, pp. 216–53. Thessaloniki: Aristotle University.

Hoey, M. (1993) A common signal in discourse: how the word 'reason' is used in texts, in J. Sinclair, M. Hoey and G. Fox (eds) *Techniques of Description — Spoken and Written Discourse*, pp. 67–82. London: Routledge.

Hoey, M. (1994) Signalling in discourse: a functional analysis of a common discourse pattern in written and spoken English, in M. Coulthard (ed.) *Advances in Written Text Analysis*, pp. 26–45. London: Routledge.

Hoey, M. (1996) Cohesive words: a paper of consequence, in *Words: Proceedings of an International Symposium*, Lund, 25–6 August 1995, ed. Jan Svartvik, Stockholm.

Hoey, M. (1997a) Lexical problems for the language learner (and the hint of a textual solution), in *Proceedings of the 5th Latin American ESP Colloquium*, Merida, Venezuela.

Hoey, M. (1997b) From concordance to text structure: new uses for computer corpora, in *PALC '97: Proceedings of Practical Applications of Linguistic Corpora Conference*, University of Lodz.

Hoey, M. (1997c) The interaction of textual and lexical factors in the identification of paragraph boundaries, in M. Reinhardt and W. Thiele (eds) *Grammar and Text in Synchrony and Diachrony in Honour of Gottfried Graustein*, pp. 141–67. Vervuert Verlag.

Hoey, M. (1998) Some text properties of certain nouns, in T. McEnery and S. Botley (eds) *Proceedings of the Colloquium on Discourse Anaphora and Reference Resolution*. Lancaster: University of Lancaster.

Hoey, M. (2000) A world beyond collocation: new perspectives on vocabulary teaching, in M. Lewis (ed.) *Teaching Collocation*. Hove: LTP.

Hoey, M. (2001) *Textual Interaction*. London: Routledge.

Hoey, M. (2002) Lexis as choice: what is chosen? Paper given at International Systemics Congress, University of Liverpool, July.

Hoey, M. (2003) Why grammar is beyond belief, in J-P. van Noppen, C. Den Tandt and I. Tudor (eds) *Beyond: New Perspectives in Language, Literature and ELT*. Special issue of *Belgian Journal of English Language and Literatures*, new series 1: 183–96.

Hoey, M. (2004a) Lexical priming and the properties of text, in A. Partington, J. Morley and L. Haarman (eds) *Corpora and Discourse*, pp. 385–412. Bern: Peter Lang.

Hoey, M. (2004b) Language as choice: what is chosen? in G. Thompson and S. Hunston (eds) *System and Corpus: Exploring Connections*. London: Equinox.

Hoey, M. (2004c) Textual colligation: a special kind of lexical priming, in *Proceedings of ICAME 2002: The Theory and Use of Corpora*, the 23rd International Conference on English Language Research on Computerized Corpora of Modern and Medieval English, Göteborg.

Hopper, P. (1988) Emergent grammar and the *a priori* grammar postulate, in D. Tannen (ed.) *Linguistics in Context: Connecting Observation and Understanding*. Norwood, NJ: Ablex.

Hopper, P. (1998) Emergent grammar, in M. Tomasello (ed.) *The New Psychology of Language*, pp. 155–75. NJ: Lawrence Erlbaum Associates.

Hudson, R. (1984) *Word Grammar*. Oxford: Blackwell.

Hunston, S. (2001) Colligation, lexis, pattern, and text, in M. Scott and G. Thompson (eds) *Patterns of Text*, pp. 13–33. Amsterdam: John Benjamins.

Hunston, S. and Francis, G. (2000) *Pattern Grammar*. Amsterdam: John Benjamins.

Jones, S. and Sinclair, J. M. (1974) English lexical collocations – a study in computational linguistics, reprinted in J. A. Foley (ed.) *J. M. Sinclair on Lexis and Lexicography*, pp. 21–54. Singapore: National University of Singapore.

Jordan, M. P. (1980) Short texts to explain problem-solution structures – and vice versa, *Instructional Science*, 9: 221–52.

Jordan, M. P. (1984) *Rhetoric of Everyday English Texts*. London: George Allen & Unwin.

Krashen, S. D. (1981) *Second Language Acquisition and Second Language Learning*. Oxford: Pergamon.

Krishnamurty, R. (2002) Corpus, collocation, and lexical sets, in B. Hollosy and J. Kiss-Gulyas (eds) *Studies in Linguistics*, vol. VI, part I (a supplement to the *Hungarian Journal of English and American Studies*). Debrecen: University of Debrecen.

Krishnamurty, R. (2003) Language as chunks, not words, in M. Swanson and K. Hill (eds) *JALT 2002 Proceedings*, pp. 288–94. Tokyo: JALT.

Labov, W. (1972) *Language in the Inner City: Studies in the Black English Vernacular*. Philadelphia, PA: University of Pennsylvania Press.

Labov, W. (1975) *What is a Linguistic Fact?* Lisse: Peter de Ridder Press.

Lakoff, G. and Johnson, M. (1980) *Metaphors We Live By*. Chicago: University of Chicago Press.

Langendoen, D. T. (1968) *The London School of Linguistics: A Study of the Linguistic Theories of B. Malinowski and J. R. Firth*. Cambridge, MA: MIT Press.

Leech, G. (1974) *Semantics*. Harmondsworth: Penguin.

Lewis, M. (1993) *The Lexical Approach*. Hove: LTP.

Longacre, R. E. (1968) *Discourse, Paragraph and Sentence Structure in Selected Philippine Languages*. Dallas, TX: Summer Institute of Linguistics Publications.

Louw, B. (1993) Irony in the text or insincerity in the writer? The diagnostic potential of semantic prosodies, in M. Baker *et al.* (eds) *Text and Technology*, pp. 157–76. Amsterdam: John Benjamins.

McCarthy, M. (ed.) (1988) *Naturalness in Language*. Birmingham: University of Birmingham.

McCarthy, M. J. (1998) *Spoken Language and Applied Linguistics*. Cambridge: Cambridge University Press.

McEnery, T. (2003) Unpublished conference paper.

Macmillan English Dictionary for Advanced Learners (2002) Oxford: Macmillan.

Macmillan Essential Dictionary (2003) Oxford: Macmillan.

Marín-Arrese, J. I. (2003) Evidentiality and epistemic modality in the discourse of fact and opinion in English and Spanish: a comparative corpus study, paper given at XII Susanne Hübner Seminar 'Corpus Linguistics: Theory and Applications for the Study of English', Universidad de Zaragoza, 19–21 November.

Morgan, J. L. and Sellner, M. B. (1980) Discourse and linguistic theory, in R. J. Spiro (ed.) *Theoretical Issues in Reading Comprehension: Perspectives from Cognitive Psychology, Linguistics, Artificial Intelligence and Education*. Hillside, NJ: Lawrence Erlbaum.

Neely, J. H. (1977) Semantic priming and retrieval from lexical memory: roles of inhibitionless spreading activation and limited capacity attention, *Journal of Experimental Psychology: General*, 106: 226–54.

Neely, J. H. (1991) Semantic priming effects in visual word recognition: a selective review of current findings and theories, in D. Besner and G. W. Humphreys (eds)

Basic Processes in Reading: Visual Word Recognition, pp. 264–336. Hillsdale, NJ: Lawrence Erlbaum.

O'Halloran, K. and Coffin, C. (2004) Checking overinterpretation and underinterpretation: help from corpora in critical linguistics, in C. Coffin, A. Hewings and K. O'Halloran (eds) *Applied English Grammar: Functional and Corpus Approaches*, pp. 275–297. London: Hodder-Arnold.

Oxford English Dictionary (1995) 2nd edn. Oxford: Oxford University Press.

Parsons, G. (1995) Measuring cohesion in English texts: the relationship between cohesion and coherence, Ph.D. thesis, University of Nottingham.

Partington, A. (1998) *Patterns and Meanings: Using Corpora for English Language Research and Teaching*. Amsterdam: John Benjamins.

Partington, A. (2003) *The Linguistics of Political Argument: The Spin-doctor and the Wolf-pack at the White House*. London: Routledge.

Partington, A. (2004) 'Utterly content in each other's company': some thoughts on semantic prosody and semantic preference, in A. Partington, J. Morley and L. Haarman (eds) *Corpora and Discourse*. Bern: Peter Lang.

Partington, A. and Morley, J. (2002) From frequency to ideology: comparing word and cluster frequencies in political debate, paper given at the 5th TALC (Teaching and Language Corpora) Conference, Bertinoro, Italy, 26–31 July.

Pike, K. L. and Pike, E. G. (1982) *Grammatical Analysis*, 2nd edn. Summer Institute of Linguistics Publications No. 53. Santa Ana: Summer Institute of Linguistics.

Pinker, S. (1994) *The Language Instinct*. New York: HarperCollins.

Pinna, A. (2003) The discourse prosody of some intensifiers in G. W. Bush's presidential speeches, paper given at XII Susanne Hübner Seminar 'Corpus Linguistics: Theory and Applications for the Study of English', Universidad de Zaragoza, 19–21 November.

Quirk, R. Greenbaum, S. Leech, G. and Svartvik, J. (1972) *A Grammar of Contemporary English*. London: Longman.

Quirk, R., Greenbaum, S. Leech, G. and Svartvik, J. (1985) *A Comprehensive Grammar of the English Language*. London: Longman.

Rappaport, G. C. (2001) The geometry of the Polish nominal phrase: problems, progress and prospects, in P. Banski and A. Przepiórkowski (eds) *Generative Linguistics in Poland: Syntax and Morphosyntax*. Warsaw: Polish Academy of Sciences.

Renouf, A. (1986) Lexical resolution, in W. Meijs (ed.) *Corpus Linguistics and Beyond: The Proceedings of the 7th International Conference of English Language Research on Computerised Corpora*, pp. 121–31. Amsterdam: Rodopi.

Rodgers, P. C. (1966) A discourse-centred rhetoric of the paragraph, *College Composition and Communication*, 17(1): 2–11.

Schegloff, E. A. (1972) Sequencing in conversational openings, in J. Gumperz and D. H. Hymes (eds) *Directions in Sociolinguistics*, pp. 346–80. New York: Holt, Rinehart & Winston.

Schegloff, E. A. and Sacks, H. (1973) Opening up closings, *Semiotica*, 7(4): 289–327.

Scott, M. (1999) *WordSmith Tools, Version 3*. Oxford: Oxford University Press.

Sinclair, J. M. (1972) *A Course in Spoken English: Grammar*. London: Oxford University Press.

Sinclair, J. M. (ed.) (1987) *Looking Up*. London: Collins.

Sinclair, J. M. (ed.) (1990) *Collins Cobuild English Grammar*. London: HarperCollins.

Sinclair, J. M. (1991) *Corpus, Concordance, Collocation*. Oxford: Oxford University Press.

Sinclair, J. M. (1992) Trust the text, in L. Ravelli and M. Davies (eds) *Advances in Systemic Linguistics: Recent Theory and Practice*, pp. 1–19. London: Pinter.

Sinclair, J. M. (1993) Written discourse structure, in J. M. Sinclair, M. Hoey and G. Fox (eds) *Techniques of Description*. London: Routledge.

Sinclair, J. M. (1996) The search for units of meaning, *Textus* IX: 75–106.

Sinclair, J. M. (1999) The lexical item, in E. Weigand (ed.) *Contrastive Lexical Semantics*. Amsterdam: John Benjamins.

Sinclair, J. M. (2004) *Trust the Text: Language, Corpus and Discourse*. London: Routledge.

Sinclair, J. M. and Coulthard, R. M. (1975) *Towards an Analysis of Discourse: The English Used by Teachers and Pupils*. London: Oxford University Press.

Sinclair, J. M. and Renouf, A. (1988) Lexical syllabus for language learning, in R. Carter and M. McCarthy (eds) *Vocabulary and Language Teaching*, pp. 197–206. Harlow: Longman.

Smith, F. (1985) *Reading*, 2nd edn. Cambridge: Cambridge University Press.

Stern, A. (1976) When is a paragraph? *College Composition and Communication*, 27(3): 253–7.

Stubbs, M. (1995) Corpus evidence for norms of lexical collocation, in G. Cook and B. Seidlhofer (eds) *Principle and Practice in Applied Linguistics*, pp. 245–56. Oxford: Oxford University Press.

Stubbs, M. (1996) *Text and Corpus Analysis*. Oxford: Blackwell.

Sutherland, S. M. (1985) A description of description: a study of information patterning in descriptive discourse and its implications for the EFL classroom, unpublished MA dissertation, University of Birmingham.

Swales, J. (1981) *Aspects of Article Introductions*, Aston ESP Research Report No. 1. Birmingham: Language Studies Unit, University of Aston.

Swales, J. (1990) *Genre Analysis: English in Academic and Research Settings*. Cambridge: Cambridge University Press.

Tognini-Bonelli, E. (2001) *Corpus Linguistics at Work* (Studies in Corpus Linguistics, 6). Amsterdam: John Benjamins.

Tucker, G. H. (1996) So grammarians haven't the faintest idea: reconciling lexis-oriented and grammar-oriented approaches to language, in R. Hasan, C. Cloran and D. G. Butt (eds) *Functional Descriptions: Theory in Practice*, pp. 145–78. Amsterdam: John Benjamins.

Upton, T. and Connor, U. (2004) Investigating stance in the rhetorical moves of grant proposals, paper given at AAAL, 2004, Portland, Oregon, 1 May.

Wang, S. (forthcoming) Corpus-based approaches and discourse analysis in relation to reduplication and repetition, *Journal of Pragmatics*.

Wang, S. and McCarthy, M. (2004) Corpus-based analysis and discourse analysis of fixed expressions: fixed, flexible or free formulation, paper given at the 2nd Inter Varietal Applied Corpus Studies (IVACS) International Conference on 'Analysing Discourse in Context', The Graduate School of Education, Queen's University, Belfast, Northern Ireland, 26 June.

Webster's New International Dictionary of the English Language (1928) London: G. Bell & Sons Ltd.

Whitsitt, S. (2003) A critique of the concept of semantic prosody, unpublished manu-script, Scuola Superiore di Lingue Moderne per Interpreti e Traduttori dell'Università di Bologna a Forlì.

Williames, J. (1984) An enquiry into the interactive nature of written discourse: the example of the newspaper argument letter, unpublished MA dissertation, University of Birmingham.

Williames, J. (1985) The interactive nature of the newspaper letter, *MALS Journal* (new series), 10: 108–40.

Williams, G. C. (1998) Collocational networks: interlocking patterns of lexis in a corpus of plant biology research articles, *International Journal of Corpus Linguistics*, 3(1): 151–71.

Williams, T. H. (1963) *Lincoln and His Generals*. New York: Knopf.

Willis, D. (2003) *Rules, Patterns and Words: Grammar and Lexis in English Language Teaching*. Cambridge: Cambridge University Press.

Willis, J. (1998) Concordances in the classroom without a computer: assembling and exploiting concordances of common words, in B. Tomlinson (ed) *Materials Develop-ment in Language Teaching*, pp. 44–66. Cambridge: Cambridge University Press.

Winter, E. (1974) Replacement as a function of repetition: a study of some of its principal features in the clause relations of contemporary English, unpublished Ph.D. thesis, University of London.

Winter, E. (1976) Fundamentals of information structure: pilot manual for further development according to student need, unpublished manual, Hatfield Polytechnic.

Winter, E. (1977) A clause relational approach to English texts, *Instructional Science* (special edition), 6: 1–92.

Winter, E. (1979) Replacement as a fundamental function of the sentence in context, *Forum Linguisticum*, 4(2): 95–133.

Woolard, G. (2004) *Keywords for Fluency – Upper Intermediate*. Hove: LTP.

Young, R. and Becker, A. (1966) The role of lexical and grammatical cues in paragraph recognition, in *Studies in Language and Language Behaviour, Progress Report No 2*. Ann Arbor, MI: Center for Research on Language, University of Michigan.

Index

abstraction 160–1
academic texts 10, 133
accountant 64, 65–8, 66t, 67t
actor 64–8, 66t, 67t
actress 64–8, 66t, 67t
agency and social structure 8
ago 120–1, 121, 123, 176–7
allusion 12
ambiguity 82, 110–13
antonyms 79
architect 64, 65–8, 66t, 67t, 154
army 118–19, 172
around the world: colligation 77–9;
    collocates 74–6, 75t; (in)definiteness
    78, 78t; semantic associations 76–7
as a 141
aversion 45, 46t, 48–9, 49t, 55–7, 56t,
    57t

Baker, P. 9–10, 19, 23
Bank of English 24, 86
Barlow, M. 63
Bastow, T. 19, 21, 23, 130
Bawcom, L. 68
Becker, A. 134
Bell, A. 132
Berry, M. 49, 53
Biber, D. *et al.* 45
Bill Bryson sentence 5–6; co-hyponymy
    65; collocation 5–6; priming prosodies
    166, 167f; Relational processes 41–2;
    semantic association 16, 18, 23, 31–2;
    textual colligation 148–50; textual
    collocation 124–8; textual priming
    114–15, 124–8

British National Corpus x, 14, 112
Bryson, Bill *see* Bill Bryson sentence
Butler, C. 7

Campanelli, P. 64
carpenter 64, 65–8, 66t, 67t
Carter, R. 152, 169
Carter, Rev. T. T. 68
cause 22–3
CDEL (*Collins Dictionary of the English
    Language*) 30–1
Channell, J. M. 64
children, writing for 21
Chomsky, N. 1, 2, 8, 153, 184
co-hyponymy: abstraction 160–1;
    colligation 65–7; collocation 64–5;
    metaphorical uses 67, 67t; priming
    hypothesis 13; semantic association 64,
    67–8
co-texts 9–10
Coffin, C. 23
coherence 117
cohesion 4, 116–17; *see also* textual
    collocation
cohesive chains 117–18, 174–5
cohesive links 117, 118
colligation: *around/round the world* 77–9;
    co-hyponymy 65–7; concept 42–3;
    conclusions 61–2; *consequence* 44–58,
    71–3, 83–5, 154; definition 13, 43–4,
    84–5; *immunity* 107–8, 107t; *reason*
    43, 59–61, 61t; SKILLED ROLE OR
    OCCUPATION 64–8, 66t; synonymous
    expressions 77–9; synonymy 71–3;
    see also textual colligation

colligational nesting 58–61, 58*f*
Collins COBUILD English Language Dictionary 30, 43, 81, 157
Collins Dictionary of the English Language (CDEL) 30–1
collocates (definition) 13
collocation: analysis 4–5; *around/round the world* 74–6, 75*t*; Bill Bryson sentence 5–6; co-hyponymy 64–5; concept 2–3; *consequences* 33, 34, 35, 35*t*; *immunity* 105, 106*t*, 108; lexical repetition 117, 121, 122; and naturalness 2–5, 6; optimum spans 4–5; pervasiveness 3, 5–7; and pragmatic association 27–9; priming as explanation 7–12; psychological definitions 4, 5; and semantic association 16–20, 33; statistical definition 3–4; subversiveness 7; synonymous expressions 74–6, 75*t*; textual definition 3; *see also* colligation; textual collocation
collocative meaning 4
Complement (definition) 45
Connor, U. 133
consequence: ambiguity 111–13; meanings 44; (= result) *vs.* (= importance) 82, 83, 87–8, 87*t*; textual colligation 52, 130–1; *see also* consequence (= importance); *consequence* (= result)
consequence (= importance): colligation 83–5, 84*t*; *of consequence* 86; pragmatic association 85–6; primings with respect to Theme 86–7; *vs.* (= result) 82, 83, 87–8, 87*t*
consequence (= result): colligational description 44–58, 71–3, 154; colligational primings in the nominal group 48–9, 49*t*; colligational primings when Subject 55–8, 56*t*, 57*f*, 57*t*, 58*f*; colligations in the clause 44–8, 46*t*; collocates 33–4, 34*t*, 35, 36–7; *as a consequence* 50, 51, 53–5; *in consequence* 50, 51, 52–3; (in)definiteness 55–7, 56*t*, 57*t*, 71–2*t*, 71–3, 73*t*; grammatical category 154–5; primings with respect to Theme 49–55, 50*t*, 52*t*, 130–1; semantic associations 24–6, 36–7,

68–71, 69*f*; *vs.* (= importance) 82, 83, 87–8, 87*t*
consequences: collocates 33, 34, 35, 35*t*; textual priming 130–1
construction grammar 2, 63
contexts 9–10, 178
corpora x; analysis 52; as evidence of priming 14–15; importance of 150
corpus linguistics *vs.* generative linguistics 152–3
creativity: Chomskyan creativity 153; literary creativity 153, 172–7; and naturalness 6, 152, 153; priming conflict 170–2; and semantic association 16, 17; types 153, 169; unintended creativity 152, 169–70

Danks, D. 159
Darnton, A. 21
Davies, F. I. 49
definiteness and indefiniteness 55–7, 56*t*, 57*t*, 71–2*t*, 71–3, 73*t*, 78, 78*t*
determiner phrase hypothesis 167–8
Dickens, Charles 172, 173–5
dictionaries 1, 30, 81, 182–3, 186
discourse 10, 162–4, 164*f*, 165*f*
domain-specificity 9–10, 13, 19–20, 133, 180, 182
Doyle, P. G. 3, 5
Drescher, N. 29
drinking problem hypotheses 82, 130; hypothesis 1: (*consequence*) 82, 83, 87–8, 87*t*; hypothesis 1: (*reason*) 82–3, 88, 92–104; hypothesis 2: (*immunity*) 82, 104–8; hypothesis 3: ambiguity 82, 110–13

E-language 8
Editor, The 169–70
education 11, 30, 180, 182
emergent grammar 9
Emmott, C. 12, 122

Fillmore, C. J. *et al.* 152, 161
Firth, J. R. 3, 10, 22, 42
folk tales 21
Francis, G. 2, 43, 63, 154, 161
fundamentally 143

Garcia, P. 29
gay 121
generative linguistics *vs.* corpus linguistics
    152–3
genre-specificity 9–10, 13, 19–20, 133,
    182
Giddens, A. 8
Gledhill, C. J. 133
Goldberg, A. E. 63, 161
grammar: construction grammar 2,
    63; emergent grammar 9; linguistic
    levels 164*f*; multiplicity of 47–8; and
    priming 38–42, 159–62, 163, 181;
    traditional view 1–2; *see also* colligation
grammars 182–3, 186
grammatical categories 13, 84, 154–6
grammatical functions 154
grammatical notes 186
grammatical priming 155
Guardian x, 14, 24, 26, 44, 50, 132,
    139, 149, 155, 169–70

Had X been 142–3, 147
Halliday, M. A. K. 4, 9, 38, 40, 42–3,
    45, 49, 84, 84*t*, 96, 116, 130
Hanks, P. 30
happen 22, 23
harmonising primings 11, 180–3
Hasan, R. 4, 116
he 140–1
Higgins, J. 186
his 140–1
Hoey, M. 3, 5, 43, 55, 86, 115, 120,
    134, 135, 163, 164*f*
Hopper, P. 9
Hudson, R. 2
Hunston, S. 2, 63, 123–4, 154, 161
hyponym-superordinate relation 64
hyponymy *see* co-hyponymy
hypotheses 12–14

I know 150
I-language 8
idioms 51
illustrate 143–4
immunity: colligations 107–8, 107*t*;
    collocations 105, 106*t*, 108; definition
    105; semantic associations 105, 106,
    106*t*, 107, 108

inflectional languages 159
intelligibility 181
interaction 163, 164*f*
intonation 188
intuition 29–31, 133
it 141

James, Z. L. 38
JOB/WORK ROLE 141, 145
Johns, T. 186
Jones, S. 4, 116
Jones, Sir William 3

knock-on 68–9, 69*f*
Krashen, S. D. 187
Krishnamurty, R. 8, 79

Labov, W. 181
Langendoen, D. T. 42
language acquisition 160–1, 178, 180,
    188
language change 9, 188
Leech, G. 4, 5
lemmas 5, 35
lexical co-occurrence 3
lexical items 156–8
lexical priming 8, 163–4, 165*f*
lexical repetition *see* repetition
lexis 1–2, 9, 115, 164*f*
literary creativity 153, 172–7; Dickens
    172, 173–5; Tennyson 172, 176;
    Thomas 172, 176–7
literary traditions 182
Longacre, R. E. 133
Louw, B. 4, 22, 23–4, 25

McCarthy, M. 150, 164
McCarthy, M. J. 123
*Macmillan English Dictionary for Advanced
    Learners* 105
Macmillan Essential Dictionary 69
Marín-Arrese, J. I. 29
mass media 182
matching relations 20, 21
Material processes 40–1, 40*t*, 44
me and you 179–80
men and women 19–20, 23, 130
mental concordance 11–12, 14–15
metaphor 67, 67*t*

Morley, J. 29
morphological priming 74
morphology 163, 165*f*

names 18; *see also* PERSONAL NAME; PLACE
    NAME; SURNAME
native *vs.* non-native speakers 181,
    184–6
naturalness 2–5, 6, 152, 153
nesting 8, 10–11, 17, 19, 29, 154–5,
    159; colligational nesting 58–61;
    definition 58*f*
node word 4–5
nouns 44, 49, 167–8

Object (definition) 45
of 156
O'Halloran, K. 23
orthographic strings 171
Oxford English Dictionary 3

paragraphing: earlier theory 133–4;
    experiment 1: 134–45, 136*t*, 137*f*,
    137*t*, 144*t*; experiment 2: 145–8,
    147*t*; length 142–3, 148; lexical
    factors 138–45, 144*t*; matrix analysis
    135–6, 136*t*; organisational factors
    136, 137*f*, 144–5, 144*t*; students'
    analyses 136–8, 137*t*, 139–40,
    144–5, 144*t*, 147*t*
Partington, A. 3, 4, 29
PERSONAL NAME 122
phonic substance 163, 164*f*, 165*f*
phonological priming 180
phonological strings 158–9, 171
phonology 22, 163–4, 164*f*
Pinna, A. 29
PLACE NAME 18, 115, 118, 124–5,
    126–8, 148, 166, 167*f*
plagiarism 12
planet 121–2
poetry 172, 176–7
polysemy: and definition 81; priming
    hypothesis 13; and textual priming
    121; *vs.* vagueness 108–10
PONDER 41–2, 44
pondered 41–2
pragmatic association: and collocation
    27–9; *consequence* 85–6; definitions 13,

26; and nesting 29; *reason* 28; role of
    intuition 29–31; *sixty* 27–8
preference 45, 46*t*, 48–9, 49*t*, 55–7, 56*t*,
    57*t*
priming: conflict 170–2, 178–80;
    corpus as evidence of 14–15; cracks
    11, 160, 178–80, 184, 186; discourse
    and text 162–4, 164*f*; as explanation
    of collocation 7–12; and grammar
    38–42, 159–62, 163, 181;
    harmonising 11, 180–3; hypotheses
    12–14; nesting 8, 10–11, 17, 19;
    productive primings 11, 12; properties
    9–12; receptive primings 11–12;
    reflexive primings 160–1; transitory/
    permanent primings 12
priming drift 9, 65, 155
priming prosody 165–8, 167*f*
productive primings 11, 12
PRONOUN 140–1, 142, 145–8
prosodic phonology 22

question 45, 46*t*, 48–9, 49*t*, 55–7, 56*t*,
    57*t*
Quirk, R. *et al.* 45

reading 10, 21
reason: ambiguity 110–11; (= cause)
    88–92, 89*f*, 91*f*, 91*t*, 92*t*, 96*t*, 100*t*;
    (= cause) *vs.* (= rationality, logic)
    82–3, 88, 92–104, 130, 176;
    colligation 43, 59–61, 61*t*; with
    for and *as* 92, 103–4; possessive
    deictics and Theme 90, 99–101, 100*t*,
    101*t*, 110; pragmatic association 28;
    (= rationality, logic) 88–9, 89*f*, 90,
    91, 93*t*, 95*t*, 96*t*, 97*t*, 100*t*, 109–10;
    reason, no, any 91, 95–9, 96*t*; *reason,
    the* 89, 92–3*t*, 92–5; and Subject with
    BE 90, 101–3; *there*/PRONOUN + BE +
    reason 90, 103; vagueness 109–10
reasons 101, 101*t*
recent 10, 133
receptive primings 11–12
reduplication 164
reflexive priming 160–1
Relational processes: Bill Bryson sentence
    41–2; definition 40; priming for 42;
    winter 40–1, 40*t*, 44

religious traditions 182
Renouf, A. 5, 35
repetition 21, 117, 121, 122, 164
result 69–73, 71–2*t*, 73*t*
Rheme (definition) 52–3; *see also* Theme-Rheme analysis
round the world: colligation 77–9; collocates 74–6, 75*t*; (in)definiteness 78, 78*t*; semantic associations 76–7
ruin 174

scientific texts 5, 133
Scott, M. 116; *see also* WordSmith
second language acquisition: data 184, 186–7; L1 interference 183–4; language activity 187; primers 184; production *vs.* reception 187; shortcuts to priming 185–6; social context 184; speaking *vs.* writing 187; word lists 184; *see also* native *vs.* non-native speakers
self-reflexivity 11, 179, 180, 181
semantic association: *around/round the world* 76–7; Bill Bryson sentence 16, 18, 23, 31–2; co-hyponymy 64, 67–8; and collocation 16–20, 33; *consequence* 24–6, 36–7, 68–71, 69*f*; constant/variable patterns 20–1, 20–1*t*; and creativity 16, 17; definition 13, 24; formulation 63–4, 67, 68; grammatical flexibility 31–7; *immunity* 105, 106, 106*t*, 107, 108; role of intuition 29–31; and semantic preference 24; and semantic prosody 22–3; synonymous expressions 76–7; synonymy 68–71; *train* 64, 68; *see also* repetition; textual semantic association
semantic preference 24
semantic priming 8
semantic prosody 22–3, 163
semantic sets 63–4, 68, 79
semantics 1
Sinclair, J. M. 2, 3, 4, 5, 7, 22, 24, 30, 35, 43, 45, 51, 81, 116, 122, 152, 154, 156, 157–8, 163, 166
sixty 27–8, 123, 131–3
SKILLED ROLE OR OCCUPATION 64–8, 66*t*
Smith, F. 10
speech turns 150

Stubbs, M. 4, 5, 8–9, 22–3, 24, 35, 157
Subject (definition) 45
SURNAME 139–40, 142, 145–8
Sutherland, S. M. 126
syllables 159
synonymous expressions sharing a word 74–80; colligation 77–9; collocates 74–6, 75*t*; (in)definiteness 78, 78*t*; semantic associations 76–7
synonymy 79; colligation 71–3; priming hypothesis 13; semantic association 68–71
syntax 163–4, 164*f*

tagmemics 2
tea 108–9
Tennyson, Alfred, Lord 172, 176
tense choice 38–40, 39*t*, 42
text 163–4, 164*f*, 165*f*
textual colligation 150; Bill Bryson sentence 148–50; claim 115, 129–33; *consequence* 52, 130–1; definition 13; *men and women* 130; *sixty* 131–3; Theme-Rheme analysis 130; *see also* paragraphing
textual collocation: Bill Bryson sentence 124–8; claim 115, 116–22; definition 13; negative priming for cohesion 119–20; positive priming for cohesion 118–19; priming for cohesive links/ short chains 120–1; priming for type of cohesion 121–2
textual priming: academic texts 133; Bill Bryson sentence 114–15, 124–8; claims 114–16; *as a consequence* 55; *consequences* 130–1; and polysemy 121; *see also* textual colligation; textual collocation; textual semantic association
textual relations 20–1
textual semantic association 13, 115, 122–4, 126–8
the 150
The + ADJECTIVE + *SIDE* 123, 148
Theme (definition) 49
Theme-Rheme analysis 130
thesauri 1
Things 149–50

Thomas, Dylan 172, 176–7
Tognini-Bonelli, E. 5
train 64, 68
travel writing *see* Bill Bryson sentence;
    Dickens, Charles
Tucker, G. H. 79

Upton, T. 133
use (n.) 45, 46*t*, 48–9, 49*t*, 55–7, 56*t*,
    57*t*

vagueness 108–10

Wang, S. 164
in war 142, 145–6, 148
Webster's New International Dictionary 3
Whitsitt, S. 23
Williams, G. C. 5
Williams, T. H. 134–5
Willis, J. 186

winter: grammatical category 155;
    Material processes 40–1, 40*t*, 44;
    priming prosody 166; Relational
    processes 40–1, 40*t*, 44; tense
    choices 38–40, 39*t*; textual
    collocation 125; *that winter* 32–3,
    33*t*, 38–40, 39*t*, 40*t*; *during the
    winter* 32–3, 33*t*, 38–41, 39*t*, 40–1*t*;
    in winter 6, 32–3, 33*t*, 38–41, 39*t*,
    40–1*t*, 44, 115; *in the winter* 32–3,
    33*t*, 38–41, 39*t*, 40–1*t*
Winter, E. 20
Woodham-Smith, Cecil 176
word: meanings 81; *vs.* lexical item
    156–8; *vs.* phonological string 158–9;
    see also polysemy
word formation 159
WordSmith x, 33–4, 34*t*, 35*t*, 65, 75

Young, R. 134

KU-281-515

Author's Note

This book is based on more than ten years of research. I first played *Grand Theft Auto* in 1997 and began reporting on its creators, Rockstar Games, two years later. As the franchise boomed, I chronicled game culture and industry for publications that included *Rolling Stone*, *Wired*, the *New York Times*, *GamePro*, and *Electronic Gaming Monthly*, as well as in my first book, *Masters of Doom*.

My reporting took me across the country and around the world—from the offices of Rockstar in New York to the streets of Dundee, Scotland, where *GTA* began. There were long days and endless nights at game conventions and start-ups. I spent hundreds (thousands?) of hours playing games. I played *Pong* with Nolan Bushnell, the founder of Atari, and, for one particularly awesome afternoon in Lake Geneva, Wisconsin, rolled the dice with Gary Gygax, the cocreator of *Dungeons & Dragons*.

As the industry grew, I saw the controversies rise over violent video games—especially over *GTA*—and covered both sides of the disputes. I sat with a crying mother in a tiny town in Tennessee, where her sons had just murdered one person and maimed another—and triggered a $259 million lawsuit against Rockstar and others for allegedly inspiring the crime with *GTA*. I went to Coral Gables, Florida, to visit *GTA*'s chief opponent, Jack Thompson, at his home.

I spoke with leaders from the Entertainment Software Association in Washington, D.C., and went behind closed doors at the clandestine Entertainment Software Ratings Board in New York to see how games are rated. In Iowa City, I sat in a small stuffy room hooked up to electrodes while I played *Grand Theft Auto*—and university researchers studied my brain. Yeah, it was strange.

Though all of these adventures don't appear explicitly in this book, they inform it. This is a work of narrative nonfiction, a recreation of the story of *GTA*. The scenes and the dialogue are drawn from hundreds of my own interviews and firsthand observations, as well as thousands of articles, court documents, and TV and radio reports. The *Rolling Stone* reporter who appears in the book is me.

Over the years since I first visited Rockstar Games, I've interviewed many people at the company including each of the cofounders. Though the current helm at Rockstar declined to participate in this book, I was able to draw freely from my previous interviews with them and speak extensively with those who have left. A few sources didn't want to be identified, due to personal or professional concerns. Others were reluctant to talk, then eager, or eager, then reluctant. In the end, the vast majority went on the record. A funny thing happens when you write a book like this. People start to realize and appreciate that they are part of a larger story, not only their own, but everyone's.

Jacked

The unauthorized
behind-the-scenes story
of **Grand Theft Auto**

DAVID KUSHNER

Collins

Published in 2012 by Collins
An imprint of HarperCollins Publishers
77-85 Fulham Palace Road
London W6 8JB

www.harpercollins.co.uk

First published in the USA by John Wiley & Sons, Inc., Hoboken, New Jersey, 2012

10 9 8 7 6 5 4 3 2 1

Text © David Kushner 2012

The author asserts his moral right to be identified as the author of this work.

A catalogue record for this book is available from the British Library.

ISBN: 978-0-00-743485-5

Printed and bound in Great Britain by Clays.

All rights reserved. No parts of this publication may be reproduced, stored in a retrieval system or transmitted, in any form or by any means, electronic, mechanical, photocopying, recording or otherwise, without the prior permission of the publishers.

MIX
Paper from
responsible sources

FSC **FSC™ C007454**
www.fsc.org

FSC™ is a non-profit international organisation established to promote
the responsible management of the world's forests. Products carrying the
FSC label are independently certified to assure consumers that they come
from forests that are managed to meet the social, economic and
ecological needs of present and future generations,
and other controlled sources.

Find out more about HarperCollins and the environment at
www.harpercollins.co.uk/green

Contents

AUTHOR'S NOTE   v

PROLOGUE: Players vs. Haters   1

1   The Outlaws   5

2   The Warriors   11

3   Race 'n' Chase   20

4   Gouranga!   27

5   Eating the Hamster   36

6   Liberty City   46

7   Gang Warfare   55

8   Steal This Game   65

9   Rockstar Loft   74

10   The Worst Place in America   80

11   State of Emergency   89

12   Crime Pays   101

13   Vice City   111

14   Rampages   124

15	Cashmere Games	134
16	Grand Death Auto	142
17	Boyz in the Hood	159
18	Sex in San Andreas	170
19	Unlock the Darkness	186
20	Hot Coffee	201
21	Adults Only	216
22	Busted!	222
23	Bullies	230
24	Flowers for Jack	247
25	New York City	259

EPILOGUE: Outlaws to the End — 271

ACKNOWLEDGMENTS — 279
NOTES — 280
INDEX — 292

Prologue

Players vs. Haters

MAIN OBJECTIVE	■ Go to Capitol City.
PREREQUISITE	■ Complete "Rockstar" mission.
FAIL CONDITION	■ Feds give you Wanted Level, then you are Busted!

How far would you go for something you believe in?

One winter day, Sam Houser was going farther than he'd ever imagined or feared—all the way to Capitol Hill to answer to the Feds. The thirty-four-year-old had achieved the universal dream: rising from nowhere to make his fantasies real. Yet now reality was threatening to take it all away.

A scrappy Brit running an empire in New York City, Sam cultivated the image of the player he had become. Scruffy hair. Shaggy beard. Eyes hidden behind aviator shades. Gripping the wheel of his jet-black Porsche. Buildings towering. Taxis honking. Flipping stations on the radio. Pedal to the metal as the world blurred like a scene from the video game that made him so rich and so wanted: *Grand Theft Auto.*

GTA, the franchise published by Sam's company, Rockstar Games, was among the most successful and notorious video games of all time. *GTA IV* alone would smash the Guinness Record to be the most profitable entertainment release in history—leaving every blockbuster superhero movie and even the final Harry Potter book in its pixilated wake. Players bought more than 114 million copies and shelled out over $3 billion on the titles. The juggernaut helped make video games the fastest-growing segment of the entertainment business. By 2011, the $60 billion global game industry would dwarf music and film box office sales—combined.

GTA revolutionized an industry, defined one generation, and pissed off another, transforming a medium long thought of as kids' stuff into something culturally relevant, darkly funny, and wildly free. It cast players at "the center of their own criminal universe," as Sam once told me. You were a bad guy doing bad things in fictional cities meticulously riffed from real life: Miami, Vegas, New York, and Los Angeles.

For the mad frat of Brits who invented the game, *GTA* was a love letter from England to America in all of its fantastic excess: the sex and the violence, the money and the crime, the fashion and the drugs. As the game's phenomenally talented art director Aaron Garbut once told me, the goal was "to make the player feel like he's starring in his own fucked-up Scorsese-directed cartoon."

Ostensibly, players had to complete a series of missions for a motley crew of gangster bosses: whacking enemies, jacking cars, dealing drugs. Yet even better, players didn't have to play by the rules at all. *GTA* was a brilliantly open world to explore. There was no high score to hit or princess to save. Players could just steal an eighteen-wheeler at gunpoint, crank up the radio, and floor the gas, taking out pedestrians and lampposts and anything else dumb enough to get in the way of a good time. The fact that players could also hire hookers and kill cops made it controversial and tantalizing.

More personally, *GTA* made Sam Houser the rock star of his industry. Sam was passionate, driven, and creative, and *Time* ranked him among the world's most influential people, alongside President Obama, Oprah Winfrey, and Gordon Brown, for "creating tapestries of modern times as detailed as those of Balzac or Dickens." *Variety* called *GTA* "a hit-machine arguably unparalleled in any other part of the media business." The *Wall Street Journal* dubbed Sam "one of the leading lights of the video game era. A secretive, demanding workaholic [with] a temperament and a budget befitting a Hollywood mogul." One analyst compared his company to "the kids on the island in *Lord of the Flies*." But the hard work and long hours were all in service of Sam's ultimate mission: to take this maligned and misunderstood medium, video games, and make it as awesome as it could be. But no one had anticipated that making a game about outlaws could seem so outlaw for real. And that's what was bringing him to Washington, D.C., on this cold day.

After years of blaming *Grand Theft Auto* for inspiring murder and mayhem, politicians had what appeared to be a smoking gun: a hidden sex mini-game in the new *GTA*. The discovery of the scene, dubbed Hot Coffee, exploded into the industry's biggest scandal ever, the Watergate of video games. Rockstar blamed hackers. Hackers blamed Rockstar. Politicians and parents wanted *GTA* banned.

Now everyone, it seemed—from the consumers who filed a multimillion-dollar class-action suit over the game to the Federal Trade Commission investigating Rockstar for fraud—wanted the truth. Had Rockstar purposely hidden porn in *GTA* to cash in? If the company had, its game might be over. As Sam's rival, moral warrior attorney Jack Thompson, warned, "We are going to destroy Rockstar, you can count on that."

How did this all happen? The answer is the story of a new generation and the game that defined it. As media theorist Marshall McLuhan once said, "The games of a people reveal a great deal about them." It's hard to understand those who came of age at the turn of the millennium without understanding *GTA*. *Grand Theft Auto* marked the awkward adolescence of a powerful medium as it struggled to grow up and find its voice. It was an artifact of the George W. Bush era and the fight for civil liberties.

The fact that it hit during one of the most volatile chapters in the history of media was no accident. It symbolized the freedoms and fears of the strange new universe dawning on the other side of the screens. *GTA* seemed to split the world into players and haters. Either you played, or you didn't. For the players, jacking a car in the game was like saying, This is our ride now. This is our time behind the wheel. For the haters, it was something foreboding.

As Sam sat before the FTC investigators, the moment brought to mind an e-mail he had sent to a colleague when faced with compromising *GTA*. "The concept of a glorified shop (walmart) telling us what we can/can't put in our game is just unacceptable on so many levels," he wrote, "all of this material is perfectly reasonable for an adult (of course it is!), so we need to push to continue to have our medium accepted and respected as a mainstream entertainment platform. We have always been about pushing the boundaries; we cannot stop here."

1
The Outlaws

```
                    CONTROLS
        Forward    [↑]    up arrow
        Backward   [↓]    down arrow
            Left   [←]    left arrow
           Right   [→]    right arrow
  Enter/Exit vehicle [ENTER]  enter
          Attack   [CTRL]  ctrl
```

G rim city. Aerial view. A man in black runs along a river as a red sports car chases after him. Suddenly, a white convertible peels up in his path. "Over here, Jack!" shouts a beautiful young British woman behind the wheel. Jack leaps into her car, and she floors it. She has long auburn hair and stylish silver-framed shades. "You didn't know you had a fairy godmother, did you?" she asks, coyly.

"So where are we going, Princess?" Jack asks.

"To the demon king's castle, of course." She shifts into high gear, speeding through a parking garage to safety.

In 1971, there was no cooler getaway driver than Geraldine Moffat, the actress in this scene from *Get Carter*, a British crime film released that year. Critics dismissed it, saying, "One would rather wash one's mouth out with soap than recommend it." Yet as is often the case with anything new and controversial, the fans won out in the end.

The scene of Moffat lounging nude in bed with Michael Caine—a Rolling Stones album propped on the nightstand beside them—epitomized how hip movies could be. *Get Carter* became a cult classic, and Moffat, one of London's most fashionable stars. She married Walter Houser, a musician who ran the hottest jazz club in England, Ronnie Scott's.

Shortly after *Get Carter*'s release, Moffat and Houser welcomed their first child, Sam. The boy's brown eyes sparkled with possibility. Every kid determines to be cooler than his parents, but when your mom's in gangster flicks and your dad's hanging with Roy Ayers, that's no easy game. Sam found inspiration in movies like his mom's. He became fascinated by gangs, the grittier the better. He'd trudge down to the local library, checking out videotapes of crime films: *The Getaway, The French Connection, The Wild Bunch, The Warriors.*

One day at Ronnie Scott's, the great jazz musician Dizzy Gillespie asked young Sam what he wanted to be when he grew up. The boy resembled his mother—the heart-shaped face, the wide flat bushy black eyebrows. "A bank robber," Sam replied.

WAVES CRASHED the sands of Brighton, the beach town south of London, but Sam wasn't interested in the shore. His parents had taken him and his stocky brother Dan, two years younger, here to play outside, breathe the fresh air, and listen to the gulls. Instead, Moffat found Sam banging at a tall, psychedelically illustrated cabinet. Sam had discovered video games.

At this time in the early 1980s, games were in their family-friendly golden age. Innovations in technology and design brought a hypnotic new breed of machines into arcades and corner shops, from *Space*

Invaders to *Asteroids*. The graphics were simple and blocky, the themes (zap the aliens, gobble the dots), hokey. One of Sam's favorites was *Mr. Do!* a surreal game in which he played a circus clown, burrowing underground for magic cherries as he was being chased by monsters. The news shop near his house had a *Mr. Do!* and Sam would eagerly fetch cigarettes there for his mom just so he could play.

Sam's parents bought him every new game machine for home, from the Atari to the Omega and the Spectrum ZX, a popular computer coming out of Dundee, Scotland. Dan, more interested in literary things, didn't take to games, but Sam always shoved a controller into his hands anyway. "I don't know the buttons!" Dan would protest.

"It doesn't matter!" Sam replied, "You have to play!"

When Dan didn't comply, he suffered big brother's wrath. Sam later joked of having once fed Dan poison berries, sending him to the hospital. The terror subsided when Dan outgrew him. Dan proved his power by leaping onto Sam below from a balcony of their house, which resulted in a fistfight—and Sam's broken hand. One of Sam's favorite games didn't require an opponent at all. It was a single-player game called *Elite*, and it was his world alone to explore. *Elite* cast the player as the commander of a spaceship. The goal was to trick out your ship however you could—mining asteroids or looting. Sam reveled in the pixilated rebellion, being what he called a "space mugger." Video games, perhaps because they were still so new, had long been seen as a second-class medium, and gamers, as a result, felt a bit like outlaws, too. Now Elite was letting them live out their bad boy dreams, if only on screen.

The game wasn't the prettiest or most realistic, but it offered something tantalizing: freedom. At the time, most titles kept players in a box—sort of like moving through a scripted shooting gallery—but *Elite* felt radically open. Players could chose from an array of galaxies, each with its own planets, to explore. It had become a phenomenon around England, selling hundreds of thousands of copies and earning its collegiate creators a following. *Elite* was so immersive, so transporting, it epitomized the essence of what a game, for Sam, could do: transport you to another world.

ONE BY ONE, the boys inched uniformly down the line—taking their plates of, say, shepherd's pie, or steamed jam sponge and custard. They looked as neat and orderly as their trays. The dark blazers with the badges. The crisp white button-down shirts and dark ties. The charcoal pants and dark socks. The black leather dress shoes. All of the boys identical, almost, except the one seen around school with the Doc Martens boots poking out from under his slacks: Sam.

If Sam wanted to escape the real world, he would have to start here at St. Paul's, the storied prep school on the River Thames. Since the 1500s, St. Paul's had weaned some of the brightest young minds in the country, from Milton to Samuel Johnson. Now Sam and Dan, like many of the privileged young sons of London, had come to learn the finer things across forty-five leafy acres in Hammersmith: playing cricket on the lawns, studying Russian history, listening to the orchestra perform.

Yet as Sam's unconventional choice of footwear proved, he had little interest in playing by the rules. Brash and iconoclastic, he was already living the rock-star lifestyle. He wore his hair long, let his shoes scuff, and was occasionally seen leaving school in a Rolls-Royce. By their teens, he and his brother dispensed of their dad's music for something more vital: hip-hop.

Specifically, they dug Def Jam Recordings, an American music label already become legendary among hip kids in the know. Founded by a punk rocker named Rick Rubin in his New York University dorm room, the company had become the coolest and shrewdest start-up for the burgeoning East Coast rap scene. Rubin, along with his partner, club promoter Russell Simmons, began putting out singles from the freshest acts in the five boroughs. As a white Jewish kid from Long Island and a black guy from Queens, they were a unique and potent mix. They fused their love of rap and rock into acts with a decidedly mainstream flair, from a cocky kid named LL Cool J to a trio of bratty white rappers, the Beastie Boys.

They had more than great taste, though. Def Jam pioneered a new generation of guerrilla marketing. Simmons and Rubin had come from the urban underworld of street promotions—do-it-yourself campaigns used in both punk rock and rap to create word-of-mouth buzz. Simmons called it "running the track," promoting each artist in as many ways as possible. They slapped stickers—bearing the iconic Def Jam logo, with its big letters D and J—on lampposts and buildings. They threw parties around New York, producing elaborate concerts with over-the-top props—such as the huge inflatable penises at the Beasties show.

Devout fans like Sam consumed not only Def Jam records, but the lifestyle. When Rubin's single "Reign in Blood," for the heavy metal band Slayer, came out, Sam hungrily bought it—slipping out the Def Jam patch that he wore like a badge of honor. Sam had taken on a way of ranting about his fixations. His mouth would motor, words firing like *Missile Command* bullets, hands gesturing, head swaying, as though he couldn't contain the sheer awesomeness of his pop culture love.

"For me, a guy like Rick Rubin is such a fucking hero," started one of his breathless rants, "to go from pioneering in that world to doing hip-hop and to doing the Cult. When he did that album *Electric*! When you can hear Rick Rubin and his sharp hip-hop street production coming out of these rockers from Newcastle! For me, seeing someone like him suddenly being in rock and the hardest form of rock—Slayer!—I was, like, 'These guys don't get any better, it doesn't get cooler than that.' And he kept on delivering . . . People like that inspire me so massively."

Even better, Def Jam hailed from New York. Sam deeply admired the city, the fashion and culture and music. By day, he wore the stiff uniform of St. Paul's, by night he fashioned the uniform of NYC. He sat in his room, piled with vinyl records and videotapes, weaving chunky shoelaces as the rappers in New York did. It wasn't just a superficial love of fashion, it was about underdogs on the fringes who revolutionized a culture.

For Sam's eighteenth birthday, his dad took him to New York. On arrival, Sam bought a leather jacket and Air Jordan Mach 4 sneakers, as he'd seen on MTV. He roamed the open world downtown, soaking in the sights and the sounds. The yellow taxis. The rising buildings. The surly pedestrians. The hookers in Times Square. "From that point I was chronically in love with the place," he later recalled.

For lunch one afternoon, Sam's dad took him out with his friend Heinz Henn, a marketing executive for BMG, the music label for the German company Bertelsmann. BMG, Henn explained, was struggling to cash in on youth culture. As Sam sat there listening, he couldn't contain himself for long. "Why is everyone in the record business so old?" he asked. "Why don't you have young people working in this business?"

Henn eyeballed this rich white kid dressed like Run DMC, then spoke to Sam's dad. Who was this hot-tempered but very self-assured boy? "Your son is an utter lunatic," Heinz told him, "but he has some good ideas."

Sam had just scored himself a job.

2
The Warriors

**RANDOM CHARACTER UNLOCKED:
JACK THOMPSON**

Follow the *"J"* icon to Beverly Hills. Find Jack
Thompson. Forty-one-year-old from Miami.
Attorney. Golfer. Expectant dad.

'm 'bout to bust some shots off. I'm 'bout to dust some cops off."

It was July 16, 1992, as the performer rapped onstage in Beverly
Hills, but this wasn't Ice-T, the artist who wrote these lyrics. It was
the square-jawed superstar actor Charlton Heston. Though best known
for his portrayal of Moses in the Ten Commandments, Heston brought
his booming voice to the Regent Beverly Wilshire Hotel for a higher
cause today: getting this song, "Cop Killer," banned.

The occasion was the annual shareholders meeting of Time Warner,
which owned the label that put out this record. Since the release of
the track in March, "Cop Killer" had become a national controversy,
decried by police groups and President Bush. Ice-T, who had written it
in the wake of the recent Rodney King riots, defended it as an honest

wake of the recent Rodney King riots, defended it as an honest portrayal of a character fed up with police brutality.

Yet the shareholders in the crowd today seemed to be believing everything Heston had to say. As he bellowed the refrain—"Die die die pig die!"—one man watched the performance in awe: Jack Thompson. Born-again and Republican, Thompson had the readiness of a schoolboy dressed for a yearbook photo. He wore his suits crisp, his prematurely graying hair neatly combed at the part, his blue eyes twinkling. He could feel the electricity of the moment. Heston had, as Thompson later put it, "lit the fuse on the culture war." And this young warrior was ready to fight.

Compared to the NRA supporter onstage, however, Thompson hardly seemed like the warring kind. Growing up a scrawny straight-A student from Cleveland with a debilitating stutter, Thompson was so myopic that he'd run across the Little League field chasing balls that didn't exist. His fellow players hated him. "It was fairly traumatic," he later recalled. One day he acted out. He went into his garage, poured gasoline on the floor, tossed gunpowder caps around, and started pounding them with a hammer until they exploded in flames.

Thompson survived the prank but enjoyed the heat. An eighteen-year-old Robert Kennedy acolyte and liberal, he got his tires slashed and life threatened after leading a student protest to desegregate housing. He listened to Crosby Stills and Nash, and hosted a radio show at Dennison University.

But Jack had a Ripper growing inside. When a Black Panther student replaced the school's American flag with a Black Power flag, Thompson confronted him. "What are you doing?" he asked. "We share the American flag!" The guy pulled a machete on him. Thompson recoiled, literally and philosophically. "It was a radical time, and you had to choose sides," he later recalled. "I became a conservative over the lunacies of political correctness."

With a William Buckley book tucked under his arm, Thompson entered law school at Vanderbilt University, alongside classmate Al Gore.

He preferred playing golf to attending class and, despite graduating Phi Beta Kappa, flunked the bar. After moving to Miami and feeling like a failure, he accompanied a friend to a church service where everyone was dressed in shorts and T-shirts. Thompson felt at home and became born-again. Before retaking the bar, he prayed and, when he passed, took it as a sign from God to go on a crusade.

In 1987, after hearing a local shock jock on the air, Thompson hit the law books. With painstaking research, he discovered a little known fact at the time: the Federal Communications Commission had the power to regulate the airwaves for obscenity, and this station, in many ways, seemed to violate the standards. After Thompson took the unusual measure of filing a complaint with the FCC, the shock jock angrily broadcast his name and phone number. Death threats, unwanted pizza deliveries, and the local press followed, transforming Thompson into an overnight rock star of Miami's right.

Confident, unflappable, and speedy with a sound bite, Thompson deftly played his part, faxing complaints to corporate sponsors until ads began to get pulled from the air. Despite the radio station's legal proceedings against him, Thompson won the right in court to continue lobbying advertisers and the FCC under First Amendment protection. His hard work paid off in historic proportions when the FCC fined the shock jock's station for indecency—the first time ever for such levies. Thompson took it as more divine purpose. "God's people were going to be warriors with me through prayer," he later wrote in his memoir.

Yet he already had others warring against him. Acting on the radio station's assertion that Thompson was obsessed with pornography, the Florida bar convinced the state's Supreme Court to determine whether Thompson was mentally ill. Faced with losing his license to practice law, Thompson underwent psychiatric testing. The test results concluded that he was "simply a lawyer and a citizen who is rationally animated by his activist Christian faith." As Thompson later liked to joke, "I'm the only officially certified sane lawyer in the entire state of Florida."

Empowered, Thompson assumed higher-profile battles. He took on incumbent Dade County state attorney Janet Reno for prosecutor, publicly challenging her to declare her sexuality. He made his name nationally by spearheading an obscenity conviction of rap group 2 Live Crew for their album *As Nasty as They Wanna Be*. With the controversy fueling demand for the record, however, the group's leader, Luther Campbell, laughed all the way to the bank.

Thompson was on his way, though—right to Charlton Heston's side at the shareholders meeting over "Cop Killer." With the impossible task of following Heston onstage, Thompson warned, amid the boos of protesters, that "Time Warner is knowingly training people, especially young people, to kill. One day this company will pay a wicked price for that."

Thompson returned to Miami for the birth of his first son, whom he and his wife named John Daniel Peace. Three weeks later, on August 24, 1992, Hurricane Andrew bore down. As his windows rattled and lightning slashed the sky, Thompson braced himself at the door in a scuba mask, holding it tight so that the glass wouldn't blow through. His wife stood behind him holding little Johnny in a blanket. Thompson relished the biblical imagery and equated it to his own fight against what he called the "human hurricane" of rappers, pornographers, and shock jocks.

He survived the storm—and won the battle against Ice-T, who was dropped from Time Warner soon afterward. The ACLU voted Thompson one of 1992's "Censors of the Year," a title that made him proud. "Those on the entertainment ship were laughing at those on the other vessel," he later wrote. "I felt that I had grabbed the wheel of the decency ship and rammed that other ship, convinced that the time for talk about how bad pop culture had become was over. It was time for consequence. . . . it was time to win this culture war."

"COME ON, come on, come on, come on, take that, and party!"

Sam Houser stared into the smiling white faces of five clean-cut boys singing these words onstage. The group was Take That, a chart-topping boy band from Manchester, Britain's answer to New Kids on the Block. In his new job as a video producer for BMG Entertainment, Sam was directing their full-length video, named for their debut hit, "Take That & Party." For a kid weaned on crime flicks and hip-hop, this scene couldn't be further from his more rebellious influences. The videos showed the boy band break-dancing, chest-bumping, and leaping from Jacuzzis. But it was a job—a creative job that fulfilled Sam's lifelong ambition of working in the music industry.

By 1992, Sam had successfully retaken his lackluster A-Level tests and enrolled at University of London. Between classes, he headed over to intern part time at BMG's office off the Thames on Fulham High Street. After his fateful lunch in New York, Sam had gotten his break interning in the mailroom at BMG—an accomplishment he took to heart, considering the obnoxious way he got in. Yet it epitomized his style: risking everything, including pissing people off, if it meant achieving his goals. "I got my first job by abusing senior executives at dinner tables," he later recalled.

Sam already had his eyes elsewhere: the Internet. Though the World Wide Web had not yet become mainstream, Sam saw the opportunity to bring the kind of DIY marketing approach pioneered by Def Jam into the digital age. He convinced the BMG bosses that the best way to promote a new album by Annie Lennox was with something almost unheard of at the time, an online site. They relented, and Sam got to work. When *Diva* hit number one on the UK charts, it bolstered his cause.

BMG soon made waves in the industry by partnering with a small CD-ROM start-up in Los Angeles to create what the *Los Angeles Times* heralded as "the recording industry's first interactive music label." The newly formed BMG Interactive division saw the future not only in music CD-ROMs, but in a medium close to Sam's heart, video games.

In 1994, the game industry was bringing in a record $7 billion—and on track to grow to $9 billion by 1996. Yet culturally, games were at a crossroads. Radical changes had been sweeping the industry, igniting a debate about the future of the medium and its effect on players. It started with the release of *Mortal Kombat*, the home version of the ubiquitous street fighting arcade game. With its blood and spine-ripping moves, *Mortal Kombat* brought interactive violence of a kind never seen before in living rooms.

Compared to innocuous hits such as the urban-planning game *SimCity 2000* or Nintendo's *Super Mario Brothers All-Stars*, *Mortal Kombat* shocked parents and politicians, who believed video games were for kids. The fact that the blood-soaked version of the game for the Sega Genesis was outselling the bloodless version of the game on the family-friendly Nintendo Entertainment System three-to-one only made them more nervous.

The *Mortal Kombat* panic reached a sensational peak on December 9, 1993, when Democrat senator Joseph Lieberman held the first federal hearings in the United States on the threat of violent video games to children. While culture warriors had fought similar battles over comic books and rock music in the 1950s and over *Dungeons & Dragons* and heavy metal in the 1980s, the battle over violent games had an urgently contemporary ring. It wasn't only the content that they were concerned about, it was the increasingly immersive technology that delivered it.

"Because they are active, rather than passive, [video games] can do more than desensitize impressionable children to violence," warned the president of the National Education Association. When a spokesperson for Sega testified that violent games simply reflected an aging demographic, Howard Lincoln—the executive vice president of Nintendo of America—bristled. "I can't sit here and allow you to be told that somehow the video game business has been transformed today from children to adults," he said.

Yet video games had never been only for kids in the first place. They rose up to prominence in the campus computer labs of the 1960s and the 1970s, where shaggy geeks coded their own games on huge mainframe PCs. From there, the *Pac-Man* fever of home consoles and arcade machines lured millions into the fold. By the early 1990s, legions of hackers were tinkering with their own PCs at home. A burgeoning underground of darkly comic and violent games such as *Wolfenstein 3-D* and *Doom* had become a phenomenon among a new generation of college students.

At the same time, Sam's peers were riding a gritty new wave of art. Films such as *Reservoir Dogs* and music like Def Jam's shunned cheesy fantasy for gutsy, pop-savvy realism. These products were bringing a lens to a world that had not previously been portrayed. When Los Angeles erupted in riots after the Rodney King beating, Sam watched—and listened—in awe to the music that reflected the changing times. The fact that Time Warner had dropped "Cop Killer" only seemed to underscore how clueless the previous generation had become.

Now the same battle lines were being drawn over games. To ward off the threat of legislation as a result of the Lieberman hearings, the U.S. video game industry created the Interactive Digital Software Association, a trade group representing their interests. The industry also launched the Entertainment Software Ratings Board to voluntarily assign ratings to their games, most of which fell under E for Everyone, T for Teen, or M for Mature. Less than 1 percent of the titles received an Adults Only or AO rating, the game industry's equivalent of an X—and, effectively, the kiss of death because major retailers refused to carry AO games.

Yet with *Mortal Kombat* still burning around the world, the media eagerly fanned the flames. Nintendo, which ruled the industry, had sold a Disneylike image of gaming to the public, but this was now in jeopardy. Video games were "dangerous, violent, insidious, and they can cause everything from stunted growth to piles," wrote a reporter for the

Scotsman, ". . . an incomprehensible fad designed to warp and destroy young minds."

While the medium was being infantilized by politicians and pundits, however, one of the biggest corporations in the entertainment business was taking up the fight. In 1994, in Japan, Sony was working to release its first-ever home video game console, the PlayStation, built on the idea that gamers were growing up. Phil Harrison, a young Sony executive tasked with recruiting European game developers, thought the game industry was being unfairly portrayed as "a toy industry personified by a lonely twelve-year-old boy in the basement." Sony's research told another story—gamers were older and had plenty of money of their own to spend.

The problem with reaching these players started with the hardware. Sony found that although children had no problem pretending their blobs of brown-and-peach pixels were Arnold Schwarzenegger, adults needed more realistic graphics to suspend disbelief and engage. The answer: CD-ROMs. Unlike the cartridges used by Nintendo, a CD-ROM could hold more content—including full-rendered video—and offer games that were more like what Harrison described as "sophisticated multimedia events." Combining a high-end graphics machine with an entertainment console was sending a clear message to the industry: it was time for the medium to become more mainstream and grow up.

Sam couldn't agree more. With the new BMG Interactive division pursuing game publishing, he desperately wanted in. Games were the future, he was sure, and he saw this as a medium through which a guy like him could finally leave his mark. The challenge was to change the meta-game, to bring the experience into a new era, just as the films and the music he loved had redefined their own industries.

Sam urged the BMG brass to give him a break. "I want a go at this," he told them. "I want to get involved. I'm not involved, but there's a lot of things I can bring to this situation." Once again, his doggedness paid off. After graduating from college, he got transferred to the Interactive Publishing division. The game industry worked similar to the record industry. Just as labels put out CDs created by bands, publishers put out software created by developers. They oversaw the production of the game, doling out editorial direction while handling the business, marketing, and packaging. Developers dealt with the front-line creation of the games, from the art to programming.

Hits paid for flops, and if one out of ten games scored, that was enough. BMG's early games (a backpacking title, a golf simulator), however, fell on the losing side. Yet Sam never gave up hope. Maybe he was crazy. Or maybe, somewhere out there, someone was making a game crazy enough for him.

3
Race 'n' Chase

FRIEND PROFILE:
DAVE "CAPO DI TUTTI CAPO" JONES

Joining Jones for the following activities goes toward 100 percent completion of the game.

ACTIVITIES ■ Fishing
■ Programming
■ Driving (fast)

Special Ability: Game Design
Call Jones and ask him to make you a computer game. You can pick up the game and sell it for cash.

I t would be a grand theft. Stealing the high score in another gang's territory. Dave Jones couldn't help himself, though. He could see the *Galaga* machine flashing inside the fish-and-chips shop like a beacon. The tall black cabinet with the red-eyed, bug-shaped alien warlord on the front. The spiraling electronic theme song. He wanted to touch it. Slip his coin in the vaginal slot, and pound the buttons. Zap the invaders, get the high score, and put his initials at the top.

Yet this was not the part of Dundee, the industrial town north of Edinburgh, Scotland, where he lived. This was Douglas, one of the rougher neighborhoods in a city known for being rough. Once famous for its jute, marmalade, and the invention of Dennis the Menace, Dundee's economy had tanked by this time in the early 1980s, taking its working-class residents down with it. Teenage gangs with names such as the Huns and the Shams prowled the street, looking for a fight like some Scottish version of *The Warriors*. Anything could set them off. The wrong look. The wrong football jersey. And especially a gawky, carrot-topped geek in glasses like Jones.

Still in grade school, Jones lived with his parents across town near his dad's small newspaper shop. When he wasn't fishing for salmon in the River Tay, he played *Space Invaders* at the greeting card store near his bus stop. Every day before and after school, he'd make sure to keep the top score.

As he passed through Douglas on an errand, he couldn't resist having a go at the *Galaga* machine. His coin dropped inside with a satisfyingly metallic plunk. Jones positioned his right pointer finger over the smooth red convex plastic button. He gripped the stick. Hit Start. The onslaught of alien insects on screen began. In a flurry of taps, Jones obliterated the invaders and took the top score—entering his initials for all to see. Who was the real player now?

But the local toughs lurking outside had seen enough. Just as Jones stepped out the door, the gang surrounded him. *Who comes here and sets the high score on our turf?* Jones ran down the gray cobblestone streets, past the old ladies with their bloated plastic shopping bags, past crusty men smoking unfiltered cigarettes under the overcast sky. The gang tackled him to the ground. As the blows came, he could do nothing but wait for the punches to end. Wait and hope that he would be alive long enough to limp back to the safety of his neighborhood and his own machines.

AS JONES AND HIS OWN GANG of Scottish geeks knew, something electric was coursing over the cobblestone streets of Dundee. A computer revolution had begun. It started at the big brown Timex plant in town, which was churning out the UK's first popular wave of home computers, the Sinclair ZX81 and the Sinclair ZX Spectrum.

The Spectrum, with its jet-black keyboard and rainbow streak on the side, looked like a control panel to another world. All you needed to know was the code, and you were in. Word had it that Spectrums were "accidentally" falling off delivery trucks—and winding up in the hands of aspiring hackers.

Jones's high school was among the first in the United Kingdom to offer computer studies, a course that he immediately took. Gifted at math, he taught himself to program and build his own rudimentary machines. On graduation, he scored a job at the Timex plant as an apprentice engineer, but what he really wanted to do was make games. A homebrew computer game scene was percolating from San Francisco to Sweden. Gamers made and distributed their own titles on Apple II and Commodore 64 machines. Jones joined a ragtag gang of computer coders called the Kingsway Amateur Computer Club, who met at the local technical college.

With cuts facing Timex, the company offered Jones £3,000 in voluntary redundancy pay—which he happily blew, in part, on a state-of-the-art Amiga 1000 computer (much to the envy of his pals). Though Jones had begun to study software engineering at the local university, his professors and family thought he was nuts. "This is never going to take off," they told him. "You're never going to sell enough games to make a living."

Yet Jones believed in his dreams. With his grades plummeting, he spent late nights in his bedroom at his parents' house, hatching his plan. While the homebrew scene was dominated by fantasy and sci-fi games, Jones wanted to bring the fast action of arcade hits such as *Galaga* to home machines. His first game, a kill-the-devil shooter called *Menace*, was released in 1988 and sold an impressive fifteen thousand copies, earning critical acclaim and £20,000—enough for this car fanatic to buy a 16-valve Vauxhall Astra.

To capitalize on the buzz, he left school and started his own game
company, DMA Design, a reference to a computer term, Direct Memory Access. Jones hired friends from the computer club and moved the
team into a two-room office on the second floor of a narrow red-and-
green building, just above a baby accessories shop called Gooseberry
Bush. Pasty-faced with polygonal hair, they looked like extras from a
Big Country video. By day, they'd code; by night, hit up the local pubs
or compete in games at their office. It was *Animal House* for nerds. They
trashed the office so much that Jones's wife insisted on coming over to
clean the toilet.

This wasn't just fun and games, though. DMA exemplified the DIY
spirit of the times: all you needed was a computer and a dream. Jones
was on a mission to make games as cool and fast as his sports car. "We
have three to five minutes to capture people," as he once said. "I don't
care how great your game is, you have three to five minutes." The edict
worked again. *Blood Money*, billed as "the ultimate arcade game," came
out in 1989 and sold more than thirty thousand copies in two months.
Jones felt elated. He was on his way.

In the competitive arena of game making, developers would compete to exploit the latest, greatest programming innovations. One day, a
DMA programmer discovered how to animate as many as a hundred
characters on screen at a time and made a demo for the team. Jones
watched in awe as a line of tiny creatures stupidly marched to their
deaths—smashed by a ten-ton weight or incinerated in the mouth of a
gun. It was just the sort of dark Scottish humor that got everyone laughing. *Let's make a game out of that!*

They called it *Lemmings*. The object was to save the creatures from
dying. Jones's crew devilishly dreamed up the most punishing fates for
the little beasts: falling into holes, getting crushed by boulders, being
incinerated in lakes of fire, or getting ripped to shreds by machines. To
survive, you had to assign each creature a skill, from digging to climbing,

building to bashing. With more than 120 scenes of zig-zagging creatures, the game didn't only play—it teemed with life.

Lemmings was released on Valentine's Day 1991 with a warning label:
"We Are Not Responsible For: Loss of sanity. Loss of Sleep. Loss of
Hair." Lemmings became an immediate hit, selling fifty thousand copies
on its first day alone. The game would go on to earn DMA more than
£1.5 million, selling nearly 2 million copies worldwide. "To say that
Lemmings took the computer gaming world by storm would be like saying that Henry Ford made a slight impact on the car market," one
reporter wrote.

Just twenty-five, Jones was one of the wealthiest—and most
famous—game designers on the planet. His journey from drop-out to
millionaire made him one of the industry's biggest success stories.
Ecstatic, he treated himself with his flashiest sports car yet, a Ferrari.
Jones hit the road, speeding through the grim city past the gangs. If only
there was a game in that.

"FUCK! Fuck! Fuck!"

It was just another day at DMA, and the biggest and most pungent
coder on the team was having one of his tantrums again. Game making
could be a mind-numbing craft—fashioning living worlds from abstract
code—and sometimes this guy had to blow off steam. But as he stood
banging his head against a wall and shouting, he saw a sprightly Japanese
man beside him. "Oh, my God," muttered another coder nearby, "that's
Miyamoto!"

Sure enough—it was him, Shigeru Miyamoto, the elfin genius of
Nintendo, the inventor of Mario. Not long before, it would have been
unthinkable that the biggest name in gaming would grace this little
indie start-up in Dundee. Yet with the extraordinary success of Lemmings,
Jones had scored a multimillion-pound contract to create two games for
the Nintendo 64. "We think David Jones is one of the very few people

in the world that are in the Spielberg category," Howard Lincoln, now the president of Nintendo of America, told the press. Miyamoto, who took the screaming coder in stride, had come to experience the magic of DMA firsthand.

Flush with cash, DMA had moved to a 2,500-square-foot office in a mirrored, militaristic building inside the Dundee Technology Park on the west end of town. Jones invested £250,000 in outfitting their rooms with the best technology they could buy. DMA was said to have one of England's biggest installations of refrigerator-size Silicon Graphics computers—so big that the minister of defense expressed security concerns. DMA needed the muscle power to bring Jones's geekiest dream to life: "a living, breathing city."

Virtual worlds were the stuff of science fiction but still not much of a reality in gaming. The appeal was obvious. Real life could be unpredictable and frustrating, but a synthetic world was something you could control. Jones had, as he put it, "a fascination with how alive and dynamic we could make the city from very little memory and very little processing speed. How could we make something living inside the machine?"

Jones set his team free to come up with their answers. Programmer Mike Dailly engineered a cityscape from a top-down point of view. Another DMAer coded dinosaurs running through the streets. Another replaced the dinosaurs with something cooler, more contemporary, and closer to the boss's heart: cars. As Dailly watched the little virtual cars speed through the city, he thought, "We have something."

Jones liked the concept of *Cops and Robbers*—casting players as the police out to bust the bad guys. "Cops and robbers is a natural rule set that everybody understands," he said. "They know how to drive a car. They know what a gun does." Thinking *Cops and Robbers* too generic a title, they renamed it *Race 'n' Chase* instead.

Walking into DMA was like seeing a bunch of grown men playing with a Hot Wheels set—except on their PCs. From the overhead view onscreen, tiny pixilated cars cruised the streets, blips of people climbed

onto buses and trains that stopped along their routes. Jones pushed for a
more and more realistic simulation. Though cars could speed down the
street, they had to stop at traffic lights that blinked from red to green.
Jones watched gleefully as his little world teemed with life.

When a demo was ready, he took the game to a prospective publisher in London, BMG Interactive. The company wooed Jones heartily,
eager to get into business with the UK's boy wonder of gaming. Jones
left with a deal to deliver four games over the next thirteen months for
Sony, Sega, and Nintendo. He retained ownership and received an estimated £3.4 million. "They will treat computer companies in the same
way that they treat their music companies," Jones effused to a reporter.

Back in the BMG office, Sam and the others booted up *Race 'n'
Chase*. There was just one problem: the game kind of sucked.

4

Gouranga!

WEAPONS

NERF CROSSBOW. The Crossbow takes three Basic Arrows or five Mega Darts, with a maximum firing distance of forty-one feet and one shot per 2.28 seconds. The range makes this killer ideal for long-range battles.

NERF BALLZOOKA. This blaster pumps out a whopping fifteen ballistic balls in just 6 seconds, with a maximum distance of thirty-four feet. Rate of fire is an impressive one shot per .37 seconds. It will have your enemies screaming, "It's raining balls!"

If you took a job at BMG Interactive, you needed to be properly armed. At any given moment, the Nerf guns would be drawn, unleashing a flurry of bright-yellow foam darts and balls across the room. The playful atmosphere went with Sam's new territory. He was making only £120 a week, but he was living his dream. As the English oddballs of the German music conglomerate, the gamers relished their outsider status, having taken over a backroom of the company's London headquarters.

They had reason to get their game on. By 1996, a new era in video gaming had dawned, thanks to the success of the Sony PlayStation. After releasing the new PlayStation console in Japan in December 1994, the company had sold five hundred thousand machines in the first three months. Sony called the £300 million debut "our biggest launch since the Walkman."

Sony hired the stylish Chiat\Day ad firm to handle the U.S. release. In England, they marketed the machine to an edgier, hipper demographic—"the cool kids of London," as Sony's Phil Harrison put it. The company created a promotional lounge at the Ministry of Sound nightclub, filling it with PlayStations and sleek displays. Fliers got passed out to clubgoers with the words "More Powerful Than God." Sony was on its way to sales of more than 8 million PlayStations worldwide for the fall of 1996.

So much for *Pac-Man* and *Donkey Kong*. Games were becoming edgier, and Sam had a kinetic new colleague who shared his passion, Jamie King. A slim, handsome twenty-six-year-old with a nervous excitability, King was a fledgling music video producer who'd been introduced to Sam through a mutual friend. King could keep up with Sam's encyclopedic passion for pop culture. They shared a love of John Cassavetes and the French black-and-white gang flick *Le Haine*, fashion and art, Tribe Called Quest, and JVC Force. King, brought on as an intern, quickly proved he could keep up with Sam's indefatigable work ethic, too.

What they needed to work on now more than anything was this new game: *Race 'n' Chase*. Though it had technical chops, it was missing something crucial: balls, preferably as big as the yellow ones flying around the room. On his screen, Sam looked down on the virtual city, the buildings rising in chunky colored blocks. Little cars puttered along gray streets with white hash-mark lines. Traffic lights blinked from yellow to red. Antlike people paced the sidewalks. Sam pressed one button on the keyboard, and the door of a car swung open. He pressed another, and it closed.

Senior producer Gary Penn—a former journalist with a streak of Johnny Rotten and a taste for bright green socks—felt dejected. "This is a fucking simulation," he said, bemoaning the game's "stupid details." Up in Dundee at DMA, the developers were starting to agree. By casting the player as the cop, they realized, they had cut out the fun. Some dismissed it as *Sims Driving Instructor.*

When an unruly gamer tried to drive his police car on the sidewalk or through traffic lights, a persnickety programmer reminded him that the stop lights needed to be obeyed. Were they building a video game or a train set? Even worse, the pedestrians milling around the game created frustrating obstacles. It was almost impossible to drive fast without taking people down, and, because the player was a cop, he had to be punished for hit-and-runs.

Race 'n' Chase hit a road block. There was just no way to have a fast and furious arcade-style game while playing by the rules. The DMAers stared at the screen, as the cars and the people raced around. Maybe there was another solution, they realized. Instead of having to avoid all of the pedestrians, what if you got points for running them over? What if you were the bad guy instead?

VIDEO GAME DEVELOPMENT is a highly collaborative work in progress, with constant feedback along the way. As the publishers of *Race 'n' Chase*, Sam and the others at BMG would frequently get new iterations—or builds—of the game to evaluate and comment on. The developers would then go off and implement necessary changes.

One day a new build of *Race 'n' Chase* arrived for Sam and the others to try out. At first, it seemed the same. With the top-down perspective, the gamer felt as if he were hovering over a city in a balloon, looking down on gray and brown rooftops. Puffy green trees poked of out of green parks. Horns honked. Engines roared. When you tapped your forward arrow on the keyboard, you saw your unnamed character, a tiny guy in a yellow long-sleeved shirt, stride across the street.

With a few more taps of the arrow keys, you maneuvered the character toward a stubby green car with a shiny hood, then tapped the Enter key. That's when it happened. The door flew open, and the driver—some other little dude in blue pants—came flying out of the car and landed on the pavement in a contorted pile. He got jacked. As you held down the forward arrow, the car careened forward, supple to the flick of the side arrows—left, right—with a satisfying *vroooom*. You headed toward a flickering traffic light. Why stop? This was a game, right? A game wasn't life. A game takes you over, or you take over it, pushing it in ways you can't for real.

So you drove through the light, squealing around a corner. As you took the turn too wide, you saw a little pedestrian in a white long-sleeved shirt and blue pants coming too close, but you couldn't stop. Actually, you didn't want to stop. So you just drove. Drove right into the ped—only to hear a satisfying *splat*, like a crushed grape with a wine-colored stain on the sidewalk, and the number "100" rising from the corpse. Score! This wasn't the old *Race 'n' Chase* anymore.

The moment that DMA let players run over pedestrians—and be rewarded with points, no less—changed everything. Instead of cops and robbers, the game became robbers and cops. The object was to run missions for bad guys, such as jacking cars, the more the better. The leap was radical. In the short history of games, players had almost always been the hero, not the antihero. You were the heartsick plumber of *Super Mario Bros.*, the intergalactic pilot of *Defender*, the glacial-paced explorer of *Myst*. One obscure arcade game from the 1970s, *Death Race 2000*, let players run over virtual ghosts, and it got banned. Nothing put you behind the wheel to wreak havoc like this. As Brian Baglow, a writer for DMA, said "You're a criminal, so if you do something bad, you get a reward!"

Sam loved it. He had always been drawn to rebels, and now he was pushing games to be more rebellious too "Once we made you able to kill policemen, we knew we had something that would turn heads," he later recalled. Yet this wasn't about manufacturing controversy. In fact, that didn't enter their minds. The game—with its ugly top-down view—was clearly so cartoonlike and absurd, someone would have to be crazy to take it for the real thing. The focus instead was on milking the tech to make it as insanely fun as possible.

Ordinarily, game making was a machinelike system carried out by artists, programmers, and producers. A designer would come up with the overall idea, then producers would dispatch programmers to code the engine—the core code that drove the game's graphics, sounds, physics, and artificial intelligence. Artists would create models of objects in the world and fill in the details of the scene with objects and textures.

But at DMA, the system had become a free-for-all. The developers scurried back to their desks in Scotland, to come up with crazy shit. DMA's nearly one hundred employees had taken over two nearby buildings, including one that housed a £500,000 motion-capture studio that no one had quite figured out what to do with. The *Race 'n' Chase* team worked separately in their own back section and quickly became the rebels of the group.

Up front, where coders worked on *Lemmings* sequels and other titles, bookish geeks toiled quietly at their desks. Yet the thump of rock music could be heard blasting from behind the wall in the *Race 'n' Chase* room. Back there, a dozen or so members of the team had transformed their corner into their own bad playground. A team of seven musicians had set up real instruments to record a soundtrack for the title (far removed from the electronic soundtracks popular at the time).

DMA's screaming gamer, in particular, was not real concerned about his hygiene. One day, someone stuck air fresheners under his desk. The next, little pine-tree fresheners hung from his lamp. Finally, he came back to find his entire desk covered in variations of air-freshening aids. For fun, they'd leave rotten food in one another's desks over the weekend.

With so much freedom to play and design *Race 'n' Chase*, anything was game. The developers included references to *Reservoir Dogs*, James Bond films, *The Getaway*, and chase scenes from the *French Connection*. They reported back to the meeting a week later, where Jones would shape the overall vision to go where no game had gone before. If someone brought him a feature he'd never seen in another game, he gave it his full backing.

He had Sam's and Penn's complete support, too. Sam had grown from an iconoclastic kid to a renegade businessman. "Fuck it," Sam would say. "Just put it in the game, I don't give a shit what people think!" He had a goal to push games into new terrain and wouldn't let any obstacle get in his way. He knew what he was up against: a surprisingly monolithic industry that had grown comfortable with formulaically heroic tales that, by and large, lacked originality.

He had refined his own style in working with DMA to produce the game. "If the game isn't coming together properly, I'll apply focus, drilling it in and pushing it through," he once told Dan. "I don't lay down the law, I'll just go in with enthusiasm and energy and do it in a pleasant but aggressive way. I don't take no for an answer. I don't do it by being difficult. I do it by putting the right effort in."

The simplest thing Sam wanted was clear: freedom. Just like *Elite* and the other games he had loved as a kid, the newfangled *Race 'n' Chase* seemed like more than just a game. It was, most important, a world. The game takes place within three fictional cities, each modeled after a real town. Jones, the savvy entrepreneur, wanted to choose cities that would have the most impact on the market—and that meant the United States.

There was palm tree–lined Vice City, based on Miami; hilly San Andreas, based on San Francisco; and gritty Liberty City, based on New York. To receive a new mission, players had to stroll up to ringing telephone booths in town. A mob boss, say, Bubby, would then explain the mission, described in a subtitle on the bottom of the screen. You'd have to go, say, steal taxis or kill rival gangsters. One mission, taken from the movie *Speed*, required you to drive a bus at more than fifty miles per hour; otherwise, it would blow up.

The thing was, some play testers didn't want to do the missions at all. Given the bad-boy nature of the game—cars to steal, pedestrians to crush—they had more fun recklessly joyriding around. Baglow, who oversaw the play testers, would politely tell them it was time to stop driving and go answer a phone for a mission, but he could sense their disappointment over being restricted from simply joyriding around.

Penn, the producer at BMG, thought the game should let players do what they wanted. "It's a virtual space," he fumed, "you're allowed to do what the fuck you like!"

THE AMAZING THING about creating a video game was that you could code your own solutions out of thin air. You didn't need to reshoot a massive scene of a movie with thousands of extras, you could just think and type. Gary Foreman, the thoughtful young programmer in charge of the technical production for BMG, came up with a solution for the mission structures on his own. There was no technical reason why the missions had to progress in a linear fashion. "Can't we just make it so you can answer *any* phone?" he asked.

Why not, in other words, just let the players proceed along their own paths, at their own pace—answering a phone whenever they wanted to or simply speeding off and having fun? This wouldn't be the first time that a game would let players freely roam in an open world or a sandbox. Games such as *The Legend of Zelda* offered degrees of undirected exploration. The *Race 'n' Chase* team also reminisced about an old Spectrum game called *Little Computer People*, which let players roam a two-story house doing random chores. Yet bringing that kind of freedom to a criminal world would break down the fourth wall as nothing ever had before.

Sam knew this sort of DIY freedom was revolutionary for the medium. "The problem with other games is that when you hit a point that's frustrating, you can't get past it," he once said, but in *Race 'n' Chase*, "when you hit a point that's tough, just go do something else. That's fucking great!" Even the audio became freer. If players could drive anywhere in the cities, why not have different radio stations in their cars, too? Such as country music when you steal a truck. Late into the night, the musicians stayed up recording the different radio tracks.

Jones had his worries about creating such an open-ended game world. Games were all about having an object, a purpose, a goal—shoot the aliens, get the high score. How would gamers respond to something as unrestricted as this? He hatched an idea of how to give them some focus: setting a goal of accumulating one million points. When he looked at *Race 'n' Chase*, the cars zipping around from here to there, he thought of a different model for the game: pinball. "Pinball, for me, is the ultimate," he said. "You have two buttons, and that's it. It's just superb for teaching players about getting feedback and hooking players for hours."

Race 'n' Chase could be similar, encouraging players to rack up as many points as possible—even by running people over. Not everyone dug the increasingly untamed direction of the game, though. One programmer stubbornly insisted on continuing to play the game as a simulation—and others walked by to find him dutifully stopping at the traffic lights in the game. Yet they realized that was the beauty of what they had created. You had the freedom to do anything, good or bad.

The only limitation was your "wanted" level. If you caused enough mayhem, a cop's face would appear on a meter at the top of the screen. Police cars would give chase if they spotted you. Commit more egregious crimes, and your wanted level increased. Now an in-game APB was put out on you. At wanted level three, police would begin to set up roadblocks. If you got busted, you got carted off to jail, and your weapons were confiscated. Yet to keep all of this from happening too frequently and ruining the game, Baglow suggested that there be Respray Shops, where you could pull in the car and get a new coat of paint.

Their living, breathing world teemed with life. DMA programmers would sit at their PCs and pull back the camera on the game, just watching cars drive on and off the screen. "The good thing about [the game]," said one coder at DMA, "is that you don't have to go down a predetermined path. And there's nothing as much fun as spinning a car over your friend's head six times."

They weren't only running over one another, however. Baglow, DMA's writer and PR guy, had an idea of other people they could mow down in the game. The inspiration came from his own real-life travels. Whenever he passed through London airport, he always got hassled by Hare Krishnas, urging him to be happy. "Gouranga!" they'd say, a Sanskrit expression of good fortune. Baglow hated it. Then a lightbulb went off over his head.

Back at BMG, a new build of the game arrived. King slipped it into his PC and began to play. As he tore down the road, he could see a line of small orange-robed figures moving down the street. The closer he came, the louder he could hear them chanting and drumming. Holding down his forward arrow, he careened toward them, plowing down each one as a point score floated up above them. As he smashed the last one, a bonus word flashed onscreen: "gouranga!"

"Dude!" King exclaimed, "I'm running over Hare Krishnas!" The BMG crew marveled at this wicked weird world the gang in Scotland had created. *Race 'n' Chase* had come a long way from the geeky simulation that DMA had submitted a year before. It was time to give it a new name, something that captured its outlaw spirit: *Grand Theft Auto.*

5
Eating the Hamster

WANTED LEVEL

Grim city. Aerial view. A blaring police car tore through narrow streets in pursuit of two cars. Inside the vehicles, the gangsters seemed young, dressed in black suits, white shirts, black ties, and shades. They leaned out their windows, waving guns in the air. The cars passed phone booths and restaurants, buses and pedestrians.

It looked like something out of a video game, but this was real life. Down by the docks along the river in Dundee, the cop pulled the car over. When he approached, he saw one of the blokes holding a video camera. "We're making a promotional video for a computer game called *Grand Theft Auto*," said Baglow, the diminutive DMAer with short blond hair and glasses. The get-ups and the toy guns had been inspired by *Reservoir Dogs*, and, as Brian Baglow and the other geeks from DMA in the cars explained, they were just making the video for fun. The cop arched his brow. *Grand Theft Auto?* What kind of crazy game was that?

Though the cop let the guys off, he had reason to be dubious. As *Grand Theft Auto*—or *GTA*, as the crew had begun to call it—developed, the darkly comic urban action game couldn't be more different from the biggest title around: *Tomb Raider.* Released in the fall of 1996, this action adventure of swashbuckling Indiana Jane, Lara Croft, had become gaming's greatest phenomenon in years. It milked the muscle power of the PlayStation like nothing else, with players jumping and swimming and shooting from mountains to crypts. Lara, with her big breasts and almond eyes, was eye candy personified.

This couldn't have come at a worse time for *GTA*. Games were often judged by appearance alone, and compared to glitzy *Tomb Raider*, the top-down, 2-D racing scenes couldn't look more outdated. The brass at BMG wanted to cut the game. Or, as Penn put it more bluntly, "they were trying to kill it every fucking month." Jones remained defiant. "Gameplay! Gameplay! Gameplay!" he said. "Graphically, it may not be at the cutting edge, but I believe this is going to change the world."

Luckily for Jones, he had BMG's crew of Nerf gun–wielding players on his side—along with a new member of the BMG team, Sam's younger brother, Dan. Fresh from studying literature at Oxford, he'd begun to compose questions for what would be a hit trivia video game, *You Don't Know Jack.* Dan shared Sam's passion for *GTA* and how it defied the wizards-and-warriors fare usually associated with the industry. "Here was a game that was commenting on the world," he later said. "It was like being in a gangster movie, rather than a game."

The decision to focus on gameplay over graphics was well thought out. As with any creative endeavor, making a video game was all about the allocation of resources. A computer had limited processing abilities. Rather than spending that currency on power-sucking eye candy, DMA took a counterintuitive approach: putting the power toward the city's

action, physics, and artificial intelligence instead. They shared the stub-
born conviction that players would agree. "It doesn't matter what it
looks like. If it is a compelling and fun experience," King said, "people
will play it."

The Nerf gang succeeded at keeping BMG at bay, while assuring
Jones to stay on target. Yet privately, they were starting to sweat. Something about *GTA* was amiss. The cars drove unresponsively. The story
seemed clichéd and uninspired. Worse, the game kept crashing—freez-
ing to a halt mid-play. It was, as Penn distilled, "a fucking mess." When
the DMA guys sent around an unofficial in-house survey to see which
game they thought was most likely to fail, *GTA* topped the list.

THE PHONE RANG URGENTLY, as it always did, at Max Clifford Associates. In the United Kingdom, publicists didn't get much bigger or more
controversial than Clifford. Having built his career representing everyone from Frank Sinatra to Muhammad Ali, the quick-witted, silver-
haired Clifford had become, as one journalist put it, "a master manipulator of the tabloid media, the man many Tories blame for discrediting
their government with a string of well-publicized scandals."

Perhaps most notoriously, Clifford resurrected fledgling singer
Freddie Starr's concert tour in 1986 by planting the sensational headline
"Freddie Starr Ate My Hamster" in the *Sun*. Like the rumor of Ozzy
Osbourne biting off the head a bat, the story generated so much attention that it sold out Starr's tour. Clifford pioneered a new game of jour-
nalism in which publicists could feed the most outrageous stories to a
willing and hungry press.

On this day in 1997, however, the caller from BMG Interactive didn't
want to publicize a celebrity or a politician. He needed help promoting
an upcoming computer game, *Grand Theft Auto*. Could Clifford feed
their hamster to the press? The decision by the marketing team at BMG
Interactive to hire such a powerful publicist—let alone a specialist in

scandal—was unheard of in the game industry. BMG, with roots in the music business, thought a bit of rock-and-roll flair might do justice to their little punk game.

Yet as Gary Dale, the avuncular head of BMG Interactive, made clear, they had to get it just right. *GTA* was clearly going where no game had gone before—portraying an over-the-top criminal underworld of carjacking, Krishna-killing, drug-dealing, and chaos. It made Lara Croft look like the Church Lady, and the parent company wasn't willing to go to hell for its deeds. "Bertelsmann is a very large private company," Dale told Clifford, "and we want to check out that we can manage the nature of the content in the right way. This is a new area. We want to get advice from a corporate responsibility point, and make sure we get the right positioning on the game and the right messaging on the game."

Blunt and opportunistic, Clifford urged BMG to forget about convention and embrace *GTA*'s criminality in all of its glory. "If it's part of the game," he said, "it's part of the game. In the same way in the music and the movie business, the rating system governs what's legal or illegal. As long as it's complying with that, my advice to you is don't shy away from the fact. It won't appeal to everybody, but it will appeal to some."

Clifford recommended not only owning up to the violence, but cooking up the most outrageous hamster possible—and shoving it down the media's throat. What better way to get people talking? Clifford said he "knew there would be the wonderful elitist members of the establishment that would take and find something like this absolutely repulsive."

Dale relayed the news to his team. "The advice from PR was as long as you're legal, you shouldn't back away," he said. Sam loved the plan. *GTA* needed a marketing plan as brash and bold as the game. Jones, however, wasn't so convinced. He didn't want controversy for controversy's sake. Sam and the others at BMG seemed more intent on being

rock stars, but Sam argued it was more about pushing boundaries.
"Look," Sam said, "you're pushing the envelope for gaming."

"Yeah," Jones said.

"Apart from this, games have been seen for kids. Here's one doing
something different, like movies. We can actually use that as a marketing
angle."

Jones wasn't so sure and had an additional concern. Looking to
grow his business, he was striking a deal to merge DMA with a publisher called Gremlin Interactive. As word spread that the company was
going to float itself on the market, the press put the value at £55 million—and heralded Jones as UK's next digital titan. Jones didn't want to
rock the boat. Others at DMA shared his ambivalence about hiring
Clifford to promote GTA on controversy alone.

When Jones met Clifford, he marveled at the assuredness of his plan.
Clifford told him how he'd put the word out to his high-powered contacts in politics, telling them to plant the bug in the appropriate ears.
"We'll encourage the right people that it would be good for them to
speak out on how outrageous this is and criticize it," Clifford said. This,
he promised, "would get publicity and, most of all, encourage the young
people to buy."

Yet, as Jones later recalled, he began to grow skeptical the more Clifford
talked. "It was like…I offer a three-month plan, what I'll say is, 'I'll feed
these stories—Shock! Horror! You should see this!—into the ear of a lord
somewhere, that there's this game developed in Scotland which is utterly
despicable and encourages people to drive over pedestrians and kill them!'
He'd say these things, and then, at the end of three months, 'You'll be in
prime time.' And I was, like, 'Yeah, right.'" His skepticism about Clifford
didn't last long, though. "Everything he said came true," Jones later said.

It started while the game was still being developed, six months
before its release. On May 20, 1997, Lord Campbell of Croy, the former
Scottish secretary and a member of the cross-party Consumer Affairs
Group, spoke in the House of Lords about a scandalous new computer

game called *Grand Theft Auto.* The game, he explained, had hit-and-runs, joyriding, and police chases. "There would be nothing to stop children from buying it," he warned. "To use current terminology, is this not 'off message' for young people?"

"The government is very concerned about violent computer games, as are the public," concurred Junior Home Office minister Lord Williams of Mostyn. "All computer games which encourage or assist in crime, or which depict human sexual activity or acts of gross violence, must be passed by the BBFC [British Board of Film Classification], which can refuse classification. If there is a refusal, that automatically makes supply illegal.

"I do understand that the general description which you attached to *Grand Theft Auto* is correct," continued Lord Williams. "One has to bear in mind very carefully the vice of these computer games. It deals not only with the sort of activity you referred to but also to acts of gross violence."

"We simply cannot allow children and young people to be given the idea that car crime or joyriding is in any way an acceptable or an enjoyable thing to do," added Lord Campbell, who called on the BBFC to examine *GTA* and determine whether it should even be legal to release. It wasn't bluster. The BBFC had recently refused to rate *Carmageddon*—a darkly comic destruction-derby title marketed as "the racing game for the Chemically Imbalanced"—unless it toned down the violence and gore, all but ensuring that it wouldn't be carried at major retail stores.

With the politicians' debates making headlines, Clifford's carefully scripted battle over *GTA* played out in the tabloids on cue. "Criminal computer game that glorifies hit-and-run thugs," the *Daily Mail* hyped. "Imagine yourself being an up and coming low-life car thief, stealing exotic cars, and then add murder one, cop killing, car-hacking, drug-running, bank-raids and even illegal alien assassination!"

Despite the aging demographic of the industry, the sheer mention of the word *games* set off a load of critics who feared *GTA* would corrupt kids' impressionable minds. A spokesperson for the Scottish Motor Trade Association said, "It is deplorable to open young minds to car crime in this way." "This game is sick, and parents should refuse to buy it for their children," said a spokesperson for a group called Family and Youth Concern. "But even that may not be the solution, because children will still get their hands on a copy. This kind of material is dangerous and will make children think it is OK to rob cars and kill."

As the press spread, BMG and DMA rode the back of Clifford's hamster. "Once those quotes got quoted, we were happy to have them out there because, of course, they generated interest in the game," Dale later said.

To keep the controversy brewing, they launched a radio ad campaign featuring excerpts of the House of Lords debate. At a video game convention, they left fake parking tickets on cars that read "Penalty: For Having a Flash Car is to have it nicked and driven in a high-speed car chase with gunplay involving the Police until it is spectacularly written off. You have been warned." The *GTA* logo appeared below in red-and-orange letters with a trail of flames, along with the tagline, "it's criminal not to." A *GTA* promotional poster showed a car careening in the street. A list of crimes was printed along the side: "Murder, drug busts, hijacking, smuggling, bank raids, police bribes, road rage, bribery, extortion, armed robbery, unlawful carnal knowledge, adultery, pimping, petty thievery, and double parking!" The penal code for *Grand Theft Auto* appeared on the game's cover. Said Baglow, "The BBFC didn't really get the joke."

Yet the joke was also on him. One night he was driving home when he brushed against a tree. It was a minor fender-bender for his beat-up old car. When Clifford heard about it, however, a sparkle of possibility flashed in his eyes. Baglow later cracked open the *News of the World* to find the story that had been entertainingly spun.

"Sick car game boss was banned from driving," it read. "The computer buff behind the sick car-carnage game *Grand Theft Auto* was once banned from the road after writing off a car. Programmer Brian Baglow was at the wheel of his high-powered Ford Fiesta XR2 when it careered out of control and smashed into a tree. Baglow was arrested and taken to court, where he received a year-long ban for careless driving. 'It was unfortunate, but you learn,' said the businessman, who stands to make a fortune from the game this Christmas."

While Baglow laughed off the controversy, Jones wasn't taking it so well. When asked how he felt about the press, he said, "Good and bad." Clifford, in a way, had done his job too well. Jones couldn't believe how many people were willing to criticize an unfinished game that they had yet to even see. He wasn't the golden boy of *Lemmings* anymore.

The press lamented that "the computer genius who developed the best-selling *Lemmings* was at the centre of a storm . . . over a new game which encourages players to steal cars and knock down pedestrians in a hit-and-run joyride." As the *Sunday Times* later put it, "It is quite a shock to realize that the charming naivety of *Lemmings* and the Grand Guignol bloodthirst of *Grand Theft Auto* were both developed by a reticent Dundonian, Dave Jones."

With the BBFC threatening to refuse classification, the game developers had a serious problem on their hands, potentially causing them to miss the lucrative holiday season. BMG commissioned a psychologist from Nottingham Trent University to study the game, which he ultimately approved for adults. Baglow defended the game's wanted levels to the press. "We are being moral," he said. "Every time the player does something illegal, that increases the determination of the police to catch them, and they will be caught. In fact, we stress that crime does not pay."

Finally, just before the game's release, came the ruling on *GTA*. "We are confronted with new problems and new forms of violence," the BBFC said in a statement. "This kind of video has already provoked concern in Parliament and government. They involve the player in potentially criminal behavior and the infliction of violence on innocent parties. Such subject matter is unprecedented." But not something to ban. The game would be rated for players eighteen and over.

Max Clifford had scored big time and soon let the cat out of the bag. "We got it across to twelve to thirteen million people because it's controversial," he said. "Do you think the *News of the World* would have come out with a piece like they did just because it was a great game? I don't."

Jones tried to transform the controversy into a teaching moment. In the final weeks leading up to the release, the team had been coding around the clock to improve the handling of the cars (each of which now drove with the appropriate physics, like big vehicles with sluggish maneuvering) and work out the bugs. He didn't want their achievements to get lost in the noise. "People assume that computer games are for kids, and that's very wrong," he said. "The trouble is when people judge games on hearsay and out of context. *Grand Theft Auto* is all in the best possible taste."

ON NOVEMBER 28, 1997, gamers in England got their first spin at *GTA*. The plan was to release it first in the United Kingdom, then, some time later, in the United States. By now, however, the release of *GTA* seemed like an afterthought to the hype, with it having already been declared, as the *Guardian* put it, "the most controversial game in a decade." This left DMA and BMG with the unenviable by-product of such an elaborate PR campaign: living up to the buzz. The cheeky tagline under DMA's credit read "Disgusts Governments, Policemen, and Parents."

Yet it didn't take long to get the verdict. As *GTA*'s producers feared, some players thought it paled in comparison to games such as *Tomb Raider*. One player dismissed its "horrendous game play due to the crappy controls. Graphics are terrible. I've seen better on 8 bit systems. When you answer the phone, it sounds like you are talking to a chipmunk."

The guys at BMG found such criticisms infuriating. "What the fuck does that mean?" Dan once said. "If it's fun to play, it doesn't matter how it looks!" Yet as more reviews came in, there were plenty of gamers who didn't care about the graphics at all. "Though not up to the moral standards, *Grand Theft Auto* is great fun, in a twisted sort of way," wrote one gamer in a review. "*GTA* is quite addictive, as there is so much freedom in the way one can accomplish the different missions." "*GTA* is a gas," another effused. "You find yourself becoming immersed in the role of being the best criminal in the city."

Across the United Kingdom, a small but passionate cult following began to form. One day, the guys at DMA found a website where gamers had assembled a timetable to keep track of the trains that randomly pass through the cities of *GTA*. A story spread that a shopkeeper had come back to find that his store had been broken into, and all of the copies of *GTA* had been stolen. Though the numbers were modest, the game sold steadily out of the gate, churning more and more copies out by word of mouth, while others would have long gone by the wayside. *GTA* was moving about ten thousand copies a week. Before long, total sales were approaching five hundred thousand—at roughly £50 a clip—bringing revenues of £25 million. Considering that the game cost roughly £1 million to make—largely, the cost of salaries—the game more than earned its right to a sequel.

Though Sam wasn't in a position yet to get rich off the game, he seemed vindicated. The twenty-seven-year-old had long admired Rick Rubin—an iconoclast who changed the music industry on his own terms. Maybe Sam could do the same for video games. This little Scottish outlaw fantasy had finally put him in the driver's seat, and he knew just where he wanted to go: Liberty City.

6

Liberty City

MAP 01: POINTS OF INTEREST

LANDMARKS
      Statue of Liberty D4
      Def Jam Recordings C3

RESTAURANTS
      Radio Mexico............................E1
      Balthazar F4

ENTERTAINMENT
      Angelika Film Center D9
      Body&Soul.............................E2

Just as Sam was riding high on the success of *GTA*, he hit a new obstacle: BMG Interactive was being sold. The division had been bleeding cash. Though still relatively green in business, Sam saw examples of mismanagement—such as opening offices in twenty-seven countries around the world. The executives of the German conglomerate were souring on video games. With buzz building about the nascent Internet, Bertelsmann had turned its sights on television and the Web.

Dale, BMG's head, tried to convince the company to stay in the game business, but to no avail. "Bertelsmann ultimately decided they didn't want to be in the video game business," he later recalled. "Games just weren't part of the strategy."

With the Interactive division on the block, Sam panicked. "I gotta put the food on the table!" he said. His heart sank as he looked for opportunities with more corporate publishers. Sam felt too iconoclastic to fit in. "They didn't want nutters like us," he later said.

Then he met a nutter just as bold as him: Ryan Brant, a young guy in New York City who was considering buying BMG Interactive. They had plenty in common. Like Sam, Brant had been born into a glamorous family steeped in popular culture. His father, Peter, owned the magazines *Interview* and *Art in America* and cofounded the tony Greenwich Polo Club. Unlike Sam's mom, who had merely acted in gangster films, Brant's father had actually served time for tax evasion. Brant's stepmother was the supermodel Stephanie Seymour.

After graduating from the prestigious Wharton School of Business, Brant, a wiry guy with close-cropped hair, wanted nothing to do with his father's world of old media. In New York, Internet start-ups dotted the downtown area newly dubbed Silicon Alley. Brant knew exactly which part of the high-tech industry he wanted to crash: video games. At the time, the game industry was dominated by big publishers such as Electronic Arts and Activision and then a number of smaller companies. Yet Brant saw opportunity. In 1993, at the age of only twenty-one, he used a $1.5 million investment from his dad and other private investors to found Take-Two Interactive, his own game publisher.

Brant, who had grown up hobnobbing with downtown celebrities, decided to differentiate himself by putting out CD-ROM games that resembled B-movies. He wanted to cast real stars, a practice still largely unheard of in the mainstream game business, and combine them with adult subject matter, cinematic pretensions, and a deliberate, if ham-handed, edginess. *Hell: A Cyberpunk Thriller* starred cult actor Dennis Hopper and sold three hundred thousand copies worldwide, earning Take-Two $2.5 million in profits. For a game called *Ripper*, Brant spent $625,000 of its $2.5 million budget to cast Christopher Walken and *Indiana Jones* heroine Karen Allen. "I want to create the best possible software," Brant told *Forbes*, "and make as much money as possible."

Brant showed an Ivy League prowess for figuring out how to cash in, completing an initial public offering that raised $6.5 million for the company. Yet he knew he couldn't remain stagnant for long. One morning, he woke up with the terrifying thought: "We're going to get killed here unless we get bigger." He began to gobble up distributors from the United States to the United Kingdom and Australia to provide both an outlet for his games and another stream of revenues. By 1997, with a number of games on the market, the company's revenues neared $200 million, with more than $7 million in profit.

With licensing deals in place for Sony and Nintendo, Brant needed to shore up his publishing resources, and that's what led him to BMG Interactive. Jamie King, the BMG producer, thought that Brant was "ballsy as fuck," a newbie willing to take on the big boys at Activision and EA. Sam desperately wanted in and pitched Brant on his vision of the future of games. "I gave a very energetic pitch to him, where I must have sweated through three layers of clothing in my own insane sweaty way," Sam later recalled, "and everyone in the office is like 'Who the fuck was that guy?'"

The pitch worked. In March 1998, Brant paid $14.2 million in stock for BMG Interactive. The deal gave him staff and the rights to *GTA* and other games. Promoted to Take-Two's vice president of worldwide product development, Sam would now be in charge of both the development subsidiaries and third-party developers, including DMA Design and Jones, who would continue work on the *GTA* games in Scotland. Yet there was one catch: Sam had to move to New York.

Everyone wants to live a dream life, working at a job that isn't a job at all but a passion. Making video games in New York City, for Sam, felt like a dream come true. Eager to convince his friends to join him, Sam broke the news to his peers at BGM. "I gotta go to New York," he told King one day. "You want to come?"

King's mind raced with images of a past trip to New York. He had been staying at a model's apartment in the Village and roamed Fifth Avenue in the snow while listening to Pharcyde on his headphones—determined to one day live here. Did he want to come to New York and oversee game production? "Done!" King replied. "I'm there! Just book the fucking ticket!"

Then Sam made a call to his other key buddy: Terry Donovan. A childhood friend from St. Paul's, Donovan was a towering Brit who'd grown up in the same kind of pop culture trend–setting family as Sam and Dan. His father had directed the iconic video for the Robert Palmer hit "Simply Irresistible." Donovan wore his lineage with rock star pride, boasting of his early brushes with greatness. "My first drug experience was at age seven, sitting in my living room with Mick Jagger, smoking a spliff," he once said.

These days, Donovan had been working as head of artist relations at Arista, putting out dance, trance, drum, and bass records. He'd also been deejaying around town, marketing himself and the clubs. Though his only work with computers was getting his PC to write "terry is cool" as a schoolboy, Donovan listened intently to Sam's pitch. "You gotta come out here because we're starting a new label within the Take-Two family," Sam told him. "It's almost like an independent, we're going to try doing our own stuff from BMG, try and make games that are more modern, more accessible." Donovan, who would oversee marketing, was in.

Gary Foreman, BMG's quiet tech whiz, got the pitch to be technical director at Take-Two. When he told his erudite gamer friends at home about his opportunity with Take-Two, however, they scoffed. Compared to *GTA*, the games that Take-Two made seemed cheesy and lame. "Take-Two?" they told Foreman. "What have you done? Are you kidding me?" No matter, he was in, along with the others. It was time to move to Liberty City for real.

SAM AND THE OTHERS WEREN'T the only British invasion coming to the States in 1998. So was their prized game, *GTA*. By now, Clifford's hamster had grown into a Godzilla-size monster, thanks to the British media. *GTA* madness had even spread to Brazil, which banned the game outright, ordering all copies to be taken off the shelves. Violators faced up to $8,580 in fines.

After hearing about *GTA* on the Internet, gamers in the States were rabidly awaiting its release. An early *GTA* website, launched by a fan at the University of Missouri, went viral online. Players added news and tips about the game, spreading the word until the site had more than a hundred thousand visitors. Sam and the others made it the official hub for the game. Reports came in that hackers were copying the game and distributing it online, a practice that had yet to really break beyond the indie underworld. When the press caught wind, they hyped the real-life criminality of the game. "A top-selling Scots computer game is being stolen . . . by teenage nerds in America," wrote the *Sunday Mail*.

Although Take-Two had purchased the rights to release the PlayStation version of *GTA* later in the year, the game arrived in the States first on PC. A small start-up in Connecticut called ASC Games, which had released a bowling title and the Jeff Gordon racing game, secured the rights. ASC followed BMG's lead by milking the controversy to fuel sales. The company hyped the game in a press release titled "Amidst Storm of Controversy," and irreverently promised "to unleash a crime wave on America."

On its release in the United States, the U.S. press heralded *GTA*'s inventiveness and rebellious spirit. Official *PlayStation Magazine* called it "one of the most original, innovative, technically impressive and controversial PlayStation releases ever." *Computer Games Magazine* effused,

"The game's gleeful embrace of anarchy is a refreshing change from the normal do-gooder activities found in most games. Crude and profane, this brilliant little game allows us all to get in touch with our inner Beavis." *GameSpot* said, "It won't win any awards. [But] Wanna-be socio-paths who can deal with the shortcomings will have a lot of fun."

Yet ASC quickly experienced the real battles that followed *GTA*. The ASC publicist handling the game learned this firsthand when he demonstrated the game for *Entertainment Weekly*. As he watched the writer, who seemed entranced with the experience, he figured he could count on a high score. He was wrong. The review came out with the lowest—and rarest—letter grade yet, an F. *GTA* got slugged off as a "shock-schlock game . . . as monotonous as it is discomforting (you earn brownie points with your Mob boss, though), leaving you with out-dated graphics and a game that's guilty but hardly a pleasure."

The publicist called up, begging for an explanation. "Why the bad review?" he asked.

"The editors," he was told.

"Why?"

"Because of the content. The content's so awful, I couldn't give it anything higher than an F."

By the time the game came out for PlayStation in the summer of 1998, however, even the worst review couldn't slow it down. *GTA* had arrived in the United States, and so had the unlikely stars behind it.

THEY CALLED IT THE COMMUNE. It was a ground-floor apartment on Water Street in the South Street Seaport area of Manhattan. Practically no windows. A cave of darkness. This was where Sam, King, Foreman, and Donovan moved in—along with Sam's three cats—when they landed in New York in the summer of 1998.

Just to be in Manhattan was electrifying, especially after so many years idolizing the States. The honking horns. The *Noo Yawk* accents.

The salty smell of hot dogs wafting up from street vendors. The Empire State Building, and the Statue of Liberty. All of the great restaurants, from the dive Radio Mexico down the street to the trendy Balthazar in SoHo. The guys spent hours flipping through the channels on TV, just watching the wonderfully American excess pipe in: sensational crimes on local TV, the game show models, Bill Clinton and Monica Lewinsky, pornographer Al Goldstein on public access flipping off rivals with a big "Fuck You!"

"I can't believe what's being pumped into the living room," Donovan said.

"We're here!" King effused. "We work on the games, they're risky and ambitious, we don't know what we're doing! It's exciting. It's amazing. Now we're here in games industry and totally high profile, whether we like it or not."

They were young, far from home, with no real clue how to run a video game company, but they had something crucial: the dream and the drive. Working out of a cramped office in SoHo, the guys began mapping out plans for a *GTA* mission pack set in London in 1969, along with a formal sequel, *GTA2*. At night, they'd return to the Commune to stay up late playing video games and plotting their future. Sam's job was to oversee the company's publishing efforts in the United States, including games beyond *GTA*. He also had a personal mission of his own: "to bring our attitude, try to make games that felt more relevant to the audience that was playing them."

The guys knew just how they wanted to do it, by starting their own video game label—"a hip, happening label, more about lifestyle, not toys or technology," as Donovan once described it.

"Take-Two has an identity, EA has their identity," King agreed, "it's important that we have our own identity, and let consumers know what we stand for, a certain kind of branding." As Baglow, who had come from DMA to handle PR for Take-Two, said, they wanted to create "an outlaw label," something that reflected the renegade spirit of *GTA*.

Sam phoned his brother Dan, who was still in London but planning to join them in the States soon to work at Take-Two and oversee the writing of the games. Dan, like Sam, was sick of an industry telling grown men to play the roles of elves and wanted something more. He was convinced, as he said, "that there was this huge audience of people who play console games in particular and who were very culturally savvy and culturally aware, but who were being fed content when playing games they found slightly demeaning."

They wanted to make the games that they wanted to play. To do this, they didn't want to model themselves on other game companies such as EA, which they considered a crass, sequel-spewing machine. Their goal, as King later put it, was simple but bold: "to change everything."

ONE DAY SAM and the others piled into a car for a road trip to Six Flags Great Adventure, the theme park in Jackson, New Jersey. The guys loved roller coasters almost as much as hip-hop and wanted to celebrate their new move with a day on the rides.

GTA was on its way to selling more than one million copies worldwide. They still weren't rich, but they were emboldened. They wanted to brand themselves while they were hot, so that consumers knew they weren't just buying into a game but a lifestyle. They just needed a name. They would still remain part of Take-Two Interactive but as a branded label. Grudge Games was Donovan's favorite, suggested because they were, as Sam once put it, "world-class grudge bearers."

"Minimum ten years," Dan said.

When they had run the idea by Brant, though, he balked. "You know, guys," he said, "I know where you're going with that, but it's a little on the negative side."

During a recent trip to London, Sam had tossed out the name Rockstar. "I like everything, from the Keith Richards it evokes to the campiness it evokes," he later said, "and everything in between. . . . at the end of the day you can't fuck with Keith Richards!"

"It's a nod to the past and a snipe at it at the same time," Donovan agreed. "And also, in a weird way, a snipe at the lameness of the present. In some ways, the golden age of the rock star is done. Not many Keith Richards around now. Now they're drinking herbal tea!"

Foreman had one concern about calling themselves Rockstar: they had better deliver. "People will make fun of us," he said, "we'll get shit, but then pressure would be on. We'll have to live up to it. We have to make sure our games are really, really good." Yet that, for them, was a given. Now the cofounders of this label simply had to make it official.

Over in the midway at Six Flags, they saw a vendor selling wooden plaques. For a few bucks, visitors could have their own messages burned into the wood, such as "Bon Jovi Rulez!" As the acrid smell of sizzling carbon filled the air, they watched the carny etch their new name into the wood: Rockstar Games.

They decided to burn one more sign for good measure. Something they could hang next to this one in the Commune back in New York. A phrase to remind them forever of this day when their mission began. A cheeky message, perhaps, for anyone who might ever try to stop them.

"Fuck Off Cunts," it read.

7
Gang Warfare

> **RESPECT-O-METER**
> Who presently tolerates you and who wants you
> dead. Depending on who you're working for, you
> either have respect with a gang or you don't. If
> you've got it with one gang, then head to their neigh-
> borhood and get yourself employed. If you don't,
> you better mind where you stray. Find yourself in the
> wrong area with no respect and you'll get a pretty
> harsh hello.

Fuck off! Go home! Go back to England!"

It didn't take long for Sam and his gang to read how their competitors felt about their calling themselves Rockstar. Game development companies, whose employees are predominantly male, are a
unique breed of frats—brainy, creative, self-effacing members who are
expected to be comfortable in their underdog status. They'd sooner
compare themselves with Napoleon Dynamite than Keith Richards.

After Sam announced his label's name in a December 1998 press
release—"the Rockstar brand will finally deliver an elite brand that

people can trust," he promised—the flames hit the online gaming forums. Game developers bristled over the cocky New Kids On The Block. The fact that these Brits were in New York City, far from the hub of game development on the West Coast, only made them more outcast.

Yet characteristically, the antagonism only emboldened the guys further. King, always ready to burst into a stream-of-consciousness rant similar to Sam's, fumed about how no one seemed to get their sense of mission or irony. "Rockstar came from growing up and being in awe of all the rock stars and the musicians and the hip-hop artists having limos, trashing hotel rooms, having stories like you snorted a fucking load of ants because you were so high!" he'd say, breathlessly. "The glamour! The photography! The backstage! The groupies! The T-shirts!"

It was as if the other developers actually liked being dismissed as nerds. "Everyone's saying we're a bunch of geeks in a garage on a Saturday night who should be out dating," King went on. "Fuck you! We've got *Grand Theft Auto* coming! It's a wake-up call to everyone. Games are going to be cool!"

The plan started with their office. The team moved into 575 Broadway, a gorgeous red brick building in SoHo over the Guggenheim Museum annex. They arrived to work from the Commune, walking from the subway past models, hipsters, and artists. Upstairs, they took over a rundown loft with glassed-in offices in the back.

Sam hung up a poster of his idol, the late movie producer Don Simpson, who made the blockbusters he'd worshipped as a kid: *Top Gun*, *Beverly Hills Cop*, *Days of Thunder*. Simpson personified the kind of high-concept entertainment that they wanted to bring to video games. The fact that he died young, a drug-addled sex fiend, only made him more of an antihero to the team. "When you have a vision and you're creating something new, no one's going to understand that," King later said. "Everyone's going to throw obstacles in your way, and you must overcome that. People like Don Simpson are an inspiration because they did it. They're pioneers, and fuck everyone else." That's the kind of game makers they wanted to be.

With their office in place, they needed a logo for their label—as iconic as Def Jam's. When they marched into Take-Two's office to unveil their plan, however, they drew blank stares. "We want to make stickers, and we want to make T-shirts!" King said.

The guys in suits just stared back blankly. "Why?"

"What do you mean why?" King responded. "Because it's cool!"

Sam shared King's frustration with his new corporate parents. "What the fuck am I doing here?" he asked Dan. "Take-Two isn't even in the top twenty-five game publishers. They're nobodies. All they have is a few corporate guys and a couple of accountants. That's it." Yet their ambitious boss, Ryan Brant, insisted on giving the boys their freedom, despite being a subsidiary of Take-Two. Rockstar commissioned a gifted young artist named Jeremy Blake to design the logo. After several iterations, they decided on the winning one: a letter R with an asterisk, R*.

As they battled to brand their identity under the corporate parentage of Take-Two, Rockstar began to build its team. As president of Rockstar Games, Sam would oversee the vibe and the vision of their products. He began hiring people who shared their mission to change the gaming culture and industry. All that it took was a few minutes with Sam for prospective employees to fall under his spell. Who was this shaggy, bearded Brit, spitting and ranting about making games cool? As one early hire said, "I bought into his vision and charisma."

Yet if you wanted to join the game industry's most elite gang, you had to play by its rules. Baglow, the former writer and publicist for DMA, learned this quickly after he showed up in New York to head Rockstar's PR. Accustomed to the more typically geeky office culture back in Dundee, Baglow had simply bought a bunch of T-shirts to wear to work at Rockstar, a different color for each day. Donovan, mountainous and chrome-domed, looked down at Baglow as if he were a lowly Hobbit. "Fucking hell, mate, are you just changing your texture map?"

he joked, referring to the graphic scheme used to color objects in video games.

The next day, Sam and Dan took Baglow along to the hip shops on Broadway, buying him a wardrobe they felt was more worthy of their new international PR manager: Dockers, hoodies, and a gray T-shirt with their logo and the words "Je Suis Un Rockstar" on the back. "I look more like a Long Island white boy than a dick from Dundee," Baglow quipped, after he donned his new garb. Baglow was told he had to, as he put it, "learn the Rockstar way."

The Rockstar way didn't end with the wardrobe. It was built on attitude, as Baglow learned one day during lunch. He had come back into the office with a bag from a nearby Chinese take-out place. Sam snarled at the sight of the restaurant's name on the bag. "Oh, no!" he snapped, "you're not getting that!" Baglow learned that the restaurant had done something inexplicable to piss off Sam and had landed on the boss's burgeoning black list. "There are places we can't go because Sam had a bad experience," another Rockstar explained to Baglow.

Though they had only about a dozen employees, the sense of loyalty was already tight. King started to call themselves the 575ers, for their Broadway address. With Sam leading by example with his passionate work ethic, they labored into the night, cast in the bluish glow of their screens. Later they'd head to their favorite bar, Radio Mexico, as alive and electric as the city outside, to guzzle cervezas and fried cheese balls.

WITH THE ROCKSTAR BRAND and team in place, they set about on their most important job of all: publishing the kind of games they wanted to play, no matter how strange they appeared to the rest of the industry. Their inexperience, relative to the corporate giants who ruled the business, only made them feel more empowered. Yet they felt that the stakes were high anyway, and their dreams were theirs alone to lose.

Rockstar wasn't limiting itself to *GTA*. The company had *Monster Truck Madness 64* for the Nintendo 64 in the works, as well as *Thrasher! Skate and Destroy*, inspired by the skater magazine. *Thrasher!* gave an early hint of the cultural mash-ups Rockstar wanted in its games. Instead of the standard arena rock soundtrack, Rockstar licensed vintage hip-hop such as "White Lines" by Grandmaster Flash and, even more unusually, released a promo on 12-inch vinyl with a Japanese logo.

By 1999, *GTA* had sold more than a million copies worldwide but remained little more than a culty underground anomaly. PC gaming was still dominated by the fantastical fare of D&D knock-offs (such as *Asheron's Call* and *EverQuest*) and first-person shooters (*Quake, Unreal Tournament*). Console titles, even more mainstream, stuck to the predictable worlds of zombie killers (*Resident Evil*), cutesy gorillas (*Donkey Kong 64*), and movie tie-ins (*Star Wars Episode 1: The Phantom Menace*).

Rockstar, however, refused to give up on its quirky urban satire. Next would come *Grand Theft Auto: London 1969*, a mission pack of extra levels for *GTA*. Sam relished the opportunity of doing bobbies and robbers in his hometown, sort of a virtual *Get Carter*. "London in the sixties was slick, glamorous and cool but with an ever-present undercurrent of ultra-violence," he said, when announcing the game.

Of course, he could press more buttons back home, too. When Matt Diehl, a reporter from *Spin* magazine, interviewed Sam about the game, he found a long-haired, frenzied Brit with a White Album beard. "You're running bagfuls of speed to a Member of Parliament's hooker," Sam effused, "and there's both female and male prostitution!" It was all part of his master plan. "We're about doing games that have relevance," he went on. "Most games let you be Tommy the Dancing Leprechaun who slays the dragon. You can't go to the pub and say, 'Wow, I just slayed the dragon, man! But if you say, 'I just carjacked fifty-five cars and ripped off drags, *that's* relevant."

At the same time, Rockstar began work on a full-blown sequel, *GTA2*. Taking a cue from *Blade Runner*, they set the action in the seedy near future of an unnamed city in America. There'd be a sleazy Elvis Presley bar called Disgracelands and an overrun mental institution. Instead of only police chasing the player as his wanted level increased, there'd be the FBI and the National Guard on the trail, too.

Yet what most excited Sam and the others were the gangs. Instead of random people roaming the streets, seven identifiable groups of criminals ruled the three districts of *GTA2*. As the player answered phones in different areas, nearby gangs would send him off on missions to complete. Each gang had its own symbol and style, just as in *The Warriors*: the Loonies, symbolized by a winking happy face, were glee-fully violent hoods who doled out brutal jobs of killings and explosives; the Rednecks were represented by a Confederate flag and pickup trucks; and the Krishnas were back, chanting outside their temple.

Depending on how players impressed or pissed off the gangs, they would reap either the reward or the sorrow. Rockstar swiped the tagline from mob films, "Respect is everything." For the 575 crew, the game felt vividly autobiographical, as King said, "from growing up in gang culture and going through thick and thin as teenagers, to the way we were a gang at Rockstar like the gangs within these games."

With Rockstar now driving the future of *GTA*, the pressure mounted on Jones and the gang back in Dundee. Gone were the free-form days of anything-goes development and the luxurious four years they spent making the first *GTA*. Rockstar, for all of its employees' youthful glee, still had a taskmaster parent behind-the-scenes: Take-Two. Their urge to rebel brought tensions to the fold.

As a public company with milestones to meet, Take-Two demanded a specific date for *GTA2*'s release: October 28, 1999. This gave DMA a little more than twelve months to make the game, with a budget of about $1 million. Making a successful game took an enormous amount of time and effort, because the developers literally had to code—and test—a believable world from the ground up. Six-day workweeks (known in the industry as "crunch time") became the norm. Gone was the time when Jones made games on his own; the development team had grown to thirty-five people.

Despite Sam's rebellious tastes, he always worked as hard as—if not harder than—any guy in a suit up at Take-Two. This is what gave him his edge, having the vision of an outlaw but the work ethic of a Puritan. To show solidarity during crunch, Sam and the others would shave their heads (then let their hair grow long again after a game shipped).

The staff sat hunched at their desks by 8 a.m. and left at 10 p.m., with Sam always the first to arrive and the last to leave. Rockstar producer Marc Fernandez later compared it to the way an NFL quarterback leads a team by example. "Sam wanted everyone to know that no one worked harder than him," he said. "You couldn't really question his critique because he was out-proving you every single day."

The tighter they became in New York, the more a sense of gang warfare emerged between Rockstar and DMA. "They were feeling that Dundee is this backwater place," DMA producer Paul Farley later recalled. "There was definitely friction."

Jones had other reasons to feel disenfranchised. DMA was changing hands again. French publisher Infogrames was acquiring Gremlin Interactive, the company that Jones had merged with in 1997, for an estimated £24 million. Infogrames wanted to become "the Disney of videogames," Jones said—and how could the Disney of games be associated with *GTA*?

"OH, NO," said Jack Thompson, as he tuned to CNN. It was just before noon on April 20, 1999, and the aspiring culture warrior was inside his Spanish-tiled home on a quiet suburban street in Coral Gables. His young son, Johnny, played in the background. With his wife, a successful attorney, paying the bills, Thompson had become a stay-at-home dad, caring for Johnny—as he kept one eye trained on the moral decay of America and his next call to action.

It didn't take long to find it. Thompson watched in horror as terrified teenagers poured from Columbine High School. As the shootings unfolded on TVs around the world, millions of concerned parents desperately tried to make sense of this incredibly senseless crime. They needed something to blame, something controllable, something to assure them that this would never happen in their families. Thompson had just the answer: video games.

Since his high-profile victories over rappers 2 Live Crew and Ice-T, Thompson had become an unusually potent crusader who built on three powerful traits, a savvy knack for media sound bites, a Vanderbilt-trained understanding of the law, and, perhaps most important, a tireless ability to fight. Thompson's best friend was his fax machine, which he used to flood the media with press releases about his latest cause.

Now he had the game industry in his crosshairs. It started in March 1998, after fourteen-year-old Michael Carneal opened fire on classmates during a school prayer group in Paducah, Kentucky. When Thompson learned of Carneal's passion for violent games such as *Mortal Kombat* and *Doom*, he worked with the attorney for three of the victims to file a $130 million lawsuit against the companies behind the titles.

"We intend to hurt Hollywood," Thompson announced at a press conference. "We intended to hurt the video game industry." The press ate his hamster on cue. Thompson went on national TV to warn *Today Show* host Matt Lauer that the Paducah shooting would not be the last of its kind. Seven days later, Columbine happened—making Thompson an even more credible media darling.

Within moments of the shootings, he had the sheriff's department near Columbine on the phone. "Because of my research on the Paducah case," he said, "I have reason to believe that school shooting—and now possibly this one—was the result of a teen filled up with violent entertainment and trained on violent entertainment, video games, to kill." The media erupted the next day with news that Eric Harris and Dylan

Klebold had been inspired by the game *Doom*, copies of which had been found at their homes.

For Doug Lowenstein, the staunch head of the game industry's Interactive Digital Software Association in Washington, D.C., Thompson had fired a devastating blow. Since the *Mortal Kombat* hearings of 1993, he had been successfully lobbying politicians to keep regulation at bay. A former journalist from New York City, Lowenstein had the First Amendment, as he said, "deep in my DNA" since his days working on his high school paper. He believed that it protected both Nazis to march in Skokie and developers to put out violent games. "That's the essence of free expression," he said. "You can't compromise on free speech."

Articulate, intelligent, prematurely balding, and dressed in a business suit, Lowenstein presented a safely grown-up face for the industry that was still considered for kids. Yet in recent years, his successes in Washington had a downside. The industry had been coasting since the Lieberman hearings, regulating itself with its voluntary ratings board, the ESRB, and staying outside the fray of cultural debate—but not anymore.

"Columbine fundamentally transformed everything," he later recalled. "Suddenly, everything was back to square one, and the worst and most negative stereotypes about the industry were not only revisited, but in a way reaffirmed. You had never been in battle, but now you're fighting a war."

Lowenstein knew exactly what was on the line: a state and federal push for regulation. Sure enough, Lieberman called for an investigation into the game industry shortly after Columbine. President Clinton soon took up the call, ordering a federal investigation into game ratings and marketing. For Lowenstein, the stakes went beyond games. "Once you [accept] the principle that violent depictions can be regulated and restricted as obscenity can be," he said, "you've opened the door to most pervasive and extensive government censorship that we've ever seen in this country."

Yet as Thompson made the rounds on TV, Lowenstein began to feel that he was losing the battle in the most influential arena: the press. Just one week after Columbine, Lowenstein went on the defensive when *60 Minutes* grilled him during a lead segment on violent games. The show then cut to the story of Paducah and Lowenstein's new nemesis: Jack Thompson, who sat alongside Mike Breen, the attorney for the victims in Paducah.

There on the most popular news program in the United States, Thompson, his graying hair neatly combed, had his biggest platform yet. This was his moment to take his culture war to a wider audience than ever before, to send a message to the players of the game industry that he was gunning for them. "What would you say to critics who feel that this is a frivolous lawsuit against defendants who have very deep pockets?" Ed Bradley asked.

"Hold on to your hat," Breen replied.

"And your wallet," Thompson said.

8

Steal This Game

THREE WEEKS INTO THE FUTURE
The city is on the edge of collapse, with law and order beginning to break down completely. People are running wild, half-addled on good-additives and semi-legal pharmaceutical pills. A giant corporation controls every aspect of society, from entertainment to organ transplants. . . . Things are going to get way out of control.

Get away from me!" screamed the half-naked man in the cage, as he struggled to remove the collar from around his neck.

"Shut up, you freak!" shouted his master—an ape chomping a cigar—as he yanked the collar tighter.

The scene came right out of *Planet of the Apes* but wasn't taking place in the movie. It was unfolding live inside the Los Angeles Convention Center. Pasty young guys jostled to photograph the women in leather bikinis inside the cage. A newscaster with spiky blond hair interviewed one of the actors dressed as a gorilla. "Chasing humans has always been my most favorite," the gorilla explained, as a comely slave stroked its mane. "I like to run them down in the cornfields, yes!"

This promotion for a new *Planet of the Apes* video game was among the featured attractions of the Electronic Entertainment Expo, or E3, the video game industry's annual carnivalesque trade show. For three days in May 1999, more than seventy thousand wide-eyed and sore-thumbed players from the real world descended here to check out the latest, greatest games. More than nineteen hundred titles from four hundred companies flashed on giant screens in booths designed like Hollywood sets.

Publishers spared no expense to dazzle players and outdo one another. Gamers crammed into Electronic Arts' giant booth to watch macho men Diamond Dallas Page and Sting hurl each other across a ring as part of a promotion for a new World Championship Wrestling game. The child star of the new *Star Wars: Episode 1* film hyped the tie-in game. Throughout the sprawling two floors of the convention, seemingly every stripper in L.A. had been hired to work as a so-called booth babe—including a gun-wielding Lara Croft. Even David Bowie, one of the many stars promoting a game at the E3, professed himself a fan. "Of course, I play *Tomb Raider*," he said. "Like every other hot-blooded male, I was in love with Lara."

Video games were sexy, and celebrities and publishers wanted to cash in. The allure of new technologies electrified the air. With the Internet booming and Wall Street soaring, the dot com bubble was churning out legions of young millionaires. Bill Gates's worth alone topped $100 billion. Video games were the fastest-growing form of entertainment in the world. In the previous three years, the industry had grown by an astonishing 64 percent—on target to gross more than $7 billion in the United States alone and surpass total box office movie sales.

Yet despite the boom, as everyone here knew, video games had never seemed more misunderstood. With less than a month having passed since Columbine, video games had landed in the crosshairs of the culture war. Thompson's crusade had reached Capitol Hill, where Senator Sam Brownback effectively put the business on trial in a Senate Commerce Committee hearing. "A game player does not merely witness violence, he takes an active part," he warned, "the higher your body count, the higher your score." The Feds passed an amendment to the juvenile crime bill in the Senate on the marketing of violent games to kids.

Lowenstein methodically countered the claims, pointing out the vast number of adults (and moms) buying games. "Video games don't teach people to hate," he told *Time*. "The entertainment-software industry has no reason to run and hide." Yet journalists at E3 couldn't find many industry people to talk to. Those who went seeking comments at an E3 panel called "Ethics in Entertainment: Will the Medium Ever Reach Maturity?" found an empty room.

Among the no-shows were the guys from Rockstar Games, who were more concerned about making a splash of their own. To mark the debut of their label at E3—the trade show that epitomized the very corporate industry they were taking on—Sam and the cofounders sauntered past the Pokemon mascots and the furry apes in tracksuits designed by Hanes, the graffiti artist behind the original Tommy Boy record logo, and emblazoned with the R* logo. The fact that few, if any, gamers at the show appreciated the fashion statement was beside the point. "It didn't matter to E3, but it mattered to us," King recalled. "We're an art house! We're an art collective! We were obsessed."

They had earned the swagger. *GTA: London 1969* had debuted at number one on the UK game charts, followed by the original *GTA* at number two. And even more, *GTA* had been in the top twenty for the entire seventy-five weeks since its release, an astounding figure in an industry that usually saw games quickly fall off the charts. "The *Grand Theft Auto* franchise has proven to hold a longevity that is unusual to find in a video game series," puffed Sam in a press release. They had even struck a deal to bring *GTA* to the family-friendly Nintendo 64 and Game Boy systems.

With *GTA2* due in October, Rockstar's British invasion had just begun, but its strategy wasn't merely to promote the games at E3. It was to sell Rockstar as a brand. For Sam, it was a way to evoke the kind of obsession for music he felt while growing up. "People have the same passion toward the game as certainly I would have to Adam Ant or David Bowie or to Abba," he later said. "People are frenetic about it and want to feel the same passion is going on behind the scenes."

Rather than demean themselves by joining the circus on the main floor, the guys at Rockstar seeded *GTA2* like a Def Jam street campaign. *GTA2* stickers got slapped on anything that stood. One of Sam's decrees was no longer to refer to the game by its full name but rather by its cryptic acronym. T-shirts were printed up with only the *GTA2* logo on the front. *GTA2* took swipes at other games, too—such as when players would get a message on their pagers in *GTA2* from a Lara, thanking them for the hot time last night. Fake pills embossed with the *GTA* logo were reportedly found by gamers in small plastic bags around the halls though, adding to the mystery, there was no evidence that Rockstar was behind the ploy.

Across the street from the convention, Sam and the cofounders partied with another group of rebellious game makers from Take-Two Interactive called Gathering of Developers—or GOD for short. GOD had transformed a parking lot into a rock-and-roll happening called "The Promised Lot." Beer flowed. Bands played. Strippers cavorted in Catholic school skirts. King hammed it up in a photo with a fake-boobed dude in the Catholic girl get-up, pretending to chop up a pile of coke with a gold American Express card.

To get a demo of *GTA2*, reviewers had to make a special appointment to meet with Rockstar behind closed doors. The preview couldn't have been more different from the *Dungeons & Dragons* fantasy of the massively multiplayer online role-playing games out on the floor.

Gamers zipped around the cyberpunk streets of *GTA2*, running missions and road-killing pedestrians.

Publicist Brian Baglow, now rechristened as Rockstar's "lifestyle manager," made the rounds, hyping the new features—Gangs! Better missions! Better graphics! With Sam's ambitions growing, Baglow desperately tried to fill his boss's burgeoning appetite for rave reviews. Sam didn't want only the game press; he insisted on reaching hipster magazines such as *Face* and *Dazed and Confused*.

Press members would be led into an interview as if they were meeting Oasis. Sam and Donovan would then take over, celebrating *GTA2*'s gangs and grit. "You can sit and watch gang wars taking place while you're around the corner having a cigarette," Sam would say, "and he does actually smoke in the game." While other publishers shied away from the post-Columbine furor, Rockstar hit it head on. "Our responsibility is to 99.9 percent of the population who aren't actually planning to murder anyone in the next two weeks," Donovan said.

Even more unusual for a game company, Rockstar showed off a short live-action film it had shot to promote *GTA2*. With no budget and with King producing, the team approached it like their own indie *Goodfellas*. For props, Foreman and King had tracked down an underground weapons shop in New York. When the gun dealer flipped on the light, Foreman and King looked around to see shelves of MP5s, M16s, and M60s. "Most people making games didn't get to do this kind of stuff," Foreman later deadpanned.

They shot the film in Brooklyn with a small cast and crew, only to have the sky open up in a torrential downpour. Without the proper know-how or permits, the locals freaked out on the guys, throwing them out of locations. Sam and Donovan finally showed up in a huff, furious to find that King had spent $150,000 and counting. Donovan eventually got into the spirit, letting himself get tied to a chair, dressed as a Hare Krishna, as thugs pretended to pummel him senseless. Dan e-mailed a photo of the scene to the *GTA* fansite Gouranga! which promptly posted it online.

Gamers at E3, however, watched the film dubiously. Who did these self-described Rockstars think they were? *GTA*, despite its cult success, was far from a mainstream phenomenon. Compared to the other games at the show—such as Sony's ultrarealistic *Gran Turismo*, showcased for the upcoming 128-bit PlayStation 2 system—*GTA2* looked outdated. One writer dismissed it for having "chess-like 2D graphics."

Undeterred, Rockstar continued its outlaw campaign for *GTA2* beyond E3. Increasingly confident, Sam and the cofounders insisted on doing it themselves, rather than take the standard route of farming it out. "This is a cultural product and we understand how to present it better than an advertising agency ever could," Dan said. Sony, after all, had been brazen with its own outlandish campaigns—which included ads that showed a hip young couple with PlayStation controller button nipples.

Yet Rockstar's overconfidence got the better of Sam and the cofounders when they pushed the controversy too far. The cover of the game showed a car against a black background with the tagline "Steal This Game" underneath. They took out Steal This Game ads on billboards and buses and TV commercials and planned to launch it at a football match in the United Kingdom. They even sponsored a *GTA2* promo with the Monster Truck tour. Retailers didn't get the joke, questioning why they'd want to encourage people to shoplift. "If you run this ad," one threatened, "I'm not buying any games."

Donovan's marketing team tried to salvage the ill-conceived campaign as best they could, spending a fortune on stickers that they slapped over the Steal This Game ads with the word *Censored*. When Baglow questioned the plan, he was told it was guerrilla marketing in action. "It's not guerrilla marketing," he replied. "It's a fuck-up."

The problems didn't end there. As Baglow later recalled, word spread around Rockstar that a website called "Fuckstar" had been set up online by a disgruntled former employee. When the team booted up the page, they found a vandalized version of the Rockstar logo—along with the sound of a toilet flushing. Sam and Dan hit the roof.

After hiring an investigator to look into the matter, they realized they were the ones being had. Unbeknownst to them, a *GTA2* marketing exec had planted the fake site as part of an elaborate ruse intended to build buzz for the game. The plan was to leak word that a Rockstar employee had nearly been killed by real gangs while doing research for *GTA2*—but that Rockstar covered up the mess. In retaliation, the scorned Rockstar had supposedly set up this vengeful site, Fuckstar. The elaborate hoax had been kept from the Housers to try to give it legs, but it proved to be yet another misconceived disaster.

For Baglow, the marketing mishaps demonstrated how easily Rockstar could go off the rails. "During *GTA2*, we engaged PR and tried to court controversy, but it was not the slick PR machine that everyone imagined," he later said. "It wasn't the shadowy masters behind the scenes engineering controversy. It was more like things came out, and then we were, like, 'Oh, shit.'"

DAVE JONES had been called a lot of names since he started making games. Genius. Boy wonder. Spielberg. Yet while Rockstar was busy courting trouble with *GTA2* in the United States, he earned a new moniker: sheep abuser. It had happened on the release of a quirky new DMA game called *Tanktics*. The game challenged players to create tanks from bizarre found parts—including sheep, for power.

When word of *Tanktics* got out, animal rights groups protested. "I am sure they could have thought of something else to make the game exciting," said a spokeswoman for one. "It has yet to be shown that a serial killer started by abusing animals in a computer game," a DMA producer responded.

Had it really come to this? Yes, Jones was rich. He had a Ferrari with a vanity plate in front. He saw *GTA* ruling the charts, and geeks were wearing their Rockstar tracksuits around Dundee (one guy gave one to his mother, who was seen sporting a velvety blue get-up while walking her dog). Yet Jones didn't want to be a rock star. He hated the press, the attention, and just wanted to make the next innovative game.

One day, he called in a reporter to show him his dream project: a virtual city. It was something he had wanted initially with *GTA* before the game had gone deep into its criminal direction. Now he was bringing it back. Unlike *GTA*, this world would let players be anyone they choose, from a cop to a businessman. He compared it to "a computerized version of the film *The Truman Show.*"

This as yet untitled game represented the underlying tension between Jones and Sam. Privately, Jones felt that despite their Rockstar posturing, they were increasingly demanding corporate executives at heart. If Rockstar was supposedly the rebel child of Take-Two, the guys seemed more like their parents instead. "There was definitely tension there," he later said. "Should we be making a game to a deadline, or should we be making it to a quality bar?" *GTA2* was proof: a lackluster sequel, in his opinion, that had been rushed out to cash in on the first.

But as far as Rockstar was concerned, they weren't demanding at all. They were just trying to make the greatest possible games. Since Jones had sold his company, the guys in New York were losing patience and wanted to take *GTA* into a new direction: 3D. During a trip to DMA, Sam had become elated when he saw a coder toying around with what the guy called a 2.5D version of the game. Sam's eyes widened as the top-down view on *GTA* suddenly shifted in an isometric way, buildings lengthening, streets receding, until he felt immersed inside it. "Oh, man, if we do this in proper 3D," he said, "it's going be insane!"

He got his chance soon enough. In September 1999, Take-Two bought DMA from Infogrames for $11 million in cash. Rather than enduring a new corporate boss, Jones took the money and vowed to start his own indie company devoted to making the next great franchise—whatever that might be. In the aftermath of the split, Jones and Sam battled over hiring the remaining developers at DMA—with Sam winning the core developers in the end. Take-Two secured the rights for the future *GTA* games and a core team, whom they moved out of Dundee to the hipper locale of Edinburgh for good. This was Rockstar's game now.

9
Rockstar Loft

MESSAGES

Some of your contacts don't like to meet in person
and will give out instructions on certain payphones
around the city. These payphones will appear on
your radar when they want to employ your special
services.

How did you hear about Rockstar Loft? Why do you want to go? If
you could take someone, who would it be? What is it you don't
enjoy about current nightlife in New York? What's the best movie
you've seen in the last two years? Who is your favorite DJ? What has
been the best moment in your life so far?"

Across New York City in the fall of 1999, club kids stood at payphones, answering each of these seven questions as best they could.
They had been lured there by calling a number advertised on fliers that
promoted a mysterious new monthly party called Rockstar Loft. They
figured they were phoning to get the secret location of the bash, but as
they listened to the young person on the other end of the line ticking

off interview questions, they realized that whoever was behind this party had a different mission in mind.

The mission was clear to Rockstar Games the moment the guys decided to launch this event. The idea had come after they moved to New York and became disappointed by the club scene. "I realized there wasn't too terribly much to do in the evenings," Sam sniffed. Similar to the game industry, the club scene wasn't hip enough for their tastes. So they decided to do a party of their own with the help of a famous promoter.

Though it seemed odd for a game company to get into party promotion, the strategy gelled perfectly with the guys' unique ambitions. They wanted to build Rockstar as a lifestyle brand that included a clothing line coming from hip label Haze (baby-T shirts for the ladies and pinkie rings for the boys, available at Urban Outfitters around the United Kingdom) and a tour of the *GTA2* movie at film festivals.

The Rockstar Loft interview process was meant to weed out the players from the punks. "Fatboy Slim would be the wrong answer" to the favorite DJ question, Donovan told Zev Borow at the *New Yorker*. "You could have someone who says *Cool Hand Luke* and someone who says *Notting Hill*," he said, "but the person who says *Notting Hill* could still actually be party-worthy." As Sam added, "The worst thing people can say is 'I'm so-and-so, and I own this company or run this record label, so I deserve to be invited.' We've made a lot of those people very angry."

Sam, shaggy and bearded, and Donovan, tall and bald, were deftly cultivating their public image to personify their games. When hipster magazine *Raygun* paid a visit, Sam and Donovan hammed it up for the photographer, posing on the rooftop in matching blue T-shirts and shades, Sam caught in mid-howl. Sam held up a copy of the game trade magazine with two stiff dudes in suits on the front. "*This* is the game business," he said, derisively, then pointed to himself and Donovan, "this isn't the game business." Donovan added, "Part of what we're trying to get away from is the lone, girlfriendless, pizza-ordering fat guy in the basement. We're just raising the tone of the entertainment to a point that we feel comfortable with."

For the launch of *GTA2* on October 25, 1999, Sam took his show on the road back to London. During an interview with Steve Poole at the *Guardian*, he seemed energized to be back where it all began—his childhood, St. Paul's, BMG. As he drowned a plate of fries in ketchup at a diner, Sam played the part of being a Rockstar to the fullest. He told Poole how he'd been out to a bar in New York and got to chatting with a girl. "There's this game my friends are playing, and they're all talking about it. I wonder if you can help me?" she told him.

"What's it called?" he asked.

"*Grand Theft Auto*," she said.

Sam started dating her. He insisted that even the cops were groupies. "I met the NYPD," he went on, "and they said, 'We think your game's all right.' And I said, 'What about the fact that you kill cops?' and they said, 'Well, you know what? There's a lot of people out there trying to kill cops, and we'd rather they did it in your game than on the street.'"

This felt like their first moment in the sun, and they were basking in it for all it was worth. To celebrate *GTA2*, Rockstar threw a big party in the East End of London. Word spread that Rockstar had invited convicted criminal Freddie "Brown Bread Fred" Foreman to the bash—only to be turned down. The game was apparently too controversial for the man. "As far as I can ascertain," Foreman said, "the video encourages our youth to rob, steal, and murder indiscriminately, and that is something I'm totally opposed to."

The hype seemed to work. The *GTA2* demo was downloaded more than a million times in only its first three weeks. Take-Two announced it would be shipping 1.2 million copies of the game, estimated to bring in $33 million in revenues by the time the company's fourth quarter closed on Halloween.

Sam jetted back to New York in time for the first Rockstar Loft party on Saturday, October 30, 1999. Out of thousands of applicants, only five hundred had made the cut. The chosen ones rushed the secret location in Chelsea, brandishing their pink tickets. Inside, they heard a Parisian DJ cherry-picked by Donovan. Sam and the rest partied late into the night.

Yet the hangover was harder than they expected. When the *New York Times* dismissed the Loft as "The Anti-Elitist Elitist Party," complaining about the surly doorman and the fruit plates, Sam steamed. "It took one article for me—one journalist to say a bunch of dot com yuppies in Ralph Lauren T-shirts in our parties, some really snippy irrelevant bitchy remark," he said. But the experience focused him. They were Rockstar *Games*, after all, not Rockstar Parties. And games were what they had to create. "That other stuff was very important to us until we figured out how hard being a game publisher is, how much time that takes," Sam later said. "Then we suddenly realized, we've got serious proper jobs here."

AFTER THE INITIAL RUSH of *GTA2* was gone, reality quickly set in. Sam got an unexpectedly forlorn visit from two suits at Take-Two, and they weren't happy about *GTA2*. Apparently, the Rockstars had made a youthful miscalculation about the level of their success. The numbers told a more tempered story. The reviews were middling; the sales, disappointing. Sam despaired that another game, *Driver*, seemed to get better reviews just because of the graphics.

Rockstar had erred in its ways—celebrating prematurely, and losing focus. Yet the guys had the gumption to own up to their slip-up and tried to make it a teachable moment. "That was a humbler," Sam told Dan, "don't count your fucking chickens. Don't take anything for granted. That's what we learn from this." If *GTA2* didn't meet their high expectations, then it was time for them to push their games harder than ever before.

There would be no rest. After building Take-Two up from nothing to become a top-twenty publisher, founder Ryan Brant had his sights set on crashing the top ten. He had just the guy to handle the business side, while Sam oversaw the games: Take-Two's new president and director, Paul Eibeler. A street-smart jock from Long Island with a thick New York accent, Eibeler had started out marketing nail-guns for Black & Decker, before getting into software. He brought a pragmatism to whatever he did, looking at office staplers and video games both as consumer products.

Take-Two continued to innovate. Eibeler landed a creative PR deal to get their games promoted in movie theaters around the country. Brant successfully took Take-Two public, using the money to buy smaller companies—from DVD distributors to smaller game publishers. They invested in a small developer called Bungie, owning around 19 percent of the company, which was working on two titles at the time, a shooter called *Oni*, and a little sci-fi game called *Halo* (a demo of which was already blowing the guys away).

With his parent company prospering, Sam's cockiness soared. One day, he showed up at Rockstar's office wearing a T-shirt for EA Sports—the label of Electronic Arts that churned out *Madden* sequel after sequel and represented the corporate machine the game industry had become. "I'm going to work for EA!" he joked.

With his infectious passion, Sam attracted a dream team of employees. He had, as he once put it, "a philosophy of hiring very slowly and hiring people extremely talented and those fit in with our culture and committed to the hard work and the insanity." Few were as committed as Sam's most dogged prodigies: Jeremy Pope and Marc Fernandez.

Pope, a slight and affable young game tester, accepted a pay cut just to be part of Rockstar's renegade band. "We're going to take over," Sam told him, "we're going to be the Def Jam of video games, and no one going to stop us!" Late at night, they'd pop in the latest PlayStation game and crack up. "Can you believe it?" Sam would say. "People are still making games for kids. We want to make games for adults, games that we want to play."

Fernandez, an aspiring filmmaker at nearby New York University, shared a love of film, a clincher for Sam—despite the fact that he preferred mainstream fare over Fernandez's artier tastes. "The real fun shit is *Top Gun*! *Beverly Hills Cop*!" Sam told him.

"Why?" Fernandez said.

"Because it taps into the mainstream," Sam replied. "And if you can create art that communicates to everybody, it's much better than creating art that communicates to five people." Sam reveled in the details of director Michael Mann's action sequences in *Heat*, such as the opening shot of the armored car whizzing across the street. "I want to translate this kind of craftsmanship into a video game," he said.

Sam put Fernandez and Pope on the franchise closest to his heart, *GTA*. Fernandez became the self-described "details guy," in charge of cultural research. This meant everything from making sure that car doors swung open the right way to roaming the streets of Chinatown, taking shots of storefronts for inspiration in the game. Pope would oversee countless hours of play-testing of the game.

Once again, Rockstar would publish the next *GTA* as a subsidiary of Take-Two, overseeing the production and marketing of the game, while the day-to-day development would be handled by the twenty-three coders and artists at DMA in Edinburgh. Sam knew how to bottle the lightning that made *GTA* magic in the first place: by fostering a highly collaborative work environment. As he later said, "Everyone working on the project, from the most junior to the most senior, everyone's opinion is of equal value." They were all Rockstars here.

10
The Worst Place
in America

OVERVIEW
Liberty City is a complete physical universe with
laws, rules, standards, ethics, and morals. They are
yours to shatter.

The moment the boxes arrived at 575 Broadway, the Rockstars hungrily ripped them open. They hurled the packaging to the side and pulled out the little black stealth tower with the ribbed spine down the middle. Each resembled a mini monolith from *2001*, and they were the Neanderthals hooting and hollering and clanging bones. As they plugged in the objects and listened to the hard drives rev to life, they sighed deeply. "Oh, my God," said Sam, "how are we going to do this?"

They had just received the PlayStation 2 development kits, the hardware with which they would create games for Sony's next-generation machine. In the game business, the big three console makers—Sony, Microsoft, and Nintendo—advanced their industry and competition by releasing new platforms every three to five years or so. Players and developers breathlessly awaited this dazzling showcase of new technologies.

Coming in 2000 (first in Japan, then other countries), the PS2 promised the most living, breathing worlds yet. A powerful new central processing unit, nicknamed the "emotion engine," meant uncanny artificial intelligence, characters, and creatures who would move and think more like actual animals. A breakthrough graphics chip would generate more dynamic images in real time, bringing a greater realism and fluidity to the scenes.

Because the PS2 could support DVD-ROMs, instead of only CD-ROMs, games could now store and stream troves more data—animations, music, environments. "Imagine a truck rolling into the level," Phil Harrison of Sony told Sam enthusiastically, "and the back of the truck bursts open and suddenly fifty people are leaping out of the truck at you!"

With the PS2 in his tool shed, Sam knew exactly what kind of world he wanted for the next *Grand Theft Auto*: 3D. In video games, the term *3D* didn't mean the same thing as in movies—with exploding watermelons flying off the screen when the viewer wore stereoscopic glasses. Instead, it was a misnomer, shorthand for the sort of vivid, deep, and immersive worlds popularized by games such as *EverQuest* and *Tomb Raider*. Although Jones had always trumpeted gameplay over graphics for *GTA*, no one stood in Sam's way anymore. Even better, they didn't need to spend long hours developing a new software engine for the game. They could simply license one—called Renderware—that would be perfect for *GTA*.

Sam had begun to develop a vital skill for success: intuitively knowing how to exploit the future without losing sight of the past. More important, he trusted himself to make the right call without second-guessing his gut. For the next *GTA*, that meant staying true to what made the franchise so special in the first place—the freedom, the choices, the central idea of casting players as outlaws and giving them choices for how to behave. By marrying *GTA* with PS2, Sam had a new mission with which to push their games: "to make the first interactive gangster movie," as he said.

GTA III would be the first of a proposed trilogy based on each of the three cities established in the first game: Liberty City, Vice City, and San Andreas. They'd start with Liberty City, all the more perfect because it was based on their new home, New York. Around the office, Sam ranted about the movies and the TV shows he wanted to emulate: *The Getaway. Heat.* HBO's new mob hit, *The Sopranos.*

Yet at the same time, Sam was also pushing himself to go beyond the limits of film. He swore off the experiments with live-action sequences, as they had tried in *GTA2.* "I'm not going to fuck with video, I'm not going to fuck with film," Sam told Fernandez. "I'm going to do everything within the world of the game engine."

To bring the 3D world to life, they rented out a motion-capture studio in the Brooklyn Navy Yard. Actors would be filmed performing the parts, then the scenes would be translated into animations within the game. Rockstar hired a fearless young Iranian-born director named Navid Khonsari to direct the scenes. Before Khonsari went out, Sam and Dan kept repeating their mantra for *GTA III*: "real, real, real."

A stylish guy with close-cropped hair and rectangular glasses, Khonsari knew this meant nailing the most iconic moment in the game: the carjacking. He molded a car out of sandbags and gymnast bars, piecing them together like Legos. He added weights to the bars, to make the doors feel heavy to open. When the actors came into the studio, he quietly told the driver to hold onto the steering wheel for dear life. Then he secretly told the other actor to yell at the top of his lungs when he ran up to the car. Khonsari watched with glee as the scene unfolded, with the driver freaking out—as expected—at hearing the unscripted scream.

Soon afterward, Sam, Dan, King, Donovan, and the rest gathered nervously to see an early prototype of the carjacking scene. Despite their bravado, they still smarted from the insults over the early *GTA*'s graphics and hoped they could finally leave Lara Croft in the dust. Onscreen, the silent scene appeared in wireframe form because the rest of the art had not yet been completed. An orange car appeared, with two men inside. Suddenly, a blue wireframe man stepped up to the side, yanked open the door and pulled the passenger out, then tossed him to the ground. The driver then fled in a panic, as the carjacker took the wheel. "Holy shit!" King exclaimed.

It worked. They weren't just looking down on Liberty City anymore, they had been teleported inside it. They watched the carjacker over and over again, grabbing the wheel and taking off just as Rockstar was determined to drive their industry.

THE ONLY THING more empowering than playing a video game was creating it. Reality was imperfect, but the simulation could be controlled. You could put in what you wanted and leave out the rest. You started with a city of your choice, then filled it with the people you designed. The cars you wanted to drive. The shops you wanted to frequent. The music you wanted to hear. And when the weather wasn't up to snuff, you could change that to your liking, too. No matter how much freedom players had in your game, they were living in your world.

GTA III started with Liberty City, which would be "the worst place in America," as the Rockstars labeled it, in the best possible ways. They would simulate New York City—not the actual one outside their door, but the larger-than-life fantasy that, in some ways, was more real. They broke Liberty City into three areas: an industrial section, similar to Brooklyn and Queens; a commercial center that resembled Manhattan; and burbs that looked like Jersey. As players drove around, they'd pass seedy and awesome places: the fish market and the Laundromat, the ammo shops and the Pay 'n' Sprays, the Italian restaurants and the busy streets.

With so many places to go, they coded the transit system with which to get there: the tunnels and the trains and the bridges and the boats. Using the Renderware engine, the PS2 created lavish blue waves that crashed and rolled with lifelike physics. The water reacted to the stimulus, too, creating weather systems of storms and rains. A thick Bergmanian fog rolled into a makeshift city block running on the PC screen. And with weather, that meant they could cycle through different times of the day—with missions in the daylight and at night. When the sun set over Liberty City, the creeps would hit the streets.

The muscle power of the PS2 transformed the experience of exploring in the game. The physics of the cars changed, based on the size of the rides, with even greater precision than in the early iterations of the games: the sluggish minivans, the nimble sports cars, the cabs and the ambulances and the ice cream trucks. With eighteen collision points on each car, the vehicles smashed and crumbled even more realistically, too. In the past they'd had only a handful of speaking characters in the games, but this time they'd have more than sixty. That meant scaling up from ten thousand to more than a hundred thousand lines of dialogue, from a pedestrian shouting, "Haven't you got respect for your elders?" as he got shoved, to a driver in a fender bender screaming, "Watch the wheels, gringo!"

As the city teemed to life, so did the story. Dan drew from his literature studies at Oxford, meticulously shaping the narrative of the game. The action began with the player cast as a nameless crook getting freed from a police truck on his way to prison. From there, he'd have to work his way back up through the underworld, running more than eighty missions for increasingly powerful bosses and gangs.

Rockstar wasn't limited to dispatching in-game missions over clunky phone calls anymore. This time, players would get jobs by meeting a motley crew of gangsters in person. For continuity, Rockstar scripted cut-scenes, interstitial cinematic shorts sandwiched between the missions to, say, burn down an enemy's hangout or whack a rival.

Compared to *GTA* and *GTA2*, the cinematics added a layer of drama and intrigue. It was one thing to pick up a phone, and another to sneak through the back door of a sex club to get a job.

To provide voice-overs for the parts, they continued to pioneer the use of celebrities, and hired some of their favorite character actors: Michael Madsen, Kyle MacLachlan, Debi Mazar. One day on set, they marveled when one of their biggest heroes walked in the door, Frank Vincent. The silver-haired tough guy had been in three of their favorite Scorsese flicks ever: *Raging Bull*, *Goodfellas*, and *Casino*, as well as *The Sopranos*. Now he was here to do dialogue for a mob boss named Salvatore Leone in their game. He took one look at these scruffy Brits and said in his thick New York accent, "I don't know shit about video games. I don't know what the fuck this is." Khonsari reassured him, "It's no different than a movie."

Balancing the nearly eighty missions with the open-ended freedom wasn't an either/or proposition. "I thought people would like to do both," Dan said, "[have] some time hanging out . . . and sometimes following the game through its path." There had always been a built-in sort of morality to *GTA*, with a player's wanted level rising according to his crimes. In *GTA III*, players didn't even have to be the bad guys at all. They could drive an ambulance or a cab around town, completing little mini missions that boosted their standing. The choice to pursue good or evil was in the paws of the gamer.

For King, the open world of *GTA III* felt not only freeing but autobiographical. "It was about kind of mirroring what life is for us growing up," he later said. "You are running around and, whether you like it or not, you are living on the other side of the fence. So instead of rescuing the princess at the end of the dungeon, you're driving cars and listening to music that's engaging."

Buoyed by the increased fidelity of their cheeky outlaw world, Rockstar turned up the volume on the sex and violence, too. Coders wrote a script that allowed players to snipe limbs off pedestrians, leaving them in puddles of blood. One day, Pope booted up a new build of the game when he noticed a new pedestrian on the side of the street—a hooker in thigh-high fishnet stockings and a bra underneath an open shirt. There had never been anything like this in a game before. When he pulled his car up, she leaned over. He let her climb in his car, then he drove off to a side street and waited. He saw his money go down, representing her taking his cash. Slowly the car began to rock, as his health meter soared.

Yet it didn't take long to make a certain leap of logic. In the game, players could beat up pedestrians and steal their money. So why not steal the cash back from the hookers after they had sex? Soon enough, a player at the office had pulled the hooker back out of the car after their tryst and pummeled her into a bloody heap—as his cash refilled. "Wow," Pope thought, "people will love this."

No matter how edgy *GTA* became, Sam stood by it. "You often can feel like you're doing things nobody is going to appreciate since the games are full of thousands of arcane details," he confided to a game reporter one day. "If you start thinking, 'Is this one really important?' you have to kill that in your head.'"

IT WAS A GRAY day inside Liberty City. Rain poured down on the Callahan Bridge, casting the buildings in a wispy haze. Cars streamed up and down the highway—the buses and the police cars, the sentinels and the patriots. Sam knew just which one he wanted, the blue banshee with the white stripe down the middle. He jogged up beside it, then tapped the triangle button on his controller as he ripped open the door and tossed the driver to the side. "He's taking my car!" the driver cried, as Sam held down the X button, flooring it.

Tapping the rectangular button with his left pointer finger, he flipped through the stations. There were nine of them now, one for every mood. *Click.* The subtitle "Double Clef FM" on top of the screen. The strains of opera. *Click.* Flashback 95.6 with Debbie Harry singing

"Rush, Rush." *Click*. Game Radio FM, underground hip-hop. Royce rapping "I'm the King." Sam tapped the X button and accelerated.

He wasn't just playing, he was observing. This was his world and it had to be perfect. His eyes and ears scanned every detail rushing past him in the game. The hum of the accelerator. The squeal of the tires and little black tire tracks when he took a corner. The splat of pedestrians under the wheel. The way the hood flew up off the front, exposing the metallically intestinal engine, followed by a terrible stream of smoke.

The guys at DMA had coded the physics to let players drive over lampposts, knocking them down to the ground so that nothing would stop their pace. Sam clipped the lampposts like pathetic sprigs, as his wheels jumped a curb for a short-cut through a green, tree-lined park. "I'm an old lady, for Christ's sake!" shouted a ped as Sam raced by.

Once he hit the highway, that's when he did it. Tapped the Select button to change the camera view of the action, which the DMA guys had coded for the first time into *GTA*. *Click*. First person POV, as if he were strapped on the hood of the car. *Click*. Third person, overhead looking down on the ride. *Click*. His favorite, Cinematic mode. It appeared as if the camera were saddled on the lower left side of the car like a chase from a film. As Sam tore through the town, the camera automatically switched to other cinematic angles, as if some brilliant invisible William Friedkin was directing.

"This is the future of moviemaking," Sam believed. "Because here's my set, I can go anywhere and put my camera anywhere. I can do anything again and again and again from any angle I want." The more he played *GTA III*, though, the more he felt something inside him change. He was twenty-eight now. A man living his childhood fantasy. Long after he first saw Michael Caine and his mom zooming down the streets in *Get Carter*, he had been fascinated by action films. Now as a pedestrian flew over the hood of his car, and the sun beamed down in its simulated brilliance, he was the star of his own revolutionarily cinematic game.

He wasn't merely watching a movie, he was inside it—and this realization made him feel as if he'd never be able to watch a movie the same way again. Games weren't about one person's authorial vision. They were stories told by a new generation of creators and players in a language all their own. "To me, as a film nut, there was something about *GTA III* that just drew a line in the sand between games and movies," Sam recalled, "and it felt like this is us taking over now."

11
State of Emergency

> **GETTING AROUND**
> Liberty City is full of many different kinds of cars and
> vehicles, all of which are yours for the taking . . .
> approach the car and press the triangle button. Be
> warned, while some drivers will be scared and hand
> over their vehicle without too much resistance, oth-
> ers may not be too happy about it and will put up a
> fight.

A car cut past the palms of Miami, Florida. City of vice. The drug
dealers in the art deco alleyway. The players in their fancy cars.
The rollerblading models, women and men in thongs. The depravity
pulsed like neon outside Jack Thompson's window as he made his way
home, but the nearness only served to remind him of his fight.

He had come a long way since his crusade began, besting rappers 2
Live Crew and Ice-T and taking his battle against violent video games
to court and *60 Minutes*. Every time he walked into his house, he knew
why he was on this mission: his son, Johnny. As a stay-at-home dad,
Thompson had enjoyed a frontline view of Johnny's childhood. When

he looked into the eyes of his boy, he saw a future he desperately wanted to protect. Although most parents shared that feeling, Thompson gave his life over to that fight.

Despite coming from completely different worlds, Thompson had something fundamental in common with Sam Houser. They were both obsessed with the same kind of game. Thompson was as committed to destroying the new generation of violent games as Sam was to creating them, and neither of them would let anyone or anything stand in their way.

While Rockstar brought *GTA III* to life, the controversy over violent video games had reached a new peak. Videos and diaries of the Columbine killers surfaced, including one shot of Eric Harris comparing his rampage to the video game *Doom*. Thompson made the rounds, warning viewers on *NBC News* about the causal link between violent games and school shootings. He was playing to a powerful and vulnerable audience—other moms and dads. No matter what side of the political spectrum, so many of them shared the same concern that a strange new world online was spinning out of control. The Internet and video games had become synonymous with sex and violence, respectively.

Even more daunting was the fact that so many parents didn't know how to gain access to these worlds well or at all. The fact that their kids were seemingly running free behind the wheel only made it seem more out of control. This was not a stereotype of out-of-touch adults. These were decent people with sympathetic desires: to protect their kids, just as Jack wanted to protect his boy. Based on the escalating number of media requests, Thompson knew he had struck a nerve.

He realized this when Tom Brokaw asked the presidential candidates about the Columbine tapes during the 2000 Republican primary. "Do you think that the gun industry, the video game industry, and Hollywood have any role in what happened?" Brokaw said.

"There is a problem with the heart of America," replied Texas governor George W. Bush. "One of the great frustrations in being governor is I wish I knew of a law that'd make people love one another, because

I'd sign it." Though a fellow Republican, Thompson felt his stomach twist. "If a presidential candidate was not troubled enough by the entertainment industry's role in Columbine to want to do something about it," he later wrote, "he would also not be troubled by the overall coarsening of our current culture."

Ironically, he thought, the Democrats had waged a stronger fight against games. President Clinton had called for an FTC investigation into the marketing of violent entertainment to children. The committee on the Judiciary for the U.S. Senate released findings that accused the entertainment industry of marketing harmful products to kids—85 percent of thirteen- to sixteen-year-olds, it determined, had been able to buy M-rated games.

Thompson's blood boiled. What could he do? Lawsuits were still unproved. A federal judge had dismissed the suit filed against a group of entertainment and computer game companies by the families of three girls killed in Paducah—despite Thompson's efforts to link the violent media with Carneal's rampage. "We find that it is simply too far a leap from shooting characters on a video screen (an activity undertaken by millions) to shooting people in a classroom (an activity undertaken by a handful, at most)," the judge wrote. A $5 billion suit filed on behalf of the families of Columbine victims was pending against companies that included Nintendo of America, Sega of America, Sony Computer Entertainment, AOL Time Warner, and *Doom*'s creators, id Software.

Thompson looked to another Democrat, vice presidential candidate Joe Lieberman, dubbed "Mr. Clean" by *Entertainment Weekly* magazine, to engage a political response. Lieberman's Twenty-First Century Media Accountability Act would standardize ratings in the software and movie industries so that parents could better protect their kids from what Thompson's ally, former army ranger Lieutenant Colonel Dave Grossman, called "murder simulators." Retailers who sold violent games to kids would face $10,000 in fines.

Although the Interactive Digital Software Association reported that the majority of game buyers were older than seventeen, the politicians threatened to legislate. "We're trying to do everything we can to keep those games that are not suitable for kids out of the hands of kids," said Senator Herbert Kohl, the cosponsor of the Media Accountability Act. Presidential candidate Al Gore, in a page-one story in the *New York Times*, gave the entertainment industry "six months to clean up their act," he said, or else. "If I'm entrusted with the presidency," Gore said, "I am going to do something about this."

Doug Lowenstein, the game association leader, argued that the industry had long been addressing this concern through its voluntary Entertainment Software Ratings Board, which evaluated and rated game content. "The FTC's own data says that in more than 80 percent of cases, parents are involved in the purchase or rental of games," he said. "Parents are engaged and that's where responsibility has to lie."

Thompson heard it all and seethed. Slowly but surely, he was building a file on medical research about violent games: a Kansas State University scientist who used functional magnetic resonance imaging to scan the brains of young kids and found that violent images triggered traumatic memories, a cover story in *Contemporary Pediatrics* on "How Violent Games May Violate Children's Health," and more. He would not sit around and wait for legislation to protect Johnny or wish for a law to make people love one another. He would play this game the only way he knew how: by fighting to the end. "Others in the decency war are tipping windmills," he said. "I'm out to destroy them."

DUST SWIRLED as Jeeps tore through the desert. Inside the cars, young men in camouflage clutched their 9-millimeter Glock handguns tightly as they aimed out the windows. *Bam! Bam! Bam!* They fired at their targets into the heat. Yet these weren't soldiers on a mission. They were gamer journalists on a junket. With competition heating up, game publishers were engaged in a meta-war to win the press. All-expense-paid trips like this had become more commonplace and outrageous. Reporters got flown to Disney World, to Alcatraz. Some got to barrel-roll in an F-14.

Today, Rockstar Games had taken them here to the Arizona desert to promote its upcoming racing title, *Smuggler's Run*. The game, which challenged players to smuggle cargo in dune buggies and rally cars, was due as a launch title for the PS2 in October. To pump up the reporters, Rockstar devised this adventurous trip, including the reporters' very own drive-by target shooting.

While work continued on *GTA III*, the guys at Rockstar were busy mastering their meta-game as bad-boy marketers. It wasn't just for fun; for Rockstar, selling games was all about style. They got their share of associated press, only not in the ways they intended. Word had begun leaking out about another Rockstar title in development called *State of Emergency*. Sam signed up the title at the 1999 E3 show, when a raffish for Rockstar, Scot named Kirk Ewing gave him a one-sheet write-up and a punk rock pitch. "It's called *State of Emergency*," Ewing said, "the citizens are revolting."

Ewing figured that'd be enough for Sam. Growing up in the Scottish game industry that emerged out of DMA, Ewing was one of a generation of developers energized by *GTA*'s fuck-it-all attitude and success. Inspired, he and a friend dreamed up a freeform game based on one of his old favorite pastimes, a bar fight. The game had started out as a kind of entertaining physics experiment. Ewing focused on simulating the fluid dynamics of crowd movement, the visceral thrill of autonomous objects hurling around.

Yet in the long months of development under Sam, the game had grown into something more primal, as Ewing put it, "a massive beat 'em up." Gamers played an urban dude who was unleashed into a mob where every character had to pummel his way to survival. Sam loved it. "This is it!" he told Ewing. "This is the natural evolution of what's going on. It's going to be massive!"

Picking up the ball, the guys at Rockstar began hyping *State of Emergency* to the press as a "social disturbance simulator," but then a real social disturbance unexpectedly got in the way. One day in May 2001, shortly after receiving a demo of the game, a reporter from the *Tacoma News Tribune* in Washington called a Rockstar publicist and said, "Hey, I just played *State of Emergency*, and it looks like the Seattle riots." He was referring to the uprising that had occurred during the World Trade Organization convention in November 1999, a violent clash from which the city was still reeling. The Rockstar PR guy, not thinking much of the observation, said, "Yeah, it probably does look like that."

The next day, Sam and the rest saw the page-one headline: "*Video Gamers* Can *Experience WTO All Over Again—PlayStation 2*" from the Tribune. The story said how "the game borrows heavily from, and adds significantly to, the World Trade Organization riots in downtown Seat-tle in the fall of 1999." It quoted appalled politicians. "If you want your child to become a violent anarchist, this is a great training game," said Representative Mary Lou Dickerson sarcastically. The reporter added, "A spokesman for Rockstar, who asked to remain anonymous, admitted last week the game had strong ties to the WTO riots."

Back when Max Clifford fed his hamster about *GTA* to the press, this kind of coverage had been a dream—purposely drummed up to fuel controversy and attention. Yet times had changed, in the United States especially. Extreme content in a video game could dramatically lower sales, because high-profile retailers such as Wal-Mart and Best Buy refused to shelve certain games, especially those with Adults Only ratings.

Despite Rockstar's best efforts to deflate the WTO rumors, however, the story spread fast around the world, getting picked up by Reuters, among other media outlets, which said, "Thanks to Rockstar Games . . . would-be hooligans can vent their anti-corporate venom by punching out riot cops and looting storefronts from the comfort of their own sofas." With the next E3 video game expo in Los Angeles days away, the guys at Rockstar had bigger concerns: unveiling their outlaw fantasy, *GTA III*, to the world.

HIGH ABOVE THE SUNSET STRIP in Los Angeles, the party raged. It was taking place in the presidential suite of the Château Marmont, the ultra-hip hotel off Sunset Boulevard where John Belushi famously overdosed. The usual celebrities weren't inside, though. This was Rockstar's party now, just one of several suites the guys took over during the E3 convention in May 2001 when *GTA III* would be revealed.

By day, they played ping-pong out by the pool, as models cut through the turquoise blue water. By night, they brought the bash to the top floor. They were Rockstars, with a fleet of blacked-out Mercedes downstairs waiting to whisk them off to any club. Ewing later recalled "going from that party to a tour of L.A. at 120 miles per hour. I felt like the president."

The pressure was on to stand out. Despite selling more than 4.5 million copies of the *GTA* games, Rockstar had to prove its muster. *GTA* was still considered a cult franchise, and the guys were angling to go mainstream. Moreover, they even had imitators to contend with, as other crime racing titles such as *Driver* and *Crazy Taxi* had watered down the market. Going into the convention, they figured that two acclaimed Japanese games were destined to beat them, no matter how well they showed: *Devil May Cry*, a demon-fighting game, and the stealthy action title, *Metal Gear Solid 2*.

This time, instead of matching tracksuits, they arrived at the show wearing matching Pantone T-shirts with a picture of Don Simpson in T-shirt and jeans on the front, a tiny Rockstar logo, and Simpson's prescription drug bill on the back. They sauntered past giant screens of wizards and warriors, the pro skaters on the full-size ramps promoting the latest Tony Hawk games, past the light sabers and the Pokemons and the portly guys with digital cameras shooting every scantily clad "booth babe," as the gamers called them, in dominatrix gear.

The Rockstar booth went for chilled understatement. It looked like a Miami lounge, white curtains and couches and a clipboard-wielding PR lackey keeping out the riff-raff. PlayStation 2 stations had been set up around the lounge, showing *State of Emergency*, *GTA III*, and other Take-Two games. Donovan worried about the difficulty of distilling a pitch on *GTA* to the necessary thirty seconds. "You had to experience the whole thing because it was so personal," he said.

Donovan stalked the booth like an NBA center, hyping *GTA III* as the necessary alternative to the geeky role-playing games such as *EverQuest* that populated the show. "I think the video game industry was actually crying out for us," he told a reporter from *Wired*. "We don't make games about Puff-the-fucking-Magic Dragon." He insisted that *GTA III* was meant for a new generation.

Yet despite all of Rockstar's cockiness, the gamers weren't listening. Sam and the guys watched as players dutifully tried *GTA III* for a few moments—and walked away. Some people recoiled as they watched the scenes of the main character sniping off pedestrians' heads from rooftops. Gamers had seen blood and gore before, but not in such a realistic setting—and they didn't know what to make of it. "Are you kidding me?" one said in disgust to Pope. Even Phil Harrison of Sony left nonplussed. "It looked like a mess," he later said.

There was one Rockstar game getting plenty of attention, however: *State of Emergency*. Crowds formed around the demo, as they maneuvered the stocky little fat guy in the wife-beater undershirt and the baggy shorts. Gamers hooted and hollered as the guy threw chairs at passersby, while buildings burst into flames from the riot. Maybe the press from the WTO connection had paid off, after all. Pope heard one of *State of Emergency*'s developers snipe, "No one cares about your game. Everyone's talking about our game."

As Pope noticed by the dour expression on Sam's face, the boss man seemed furious. *State of Emergency* was Sam's game but not his baby. The response only made him more convinced about ensuring *GTA III's* success. He would work harder than ever before, and he expected everyone on his team to do the same. Pushing boundaries would take all of their energy, together. Their fight was inherently sympathetic, they thought, because they had the cause of every gamer at stake. "Well," Sam said, "we'd better put the fucking hammer down now."

GTA III did manage to pique the interest of one very important player at E3, Doug Lowenstein, who came by for a look. Still reeling from the Columbine fallout, the game association president worried about any products that would add more fuel to the fire. The second he saw cars getting jacked in *GTA III*, he knew he was in for a fight. "This is going to be a problem, this is going to be controversial, this is going to trigger negative attacks on the industry," he thought. "Oh shit."

"OKAY," 8-Ball said, "let's do this thing!"

It was another overcast day in Liberty City, and Sam was playing *GTA III*. He had maneuvered his character to see 8-Ball, an African American bomb expert and buddy inside *GTA III*. Despite his neatly shaved head and natty blue-and-white jacket, 8-Ball didn't look so good. His hands were wrapped in bandages, the result of a fiery ambush by the Colombian Cartel, but now he was coming to Sam's aid.

Sam was running through a mission called Bomb Da Base. The goal, as laid out in a cinematic cut-scene from Salvatore Leone, was to take out the cartel's center of operation: a boat on the docks being used to churn out a drug called SPANK. "I'm asking you to destroy that SPANK factory as a personal favor to me, Salvatore Leone," the Don explained from a leather chair in his well-appointed home.

Sam had just sped through the streets, taking out a few peds along the way, past the hookers and the ammo shops, just to get to his accomplice who had the fire power he needed. "I can set this baby to detonate," 8-Ball said, "but I still can't use a piece with these hands." 8-Ball waved a gun ineffectually in the air. "Here, this rifle should help you pop some heads!"

Ever since playing a game called *Star Fox 64* on the Nintendo 64, a shooter that had him fighting to protect his wingmen, Sam had dreamed of creating in games the kind of sympathetic characters one finds in movies and novels. Such emotions had been largely elusive in the industry.

Yet as he stood on the rooftop later, watching 8-Ball detonate the bombs on the SPANK factory after he clipped the cartel, Sam felt ecstatic. The ship exploded into flames, as 8-Ball fled in safety. A cool wave of relief washed over Sam, knowing his friend was okay. The emotion was real. *GTA III* had successfully brought the feeling to life.

But reality was about to get in the way. At 2 a.m. on September 11, the *GTA* fan site Gouranga.com posted a chat transcript between fans and Dan Houser. "Q: Will we be able to hijack things besides cars?" one gamer asked. "A: Boats . . . tanks . . . ambulances, taxis, buses, ice cream vans," Dan replied. "Just not the big stuff—choppers . . . jumbo jets and oil tankers, you are a criminal, not an airline pilot."

Seven hours later, Sam stood at his apartment window, watching an awful black cloud of smoke choke downtown where two planes had just flown into the World Trade Center. Amid the fear and disgust, he couldn't help feeling as if he were in a movie. "It was the most real action-movie thing I'd ever seen because it fucking well was real," he later recalled.

With Rockstar's offices only a mile away from the site, the company reeled. "Everyone had someone who had an uncle or brother" who was impacted by the attack. Eibeler later recalled, "and for a young company it was devastating." When Pope walked into the office for the first time soon afterward, he had to flash his ID—strangers wouldn't be allowed into Rockstar anymore. As he made his way through the loft to the back, he wondered who the closely shorn guy was sitting at Sam's desk—until he realized it was Sam. Sam told Pope he had shaved his long hair clean because he didn't want anyone to get the wrong idea. "Those fucking terrorists," Sam muttered. "I don't want to look anything like those terrorists!"

Neither could their games. As the city reeled from the attacks, Sam and Dan wondered whether they should even release *GTA III* at all. Maybe it was too soon. "This beautiful city has been attacked," Sam thought, "and now we're making a violent crime drama set in a city that's not unlike New York City. My God, I'm terrorized where I live, and on top of that, we've got this fucking crazy game that is not exactly where people's heads are at right now."

Instead of shelving the game, they, along with Sony, decided to make changes instead. No more sniper rifle shots to the limbs with body parts flying—too gory. No more buildings that looked like the World Trade Center in the game. Sam e-mailed Gouranga.com apologizing for the added delays. "Rest assured the game will be phenomenal," he told them. "As ever, we really appreciate your continued support."

As they tried to recover from 9/11, people across America flipped on their TVs looking for escape. Some caught an unusual ad. In the background, a soprano sings the Italian aria "Mio Babbino Caro" from the 1918 opera *Gianni Schicchi*. Lyrical cut-scenes play on top, like an animated trailer for a mafia film the viewers have never seen. A sleek blue-and-white sports car peels around a corner. A foot chase of a guy with a shotgun running after a woman—until she turns and shoots him down. Then the title fades in on red lowercase, "*grand theft auto III*."

The ad promised something strange and new: less a game and more like a film you could control. Viewers watched the stoic antihero in his black leather jacket, walking through a lavish home as the Don, Salvatore Leone, puts his arm over the antihero's shoulder and makes a pact. This was the cut-scene setting up the "Bomb Da Base" mission, the one that had inspired Sam not long ago. Leone's promise was, in effect, the promise of Rockstar and the new era of gaming they wanted to usher in.

"If you do this for me, you'll be a made man," Leone says, "anything you want."

In living rooms around the country, on sofas and chairs, in bedrooms and dorm rooms, a generation of players clutched their Mountain Dew cans tightly, and said, "Hell yeah."

Bring it.

12
Crime Pays

WANTED LEVEL

"Please welcome Colin Hanks!"

It was January 16, 2002, and Jon Stewart, the host of the *Daily Show*, eagerly greeted his next guest. Hanks, the boyish twenty-four-year-old actor and son of star Tom Hanks, was in town to promote his latest film, *Orange County*. Yet what he really wanted to talk about was a new video game, *Grand Theft Auto III*, the mention of which elicited a burst of applause from one gamer in the crowd. "He knows what I'm talking about!" Hanks deadpanned.

Stewart sank his head in his hands, laughing, as Hanks recounted his adventures with mobsters and hookers. "If you want your money back when she gets out of the car, you run her over," Hanks continued, "problem solved!"

Stewart replied, "Now I know what to ask for, for the holidays!"

He wasn't the only one. *GTA III* was an immediate sensation. Game reviewers raved. *GameSpy* called it "an insanely well-made and fun game to play. . . . proof of the power behind the PS2's hardware." *GamePro* magazine said it "makes an offer you can't refuse: Live a life of crime and reap the rewards that come with it." *Game Informer* said it "shatters the standards set by its predecessors." *Entertainment Weekly* deemed it "every bad boy's dream (and every parent's nightmare)."

Players swapped tales of their adventures in the game as if they had taken place in real life. "The first few days," posted one online, "I did nothing but run around the city stealing cars and running over hookers." Though women played the game, *GTA III* was undeniably the stuff of dudes—raucous, enraged, frenzied. The game gave even the most powerless person a way to unleash his most violent fantasies, but in a world made from pixels where no one real got hurt. The most common reaction to flattening a pedestrian during the game wasn't a gasp, after all, it was laughter. To suggest that the game could cause players to run over people in real life would only make them laugh harder.

A commentator on National Public Radio swooned about driving aimlessly within the game with the radio cranked while the sun set on the horizon. "You become like Emerson's transparent eyeball," he gushed, "seeing everything, consisting of nothing." For Dr. Henry Jenkins, the director of comparative media studies at the Massachusetts Institute of Technology, *GTA III* marked a new frontier. "Now that we've colonized physical space," he said, "the need to have new frontiers is deeply in the games. *Grand Theft Auto* expands the universe."

Fueled by reviews and word-of-mouth buzz, *GTA III* became the fastest-selling, highest-grossing title for PlayStation 2 with more than six million games sold around the world. Take-Two's stock soared from $7 a share in October 2001, three weeks before the launch of *GTA III*, to almost $20 a share in January 2002. At one point, Rockstar held the top spots on the game charts, with *GTA III* number one, followed by its dark thriller, *Max Payne*. Including these two games and *State of Emergency*, Rockstar soon had three titles in the top ten.

GTA III permeated the culture at large, just as Sam had always dreamed. The shout-outs on the *Daily Show.* Mix-tapes in New York with *GTA* sound bites. Even ecstasy pills allegedly floating around clubs with the Rockstar logo, not a company PR campaign but simply an act of love, it seemed, from fans. Rockstar also, got its due from the peers who once mocked them for having the audacity to name themselves Rockstar. When Rockstar producer Jeronimo Barrera, dressed in a zoot suit, accepted the trophy for game of the year from the industry's Game Developer's Choice Award, he said, "This is to show that video games don't have to be about hobgoblins and dwarves!"

GTA III's success helped propel the U.S. game business to a record $9.4 billion in sales for 2001, a 40 percent increase from the previous year—and enough to dwarf the $8.38 billion in film box office sales. Sony, which had signed the *GTA* franchise exclusively to its consoles, rode the success to the top of the industry, outperforming rivals Microsoft and Nintendo, who had just released their new consoles, the Xbox and GameCube, respectively, in November (Xbox, ironically, was riding high on the success of *Halo*, the sci-fi shooter Take-Two had relinquished to Microsoft, after the company bought the game's creators, Bungie). Before long, Sony had shipped almost 30 million PS2 systems.

Sony's Phil Harrison marveled at *GTA III*'s huge reorders and crossover success. Like Sam, he had long wanted to expand the market for gamers, and Rockstar had tapped into something broad. "It demonstrated that Rockstar was thinking quite deeply about culture and the way that people would play the game," he said. "*GTA* probably defined the zeitgeist better than anything else."

In Japan, home to Sony's headquarters, *GTA III* represented a seismic shift within the country's storied game culture and industry. Nintendo's two decades of family-friendly rule seemed quaint compared to the naughty new age of *GTA III*. Yet the changes raised eyebrows at Sony, too. Government ministries began to question Sony's execs. At a dinner party, the wife of Sony's founder was said to have admonished the PlayStation group over *GTA III*. "Oh," she said, "I hear your games are very violent."

Harrison and others in the West did their best to reassure their counterparts in Japan. "Look," Harrison would say, "if we're going to be a full-spectrum entertainment platform, we're supposed to have everything from Mickey Mouse to Mickey Rourke. We have to have a complete spectrum of entertainment on the platform if we're going to be truly mass market." Japan formed its own Computer Entertainment Ratings Organization, similar to the ESRB in the United States, to help monitor the new generation of games.

As outrage spread over *GTA III*—particularly, the hooker cheat— the game became a lightning rod around the world. It exposed the bias and confusion reserved for this young medium. Though similar battles had played out before—over pinball, comic books, rock music, and *Dungeons & Dragons*—this meant little to the public at large. Still viewed as a children's toy, video games were deemed an unacceptable forum for adult content. Although people clearly understood the difference between movies and TV shows meant for children or adults, video games didn't get the same consideration. The fact that *GTA III* was explicitly and voluntarily rated M for Mature (with a mandatory label on its ads and covers) fell flat.

In Australia, the Office of Film and Literature Classification Board, the country's federal body responsible for rating media products, denied it a rating due to its depiction of what it classified as "acts of sexualized violence." *GTA III* was not only illegal to sell, but illegal to view. Retailers faced up to two years in jail and tens of thousands of dollars in fines for even displaying it. Players were told to bring the games back to the stores or face criminal charges if they were to show the game to others.

In England, the director of a child advocacy group called Children Now warned that games threatened to desensitize kids to violence. A psychologist at the University of Northumbria said "newer breeds of increasingly sophisticated games encourage solitary behaviour and tendencies towards rebellion." When the National Institute on Media and the Family, a nonprofit child advocacy group in the United States, released its annual Video and Computer Game Report in December 2001, *GTA III* was picked as the number-one game for parents to avoid. "We have enough violence in the real world," said Senator Kohl. "We don't need to wrap it up in a bow and give it to children as a present."

U.S. representative Joe Baca, a Democrat from Southern California, introduced the Protect Children from Video Game Sex and Violence Act of 2002, which would make it illegal to sell an M-rated game to anyone under seventeen without permission from parents. "We saw what happened in Columbine," Baca warned on CNN. "These are kids that are being programmed. They play the video games, they take the action and the character; they began to play that character, and then they began to commit those particular crimes. It's a shame when we have *Grand Theft Auto III*. We have another one as well—we have the *State of Emergency*. We look at a lot of the gang-by shooting that goes on, the riots that are going on in the immediate area. We have got to stop this."

Over at the IDSA, Doug Lowenstein tried in vain to counter what he called "the exaggerated claims of ideologically oriented politicians and media critics who favor putting government, not parents, in charge of the entertainment used by our kids." Yet he refused to jump to the defense of the industry's most controversial publisher. "We shouldn't be spokespersons for the Housers," Lowenstein later said. "That's their game."

CHEESE BALL! Cheese ball! Cheese ball!

It was late one cold November night at Radio Mexico, the dive bar and restaurant downtown in New York City. Multicolored balloons with streamers bobbed against the low ceiling. Holiday lights wrapped the windows. Dozens of partying twenty-somethings in hoodies and trucker hats jammed inside, but the door was firmly closed to anyone passing by.

In honor of Sam's twenty-ninth birthday, Rockstar was celebrating its most awesome tradition: the annual cheese ball–eating contest. The object was to devour more gooey, greasy, deep-fried, chili pepper–sauced, baseball-size globes of fat than anyone else. It wasn't easy. In addition to packing down the lard bombs, competitors had to endure chaos around them.

While they ate at a center table, Rockstars waved fistfuls of cash as if they were betting on horses. Wagering was encouraged; screaming, the norm. Dan, the announcer, shouted through a bullhorn so that he could be heard above the wailing sirens. The winning ball guzzler got $2,000, two plane tickets anywhere—and serious bragging rights, especially when the record count hit twenty-four. Some competitors wore yellow head-bands scrawled with the words "Eat Strong." In between cheese balls, they had to eat rounds of jalapeño poppers. Buckets were left around the room for vomiting, and they got used. Casualties rinsed with tequila and lime.

Afterward, they passed out awards—such as "Most Likely to Fuck Someone in the Office," "Most Likely to Be in the Office at 4 a.m."—made from medallions with the Rockstar logo. "Despite the industry's reputation as being male-dominated, Rockstar was about an equal mix of guys and girls, all young, and all more than willing to get shit-faced on any night of the week," Rockstar producer Jeff Williams later recalled.

On the heels of *GTA III*, it was a good time to be a Rockstar. Money and drinks flowed. It was the ultimate private club, where mem-bers called one another militaristically by their last names. As a sign of faith, employees each received a pewter ring with the Rockstar logo. They also received real U.S. Army jackets, personalized with the Rockstar logo and their street number, 575, on the back. They wore them with pride, sauntering through game conventions as fans cleared a path.

Few felt more empowered than Fernandez and Pope. "Imagine a company where a hundred people felt like they were in the Beatles," Fernandez recalled. Pope credited Sam. "It's easy to see his genius in all this," he went on. "He really understands you really have to have all the style in world, but have to marry that with really hard work and strong technology. He understands you need the whole package."

Weathering the controversy over *Grand Theft Auto*, however, was proving more difficult. Though they put out perfunctory statements assuring the public that the company "makes every effort to market its games responsibly, targeting advertising and marketing only to adult consumers," they tried to stay out of the sociopolitical debate. "I didn't think we could win," Eibeler recalled. Khonsari, GTA's director, got an e-mail telling him to lie low as the press descended on the hooker story. "This is going to blow up," he was told. "Just keep your head down and don't talk to the press."

The nuances of the hookers in the game were lost on the general public. GTA didn't require you to kill a prostitute to increase your score or anything like that. Players who robbed and murdered the women were simply doing it of their own accord. It was, as King later put it, "an inadvertent consequence of sandbox gameplay. It was in the user, it was in his mind. What does this say about him?" At the same time, King knew that Rockstar was pressing buttons. "We put ourselves out to be the next poster child of this medium," he said.

No matter how erudite the founders of Rockstar were about American pop culture, they failed to take something essential into account: how puritanically people would view their games. This extended to their own peers. To their dismay, Jason Rubin, the cofounder of Naughty Dog, makers of the kid-friendly and best-selling Crash Bandicoot franchise, told the *Los Angeles Times* that selling *GTA III* was "like selling cigarettes to kids."

Though some on the outside might find it hard to believe, the attacks wounded the inner circle of Rockstar. They knew they were giving millions of people an entertaining outlet but couldn't help but wonder if they were crossing some dangerous line. "Are we doing something that's morally wrong?" King wondered. "We were always questioning ourselves and criticizing ourselves," he later recalled.

When a reporter for *Rolling Stone* came by the office for a feature on Rockstar, however, the cofounders dismissed any notion of responsibility. Ragged and unshaven as they sat in a back room, Donovan and the Housers took their critics to task. "If you realize PlayStation owners aren't all ten," Donovan said, "there isn't some kind of social responsibility to have a redeeming social value."

"Why are we having this conversation?" Dan asked rhetorically. "It's insane. We get dragged into these stupid conversations about, 'Are you brainwashing children?' or whatever rubbish it is that month. It's like, 'How can we as adults be having this conversation when we both know that you're talking crap?' It's just not even complicated.

"If this was a movie or TV show and was the best in its field, you'd give it loads of awards and put those award shows on television," Dan went on. "I genuinely don't aspire to that, but I do aspire to not being called an asshole for doing the same thing in a video game. So what you're really saying is, 'It's not the content, it's the medium.' You've proven that by your actions in other areas. So what is it about the medium you don't like? Because maybe we should challenge those ideas. It's not what you think it is to a lot of people. To us, it's way of experimenting with nonlinear interactive storylines."

When asked about the violence, Sam threw his weight behind the Entertainment Software Rating Board (ESRB). "We adhere very strictly to the ratings system and take the ESRB guidelines on marketing mature-rated product very seriously," he said. "What are the alternatives? Censorship? I sincerely hope not."

To ask games to be socially redeeming was missing the point. "What's socially redeeming about a fantasy world in which someone pats you on the back when you've done something well?" Dan asked. "That's just patronizing." Sam shifted in his seat, as if trying to contain his outrage. They were not shallow shock jocks, they were hard-working artists and producers, they felt, and what was wrong with that?

"I tend to try avoid talking too much about the violence because that's what it all gets boiled down to at the end of the day," Sam said. "But when you do something wrong in the game, the police come and get you. . . . You don't just run around on a rampage and just carry on, carry on, carry on. You do commit crimes, and the police are on you. You commit more, and they're on you more, and you commit more, the FBI will turn up, the SWAT will turn up, and then the army turns up. If that doesn't reinforce a moral code in a game, I don't know what does."

"HAVE YOU seen the *New York Times*?"

One day at Rockstar, Jamie King got this message from his dad. King had a good relationship with his father, who took pride in his son's accomplishments in the game industry. Yet his dad had phoned to warn him that maybe something seriously outlaw was taking place behind the scenes.

The headline of the *Times*'s page-one business section story read, "Hit Video Games Overshadow Company's Woes." King read on. "Can looting, drive-by-shootings, random beatings, prostitution and drug dealing compensate for accounting irregularities? Maybe—if the mayhem has really great graphics. . . . Take-Two, which has emerged as a leader in the game software market, admitted early this year...to having misstated seven quarters of financial returns. The Securities and Exchange Commission forced a three-week halt in the trading of its shares and is continuing to investigate. And at least five shareholder lawsuits are under way against Take-Two."

Reports found that Take-Two had overstated revenues by $23 million in 2000. According to one analyst, this resulted in a sizable increase in reported profits for the year—a figure of $24.6 million, instead of the now-revised figure of $6.4 million. Another analyst said that the actions constituted fraud. Given Take-Two's extraordinary success since Brant entered the game industry, the financial community found the SEC investigation especially foreboding.

"With all this stuff about Enron and corporate responsibility, there's a wrong message here," said one hedge fund manager who lost money on Take-Two stock. "It says, 'Who cares about the past, now that we have a good game.' It says, 'Crime does pay.'"

Eibeler and the other execs tried to keep Rockstar as separate as they could from the problems, but it wasn't easy. "Keep your head down," Eibeler told them, "business is great, look at the success." Yet privately, he felt the strain. "While the company was performing extremely well, financially we were under a real cloud," he later said.

Though Sam kept his team insulated from Take-Two, the underlings weren't entirely surprised by the investigations. There had been a revolving door of Take-Two executives, after all. The problems hit especially hard on the two Rockstar cofounders in the shadows, King and Foreman. Since launching the company with Donovan, the Housers, and King, Foreman felt a split forming between the founders. It had started with the press and the positioning of Donovan and Sam as the faces of Rockstar. Foreman, shy by nature, had been happy to let them have the spotlight, but cracks were starting to show that he could no longer ignore.

Foreman would later recall the day when Sam came up to him enthusiastically and said, "Within a couple years, we can all be millionaires! It will be amazing!" Then Sam amended his comment. "You know," he added, "I'm not going to stop until I get a billion."

As Foreman watched him walk away. he thought about Sam's incessant passion for pushing boundaries, for pushing games, for getting the most out of whatever he could. "Knowing him," he thought, "a billion won't be enough."

13

Vice City

TONY: You be happy. I want what's comin' to me
when I'm alive, not when I'm dead.

MANNY: Yeah, what's comin' to you, Tony?

TONY: The world, man, and everything in it.

As Sam watched Tony Montana drive down the neon streets of
Miami, he couldn't get enough of *Scarface*. The film still blew him
away—Al Pacino's incredible portrayal of this Cuban refugee's ascent,
and descent, into becoming the king of the coke trade. The drugs. The
violence. The cojones. The way Montana didn't take shit from anyone
and always stuck to whatever he thought was right. Just as Sam had to
keep his head down and work on his games, despite the mounting pressures around him. "*Scarface* is the ultimate, right?" Sam once said,
"Montana is the ultimate."

So, he thought, was Miami in the eighties. He considered it to be
"hands-down the grooviest era of crime because it didn't even feel like
it was crime. You had Cuban hit men coming across and gunning people

down in the street, but it was still celebrated in a sort of haze of cocaine and excess and Ferraris and Testarossas, and it was a totally topsy-turvy, back-to-front period of time. It was everything that was crazy about the eighties, and it was in America so it was crazier." What better time and place to set a game?

With *GTA III* racking up awards, sales, and controversy, Sam could feel the anticipation growing for the next game. The one thing he knew he didn't want to do was a listless sequel, as the other publishers did. At the same time, however, Rockstar was a subsidiary of a public company, and Sam had the added pressure—and tension—of pleasing his corporate parents at Take-Two. But could he top himself? "You gotta repeat the impact of *GTA III*," he said. "That's scary."

Although they had already mapped out the idea of having the next game set in *Vice City*, the Miami-themed locale from the first *GTA*, they still had to figure out the era. In New York at the time, the eighties were making a comeback. At clubs, INXS and New Order thumped from the speakers, and cocaine was making a comeback, too. For Dan, the time period "glorified values we felt the game could satirize very effectively—greed, the love of money, bad clothes . . . and the music was something we were all interested in, as it was a time when we were growing up and first getting interested in such things." Bolstered by the success of *GTA III*, he was finding his voice as a writer—not a novelist, not a screenwriter, but a writer of games. Someone who could carry a narrative over cut-scenes, picking the right moments to unleash the player into the fictional world.

When Sam went around the Rockstar loft effusing about setting *GTA:Vice City* in the eighties, however, some people didn't get it. "What are you on about?" he recalled one employee asking.

"No, no, no," Sam insisted, "it's so slick!"

"The eighties, man?" another said. "That's a rough one, isn't it?"

"Yeah, of course it is!" Sam replied. "But that's all the more reason to do it!"

Sam had one key believer on his side: Co-founder Jamie King. With his ready enthusiasm and charm, King had assumed a key role within the company, acting as a buffer between Sam's full-throttle passion and the team's pressure to deliver. When he heard team members questioning *Vice City*'s direction, he'd say, "It should be fucking Flock of Seagulls!" and that they needed to trust Sam. So they set about winning over the skeptics instead. Sam rented out a movie theater nearby and took the team to a private showing of *Scarface*. They watched *Apocalypse Now Redux*. *Miami Vice* episodes were not on DVD, so Sam surfed eBay and snatched up every VHS copy of the show he could find between the seasons of 1984 and 1989.

At lunch, he'd rush home to pop in another cassette and watch an episode or two. He reveled in how perfect the series was for a game—from its action scenes to its missionlike structure. *Vice City* wasn't just a game about the eighties, Sam insisted, it was specifically 1986—the peak of the decade, as far as he was concerned. Sam and Dan had Fernandez build a web system and populate it with all of the cultural research he could find: photos of parachute pants, DeLoreans, pink-lensed aviator shades. Sam was exacting in his details. He didn't want just any Ferrari in the game, he wanted the Ferrari Spider GTB from 1986 with one side-view mirror, not two.

Ewing, the scruffy producer of *State of Emergency*, walked into the Rockstar loft one day to find Sam sketching on a white board like some inspired mad scientist. Ewing saw all kinds of seemingly random but hilarious eighties terms scrawled on the board: *Flock of Seagulls, Miami Vice, cocaine*. Lines and arrows pointed from these words to the center of the board, where Sam had drawn the word *Arnold*, referring to Gary Coleman's character from the hit eighties sitcom *Diff'rent Strokes*. "It was as if Arnold had become a fulcrum of understanding," Ewing recalled. "It was just a little window into Sam's mind and how he was pulling cultural threads into a product."

Sam's gospel took hold. Employees started walking around the loft in Members Only jackets. Rockstar flew the DMA developers, now renamed

Rockstar North, from Edinburgh to Miami and checked everyone into snazzy hotel on Ocean Drive. They stood out front, thirty pale Scots with cameras around their necks. "Live and breathe this place," Sam told them, "learn this place, this is what we're going to put on the screen!" Oh, and one more thing. "Get me neon!" he said. "I've got to have neon!"

The weather at first was stormy and gray, just the kind to send the Scots into a pub. When the clouds parted, the guys took to the streets, snapping photos of the buildings, the palms, the sunsets. By the end of the week, they had hundreds of photos—and thirty really bad sunburns. Since leaping into 3D with *GTA III*, they could simply focus on refining the technology—rather than reinventing it—for *Vice City*. The goal was to use the tech to make the world teem even more actively with life. They'd stream scenes faster to immediately immerse gamers. They'd tweak code so that pedestrians moved more believably. A refined physics engine let them expand the choice of vehicles, such as mopeds that drove with just the right feel and degree of nimbleness.

Perhaps most important, the game's new lighting system gave them a broad and expressive palette to render *Vice City* in all of its sunny, neon glory. Most action games came in depressing shades of grays and browns, but *Vice City* would burst with color. They populated the palm-lined streets with exaggerated characters like those out of R. Crumb or Felix the Cat. Curvy women in bikinis on skates. Greasy dudes in ball-hugging briefs. Hustlers in baby-blue Don Johnson leisure suits. "Ours is kind of the look Walt Disney might have gone for if he was more of a psychotic substance abuser with authority issues," said Aaron Garbut, the art director at Rockstar North.

Rendering this detail took countless all-nighters. The introduction of planes and helicopters meant the scenes had to be viewable from the sky, as well as from the street. They weren't merely giving players a richer, more vibrant world than in *GTA III*, they were creating a stronger sense of place. In *Vice City*, the player was cast as Tommy Vercetti, a small-time hood who would complete missions for the warlords and the drug kings in town. This time, the player would get his own apartment on a virtual Ocean Drive. He'd walk inside the shiny Miami lobby and up to his room. These kinds of tropes were usually the domain of role-playing games, the idea of living in a simulated home, but it all fit in with Sam's mission to bring games to life. "It's giving the people a sense of owning something," he said, ". . . it's there and it's real."

Nothing would be more real than *Vice City*'s radio stations. This time they had nine, from the metal of V-Rock to the Latin sounds of Espantoso. Dan, who also wrote the satirical radio commercials, sat for hours listening to FM radio ads from the 1980s—the goofy voice-overs, the jingle singers—culled from ad agencies. They spoofed slasher flicks and donut dealers, self-help gurus and hairstyling products ("May cause dry mouth, dilated pupils, paranoia, heart palpitations and nose bleeds, plus your hair will be great!"). They also poked fun at the low-resolution eighties games they had grown up playing ("*Defender of the Faith . . .*" save the green dots with your fantastic flying red square!").

One morning, Fernandez's phone rang in his apartment on Spring and Elizabeth, just a couple blocks from the Rockstar loft. "Hello?" he said.

"Fernandez!" It was Sam. "Meet me downstairs!"

Fernandez was happy to be at his boss's beck and call. He considered Sam a true genius, a producer on the scale of Bruckheimer or Geffen. He loved how Sam promised Take-Two he'd sell ten million copies of the game. Sam had the nerve to stand up to the corporation and maintain their leverage over their "parents."

Fernandez also appreciated how much Sam valued him and Pope. Not long before this, Sam had come over to Pope's East Village apartment to check out his new surround sound system. They had drinks and watched *Lord of the Rings*, as Sam effused, "Your standard of living is better than mine!" In fact, Sam treated himself to a new Porsche and gave Dan a Rolex. He was buying a house in the West Village and wanted Pope to help him set up his home theater. They were friends.

When Sam's call came to Fernandez that day, Fernandez quickly brushed his hair, no time for coffee. Outside, he found Sam at the ready. In his hand he held a chunky white device with a screen and a sleek dial. "What's that?" Fernandez asked.

"An iPod!" Sam said, referring to the new device from Apple. Sam began to walk up briskly toward West Fourth Street, and Fernandez trailed after him. "Fernandez!" Sam told him, "let's drive around the city and listen to the songs I'm thinking about for *Vice City*."

At the garage, the driver pulled out Sam's Porsche. Sam shot straight for the FDR Drive, the long stretch of highway on Manhattan's East Side. He reached for the iPod, which he had hooked up to his car stereo. "Let's see which one of these songs feels the best when you're driving fast," Sam said and hit the gas. He pressed a button, triggering "Crockett's Theme," the theme of *Miami Vice*. The pulsing synthesizer. The drums coming in. Then the weird sort of coke come-down chords, the strange almost Japanese plucking of a simulated harp. "This is the vibe of the game," Sam said.

Fernandez leaned back as the golden city and more songs blurred. Teena Marie. Slayer. Phil Collins. As each played, he scribbled down the name, and they assigned it a rating for how well they thought it would fit. When one song in particular came on, Sam turned it up, and something came over his face. This was a song from his childhood, one that Dan and he had listened to back in the day. "More than this," Bryan Ferry crooned, "you know there's nothing more than this."

IT WAS EARLY one Sunday morning when Fernandez heard his phone ring again. He rolled over, pressed it to his ear. "Hello?"

"The build is here!" Sam said. "Come check it out."

Fernandez and Pope followed Sam inside the loft and booted up the first build of the game. With a scheduled release date of October 2002, the guys had only had a total of ten months to make *Vice City*—with seven left to go. As the simulation based on Ocean Drive spread onscreen, Fernandez hopped into a Ferrari GTB and hit the road, watching the beach roll by. "Wow," he said, "this is it."

Pope climbed to a rooftop in the game and just sat there. Sat there looking out over the water, as the sun set in crimson and orange over the copper-blue waves. The palm trees swayed, and seagulls fluttered by. My God, he thought, it's beautiful.

Sam loved to just drive, cruising around the maps to get the vibe of the game, the perfect little world the team had created in a box. He jacked a motorcycle and hit the road, popping wheelies as he drove by the neon storefronts. Over the roar of the engine, as he heard "99 Luftballons" play, he felt something strange begin to shift. The screen on his computer monitor rippled in waves, like glass turning to jelly until there was no glass anymore. There was just him, inside the game, not in a crazy way but real. He thought it felt "like crossing a line between the reality and the fiction."

Yet he also felt gripped with anxiety. What if this didn't sell? With a budget of $5 million, *Vice City* was their biggest title yet. The script alone dwarfed the average game or movie: 82 cut-scenes, 200 pages, and another 600 pages of pedestrian dialogue, and 300 pages of radio scripts. They were squeezing every last bit of possible content onto the DVD. Sam and Dan wanted to push the celebrity voice-overs as no game had before. "We thought what's cool about TV shows are all the guest stars showing up," Dan said, "like sports stars in an episode of *Magnum, PI*."

"Like a fallen sports star and now doing other things, things like in *Miami Vice*, always guest starring Phil Collins or Frank Zappa," Sam concurred. As King said, they just wanted an excuse to meet these stars. They started with Vercetti, who, unlike the star of *GTA III*, would now have a voice. To inject personality into such a big world, they needed just the right actor—Ray Liotta, whom they'd been obsessed with since *Goodfellas*.

King hit the phones, hustling with his usual determination and style. It wasn't easy. King kept getting told that Liotta was looking to change his reputation and do a family film. Finally, he got through to a sympathetic young Hollywood agent. Next thing he knew, they were sitting at Peter Luger's Steakhouse in Brooklyn with Liotta himself, drinking and laughing and effusing about how much they loved his films. Then suddenly Liotta went cold for no reason, staring them down. "Why the fuck are you laughing?" he snapped.

The guys gulped. Liotta cracked up. "I'm fucking with you!" he said.

"He totally *Goodfella*ed us!" King said.

Liotta signed on, but the *Goodfellas* shtick wasn't entirely an act, as Khonsari later recalled after taping the voice-over session. Liotta limped in, bitterly sore from a basketball game. "The last fucking video game I played was Pong," he said wearily.

What the hell? Khonsari thought. Khonsari's dad was a doctor, and here was this Hollywood tough guy—who was getting paid half what his dad made in a year? And he was copping an attitude? "Look," Khonsari said, "I don't really give a shit what you do outside this, I mean, I loved you in *Goodfellas*, but this is a job, and you gotta do this." Khonsari got him a big cup of Starbucks, and he calmed down and got into the part.

Before long, a parade of their favorite celebs began pouring in to tape parts in the game: Peter Fonda, Dennis Hopper. Starring in *GTA* was a badge of honor for the actors, a sign of hipness. The Rockstars couldn't contain their glee. "I'm sitting next to the Six Million Dollar Man!" King said, as Lee Majors arrived for his part.

For *Vice City*'s porn star Candy Suxxx, Khonsari suggested adult star Jenna Jameson and offered her $5,000 for the part. It'd be an easy gig for her, something she could do when she was in town for the Howard Stern radio show. Turned out, her boyfriend was a huge *GTA III* fan—done deal. For *Vice City*, Khonsari motion-captured a scene of Candy on her back, having implied sex with a fisherman who joked about his twelve-inch fish. "Yeah," he said, "it's regulation, baby!"

Still, the guys tittered nervously like school kids when Jameson came to the studio to read her part. Dan took one look at her in her tight blue jeans and black shirt, and began to "feel very English," as he said, and embarrassed. It didn't help that she showed up at the session with her father. "Look, I have no problem with her father," Khonsari whispered to Dan, "but I do not feel comfortable making her moan and groan as if she's getting banged."

With Jameson's father glowering, the time for the orgasm came in more ways than one. "Oh, hello, Jenna," Dan said, awkwardly. "So could you sound like you're excited?"

She eyed him dubiously. "What do you mean?"

"Sound like you're happy! Like you're having a great time!" He snapped his fingers. "Sound like you're eating a chocolate bar!"

"So it's supposed to be kind of like sex?" she deadpanned, "or like I'm eating a chocolate bar?"

"Yes, like you're having sex," Dan said, "that would be perfect!"

She obliged.

Nothing prepared them for their visit with Burt Reynolds, who played Avery Carrington, a real estate mogul in the game. Since the guys had grown up on the actor's campy and macho classics—*Smokey and the Bandit, Deliverance*—they were psyched to work with him. Reynolds showed up ready to work and be treated like a star. Khonsari could see the disdain in his eyes, the attitude so many other actors copped about the medium. "They look at you like 'Who the fuck are you?'" he recalled, "'You're game guys.'" Khonsari had no qualms about putting actors in their place. "If you want me to break it down to you," he'd say, "these games gross over half a billion dollars, more than all of your movies put together!"

Yet with Reynolds, he lost his nerve. Khonsari recalled how, after Reynolds cut his scene, Dan asked politely for another take. "Hey," Dan said, "can you say that line again?"

Reynolds stared him down and muttered, "Say that again?"

"Can you do the line again?" Dan repeated.

"You know, you need to give people an 'atta boy.'"

"An 'atta boy'?"

"Yeah, people do something good, you gotta give them an 'atta boy.'"

Khonsari and Dan shifted uncomfortably, having no clue what Reynolds was talking about at first—then realized he wanted a bit of acclaim before he did anything again. He wanted a "that a boy." They redid the line, but Khonsari thought that Reynolds's attitude only got worse. The studio grew hot, so hot he was sweating through his clothes. Unbeknownst to Reynolds, his manager had gone out to buy him a dry shirt. When the shirt arrived, Dan innocently approached Reynolds. "Oh, your shirt's here," he said.

Reynolds didn't know the shirt was coming and must have thought Dan was insulting him for being sopping wet. "There's going to be two hits here," Reynolds told him, "me hitting you and you hitting the floor!"

Dan flipped, ready to cut Reynolds out of the game entirely. Khonsari intervened. "We got the performance," he told Dan. "He's a total cock, but let's move on."

"GO GET ME COVERS!" Sam shouted. "I want covers!"

It was closing in on the release date of *Vice City*, and Sam wanted his public relations team to deliver not just rave reviews, but magazine covers. It was a song-and-dance that began months before a game's release, because the magazines had to go to press in time to run with the launch. "There'd be lot of pressure on the PR guys to deliver good reviews," Rockstar senior product marketing manager Corey Wade recalled. This would consist, he said, of "massaging those relationships and doing whatever you have to do to beef up a review."

Dan "Shoe" Hsu, the editor of *Electronic Gaming Monthly*, a top gaming magazine, described the relationship with Rockstar as "a constant fight" because the company would jockey for sympathetic reviewers. Hsu was still smarting from the Rockstar backlash over the magazine's *GTA III* review, which, despite raving about the game, suggested it would be highly controversial. He then fielded an angry call from Rockstar. "They were really upset," Hsu recalled, "and wanted to control the message and control the heat."

Press got flown down to Miami to check out *Vice City* at the Delano Hotel. Rockstar rented a mansion by the water and showed what the guys called a "vibe reel" of eighties TV shows and films. In addition to the usual plans for ads and trailers, Rockstar rolled out a series of fake eighties websites online. No expense was too great. Recently, to promote *Midnight Club 2*, Rockstar had taken media members drag racing in San Diego.

As word spread among gamers, demand began to reach a fever pitch. At Multimedia 1.0, a video-game store on St. Mark's Place in the East Village of New York, gamers were calling nonstop for *Vice City*. People were coming in and buying anything with a Rockstar logo—games, shirts, stickers. There was a police precinct near the shop, and officers kept coming in and asking for the title. They told the owner they loved to shoot the cops. When he saw a police van outside with the Rockstar logo, he didn't know if a cop had put it on there or someone from Rockstar had.

Yet the hype and the marketing also jacked up the pressure around the office. Random outbursts became commonplace. One day, Foreman read on some online gamer discussion board how they said the trees in *GTA III* looked terrible. He saw Sam's face redden in anger and went over to console him. "Look at these people," Foreman said, "if they're sitting around looking at the trees, think about how much they're actually missing. It's just not relevant. It's easy to take something in isolation and get beaten up about it. But the reality is that *GTA* is not about the trees. It's everything in there. Not one thing in there is that great. You have to take it as a whole."

Little garnered as much attention as the screenshots. Unlike the film or TV industry, which can rely fairly heavily on trailers and buzz, game makers rely hugely on still images sent out in advance of a game. Magazines would jockey just to be the first to feature new images from a game. One screenshot could become the basis of a marketing campaign. They'd pore over a good five hundred stills simply to choose one to send out to the press. "We have to do it better or have to do it different," Donovan insisted.

The closer the launch of *Vice City* loomed, the more obsessed the team in New York became. Hours shifted from 9 a.m. to 5 p.m., to 11 a.m. to 3 a.m. The developers in Edinburgh shared the intensity and the stress. "Luckily, we have a healthy supply of *Grand Theft Auto III* promotional baseball bats that we can use to hit things when the going gets tough," joked Rockstar North art director Aaron Garbut. Pope recalled the time one executive take a whack at another's desk. "It's led to quite a few embarrassing and possibly worrying incidents with our cleaners," Garbut said. Employees reported seeing others roaming the loft with (unloaded) rifles and shotguns, weapons used for art in the game—but good props when they wanted to storm into someone's office and make a point. "It was comedy," Foreman recalled, "it was rock and roll."

Perhaps no one at Rockstar had to let off as much steam as the game testers. The dozen or so players occupied a front part of the loft. A foosball machine and a vintage *Asteroids Deluxe* arcade game awaited play. Packages of Throat Coat and other cold and flu remedies lined the shelves. Bikini centerfolds smiled seductively from the walls. The testers needed all the encouragement they could get.

For a typical game, they spent about thirty thousand cumulative hours playing through the action and checking for bugs. The process could start months before a game's release. The game testers took out their stress by inventing demonic ways to test the PS2 hardware. Once, they chucked the console out their third-floor window. Another time, they blasted it for hours with a hair dryer. Then they hurled it into a freezer ,where it iced over for a weekend. Such lengths were necessary, given the increased demands—and creativity—of players. "The gamers today are highly intelligent and are absolutely going to take your game apart," King told a reporter one day, "and they will savage you. That makes our job harder."

Around the office, the violence, or threats of violence, had become a running joke. When asked to describe his ultimate video game, Sam quipped, "It'd be a fully networked online world, so that I could drive over to Terry's house and smash the shit out of it and get out of there!"

Even celebrities would not be spared Rockstar's wrath. After word circulated that Liotta was bitching about being underpaid for the game, Sam bristled. "It's like, be cool," he later told a reporter from *Edge* magazine. "You know? I hate that—it's so cheesy. Like he's saying, 'Next time I'm really going to pin it to them.' Well, how about we just killed off your character? So he doesn't exist—there is no next time. That's how we handle that."

14
Rampages

```
                      RAMPAGE #28
        DISTRICT:      Little Havana
        LOCATION:      On top of the lower rooftop
                       of the West Haven Com-
                       munity Healthcare Center
        RAMPAGE:       Gun down 20 gang mem-
                       bers in 2 minutes
        WEAPON:        Sniper Rifle
```

Palm trees, blue skies, golf courses. Jack Thompson had every reason to feel sunny as he drove his son to school one morning in October 2002. Yet as he pulled up to his boy's school and watched him run into the building, he felt his stomach twist. Images flashed through his mind. Kids with guns. Blood. Tiny bodies. Paducah. Columbine. And now the Beltway sniper.

During the last few weeks, an unknown sniper had randomly shot ten people dead in the suburbs of Washington, D.C. The country roiled in fear and horror as reports played out on national TV and the Internet. Everyone was looking for a reason behind this most unreasonable act of violence. Once again, Thompson had his reason ready to serve: video games.

Stern and narrow-eyed, he had grown more and more adept at evangelizing the gospel against violent games. While the snipers rampaged, Thompson made the rounds of the biggest shows on TV. On October 11, he appeared again with Matt Lauer on the *Today Show*, positing his theory that the sniper had been trained on video games. "The one-shot methodology is indicative of a video game," he said. Three days later he was on CNN, arguing that investigators who had been seeking leads in the military community should instead be looking at gamers. "The haystack that this twisted needle might be in may indeed be the video game community," he warned.

On October 22, he found a captive audience in Phil Donahue. "So you've really become an expert on video games, haven't you?" Donahue asked.

"Well, I'm afraid I have," Thompson replied stoically. "And I'm a father of a ten-year-old. Every day I drop him off, I know there's a possibility that there might be some sociopath who has trained on these games."

After the snipers were caught, news broke that the fifteen-year-old shooter, Lee Boyd Malvo, had in fact, according to one witness, trained on video games such as *Halo*. "Malvo liked playing in the sniper mode, and John Muhammad would coach Malvo on how to shoot in the sniper mode," the witness said. He added, "Malvo was really into the game and would often get angry while playing it."

Back at his home, Thompson quickly fired off a press release. "It is time for this greedy industry to pay for its mayhem," he wrote. Thompson's battle was all the easier to wage because he lacked one obvious opponent: the game makers. Back in Washington, Doug Lowenstein of the Interactive Digital Software Association watched Thompson's campaign in horror but rarely went on the air to respond. "I got criticism for not going on every show Jack Thompson was on," Lowenstein later said.

Secretly, however, he was playing a meta-game against Thompson on his own. "I was always managing a calculus," he recalled.

The stakes of this culture war, he knew, were rising, despite the dismissal of Thompson's Paducah suit and the death of Senator Baca's "Protect Children from Video Game Sex and Violence Act." In St. Louis, an ordinance to ban the sale of violent games to anyone under eighteen succeeded in withstanding the industry's argument that it defied the First Amendment. Senior U.S. district judge Stephen Limbaugh ruled that games did not constitute speech and therefore didn't deserve such protection.

Lowenstein feared that engaging Thompson would only make things worse and would give him the ammo he was seeking for future legal actions. "I knew what he wanted me to do was be in a forum where he could have me say something and slap a lawsuit," Lowenstein said. So Lowenstein chose to sit back and watch. He wasn't the only game executive who remained silent. "No one in the industry wanted to be a point person or target," Lowenstein said.

As a result, Thompson was left to speak out, unopposed, and had a profound impact on shaping popular opinion about video games. Elevated by the press and bolstered by his predictions, Thompson quickly found a new target of his own: *Grand Theft Auto*. It happened during a packed press conference in Washington. David Walsh, the head of the National Institute on Media and the Family, was joined by senators Lieberman and Kohl to present the annual Video Game Report Card. This had not been a good year for the industry, they said—and cut to a tape. On the screen, footage of a game appeared: a car bobbing up and down. A prostitute walking out of the vehicle, only to get beaten to death with a bat and left in a bloody pile. *Vice City*.

"Women are the new target of choice in the most violent video games," Lieberman said. "This relatively small but highly popular minority [of games] is not pushing the envelope, they are shooting, torturing and napalming it beyond all recognition and beyond all decency."

"These games are phenomenally popular with kids," added Walsh. "Anyone who says that the only people playing these kinds of games are adults are not talking with kids. By and large, parents are very uninformed. . . . What do we think *Grand Theft Auto: Vice City* teaches our fourteen-year-olds?"

GTA enraged Thompson. The sex. The violence. And being set in a fictional Miami, his hometown, no less. How dare they peddle this filth to children? He knew just how he would fire back with the help of his own son. One day, he went up to his son, Johnny, and asked him for a favor. He had a suspicion that the Best Buy chain, among others, was selling this game to kids despite the M-rating, and he wanted to prove it. "It would be useful at this point, Johnny," he said, "to be able to say whether or not Best Buy, which claims to be the most reasonable on this issue, is selling it."

Thompson drove to the Best Buy parking lot and handed Johnny $60 to buy the game. He gripped his video camera and told his son he'd be waiting outside. Thompson watched Johnny head into the store as he positioned himself outside the glass door. He palmed his camera and stared through the viewfinder, thumb hovering over the record button. He waited, watching the people come and go by the registers, checking out in the lines to head back into the Miami heat. Waited until he saw his little boy walk up to the clerk with the black plastic case in hand.

Thompson hit record, zoomed in, and could see it: the lower case *Grand Theft Auto* logo and the pink neon subtitle, *Vice City*. He crouched lower, just at the right angle to film the transaction. He could feel his throat constrict and heart race as his son handed over the game. The clerk eyed the boy. Then he took his money and sold him the game. Busted! "Everyone knows what's in this game, and it's the sexual content that gets them in trouble," Thompson told Johnny.

Using this evidence, he could go after the retailers for illegally selling sexual content to minors. He could use the tape to prove their negligence. Thompson examined the video game box in his hand. The cover was broken into frames like a comic book—flaming cars, a girl in a pink bikini, a black guy with a big gold chain and a gun. He eyed the tiny little logo in the bottom-right corner, the yellow square with the letter R and the star. Rockstar Games? Get ready to be Jacked.

CHEESE BALL! Cheese ball! Cheese ball!

Another year, another cheese ball–eating contest at Radio Mexico for the players at Rockstar Games. Tequila poured. Bets flew. Vomit buckets spilled. In what was also now an annual tradition, valued employees received a new company jacket. This time it was a military green bomber jacket, stitched with the word *Rockstar* on the front and the company's crest (including the logo and a set of brass knuckles) on the back. Surrounding the crest was the phrase, in Latin, "to pulverize our enemies."

The company's faithful crew had more reasons than ever to celebrate. *Vice City* was on its way to becoming the best-selling video game of all time. The success came out of the gate, when it moved an astonishing 1.4 million copies in its first two days (more than most developers sold in a lifetime), making it the fastest-selling game ever.

At the same time, *GTA III* continued to break records. Costing less to make than many indie films, the game has sold more than 8 million copies, generating roughly $400 million in its first year and eclipsing even that year's blockbuster film *The Matrix*. The *GTA* juggernaut bolstered Take-Two, still under an SEC investigation, and the game industry, which hit a record $10.1 billion in revenues for 2002, up 10 percent from the previous year.

Vice City wasn't only a commercial hit, but a critical phenomenon, too. The game received raves from the most influential magazines and websites. "The depth and gameplay variety is through the roof," gushed *PlayStation* magazine. *Entertainment Weekly* voted it game of the year, saying, "the reason *Vice City* blows every other game away isn't that it's a driving, shooting, action, or simulation game, but that it's all four combined into a criminally stylish package." *Vice City* racked up the industry's top awards. "Hopefully, this time around, both parties will begin to ignore the controversy and recognize *Grand Theft Auto: Vice City* for what it really is," wrote *Game Informer*, "a brilliant video game."

In the wake, the industry recently ruled by Mario and *Tomb Raider* desperately rushed to emulate Rockstar's new ruling style. As one game analyst put it, "They're not afraid to release titles like *Grand Theft Auto*, which is something that not many people would release before. Now everybody's moving to copy it." Plumbers and Indiana Janes were out. Sex and violence were in. A new game called *The Getaway* grabbed headlines for its car-chasing violence. And another, *BMX XXX*, boasted lap dances—allegedly shot using motion capture of real strippers.

"You wouldn't expect your average child's Christmas list to include a lap dancer, a series of savage murders or an armed hold-up," warned the *Daily Record* in Glasgow. "But that's what most teenagers are wishing for this year—in the shape of some of the best-selling computer games of all time."

With its success growing, the Rockstar brand was cooler than ever. Emulating the DIY marketing of the recording artists they grew up admiring, the guys at Rockstar promoted its games by plastering stickers all over the city. It had become a badge of hipness to wear a T-shirt with the company's logo or to blast *Vice City*'s nine-CD box set soundtrack (a packaging coup unheard of in the game business) in your car. *GTA* was parodied on *Chappelle's Show* and name-checked on a hip-hop track by rapper Cam'ron. New York disc jockeys Opie and Anthony began to effuse about *Vice City* on the air each day.

When asked by *Rolling Stone* whether he planned to go even further with the content of future games, Sam said, "The answer to that is yes. At the end of the day, there's enough people in this country that would like to see us sort of thrown out or locked up than doing what we do, but my answer is, we're on it, one step at a time kind of a thing. Look at the trouble we got into for the prostitute thing. You'd be amazed at how conservative people are."

Rockstar had not only achieved the cultural cachet that Def Jam had in the 1980s, it had surpassed it in a new medium for a burgeoning generation. In fact, even Def Jam itself had come calling. After reading the *Rolling Stone* profile of Rockstar, in which they discussed their admiration of the label, Def Jam president Kevin Liles got Donovan on the phone. "You want to be like us?" he asked, dubiously. "I gotta know who the fuck you are." The two met, and Liles said, "Let's figure out some shit to do together."

For the Brits who grew up dreaming of New York in their bedrooms in London, the fame felt mind-blowing. Gamers who found out their identities would stumble up to them and fawn, "Oh my God! You're the coolest people in the world!" When SoHo House, an exclusive new club, was recruiting members for its opening in mid-2003, the club's representative made a beeline for King, whom she met through a mutual acquaintance. "Oh, you're Jamie King! And you work at Rockstar Games!" she cooed. "And you're at the helm of something which is an extraordinarily exciting new venture." King didn't merely join, he became an investor.

As Take-Two's revenue topped $1 billion, there was plenty of cash to go around. As one Rockstar recalled, "Once stock options came in, people were making money and buying houses." The company gobbled up more game development houses to complement its satellite studios in Vienna, San Diego, and Vancouver. While dozens of fresh employees milled about the loft, veteran Rockstars—the "575 crew," as King proudly called them—such as Pope and Fernandez felt that a new era had begun. Yet it wasn't entirely the one they expected.

Maybe it was just the hangover of the seventy-hour work weeks of *Vice City* finally setting in, but when Pope looked up wearily from his new desk one day, he thought they weren't the same happy family anymore. As if in slow motion, he watched the Brits parading around the loft in cashmere sweaters with tiny R★ logos sewn fashionably over the breast.

Sam had always made such a big deal out of the Rockstar gear, doling out army jackets and rings to everyone as a sign that they were all part of their gang. But in the eyes of Pope, the fancy sweaters seemed to be reserved for the Rockstars at the top. The cashmere gamers were a gang of their own.

BANG! BANG! BANG! POW! Foreman looked up at the horrific smashing sounds coming from Sam's office and waited for the inevitable words to follow. "I need a new phone!" Sam shouted to him. Foreman pulled out an equipment purchase order and filled out yet another request for one of Sam's broken phones.

As Rockstar's reputation grew, such rampages were becoming more routine. Foreman later recalled. "He'd flip out if someone told him something he didn't want to hear. We replaced his phone an awful lot of times." Foreman hated the favoritism shown in the cashmere sweaters. Though he, as a cofounder, received one, he felt ashamed to wear it. "It was a 'fuck you' to everybody," he said.

Even the military jackets and the rings didn't seem so glamorous anymore. One day Pope looked at the Rockstar ring on his finger and felt like a chump. "We've been manipulated so a five-dollar ring means everything to you," he realized. "There was rivalry, but it was never articulated. It was a dividing line."

But what some saw as runaway egos could also been seen as merely more determined image control. So what if a boss wore different swag, or got pissed off when something didn't go right? If games were the new rock and roll, then such antics went with the territory. Rockstar also understood that part of their allure was their enigma, and they were dead-set on preserving it—by any means necessary. Though the game industry was big on sharing knowledge at conferences and events, Rockstar limited the exposure. Foreman found this out firsthand when he told Donovan he'd been asked to speak on a panel about game development. "No, you can't do it," Donovan told him.

"Why?"

"We don't do that."

"I won't even mention Rockstar, aside from my intro, that I'm CTO of Rockstar. It will be a generic talk."

"We don't do that."'

Foreman thought he knew why they had kiboshed it. Because of "the fear that you may talk about something that was outside of their control," he later said. "They never wanted the world to know the secrets." Yet for him, the secret was obvious and nothing to hide. Rockstar's success was built on hard work and dedication, more than anything else. "The secret is to be really, really passionate about what you do and put in a lot of effort to realize it," Foreman said. "That's it." All of the broken phones and the tantrums fed these amazing games. "No matter how messed up it might be," Foreman recalled, "it worked."

The cashmere gang wanted to control real life the same way they controlled their games. They would sit at their computers, anxiously waiting for the reviews of their newest games to be posted online. They wanted everyone to see the games to be the masterpieces they imagined. "The magic that I see in this game in particular, I don't think has been captured in words on a piece of paper," Sam once griped.

The guys who once considered calling their company Grudge Games proved they could still live up to that moniker. Negative press drew a backlash from Rockstar, in which ego trumped economics. Not only would writers get their access to the company cut off, but Rockstar would boycott ads in the offending publication. "They were crazy about the media in general," Dan's assistant, Gillian Telling, later said. "They'd get a 9 out of 10 score and call them up and threaten to pull ads forever."

Pope and Fernandez needed a break, and bad. One night, with *Vice City* done, they and some others went to celebrate at a nearby restaurant. After going straight from *GTA III* into *Vice City* without a stop, they relished the chance to unwind. Yet no sooner did their drinks arrive than Pope's phone rang. "Come back to the office!" Sam exclaimed enthusiastically on the other end of the line. "Let's talk about San Andreas!"

15
Cashmere Games

> **PERSONAL SAFETY**
>
> There isn't a neighborhood in the entire state of San Andreas that we would categorize as "safe," so we recommend carrying a weapon at all times. Actually, 2 is better. Visit the local Ammu-Nation superstore (see map for details) soon after arrival for firearm supplies.

Grim city. First-person point of view. Gazing out a car window. Dead palms. Broken doors. Graffitied storefronts. Dudes in bandannas and baggy jeans. Random snippets of pedestrian dialogue:

"Never gonna get it, never gonna get it, beyatch!"

"These clothes? Yeah, they're tight!"

"Hey, homie, you've been hitting the weights?"

"Where the fuck am I?" wondered Fernandez, as he made his way through a dangerous part of East Los Angeles. He was here as part of his cultural research for *GTA: San Andreas*, soaking up details they might use in the game. Stout and dark-haired, he was sitting in the passenger seat of a slow-moving car driven by a bald Mexican American with ripped, tattooed arms. Fernandez pointed a microphone out his window as he rolled, recording passersby whom he heard over his headphones:

"Now, when I slap you, don't trip!"

"You smell like *pasulo!*"

Though a Latino from Miami himself, Fernandez felt nervous and out of place here in this 'hood. He could pass for the guys in the street, but he was a geek at heart. At least he had someone who knew this area behind the wheel, Estevan Oriol, the former bouncer and hip-hop tour manager who now ran one of the hippest clothing lines in the area, Joker Brand. Who better to show him around?

With *Vice City* topping the charts, the pressure had immediately set in on Rockstar to raise the bar once again in *San Andreas.* "Man, how the hell are we going to follow this one up?" Sam asked. "What's after Miami in the eighties? Well, of course, the Bloods and the Crips and the L.A. early-nineties gang-banger culture!"

San Andreas had been established in the first *GTA* as a San Francisco–like town, one of the three cities that included Liberty and Vice. For the stand-alone version of *San Andreas,* Rockstar knew exactly where and when to set it: in the era of hip-hop West Coast culture they had grown up admiring. The game would cast the player as a young gang member trying to find his way back through the hood. It would be biggest *GTA* so far: more than two hundred hours of gameplay in a virtual world almost five times the size of *Vice City.* It wouldn't be only one town; it would cover an entire state.

Over inspired late nights in New York and Edinburgh, they mapped out their vision. They would have three cities in one game—a mock Los Angeles, San Francisco, and Las Vegas. With vast distances to travel through hills and forests, over bridges and mountains, San Andreas would feel epic. Sam didn't merely want it set in the early 1990s, he wanted it to render 1992, the era of Rodney King and films such as *Colors, Boyz in the Hood,* and *Menace II Society.*

Gangs had always been central to the evolution of *GTA*—from Dundee to *The Warriors* and the real-life gang that Rockstar had become. For the guys, rendering the gangs of San Andreas fulfilled their ultimate dream. "We aren't just a bunch of marketing guys who think we can make a buck," King said. "It was more about 'That's fucking cool! Look at the way they're dressed! Look at their cars and look at what they go through every fucking day! Amazing!' That's us living out our fantasy of being able to engage in it with a video game. . . . We were all wannabes." He went on, "But then, we were from England. What do we know?"

To boost their credibility and realism, they hired the best consultants they could find—Oriol and his Joker brand partner, the famed tattoo artist Mr. Cartoon. After recording pedestrian dialogue for the game, Fernandez was going with Oriol to talk with a friend who had been shot. They made their way through the neighborhood, down a narrow street, when suddenly a car came toward them from the other direction. There was nowhere for them to go. Fernandez's heart pounded. Then the car stopped, and a gangbanger got out and headed toward them. "Lower the window!" Oriol shouted to another guy in the car with them. "Lower the window!"

Fernandez panicked, imagining a gun fight. "Don't lower the window!" he said.

"Lower the window!" Oriol repeated.

"Don't lower the window!" Fernandez shouted back. As Fernandez feared for his life, the window came down, but this passerby wasn't looking for a fight. He was just a friend of Oriol's and wanted to say hi. Fernandez felt like an asshole. "What the fuck am I doing?" he thought. "I'm making a video game. I can look at movies and see this shit!"

"HEY! HEY! Get a grip! Calm down!" James Earl Cash pounded against the door of the execution chamber, ignoring the disembodied voice that came from the speakers overhead. A young con sentenced to death, the last thing he remembered was being pinned down to a gurney and injected with a lethal cocktail. Now he was desperately trying to escape. Suddenly, the door cracked open with a blade of light. "You've had an unexpected reprieve," the voice said. "Do exactly as I say, and I promise this will be over before the night is out."

This was the opening scene of *Manhunt*, another Rockstar game in production in early 2003. *Manhunt* cast the player as Cash, a pawn in a sick game of his own. A twisted movie director had hired gangs to hunt and kill Cash, chronicling the chase with surveillance cameras for the ultimate snuff film. Now Cash had to use any means necessary—wires for strangling, glass shards for throat-slitting, bats for pummeling—to survive.

Unlike *GTA*, which was, at its core, a driving and action game, this fell under the genre of survival horror, popularized by the zombie franchise *Resident Evil*. Survival horror games thrived on suspense, the chilling feeling of being stalked down alleyways by murderous beasts. Yet once again, Rockstar had flipped the script, bringing games into a contemporary reality. The player wasn't only being hunted, he was hunting, too, sneaking around corners with a plastic bag to pull over an unsuspecting gang member's head.

There would be no zombie fantasy to relieve the tension of the violence. These victims were vividly human. The brutal ways in which they could be killed—the spray of the arteries when cut with a sickle, the bone-crunching snap of a twisted neck—were unheard of in the industry. If the politicians freaked out about the cartoonish spine-ripping move from *Mortal Kombat*, what would they make of this?

For Pope and some others at Rockstar, the grimness of the game evoked a starker reality of their own. Life around the loft was changing. A darkness drifted in the air. A sense of being like Cash, trapped with some all-powerful director calling the shots as they struggled to survive. Sam's joke of wearing EA Sports shirts to mock the corporate game machines didn't seem so funny anymore. "In a way, we were becoming that," Pope later said, "a big nameless faceless machine that turns out these titles. You're just one cog in a huge corporation. . . . We were churning out *GTA*s as fast as we could."

The tensions mounted the day they went from completing *Vice City* to starting *San Andreas* with no break. Promises of a party to celebrate *Vice City* came and went. Foreman worried that the company had descended into "constant crunch mode," with days going into seventeen hours. He felt that they were working so hard, they never had time to enjoy their success. Pope began working so long, dreams blended with reality. He'd go back to have nightmares about blowing off people's limbs while staring down a rifle scope.

One producer who had been there since 1999 thought the company was taking on "shades of Miramax," the legendary but volatile film company *Manhunt* became especially divisive. "There was almost a mutiny at the company over that game," as Rockstar producer Jeff Williams later blogged, "…there was no way to rationalize it. We were crossing a line." And the powers-that-be didn't take kindly to being told otherwise. "Every day, someone would say something they didn't like about a game," Pope recalled, "and they'd tell them, 'You're a fucking idiot.'"

It wasn't just only the underlings getting pawned, it seemed to Pope, it was one of the founders himself: King. As the person in charge of juggling the games and overseeing the day-to-day production, King carried a great deal of weight. Pope watched in dismay as King appeared to buckle from the constant stress.

Pope felt a chill. "If that could happen to Jamie," he thought, "it could happen to me." In confidence, he approached Fernandez, his best friend at the company and, like him, one of the closest guys to Sam. Fernandez had been entrenched in researching *San Andreas*. He had traveled from L.A. to Vegas, where he stealthily recorded the dialogue of players at gambling tables. As Pope poured out his frustrations to Fernandez, however, his friend didn't entirely see eye-to-eye.

For Fernandez, Sam was more bark without bite. He told Pope how much Sam's passion inspired him, how Sam gave him this feeling he could do anything. To Fernandez, the rampages were part of Sam's overarching obsession with quality. "That's the only reason the games are so good," he once said. Anyone who got on Sam's case for his outbursts was missing the point. "Make great games, forget about the bullshit, and we'll triumph, that's his philosophy," Fernandez said. "It's the ideal way any company should be run."

Pope wouldn't listen. "When the novelty of working for a cool company in SoHo in a loft wears off, then it's all downhill from there," he said. "And then they keep you around with money or little trinkets." What was happening? he wondered. To their games? To Sam? Massively multiplayer games such as *World of Warcraft* were all the rage, and Pope was among those at the office who wanted Rockstar to take a shot at the genre. Yet whenever Pope brought it up, he just heard Sam mutter derisively about orcs and elves.

Pope had had enough. One day he stormed into Sam's office. His boss had taken up yoga, and Pope had sometimes seen him doing handstands in the back. Maybe Pope was overreacting. "I'm not happy here," Pope said.

"Why?" he recalled Sam replying.

"There's too much being asked of us. We were never given a break. It was one thing to go right into *Vice City*, but then we went straight into *San Andreas*."

"It's hard. We have to keep grinding. We're going to lose our edge if we don't keep this up."

"You've kind of already lost touch."

"What are you talking about?"

"You're not playing games anymore. You're off in your office making decisions."

"I'm still involved! Who are you to tell me?"

"I'm not the only one who feels this way."

SAM SAW a rubber band on the floor. Alone. Discarded. Coiled. And he just had to stop everything to pick it up. Shove it in his pocket like Mario collecting brightly colored coins. It was a habit that Fernandez had been observing for a while: Sam randomly picking up rubber bands. When Fernandez asked him about this, Sam told him it was just a good luck superstition. Fernandez took it as something else, an example of how granularly aware Sam was of the details around him—even if that obsession with detail had sometimes been lost on others.

But the passion was clearly paying off. Now thirty-two, he was living his Rockstar dreams. His games were bringing pleasure to millions of people around the world. Take-Two had $1 billion in revenues after *Vice City*, and they were only set for more.

He was proving the old skeptics wrong. "You go out here, and people were like 'What are you talking about? How can you say games are cool?'" Sam recalled. "That whole sort of teenager in the bedroom with the bottle-top specs, that hung around the game industry neck like a fucking albatross." Yet now, thanks in large part to Rockstar, games were growing up, along with their fans. "People now accept it is a new medium," he said. "It's something that can be appreciated. It's not just something reserved for weirdos."

It was all the more reason, then, that he seemed shocked to hear a rumor that Pope was quitting. Sam approached him and said, "I'm hearing you're going to leave."

"Yeah, I'm really unhappy," Pope said. But Pope wasn't going alone. He and Fernandez had decided to start their own company, along with some other employees on staff. They even had their own idea for a title, inspired by their time at Rockstar. Players would have to battle a cult leader similar to David Koresh. "Instead of carjacking," Pope said, "it'll be mind jacking!" Their working title, *Whacko*. And the name of their start-up would be the biggest fuck-you of all to Rockstar: Cashmere Games.

Despite Fernandez's deep admiration for Sam, he felt bullish enough to think he and Pope could replicate Rockstar's success on their own.

Leaving the mentor and friend who inspired him so much wouldn't be easy. As Pope said, "They don't take you leaving kindly, they treat it like the mob, like you abandoned the family." Fernandez felt his heart sink, his stomach twist, knowing there was no turning back. "My biggest regret is that Sam's such an influential guy," Fernandez later said. "It's the worst part of leaving Rockstar. Maybe that's the decision you have to make."

Sam seemed devastated by the news, so much so that he went to Fernandez's apartment to plead with him to stay. "I'm asking you one more time," Sam told him, "are you leaving or staying?"

"I'm leaving," Fernandez said.

Sam took one last look at him, then turned and walked away.

This game was over.

16
Grand Death Auto

WANTED LEVEL

★★★☆☆☆

The bullets came from nowhere, and there was plenty of nowhere in Newport, Tennessee. An hour east of Knoxville, the country town of 7,200 was little more than a pit stop on the way to nearby attractions such as Dolly Parton's Dollywood theme park and the Life of Christ Experience in 3-D. Like most people who make it to these parts, Aaron Hamel and his cousin Denise "Dee Dee" Deneau were just passing through. Quickly.

It was around 8 p.m. on June 25, 2003, and the sun was still shining at the end of what Hamel called "a perfect day." The two were driving back to Knoxville in his red Toyota truck after hiking in Black Mountain, North Carolina. Hamel, a forty-five-year-old registered nurse and nature lover, had recently relocated from Ontario, dreaming of buying a log cabin in the woods. The previous day, he had gotten a callback from a juvenile detention facility where he hoped to work. "I think I could make a difference and help these kids," he told his cousin during their hike.

Driving among the semis on Interstate 40, Hamel admired the rolling hillside. "Oh, Dee Dee," he said, "look at the beautiful flowers—" As Deneau would later recall, Hamel didn't have time to finish the word before the window shattered. Blood and broken glass sprayed Deneau's lap. With blood pouring from Hamel's head, their truck sped out of control over the median into oncoming traffic and smashed into a guardrail.

Coming up behind them in a white Mazda west on I-40, a tourist from Roanoke, Virginia, nineteen-year-old Kim Bede, and her boyfriend Marc Hickman heard the crash. They assumed someone had blown out a tire. Another bullet proved them wrong. It pierced the passenger side of their car, shattering Bede's hip. Then the shots stopped, and Newport fell quiet again.

When the cops arrived, Hamel was dead. Bede was gushing blood, fragments of bullets in her spine. The woods under the faded billboards along the highway were shrouded in darkness. As word spread around the small town, investigators scoured the brush with spotlights and heat-seeking equipment, looking for a trace of what they feared might be a replay of the Beltway snipers. "We don't know if it was road rage, a sniper, or what," a deputy told reporters that night.

It didn't take long to find the answer. Lurking anxiously in the bushes was a lanky, quiet fifteen-year-old named William Buckner, with his short, hyperactive thirteen-year-old stepbrother, Josh. The two had been stepbrothers for only a brief while but had instantly bonded after growing up in unstable families. They had no prior records, had clean slates at school, and seemingly had no reason to have fired the deadly shots. Yet after breaking down in tears and confessing to the crime, the boys volunteered a reason of their own: *Grand Theft Auto III.*

During Will's deposition, he revealed that he had been playing the game at home. When asked whether he thought the game "had some impact on you related to this shooting," Will said, "in some way, yes."

"How so?"

"I think it gave us the idea in a way."

After word of the *GTA* connection hit the press, the phone in the Buckner home rang. Donna, Will's mother, answered. "My name's Jack Thompson," the caller said, "and there might be an explanation for why your boys did this."

NEWS OF THE Buckner shootings had come at a busy time for Thompson. After filming his son on a sting buying *Vice City*, his obsession with *GTA* rivaled Sam's. Since launching his campaign against the game industry, Thompson had made more than fifty television appearances on all of the biggest shows, including seven visits to the *Today Show* alone.

As well as Sam played to the gamers, Thompson played to the emotions of the general public. No matter how much people believed in protecting the First Amendment, something inside them couldn't rule out the possibility that violent games might be harming their kids. Despite scientists and researchers debating what, if any, impact games had on aggression, Thompson cited studies that effectively stoked fears. "There has been a wealth of research to show that children's brains process these video games in a different way from adults'," he said. "They cannot differentiate between fantasy and reality, so they play these games and then think if they do the same thing in reality, it's okay, there will be no consequences."

His campaign was working. Across the world, *GTA* was being linked with more crimes. In Oakland, a gang called the Nut Cases made waves for allegedly emulating the game. According to a story in the *San Francisco Chronicle*, "They got high and played video games during the day, the young men later told police. Their favorite was one called *Grand*

Theft Auto III, in which players win points for committing violent crimes. When darkness fell, they told investigators, they did it for real on the streets of Oakland."

Thompson cited the recent case of Dustin Lynch, a fifteen-year-old boy from his home state of Ohio who had stabbed and bludgeoned a girl to death just weeks after *Vice City*'s release. Thompson learned that Lynch had been playing *GTA* prior to the killings, and he convinced the girl's father to sue Rockstar. "We're not arguing the game was the sole cause of [the] murder," Thompson said. "The game had something to do with it."

Though the threat of a lawsuit fizzled, Thompson spread his gospel from newspapers to an appearance on *Good Morning America*. It was an effective strategy: filing a suit was enough to get him press—perhaps his most effective weapon at shaping the public's perception of video games. Whether he won or lost a case or saw it dismissed didn't matter. With Rockstar and the game industry all but silent, he waged his war virtually unopposed.

"I'm a father and a Christian and a lawyer, and I love the kind of world I grew up in during the fifties, where we shot baskets, not people," Thompson told *Philadelphia Weekly*. "But I'm not trying to take away the constitutional right of adults to view or consume this material no matter how objectionable I might find it personally. I'm trying to stop them from marketing this filth to minors."

The more Thompson battled, the more difficult the struggle became for Lowenstein, the game industry's spokesperson. Despite *GTA*'s "M For Mature" rating, a recent survey by the Gallup Organization of 517 teens, ages thirteen to seventeen, found that 60 percent had played a *GTA* game. Still reeling from the debate over Columbine and the threat of federal legislation over the marketing of violent games, Lowenstein tried to steer away from Thompson's rhetoric. "I have no doubt that Mr. Thompson is quite passionate and committed to his cause," he said. "We're just as committed to ours."

In addition to standing by the industry's rating system, he cited a recent FTC study that found that parents were the ones purchasing games, including M-rated ones, for kids more than 80 percent of the time. Lowenstein urged parents to pay more attention to what they were giving their kids. "If a twelve-year-old has *Grand Theft Auto*," he said, "chances are he got it from Mom and Dad."

Lowenstein felt bolstered by a recent ruling by the 8th U.S. Circuit Court of Appeals, which ruled against St. Louis County's attempt to ban violent game sales to kids. "If the First Amendment is versatile enough to shield [the] painting of Jackson Pollock, music of Arnold Schoenberg, or Jabberwocky verse of Lewis Carroll," the court ruled, ". . . we see no reason why the pictures, graphic design, concept art, sounds, music, stories and narrative present in video games are not entitled to similar protection."

Yet this wasn't swaying the skeptics. In April 2003, the governor of Washington proposed to ban the sale of violent games to minors. Lowenstein felt increasingly frustrated with his meetings on the Hill and how routinely politicians would sacrifice the First Amendment in the name of protecting children. "I know this is a bad bill," he recalled being told by one governor, "but I have to sign it."

Where were the game developers to fight back? "Rockstar and all the other ones had their heads in the sand," Lowenstein said. The developers suffered from a "victim mentality for being singled out," he went on. "The problem was the industry wasn't willing to understand the fundamental instincts of parents to care about their children."

While many gamers shrugged Thompson off as a clown, they failed to realize the extent to which he was influencing the public conversation on video games. "He used media effectively, locally and nationally, and inspired politicians to take up his cause and push legislative remedies that we're fighting," Lowenstein later said. "To give the devil his due, if there was no Jack Thompson, there would have been far fewer bills we'd be dealing with."

Thompson had just begun. On October 20, 2003, he filed a $246 million lawsuit on behalf of the Buckners' victims against Sony Computer Entertainment America, for marketing *GTA III*; Wal-Mart, for selling it; and Rockstar, for creating and publishing it. "If they're going to continue to market adult-rated games to children with these horrific consequences," Thompson told the press, "then we're going to take their blood money from them and send a message to their boards that they have to stop this practice or there will be other suits on behalf of other people killed by these games."

"I DIDN'T REALIZE the highway was this close," said Wayne Buckner, Josh's father and Will's stepfather, as he walked to the spot on the hill where his boys had shot at the cars that night. He was surrounded by trees and tall brush as the cars and the trucks sped by on I-40 below. Wayne was a tall, gray-haired fifty-six-year-old in a golf-course vest, blue jeans, and a baseball cap. "I saw this area in the police diagram," he said, making his way tentatively around the brush, "but this is the first time I've come here. My wife doesn't want to know where this spot is."

In his mind's eye, Wayne had pictured the boys standing much farther away from the road, so far that their bullets would not have easily hit the cars. As we looked down at the highway, though, we were close enough to make out the passengers behind the windows. Wayne's eyes welled up. "It's pretty sad," he said. The path in the weeds that Will and Josh cut with machetes was still discernible. A deflated inner tube they once used to ride down the nearby creek rested against a tree. Pigeons roosted in a rickety liquor billboard a dozen feet away.

It was the birds that first took the blame after the boys were caught that night. Josh told Wayne that they had been shooting at the pigeons and must have accidentally hit the cars in the process. "He said the birds always fly off this billboard toward the interstate," recalled Wayne. When the birds suddenly abandoned their roost above us, however, not a single one flew toward the road. "I really wanted to believe him," Wayne said.

The Buckners lived in a split-level brick house on the side of a golf course. The golf cart Will and Josh used to ride sat near the garage, where a basketball net hung. In the backyard, the yapping dogs now had free rein in the impressive treehouse Wayne had built for the kids. Inside the living room, Wayne's wife, Donna, lit a cigarette. A petite and pretty thirty-seven-year-old in a powder-blue sweater, she had dropped to a painfully thin eighty-five pounds since the incident. "I just can't get my appetite back," she said. Wayne excused himself to hit the greens. "He plays too much golf," Donna grumbled quietly.

Since the shooting, Wayne and Donna had struggled to survive and make sense of this most senseless of acts. Though their sons were found to be reckless, not murderous, that hadn't made their soul-searching any easier. Ultimately, that search led them to one answer: *Grand Theft Auto III*. "Will and Josh wouldn't have done this if they hadn't been playing that game," Donna said, as she showed a visitor family photos. "They aren't serial killers. They're good boys."

Though taken during better times, the shots didn't exactly convey adolescent bliss. In one, Josh and Will sat expressionlessly on either end of a black futon facing a giant television screen. Josh, a small, wiry kid with uneven sandy blond bangs and a spotty complexion, leaned against an 8-ball pillow in a yellow Fort Lauderdale Surf Sport T-shirt. The stoic look on Will—who was wearing baggy tan shorts, a yellow Hawaiian shirt unbuttoned over a black Nike tee, a dog-tag necklace, and a half-dozen bracelets on his arm—revealed, if anything, a desire for his mother to hurry up and shoot already.

In a picture taken on a family trip to the beach, Will stood awkwardly in a blue T-shirt and long blue shorts, bony white arms crossed around his chest, next to Josh in a bright red shirt, arms stiffly down, staring forward; Wayne and Donna were clear across the frame. No one was touching. "I don't see how we could ever be a family again after this," Donna said, as she sparked another cigarette. When asked how much they felt like a family before the shooting, she exhaled and said, "Somewhat."

Will and Josh had both had unstable lives from the start. Born to Donna several weeks premature, Will suffered a cerebral hemorrhage at the age of one month, leaving him slightly brain damaged. Though able to function normally, he was slower than average, with an IQ of 91. His dad, a factory worker, had little patience for the boy, said Donna, and even less after she divorced him, when Will was three years old, for fooling around with her friend. "He never wanted anything to do with him," she recalled. "Will begged him to come over and visit, but he just wrote him off." Years later, when she took Will to see his father on his deathbed, he wouldn't acknowledge his son. "Will always thought his father hated him," she said.

Donna's second marriage was equally difficult for Will. When Will got up at night to pee, her husband would berate the boy for waking him. Will began to wet the bed. Donna soon divorced again. Though Will loved the outdoors, he became more shy and reclusive at school. "He was something of a loner," Donna said. Yet he rarely acted out. The worst thing he ever did was to write the word *Fuck* on the kitchen floor with a felt-tip marker. When Donna met Wayne and his young son, Joshua, in 2002, while working as a bookkeeper at the club where Wayne golfed, Will was ready for a friend.

So was Josh. Though outgoing and energetic, Josh had had his share of trauma. He was born to a mother, Sandy, who suffered from congestive heart failure. Often sick, she was unable to provide readily for Josh, retreating to her books and her soap operas while her son fended for himself. She died when he was eleven.

As the hospital bigwig and an active officer of the chamber of commerce, his father, Wayne, kept busy and had little time for Josh, who was literally bouncing off the walls. In the first grade, Josh was diagnosed with attention deficit hyperactivity disorder and began a lifetime of medication. The drugs made him sluggish but seemed to help to some degree. Josh was warm with friends and family, giving big and frequent hugs. Popular with the girls, he was the only boy invited to his friend's slumber party. "He was like a little puppy dog," his friend's mother recalled.

Still, Wayne had the impression that Josh was suffering. "After his mother died," Wayne said, "he was on the run all time." Josh never let on how he was feeling, as he stayed up late playing video games or listening to his Eminem CDs. "He keeps it all inside," Wayne said. "Anything bad happens, he laughs it off."

Late one night when Josh was around eleven, Wayne heard a strange sound coming from his son's room. He walked down the hall and opened the door. The room was painted bold yellow and plastered with posters of sports cars. A Lava Lite sat near a small desk, a student Bible, an enormous boom box. A big black sign read Go Away. Wayne half-expected to find that Josh had pulled the blankets from his bed and was sleeping on the floor, a habit his son had taken to without explanation. Tonight, Josh wasn't there. He was curled up in his closet, crying. He said he wanted his mommy.

When Donna and Wayne married, it seemed as if Will's and Josh's hard times might finally be behind them. The boys hit it off so well that bringing the two families together was easy. They both dug 50 Cent and Tony Hawk and the PlayStation 2. After the wedding, Will and Donna moved to Newport to live in Wayne's house. Buoyed by the prospect of good times, the parents transformed the basement into the kids' ultimate playpen: a giant screen TV, a foosball table, posters and pennants of race cars, their very own microwave. Will slept here on a futon under a blanket with the words *Hot Hot Hot* written in flames.

Video games were among their favorite distractions. Paul Buckner, Josh's nineteen-year-old stepbrother from Wayne's previous marriage, gave Josh *GTA III* for his birthday. "When I came downstairs, I'd just see them crashing in their cars," said Donna. "I didn't know you could kill prostitutes and stuff like that." The violence she witnessed, though, was enough to give her pause. "You realize this is virtual reality, not reality," she told the boys. They nodded and returned to their game.

Though they had a great time together, things were more difficult, particularly for Will, when they were apart. Because Will was older, he had to go to a different school than Josh and manage on his own. After classes, Will's guidance counselor, Karen Smith, often saw him outside her window, wandering the parking lot. "He'd be off by himself," she said. "He was a bit of a loner," said his driver's education teacher. "He only had a couple of friends. I told him to watch out, because there were other kids here who were taking advantage of him." Girls would ask Will for money, and wanting to be liked, he'd hand over the cash, never to be repaid.

After school and on weekends, Will fell eagerly under Josh's wing. Although Josh was younger and smaller, he was the town veteran and eagerly assumed the role of Batman to Will's older and taller Robin. And Will, somewhat slow by nature, needed all the help he could get. "Will is a little more down-the-stream relaxed," said one friend, "and Josh is the hard-core whitewater rafter."

To prove his loyalty, Josh steered Will into the arms of his ex-girl-friend, Amanda Hetherington—a smart and iconoclastic thirteen-year-old with long dark hair and blue paw prints painted on her fingernails. Amanda wrote moody poetry, listened to Marilyn Manson, and was known as one of Newport's only female skaters. She was a cheerleader but the sort that would be portrayed by Christina Ricci. She hated it. "It's just something to do," she said.

On weekend nights while watching horror movies, Will and Amanda bonded over their disdain of Newport. "There's nothing to do here but stare at the dots in the ceiling," Amanda said. Although differ-ent, they shared a feeling of being outcasts among the ruling kids of Cocke County. "The rednecks have power over everyone here," Amanda lamented. She thought it was cute that Will refused to wear a jacket emblazoned with the name of the school's embarrassing mascots, the fighting cocks.

Back at home, it began to seem that Josh was leading Will into more than just a new relationship. He was leading him into trouble. One day, out by the creek behind their house, the two went out shooting with their pellet rifles. Wayne, in one of his father-son bonding excursions, had taken the boys out target shooting with his .22 rifle. They spent the day shooting at cans floating down the water. This time, Josh struggled to aim at his target. When he fired, a pellet flew at a rock, bounced back, and lodged in Will's neck.

Yet it didn't deter them. One day later, about six months before the fatal shootings, Wayne caught the boys sitting in his bedroom, cleaning his .22 rifles that they had taken from his closet. "You do not ever, ever do that," admonished Wayne, who seldom raised his voice with the boys. He grounded them for a week and dead-bolted his bedroom door whenever he left the house. When he was home, it would remain unlocked.

WHEN YOU'RE A teenager without a driver's license, it doesn't take long to get bored. In Newport, you get bored hanging out in the parking lot at Wal-Mart, waiting for the cops to tell you to beat it. You get bored cheering the Fighting Cocks, watching *American Idol*, and swilling soda at the tiny movie theater. You even get bored playing *GTA III*, which is what happened to Will and Josh that night in June.

The summer of 2003 had started on a bad note. Josh failed seventh grade. It turned out that he had not been turning in his homework during the school year. Wayne and Donna went in for a meeting with the teachers and Josh, but he offered no explanation. As Wayne recalled, "He just said he didn't feel like turning it in." While Amanda, Will, Sarah, and his friends would be moving on, he would be staying behind. Despite the recent breakdown over his mother, Josh was back to his ways of denial. "He just laughed everything off again," Wayne said.

Will, on the other hand, had every reason to look up. After months of biding his time, he was one month from turning sixteen and getting his driver's license. He and his mother, Donna, had even made plans to get him his own car, a used Mustang that he couldn't wait to get his hands on. With his own wheels, the invisible walls of Newport would finally come down. He could pick up Amanda himself, take her to the skateboard park, maybe even cruise up to Dollywood to soak in the Big Bear Plunge rafting ride—but he would never get the chance.

After a few rounds of *GTA III* that night, Josh felt the boredom set in. "Hey," he said to Will, "let's go shoot at the sides of trailer rigs for real." It was doable. Wayne and Donna were home, which meant their bedroom door would be unlocked. They went upstairs. Their parents were watching TV. They asked if they could go ride the four-wheeler. Donna looked outside. The sun was still out. "OK," she said, "but you gotta be in before dark."

The four-wheeler didn't go anywhere that night. Will and Josh sneaked the .22 rifles from their parents' bedroom closet and hit the trail across the street. It's a steep incline down to the creek. They passed the rickety pump house, making their way down the path they'd cut with Wayne long before. Up the trail, they could hear the semis speeding down the highway. Pigeons fluttered from behind a faded billboard. The boys took a few shots at the birds but, despite the short distance, missed. The trailer rigs would be easier to hit.

They crossed a rickety wooden fence that separated the path from the hill overlooking I-40. Will faced west down the road. Josh ran a short distance along the hill and faced east. They didn't say anything to each other. They just started firing. Will thought that if he actually hit a rig, the bullets would simply bounce off the side. After more than twenty shots, though, they hadn't hit anything. Yet Will had a few bullets remaining, and he fired them away. Then they heard the rubber squeal.

After they saw the red truck careen over the median, they ran, assuming they had accidentally shot out a tire. Wayne and Donna were

still watching TV when they came back home, and the boys quickly put
the guns back in the closet. Their minds and hearts were racing. From
the house, Will and Josh could hear the police sirens. When they asked
whether they could go back outside and hit golf balls, Wayne and Donna
didn't think anything of it.

An hour later, Will and Josh were nowhere to be found. Calls to the
walkie-talkies they carried went unanswered. Wayne got in the truck
and drove up the road. Donna grabbed a flashlight and hit the trail, fearing they had some kind of accident. Desperate, she called 911 and
reported the boys missing. The cops called her back. "We have your
boys right here," she was told.

While investigating the scene of the shooting, a cop saw Will and
Josh standing up on the hillside. "It's not a place you expect to find kids
around," said the district attorney who would prosecute the case. "The
officer began talking to them and getting unusual answers."

When the boys were released to their parents, they said they had
been out shooting pigeons with their pellet guns, and when the
pigeons flew over the highway, they might have accidentally shot the
cars. But their parents knew enough to realize that a pellet couldn't do
that kind of damage. Two days later, during questioning in a polygraph
test, Will and Josh broke down and confessed. "They said they'd gotten
the idea from playing the game," the district attorney said. The Buckners were ordered to turn over to the police their guns and their copy
of *GTA III*.

As the sensational news of the video-game killers hit, the national
media descended on the small town. Josh would be the youngest person
tried for homicide in Newport history. In written statements, the boys
expressed remorse. "I will always hate myself for what happened," Will
wrote. "If I could give my life to bring him back, I gladly would. I know
what I did was stupid. I didn't think anyone would get hurt. . . . I am so
so sorry, and no matter how long the judge gives me, it won't be long
enough because I will still hate myself." Josh wrote, "I am sorry. . . . I hate

that it happened. . . . I know what it is like to lose someone because I lost my mother when I was eleven. And it has been hard without her."

On the day that the boys were being led into the courthouse, Amanda rushed down to get a glimpse. Will saw her long dark hair in the crowd and blew her a kiss as the cameras rolled. She knew they would never want to hurt anyone, but rejected the idea that the game was to blame. "I don't think it would persuade them to do this," she said. "I mean, my aunt plays that game."

Amanda has been writing poems for Will. "Hold my hand," one read, "make me stop crying. By myself I feel like dying. I can be strong if you stay. We can be together, we'll be okay. So here we are, together at last. We'll be okay, forget the past." Yet she hadn't brought herself to ask Will and Josh why they fired the shots that night. "I don't want to know the reasons," she said, picking at her food. "It freaks me out."

THE SUN WAS coming down over the barbed-wire fence surrounding Will and Josh's gloomy new home, a juvenile detention center outside Newport. Behind the two-story chain-link fence that encircles the brick buildings, a stocky guard slowly led a group of prisoners across the pavement. Two rows of tough kids—murderers, sex offenders, drug dealers—walked single-file behind him.

Outside the fence in the parking lot, Wayne and Donna were finishing their last cigarettes before walking inside to see their sons. In Tennessee, kids under the age of sixteen cannot be tried as adults, and they must be tried before a judge, not a jury—which meant that a determination in the Buckner case came quickly. After listening to the evidence and evaluating a psychological assessment of the boys, the judge determined that the boys had done something extraordinarily stupid but without murderous intent.

Will and Josh pleaded guilty to reckless homicide, reckless endangerment, and aggravated assault and were sentenced to a nearby juvenile detention center. According to state law, they could be detained only until the age of nineteen. With good behavior, however, they could get out much sooner—as soon as one year. Deneau called the sentence a "slap on the wrist."

Despite many attempts, lawsuits against the makers of violent games seldom get very far, and the Buckner case proved no different. After Thompson filed his suit in a Tennessee state court, the defendants moved it to federal court. The victims' attorneys responded by dismissing the suit altogether. Buoyed by the press and the attention, however, Thompson felt even more resolved in his mission. "The goal is to destroy the video game industry," he said. The damage had been done. After a dozen unexplained shootings later took place on an interstate highway in Columbus, Ohio, a suburban Wal-Mart pulled *Vice City* from the shelves—just in case.

For the Buckners, however, it was too late. Donna and Wayne had been coming promptly for each allotted visit—one hour every day except weekends and Fridays. Over on the basketball court behind the fence, we could see Josh braving the cold to squeeze out a few more minutes of hoops. Despite the chill, he was wearing only a green short-sleeved T-shirt and long baggy black shorts. As a couple of taller kids hogged the ball, he lagged behind them, quickly rubbing some heat along his arms with his hands before they turned around. "I worry about him in there," said Donna. "He's a lot smaller than the other kids."

Life inside the juvenile center was hard for the boys from the start. Will and Josh were assigned to separate 6-by-8-foot cells. They spent the days taking classes. Lights out by 6:30 p.m. Their parents couldn't get them anything to help them fill the time. When they requested Bibles for the boys, they were told no; kids use pages of the Bibles to roll smokes.

Josh soon stopped taking his ADHD medication because the other kids were stealing it from him. Josh, however, had been known to willfully decline the medication in the past. With his hyperactivity unleashed, he started getting into trouble, talking out of place, and showing up at visitors meetings without wearing his requisite uniform. One day he was caught piercing the tongues of a bunch of other kids with a thumbtack.

Will soon stopped playing follower to Josh's leader. Unlike Josh, Will had few infractions. He began to do well in school and was on the fast track to getting out. Will was transferred to a much less punitive group home facility. Josh soon began shaping up his act and was transferred to a separate group home. With good behavior, the two could eventually take the next step and be released for good. If and when that happens, however, the stepbrothers would not be sharing a house again.

According to Donna, "The judge doesn't want the boys back together." When Will walks out the door, she said, she plans to move with him out of state, leaving Wayne and Josh behind. It doesn't seem as though there will be love lost between the boys. "Josh is going to pay for some of the things he's done in here," Will told his mother without elaboration.

That was not all that had changed in Will's mind, Wayne and Donna learned after they passed through the metal detectors to see him that cold February night. With guards standing watch, Will sat at the table in his uniform, exchanging greetings with his parents. After a bit of small talk, Donna looked him in the eye. "You've had a lot of time to think about what you've done," she said. "Do you still think it was a video game that made you do this?"

Will sat up and became emphatic. "It wasn't the game that made us think to go out and do this," he said bitterly. "We wanted to do this. The idea was to act out the game. But the game didn't reprogram our minds." When asked to elaborate, he just repeated that phrase: "The game didn't reprogram our minds." He said he wished the lawsuit against the game's makers had never happened in the first place. With Will's time up, the guards came and took him away.

As Donna lit a cigarette outside, she said she was surprised that Will was backpedaling from blaming the game. Yet she also wondered whether he wasn't backing off for another reason: "Because the kids inside there are fans of *Grand Theft Auto*, and they told him if he gets the game pulled from the shelf, they're going to beat him up."

17

Boyz in the Hood

WANTED LEVEL

★★★★☆☆

J amie King felt the AK-47 burning in his hand with every shot he
fired. Tall and lanky with longish brown hair, he crouched in a gun
range in Las Vegas, firing off weapons during a research trip he'd orga-
nized for *GTA: San Andreas.* The idea of this one, ostensibly, was to take
artists and programmers from Rockstar North to Vegas—which would
be simulated and satirized as the city of Las Venturas in the game. Scots
had roamed the neon streets with digital cameras and audio recorders,
chronicling the garish steakhouses and the gaudy nightclubs for
inspiration.

Coming to Vegas was also an excuse to shoot some really big guns.
Rows of pasty coders stood beside King, nervously handling their
weapons. Most hadn't handled guns before. In fact, some even refused
to come inside—for fear of getting Dick Cheneyed in the glasses. King

told the guys to listen closely to every shot, feel the recoil of the weapons in their hands. This was the level of authenticity he and the other cofounders of Rockstar demanded.

As King unloaded the gun, he needed to blow off steam. Despite clawing their way to the top of the $10 billion video game industry, Rockstar, privately and publicly, was under fire. Behind closed doors, the company was still reeling from the shocking departure—or betrayal, as Sam might have it—of Sam's key men, Pope and Fernandez, who, even worse, took a handful of other Rockstars with them. When word came that Pope and Fernandez were calling their new start-up Cashmere Games, it only mocked Rockstar more.

The pressure grew on King. The company now had five Rockstar-branded studios around the world churning out games. As production coordinator, King was constantly traveling between them, trying to keep the process going. Yet everywhere he landed, he'd hear complaints and moans. Then he'd be dealing with pressure in New York, racing to complete games at the eleventh hour or hopping into Brant's Porsche to run urgent missions for the team.

In a way, King thrived on the drama, but the work was whittling away at his soul. Still, he had plenty of other problems to manage. While internal strife grew, the fallout of the media frenzy over *GTA* continued to grow. On any given day, the Rockstars would open an e-mail that read something like, "You should be taken out into the streets and stoned to death."

The Rockstars knew who was chiefly responsible for stirring up the storm: Thompson. His name echoed down the halls like exclamation points in a comic book word balloon. Every day it seemed as if a new crime was being blamed on the game. Eibeler fumed. "You realized it made no sense at all, and it was a pretty tough stretch," he recalled, "but if you were sued, you had to deal with it."

Any time Thompson spoke out, it seemed, dozens of in-bound calls came to the Rockstar publicist's phone. The company's PR consultant, put out the flames as best he could. "Be responsible, don't engage," was his mantra. On the calls, he stuck to his script. "We're rated," he told the press, "we don't support selling the game to anyone under eighteen."

Eibeler worked the political lobby behind the scenes. Take-Two sponsored a baseball game between Republicans and Democrats in Washington, D.C. Eibeler made the rounds on the Hill and encountered the same pattern. Whenever he walked into a congressman's office to meet with the chief of staff, there would be a young guy at the door. "Take-Two! You guys are rock stars! *Grand Theft Auto* is the greatest game ever made!" Then he'd get back to the chief, who would say, "We gotta be careful about the effect on children."

"The average age of a gamer is twenty years old," Eibeler always replied, to no avail. He went back to NYC, only to see the same politicians grandstanding against video games on TV. "They'd all be receptive" at first, he said, "but in reality all politicians love a sound bite."

As Eibeler fought on the frontlines, Rockstar's founders privately reeled over Thompson's campaign against them. Here they were in a country teeming with protests over the war in Iraq, and people were getting up in arms about a video game? "It's weird that every day someone was speaking out against you," King later said of Thompson. "Thankfully, a lot of what he said was ridiculous."

King believed that their games were cathartic. "We're human beings," he said. "We're the only species on the planet that commits genocide on our own race. We are barbaric. We are warring nations." Rather than "suppress it and then have outbursts that are catastrophic, put it in the living room, and allow you to engage in it . . . in a video game exercise, those feelings of frustration and anger. See it for what it is, laugh about it, smile and have fun. Versus 'I don't have an outlet I don't have a video game I don't have a book, I don't have a film I don't have anyone to talk to, I'm feeling alone, I'm getting trapped, and I'm building up, building up so I express them through some extreme fashion.' For whatever reason we often as human beings don't like to confront things that are uncomfortable."

Yet they also wondered, What if Thompson was right? What if the games were having some kind of effect? They had made a game casting players as bad guys, and now they were being painted as bad guys themselves. "Are we bad people?" King once asked the others. "Are we wrong?" Then, after a beat, he said, "Fuck that. This is our lives!"

DAYCARE CENTER pedophiles. Travel club scam artists. Shady tow truck companies. Newscaster Arnold Diaz had exposed them all in his running "Shame on You" feature on the local CBS-2 news show in New York. On November 6, 2003, he inducted his first video game maker into the hall of shame: Sam Houser. "While much of *Vice City*'s violence is random and indiscriminate," Diaz said, "'Shame on You' found as you get deeper into the game, it takes an ugly, racist twist. Players are instructed to exterminate an entire ethnic group!" With that, he cut to a *GTA* gamer, who said that "My mission in the game is to kill the Haitians."

"That's right, 'kill the Haitians,'" Diaz said. Though *Vice City* had been out for more than a year, the media was still looking for new ways to exploit the controversy, and Diaz had seemingly happened on a fresh new shocker. "Just read the game's dialogue," he said, quoting from the game script. "'I hate these Haitians. We'll take them out, we'll take these Haitians down."

It was true, sort of. The words were spoken by Umberto Robina, the Cuban kingpin in *Vice City*, in a cut-scene preceding the twentieth mission in the game, "Cannon Fodder." As in every *GTA* game since *GTA 2*, *Vice City* depicted wars between rival—and stereotypical—gangs: rednecks, metalheads, bikers, and, yes, ethnic groups such as Cubans and Haitians and Italians, too. Robina was sending the player, Tommy Vercetti, on a mission to take a crew of armed Cubans into the Haitian gang's enclave—and attack. But when Umberto said, "Take my boys over there, and then we'll take these Haitians down!" he wasn't talking about taking *all* Haitians down, he meant only the drug-dealing gang.

Yet what was clear to Rockstar and its fans was lost in the ratings war of the evening news. "Why is Rockstar Games, the maker of '*Grand Theft Auto*: *Vice City*,' using the killing of Haitians as entertainment?" Diaz asked his viewers. "The company is based right here in New York City. Its president, Sam Houser, is ranked as one of the entertainment industry's most powerful people. But he's hiding, refusing to speak with us at all, refusing to even acknowledge the community's concerns about the game. . . . So into the CBS 2 'Hall of Shame' we induct Rockstar Games and its president, Sam Houser, for cashing in on racism and violence."

Within days, the Haitian Centers Council and Haitian Americans for Human Rights put out a press release saying that Rockstar and Take-Two "advocate the killing of Haitians as entertainment. . . . Players are instructed to kill all Haitians, who, in the video game, are stereotyped as thugs, thieves and drug dealers." Politicians warned of people emulating the game's violence in real life. On November 25, 2003, Haitian American protesters stormed City Hall. "We believe that it was the purposeful intent of Rockstar Games Inc. to create a product that was controversial in order to increase sales," said the group's leader, who called for an international boycott of the game.

Powerful people were listening. Haitian president Jean-Bertrand Aristide was reported to have been talking with U.S. authorities about the matter because, as his government spokesperson said, "This racist game is psychologically extremely dangerous and is an incitement to genocide."

Once again, this game that had intended to satirize America instead struck a nerve. It didn't matter what was or wasn't in the game because the controversies weren't really about the game at all. They were about the fears—first violence and now racism—that the games unleashed, and Rockstar had no choice but to respond.

"We empathize with the concerns of the Haitian community, and we are giving serious consideration to them," a Take-Two spokesperson said in a statement. "There was no intention to offend any ethnic group." He compared the rivalries in *Vice City* to *West Side Story*, but the press wasn't buying it. As the Haitian storm grew, it only swept more of Rockstar's battles into the public eye, including Thompson's $246 million suit from the Tennessee shootings. U.S. senator Carl Andrews, a New York Democrat, proposed a bill banning the game. From Boston to Florida, more rallies waged.

During a December visit to a Haitian church in East Flatbush, New York City mayor Michael Bloomberg told the crowd that he'd sent a letter to Rockstar condemning the game. "It's disgraceful, it's vulgar, it's offensive," Bloomberg said of *Vice City*. He promised "to do everything we possibly can" to have the "kill the Haitians" line removed. "This type of hate has no place in our city, and as a mayor I will not tolerate it."

Bloomberg delivered. Two days later, Rockstar put out an apology to the Haitian groups. "It was not our intention to target or offend any group or persons or to incite hatred or violence against such groups or persons," the statement read. For a secretive company that rarely, if ever, spoke out about its own controversies, the statement was revealing and significant. In rather patronizing tones, it showed how desperately the cofounders wanted to school the haters. It also demonstrated their fondness for blaming the media for their problems.

"Contrary to what some may believe," the statement read, "it must be recognized that videogames have evolved as an adult medium, not unlike literature, movies and music. The fact that the game is popular does not mean that it will encourage players to act out hatred or violence against any group or persons in the 'real world.'. . . We believe that recent media coverage has taken certain statements made in the game out of context, and has blown it out of proportion by mischaracterizing the nature of the game play, as well as the actual portrayal of persons and groups in the game.

"As with literature, movies, music and other forms of entertainment, we have strived to create a videogame experience with a certain degree of realism, which we believe is our right. Nevertheless, we are aware of the hurt and anger in the Haitian community and have listened to the community's objections to certain statements made in the game."

Rockstar promised to remove the controversial kill-the-Haitians line from all future versions of the game, but protesters said they wouldn't rest until all 10.5 million copies of the game had been pulled from the shelves. To show their resolve, they rallied outside Blockbuster and Wal-Mart stores around the country. On December 15 at 10 a.m., a hundred of them gathered outside the offices of Rockstar Games, chanting, "They say kill us! We say fight back. Rockstar, racist!" When a reporter asked a protester why she would come here on such a wintry day, she said, "I'm outraged against Rockstar for stepping over Haitians to make money. I don't feel the cold."

WHILE THE HAITIAN controversy raged, little did the outside world know that Rockstar was already probing deeper into America's racial tensions with the next *GTA, San Andreas.* The plan had been hatched late one night early in the brainstorming sessions as Sam and King talked in the game-testing area. They were making a game about California in the nineties, about gangs, so casting the main character seemed like a no-brainer. "We should have a black lead," King said. "That would be cool."

In the game industry, however, this wasn't cool yet at all. Other than sports titles, games were still like music videos in the early eighties, bereft of African American leads. Sam saw the chance to innovate once again by breaking down the color barrier, too. "It was something of a risk," Sam later recalled. "It was certainly left field for the industry at that time, but, you know, I'm proud to do things like that, and anyone who has a problem with that, we don't want you buying the game anyway, mate, quite frankly."

San Andreas would follow the story of Carl "CJ" Johnson, a gang kid who fled Los Santos, their fictional Los Angeles, after the drugs and the shootings became too much for him. Yet as with the other *GTA*s, fate would draw him back. When CJ learns that his beloved mother has died as an innocent victim of gang warfare, he comes back to his old neighborhood for her funeral and for vengeance. CJ's odyssey will ultimately lead him around the state of San Andreas, taking on the gangs.

Compared to the more raucous thrills of the earlier *GTA*s, CJ's conflicts and struggles would bring a new depth and complexity to the franchise and the game industry. *San Andreas* would still be satiric, but Sam, Dan, and the rest were dead serious about the awful world of gang consequences they were portraying. For added authenticity, they continued the street research that Fernandez had begun in L.A. before he quit. Khonsari flew out to L.A. to hook back up with Mr. Cartoon and Esteban and start casting the game. He cruised South Central, snapping photos of barbershops, houses, and hangouts to use in-game.

One day, he set himself in the Second Hand studio owned by Dr. Dre to begin casting the game. Because of their success, Rockstar was more interested in discovering new talent than on relying on celebrity voice-overs. Gang members and amateur rappers streamed in, begging to be in *GTA*. "Anything you can do to get me a role," one told Khonsari. "I don't care if it's a big role, I just want to be in it!" As one of the applicants brazenly puffed on a joint, a grin spread across Khonsari's face. *GTA* had always been about authenticity, but it had never felt as real as this.

Despite their efforts, though, the fact that *San Andreas* represented a white British take on L.A. gang culture seeped through. Khonsari sat at his desk in L.A., as a gang member got stuck on a word in Dan's script. "'Rubbish?'" The extra said, "What the fuck is this? I'd never say 'rubbish!'" To de-Brit the script, Rockstar hired DJ Pooh, the screenwriter of the Ice Cube film *Friday*, as cowriter.

As work proceeded, however, one Rockstar wasn't taking too kindly to the game. He'd been at the company since 1999, an original 575er, and had seen the changes and stresses bearing down on the team. Compared to the humor of *GTA2*, *GTA III*, and *Vice City*, he thought Rockstar had entered a gloomer era. He'd grown tired of what he felt were Rockstar's "exploitative" games—none more so than *Manhunt*. "There's a difference between violence and gratuitous violence," he said.

He also had an objection that was even more personal: the African American protagonist and tone of *San Andreas*. He had grown up a white guy listening to rap, as Sam had. Yet now he had a black wife and was living in a black part of New York where people were shooting one another in the streets. "I have a problem with the portrayal of African Americans in the game," he later said. So he quit.

He wasn't the only one at the company with such concerns. Though Eibeler was impressed by the scope of the game, he worried that the black lead could be problematic, and he didn't want a repeat of the *Vice City* furor over the Haitians. To avoid problems, he suggested that they bring Lowenstein up to get an early peek at the game.

It wasn't common for the head of the Entertainment Software Association (renamed recently from the IDSA) to check up on every new video game, but with the controversy surrounding the franchise, he wasn't taking any chances on the new *GTA*. On one hand, the games had brought in money and acclaim for the industry, but at the cost of fueling the culture war over the medium. Lately, Lowenstein felt that he was making progress on the strength of the ESRB, the industry's voluntary rating board. He had met with Hillary Clinton, who seemed open to self-regulation. He didn't want the next *GTA* to put that to waste.

Despite all of the public and private jockeying over Rockstar's games, however, Lowenstein had virtually no relationship with the Housers. Instead, he dealt with Eibeler at Take-Two. Rockstar, even for him, remained an enigma. As he saw it, their attitude was "We are on our own and do what we want and everyone has to suck it up."

Rockstar had its own floor in the Take-Two building, and getting there was a game unto itself. Lowenstein watched as a Take-Two executive called someone at the desk for permission to visit. "We'd like to come down," the executive asked. Then he and Lowenstein had to wait, humiliatingly, for Rockstar security to escort them. "I couldn't believe this," Lowenstein recalled. "Literally, the head of Take-Two couldn't wander down there." As Lowenstein sat in a conference room watching *San Andreas*, he sensed tension between Rockstar and Take-Two—Sam's parent in the most literal sense.

Lowenstein greeted the demo of *San Andreas* with a certain detachment. This was never his cup of tea, as he put it, but it didn't matter. He knew the guys were pushing the medium and deserved his protection and defense. Onscreen, he watched as the nimble young black man in jeans pulled a helpless driver from a car and hurled her to the ground. As CJ sped off past the dilapidated crack houses and bodegas of this fictional Los Angeles, Lowenstein didn't think there was anything unique or newly concerning about the violence. Yet he had a whole new worry in mind.

He feared the potential impact of *San Andreas*, especially after the protest over the Haitians in *Vice City*. Rockstar, he thought, might be opening up new lines of political attacks by, as he put it, "profiling minorities in the worst possible light by focusing on gang warfare in Los Angeles." He felt particularly concerned about the possible response of the Congressional Black Caucus, whose members he had watched take a strong First Amendment defense when white politicians were attacking gangster rap. "This is the last thing we need," he thought.

Lowenstein resented what he thought was Rockstar's tendency to cut and run whenever the shit hit the fan—and then leave him there to clean it up for the industry. This time, they owed him, he figured. "I like to think that after I took a lot of hits and bullets on *GTA III*, they saw

I wasn't throwing them overboard," Lowenstein later said. "I hoped they felt I was on their side and felt I was not trying to do anything to compromise their artistic freedom."

He told them his opinion. "Listen, you guys gotta get out in front of this," he said. "This is going to be very controversial, and it makes our job that much more difficult if we don't have the company making the game trying to defuse the controversy." Lowenstein suggested that before the game's release, they take the time to prepare key leaders in the Congressional Black Caucus.

To his relief, Rockstar and Take-Two were receptive. They brought in consultants to, as a Rockstar publicist later put it, "mature our understanding of the controversy issue," so that they would "know how to respond when the heat came." As Sam returned to the production of *San Andreas*, he had something hotter than ever in mind for the world's most notorious video game: sex.

18
Sex in San Andreas

THE DATE

On a good date, you earn 5% Girlfriend Progress. Add Flowers and a kiss to bump that figure up two percentage points. You can kiss and give gifts as much as you like on a single date, but they won't help beyond the first attempt. Girlfriend Progress (displayed in percentages) can be viewed in the "Achievements" option under "stats" in the Pause Menu.

It's always weird going back to the old neighborhood, but it sure feels strange the morning of Carl Johnson's return.

Under a blue sky, he pedals his yellow BMX bike down the familiar city streets, past the Ideal Homies Store with its guns and jeans, past the yellow cabs and the vintage vans, past the brothers on the corner in their baggy pants, over the narrow bridge and around the bend by the tall chick in the thigh-high stockings and the halter top, down Grove Street along the small rundown houses behind chain-link fences, garbage outside and muscle cars in the driveway, until he comes to a stop outside a brown dilapidated home with palmettos shooting through the broken slats of a wooden fence out-side. "Home," CJ says to himself, "or at least it was before I fucked everything up."

The moment he opens the paint-chipped front door and steps inside, he feels off-balance. He eyes the empty living room with fading blue wallpaper. The stairs leading up to his old bedroom. Worse, the home has been vandalized. Precious mementos scattered. He staggers dizzily, mouth agape, as he reaches for the framed photo of his dead mother on the floor. He props the photo gently up on a table, then pulls up a chair and stares at her face, head in hands.

This is the opening mission of *GTA: San Andreas*, and the gamers at Rockstar were watching CJ arrive at his home in Los Santos. With the staff growing, they had moved to a bigger office at 622 Broadway with foosball tables and arcade machines, but there was little time to play. By the middle of 2004, they were busy testing *San Andreas*, scouring for bugs in the software, then fixing the art and the code. As the cinematic sequence played, they found something new in the pixilated world—emotion. It was a feeling, something real and strange and evocative of the films they'd loved, something few would associate with *GTA* or video games at all: tenderness.

As Khonsari, the director of this and other cut-scenes in the game, watched CJ mourn, he felt particularly moved. For years, he had been making films in which he tried to evoke emotions from viewers, and now they were bringing this power to video games. He realized that video games might go even further than films, because of how they cast and immersed the player in the action firsthand.

Sam couldn't agree more. For *San Andreas*, he wanted to immerse players in their characters more than ever before. Rockstar achieved this in a most unexpected way—by transforming *GTA* into a kind of role-playing game, the genre Sam had disparaged for so long. RPGs, which dated back to *Dungeons & Dragons* pen-and-paper games, were built on personalization. Players chose their own characters at the onset—say, wizards or warriors—and assigned levels of intelligence and strength that could be augmented throughout the game experience. Although most common in fantasy RPGs, customization had become more fashionable in the industry, with even sports titles hyping their ability to let players create their own likenesses in the game.

Once again, Rockstar's innovation was to bring such features into an open and contemporarily realistic world. In *San Andreas*, players could buy a choice of tattoos and haircuts (afros and Jheri curls). They could change their bodies, eating pizza and burgers to get fat or salads to stay lean. They could go to the gym and pump iron to get ripped. The more they drove their vehicles, the higher their stats and skills would soar. *San Andreas* even included dating, letting the player win the hearts of girlfriends with flowers and kisses. Sam thought the leisure time activities were a way to further connect a player with the game and personalize the experience, but he worried that the role-playing elements might prove too geeky for *GTA*'s hardcore fans. "What are we doing here?" he wondered. "We've made *GTA* uber-nerdy in a way with this stuff—will people get it?"

Gamers had better. With more than 32 million *GTA*s already sold, the shareholders of Take-Two wanted another hit. As Sam said in the press release announcing the game in March 2004, "We have put an enormous amount of pressure on ourselves to ensure we do everything possible to exceed people's expectations."

They decided on one more powerful way to blow gamers away: with sex. Although violence had long been an acceptable, if not controversial, part of games, sex remained taboo. Early computer games such as *Custer's Revenge* and *Leisure Suit Larry* toyed with bawdy (and dumb) soft porn, like bad jokes from episodes of *Benny Hill*. Later, hits such as the cheeky shooter *Duke Nukem* and even Rockstar's own *Vice City* put strippers in the action.

Because games were still thought of as a children's toy, however, M-rated games couldn't get away with the kind of content one would see in an R-rated film. Nudity would likely earn a game the Adults

Only rating, banning it from mainstream retail—and costing millions in losses. This infuriated Rockstar, but Sam wasn't going to sit idle anymore.

Early Wednesday morning, July 14, 2004, he fired off an e-mail to Jennifer Kolbe, the director of operations for Rockstar, copying Donovan and Dan:

> [J]ennifer, how are we going to handle the approval of certain bits of content in sa [*San Andreas*], we are keen to include new functionality and interaction in line with the 'vibe' of the game. to this end, in addition to the violence and bad language, we want to include sexual content, which I understand is questionable to certain people, but pretty natural (more than violence), when you think about it and consider the fact that the game is intended for adults. Here are some examples of content that will be displayed graphically:
>
> - blowjobs
> - full sex (multiple positions)
> - dildo sex (including being able to kills [*sic*] someone with a dildo)
> - whipping (being whipped)
> - masturbation (one of the characters is compulsive; this MUST be kept)
>
> all of these items are displayed both through cutsecnes [*sic*] and in-game. I know this is a tricky area but I want to find a way for this work; the concept of a glorified shop (walmart) telling us what we can/can't put in our game is just unacceptable on so many levels. All of this material is perfectly reasonable for an adult (of course it is!), so we need to push to continue to have our medium accepted and respected as a mainstream entertainment platform, we have always been about pushing the boundaries; we cannot stop here. . . . how do we proceed with this? we really don't want to cut these areas. please advise.

Kolbe wasn't encouraging. "There are clearly two issues I need to deal with," she replied. "1. The ESRB and how far we can push the content envelope before the game turns from a Mature to an AO, which would traditionally eliminate us from about 80% of our distribution channels (in all likelihood, the fact that we are talking *San Andreas* would probably reduce the number to about 60%). What I know for certain is that any type of sexualized violence immediately brings a game over from a M to an AO and based on this, out of all the content you have listed below the only one that would seem likely to fall into this category would be killing someone with a dildo, as ridiculous as that sounds. I will do some checking and find out how this line has been drawn historically and where we can push it."

That wasn't all. "Second issue," she wrote, "is with retail and how to raise the level of content and still stay within the boundaries, both vague and clear, that have been set by the more conservative retailers, within the m category, there is a line we can cross that will preclude us from being carried in places like wal-mart and best buy; both have gone on the record to say that a game featuring full frontal nudity is a no-go but as we with *Vice City* and the candy suxxx scenes, there is a level of content that is allowable depending on its context and depiction within the game. as with everything in the *Grand Theft Auto* series, we have always argued that everything is done within the context of the storyline and I think the same has to be said here.

"In short order, I need to do A LOT of research on the games that currently exist in the AO category so that I can put together a cohesive list of boundary crossing content as a reference for the existing content in *San Andreas*. If the AO games are as hardcore and gratuitous as I have heard they are, then a strong case can be made for the fact that we are still within Mature territory because while the sexual content in *San Andreas* is part of the storyline, it certainly isn't the whole game."

Sam's eyes ran over her last sentence, the requisite throwing of the bone. Yes, she heard him. "The directive here is very clear," she had written, "we need to push the boundaries as hard as we can so that the integrity of the game is not compromised but still maintain our level of distribution so that sales are not affected." Sometimes the hypocrisy of Sam's adopted homeland was mind-numbing. Sam would marvel at states such as Utah and the reign of the Mormons. Had the game industry come to this? Were they living in a virtual Utah?

"We need to move VERY fast," Sam replied to Kolbe. "There is nothing planned than an adult (M-rated) can't handle. Even if it is an AO (which it shouldn't be), why should this reduce our distribution so much. We have to have retail tell us what games to make? That's nonsense. Sim-Moorman (sp?) is our new idea. Freedom of speech? Isn't that how the country is justifying the invasion of Iraq and other places? We must expose such flagrant hypocrisy. Boundaries need to be stretched. This is key. Ultimately it looks nothing like the real world, so if movies do it, which are obviously more realistic, it just doesn't make sense if we can't."

Donovan spent weeks researching Sam's requests, going over the sex scenes in the game, and scouring the rules around the world for just what could and couldn't make it in. Sam tried his best to reassure the developers in Scotland. "As you know, sex is more of an issue than murder [in the United States]," he wrote in an e-mail to Rockstar North, ". . . so we're going to have to be as smart as possible. We're definitely going to have to do a separate version for Wal-Mart. Therefore whatever content we do agree on needs to be easily removable. . . . We'll do whatever we can to keep this stuff in. It's going to be tough but we love a good battle."

PHIL HARRISON cut through London one summer morning on his way to work. Now senior vice president of product development at Sony Computer Entertainment Europe, he had become one of the most iconic stars on the PlayStation team. Tall, bald, and incisive, he was the kind of game executive whom gamers readily called one of their own. Like Sam, he shared the passion to make games mass market. With the success of *GTA*, he was now on a new mission—to make games not only for adults, but for the entire family, too.

The answer was the EyeToy, a motion-sensing camera that would let players interact with games without the use of a controller. All they had to do was wave their hands. In one game, bubbles appeared to line the TV screen, and kids competed to wipe them off simply by waving their hands in the air. "It was something the whole family could play," Harrison said. "We got quickly into the idea of removing the game controller from the equation. It was a huge boost to people. If you hand a controller to a nongamer, it's like you've handed them a live grenade."

Released a year earlier, in the summer of 2003, the EyeToy sold more than 2.5 million copies by year's end. Other family-friendly games such as SingStar (a karaoke game) helped expand the market even more. For Harrison, it represented a triumph—proof that between *GTA* and the EyeToy, there would be games for everyone. When his sister phoned him on the way to work, she could have been doing it to congratulate him, but she wasn't. "Have you read the *Daily Mail* this morning?" she asked.

"I don't read the fucking *Daily Mail*," he quipped.

"I think you ought to read it. Go buy a copy."

Harrison saw the headline: "Murder By PlayStation." Oh shit, he thought. The story concerned a seventeen-year-old boy, Warren Leblanc, who had recently confessed to murdering his fourteen-year-old friend, Stefan Pakeerah, with a claw hammer and a knife. Now Pakeerah's mother was speaking out. She had heard through the boys' friends that the two were obsessed with playing a video game, *Manhunt*, and now she blamed it for the crime. "This game should be banned," she told the *Daily Mail*. "It promotes violence for violence's sake and corrupts young minds. . . . We owe it to Stefan's memory to take on those people who have succeeded in getting this game marketed."

Since its release in November 2003, *Manhunt* had already created a storm in the game press over its chilling but impeccably rendered violence. A barbed-wire garrote was sent out to reviewers of the game. Yet reading this story made Harrison stop in his tracks. He had seen the hamster of video game violence run through the press for years, but this story marked a new era in England. This wasn't a Max Clifford ploy. This was a real mother of a real dead boy. Harrison felt terrible for the family but furious that games were blamed. "There was a segment of the potential audience for games who would believe this headline," he later said.

The *Manhunt* controversy only exploded from there, as the story spread around the world. The game—already banned in New Zealand—got pulled from stores of the United Kingdom's largest retailer, Dixons. Before long, the United Kingdom's own answer to Jack Thompson, Leicester East member of Parliament Keith Vaz, took action. During a question session with Prime Minister Gordon Brown, Vaz called for protective measures—despite the fact that *Manhunt* had been already rated for eighteen-year-olds and over. "This is not about adult censorship," he said, "it is the protection of young children and young people."

Amid all the debate, however, there was one group conspicuously missing—Rockstar. Instead of speaking out, Donovan worked behind the scenes with Simon Harvey, a spokesperson for the British game industry, to provide any response. Harvey said in his statement, "Simply being in someone's possession does not and should not lead to the conclusion that a game is responsible for these tragic events."

Harrison struggled to move forward with his plan to bring games to families in the face of this controversy. Like Lowenstein in the United States, he couldn't help feeling that when the shit hit the fan, the bad boys of gaming lacked the courage to take a stand. "I was frustrated that nobody from Rockstar ever went on the record," he recalled. "They just went radio silent."

WHILE THE CONTROVERSY over *Manhunt* grew back in their home country, Sam and the guys at Rockstar were more concerned with *San Andreas*—and the results of Donovan's research into how far they could push the sexual content in the game. The findings weren't encouraging.

"Unfortunately, here is the situation," Donovan wrote in an e-mail to Sam on August 16, 2004, and proceeded to list the necessary changes.

"Hooker in car blow job—we need to show much less of the critical mouth to penis area.

"Hooker Stand Up Blow Job—this needs to be removed or implied.

"Sex with girlfriend—essentially this is all beyond the bounds of M and 18 ratings, and needs to be removed or implied.

"Sex shop workers need to have slightly more nipple coverage particularly for the States.

"Key to her heart spanking date scene needs to be removed, as it constitutes sexualized violence which is a huge problem.

"Blow job in back room of dealer's house is cool however.

"I wish we could include all this incredible stuff, but it just isn't feasible to get it out there at the moment. As discussed we are working on a couple different scenarios for a release of a version with this content included."

Sam clicked the attachment—four excruciating pages of explication, details, country by country, over just what kind of sexual activity could and could not be shown, given their target rating. All of Sam's ranting about Iraq and hypocrisy splintered into pixels as he read the rules in black and white. This was someone else's game. The list under each country's regulations was beautifully absurd, hilarious and horrific, and inescapably real. It started with the United Kingdom, where the target age rating was eighteen.

"Male nudity—Full frontal nudity is acceptable as long as the penis is not erect," Donovan explained.

"An erect penis should be avoided entirely or we would need it to be pixillated.

"Female nudity—Full front nudity is acceptable but only at a distance if the full body is to be shown and showing the breasts only is preferable.

"Masturbation—Can be implied but the penis should not be visible. We would be safer to show a man from the back view doing this, not with the camera angle straight on.

"Oral sex—Similar to masturbation, the act can be implied but cannot be graphic. Any close-ups would require pixilation and the BBFC might ask us to remove this in order to achieve an 18 rating. Your character should not be able to kill the girlfriend or the hooker after you have sex." And so on.

As Sam read the guidelines, he saw how each country had its own seemingly arbitrary definitions of what would nudge a game into the realm of unacceptability. Spain and Italy were fine with nudity (including erections) and "lax," as Donovan put it, with regard to sexualized violence. France was okay with male nudity (no erections) and female nudity (though, as Donovan explained, "as long as it can be considered 'erotic' and not pornographic"). While Australia didn't permit male nudity, female breasts and buttocks were fine. Spanking, across the world, was pretty much a no-no, with the exception of Spain and Italy, where it was okay if it was part of the story. Every country was cool with jacking off, as long as no penis appeared. No mentions, though, of female masturbation. Implied oral sex, no problem anywhere.

Of all of the territories, the United States was by far most restrictive—any male nudity had to be covered in shadows, and although female breasts could be shown, vaginas were off limits, and nipples had to be covered with pasties. And an inexplicit scene of CJ having sex with his girlfriend? Though acceptable across the world, it would surely garner the deathly Adults Only rating in the U.S. Then Donovan dropped the bomb. "The sex scenes that are in *San Andreas* currently are going to be considered too graphic," he wrote. They had to go.

Sam sat at his computer, watching the cursor blink as the hot flush of anger crashed in. "This is WAY, WAY more than I expected," he wrote to Donovan, pounding his keys. "Not only is it insane to edit comedy like this—look at movies and everything else—to do so is going to be a lot of work and will screw with things (eg: changing the spanking mission, which could not be more harmless/silly). Is this really as far as we can push it? I just cannot believe it."

Donovan's reply came seventeen minutes later. "That's not good," he wrote, with an audible thud. "I thought we were pretty much on the same page." What was all this, anyway—a game or something else? Some big middle finger to the world? They weren't rebellious kids in prep school anymore. They were high-paid employees of a public company. They couldn't play and control life as if it were a game. They had always fought for the right for games to grow up; maybe it was time for them to grow up instead. Why not just dial back the sex in *San Andreas*?

"Spanking is pretty much the worst thing in there," Donovan explained. "You can see her vagina and asshole or at least where they would be, and the combination with the violence is what gets people most hot under the collar. Every country bar Spain came back to us and stated sexualized violence is a no-go. It is just too easy for people to take that scene out of context and claim the game requires violence to women to complete gameplay objectives."

Sam was having none of it. He came to America to find freedom, not give it up. "Wow," he wrote back to Donovan. "We have too many sales people. We need people to fight for 'freedom.'" He fired off an e-mail to Les Benzies, producer at Rockstar North, breaking the news.

"This is a shame," Benzies wrote back.

"I know," Sam replied, "it's a disaster. we should review all our options. it feels wrong to edit our game. we need to PUSH."

And so he did, throwing off a Hail Mary appeal to Take-Two's founder, Brant. Brant, however, was desperately fighting battles of his own. Despite having grown his company to more than $1 billion in revenues, with more than $100 million in earnings, Take-Two had been overtaken by scandal. The SEC investigation into Take-Two's accounting practices was still proceeding, and, furthermore, the commission suggested that it would take civil action against Brant and two former Take-Two executives for their involvement. On March 17, 2004, Brant resigned as chair and director of Take-Two. "I believe this is the right time to make a management transition to position Take-Two for the future," he said in a statement.

There had always been explicit and implicit tension between Take-Two and Rockstar, with the latter being like the unruly kid who was trying to call the shots. Yet the fact was, Sam, despite his shaggy appearance, was always a dogged leader at heart, running his ship like a CEO. Because Brant remained as vice president of publishing, Sam didn't hesitate to reach out to him.

"Hi, Can we confirm that these are the content changes that need to be made?" Sam wrote. "As I mentioned to Terry, I was pretty much shocked by the list. The cuts are everywhere. It doesn't feel like we are pushing any boundaries now. Why bother? I really, really do not want to change this stuff. It feels SO wrong at the behest of psychotic, mormon, capitalist retailers. This is a GAME. It's COMIC. Airplane (the movie) was more offensive. Please can we not forget the edgy-ness that got us here."

Poring over Benzies's menu of possible changes—moving the camera on the blowjob scene, removing other scenes entirely, and masking others, such as sex with the girlfriend, with blocky filters—felt bad enough to Sam. Even worse was Benzies's implication that they had given up their fight. "This stuff was so cool," Benzies wrote to Sam, "we're not really pushing boundaries without it."

For Sam, pushing boundaries was his life's mission, from his rebelliousness at St. Paul's through his early days at BMG. He built his career by Captain Kirk-ing beyond where others had gone before. How many people could claim they had really done that—not just in video games, but in anything? How could they stop now?

Sam had a choice to make: fight or flight. "If you and the crew feel strongly, let's make a stand," he replied to Benzies. "Let's keep what we want in the game—OUR game. It will half our retail distribution, but who cares? The game will still sell, people will have to go and find it, but it will be the game we want. We may probably sell less this route (who knows—maybe more, in the long run?), but at least we won't have been told what to do by a load of fucking bureaucrats and shop-keepers."

Not everyone agreed. Cofounder Gary Foreman characterized the sex in *San Andreas* as "funny, schoolboy, puerile humor" but thought it had its limits. "There's no way the game's going to be approved with that in it," he said, "so take it out." Plus, he thought, what's the loss? "For me, sorry I'm not twelve anymore, it was unnecessary," he later said. "There were conversations about pushing the barriers of what we could do, but I felt personally it was, at that point, gratuitous."

When King walked up to Sam one day at Rockstar, however, he could tell that his cofounder wasn't pleased at losing this battle. Though the two had had their skirmishes, he still supported his old friend and thought the sex in the game was funny.

Rockstar had built an empire on simulated fantasies, but this time reality bore down. The struggle dripped with irony. Sam wanted to make games for adults, but an Adults Only rating would be retail suicide. He personified the awkward and interminable adolescence of his entire industry and, moreover, a generation of players. It wasn't that he didn't want to grow up; he simply wasn't allowed to. He was infantilized. No matter how mature he had become, he still had to answer to his parents at Take-Two.

There was nothing that he, Brant, or anyone could do. The bureaucrats and the shopkeepers had won. Rockstar would cut back the sex from *San Andreas*. Some moderate content could remain, such as the two-ended purple dildo hidden in a police bathroom as a weapon, but little more. Instead of seeing CJ have sex with his girlfriend inside her house, players would only make it as far as the front door.

With the game's deadline just weeks away, the sex scenes had to be removed, and fast. Sometimes instead of deleting code, which can be problematic, game developers essentially hide the content from players so that it won't be seen. It's a common and acceptable process known as "wrapping," sort of like wrapping an unwanted package in camouflage and burying it in the woods. There was nothing sneaky about it.

So one quiet day at Rockstar, a programmer tapped a series of buttons on a keyboard and took care of the job. The *San Andreas* sex scene was wrapped and tucked away into the forest of code. Because the industry didn't require game developers to disclose wrapped content, Rockstar had no reason to mention the sex scene when it submitted the new *GTA* for its rating.

This game was done.

ON SEPTEMBER 12, 2004, the mailman delivered the submission package for *Grand Theft Auto: San Andreas* to the Entertainment Software Ratings Board on Madison Avenue in New York. The nondescript cluster of cubicles was protected like Area 51. "Sorry, you can't go back there," Patricia Vance, the steely president of the ESRB, would tell a visiting reporter, as he made his way past posters of Tiger Woods and brochures of happy kids, tongues wagging as they played their video games.

Every day, game publishers sent in their products for voluntary ratings, which included E for Everyone, T for Teen, and M for Mature. Lately, however, they were under fire. Harvard University had issued a study on "Content and Teen-Rated Video Games," which found that almost half of the games included content that was not listed on the video game box. In Washington State, legislators were trying to ban the sale of M-rated games to anyone under the age of seventeen. The game industry was fighting this on the grounds that such a law would be a violation of free speech.

Despite *GTA*'s past controversies, the ESRB had no reason to scrutinize it differently from any other title. The process started with the raters: a pool of fifty Americans from all walks of life—teachers, doctors, single moms, ranging in age from twenty-one to sixty-five years old. The ESRB placed ads in parenting magazines and received about a thousand applications per year. Game-playing experience was not required.

This was why: when a game company sent in a game to be rated, it was not actually sending in playable demos; the company only sent in video footage. Publishers were required to send in what Vance called "the most extreme footage" of a game, usually two or three months prior to a game's release. The footage could last anywhere from twenty minutes to a few hours. As each of the two or three raters watched the footage, a frame count rattled off onscreen. The raters had a guide to determine which content should be flagged: from gambling and sexuality to violence and destruction. Still, gore was in the eye of the beholder. "There's no formula," Vance said. "We want raters to use their own judgment."

Once a game was reviewed by the raters, the team looked to see whether there was consensus on the evaluation—Vance said there almost always was—and the game got rated accordingly. For games sold in 2003, 54 percent were rated Everyone (E); 30.5 percent were rated Teen (T); and only 11.9 percent were rated Mature (M). Despite the debate over violent games, 70 percent of the top twenty best-selling console games were rated E or T. Vance said the ultimate responsibility resided with consumers. "If a rating doesn't give you pause, at a certain point, that's not our problem," said Vance. "We can't dictate morals or ethics. People make up their own minds."

Vance thought Rockstar had always been good about disclosing the content of its games and had no reason to think otherwise with *San Andreas*. Each rater sat in a cubicle watching footage of CJ joyriding and fighting his or her way through *San Andreas* as the hip-hop music pulsed. The raters scribbled in their notepads, forbidden from talking to one another about their points of view. Finally, they convened to discuss their ratings, with a foreman presiding, but there wouldn't be any debate. *GTA: San Andreas* was rated M for Mature. Its future would be in the gamers' hands now.

19
Unlock the Darkness

RANDOM CHARACTER UNLOCKED:
PATRICK WILDENBORG

Follow the **"P"** icon to Deventer, Holland.
Approach while Patrick's family is sleeping. Patrick
will be on the couch, laptop open.

Patrick Wildenborg took his coffee black and plenty of it. As a die-hard programmer in Deventer, a small town in eastern Netherlands, Wildenborg needed all the fuel he could get.

By day, he did computer consulting, making real-time embedded systems for traffic management and military applications. Later he'd come home to his wife and two kids, a six-year-old boy and a four-year-old girl. A burly six-foot-two-inch thirty-five-year-old with small glasses and receding brown hair, Wildenborg would stoop down to the floor to play with his kids. After dinner and when the children were asleep, he'd pour himself a hot coffee, slip out his laptop on the couch, and get his game on while his wife channel-surfed the TV.

Wildenborg's favorite way to unwind was with *Grand Theft Auto*: *Vice City*. An avid gamer since he'd played on the Commodore 64 computer as a kid, he had fallen hard for Rockstar's epic. He loved the kitschy eighties American atmosphere, the synth pop, the *Miami Vice* vibe that reminded him wistfully of his own awkward youth. But mainly he liked the freedom. "The freedom," as he put it, "to do whatever you have to do." He considered the elusive creators at Rockstar to be heroes.

Like a lot of avid players, Wildenborg quickly tore through the entire *Vice City* game, finishing it up during late nights after work in a little more than a month. Yet the moment he completed the game, he felt the sad sick itch of loss, like the afterglow of the most awesome vacation ever. He didn't want it to end. Then he found a way to make the game live on—by hacking it.

Computer game hacking wasn't new. Players had been altering the code of their favorite titles for decades. The resulting modifications, or mods, ranged from the simple and goofy (such as putting Barney in the first-person shooter *Wolfenstein 3-D*) to the wildly complex (such as transforming the sci-fi title *Half-Life* into a team-based counterterrorist game, *Counter-Strike*).

Mod makers collaborated online, often without ever meeting in person, and freely distributed their programs across the Net. They did it for love and ego but seldom for money. A few mods, including *Counter-Strike*, garnered such a cult following that game companies struck deals to publish the titles themselves. As John Carmack, the programmer of mod-friendly franchises such as *Doom* and *Quake*, once put it, mods became the default résumés for aspiring game developers.

Although allowing consumers to alter a product seemed like an anathema to many, forward-thinking game makers embraced the mod community for one smart reason: mods sold games. In order to play a mod, gamers still needed to own the original CD, which meant a longer shelf life. Plus, mod makers served as the best source of viral marketing around. As a franchise's most early-adopting, impassioned fans, mod makers played a crucial role in spreading the word about new games online.

For this reason, the savviest companies not only embraced mod makers, they cultivated them—seeding, essentially, their own hardcore fans. As Wildenborg swiftly discovered online, few were as mod-friendly as Rockstar. The strategy fit perfectly with Rockstar's DIY style. Despite the fact that creating mods violated the end user license agreement of Take-Two's games, Rockstar had been building relationships with the mod makers since its earliest titles.

Fan sites such as Gouranga.com were among the first to receive regular visits and updates directly from the Housers. By the time *GTA III* came out, Rockstar had cherry-picked its own coterie of fan sites, which the company promoted on its own page. For *Vice City*, Rockstar created a homepage for what the company described online as its "international friends." As Rockstar's welcome paragraph on the site read, these were the places "to go for all those unofficial mods."

Modders knew the relationship was mutually beneficial. As one *GTA* modder put it, "The modding scene for the *GTA* franchise has generated revenue at little to no cost for the producers or publishers. We know for a fact that there is a significant percentage of *GTA* fans who only buy the game for the PC because of the open-ended modification possibilities."

As a coder and a gamer, Wildenborg threw himself into the mod scene. He knew exactly what he wanted to create for *Vice City*. In the game, players could store only four cars in a garage—hardly enough room for the dozens of sweet rides Wildenborg amassed. After a month of caffeine-fueled nights, he created Marina Carpark—a mod that, when downloaded and installed for free—let players store up to forty cars in a sprawling lot. The feat earned Wildenborg the *GTA* mod community's respect when he released it in January 2004. "People said it was impossible, but I somehow managed," he explained, with his mixture of modesty and pride.

Wildenborg spent long hours on GTAforums.com, a popular site for mod makers of the game. The visitors were often anonymous, logging on under assumed names and rarely, if ever, meeting in person or talking on the phone. Theirs was a collaborative, obsessive group of fans. One person might come up with an idea for a mod, then another would chime in—working together to reverse-engineer the game and get at the code. "The modding community felt like a bunch of friends trying to solve a mystery," Wildenborg said.

In October 2004, the players finally got their hands on *Grand Theft Auto: San Andreas*, Rockstar's hotly anticipated new game. Wildenborg and the others delighted over having "new worlds to explore," he said. He marveled at the sheer expanse of the game, cruising through the forests in his Banshee sports car, flying in his airplane, and jumping over hills on his motorcycle. He tagged storefronts with graffiti in Los Santos, hit the casinos in Las Venturas. The story of CJ's rise through West Coast gang violence brimmed with the kind of uncanny details and encyclopedic pop culture references that made Rockstar famous. Wildenborg, like the other modders, couldn't wait to play around with the code.

With only the PS2 version of the game released, however, there was only so much they could do. Mods were primarily a computer game phenomenon because consoles were harder to crack. Until the PC version of the game came out, along with the Xbox version, next summer, Wildenborg could do little more than poke around the PS2 code.

Yet poking around was half the fun and created a sublime beauty all its own. When you went deep enough into the code, you felt as if you had left your Mountain Dew–stained desk chair for the abstract world behind the computer screen. After hours of hacking *San Andreas*, Wildenborg found himself there. It was like standing in an electric forest of trees with long glowing limbs of ones and zeroes. The ground shimmered in peppery static. Wildenborg reached down into the pixilated thicket and picked up a camouflaged package wrapped and buried out of sight. He held it in his hand as it sizzled and sparked.

What, he wondered, was this?

BY THE TIME Sam's thirty-fourth birthday (and Rockstar's annual cheese ball–eating contest) rolled around, he had reason to be elated. *San Andreas* was a hit. In its first two months, *San Andreas* sold 5 million copies at $50 a pop. The game was on its way to eventually selling an astonishing 21.5 million copies, making it the most successful PS2 title ever. When the fiscal year ended on October 31, 2004—just days after the launch—*San Andreas* accounted for 20.9 percent of Take-Two's revenues.

Fans and reviewers hailed it the company's crowning achievement. *Game Critics* called it "a stunning milestone in every aspect that matters. . . . a monumental game that has now redefined the standard against which all future games like it will be measured." *Game Informer* deemed it "extraordinary—something that I believe will define a generation and will forever change the way that we look at video games." *IGN* considered it "a terrific unending masterpiece of a game." In New York, an artist friend of Rockstar's created a so-called Delinquency Chamber inspired by the game—a free-standing installation with a built-in bong, a beer-filled fridge, and a wide-screen TV for playing *San Andreas.*

Yet not everyone dug the new *GTA.* The *New York Times* found the game "just as disturbing and annoying" as the others in the franchise. Another swipe came from Dave Jones, the ex-DMA chief who was busy working on his own upcoming action game, *Crackdown.* A few days after *San Andreas*'s release, Jones dissed the game in a lengthy profile in the *Sunday Times.* "Some of it does make you grimace," he said. "It is like watching *Goodfellas.* There are some scenes when you ask yourself, Did they really have to do that? How far will this go?"

As Lowenstein had feared, others took umbrage over what was perceived as the stereotypical black lead in the game. The *Chicago Tribune* quoted an academic who said that "even though there's a lead black character, which is in some sense progress, that lead character is in a violent, urban environment . . . engaging in gang activity, drug activity, running from police."

In an article called "The Color of Mayhem," the *New York Times* said that "*Grand Theft Auto: San Andreas*, underscores what some critics consider a disturbing trend: popular video games that play on racial stereotypes, including images of black youths committing and reveling in violent street crime." King couldn't believe it when he read comments on online forums from gamers who simply didn't want to play a game with a black lead.

Yet privately, Sam had other matters in mind. Although he was publicly elated over *San Andreas*'s success, he seemed to be still reeling from cutting the sex scenes out of the game. Then came an idea for how to win in the end—by putting a sex scene into the PC version of *San Andreas* that would be getting published in June 2005. On November 25, 2004, Sam e-mailed Benzies, urging him to "explore any additional content ideas" to determine "how hard we can push the sex stuff . . . to make it bonkers." Benzies promised, "We will get the sex stuff back to the way it was."

Two weeks later, the Rockstar designer handling the production process e-mailed a colleague about the decision to bring the sexy back to the game. Animators were instructed to dig up the old animations and make sure they were up to par. "And may I say how happy I am that they are going back in," the colleague replied.

If need be, Sam later explained in another internal e-mail, the company might put out two versions of the game, "we will do AO and M versions (as discussed)." Releasing an AO version of *San Andreas* would be more of an artistic statement than a way to cash in. Rockstar would be sending a message, as Sam wrote, that "yes we will go to places that you other f★cks wouldn't even consider."

Over at the ESRB, however, the Xbox and PC versions of *San Andreas* were no reason for concern. On January 7, 2005, the submission package from Rockstar arrived at the ESRB office without fanfare. Because the game was identical to the PS2 version, Rockstar was not required to send a new disc with the package. The reviewers simply rubber-stamped the Xbox and PC versions of the game with the same M-rating as before.

Back at Rockstar, Donovan told Sam that fear was spreading among the sales force over the sex scene plan. "They are concerned we will get a really intense backlash if we push the pc version too far," Sam wrote to Benzies on January 18.

In the computer game ecosystem, games sometimes need updates after they're released. This could be for a variety of reasons, maybe to fix a bug or tweak new content. To remedy this, game makers put out small software programs called patches, which gamers can download for free online. As part of a possible new AO-rated version of San Andreas, Rockstar could release the PC version of the game with the sex-scene wrapped away, as in the PS2 game. Then later, they could put out a patch which, when installed, would open the sex scene and, as Sam put it in an email, "unlock the darkness." There would be nothing illegal or misleading about it.

On February 7, 2005, a Rockstar designer e-mailed a colleague the possibility that "sex is going to be released as a patch, so we can fudge as much as you like." The next week, another email made sure that the "full on sex works" in the "patched version" in the PC edition of *San Andreas*.

It was time for the darkness to set in.

"YOU ARE DOING GOD'S work in battling these forces of darkness. Satan is behind them, and God is behind you." Jack Thompson would never forget these words of encouragement that a fellow culture warrior had once shared with him. He felt more blessed than ever when he found himself on *60 Minutes* taking on what for him was the darkest force of all, *GTA*.

"*Grand Theft Auto* is a world governed by the laws of depravity," correspondent Ed Bradley said by way of introduction. "See a car you like? Steal it. Someone you don't like? Stomp her. A cop in your way? Blow him away. There are police at every turn, and endless opportunities to take them down. It is 360 degrees of murder and mayhem: slickly produced, technologically brilliant, and exceedingly violent."

It was March 5, 2005, and the world's most notorious video game was in the crosshairs for a shocking series of murders in a small American town. "But for the video-game training," Thompson, graying hair neatly combed, told Bradley, "he would not have done what he did."

Thompson was referring to what happened on June 7, 2003, in the small coal-mining town of Fayette, Alabama. At 3 a.m., police officer Arnold Strickland found a young black man, eighteen-year-old Devin Moore, sleeping in a car that came up as stolen. Strickland cuffed Moore and took him back to the station for questioning. While Moore was being booked, he suddenly grabbed the Glock handgun from officer Arnold Strickland's holster and shot him dead.

Moore fled, as another cop came after him, but Moore was fast in his reflexes and unloaded three shots at the cop, killing him, too. As the boy passed the office of an emergency dispatcher, he squeezed off five more rounds, including another head shot. With the three men left bloodied and dead, Moore spotted a set of keys and took them outside, where he sped off in a squad car just before sunrise.

Three and a half hours later, police chased the dark-blue stolen police car just over the Mississippi state line. On Moore's arrest, news of the shooting spree traveled the country, and people wondered what would cause this young guy, with no prior criminal record, to snap as he did. During a court hearing in December 2004, an officer testified that as Moore was being led into the county jail, Moore said, "Life is like a video game.You've got to die sometime." And the game he liked to play was *GTA*.

When Thompson heard this news, he snapped into action. While Rockstar had become the biggest player in the game industry, Thompson had become the most notorious player hater around. He felt more confident than ever. In the previous year, he had successfully battled the most controversial radio shock-jock in America: Howard Stern. After badgering the Federal Communications Commission about Stern, Thompson managed to get Stern suspended from air time in Miami and, ultimately, fined nearly $500,000. Even Stern gave him props by calling him the "lunatic lawyer in Miami who got me off the air down there."

Now he was ready to set his sights back on Rockstar. "What we're saying is that Devin Moore was, in effect, trained to do what he did," Thompson told Bradley, who listened intently. "He was given a murder simulator. He bought it as a minor. He played it hundreds of hours, which is primarily a cop-killing game. It's our theory, which we think we can prove to a jury in Alabama, that but for the video-game training, he would not have done what he did." Thompson promised that a lawsuit would follow.

As the players of the game industry watched the segment, they reeled and fumed.

Lowenstein felt more exasperated than ever. Prior to the segment's airing, he tried to interest the producers in other angles—the demographics of games, the health benefits—but for naught. Lowenstein later recalled, "People would apologize and say, 'Listen, I'm really sorry, but the editors are telling me I have to do this story, I know it's bullshit. I know Jack Thompson is a joke. But we gotta do the story, and we're going to quote Jack.' It became increasingly appalling and irresponsible for supposedly honorable, serious journalists to knowingly feature someone they would privately admit lacked credibility only because he was good on TV."

Back in New York, Pat Vance, the businesslike president of the ESRB, and her lead publicist, Elliot Mizrahi, watched Thompson on *60 Minutes* in awe. "What's incredible is when he's on with Ed Bradley, he's measured and composed," Mizrahi later said, "but his press releases are like the ranting of a maniac."

"We don't serve Jack Thompson," Vance snapped, "we serve the public." Yet she knew she was helpless to his message. Thompson simply played the media game better than they did. "It's not a great story to say the industry has its act together," she said. Her strategy: "Stay focused, and try not to listen."

Still, the guys back in New York couldn't help but watch—and fume. "We were low-hanging fruit for the sensationalists and the extremists," King recalled. "And there was value in the IP of *Grand Theft Auto*, to the extent that someone like Jack Thompson could make it his platform. We ultimately thought it would end in tears for someone like Jack Thompson."

Yet with his phone ringing off the hook from reporters, Thompson felt more powerful than ever. Nothing could stop him, not the people who called him crazy or even the ones who had been calling him at home, threatening to kill him. He was on a mission from God. "I was enjoying this," he later wrote in his memoir, "all the while trying to remember whose victory it really was."

His son, Johnny, however, now in the sixth grade, seemed to have doubts. As a younger boy, he had dutifully joined his dad's crusade, even buying *GTA: Vice City* while his dad videotaped him stealthily outside. Yet now he was in middle school, surrounded by game players who knew he was the son of the biggest player hater around. After his dad had been invited to speak about violent games at his school, he approached his father.

"Dad," Johnny said, "I think it's great that you're on this national show, but the kids are giving me grief about it. Kids I don't even know are coming up to me and bothering me, saying things like 'Tell your dad that I'm not going to Columbine.'" He begged his dad not to deliver the speech. Thompson's heart sank as he looked down into his son's eyes. Yet after telling the school he was declining the speech, the school counselor convinced Thompson that the best thing to do for his boy was to share this message with everyone before it was too late. Thompson agreed.

On the day of his lecture, he stood before the kids, Thompson stoked their fears as deftly as he did the viewers of *60 Minutes*. He quoted passages from the bible, along with brain-scan studies on players of violent games, and he invoked the palpable horror of school shootings. "The *Grand Theft Auto* games turn the world on its head," he preached. "Bad guys are good guys. Cops are the enemy. Women are to be used and discarded. . . . If you are convinced that violent video games cannot possibly affect you, then how sure are you that they will not affect a classmate?"

Still a stay-at-home dad, Thompson had to pick up his son at the end of school that day. As he waited, he had no idea how his son had reacted to his speech. Would Johnny hate him? Was this crusade really worth it, after all? "Dad," Johnny told him, "I was proud of you." Then he drove his boy safely through Vice City, home.

ACROSS THE OCEAN, two weeks after Thompson's appearance on *60 Minutes*, Patrick Wildenborg and the *GTA* modders were feeling proud, too. Since finding the secret code hidden in *San Andreas*, they were on a mission to see what it revealed. They created a secret forum in an online chat room, where a couple of dozen modders met every day as they pursued their quest.

These weren't any ordinary files, they realized. They referred to animations left out of the game for some reason. The problem was, without the right software, the modders couldn't see what the images contained. One modder with a particularly awesome nickname,

Barton Waterduck, got to work on cracking the code. Wildenborg knew as much about Waterduck as anyone else on the forums—pretty much nothing. But Waterduck had skills. He ran the code through a crude program that converted the files into stick figure animations— not the fully realized scenes, alas, but at least a sketch of what possibly was there.

When Wildenborg downloaded the video that Waterduck had posted online, he struggled to make out the abstract images. He saw a white stick figure person. Lines for legs. The body. Arms. A head. The person appeared to be on all fours. Wildenborg lowered his laptop screen in case his kids wandered by. "It was puzzling," he later recalled. "It was pretty clear the animations were sexual."

He was right. The hidden files had suggestive names—"SEX," "KISSING," "SNM," and "BLOWJOBZ." Soon they had more proof. On March 18, 2005, at 5:05 p.m., after two months of tinkering, Waterduck posted a note to the group titled "Real SEX animations—really." He explained how he had run the animation code through a special program with astonishing results. "There he was, CJ on the pavement," Waterduck wrote, "fucking like a rabbit." He punctuated the line with a wide-mouthed, wide-eyed emoticon. "I never EVER thought they actually created real sex animations like that in a ps2 game," he wrote, "and if they took it out, well, they didn't."

Waterduck shared his code so that others could achieve the same results. The forums lit up. Finding hidden files was one allure of modding, but finding hidden sex files in the biggest video game around— that was too killer for words. "Wow," wrote one modder, "I really didn't expect Rockstar to leave that in there." He joked, "Now they are training children to kill prostitutes as well as teaching them sex moves."

Still, Waterduck had not unearthed an entire coherent scene, only random, disorganized pieces. By the next day, Waterduck had found more, he wrote, "a video of CJ with afro and a goatie and with a almost naked (?) girlfriend model, suck, fucking, slapping, slapping too hard (!), lying, sitting, standing, on knees. . . . Only different from a real porn video is that CJ has clothes on."

It was like seeing the separate elements of a cartoon but not the whole cartoon itself. With each animation, though, a bigger picture began to take shape. "The diversity and types of animations lead me to believe that it was planned to be a mini game," posted one modder, who suggested they work now to piece it together. "But we better keep that whole thing private for now," he added, "or R★ will definitely take the anims and models out of the PC version, and that's not what we want, right?"

The modders knew enough about the real-life battles of Rockstar to realize they were playing with more than laughs. By making this public, who knew what kind of Thompsonian backlash might hit their favorite pastime? "Maybe we should keep quiet about it?" suggested one concerned modder. "If we release this video, all the bitch-mom's in all the world are gonna freak and jump on the anti-*GTA* bandwagon and give R★ grief. Maybe R★ will decide to remove it for the PC version. Then again, maybe not. Maybe it'll create a sensation for the PC release."

What had Rockstar wrought? Wildenborg wondered. Why had they buried these files? "It was just a sort of treasure hunt," he later said. "I felt like a detective figuring out how stuff works." Late at night on his couch with his coffee, he obsessively pored over the files until he found something stunning—a series of commands that enabled the player to control the action firsthand. Because he was just reading code, he couldn't see the action, but the clues seemed sure enough: this wasn't some kind of sexual cinematic, it was a mini-game!

"There are two variations," he posted. "A spanking game and a shagging game." In the spanking game, he explained, players had to smack a girlfriend's booty by tapping a button on the PS2 controller to get her as stimulated as possible. A bar labeled "EXCITEMENT" measured the player's progress. "A wrongly time spank or a missed one lowers the exitement [*sic*]," Wildenborg noted. "In the shagging game, you need to move the analog stick in rhythm with the movement of the bodies to increment the exitement," he continued in broken English. He also thought he found scenes showing CJ getting a BJ while driving his car and while taking his girlfriend for a walk.

Despite all of their detective work, however, they didn't have the files they needed to bring the complete mini-games to life. "We had no proof," Wildenborg later recalled. They had to wait for the PC version of *San Andreas*, which would give them the full ability to hack completely into the code they needed. There was just one catch: although Rockstar had left the mini-game code in the PS2 game, for all the modders knew the company had removed it from the PC game. "Lets pray they left the animations in," Wildenborg posted.

A few days later, on June 8, Wildenborg eagerly flipped open his laptop on his couch. It was nearing midnight. The PC version of *San Andreas* had just come out in the States. Now, once and for all, his code could be tested to see whether the full mini-game could finally be made to work. At 11:37 p.m., a modder posted the results. "It looks like this is working Pat," he wrote. "Although I failed to satisfy her on my first attempt. But I got her on my second try!"

Wildenborg leaned forward as he finally saw the full video of the scene unfold. It started familiarly enough. CJ pulled up in his car with his date to her house as she said, "How about a little coffee?" A subtitle appeared on the bottom of the screen, "This is it, she's inviting you in for coffee! Gird your loins for love." At this point in the official version of the game, CJ and the girl would go into the house as the camera remained outside—suggestively shaking. And that would be that.

Yet with Wildenborg's code running now, the mission cut to the hidden scene of CJ and the girl inside. Her bedroom was small and messy, with a *GTA: Vice City* poster and a poster for the fictional film *Badfellas* on the wall. CJ, in his jeans and white undershirt, leaned back on her bed as she stood before him with her back to the camera. She wore nothing but a thong and a Rockstar Games baby T-shirt, just as the company sold in real life.

Then she knelt down.

The ensuing scene was more comical than pornographic, mainly because CJ remained fully clothed throughout the tryst. As the girl's head bobbed between his legs, CJ reached for the back of her head and pressed it deeper into his blue-jeaned crotch. She then lay back on the bed, as he mounted her missionary style, still completely dressed. An instructional graphic in the upper left-hand corner explained to "push the left analog stick up and down in rhythm." An "Excitement" bar graph, just as Wildenborg had found, measured CJ's progress as he thrust. There were no genitals or money shots, but the scene, in such a prudish industry, was outrageous enough. "You're a real professional, baby!" CJ gushed, over her moans. "Go on, tell me I'm the best!"

After all of that work, all of the collaboration, the modders had done it, unearthed the sex mini-game that Wildenborg dubbed "Hot Coffee"—both for the drink that the girl euphemistically invited CJ to share and for Wildenborg's own love of the stuff.

"*Zege*," he said in Dutch.

Victory.

20
Hot Coffee

> **WANTED LEVEL**
> ★★★★★☆

Milky white clouds rolled against a bright blue sky over a jagged mountain range. A glowing sun bathed the earth in honey-colored hues of amber. You felt as if you were flying over the Rockies in a smooth, silent glider. Yet this scene wasn't real. It was a simulation.

The video played on a giant screen in Los Angeles, as a sea of slack-jawed gamers gaped from their seats. It was May 2005 at the annual E3 convention, and more than seventy thousand people had come for the biggest show yet. The game industry was posting record numbers, approaching $30 billion worldwide and more than $10 billion in the United States alone. Even better, three new video game consoles were being announced this week: Nintendo's new machine, code-named Revolution; Microsoft's Xbox 360; and Sony's PlayStation 3.

At the packed Sony press conference, the company's iconic exec Phil Harrison towered onstage in a blue suit and an open-collared shirt, evangelizing the PS3's awesome processing chip, called the Cell. Technical specifications elicited fetishistic oohs and aahs from the crowd. "Even the clouds are generated procedurally," Harrison effused, as the gamers pressed their digital cameras against their eyes. The heavenly scene was, Harrison added, a "stunning example of where immersion in games will go from here on in."

If the players wouldn't take Sony's word for it, they would believe the deified game king whose face then filled the enormous screen onstage: Sam Houser. The pretaped video seemed like a dispatch from deep in Rockstar's elusive bat cave. Sam sat in a darkened room, blinds cracked ever so slightly on the window beside him. He wore a loose gray T-shirt and an unkempt beard. Dark circles puffed under his eyes, as if he'd just been pulled from an all-nighter.

"I think what we're most looking forward to creating in a PlayStation 3 game is a truly realized, truly immersive living, breathing world," he said, gesturing emphatically and evoking the old tagline from DMA. "This is what we live for," he said. "You know, every five or six years, these amazing companies like Sony come along and give you this wonderful new piece of equipment that allows you to start unlocking your vision and unlocking the dream that you've been having for however long.

"With Cell and with PlayStation 3, we feel very excited and very confident that we're going to be able to absolutely push the limits of what can be created and the experiences that we can immerse our audience in. We really know that we're going to be able to go to the next level in terms of realistic simulations and realistic immersion, combined with incredible narrative, incredible storytelling, and those two elements combined are what are going to create the experiences of the future."

Then, as quickly as he had materialized, he was gone. Gamers weren't used to hearing much, if anything, from Sam anymore. Since his early days of preening on magazine pages, he'd withdrawn so much that any interview with him was preceded by adjectives such as *reclusive* and *Pynchonesque*. At E3, Rockstar maintained the enigma, parking a fleet of jet-black tour buses with blackened windows inside the convention hall. Only conventioneers with elite invites were allowed inside to check out the company's latest games.

Despite the stealthy pretense, Sam seemed busier and happier than ever. Now married, he and his wife had recently welcomed a baby boy. Sam's days became even sunnier this month when he went to San Diego to oversee the making of a new game, *Red Dead Redemption*. The Old West adventure was a follow-up to the previous year's *Red Dead Revolver*, also developed by the team at Rockstar's San Diego studio. Though *Revolver* earned mixed reviews, Sam, an erudite fan of spaghetti Westerns and Sam Peckinpah, felt convinced that the sequel could be a brilliant way to bring the open world design of *GTA* to a fresh, but no less outlaw, American dream.

In the meantime, business was booming. Sony had recently launched its new PlayStation Portable handheld game system, and Rockstar's title *Midnight Club 3* had been the top launch title. *San Andreas* was still selling out around the world. Privately, Sam was eagerly awaiting the launch of the PC port of the game. Rockstar had still been talking about distributing a patch following the PC release, which would let gamers unlock the sex mini-game, once and for all. As an added concession to the modders, Rockstar changed the end user license agreement for the PC *San Andreas* to permit players "to construct new game levels and other related game materials." Game on.

Yet when Sam arrived at work in San Diego on June 9, 2005, two days after the PC game's release, it seemed more like game over. That morning, the SEC revealed the findings of its two-year investigation into Take-Two Interactive. The commission announced a settlement agreement under which Take-Two would pay $7.5 million in penalties (including $6.4 million in combined penalties paid by Brant, the vice president of sales and two former Take-Two executives)—but would admit no wrongdoing.

The allegations suggested an elaborate game behind the scenes. The SEC alleged that on Halloween Day 2000, executives at Take-Two recorded a single shipment of 230,000 video games for $5.4 million, its biggest sale to date, but the games were soon sent back to headquarters. To hide their return, Take-Two had disguised it as a purchase of "assorted products." As a result, the company improperly recognized $60 million in revenue from 180 different parking transactions in 2000 and 2001. To "consistently meet or exceed" revenue ensured that Take-Two, according to the SEC, met or surpassed financial forecasts and delivered "substantial bonuses" to execs, including Brant—who sold $20 million in stock along the way.

Yet the blow of the SEC news that morning was only the first punch. When Sam went online, he found another story about Rockstar blowing up on the message boards. Some dude named Patrick W had just uploaded a new mod for *GTA: San Andreas* to his homepage in the Netherlands. He called it Hot Coffee. "With this mod," Patrick W posted, "you will be able to unlock the uncensored interactive sex-games with your girlfriends in *San Andreas*. Rockstar build [*sic*] all this stuff in the game, but decided to disable it in their final release for unknown reasons. And now this mod enables these sex-games again, so now you can enjoy the full experience."

Sam grabbed his phone and stabbed the numbers for Rockstar's office in New York. Because Rockstar hadn't yet put its patch online for the sex scene, this meant that the intrepid modders had somehow reconstituted the mini-game on their own. Back in the loft on Broad-way, the phones were ringing off the hook. Rockstar's harried team of publicists looked up to find a boss looming over them.

"Don't answer the phones," he said. "This is going to get ugly."

DOUG LOWENSTEIN walked into his office of the Entertainment Soft-ware Association in Washington, D.C., on June 9 to find his assistant looking forlorn. "Oh, shit," he was told, "we have a problem."

A video of the Hot Coffee mini-game was already going viral online. As Lowenstein watched the girlfriend go down on CJ, he thought it was a joke—cartoonish, like something from a PG-13 movie. Yet he knew that while the world had long decried violence in video games, this was pushing into a new territory: sex. As the industry's chief lobbyist, Lowenstein knew the stakes better than anyone.

Since the industry developed the ESRB in 1994 in the wake of threatened government regulation, he had labored every day to win the trust of politicians. It had been costly, with hundreds of thousands of dollars wasted on related legal fees. The battles hadn't been easy, and he had put himself on the line when Take-Two and Rockstar refused to get involved in the public debate. Hot Coffee was no laughing matter. "If this undermined the political support we had, from Joe Lieberman to David Walsh and Hillary Clinton," he later recalled, "we would be in a very compromised position. This endangered the credibility of the most important shield our industry had to excessive regulatory force."

After seeing the clip, Lowenstein phoned Pat Vance, the head of the ESRB, who was also reeling from the news. Vance felt the same pressure that Lowenstein did to defend the industry's ratings from government regulation, but, she wondered, maybe this mod wasn't a problem after all. The ESRB rated games, not user-generated content, and if this was just something programmed in some basement in Holland, then it seemed beyond their purview. Even the staunchest opponents weren't lobbying to legislate what gamers did in their own homes.

If it was true, however, as the modder claimed, that "Rockstar build [sic] all this stuff in the game," then they had a potential nightmare ahead. Had Rockstar gamed the ESRB by neglecting to disclose sexual content hidden in *San Andreas* in order to get an M-rating? If so, this would confirm the worst stereotypes of the industry and would provide a smoking gun that legislators and critics such as Jack Thompson had been hunting for all these years. Like the pixilated girl in the Rockstar baby tee, the gamers would be screwed. "If the publisher put the content on the disc," Vance said, "somebody knew it was there."

"THEY FOUND IT," Sam wrote in e-mail to Les Benzies on June 13. ". . . [does] this cause any problems? Hope not as it is pretty cool."

But why stop there? Rockstar could release its patch online anyway, so that less industrious gamers could easily "unlock this gem" of Hot Coffee themselves. Donovan, as usual, expressed concern. Releasing a patch now would only fan the flames of controversy and possibly cause the game to lose the M-rating they had labored so hard to receive.

By the next day, Hot Coffee was the talk of the office. Two producers within Rockstar were gossiping about the leak, saying that Benzies seemed psyched that the sex scene had been discovered by hackers because now "we don't have to do anything ourselves," as one wrote. The other agreed that the hack was "better than an official patch" because of its cryptic nature.

Jennifer Kolbe, Rockstar's director of operations, e-mailed Donovan and Rockstar producer Jenefer Gross that same day to further explain what had happened. "[W]hen we originally created the sex scenes that Sam wanted approved, we used girlfriend models wearing underwear," she wrote. "Also present in the code (but unused by us) were fully nude girlfriend skins. The author of the mods used those skins instead of the clothed versions, making things appear even worse than we'd originally intended." She added that the unlocked scene "is the entire sex animation that was in the game previously . . . the mod unlocked everything."

In an e-mail to Donovan, Sam reiterated that deleting Hot Coffee from the game would have been too complicated. "We locked it away because there was no other way to get the game done on time—safely," he wrote. "The code is very interwoven in [*GTA*] and everything reacts to everything else," he continued. "The impact of yanking something late is too scary."

Yet Rockstar's veteran technical officer, Foreman, didn't agree. Yanking the mini-game "wouldn't take that long at all," he later said, "not even days." The fact that it wasn't removed was "laziness, pure and simple," he said. Foreman felt duped. When he had been told that the sex scene had been removed from the game, he assumed that meant it had been deleted from the disc, not merely wrapped. "We didn't question it," he later said. "If it's out, it's out."

For years, Sam had tried to play life like a video game, planning for every contingency, sculpting Rockstar's outlaw image, fighting conservatives, managing the media, plotting precisely how much they could get away with in a game. Real people—in their complexity and emotions and unpredictability—always seemed to be a source of frustration for him. No one believed in the games as he did. No one worked as hard for them as he did. No one saw the beauty in them as he did. Yet now, after one deft move by some gamer in the Netherlands, the carefully constructed world shattered. This crisis was real. Now he had to deal with it.

With Hot Coffee unleashed, Rockstar readied its PR team for the crisis. "There is some sexualized content that was removed from the released version of *San Andreas*," Gross explained to the publicists in an e-mail. "The process of removing it involves burying it deep within the code, however, with the release of the pc version, modders (people who go into the code to add things/change things to make quirky things happen), have found the hidden code and accessed it revealing the sexual content that was removed from the released version. They then post instructions for others on how to access this content."

Soon, all of Rockstar's PR and marketing people were pulled into a meeting, where they found a brash new PR guy at the table. As Todd

Zuniga, a former game journalist who had joined Rockstar as a PR manager, listened to the new PR guy map out his militaristic strategy, he couldn't help but laugh inside. Zuniga ran a humor site on the side and thought the scandal represented the height of absurdity. When he watched the Hot Coffee scene, he thought, "Look at this stupid shit. Why'd they put that in?" Even worse, the new PR guy sure didn't seem like a gamer to him and seemed to "say absolutely nothing and talk to you for an hour," Zuniga later said. "Why did they bring him in? That's kind of weird. They have no faith in anyone. They think everyone's an idiot."

As Zuniga said he was instructed, phone calls were to remain unanswered. One caller demanded an answer, however: Pat Vance at the ESRB. After talking with Eibeler, she called Lowenstein and told him the news. "They claimed it was a third party modification," Vance said. In other words, Take-Two and Rockstar implied that the content was not on the disc but something created by a gamer for fun and released online. Vance, however, wasn't going to take Rockstar's word for it. "We're going to do an investigation," she told Lowenstein.

"Do what you have to do," he said.

On July 8, Vance released a statement announcing the ESRB's official investigation into Hot Coffee. "The integrity of the ESRB rating system is founded on the trust of consumers who increasingly depend on it to provide complete and accurate information about what's in a game," she said. "If after a thorough and objective investigation of all the relevant facts surrounding this modification, we determine a violation of our rules has occurred, we will take appropriate action." What that action would be, they didn't know. Nothing like this had happened before.

With news of the investigation, Hot Coffee became the biggest scandal ever to hit the game press. This was like their very own Watergate—Coffeegate, some joked—starring the most notorious and guarded publisher in the business. "Today, one of the most popular recent game industry rumors showed signs of turning into a very real scandal," *GameSpot* reported.

Yet Rockstar seemed to be implying that the sex scene had been the creation of modders, not them. "We also feel confident that the investigation will uphold the original rating of the game, as the work of the mod community is beyond the scope of either publishers or the ESRB," the company said in a statement.

"Was the Hot Coffee code included on the game discs manufactured by Rockstar?" a writer for *GameSpot* asked a Rockstar PR representative that day.

"No," the PR rep answered.

As news of the investigation spread, politicians moved in. A young aide served up Hot Coffee to his boss, California state assemblyman and Democrat Leland Yee, one of the growing ranks of politicians who were sponsoring bills to outlaw the sale of Mature-rated games to minors. "It's outrageous," Yee said. "It tells you how to copulate a woman. That should not be in the hands of children."

Along with the National Institute on Media and the Family, Yee demanded that the ESRB slap *San Andreas* with the dreaded Adults Only rating. Rerating or altering the game would be a massive undertaking, requiring Rockstar to recall millions of products at a cost of surely tens of millions of dollars—not to mention banning it from major retailers. Yee had his own solution, AB 450, a bill to ban violent video games from being sold to minors.

Back at Take-Two, CEO Paul Eibeler struggled to keep up with the scandal. "It just spun out of control," he later said. "It was a politician's goldmine." There was a great irony at play. *GTA* was a scandal invented by a publicist in England, brought to America, where it became real. Now the people outside the United States were seeing this as a joke. Eibeler's colleagues in Europe couldn't believe the concerns in America over the scene. "The Europeans were laughing," he recalled. "You're worried about some graphics that some hacker opened up and had sexual innuendo?"

To ease the minds of the already weary Take-Two board, Eibeler sent them a memo reassuring them that "these modifications are not possible on retail Xbox or PlayStation consoles." This implied that the scene was not on the disc at all, which, of course, wasn't true—though it was unclear how much Eibeler knew at that moment. A follow-up memo from him the next day, however, acknowledged that mods had been found online for the consoles.

Meanwhile, in the Netherlands, Wildenborg's once-quiet home had been turned upside down. Within a month of its release, the Hot Coffee code had been downloaded more than one million times. Dutch TV camped outside his house. The phone rang nonstop with calls from the press around the world: CNN, the *New York Times*, ABC News. With his wife panicking as her young kids played, they soon took the phone off the hook. "We didn't know what was happening or how it would influence our future," Wildenborg later said. As a precaution, he told his boss what was going on. His boss referred Wildenborg to his lawyers—just in case.

When asked by the Associated Press about Rockstar's denial of having put the sex scene on the disc, Wildenborg lashed out. "If Rockstar denies that, then they're lying, and I will be able to prove that," he said. "My mod does not introduce anything to the game. All that content that is shown was already present on the DVD."

Wildenborg wasn't fighting off only the press, but other modders, too. Some resented Wildenborg talking smack about Rockstar. "Seriously, Patrick," wrote one modder in the online forums, "are you trying to dig them in deeper? They've denied it because they really don't want the game being re-rated as AO. If the game gets re-rated as AO, it'll hurt their sales, and they'll care less about modding in future games." The modder suggested telling the press that the content wasn't in the original game. "It might be bending the truth a little," he wrote, "but it's better than going against Rockstar."

"I don't think R★ should have to go it alone," another modder agreed. "This is every gamer in the US's problem if the soccer moms get the game b& [banned]."

"The last thing I want is to get rockstar into problems," Wildenborg replied, but ". . . If R★ denies that the content was on the disc, they basicly say I've been a liar all along (and a pr0n producer)." Yet the modders convinced him in the end. Wildenborg just wanted his life, and his hobby, back and agreed to stick by Rockstar's side. "I think the next time a journalist asks a question," he wrote, "I won't be answering his questions, but just issue a R★ friendly statement."

Together, the modders strategized on how best to distract the media. One suggested pitting them against Sam's old rival, Electronic Arts, instead. Modders, they knew, had recently created a program to make characters in the EA game *The Sims* naked. Why not just point that out—even though it wasn't analogous to Rockstar putting the sex scene in its own game? At least, it would be a diversion.

When the *New York Times* e-mailed Wildenborg for an interview, he panicked, worrying that his broken English would do him in. So he had a friend compose what he described in the modder forums as an "exceptional Rockstar friendly reply," including a dig at *The Sims*, which he sent to the paper in reply. "At the end of the day," the *Times* quoted Wildenborg as saying, "*Grand Theft Auto* is not a game for young children, and is rated accordingly."

On July 11, the day the *Times* story ran, Wildenborg's phone rang. Wearily, he answered, but it wasn't the press this time. The caller said he was from Rockstar Games. Wildenborg's heart raced. What did they want with him? He asked for an e-mail address for verification. Sure enough, when he got a reply from the Rockstar address, he knew this was real. When he phoned back, the caller told Wildenborg how much Rockstar appreciated the quote on his website and, specifically, the part where he said that Hot Coffee was only playable when the game was modified. Oh, and they wanted to give a heads up. "We're going to issue a statement tomorrow," the caller said. "You shouldn't worry too much about it."

Wildenborg hung up with a sigh. "I felt relief that not too much consequences personally, that they weren't suing," he later said. The next day, Rockstar put out a statement finally addressing the scandal in full. There would have been one way to come clean: to admit, in clear language, that the sex scene was on the disc but had been cut and not intended for release. Rockstar could say truthfully there was no intention to deceive the ESRB or pervert the minds of the world's youth at all. Yet instead of being forthright, they seemed to throw the modders under the bus.

"So far we have learned that the 'hot coffee' modification is the work of a determined group of hackers who have gone to significant trouble to alter scenes in the official version of the game," the statement read. "In violation of the software user agreement, hackers created the 'hot coffee' modification by disassembling and then combining, recompiling and altering the game's source code. Since the 'hot coffee' scenes cannot be created without intentional and significant technical modifications and reverse engineering of the game's source code, we are currently investigating ways that we can increase the security protection of the source code and prevent the game from being altered by the 'hot coffee' mod."

Game sites across the Net seized the answer. "Well, that's pretty damn clear," reported the popular blog *Kotaku*, under the headline "Rockstar Official Denies Making Hot Coffee." *Kotaku* continued, "To summarize: We had nothing to do with it. Now we just have to wait and see what the investigations into the mod in the U.S. and Australia find. I'm pretty sure it will be easy to determine who's telling the truth and who's lying and *man* is someone gonna get in trouble when they do."

The modders, however, knowing the truth, felt incensed. Despite all of their efforts, their years of loyalty, this was how Rockstar repaid them? "R★ are a bunch of fuckign [*sic*] retards," wrote one modder online. "They're now trying to demonise modding and make us out to be the bad guys. It's completely fucking stupid, and completely fucking pointless."

"They can't possibly have expected us not to find it eventually, if not Patrick, someone else later," wrote one modder of Hot Coffee. "It was just a matter of time with this one." Another wrote that "they are outright lying and trying to discredit Patrick from what I can see. I'm also sure heads will roll at Rockstar for leaving all that unused content in the game."

Within Rockstar, people were just as amazed by the press release. "You've got to be fucking kidding me," said Foreman, who read it while he was in Scotland visiting Rockstar North. Well aware of the truth behind Hot Coffee, he considered the press release "a huge miscalculation." After so many futile attempts to argue and change things, he thought it was pointless to talk with the Housers and Donovan about it now. Instead, he looked at the other gamers and cracked up. "What could we do?" he recalled. "We sat around and laughed about it."

Eibler later said, "It wasn't the best written press release." The Hot Coffee scandal confirmed all of the hysterical, overblown suspicions about *Grand Theft Auto*, and Rockstar's publicity department, which in the past had displayed an uncanny knack for building brand mystique, only seemed to exacerbate the outrage. "Blaming it on hackers was a colossal PR screw-up," Corey Wade later said. "It was a complete disaster. . . . They lied."

"They released that bullshit quote about how this is an act of hackers, which is completely comical," Zuniga agreed. "We were, like, 'This company is run by arrogant English people. What the fuck was that statement? Why don't we tell the truth?'"

Work on Rockstar's games screeched to a halt. Approval for ads and publicity plans got derailed. Screenshots sat on computers awaiting sign-off. With the statement out, talking points were drawn up for the PR team—the plan was to spin this as an attack on the game industry by political conservatives out to undermine the industry. When *Rolling Stone* called, asking whether the creators of the sex scene were at Rockstar, the PR rep bristled. "They're not within the company," he said, then began to chastise the magazine. "One of our concerns with this story is that it might add to the confusion of people who don't understand how the industry works," he said.

Zuniga couldn't believe this ploy to cast Rockstar as victims. "These people are trying to undermine video gaming?" he asked dubiously. "It's an attack on the game industry?" He knew this was far from the truth. As one journalist told him, "This isn't attack on the game industry, you fucked up."

While Take-Two tried to placate the board and Rockstar struggled to manipulate the press, Rockstar also tried to repair damage with the modders it had so unceremoniously left behind. On July 13, an e-mail allegedly from Rockstar with the subject heading "Confidential—Private Statement to the *GTA* Mod Community" unexpectedly arrived in modders' in-boxes around the world. "I'm a bit disappointed that they only want to support us in private communication," one modder responded, "but that's probably because of pr, and it's better than nothing."

"We are sure that by now you are all aware of the media furor surrounding the 'hot coffee' mod," the e-mail read. "Several long-time critics of video games are using it to renew their attacks on *Grand Theft Auto: San Andreas* in particular and video games in general. Our critics are using the opportunity to distort *Grand Theft Auto* and suggest that games do [not] deserve to be treated the same as other forms of media. Therefore, we have been forced to counter their arguments.

"Unfortunately for the gaming community, elements of the mainstream media don't cover technology or new media well, and they can be especially bad with subtle details. As we defend the game and stress the delineation between the official retail version and the alterations to the code, we want you to know we continue to respect and admire the creativity involved in creating mods. The strength of the mod community proves that *Grand Theft Auto* will always have more fans than critics, and we wanted to take this opportunity to reiterate our gratitude. We will always admire the passion and technical brilliance of the mod community. Thank you for your notes of support, and thank you for not letting the personal agendas of our critics get in the way of your enthusiasm for *Grant Theft Auto: San Andreas.*

"We are disappointed by the way the media have misrepresented *Grand Theft Auto* and detracted from the innovative and artistic merits of the game. But the biggest problem with all of this is that it serves to widen the gap between people who create and play games and people who don't. Critics create these controversies to undermine the rating system and to create a public appetite for censorship and extreme regulation. Indeed, the existence of a rating system is a fact our critics ignore as much as they ignore the fact that gaming is now an entertainment medium enjoyed predominantly by adults.

"Thank-you again for your support.

"Rockstar Games."

21
Adults Only

> **ESRB CONTENT DESCRIPTORS**
>
> NUDITY—Graphic or prolonged depictions of nudity.
>
> PARTIAL NUDITY—Brief and/or mild depictions of nudity.
>
> SEXUAL CONTENT—Non-explicit depictions of sexual behavior, possibly including partial nudity.
>
> SEXUAL THEMES—References to sex or sexuality.
>
> SEXUAL VIOLENCE—Depictions of rape or other violent sexual acts.
>
> STRONG SEXUAL CONTENT—Explicit and/or frequent depictions of sexual behavior, possibly including nudity.

When Jack Thompson heard about Hot Coffee, he saw more than steam rising from a cup, he saw a smoking gun. For years, he had been banging his war drum about game makers marketing objectionable content to kids. With Hot Coffee, there would be no speculating anymore. If the scene really was on the disc, then everything he had ever warned the world about would suddenly be justified. He couldn't be called crazy anymore. He'd be right.

Thompson called his longtime ally in the culture war, David Walsh of the National Institute of Media and Family. The more Walsh listened, however, the more dubious he became.

"You don't have to agree with me," Thompson replied, when Walsh divulged his concerns. "I'm the lawyer, you're the psychologist. You just do your research, and I'll take care of getting these games banned." Thompson urged him to move fast on Hot Coffee. "Dave," he said, "I think this is a big deal because if they put that in there, not only is it fraud, but it's distribution of sexual material to minors."

Putting his differences with Thompson aside, Walsh issued what he called a "National Parental Warning" about Hot Coffee. "While *San Andreas* is already full of violent behavior and sexual themes, the porno- graphic sex scenes push it over the edge," he warned in a statement. "Can you imagine the impact of 13, 14 and 15 year old boys literally enacting this scene?"

Thompson's phone rang later, but it wasn't Walsh. It was the office of Senator Hillary Clinton. "The senator wants to do a press conference on Hot Coffee," Thompson was told, "and we need you to prep her."

Clinton was no stranger to *GTA*. In March, she had delivered a speech to the Kaiser Family Foundation about the impact of violent media on children, which she called a "silent epidemic." She singled out *Grand Theft Auto*, she said, "which has so many demeaning messages about women and so encourages violent imagination and activities and it scares parents. . . . They're playing a game that encourages them to have sex with prostitutes and then murder them. You know, that's kind of hard to digest."

Thompson had written to Clinton soon after her speech, urging her to join his fight. "I am a Republican; you are a Democrat," he wrote. "As you know, this is not a partisan issue. . . . Senator, I believe the time has come for the United States Congress to prohibit the sale of mature-rated video games to children. I respectfully urge you to author a bill toward that end." More Columbines, he warned her, were coming.

Now with Clinton calling for his help, he jumped to duty, schooling her on the scourge of *GTA*. Emboldened, he fired off an open letter to the members of the Entertainment Software Association, including Take-Two and Sony, lauding her. "Millions of American parents should be thankful to the Senator for striking back against what can be fairly called 'Grand Theft Innocence' at the expense of our children by only some within your industry," he wrote.

Clinton sent a letter apprising the chair of the Federal Trade Commission of the ESRB investigation into Hot Coffee. "Alarmingly, it seems that no one yet knows the source of this content," she wrote. "We should all be deeply disturbed that a game which now permits the simulation of lewd sexual acts in an interactive format with highly realistic graphics has fallen into the hands of young people across the country."

Lieberman called for an independent investigation to look further into the scandal.

Clinton introduced legislation to ban the sale of violent and sexually explicit video games to children—with a $5,000 penalty for retailers who do so. "The disturbing material in *Grand Theft Auto* and other games like it is stealing the innocence of our children and it's making the difficult job of being a parent even harder," Clinton later said. "I am announcing these measures today because I believe that the ability of our children to access pornographic and outrageously violent material on video games rated for adults is spiraling out of control."

Vance raced to Washington to meet with Clinton and encouraged her to use this moment to educate the public about the ratings system. When Vance arrived, she was told she'd have ten minutes. She earnestly and deftly went through her presentation, handing Clinton brochures on the ratings system, the efforts of the ESRB. Clinton remained silent until the end, when she leaned back and said, "I just want to protect kids." Then she got up and left. The meeting was over.

Vance felt stunned. "For her to put up a wall was surprising," she recalled. "Considering her intellectual abilities, that was disappointing." Yet Vance felt that the gamers were as much to blame. "Politically, it's such an expedient issue that they don't get negative push-back from constituents," Vance added and took the gamers to task. "The consumers of video games have not been vocal about these shenanigans," she said. "They're not calling up senators to say stop with this nonsense."

With Clinton's call for legislation, Walsh and Thompson pushed to have Take-Two reveal the truth about Hot Coffee, once and for all. "I challenge Take-Two, just tell us: is it on the disc or not?" Walsh told the press. Within hours, Walsh's phone rang. The caller wouldn't identify himself but said he worked in the game industry and had inside information on Hot Coffee. "Dr. Walsh," the mysterious person said, "I can guarantee that it is on the disc."

Walsh felt as if he were suddenly in a spy movie; his heart pounded long after the mysterious caller hung up. With this tip, he began to scour Minneapolis for a computer expert to crack the code. Finally, he reached a hacker who said he was a concerned parent and willing to help. "This is what you do," the hacker told him, "reverse-engineer it."

"I don't even know what that means!" Walsh said.

The hacker said he'd do the job for $2,000. Walsh agreed. Two days later, the hacker called back. "It's on the disc," he said.

Walsh knew the ESRB was conducting an investigation of its own, and he was eager to get the news out immediately, but his lawyer advised him against it. "Don't do it," his attorney said. "You're playing with dynamite. You have to be absolutely certain. You can't take the word of an anonymous tipster. You need a second independent verification, then I could advise you to go public."

Walsh hung up, flustered. He couldn't afford to pay another hacker, so he thought of a less expensive alternative: the Geek Squad, the tech supporters for hire at Best Buy.

Walsh figured that Best Buy, one of the major game retailers in the United States, had plenty at stake in the possible rerating of *San Andreas*. He thought he might get someone there to help him out, gratis. "Here's what I know," Walsh told the Geek over the phone, filling him in on the scandal. "Are you interested?" The listless Geek said he'd have to get back to Walsh.

Yet there was no need. Back in New York, Eibeler's phone rang at Take-Two Interactive. It was Vance, who told him the ESRB had finished its investigation. "You should come up," she said. "We should meet." When he asked why, she told him they had determined that Hot Coffee, despite Rockstar's denials, was in fact on the disc. Eibeler sounded surprised. Vance thought it must not have been what his people had told him.

"We have two options," she explained. "One is to put out a statement to revoke the rating, and basically the retailers would ship the product back, and the product would be off the market. Or we can put out a statement that says we're revoking the rating, and these are the steps that Take-Two is taking." Vance preferred the second option, which would mean that the publisher, not the retailers, was assuming responsibility.

Rockstar put up a fight. The ESRB had never rated games based on a modification before, Sam and the others argued, and there was no reason to start now. They refused to accept the rerating of the game from M to AO. "Fine," Vance told them, "you're leaving us with no option but to put out a press release saying it's revoked, and we don't want to do that." She couldn't believe "the arrogance" of Rockstar, as she later put it. "They were saying we don't have the right to do it, we were saying we do."

It was undeniably ironic. For years, Sam had tried to make his games more adult. Now he was getting his wish, but not in the way he intended. On July 20, less than a day after a media watchdog group called the Parents Television Council demanded a recall of *San Andreas*, the ESRB announced its findings.

"After a thorough investigation," Vance said, "we have concluded that sexually explicit material exists in a fully rendered, unmodified form on the final discs of all three platform versions of the game (i.e., PC CD-ROM, Xbox, and PS2). However, the material was programmed by Rockstar to be inaccessible to the player and they have stated that it was never intended to be made accessible. The material can only be accessed by downloading a software patch, created by an independent third party without Rockstar's permission, which is now freely available on the Internet and through console accessories. Considering the existence of the undisclosed and highly pertinent content on the final discs, compounded by the broad distribution of the third party modification, the credibility and utility of the initial ESRB rating has been seriously undermined."

And so it was done. In an unprecedented move, the ESRB mandated that Rockstar tell retailers to cease all sales of *Grand Theft Auto: San Andreas*. The game had a new rating now: Adults Only.

22
Busted!

ANSWERS.YAHOO.COM > GAMES & RECREATION > VIDEO & ONLINE GAMES

QUESTION:

I JUST started playing GTA: San Andreas on PS2 (I know I am behind the times).... What are you supposed to do after being wasted/busted? Run somewhere? Thanks in advance.

BEST ANSWER:

When you are wasted/busted: Time advances by 6 hrs. You lose all your weapons and $100, unless you have relationships with cops and nurse girlfriends. When you are wasted your max health is somewhat reduced, say about 0.1%. When you are busted your respect increases, again about the same trifle. If you are wasted/busted while doing a mission, you fail that mission and you have to do that mission again.

As the sun beat down during the summer of 2005, Sam knew just where he wanted to go to escape the heat: Gander Mountain. Gander Mountain was a sprawling, log cabin–shaped store in upstate

New York, not far from where he and Dan had bought a rural vacation home.

Though it had been nearly seven years since they moved to the United States, Sam still marveled at the wonderful excess of this country, and nothing was quite as wonderfully excessive as this outdoors store. It looked like a prop shop from *Deliverance*: camouflaged paintball face masks, fold-to-go toilets, battery-powered, rabbit-shaped Quiver Critter Decoys. Toward the back, something caught Sam's eye: an M16 rifle. "Wait a minute," he later recalled, "Wal-Mart is going to pull our game, but you can go in there and buy a pump-action or a Glock or whatever? I don't get it."

No matter. The awful wake of Hot Coffee had begun. In response to the ESRB's rerating of *San Andreas* to Adults Only, Wal-Mart, Target, Best Buy, and Circuit City stores pulled the game from their shelves. "We hope we're sending a statement to manufacturers that they need to cooperate with the ESRB," said a Best Buy spokesperson. Rockstar would now have to remove the sex scene from the game and re-release the discs in order to receive the M-rating again—a process that would take at least until the fall. Wal-Mart alone accounted for 20 percent of game sales, a huge loss in the meantime. In total, Take-Two would spend a reported $25 million to fix, recall, and rerate the games.

Take-Two tried to save face. "We are deeply concerned that the publicity surrounding these unauthorized modifications has caused the game to be misrepresented to the public and has detracted from the creative merits of this award-winning product," Eibeler said. Yet there was no more avoiding the fact that Rockstar had been busted for the oldest trick in the book: a hidden fuck.

In July, the board of the ESRB—consisting of representatives from Sony, Nintendo, and other major publishers—met to discuss the fallout. Vance found a room full of angry faces, people angry at Rockstar because they had to, as she later put it, "clean up their mess." Hot Coffee mucked up years of lobbying and public education efforts. Vance pleaded for more power to enforce her ratings system, but the political backlash grew.

"It looks like Take-Two Interactive purposefully conned the video game industry rating board and parents across the country," Washington State representative Mary Lou Dickerson told the *Los Angeles Times*. "*San Andreas*, as a top-selling game in the country, now is in the hands of thousands of children who can practice interactive pornography. There should be legal consequences . . . so [the company doesn't] laugh all the way to the bank."

On July 26, Take-Two dropped another bomb: it was being investigated by the Federal Trade Commission. The House voted 355–21 to pass a resolution asking the FTC to see whether Rockstar had committed fraud by intentionally duping the ratings board to avoid an Adults Only label. Threatening fines, the director of the FTC's Bureau of Consumer Protection called this "a matter of serious concern."

The feds weren't the only ones pursuing Rockstar. On July 27, an eighty-five-year-old grandmother from the Bronx, New York, named Florence Cohen filed a civil suit against the company. Cohen said she had bought the game for her fourteen-year-old grandson and wanted her money back (along with unspecified damages for the false advertising and consumer deception) after learning of the hidden sex scene.

Though Hot Coffee skirted much controversy in the United Kingdom and other countries, the ratings board of Australia declared *San Andreas* illegal to sell, advertise, or distribute after revoking its rating. States that included California, Michigan, and Illinois heightened their fight to ban the sale of M-rated games to minors. "That's what tipped it for the whole industry," Yee said of Rockstar. "They lied to us." Fifty-six-year-old Yee called himself a First Amendment defender but drew the line at video games—even though he didn't know *Pac-Man* from table tennis. "When I was in grad school, computers still had lightbulbs," he said. "I used to play Ping-Pong, you know, that game with the guy eating up balls."

On October 9, flanked by Girl Scouts and seated behind a table of outdated video games such as *Postal* and *Manhunt*, California governor Arnold Schwarzenegger (the star of his own violent *Terminator* video games) enacted AB 1179: a bill that banned the sale of violent video games to anyone under eighteen. Under the new legislation, retailers such as Best Buy and Wal-Mart would be subject to a $1,000 fine for each violation.

The controversy once again underscored the bias against the medium of gaming. While politicians fretted about children confusing games with reality, they seemed to have a harder time distinguishing between the two worlds than the players did. They spoke of the games as if players were committing the crimes in real life. "You're the one who rapes someone," James Steyer, the CEO of Common Sense Media, the San Francisco–based nonprofit that provided the legal underpinnings of the bill. "You're the person who is serviced by a prostitute in the back of a car."

The next month, Clinton and Lieberman introduced the Family Entertainment Protection Act, which would, among other things, ban the sale of M-rated games to children and allow for government audits of both the game industry's rating system and retailers' enforcement policies.

As the backlash grew, acclaimed game designer Warren Spector took the stage at the Montreal Game Developers Conference and did something few in the industry had before—hit back against Rockstar and *GTA*. "*GTA* is the ultimate urban thuggery simulation, and you can't take a step back from that," he said. "But I sure wish they would apply the same level of design genius to something we really could show enriches the culture instead of debases it. . . . We are dead square in the cultural crosshairs right now."

An editorial in *GameDaily*, the industry trade, echoed the sentiment. "The video game industry is well along the road to losing the culture war in the United States," it warned. "That this could be happening at a point in which games enjoy unprecedented commercial popularity is simply mind boggling."

Yet the momentum against the players couldn't be stopped. Even the city of Los Angeles filed a suit against Take-Two, alleging that the company had violated the state's business code through deceptive marketing and unfair competition. "Greed and deception are part of the *Grand Theft Auto: San Andreas* story," said the L.A. city attorney, "and in that respect, its publishers are not much different from the characters in their story."

DARKNESS COVERED New York City, as the neon-pink Ferris wheel spun over Coney Island. A subway car slowly snaked into the station near where a gang had gathered. It looked just like the opening scene from *The Warriors*, but not exactly. It was a lovingly rendered, shot-for-shot recreation created by Rockstar for a video game version of Sam's favorite childhood film. The game, due in October 2005, cast the player as a new member of the Warriors gang, working his way up through the ranks as he battled off rival squads in scenes and settings straight from the film.

A team of fifty artists and programmers at the company's Canadian studio, Rockstar Toronto, had been laboring for four long years on the title. For Sam and Dan, it felt like coming full circle, taking the fantasy world of their childhood dreams and making it real. Sam retreated gladly into the virtual world of his games. Anything was better than dealing with the feeling of being ganged up against in real life. People were drowning in New Orleans while President Bush flew overhead, and the Feds were coming for them? "These guys are out to get us," Sam told Dan one day. "They'll garrote us whatever we do. They don't give a shit. This is crazy. They're throwing the serrated-edge boomerangs like the little kid in *Mad Max 2*."

Sam was also overseeing his most autobiographical game yet, *Bully*. Developed by Rockstar Vancouver, the game followed the adventures of James "Jimmy" Hopkins, a troubled, bald, chubby new kid on a mission to survive a boarding school called Bullworth Academy. With his monogrammed school sweater and battles with teachers and preppies, Jimmy could have come straight out of St. Paul's. Jimmy wasn't the *Bully* of the title; he was an underdog warding off the bullies with a cheeky arsenal of stink bombs and potato guns. The game mashed up tropes from sources such as *The Outsiders*, *The Catcher in the Rye*, and *Sixteen Candles* to create an archetypal high school setting. Just as *GTA* players had to ingratiate themselves with the mob, the yakuza, and the triads to advance, players of *Bully* had to win over the geeks, the jocks, and the preps.

Within Rockstar, however, the gang of developers weren't feeling so chummy anymore. After years as the self-proclaimed rebels of the industry, being treated like real outlaws didn't feel so hip. Employees hunched quietly at their desks in the office, tapping at their keys. The foosball table and the arcade games collected dust. Members of the public relations team were still twiddling their thumbs because Rockstar refused to discuss the scandal in detail with the press.

To promote *The Warriors*, Dan agreed to talk with the *New York Times* but would not address Hot Coffee. "Certainly, it's frustrating when people don't wish to understand what you do and don't wish to learn," Dan said. "Anyone who plays any of our games and wishes to criticize it, having played it, experienced it, and thought about it, they are, of course, welcome to do that. But when large numbers of people criticize something and haven't even done it, it's very frustrating. There's a large amount of the population that lives in relative ignorance and only hears scary stories about what we do."

As a cone of silence enveloped the company, veterans of the team watched in despair. Dave Jones, still working on his own action game, *Crackdown*, thought that "to leave [Hot Coffee] in there was risky and they chose to do that." Former BMG Interactive head Gary Dale, now the managing director of Capcom in Europe, thought that Rockstar's refusal to answer questions only exacerbated the problems. "That just made it worse," he said. "Someone should have publicly engaged and nipped it in the bud, early. It was allowed to drift and drift."

Behind the scenes, some were blaming Brant for not stepping up and, as a result, leaving Rockstar to reel in the chaos. "Sam was extremely frustrated," Eibeler recalled. "He felt he was being personally called out for things—and that other games were being held to different standards. It was more of a political football."

"It definitely had a lot of effect on the company," King recalled. "Distraction, waste of time, slowed our momentum down, took key resources away." They weren't so invulnerable after all. "For me, it was an education in American morals, and history," he said. "Perhaps Hot Coffee symbolized that."

Sam had spent decades warding off the culture warriors as he stuck to his mission, but Hot Coffee was slowing eating away at him. On one level, he felt his legacy under siege. "I don't want that game being remembered for Hot Coffee," he later said, fearing that it "was going to take this really beautiful piece of work and it was just going to be known for something else."

For years, it had been easy to shrug off the critics of video games as simply player haters—out-of-touch politicians and parents. It was almost Freudian. The haters represented mom and dad. Something had changed, however, in the wake of Hot Coffee and the pile-up of murders and mayhem and sensational media associated, no matter how wrongly, with GTA. That change became more evident than ever one morning when the Rockstars heard a crowd chanting outside their office on Broadway. "Hey, hey, ho ho," the protesters yelled, "Rockstar has got to go!"

As the players looked down from their windows, they didn't see a mass of middle-aged blowhards outside. They saw a sea of fresh young faces—150 children, mainly black, holding handmade signs with slogans such as "Prosecute Rockstar Games. They are felons" and "Put the Cuffs on Rockstar, Not Youth." The protesters were called the Peaceaholics and had traveled from Washington, D.C., to rally against Rockstar. "These games are training our children to be criminals," one of the group's advisers told ABC News. "Our children are being trained to be killers, murderers, rapists, drug users, drug dealers."

As the crowd swelled, Rockstars who hadn't yet arrived were advised to enter through the back door for safety. Leading the protesters was a familiar gray-haired man. He wore a white button-down shirt and a blue tie and held a bullhorn, chanting as the kids danced behind him: Jack Thompson.

At the end of many video games there is a Boss Level, when the player faces off against the most imposing foe. Yet when Thompson demanded for someone from Rockstar to come down and meet with them, no one came. To him, they were cowards. He wasn't the hater, he believed; he was fighting for love. Love for the higher power. Love for his son, Johnny. Love for the children surrounding him here. Who was the player now?

23
Bullies

WANTED LEVEL
★★★★★★

"**I** AM GOING TO FUCKING KILL YOU!!!"

That's what the e-mail to Jack Thompson said. He had received it from some anonymous gamer on the heels of his victory over Hot Coffee. "I think video games or [*sic*] freaking awesome, and they are my entire life," the player wrote, "and for you to insult them, is like telling me my life is totally worthless. For this, sir, I AM GOING TO FUCKING KILL YOU!!!"

This wasn't the only death threat in his in-box. "Everyone thinks you are insane," read another, "hence the name 'Wacko Jacko', which makes you the equivalent of a molester. Therefore you are gay. I hate you, and the world would be a better place if you were brutally murdered." And another: "This is not spam, its [*sic*] my right as a citizen to send you thousands upon thousands of emails saying the same thing until you die painfully from gun shot wounds."

Though Thompson considered himself a religious crusader, empowered by a mission from God, he knew he was mortal—and a father to boot. He couldn't take these threats lightly. A few weeks before his protest at Rockstar Games, he sought an unlikely ally for help: the game press. He forwarded the death threats to *GameSpot*, whose editors weren't taking his word. "Are you crazy?" Thompson fired back. "People are threatening to kill me."

Thompson sought an even higher power: Clinton and Lieberman. "I have had a number of video gamers threaten to kill me in the last few days in the aftermath of the success against *Grand Theft Auto: San Andreas*," he wrote to the senators. "The use of death threats in retaliation for my participation in the public square serves to prove, rather convincingly, that the violent video games are having the attitudinal effect that psychologists such as Dr. David Walsh and others who have testified before Congress say they have."

Thompson wasn't crying wolf. A sixteen-year-old gamer from Texas was later charged with harassing him. In a mass e-mail about the boy, Thompson called it par for the course in the war between the players and the haters. "'Shoot the messenger' is the video game industry's strategy," he wrote. "This time, because of the arrest in Texas, it didn't work. It backfired."

Yet that wasn't all. After so many talk shows, so many mass e-mails, so many lawsuits and diatribes against violent games, Thompson found himself battling a new opponent in the culture wars: the players, just as Sam was besieged by the player haters. It had started with flames on forums and message boards with titles such as "Jack the Fucking Video Game Ripper!" and "This man is certifiable!" Then came entire websites and blogs devoted to railing against him—StopJackThompson. com and Hating Jack Thompson Since Before It Was Cool—and the petition Gamers United to Stop Jack Thompson.

Gamers spent hours a day fighting villains, and Thompson—with his gray hair and schoolmarm ways—was a hybrid of Darth Vader, the

Teacher from *The Wall*, and Mr. Hand from *Fast Times at Ridgemont High*. One gamer made and sold Jack Thompson Toilet Paper emblazoned with his name, available for $5.95. "Wiping my butt with him may be better than he deserves," the seller wrote. One made an online comic about Thompson. "Rockstar are CRIMINALS!" spewed a manic Thompson in the strip. "They should be sent to prison, raped, then SHOT." An anonymous word balloon responded, "Er . . . for making video games?"

The salvo from gamers only made Thompson more defiant. "The amount of energy put into trying to destroy me tells me they know this is about something worthwhile," he said. Thompson made his e-mail, home address, and phone number (which, to gamers' delight, contained the prefix 666), readily available online and became famous for replying to those who contacted him. The dialogues would eventually end up online. When one game reporter e-mailed to ask for an interview, Thompson replied, "Kiss the game industry good-bye."

Thompson had a new game to kiss off, *Bully*. With little to go on other than the title, he exploited the frothing eagerness of the press by painting a foreboding version of the unreleased game. CNN was quick to give him his airtime. "Tonight, another disturbing example of our culture in decline," bellowed host Lou Dobbs. "A new video game to be released this fall encourages children who have been bullied to become bullies themselves."

"What you are in effect doing is rehearsing your physical revenge and violence against those whom you have been victimized by," Thompson warned. "And then you, like Klebold and Harris in Columbine, become the ultimate *Bully*."

In response, Thompson penned an open letter to Doug Lowenstein and the press called "A Modest Video Game Proposal." He promised to write a $10,000 check to Eibeler's favorite charity "if any video game company will create, manufacture, distribute, and sell a video game in 2006 like the following . . ."

Thompson described a game that would follow Osaki Kim or O.K., the bereaved and vengeful father of a boy who'd been bludgeoned to death by a violent gamer. Equipped with a choice of machetes and baseball bats, Kim, Thompson wrote, "hops a plane from LAX to New York to reach the Long Island home of the CEO of the company (Take This) that made the murder simulator on which his son's killer trained. O.K. gets 'justice' by taking out this female CEO, whose name is Paula Eibel, along with her husband and kids. 'An eye for an eye,' says O.K., as he urinates onto the severed brain stems of the Eibel family victims, just as you do on the decapitated cops in the real video game *Postal2*."

After taking out video game lawyers, arcades, and retailers, the player then maneuvers O.K. to his final mission, the 2006 E3 convention in Los Angeles, as Thompson wrote, "to massacre all the video game industry execs with one final, monstrously delicious rampage." He concluded, "How about it, video game industry? I've got the check and you've got the tech. It's all a fantasy, right? No harm can come from such a game, right? Go ahead, video game moguls. Target yourselves as you target others. I dare you."

The moguls didn't pick up the gauntlet, but the players did. One team of modders released a free game called *Defamation of Character: A Jack Thompson Murder Simulator*. Built as a modification of *GTA: San Andreas*, the game cast players both as Thompson and as Thompson's fictional alter ego, Banman. The ripped-from-the-headlines missions included stopping a truck full of *Bully* games from reaching a store and busting Lowenstein from putting secret sex scenes in a game. Players could even hold a press conference in the game, calling up a menu of Thompson's real quotes. Another mod team made a game more explicitly based on his proposal.

Thompson wasn't buying it. "I'm not interested and won't be commenting on the mod," he told the site *GamePolitics* in an e-mail. He added that his proposal "was intended to highlight the patent hypocrisy and recklessness exhibited by the video game industry's willingness to target cops, women, homosexuals, and other groups with some of their violent games. To be fair, though, you can't expect a bunch of gamers to understand the satire if they think that Jonathan Swift, the author of 'A Modest Proposal,' is the name of a new Nike running shoe."

Over in their self-described "fortified bunker in Seattle," Mike Krahulik and Jerry Holkins, the cocreators of the popular video game web comic *Penny Arcade*, had had enough. On October 17, they posted a response. "You know what, Jack? We're going to be the men you're not," they wrote. "You said that your insulting, illusory ten thousand dollars would go to the charity of Paul Eibeler's choice. We've got a good guess that he'd direct your nonexistant [*sic*] largesse toward The Entertainment Software Association Foundation, a body that has raised over six point seven million dollars over the last eight years. We've just made the donation you never would, and never meant to. Ten thousand dollars' worth. And we made it in your name."

Thompson wasn't amused. He faxed a letter to the Seattle police chief, urging him to "shut this little extortion factory down and/or arrest some of its employees." Krahulik and Holkins never heard from the local officers. "We should thank our stars that we have someone as impotent as [Thompson] is in his role," Holkins said after the fracas. "Our fear is that someone intelligent and charismatic should take over."

Thompson's "Modest Proposal" turned into a major backlash. In an open letter distributed widely online, David Walsh of the National Institute of Media and Family, the organization Thompson had long cited in his tirades, cut Thompson off for good. "Your commentary has included extreme hyperbole and your tactics have included personally attacking individuals for whom I have a great deal of respect," Walsh wrote in a public letter.

Thompson dismissed Walsh as "an idiot," and Walsh, in a subsequent interview, distanced himself from Thompson even more. "We're coming from a scientific and public safety perspective," he said, "not a religious one." When pressed, however, Walsh admitted that hard evidence linking violent games with violent behavior was lacking. "None of these studies are definitive," he said. "I would never say that playing a violent video game is going to make a kid act violently. What I would say is as kids have risk factors, if you add violent video games into the mix, you're increasing the chances."

Though Lowenstein had always done his best to avoid speaking directly about Thompson, he publicly refused to engage him anymore. "My comment for the record is we have no comment on the work of Jack Thompson," Lowenstein said. "By 2010, the digital generation will be in the seats of power, they'll be in editorial meetings and they will be making news decisions and what people in government and the cultural elite regard now as dangerous will be seen merely as rock and roll."

With Thompson vulnerable, Rockstar moved in against him, too. The guys' first missive came, fittingly, in a game. On October 25, the company released *Grand Theft Auto: Liberty City Stories*, a game for the PSP that became the top-selling title on that platform. Thompson surfed over to Rockstar's website promoting the game and found a surprise. Players could click on a fictional e-mail from someone named JT with a group called Citizens United Negating Technology For Life And People's Safety—or C.U.N.T.F.L.A.P.S. for short.

"The internet is unambiguous evil," read the fictional e-mail. "The only things worse than the internet are computer games and liberals. . . . Only last week, I was using the internet to look up some information for my 15 year old niece, who is a keen water skier and state wide sailor. Trust me when I say this—searching under the subject matter 'Teenage girls water sports' is not for the faint hearted."

Outraged, Thompson spammed the Net about the attack, accusing Rockstar and Take-Two of "furthering the notion that its most abiding and most effective critic, Jack Thompson, is himself a sexual pervert."

Thompson added that he "can assure the world that the only thing to which he is 'addicted' is eating entertainment industry scofflaws for breakfast—and golf."

Yet his battle with Rockstar was no laughing matter anymore. In November, Thompson went to Fayette, Alabama, to face off with Rockstar in person again. The occasion was a hearing over the $600 million civil lawsuit he filed on behalf of relatives of Devin Moore's victims against Take-Two, Rockstar, Sony Corporation of America, Wal-Mart, and GameStop, where Moore purchased *GTA: Vice City*. Moore had been recently convicted of the murders and sentenced to death, but Thompson wanted the game companies to pay.

On November 3, 2005, he and Rockstar's lawyers faced off in a Fayette courtroom. "These *Grand Theft Auto* games are unique," Thompson argued. "They are murder simulators. The only thought they convey is how to murder people and how to enjoy killing." Rockstar's team wasn't having any of it, though, and filed a motion to have Thompson removed from the case. "This isn't a street fight," said one of Rockstar's attorneys. "He's going to turn the courtroom into a circus and we can't have it."

Thompson lashed out, accusing Rockstar of labeling him a "bisexual and a pedophile," as he told the judge. Exasperated, the judge pulled out a stack of the e-mails and press releases that Thompson had been spewing across the Net.

"Why did you do this?" the judge asked Thompson.

"You said after the criminal trial to 'have at it,'" Thompson replied.

"Your idea of 'have at it' and my 'have at it' are not the same."

Days later, the judge issued an order preventing Thompson from participating in the case. "Most of these communications contained long and angry speeches by Mr. Thompson that can only be described by the court as bizarre and childish," the judge said. "If Mr. Thompson continues to inundate the court with prohibited and irrelevant communications, this court shall use its contempt power for relief."

Thompson came home to Coral Gables to find a pile of mail at his door. Among the envelopes was a package and a note: "Enclosed please find the sample you requested." Thompson removed the wrapping to find a small bottle of Astroglide Silken Secret, a "vaginal moisturizer to help relieve the discomfort associated with vaginal dryness."

The gamers! Thompson thought. He marched over to his computer, his mission command, and his fingers hit the keys. "Dear Judge," he began. Though he was off the Alabama case, he wanted the judge in the case to know that Rockstar and its fans were still "targeting me." They were the bullies, not him. "Is there any connection," Thompson wrote, "between [Rockstar] stating to its video gamer minions that I head an organization whose name refers to vaginal folds and the sending of me and my wife a vaginal moisturizer? A good question and a fair question, don't you think, Judge."

FIRST PERSON point of view. Wintry day. January 2006. Capital City. Sam stood at the steps of the Federal Trade Commission building in Washington, D.C. He was here voluntarily to answer questions for the FTC's investigation into whether Rockstar had purposely deceived the ESRB to avoid an Adult Only rating for *San Andreas*.

So it had come to this. Ten years, ago he was just a bloke in England who dreamed of invading the United States of Def Jam. Now here he was in the nation's capital, the seat of power, a stone's throw from George W. Bush himself. And for what? There was Bush and the lies and the wars and the madness, and now the United States was spending taxpayer money to investigate a game? If gamers were outlaws in the eyes of the public, they had never seemed as outlaw as this before. "I felt those people were out to crush us," Sam later recalled, "and if they could have crushed us, they absolutely would have."

Keith Fentonmiller, a senior attorney for the FTC's Division of Advertising Practices, knew it would be a touchy investigation beyond the obvious First Amendment concerns. "What hackers did was technically illegal," he later recalled, "but when you're encouraging or turning a blind eye to years of them doing this thing, it just doesn't look so good."

Sam took his seat with his three lawyers across from a trio of government investigators. The Feds had everything. A towering stack of Rockstar papers. Internal e-mails. Timelines. *San Andreas* art. Sam's head spun as he listened to their questions: *Why have you done this? Why have you done that? Why have you put that word in apostrophes?*

At one point, an e-mail of Sam's surfaced that seemed to cut to the core of his feelings. "Why are they so concerned about what we're doing in the game when we're bombing the hell out of people in Operation Enduring Freedom trying to keep our freedom," he had written, "and we're back here trying to curb the freedom that we're paying the taxes to fight for."

The clock ticked endlessly. One hour. Two hours. Four. Seven. The questioning lasted for nine hours. "It's a heavy one, right?" Sam later recalled. "It's not many game designers that have been in that position that I know of . . . which goes back to the point about having the fire for this game."

He returned to New York to a piece of the past that was, literally, in ashes. A five-alarm fire had raged through their historic old digs at 575 Broadway, which still housed Rockstar's corporate sibling, 2K Games, along with Brant Publications, Ryan's father's company. The spring collection at the $40 million, Rem Koolhaas–designed Prada store went up in flames, along with a wallpaper mural titled *Guilt Incorporated*. When word leaked that the storage closet fire was deemed suspicious, one gamer posted the absurd joke that "Jack Thompson got caught smoking a little too close to the building."

It wasn't only 575 feeling the heat. In a public relations industry's annual list of top ten PR blunders, Hot Coffee made the cut and was ranked by *Business 2.0* magazine as one of the dumbest moments in business of the year. The business site MarketWatch anointed Eibeler the Worst CEO of the Year, citing that "so far this year it has sliced earnings guidance by more than 60% to a range of 53 cents to 56 cents a share.... Congratulations, Paul! (To shareholders: condolences.)"

In a feature story in *Fortune* called "Sex, Lies, and Videogames," journalist Bethany McLean detailed the financial scandals that plagued the company around the time when Hot Coffee was discovered. This included the chief financial officer's sales of more than $5 million in shares and the chief operating officer's exercising of 20,000 in options. Brant, then Take-Two's publishing director, had reportedly taken home more than $4 million.

Take-Two's corporate drama grew with the resignation of Barbara Kaczynski—a board member and the former CFO of the National Football League, who had been brought in to chair the audit committee after the SEC investigations began. According to her attorney, "her concerns have risen significantly because of what she views as an increasingly unhealthy relationship between senior management and the board of directors."

In the aftermath of Hot Coffee, *GTA* had come to represent, for some, a broader coarsening of the culture. This went beyond games into a burgeoning and graphic genre of blockbuster horror films, such as *Saw* and *Hostel*, nicknamed "torture porn," as well as torture-happy TV shows such as *24*. The fact was, perfectly sane players did like kicking pedestrians into bloody pulps in *GTA*—and, in fact, traded clips on YouTube of killing sprees in the game.

In April 2006, the New York attorney general and leading candidate for governor, Eliot Spitzer, joined the high-profile fight against the violence and sex of video games. "Nothing under New York State law prohibits a fourteen-year old from walking into a video store and buying a game labeled 'Adult Only'—a game like *Grand Theft Auto*," he said, "which rewards a player for stealing cars and beating people up. Children can even simulate having sex with a prostitute." If elected, no one was going to simulate sex with a hooker under his watch.

On June 2, Take-Two and Rockstar entered a consent order with the FTC, without admitting wrongdoing. As part of the settlement, the company agreed to disclose all relevant content for ratings in future games and establish a system for making sure nothing like Hot Coffee ever got buried on a disc again.

For months, Sam had been fighting to keep the voices of the haters out of his mind, but the pressure was growing too great. He later spoke to journalist Harold Goldberg of panic attacks and wanting to flee the United States for good. A doctor compared his trauma to that of a car crash victim. Sam tried to lose himself in his games, flying to Edinburgh to work with Rockstar North. During a train ride back to his old home of London, however, he answered his cell phone, and the world emptied out below him. The Manhattan district attorney, he learned, was issuing a grand jury subpoena into Hot Coffee. The battle wasn't over at all.

Sam wanted out, away from the industry and the world. It was like some weird mission from Liberty City brought to life. New York City, their haven, their inspiration, had just boosted their wanted level to a maximum six stars. In *GTA*, there was always an easy fix. No matter how many cops were on your tail, you could drive into a body shop, get a fresh coat of paint for your car, and your wanted level would drop to zero. It wasn't that easy in real life.

WHERE'S JAMIE? The question made its rounds at Rockstar. Jamie King—Rockstar cofounder—was gone, and no one seemed to know why. He had simply left the office at the end of one day in January 2006 and not returned. With a number of games in production at the various Rockstar studios, it wasn't uncommon for King to be on the road, dispatching orders from New York. "Maybe he's traveling," some said.

Gary Foreman suspected that something more ominous might be in play. In the aftermath of Hot Coffee, Foreman had noticed that King seemed sullen and withdrawn. Though the two were close, they didn't discuss it, sinking back into the shells they had built to survive the chaos of the recent years. Foreman, however, became suspicious when, seemingly apropos of nothing, a Take-Two executive told him, "You know, the senior management are really big fans of yours, we're going to take care of you." Foreman eyed him dubiously. "It was surreal," he later recalled. "It was like, yeah, I've been here a long time, I built this business up, I hope you would value me."

Foreman wasn't the only one feeling adrift. On the morning of May 6 in Austria, the one hundred employees of Rockstar Vienna, the acclaimed studio that worked on games such as *Max Payne* and *Vice City*, had arrived to find security guards turning them away at the front door. Producer Jurie Hornemann quickly broke the news online. "This morning, as I came into work, I was greeted by security guards," he blogged. "It turned out Take-Two has closed their Rockstar Vienna office, effective immediately, 'due to the challenging environment facing the video game business and our Company during this platform transition.'"

With no warning, Rockstar Vienna had been closed. Even in the game industry, known for its volatility, the abruptness was unusual. As word spread in the blogosphere, gamers—including anonymous Rockstar employees—blamed Hot Coffee, in part, for the mess. "The Hot Coffee brouhaha, ridiculous as it was in many respects, did nothing to increase the popularity of Rockstar Games both inside and outside of the industry," Hornemann blogged. "Whichever way you look at it, game development has become a bit harder for everyone because of that incident."

Commentators on the blog, many claiming to be ex-Rockstars, vented angrily. "Rockstar is NOT cool after all, the employees who worked for this hypocritical company WERE! good luck to all of us!!!" one wrote. "If this is what you do to hard working employees, who the hell would or want to work for you Rockstar?" posted another. This couldn't be dismissed as sour grapes of anonymous exes. Even Scott Miller, the veteran publisher of games such as *Duke Nukem*, who had worked on the *Max Payne* blockbuster with Rockstar, chimed in.

"Other than *GTA*, a brand Rockstar did not invent themselves (they bought the IP from DMA), what have they created that's truly a hit?" he posted. "*Manhunt*? Nope. *Warriors*? Nope ... not a huge hit, and not their home grown brand. *Max Payne*? Nope ... Rockstar so far is no different than [*Tomb Raider* publisher] Eidos, in that they've had one success and everything else is on par with the same-old-same-old the rest of the industry puts out."

The downward spiral continued. In May, Rockstar released a table tennis game (inspired by their legendary matches at the Chateau Marmont) that, while technically impressive, bombed. Amid the mounting lawsuits over Hot Coffee, Take-Two stock plummeted—soon down by 13%. Then came word on King: he wasn't coming back. No one knew why, and it wasn't the only defection. *GameDaily* ran a story on the exodus at Rockstar. "When Jamie King (a Rockstar co-founder), two different directors of marketing, and others all leave within the same period that the parent company's stock is in a freefall, it smells fishy," wrote the site.

Fed up, Foreman marched into Donovan's office. "Look, you know what?" he told Donovan. "I need to make some changes here in the processes and end all this constant crunch mode." He mapped out his vision of how to impart a structure to the process, allocating more people to the teams when *GTA* titles ramped up. "These are things I want to do," he said, "but I'm really frustrated after all this time, of this thing

we built. I want to make it better. I want to take it to the next level, and
I don't have the ability to do that."

As foreman recalled, Donovan sat there nodding, staring at the floor,
but he had nothing to say. Though open communication had never
been a strength at Rockstar, Foreman found Donovan's behavior particularly odd. Foreman wondered whether maybe Donovan was simply
thinking through the impact of what he was suggesting or how life at
Rockstar might be without him. "I need to change things here," Foreman continued, "and if you're telling me I can't do it, then this isn't the
place for me anymore."

Finally, Donovan broke his silence. "Things work as they are," he
said, "we're doing okay."

Foreman felt as if he were living in some kind of alternate reality, a
reality that, he realized in that moment, he couldn't deny anymore.
"This isn't going to work," he said. He quit. As he was gathering his stuff
in his office, however, Kolbe came in. "Sam and Terry have asked me to
come in here and ask you to change your mind," she said.

"Wow," Foreman said.

"What do you mean 'wow'?"

"As much as we've been friends for a long time, wow on two things.
One, I almost can't believe they sent you here to deliver their message,
and it's really cheap, but, yeah, I can understand that they have. But also
if either of them truly meant that, one or both of them would be here
having this conversation with me."

Foreman was gone—and he immediately knew who he wanted to
track down, once and for all: King. Reaching out through a mutual
acquaintance, he asked the friend to have King call him. King replied,
and the two met at a restaurant in Chelsea. "You know I left?" Foreman
told him.

"No, you didn't," King said.

"Yeah, I did," Foreman said and filled King in on his final days. As
Foreman and everyone else had known for years, King had been strained

and unhappy. King had been burning candles at both ends for so long, he was out of wax. Like Foreman, he felt that Hot Coffee had been, as he called it, "a horrible episode for Rockstar." The years of drama had finally become too much.

"I was like, fuck it, I'd rather be broke," King later explained. King wanted to move on, and Foreman and he talked about starting their own company, one built on new franchises and new ideals— without repeating the mistakes epitomized by Hot Coffee. "What I learned from that is to be very, very upfront about what we're doing," King said.

With Foreman and King gone, it was just the beginning of the end of an era for Rockstar. One day in September 2006, Donovan walked out the door—and didn't come back. Employees were cryptically told that he was taking a leave of absence. The next month, Brant resigned from the company—followed soon by an announcement from Take-Two that the company would be restating its financial results from 1997 to April 30, 2006. Brant pled guilty to backdating stock options, paid an additional $7.3 million in penalties, and accepted a lifetime ban on serving in a management position of a public company. By the end of the year, Take-Two had lost $184.9 million.

Sam tried his best to maintain a sense of normality for his staff—in his own inimitable way. For the holiday party in December 2006, they filled a nightclub with strippers in Santa outfits and red hot pants. Festive young employees took turns swallowing shots from a giant ice luge. This was one of the great truisms of Rockstar—and the game industry as a whole. That no matter how tough things got or how many people quit, no matter how great the stress or long the hours, no matter how much they were exploited and unorganized, there was always a new generation of developers eager and willing to sign up for the promise of fun.

As Sam looked across the crowded party, no one at Rockstar personified this dedication and the promise of the future more than William

Rompf. Preppy and blond in his ever-present pullover sweater and tie, Rompf was almost like a long-lost American cousin of the Houser brothers. He had been refined in boarding school, then in the prestigious business program at NYU, and said his goal in life was to become "landed British gentry."

Yet like the Housers, he got the bug for games, transforming a time-biding postcollege job at Rockstar into a full-blown obsession. Able to find hundreds of computer bugs during sixteen-hour workdays, Rompf quickly earned his stripes, rising to the top of the quality assurance team. He earned and wore every new Rockstar monogrammed jacket with pride, happily working through the night as he heard Heart's song "Barracuda" blasting from Sam's office down the hall. Rompf would forward his boss articles from the *Economist* and anticipate the next mission. "I believed in everything," Rompf later said.

Though Rompf knew about all of the recent departures, his devotion hadn't been swayed. Fueled on shots from the ice luge, he stumbled up to Sam to pledge his support. "Dude, I fucking love you," he shouted over the music, "and I love this place."

"No," Sam replied, "I fucking love you. Don't ever leave this place. Don't ever fucking leave me."

"I'm here forever," Rompf vowed.

But the others weren't sticking around. A few weeks later, on January 12, 2007, Donovan's fate became official. He wasn't coming back. Sam later said that the emotional trauma since Hot Coffee had been too much for him. "It was very important to them that the public persona of Rockstar was one big happy family, and I think cracks started to show," Foreman later said. This seemed to clarify why Donovan was acting so oddly when Foreman had come to him that day. "It explained his behavior," Foreman said. "He was already gone."

In March 2007, shareholders themselves were done with all of the games. An investor group that included several prominent hedge funds voted to replace Eibeler and most of Take-Two's board at the company's annual shareholder meeting. Rumors began to circulate that the company might be sold. (Tellingly, the stock jumped on initial reports of both of these developments.) Many noted that potential purchasers had to balance the upside of Rockstar's immensely profitable *GTA* franchise against the downside of the many lingering SEC investigations and class actions.

Rockstar announced that Gary Dale, the former head of BMG Interactive, was returning as chief operating officer. "Rockstar is a very robust organization and has tremendous depth," a company representative said. "It has over 600 artists and developers, marketing people. . . . Sam and Dan is the leadership now, along with Gary Dale. The roles have been filled."

24
Flowers for Jack

FLOWERS

Flowers are an item found in *Grand Theft Auto: San Andreas* that are classified as weapons within the game. Flowers are placed in Slot 11 in the weapons inventory. The flowers can be used as a weapon by Carl Johnson, inflicting slightly more damage than regular fist fighting.

It was a bright blue February day in Las Vegas, as the highest rollers of the game industry milled about the glittery, palm-lined Green Valley Ranch Resort. Thin and patchy Will Wright, the cerebral creator of the best-selling computer game franchise of all time, *The Sims*, puffed on a cigarette. Spiky-haired Cliffy B, the bratty genius of the brawny shoot 'em up *Gears of War*, chatted with Microsoft execs. Lanky Phil Harrison, the PlayStation guru, schmoozed nearby.

They had come for the 2007 D.I.C.E. (Design, Innovate, Communicate, Entertain) Summit, the industry's most exclusive event of the year. A welcome reprieve from the circus of E3, this fancier and more intimate affair was when the leaders of the industry could hang out and play Hold 'Em in peace. The highlight was the annual Interactive Achievement Awards, the Oscars of the business. This year, the list of nominees signified something radical: the end of an era.

The pixilated wall between gamers and the rest of the world was fading. In the decade since the first *GTA* was released, the sheer complexity of video game controllers—all of those intimidating buttons and sticks—had alienated two generations of potential players: little kids and boomers. The average person needed only eyes and/or ears to consume every book, TV show, song, or movie ever made, but when it came to consuming games, most people were all thumbs. Or, rather, they were dumb thumbs; they were Thumbies— lacking the requisite hand-eye coordination to survive the virtual worlds.

The impact was profound, both economically and culturally. In addition to missing out on legions of customers, the Great Thumbie Divide had spawned a sociopolitical backlash that went all the way to Capitol Hill. Unable to play games, politicians and pundits instead relied on watching short and often sensational video clips—which is as unlike playing a game as watching porn is unlike having sex. Games are, fundamentally and essentially, an experiential medium. It's easy to hate the players when the haters can't play—and vice versa.

Change had come, though. It started in late 2006 with the recent release of the Nintendo Wii, a new console with motion-sensitive controllers. Instead of tapping an elaborate combo of buttons, people could play Wii Tennis simply by gripping the Wii Remote and swinging their arms as if they were holding racquets for real.

With more than six million units sold in its first four months, the Wii quickly became the fastest-selling console in the world, from the United States to the United Kingdom, and catapulted Nintendo back to the top of the industry. This despite the fact that the Wii lacked the high-definition graphics and the photorealism of its competitors. In the first six months of its release, the Wii would outsell Sony's PlayStation 3 and Microsoft's Xbox 360 combined.

At the same time, the blockbuster franchise *Guitar Hero*, played with guitar-shaped controllers, took the medium even wider. The spin-off game *Rock Band* would earn more than $1 billion. With more and more people playing casual games online and on Facebook and the recently released iPhone, the plight of the Thumbies seemed to be ending for good.

Yet it wasn't only the end of this era at D.I.C.E. It was the end of Doug Lowenstein, the president of the Entertainment Software Association, who had been the face of the industry during its awkward adolescence. Since taking his post in 1994, the year of the *Mortal Kombat* hearings, and defending it through Columbine and Hot Coffee, Lowenstein was moving on to launch a private equity trade group. Yet the game makers and the media people who crammed into the auditorium to hear his farewell speech discovered he had to settle one last score.

"The publishers and developers who make controversial content and then cut and run when it comes time to defending their creative decisions, nothing annoys me more," Lowenstein said. "If you want the right to make what you want, if you want to push the envelope, I'm out there defending your right to do it. But, damn it, get out there and support the creative decisions you make." People in the room wondered. "If you want to be controversial, that's great," Lowenstein continued, "but then don't duck and cover when the shit hits the fan. Stand up and defend what you make."

Lowenstein wasn't gunning only for Rockstar, however. He chastised the game industry for staying silent and politically inactive. When he asked how many in the room had joined the Video Game Voters Network, an activist group, and saw few hands, he snapped, "That's pathetic! . . . no matter how good we are, and we're good, we can't win the war without an army. And you're the army. And most of the people in this room who have the most at stake are too lazy to join this army."

Furthermore, he lambasted the game press for granting the most notorious culture warrior such a wide platform. "You know who gives Jack Thompson more attention than anyone else? The games press!" Lowenstein fumed. "The games press legitimizes Jack Thompson. Everyone gets so upset that Jack Thompson has so much ability. I just think it's nuts."

AS MUCH AS the gamers thought they knew Thompson, in many ways, they didn't know Jack at all. Yes, there were tiny crucifixes on his hand towels and a Bush magnet on his fridge, but there were also signs of the other version of the man. Not Jack the Ripper, but Jack the Dude.

After he spent so many years fighting against the scourge of pop culture, something surprising had happened: Thompson had become kind of hip—not hip as in cool, but hip as in aware. His pop savvy was the unlikely by-product of his obsessive immersion in his cause, surfing the channels and the video games and the radio stations for hours on end. An outsider himself, he gravitated toward black comedy. His favorite shows were *Ali G* and *Curb Your Enthusiasm*, which filled his DVR and he could quote from memory. He still had a soft spot for Frank Zappa. "I think Zappa was prescient," he said, "and I love his live album at the Fillmore East."

One hot morning in the spring of 2006, Thompson looked like a weathered fifty-five-year-old fraternity adviser. Dressed in khaki cargo shorts and a faded white polo shirt, he was unshaven with a beard grown into a Fu Manchu. He kicked back on a cushy recliner near a percolating aquarium. He had taken to saying "dude" a lot. When someone e-mailed him good news, he replied with phrases such as "way freaking kewl" typed in cherry red 36-point font.

It wasn't just the culture war keeping him young, it was his son. Johnny was going on fourteen now, an athletic kid with whom he regularly shot baskets out back by their pool. For old times' sake, Johnny still helped his dad out on his cause now and then. On the heels of *The*

Warriors video game release, Johnny dutifully headed into a Best Buy on a sting to see whether the clerk would sell him the M-rated game—while his dad videotaped the transaction from outside.

Yet Johnny had become something of a gamer, too. He begged his parents to get a Sony PSP handheld game device, along with an Xbox. One morning before he headed off to lacrosse camp, he mustered up his nerve to stake out his ground with his father. "Dad," he said, "if you don't mind, I don't think I'll tell anyone that I'm your son."

When Thompson recalled this tale a few days later, his face slackened, his eyes blinked, and his words, often gushing, halted to a stop. The fish tank burbled. For an awkward moment, he wasn't the big bad culture warrior anymore. He was just a father dealing with the bittersweet reality of a child growing up. When asked how he responded to his son, Thompson straightened his back and narrowed his eyes. "I tell him I'm sorry that he goes through that," he said, "but I'm not sorry for what I've done."

In fact, bolstered by Hot Coffee, Thompson's fight against the gamers was going strong. A group of players raised money from around the world to send a bouquet of flowers in tongue-in-cheek reconciliation to Thompson, whom the campaign organizer characterized as "a shining example of the hysterical anti-youth bias in American government and media."

Their campaign, which they called "Flowers for Jack," went viral, bringing in news and money from around the world. Thompson received the bouquet, then forwarded it to Take-Two, as he wrote in an accompanying note, "in the memory of all of the people who now lie in the ground because of your reckless design, marketing, and sale of mature-rated murder simulators to children."

Yet this wasn't just a war of roses. Thompson's battle against *Bully* was reaching a feverish and effective pitch. He spammed the Net with a screenshot of brawling kids from the game, which, he promised, "will allow teens to practice beating up their virtual classmates." To the surprise of gamers worldwide, he successfully convinced his local Miami-Dade School District, the fourth largest in the country, to unanimously issue a resolution asking Take-Two not to release *Bully* and urging parents not to buy it—despite the fact that no one had seen the unreleased game.

He wasn't stopping there. In June 2006, the Louisiana legislature passed a bill Thompson coauthored, banning the sales of violent video games to minors. Then in September, Thompson spearheaded a $600 million wrongful death lawsuit against Rockstar, Take-Two, and the Sony Corporation of America. The suit claimed that *Grand Theft Auto: Vice City* inspired a teenager named Cody Posy to kill three people one day in 2004 on the New Mexico ranch of television anchorman Sam Donaldson.

With *Bully* slated to come out at the end of October, Thompson filed a petition to prevent Wal-Mart and other major retailers from selling it on grounds that the game violated Florida's public nuisance laws. In what the *Washington Post* called a "major coup" for Thompson, Take-Two was ordered to give a judge a preview of *Bully* to see whether in fact it violated such a law. After viewing the game, however, a Miami-Dade County circuit court judge ruled against banning the sale of the games to minors, as Thompson had hoped. The game ultimately earned a Teen rating, suggested for anyone thirteen and up.

Thompson argued that the judge had erred by allowing a Rockstar employee to show him the game and thus could have navigated away from the more violent encounters. A video clip of *Bully* leaked online showing boy-on-boy kissing. "You did not see the game," Thompson told the judge. "You don't even know what it was you saw." Thompson then sent an open letter to the judge, saying, "You have consigned innumerable children to skull fractures, eye injuries from slingshots, and beatings with baseball bats."

When Take-Two sought to have Thompson declared in contempt of court, Thompson fired off another open letter in response. "You want to play hardball?" he wrote. "You want to try to throw me in jail? You have no idea what you are unleashing in doing this. You're at the brink."

On October 25 at 4 p.m. Thompson sat in a Miami courtroom for his contempt hearing. A reporter for a game site called Destructoid recorded the proceedings on a shaky camera and posted it online as a short film titled *Jack* (written in the same font as the *Bully* logo). The footage of Thompson—sitting in his suit, clutching a poster board on which he had printed the definition of contempt, and getting scolded by the judge—delighted gamers as his final comeuppance. When the judge revealed that he was personally filing a complaint to the bar against Thompson, it seemed to mark the beginning of the end.

With the specter of disbarment looming, Thompson sent another open letter to the judge, chastising him again for "the game that you unleashed on . . . kids." He wrote: "You don't care because you don't have a teen in a school as I do." Thompson refused to back down, but after threatening to sue to block the release of *Manhunt 2* and the next *GTA* game, he claimed he got a call from Take-Two to come to meet its executives in New York, once and for all.

Thompson said he flew to New York and convened with an intermediary for Take-Two's new CEO, Straus Zelnick, in what he later called "a double secret probation meeting on Central Park West." Thompson told the intermediary, "Look, I'm here to tell you to stop selling your *Grand Theft Autos* and other mature-rated games to kids, and if you do that, and tell your retailers to stop, I will call a press conference and tell them Take-Two is the most responsible bunch of people I ever met."

They weren't having it, however. "We are in a war with you, Mr. Thompson," Thompson later claimed he was told, "and we will do whatever it takes to defeat and destroy you." In March 2007, Take-Two petitioned the United States District Court for the Southern District of Florida for relief. "Thompson has a history of making multiple threats of legal action, whether substantiated or not, both against (Take-Two) as well as the retailers who purchase the video games and offer them for sale to the public," the complaint read.

After all of the years of fighting against *GTA*, Thompson was up against a wall. The efforts to ban violent games were failing, including his Louisiana law, which was ultimately declared unconstitutional. He faced charges of contempt and disbarment, and now, he was looking at hundreds of thousands of dollars in legal fees, including fees that Take-Two wanted to collect for the cases against him, if he didn't settle with the company. "I looked at it and said, this is not working," he later recalled, "so I agreed."

In a settlement reached on April 17, 2007, Thompson agreed not to sue or threaten to sue Take-Two or to direct any future communications to them through their attorneys. In short, his public war with Rockstar would cease. Boss Level complete. Game over.

IT WAS 11 A.M. at Rockstar, but what still felt like the middle of the night to Will Rompf. As one of the company's most devoted foot soldiers and heads of quality assurance, Sam's preppy acolyte was starting another sixteen-hour day testing *Manhunt 2*—the ultraviolent sequel to their controversial 2003 thriller. Yet it wasn't only the endless nights of bloody decapitations and nut-busting groin kicks that were getting to him.

For Rompf, the electric thrill of working at Rockstar had begun to fizzle dark. It started, he felt, not long after Jamie King ("Kinger," as Rompf called him affectionately) left the company. Though Rompf hadn't fully appreciated it at the time, he thought now what a buffer King had been for him—such as encouraging him to go home after a long day's work. "Things changed massively when Jamie left," Rompf recalled.

His crunch time at the office now raged unabated. Rompf was losing touch with his family, his friends, and his girlfriend. To survive, he was self-medicating. It started with late-night bong hits, then he'd down four

Tylenols and a shot of bourbon to fall asleep after arriving home at 9 a.m. following a graveyard shift, only to return hours later with the help of amphetamines.

Rompf, a diehard Marxist, never failed to put his heart and soul into his work and, even in his bleakest hours, pledged himself completely to the company. To the consternation of his friends, he had even branded himself with his devotion—getting a Rockstar logo tattooed on his wrist. But his body and mind were losing the fight.

This morning, as he slashed through *Manhunt 2*, he could feel himself begin to snap. It happened when an irritating colleague kept obnoxiously looming over his computer. "Dude, just get the fuck away from my desk," Rompf said. "I'm stressed, I'm tired, I'm working all the time."

"No way," the guy replied.

"Get the fuck away, dude," he said, gripping a pen, "or I'm going to stab you."

The words sounded alien coming from the mouth of a former volunteer for Tibet, who had once been personally honored by the Dalai Lama, but he couldn't help himself. Rompf saw the guy approaching in the reflection of his computer monitor and thrust back his hand, meaning to warn him. He realized how badly he'd misjudged the distance when he heard the guy scream and saw the tip of his pen broken off in the guy's hand. "Will just stabbed me!" the guy yelled, running off to the hospital. Though spooked by his outburst, Will stayed behind, completing his task at hand.

He wasn't the only one reeling. The climax of departures and dramas in the previous year had become almost operatic. There was the exodus of Brant, Eibeler, Foreman, King, and Donovan. The shareholder revolt. The FTC hearing. The mounting class-action suits over Hot Coffee. The games were suffering, too. Despite the brilliance of *Bully*, sales of the game fell flat. Rockstar's adaptation of *The Warriors* met a similar fate.

Now, even the reliable *GTA* cash cow was ailing. *GTA: Vice City Stories*, a spin-off for the Sony PSP handheld released in October and ported to PS2 in March, was the worst-selling game in the history of the franchise. *Manhunt 2* received an Adults Only rating by the ESRB in the United States and was refused classification in the United Kingdom. Though Rockstar begrudgingly dialed back the violence in the game to earn an M-rating, sales disappointed. For Rockstar publicist, Zuniga, the crash seemed like post-Coffee karma. "Hot Coffee pretty much did fuck Rockstar and did bring the company down in a way," he later said. "They were the bully of the industry, and they got punched in the face."

Former Rockstar producer Jeff Williams posted a lengthy blog called *Life during Wartime*, in which he exposed life inside the company. In addition to claiming that he was among those who knew about the presence of the Hot Coffee scene, he railed against the working conditions. "Every Rockstar project turned into a huge clusterfuck," he wrote. "I mainly blame this on a horrendously inefficient company structure, combined with a few individuals who thought they were hot shit but really didn't know anything about either video games or marketing. . . . Rockstar was arrogant to the point of absurdity." Later, the blog came down.

Of course, many people still worked at Rockstar and surely had differing opinions of day-to-day life there. Presumably, there were those who were quite happy and nonplussed by the drama. Maybe Rockstar was just, like many ambitious companies, a hard-crunching, late night culture. But beacause the majority of current employees at Rockstar were seldom, if at all, heard form publicly, the comments online gained a great deal of attention among the game press. As more and more ex-employees began sounding off across the Net, game industry observers smelled blood. "If you look at the content of what these guys have distributed, it's so offensive and inappropriate," said James Steyer, the CEO and founder of the San Francisco–based multimedia ratings group Common Sense Media. "It's not surprising to learn they had committed massive acts of fraud at the board and CEO level. The chickens have come home to roost for this company—and I say good riddance to these guys." *Motley Fool* CEO Tom Gardner summarized it: "You have backdated options, hidden porn, accounting issues, and mismanagement. You have management that was at best incompetent and at worst dishonest."

Such jibes were hurtful enough to Rockstar, but most devastating of all was the shocking death of Jeremy Blake, the designer who'd come up with the iconic Rockstar logo. On July 10, Blake had found his girlfriend, video game designer Theresa Duncan, dead from suicide in her apartment. One week later, he left the offices of Rockstar and took the subway to Rockaway Beach in Queens, where he was last seen wading naked into the water. His body washed up near the shore of Sea Girt, New Jersey. A second suicide at Rockstar within weeks of Blake's only exacerbated the sense of despair in the company—how could such a beloved long-time employee with a family take his own life?

To treat the bad energy in the office, the company brought in a spiritual healer. In her hand, she held a string with a crystal hanging from the end and swung it slowly like pendulum. One by one, she passed the desks of the hipsters and the gamers, their computers, their Xbox controllers, and their desk tchotchkes. She stopped at an empty desk, where she felt, as said, "pretty strong readings." The fact that this incident had been reported by the *Wall Street Journal* sent a clear message to those worried about the future of Rockstar and their parent company: a new era had begun.

As if to mark it, the company soon had its biggest blowout yet for Sam's birthday, in honor of his turning thirty-six at a trendy bar downtown. Gorgeous Belgian strippers in pigtails and cowgirl outfits poured shots down employees' throats. Out in the back, Rockstars took turns donning giant inflatable sumo wrestling suits and slamming one another gleefully to the ground.

Yet the real action was inside, where they lined up the tables again and readied the greasy cheese balls. As was the tradition, buckets were strategically positioned for puking. Rockstars reached into their wallets for fat wads of cash to bet. It seemed just like the old days—except, of course, it wasn't. With the other cofounders long gone, there were only the Houser brothers calling the shots, just as they did when they were kids in London. Now Sam and Dan had to prove to everyone that they could rise up and do what they did best: make amazing games. They knew just how to do it, by pouring everything into their fantasies and creating a new reality of their own.

Sam, dressed in a black T-shirt, and Dan, bald and beefy, dressed in white, loomed at the head of the table as the Rockstars squeezed in around them. Nauseous competitors hunched over their soiled plates at the table. As Sam grinned behind his unruly beard, Dan shouted through his bullhorn at the woozy eaters who were about to compete in the next round. "Let's move on to cheese ball fourteen!" Dan said in his thick British accent. "One minute, one cheese ball! It's easy! You've done it before! Let's go!"

25
New York City

FINALE

Now you make your final choice, a
choice that dramatically affects the overall story and how the game's final three
missions unfold.... Which outcome will
you choose: money or revenge?

I t was late one night in Brighton Beach, the Russian neighborhood near Coney Island in Brooklyn. Inside a gaudy nightclub, a group of young guys took turns at the karaoke machine, downing vodka, and poking at the jellied sturgeon on their plates. Shady mob types lingered cryptically. A security guard who'd been escorting the group said that if they came under fire, he'd be able to rescue only one person. They should decide now.

The young guys weren't mobsters. They were artists and coders sent over from Scotland to research Rockstar's most ambitious game yet: *Grand Theft Auto IV*. They had hired a cop to protect them while they roamed the city's edgier streets. In the past, the *GTA* games had emulated gangster films and lost eras, but not this time. The guys at Rockstar had set their sights on their hometown in all of its current glory: New York, present day.

Although the Liberty City of earlier *GTA*s had always been based on the Big Apple, Rockstar had never had the technology or the experience to bring the city in all of its crazy and beautiful detail to life. Now the time had come. "If video games are going to develop into the next stage, then the thing isn't to try and do a loving tribute," Dan said. "It's to reference the actual place itself. . . . If we can't do that now about New York, then when the fuck could we do it?"

With their powerful new processors and high-definition graphics, the new generation of consoles—the PlayStation 3 and Xbox 360—would let them render more astonishing details than ever before. Dan compared it to the leap from 2D to 3D, but this time they were going from low-definition to high-def. Rockstar enlisted a breakthrough new software engine designed by two graduates of the zoology department at Oxford. Drawing from both human and animal behavior, the engine—called Euphoria—combined a fluid mix of artificial intelligence and biomechanics. Characters could be built around skeletons true to human anatomy, from the way their muscles flexed down to their nervous systems. The moment Sam saw a demo of the engine, his blood raced. "That's my dream—it's happening!" he said. "It's there, let's do it!"

The heightened realism would enliven everything from the handling of the vehicles to the waves lapping up on a beach. Sophisticated physics enabled more believable reactions, such as pedestrians whose rag-doll bodies tumbled and twirled through the air when struck by a car. Enhanced animation allowed for more cinematic close-ups, so vivid that when, say, a mobster gets a bad call, his eyes narrow believably in frustration. Supple lights and shadows would bathe Liberty City, from the giant neon credit card billboard ads to the blood-orange sunsets over the skyline.

Such innovations weren't only eye candy. The new palette enabled a more sophisticated level of storytelling and design. Dan's six-page treatment told the story of Niko Bellic, a Serbian national who came to Liberty City after a wartime betrayal left his closest friends dead. Yet like many immigrants, Bellic came to find that the American Dream was more like a nightmare. His cousin Roman, a drunken loudmouth cabbie, needed Bellic to help him with petty missions to resolve some gambling debts. As in the other *GTA*s, the ensuing missions unlocked a series of lowlifes and gangsters, each with his or her own battles and plans. The deeper Bellic went, the more tangled he became in balancing his deep sense of loyalty with his need for money and revenge.

Sam and Dan, immigrants themselves, were drawn to the struggles of Niko's fish-out-of-water story. After seeing (and making) so many portrayals of Italian American mobsters, the Housers found the character of a Eastern European especially fascinating. "On one hand, he's an innocent," Dan recalled. "On the other hand, he's battle-hardened and world weary. A modern 'arriving in America' story felt very interesting to us." Sam said, "These new guys off the boat, they're coming with something to prove, and they mean business. They are fucking fearless."

To best immerse players in Bellic's world, Sam wanted to focus on packing as much dense detail as they could into their fictional New York. The task was insanely ambitious—not only to make the gangster movie they had always dreamed of, but capture the Big Apple in all of its madness. "What epitomizes New York?" Dan asked.

To find the answer, the coders and the artists from Rockstar North arrived with cameras and notebooks in hand. It remained one of *GTA*'s great and largely unappreciated ironies—that a bunch of Scots were creating the most influential simulation of America ever made. More than fifty of them scoured the neighborhoods, taking thousands of photos of the people and the places to get the right feel. Sam began to take weekly treks to Brighton Beach.

Geeks trolled the karaoke bars and the nightclubs, the restaurants and the clothing stores. They even studied the public bathrooms in Brighton Beach, watching in awe as old Russian men shaved their armpits over the sinks. On more than one occasion, they got threatened for taking photos of passersby. Some guy in Harlem warned that he'd shoot them if they didn't put their cameras away.

No detail proved too arcane or obsessive. They hung plasma TVs over the developers' desks in Edinburgh and fed them with nonstop footage of New York. They studied a library of books on the city, from the architecture to the sewage system. They pored over census data to ascertain the appropriate ethnic makeup of each neighborhood. Researchers grilled the Taxi and Limousine Commission to find the precise ratio of cabs to other cars in NYC.

They set up a time-lapse video camera aimed at the sky over the city, just to see how it changed throughout the day. They watched hours of DVDs of traffic patterns from New York, simply to get the flow of taxis and cars right. To ensure the accuracy of the types of cars in the streets, they researched auto sales reports. The audio engineers spent hours getting just the right sounds for the amount of coins in a character's pockets.

With more than 150 artists and programmers working on the game, *GTA IV* came to life. Within six months, they had built out a detailed map of Liberty City. The action would unfold over five boroughs based on the real NYC: from Algonquin (Manhattan) to Broker (Brooklyn). Each borough would feature a meticulous reconstruction of real NYC locales, the iconic Statue of Happiness, the flashing lights of the Times Square–style Star Junction, the Brooklyn/Broker Bridge, the JFKish Francis International Airport in Dukes (Queens). Though the Rockstars insisted that their pixilated city was a dream-version of reality, *GTA IV* was one of the most passionate love letters to New York City ever written.

As the story got outlined and the city mapped, artists created the characters: Bellic, with his broad forehead and bent nose, his Serbian swagger; Michelle, the vaguely ethnic girl in the fashionable pea coat, whom he dates; Little Jacob, the Jamaican smuggler, with his dreads and drugs; Trey "Playboy X" Stewart, the crack king in the rainbow hoodie. To capture the spontaneity of street interactions, they created a range of oddball passersby—crackheads and cougars, hipsters and hot dog vendors. They labored to get every detail right, from the dialogue to the fashion. To make sure the peds were dressed properly, they even hired NYC stylists to design their virtual clothes.

Dan and his team broke the narrative into cut-scenes and missions. At the core, *GTA IV* was still essentially a racing-and-shooting game, but the missions were designed to tour the player throughout the rich and wonderful Liberty City world. To whack one foe, the player needed to climb a series of ladders to the roof of a construction site, then leap over buildings as the sun set gorgeously on the town. In another mission, the player would wipe out a series of dockside Russians, chasing down coke dealers in a speedboat around the city. Along the way, the player would be given moral choices—such as revenge or deal?—that would affect the direction of the game. If you stood up Roman for a guys' night out, his respect would go down accordingly.

The action sequences were broken up by naturalistic diversions. While *San Andreas* had introduced role-playing game elements to the story, *GTA IV* expanded the richness of the open world by bringing interiors to life. A trip to a nightclub to see a review of cheesy jugglers and torch singers. A date to a bowling alley, complete with a ten pin mini-game. Owing something to the real-world scenes innovated in *Bully*, *GTA IV*'s everyday moments were sublimely banal. A player would take a long ride on a quiet subway through Liberty City at night or sit in a car wash, as the sudsy foam bathed Bellic's stolen ride.

With the expanded online capabilities of the new consoles, Rockstar had new ways to enhance its virtual world. Missions wouldn't end with the original disc. Microsoft paid about $50 million to Rockstar to distribute two additional episodes of the game exclusively over the

Xbox 360 (this along with, for the first time, having a same-day release as the PS3 version of the game). *GTA IV* would feature a multiplayer online version, too.

In the past, *GTA* players ran between phone booths and received pages, but now *GTA IV* was catching up to contemporary communications. The game included a mobile phone for placing and receiving calls and even sending text messages to crime lords and girls. There'd be an in-game Internet with more than a hundred fake websites (craplist.com, for classifieds; friendswithoutfaces.com, for social networking). Maybe best of all, they put a television set in Bellic's apartment, complete with three channels of programming that players could sit and watch (from a PBS-style "History of Liberty City" to stand-up performances by comedians Ricky Gervais and Katt Williams, appearing in pixilated versions of themselves).

As the game's work progressed, so did its size. The budget neared $100 million, the most ever spent on a game, and the development time soon spilled over three years. The environment grew to four times the size of other *GTA* games and included three cities, twelve towns, and surrounding woods equivalent to seventeen square miles. There'd be a record-breaking eighteen radio stations (such as Tuff Gong for reggae and Vladivostok FM for Russian dance tunes). In total, there were 218 licensed tracks and plans for a deal with Amazon.com to let players download in-game music directly from the site. Rockstar hired a private eye just to track down the rights to the 1979 song "Walk the Night."

They hired New York news radio personality John Montone to do the voice for a similar station in the game. In honor of the Housers' dad, Sam said, "Let's do jazz properly" in the game, too. Walter Houser suggested tracks from Miles Davis, John Coltrane, and Charlie Parker. When eighty-three-year-old jazz legend Roy Haynes heard he'd have a song in *GTA IV*, he was happy that "the youngsters are going to check that out in the game, you know, and that'll be cool." Sam and Dan even included a version of their dad playing saxophone in the game.

Rockstar hired a cast of 861 voice actors to play the parts of mobsters and pedestrians and waitresses. In all, they'd have more than eighty thousand lines of dialogue, in languages that included Chinese, Spanish, and Russian. And, yes, they'd have hookers, too, with HD-quality implied oral sex in dark alleys—though nothing that went beyond the M-rated line and there were no hidden scenes.

For *GTA IV*, Rockstar changed its once mod-friendly end user license agreement to prohibit reverse engineering and copyright protection circumvention. As longtime Rockstar Jeronimo Barrera told MTV News, "Are we going to have a 'Hot Coffee' situation? Absolutely not."

OLD CITY. Aerial view. A car cut through the city of Edinburgh. Sam had come to check on the development of *GTA IV.* It had been a decade now since the first *GTA* game, and so much had changed. This wasn't a ragtag group of nerds working in a frat over a pub in Dundee. Sam pulled up to a sleek modern building and strode into a lobby marked only by the R★ logo—and blocked by security. Upstairs, he found dozens of workers laboring in a neat, orderly office, distinguished only by a couple of arcade games—*Super Off Road* and *Super Street Fighter II Turbo.*

On one floor, three round-the-clock shifts of game testers—known in the industry as quality assurance, or QAs—filled cubicles, playing through every moment of the game, looking for inconsistencies, glitches, and programming bugs. Unlike many games that allowed players to choose difficulty levels, *GTA* didn't offer such customizations. Instead, the team would play and play and play the game, until the challenges hit the sweet spot: so that an average player could finish a mission in fewer than three tries. Too many cars in a chase scene? Remove them. Too much space to jump over between buildings? Narrow them down.

Yet Sam had his own ritualistic way of checking out the game—by immersing himself inside it. Sitting in front of a screen, he grabbed a

controller and began to walk Niko down the virtual streets. He passed
the storefronts under the overhead train track. He passed decrepit gray
buildings, tall bleak apartment complexes. Yellow cabs streamed by. The
flutter of newspapers kicking up in the breeze. The vendor pulling hot
dogs from the steaming cart.

Sam could feel it. The weight of reality. The simulated world sus-
pending his disbelief in ways he only dreamed of. This was it. He went
to jack a car, but the driver wasn't having it and started to chase him
down the street. Sam stopped dead in his tracks. "I'm not running from
you any more," he thought. "I'm going to fucking have it with you now,
mate."

As he stood there, ready to slug the guy, a car suddenly careened past
and—bam!—sent the dude flying like a pathetic ragdoll through the air.
The collision was just another random event driven by the artificial
intelligence of the game. The living, breathing world Sam had long
craved came alive before his eyes. "This is how we always wanted *GTA*
to be," he later recalled, "but it simply wasn't possible until now."

Climbing into his car, Sam knew just where he'd like to go: the
Steinway Beer Garden, a pub where Niko could swill pints of stout and,
according to a commercial, "watch drunk fat old men throw sharp
instruments around a crowded room." In real life, Sam sucked at darts,
but the mini-game of darts was one of Sam's favorite and most accom-
plished pastimes in *GTA IV*—and something he could actually win.

Sam pulled up to the walled garden of Steinway's and walked in
under the orange arch. He stepped into the outdoor patio, then walked
along a line of trees with red autumn leaves. Drinkers socialized at white
plastic tables under red-white-and-blue umbrellas that had plastic flags
strung between them. Through the front door he went, into the pub
with the lute music playing. A bartender stood behind the taps in a long
walnut-colored bar on the right, rows of booths to the left along green-
paneled walls. Down to the right in front of the bar, he saw the tattered
red, black, green, and white dart board. It was time to play.

With his left thumb over the left controller stick he aimed his dart, and with a tap of a button, he let it fly. As the Irish music played, he heard a satisfying *thwack* as the tip of the dart logged into the board. With each dart, Sam felt a bit of his real self dematerialize, cells replaced by pixels, blood by electricity, a gamer immersed in a game, until he wasn't Sam anymore. He was Niko.

Sam had always had relationships with his game alter egos before, but there was usually some impediment to his suspension of disbelief: the top-down view of *GTA* and *GTA2*; the silent protagonist of *GTA III*; Liotta's voice in *Vice City*. Yet this felt different. The technology and the design of *GTA IV* had conspired to create something magic. "Niko is a real person to me now," Sam thought.

This feeling of connection extended to relationships with other players in the game. Befriend one, and he brings you a helicopter; earn the trust of another, and he introduces you to an important contact. In a scene that Sam found particularly moving, Niko had to save Roman from a mob of fifteen angry Albanians. As Sam urgently worked his buttons while his cousin screamed for help, he felt awed by the emotions swirling inside him. "The idea of having feelings for a bunch of polygons is very profound," he later recalled.

Sam realized the implications of this one morning back in New York as he was driving over the Brooklyn Bridge. In the distance, the skyscrapers rose above the South Street Seaport, where he had lived with the others in the Commune so many years ago. They had come to America to live out their fantasies, to make the games they wanted to play, and, in turn, to make games urgent for a new generation. They had fought for this dream, from the streets of SoHo to the halls of Capitol Hill. They had been celebrated and vilified, rewarded and fined, had survived murders and marriages, suicides and births. They had even seen the tallest buildings in town crumble and fall.

Yet through it all, this amazing city remained. New York. The place he'd dreamed of as a kid sitting in his bedroom listening to Slayer. Now the city was his to share. Decoded. Replicated. Simulated. A living, breathing world on a disc that anyone could play. For weeks, he had been in Edinburgh, immersed in Liberty City, but now, as New York City towered above him, something shifted inside him. *Why doesn't this feel different?* he wondered. Then it hit him. It didn't feel different because the simulated world had come so vividly to life. "I didn't feel like I'd left," he realized, "because I'd been here the whole time."

THE STOCK MARKET crash of 2008 didn't stop gamers from buying *GTA IV.* When the game was released on April 29, 2008, it broke the Guinness World Record to become the most successful entertainment product launch of all time—bigger than any game, movie, or album.

Taking in more than $310 million on its first day alone, it eclipsed the box office champ *Spider-Man 3* and even *Harry Potter and the Deathly Hallows,* the final book in the series. Not even *The Dark Knight,* which *GTA IV* outsold five-to-one, came close. By the end of its first week, the game had sold more than six million copies for more than half a billion dollars. Electronic Arts attempted a hostile bid to buy Take-Two for a reported $2 billion but didn't succeed.

According to MetaCritic, which aggregated reviews, *GTA IV* became the best-reviewed game in history. *GameSpot* called it "the series' best by far." *Game Informer* effused that "it completely changes the landscape of gaming." *GameSpy* deemed it "an instant classic, a game unlike any we've played before. As is the case with many great books and movies, you'll want to know what happens to the characters after the game ends, and one can't help hoping that all of their American Dreams comes true." The game took nearly every major game industry award.

In the past, controversy had dogged every new *GTA,* but now (with the exception of the Chicago Transit Authority pulling *GTA IV* ads from buses for fear of inciting violence) something had changed. The mainstream press was focusing on the one thing Sam had championed all along, the game. The *Sunday Times* in London said *GTA IV* "embodies the future of entertainment" and called it "the pinnacle of a British-created phenomenon."

"The real star of the game is the city itself," effused Seth Schiesel in the *New York Times*. "It looks like New York. It sounds like New York. It feels like New York. Liberty City has been so meticulously created it almost even smells like New York." A blogger for *New York* magazine wrote, "It will finally allow us to do all the things we fantasize about doing whenever our urban surroundings impede on our ability to not be completely annoyed . . . head-butt that guy who made us miss a 6 train this morning or drive a tank through the living room of our jerk next-door neighbor with the surround sound."

Not everyone was so keen. Back in Dundee, some of the original *GTA* team thought the series had been losing its sense of humor since *Vice City*. "*GTA IV* is so dour," lamented Gary Penn. "It's become a very serious franchise," said Brian Baglow. Writing in the *Wall Street Journal*, Pulitzer Prize–winning novelist Junot Diaz admitted to be a longtime fan of the series but thought that *GTA IV* failed to rise to true art. "Successful art tears away the veil and allows you to see the world with lapidary clarity; successful art pulls you apart and puts you back together again, often against your will, and in the process reminds you in a visceral way of your limitations, your vulnerabilities, makes you in effect more human," he wrote. "Does *GTA IV* do that? Not for me it doesn't, and heck, I love this damn game."

Yet ultimately, being a damn good game was enough. With *GTA IV*, Rockstar finally had achieved its lifelong goals—to break the wall between reality and fantasy and have its medium respected as mainstream entertainment. "There was a sense that in some way movies were a higher art form and video games could aspire to be like them," Dan said. "I think now, because we and a few other companies are making products, that this isn't the case. They're just different and video games are capable of things that movies aren't."

In the United Kingdom, the first battleground over the games, *GTA IV* wasn't merely celebrated, it was fueling one of the country's most esteemed institutions: Oxford. Because the university retained a share of the company that created the *GTA IV* engine, Oxford would be making money from the game. A university spokesperson called it "a huge success."

After a decade of fights and betrayals, dreams and nightmares, the players had done it. Video games didn't seem so outlaw anymore—and neither did the industry's most influential player, Sam. The thirty-six-year-old was now living in a tony brownstone on a leafy street in Brooklyn with his wife and kids. He had even gone through the long naturalization process to become a United States citizen. After making such iconically American games, he was now an American too.

When Sam reflected on the adversity he'd overcome, it was as if he spoke for the entire generation who had grown up on his games. "It's made our resolve that much stronger," he told a reporter one day, "and in some ways I feel that some of the negative stuff had to happen to keep everybody's feet on the ground, and to keep everybody hungry and motivated. . . . the fact that, after all this time, we can still be this hungry and ambitious and driven and crazy—that's got to be a good sign. Because if they can't shake us now, then what can they do to us?"

This game was over; this mission, complete. It was time for another to begin. "What have I got left to achieve?" Sam asked. "Everything."

Epilogue

Outlaws to the End

FREE ROAM

You can choose people to enter your posse by hitting back and separately inviting each of the players. If you receive a posse invite, tap back and accept the invitation.

Perhaps more than any other entertainment product of its time, *Grand Theft Auto* defined a decade. "It was a defining creative work that represented the coming of age of a breakout industry," as Lowenstein said. Yet that decade—spanning the inception of the franchise through its crowning achievement, *GTA IV*—marked more than the awkward adolescence of the industry. It signified one of the most disruptive chapters in the history of media.

When players weren't exploring Liberty City, they were toying with powerful new tools from YouTube to Facebook, from texting to Twitter. A new world emerged on the other side of our TV and telephone and computer screens. We started the millennium thinking that tweeting was for birds. By the end of the decade, we couldn't go long without peering through the looking glass into the wonderland online. Whether you thought technology brought out the best or the worst in humanity or maybe a little of both, life would never be the same.

Neither would video games. Sam Houser's dream of seeing games get taken as seriously as films had been fulfilled. *GTA* made it possible to have the game industry's equivalent of Scorsese films: arty, funny, dark, violent, and authentic. Franchises from *BioShock*, a sort of retro futuristic thriller, to the military shooters, such as *Call of Duty*, represented, along with *GTA*, a new wave of cinematic storytelling—just made for participants with controllers in hand.

In addition to maturing as a storytelling medium, games had become a huge business. By 2010, the $60 billion global game industry was expected to hit more than $90 billion within the next five years. The stereotype of the pimply teenage boy gaming in his basement was finally fading away. A new generation of online games—nicknamed social or casual games—had become the craze. Often free to download and play, the games were cheeky and accessible, such as the biggest hit on Facebook, a farm simulator called *FarmVille*. Every day, 62 million people were harvesting virtual corn.

Mobile gaming, once a pipe dream, had millions of fingers twitching and swiping their screens. Cheap to make and easy to produce, these games spawned a new golden age of start-up development. While *GTA IV* had a team of 150 and a budget of $100 million, a mobile game hit could be made by one intrepid coder with a laptop and a dream. That was pretty much the case with *Angry Birds*, a Finnish physics game that despite its surreal premise (slingshot birds at kidnapping pigs?) became the *Pac-Man* of the iPhone generation.

With casual games seducing moms (and grandmas), consoles broadened their audience as well. Riding on the success of the Nintendo Wii, Microsoft and Sony introduced their own motion-sensing controllers—the Kinect and Move. Players didn't need thumbs that danced like Michael Jackson anymore. They could simply wave their arms—or jump or shout—to play.

Despite whispers at game conventions that the age of the block-buster might be over, the big-budget epics that GTA pioneered kept coming. In fact, it didn't take long for GTA IV's blockbuster sales record to be broken. The latest champ was the military shooter Call of Duty: Black Ops, which brought in more than $650 million in its first week alone. The game industry remained the testing ground for technological innovations, such as 3-D television, and a new wave of blockbusters was always around the corner.

As a broader range of games served a wider demographic, another seismic shift occurred in the wake of the GTA Decade: the sociopoliti-cal battle subsided. Some took it as a sign that the Bush era was over, and the Obama one had begun. "It feels at last like we're moving on from that debate," Dan said. "The audience is getting past thirty so it all becomes a bit silly."[1]

Hot Coffee, despite all of the headaches, was credited with making the game industry stronger. It pushed the ESRB to refine its submission process, ensuring that such a costly scandal would likely never happen again. "It forced us to address issues we hadn't addressed before," said Vance, who noted that stores now card 80 percent of minors buying M-rated games, as opposed to 20 percent at the beginning of the decade. Hot Coffee "gave us an opportunity to show to critics that we're not in the tank," Lowenstein said.

At the same time, the suppositions about the effects of video game violence wore thin. In a meta-analytic study called "Evidence for Pub-lication Bias in Video Game Violence Effects Literature," Dr. Christo-pher J. Ferguson of Texas A&M International University's Department of Behavioral, Applied Sciences and Criminal Justice found what he called "a systematic bias for hot-button issues" that resulted in overstate-ments and misleading findings.

"No one has shown a causal link between violent games and real world violent behavior," said Dr. Cheryl Olson, a professor of psychiatry at the Harvard Medical School's Center for Mental Health and Media.

"As with the entertainment of earlier generations," she said, "we may look back on some of today's games with nostalgia, and our grandchildren may wonder what the fuss was about."

In November 2010, the debate reached the U.S. Supreme Court, which held a hearing on the controversial California law banning the sale or rental of violent video games to minors. Protesters—including one dressed in a fake mustache and a red hat like Nintendo's ubiquitous hero, Mario—took to the steps, calling for justice. During the hearing, the California Attorney General argued that the "deviant level of violence that is presented in a certain category of video games" necessitated the law.

Conservative justice Antonin Scalia questioned whether such restrictions should apply to violent stories such as Grimm's fairy tales as well. "Are you going to ban them, too?" Scalia asked. The following June, the high court voted to throw out California's violent game ban entirely. "Like the protected books, plays and movies that preceded them, video games communicate ideas—and even social messages— through many familiar literary devices (such as characters, dialogue, plot, and music) and through features distinctive to the medium (such as the player's interaction with the virtual world)," Scalia wrote. "That suffices to confer First Amendment protection."

The hypocrisy of the war against games was not lost on many— especially when, not long before, New York governor Spitzer, who campaigned against the virtual prostitution of *GTA*, got busted for the real thing. One familiar player, however, was absent from the debate: Jack Thompson, who had come to an unexpected conclusion of his own. At first, after settling with Take-Two and agreeing not to sue or correspond directly with them again, Thompson continued to speak out. He called *GTA IV* "the gravest assault upon children in this country since polio" and, legally bound from contacting Take-Two directly, wrote an open letter to Take-Two chair Strauss Zelnick's mother instead. "Your son, this very moment, is doing everything he possibly can to sell as many copies of *GTA IV* to teen boys in the United States, a country in which your son claims you raised him to be 'a Boy Scout,'" Thompson wrote. "More like the Hitler Youth, I would say."

Yet his legal battles were soon done. On September 25, 2008, the Florida bar voted to permanently disbar Thompson because of "the extensive misconduct of respondent and his complete lack of remorse." The U.S. District Court ruled that Thompson's numerous lawsuits were "abusive and vexatious." For gamers, it was like the melting of the Wicked Witch of the West, and they flooded the Net with YouTube videos and online comics rejoicing.

Thompson soon found a higher calling than *GTA*, however. In January 2011, he revealed that he was enrolled in the online Reformed Theological Ministry to join the clergy. "As a virtual minister, Thompson will be able to seek the absolute and eternal justice he was denied over and over again," reported the *Miami New Times*. "Thirty-one years fighting with the bar and the entertainment industry is a pretty good run," Thompson said. "I'm surprised that I lasted that long."

While the conflicts of the *GTA* Decade came to a close, one question remained: the legacy and the future of Rockstar Games. Despite the success of *GTA IV*, the company could not completely escape its past. In September 2009, Take-Two announced that it would be paying $20 million to settle the class-action lawsuits from Hot Coffee—in addition to the estimated $25 million already spent to recall the AO version of the game.

Three months later, Rockstar's wall of silence shattered like never before. It happened when the self-described "Determined Devoted Wives of Rockstar San Diego employees" wrote a public blog alleging dismal working conditions for the studio working on *Midnight Club: Los Angeles* and *Red Dead Redemption*. They complained of twelve-hour-a-day, six-day work weeks that "turned [employees] into machines as they are slowly robbed of their humanity."

The wives said that "the current Rockstar management has grown a thirst for power," while failing to adequately compensate employees.

"The last *Grand Theft Auto* game made over a billion dollars of revenue," the wives concluded, "so where is the recognition and appreciation to those of whom, without them, such success would not have been made?" They vowed legal action, seeking compensation "for health, mental, financial, and damages done to families of employees."[2]

The blog triggered similar allegations by people claiming to be ex-employees of Rockstar. One compared the company to the Eye of Sauron, the fire-rimmed, all-seeing eye of the dark lord in *The Lord of the Rings*. Rockstar NYC wouldn't comment—directly, at least. Shortly after the Eye of Sauron comment, the company posted a series of psychedelic wallpaper images on its website titled "The Eye Is Watching." In one, a giant eye clutched a lightning bolt as it stared down on an exploding R★ icon. The wives weren't laughing and pursued their class-action case with more than a hundred employees from Rockstar San Diego. The blog doystig reported that in April 2009, Rockstar settled out of court with the group for $2.75 million.

The next year, similar allegations about working conditions surfaced following the release of *L.A. Noire*, a critically acclaimed detective thriller published by Rockstar and developed by Australian game makers Team Bondi—prompting an investigation by the International Game Developers Association (IGDA). "Certainly, reports of twelve-hour a day, lengthy crunch time, if true, are absolutely unacceptable and harmful to the individuals involved, the final product, and the industry as a whole," said IGDA chair Brian Robbins. Some felt it was time to unionize the game business—like other parts of entertainment industry—once and for all.

Even the Rockstar who most exemplified the selfless devotion to the company, Will Rompf, Sam's acolyte, left broken in the end. After five long years of work, he was finally crushed by the crunch time. It happened just three weeks before the release of *Grand Theft Auto IV*. One day he looked up at his friend from his desk and said he couldn't endure the stress anymore and needed to take the rest of the week off. Within hours of his leaving, he said his Rockstar e-mail had been shut off—but an uncommon practice when an employee leaves a company, lot one that seemed abrupt.

Unable to give 100 percent of himself anymore, Rompf chose not to come back. Assuming he'd be cut from *GTA IV*'s credits, despite all of his work, as was Rockstar's way, he made one last call to the company—asking a friend to be the one who removed his name. "I wanted someone I love and trust to do it," he later recalled. Eventually, Rompf got back on his feet, cleaned up, and took a job as the head of quality assurance at a major game publisher. Despite the ups and downs, however, he still had a deep-felt connection to Rockstar. "I kind of want back," Rompf later said with a laugh.

He wasn't the only Rockstar veteran with mixed feelings. Jamie King, who had launched his own company, 4mm Games with Rockstar cofounder Gary Foreman, suggested that perhaps nothing great could come without some degree of chaos. "We never believed in the easy way," King said. "You don't create something amazing that's easy." In the end, it was this obsession that raised the profile of games to the point they had recently reached. "Games are very cool now," he said, "and now even in the movies if the character is a gamer, the guy gets laid!"

Replicating the success of Rockstar, many realized, wasn't easy. Dave Jones, *GTA*'s original creator, spent more than five years creating a multiplayer online urban action game, *APB:All Points Bulletin*, only to see it shut down following disappointing sales shortly after its release in July 2010. Fernandez and Pope, who had left Rockstar to launch their own start-up, Cashmere Games, met a similar fate when their company dissolved.

Pope went on to make a very non-*GTA* game for self-help doctor Deepak Chopra. "It's taking everything that's amazing about games and doing something positive," he said. "With video games you're either creating or destroying; with *GTA* we were definitely destroying." Fernandez, a producer at another company, kept a quote of Sam's over his desk. "It says, you must always fight for greatness," Fernandez said. "If you get complacent, you're dead. If you're not fighting for greatness, you're dead."

Rockstar still had plenty of fight. In May 2010, the company released *Red Dead Redemption*, its open world Western. The game arrived in a dust storm of notoriety. In addition to having come from the embattled Rockstar San Diego studio, it was at the heart of a controversy in Australia, where a game journalist was fired after posting an alleged e-mail from Rockstar seemingly pressuring him to give the title a positive review. "I did not sign up to become a journalist to write advertorials masquerading as editorial," he said.

Rockstar didn't need his help, though. With its sweeping sunsets and old world grit (and, yeah, horse-jacking), *Red Dead Redemption* was a critical and commercial hit. The game became 2010's fastest selling title, racking up more than eight million copies in sales and numerous awards. More than anything, it proved that Rockstar wasn't a one-trick pony. As players rabidly awaited *GTA* V, which would be set in Los Santos, the fictional Los Angeles from San Andreas, it seemed like anything in the future could come. "Until we've simulated the world outside," producer Les Benzies said, "we're not going to stop."[3]

In the meantime, they had a little gift for their fans. It came on June 22, 2010, as a free bonus for buyers of *Red Dead Redemption*. Rockstar created a new pack of missions for the game, from raiding a mining camp to protecting a herd of cattle, but there was a twist. Instead of rustling on one's own, a gamer could team up online to play cooperatively with up to three others.

Gangs had always been crucial to the guys at Rockstar, from their own gang of developers to the ones they simulated in their games. Now, all across the world, posses of players hopped on their horses and rode off into the sunset together. It was a fitting finale for the ones who seemed so outcast not long ago. Yet no matter what was on the horizon, they'd never forget from where they came. The name Rockstar gave to the *Red Dead Redemption* mission pack ensured this:

Outlaws to the End.

Acknowledgments

Thanks to Connie Santisteban, ace editor (and gamer!) and everyone else at John Wiley & Sons, for seeing the potential of a book on *GTA*, and Jenny Heller, Craig Adams, and the rest at HarperCollins, for bringing this story to the UK where *GTA* began. Thanks to my agents, David McCormick of McCormick & Williams, and Matthew Snyder and Tiffany Ward of Creative Artists Agency.

I'm grateful to those others who shepherded this along the way: Mary Ann Naples, Laura Nolan, Shari Smiley, and the many editors who have assigned video game stories to me over the years. A big shout-out to Chris Baker, my longtime editor at *Wired*, for reading and commenting on the manuscript. As always, thanks to my friends and family and, especially, my dad, who I wish could have read this book.

Notes

Portions of this book are drawn from articles of mine that appeared in publications including *Rolling Stone, Salon, Wired, Electronic Gaming Monthly, and GamePro.*

I also drew from interviews I conducted over the years with people including: Dave Jones, Sam Houser, Dan Houser, Terry Donovan, Jamie King, Gary Foreman, Brian Baglow, Kevin Liles, Paul Eibeler, Jeremy Pope, Marc Fernandez, Gillian Telling, Aaron Garbut, Phil Harrison, Doug Lowenstein, Simon Harvey, David Nottingham, Corey Wade, David Walsh, Will Rompf, Gary Dale, Jack Thompson, Kirk Ewing, Bill Linn, Jeff Castanada, Colin MacDonald, Gary Penn, Lol Scragg, Mark Ette, Max Clifford, Mike Dailly, Navid Khonsari, Pat Vance, Patrick Wildenborg, Paul Farley, Todd Zuniga, Rodney Walker, Rob Fleischer, Corey Wade, Dan Hsu, Crispin Boyer, Scott Miller, Ian Hetherington, Strauss Zelnick, Leland Yee, Jerry and Mike of Penny Arcade, Luther Campbell, Warren Spector, Will Wright, Henry Jenkins, Wayne Buckner, Donna Buckner, Amanda Hetherington, Chris Carro, Michael Gartenberg, Michael Pachter, Craig Anderson, Doug Gentile, and others, some of whom wish to remain anonymous.

Prologue: Players vs. Haters

3 *"creating tapestries"* "The 2009 *Time* 100: Sam and Dan Houser," *Time*, April 30, 2009, www.time.com/time/specials/packages/article/0,28804,1894410_1893836_1894428,00.html.

3 *"a hit machine"* "Rockstar Execs Keep Low Profile: Videogame Company Creates Its Own Rockstars," *Variety*, April 18, 2008.

3 *"one of the leading lights"* "Studio Is Prize in Takeover Duel: Intense 'Grand Theft' Creator Wows Gamers—and Electronic Arts," *Wall Street Journal*, May 12, 2008, A1.

3 *"the kids"* Ibid.

3 *"We are going to destroy"* "Florida Attorney on *Manhunt* for Rockstar, Jack Thompson Seeks to 'Destroy' Take-Two Label," Posted July 30, 2004, GameDaily, http://biz.gamedaily.com/features_new/jack_thompson/.

4 *"The concept of a glorified shop"* United States District Court Southern District of New York in Re Take-Two Interactive Securities Litigation, Consolidated Third Amended Class Action Complaint for Violations of Federal Securities Laws, Exhibit B-3, Filed 9/15/08.

1. The Outlaw

6 *"A bank robber"* "Studio Is Prize in Takeover Duel: Intense '*Grand Theft*' Creator Wows Gamers—and Electronic Arts," *Wall Street Journal*, May 12, 2008, A1.

7 *Sam's broken hand* Harold Goldberg, *All Your Base Are Belong to Us: How Fifty Years of Videogames Conquered Pop Culture* (New York: Three Rivers Press, 2011), 216.

9 *"running the track"* Stacy Gueraseva, *Def Jam, Inc.: Russell Simmons, Rick Rubin, and the Extraordinary Story of the World's Most Influential Hip Hop Label* (New York: One World Ballantine, 2005), 17.

10 *"Why is everyone"* "Sam Houser: The First Global Superstar of Gaming," *Independent*, July 10, 2000, www.independent.co.uk/news/business/analysis-and-features/sam-houser-the-first-global-superstar-of-gaming-694096.html.

2. The Warriors

12 *"lit the fuse"* Jack Thompson, *Out of Harm's Way* (IL: Carol Stream, 2005), 116.

13 *"God's people"* Ibid.

14 *"Time Warner is"* Ibid., 117.

15 *"I got my first"* "At Your Leisure, Sam Houser, Video Game Designer," *Express*, October 23, 1999.

15 *"the recording industry's"* "David and Goliath Are Interacting, Bertelsmann and Upstart Plan Music Label for CD-ROMs," *Los Angeles Times*, September 10, 1993, 1.

16 *"Because they are"* David Kushner, discussion of Lieberman hearings, *Masters of Doom* (New York: Random House, 2003), 154–158.

17 *"dangerous, violent"* "You Can Run but You Can't Hide," *Scotsman*, March 19, 1994.

3. Race 'n' Chase

24 *"To say that"* "Have a Blast with the Lads from '*Lemmings*,'" *Scotsman*, December 20, 1996, 17.

24 *"We think David Jones"* "Turning a Redundancy Cheque into Millions," *Scotsman,* May 4, 1994.

26 *an estimated £3.4 million pounds* "Games Firm in £1.5m Legal Action," *Herald* (Glasgow), July 30, 1997, 4.

26 *"They will treat computer companies"* "That's Quite Some Game, Boy," *Herald* (Glasgow), May 20, 1995, 31.

4. Gouranga!

28 *five hundred thousand machines* "*Sony* Plays for Millions in Games Gamble," *Guardian*, March 19, 1995, 5.

28 *"our biggest launch since the Walkman"*   "Sega, Sony Battle New Systems Vie for Players," *Cincinnati Post*, June 20, 1995, 6C.

31 *"Once we made you able to kill"*   "Get Your Game On," *Raygun*, Summer 1999.

32 *"If the game isn't coming together properly"*   Harold Goldberg, *All Your Base Are Belong to Us: How Fifty Years of Videogames Conquered Pop Culture* (New York: Three Rivers Press, 2011), 219.

5. Eating the Hamster

38 *"a master manipulator"*   "Driving Publicity to the Max," *Scotsman*, December 3, 1997, 3.

41 *"I do understand"*   "Minister Condemns Car Crime Computer Game," *Parliamentary News*, May 20, 1997.

41 *"We simply cannot allow children"*   "Car-Theft Computer Game Accused of Glamorising Violent Crime," *Scotland on Sunday*, July 20, 1997, 6.

42 *"It is deplorable"*   "Criminal Computer Game That Glorifies Hit and Run Thugs," *Daily Mail*, November 24, 1997, 20.

42 *"This game is sick"*   "Ban Criminal Video Game," *News of the World*, November 23, 1997, 21.

42 *"The BBFC"*   "DMA's Joy-Rider Game in Dock," *Scotland on Sunday*, November 23, 1997, 1.

42 *"Sick car game boss"*   "Sick Car Game Boss Was Banned from Driving," *News of the World*, December 21, 1997, 21.

43 *"the computer genius"*   "Criminal Computer Game That Glorifies Hit and Run Thugs," *Daily Mail*, November 24, 1997, 20.

43 *"It is quite a shock"*   "Big Game Hunter," *Sunday Times*, October 31, 2004, 1.

43 *"We are being moral"*   "Car-Theft Computer Game Accused of Glamorising Violent Crime," *Scotland on Sunday*, July 20, 1997, 6.

44 *"People assume that computer games"*   Ibid.

45 *"Though not up to moral standards"*   http://web.archive.org/web/20030105021602/ www.gemonthly.com/reviews/gta/index.htm, accessed July 28, 2011.

45 *"GTA is a gas,"*   www.allgame.com/game.php?id=9363&tab=review, accessed July 28, 2011.

6. Liberty City

48 *"I want to create"*   "Game Boy," *Forbes*, May 20, 1996, 276.

48 *"We're going to get killed"*   "Fatherly Advice on Facts of Financial Life," *Crain's New York Business*, October 12, 1998, 34.

49 *"My first drug experience"*   "Drugs, Juggs, and Speed," *Spin*, July 1999, 70.

50 GTA *madness had even spread to Brazil*   "Brazil Bans Sale of 'Dangerous' Computer Game," Reuters, March 1, 1998.

50 *"A top-selling Scots computer game"*   "Game Cheats," *Sunday Mail*, March 22, 1998.

50 *"one of the most original"*   "The Complete History of Grand Theft Auto," *Games-Radar*, http://a3.gamesradar.com/f/the-complete-history-of-grand-theft-auto/a-2008042314506193050, accessed July 29, 2011.

51 *"The game's gleeful embrace"* "Grand Theft Auto for DOS," *MobyGames*, www.mobygames.com/game/grand-theft-auto/mobyrank, accessed July 28, 2011.

51 *"It won't win any awards"* "Grand Theft Auto Reviews," *GameSpot*, www .gamespot.com/pc/adventure/grandtheftauto/review.html, accessed July 28, 2011.

51 *"shock-schlock game"* "Grand Theft Auto for DOS," *MobyGames*, www .mobygames.com/game/grand-theft-auto/mobyrank, accessed July 28, 2011.

7. Gang Warfare

55 *"Respect-O-Meter"* Grand Theft Auto 2, *Manual*, 7, Rockstar Games, 1999.

55 *"the Rockstar brand will finally deliver"* "Take-Two Interactive Software, Inc. Subsidiary Rockstar Games Announces Highly Anticipated 1999 and 2000 Video Game Lineup," Business Editors, *Business Wire*, February 23, 1999, 1.

57 *"What the fuck"* Harold Goldberg, *All Your Base Are Belong to Us: How Fifty Years of Videogames Conquered Pop Culture* (New York: Three Rivers Press, 2011), 220.

59 *"London in the sixties"* "Gathering of Developers Urges Drivers to Get on the Wrong Side of the Road with *Grand Theft Auto: London 1969*," *Business and Entertainment Editors*, March 15, 1999, 1.

59 *"We're about doing games"* "Drugs, Juggs, and Speed," *Spin*, July 1999, 70.

8. Steal This Game

65 *"Three weeks into the future"* GTA2 Manual, 2.

67 *"A game player"* Steven Kent, *The First Quarter* (Bothell: BWD Press, 2000), 440.

67 *"Video games don't teach people to hate"* "A Room Full of *Doom*," *Time*, May 24, 1999, 65.

67 *"The Grand Theft Auto franchise has proven"* "Take-Two Interactive Software, Inc. Announces That Its Grand Theft Auto Franchise Is Topping European Charts," Business Editors, *Business Wire*, May 19, 1999, 1.

70 *"chess-like 2D graphics"* "Familiar Car Theme Given Better Twist," *Southland Times*, August 20, 1999, 13.

70 *"This is a cultural product"* "Dan Houser's Very Extended Interview about Everything *Grand Theft Auto IV* and Rockstar," *Variety*, April 19, 2008.

72 *"a computerized version"* "Cyber City Virtually a Whole New Way of Life," *Scotland on Sunday*, September 12, 1999, B8.

72 *"Oh, man, if we do this in proper 3D"* "*Grand Theft Auto*: The Inside Story," *Edge*, March 17, 2008.

9. Rockstar Loft

74 *"Some of your"* Grand Theft Auto III, Manual, Rockstar Games, 2001, 10.

76 *"This is the game business"* "Get Your Game On," *Raygun*, Summer 1999.

76 *"As far as I can ascertain"* "Organisers of the *Grand Theft Auto 2* Video Game Launch Reacted with Some Shock to Freddie Foreman's Dramatic Snub for Their Party Yesterday," *Sun*, October 20, 1999, 6.

76 *Take-Two announced it would be shipping* "Take-Two Interactive Software, Inc.'s Rockstar Games Division Begins Global Shipment of GTA2," *Business, High Tech and Entertainment Editor*, October 21, 1999, 1.

78 *"That was a humbler"* Harold Goldberg, *All Your Base Are Belong to Us: How Fifty Years of Videogames Conquered Pop Culture* (New York: Three Rivers Press, 2011), 228.

79 *"Everyone working on the project"* "Grand Theft Auto: The Inside Story," *Edge*, March 17, 2008.

10. The Worst Place in America

80 *"Oh, my God"* "Rockstar Envisions the Future: President Sam Houser Discusses the Upcoming Next-Gen Wars, PS2 *Duke Nukem*, *GTA*, and *Austin Powers*," *IGN*, November 1, 2000, http://ps2.ign.com/articles/087/087203p1 .html, accessed July 28, 2011.

82 *"to make the first interactive"* "Rockstar's Sam Houser Mouths Off," *IGN*, September 10, 2001.

88 *"To me, as a film nut"* Ibid.

11. State of Emergency

89 *"Liberty City is"* *GTA III Manual*, 7.

92 *"We're trying to do everything"* "Senators Vow Legislation to Curb Sale of Violent Games," *Newsbytes*, January 25, 2001.

92 *"If I'm entrusted with the presidency"* "The 2000 Campaign: The Vice President; Gore Takes Tough Stand on Violent Entertainment," *New York Times*, September 11, 2000, www.nytimes.com/2000/09/11/us/2000-campaign-vice-president-gore-takes-tough-stand-violent-entertainment.html?pagewanted=2, accessed July 28, 2011.

94 *"A spokesman for Rockstar"* "*Video Gamers* Can *Experience WTO All Over Again PLAYSTATION 2: 'State* of *Emergency' Offers a Virtual Urban Riot over Actions* of the *'American Trade Organization*," *News Tribune*, May 28, 2001, A1.

94 *"Thanks to Rockstar Games"* "Nothing Beats a Relaxing Riot," *Herald Sun*, June 1, 2001, 34.

96 *"I think the video game industry"* "Why Rockstar Games Rule," *Wired*, July 2002.

97 *"we'd better put the fucking hammer down"* "*Grand Theft Auto*: The Inside Story," *Edge*, March 17, 2008.

98 *"Q: Will we be able to hijack"* "Dan Houser Chat," cited in Gouranga! www.gouranga.com/nf-september01.htm, accessed July 28, 2011.

99 *"This beautiful city"* Harold Goldberg, *All Your Base Are Belong to Us: How Fifty Years of Videogames Conquered Pop Culture* (New York: Three Rivers Press, 2011), 232.

99 *"Rest assured the game will be phenomenal,"* www.gouranga.com/september01.htm#h426, accessed July 28, 2011.

12. Crime Pays

102 *"an insanely well-made and fun game"* "Grand Theft Auto III," cited in *MobyGames*, www.mobygames.com/game/grand-theft-auto-iii/mobyrank, accessed July 28, 2011.

102 *"makes an offer you can't refuse"* Ibid.

102 *"shatters the standards"* Ibid.

102 *"every bad boy's dream"* "Holiday Games Preview," *Entertainment Weekly*, November 16, 2001.

102 *"You become like Emerson's transparent eyeball"* "Vice City," *Rolling Stone*, November 7, 2002.

104 *"acts of sexualized violence"* "Sexual Violence 'Way Beyond' Toughest Rating," *Sunday Herald Sun*, December 16, 2001.

105 *"newer breeds of increasingly sophisticated games"* "Violence Makes Games 'Unsuitable for Children,'" *Observer*, December 16, 2001, 13.

105 *"We saw what happened in Columbine "* "Rep. Joe Baca Speaks against Computer Games," *Market Call*, CNNfn, May 16, 2002.

105 *"the exaggerated claims"* "School Shooting Reignites Game Violence Fears," Gannett News Service, May 13, 2002.

106 *"Despite the industry's reputation"* See "Life During Wartime – Working at Rockstar Games," AlphabetCityblog, web.archive.org/web/20070804084043/http://badasscat.blogspot.com/2007/07/rockstar.html, accessed July 28, 2011.

107 *"makes every effort"* "Sex, Violence in Children's Computer Games under Scrutiny," Knight Ridder Tribune News Service, February 7, 2003, 1.

107 *"like selling cigarettes"* "Video Game Maker Finds Shock Value," *Los Angeles Times*, April 7, 2002, C1.

108 *"If you realize PlayStation owners"* "Vice City," *Rolling Stone*, November 2002.

108 *"Why are we having this conversation?"* "Dan Houser's Very Extended Interview about Everything 'Grand Theft Auto IV' and Rockstar," *Variety*, April 19, 2008.

108 *"We adhere very strictly"* "Rockstar's Sam Houser Mouths Off," *IGN*, September 10, 2001.

109 *"Can looting, drive-by-shootings"* "Hit Video Games Overshadow Company's Woes," *New York Times*, May 6, 2002, C1.

110 *"With all this stuff about Enron"* Ibid.

13. Vice City

111 *"hands-down the grooviest era"* "*Grand Theft Auto*: The Inside Story," *Edge*, March 17, 2008.

123 *"It's like, be cool"* Ibid.

14. Rampages

125 *"Malvo liked playing in the sniper mode"* "Disclosures May Help Malvo's Defense; 6 Witnesses Described Teenager's Obedience," *Washington Post*, July 24, 2003, B01.

126 *"Women are the new target"* "Video Industry Gets 'F' for Christmas; Group Cites Prostitutes and Violence," *Washington Times*, December 20, 2002, A13.

127 *"Everyone knows what's in this game"* "Crackpot or Crusader?" January 31, 2003, http://money.cnn.com/2003/01/29/commentary/game_over/column_gaming/, accessed July 28, 2011.

129 *"They're not afraid"* "New York Firm Buys Carlsbad, Calif., Video Game Developer," Knight Ridder Tribune Business News, November 21, 2002, 1.

129 *"You wouldn't expect"* "FOUL PLAY; X Sells . . . the Top Video Games for Christmas Have Murder, Car-Theft and Lapdancing Assassins . . . and They're Top of Kids' Wish-Lists," *Daily Record*, December 19, 2002, 8.

130 *"Oh, you're Jamie King!"* "The Utopians," *New Yorker*, March 20, 2006, 108.

15. Cashmere Games

134 *"There isn't a"* *Grand Theft Auto: San Andreas, Manual*, Rockstar Games, 11.

135 *"Man, how the hell"* "*Grand Theft Auto*: The Inside Story," *Edge*, March 17, 2008.

16. Grand Death Auto

144 *During Will's deposition* "Metropolitan Property and Casualty Insurance vs. Wayne Buckner et al." in the Court of Appeals at Tennessee, Knoxville, December 2, 2008.

144 *"Their favorite was one called"* "Nut Cases' Wide Swath of Destruction/ Oakland Gang Ran 'Wild,' Killing, Robbing at Random, Police Say," *San Francisco Chronicle*, February 10, 2003.

156 *"The goal is to destroy"* "Wal-Mart Pulls Video Game after Highway Shootings 'Grand Theft Auto' Simulates Shootings," *Columbus Dispatch*, December 2, 2003.

17. Boyz in the Hood

162 *"While much of* Vice City's *violence"* "Vice in America," CBS New York, November 6, 2003.

163 *"advocate the killing"* "Video's No Game to Haitians/They Say It's Violent, Racist," *Newsday*, November 25, 2003, A06.

163 *"We believe that it was the purposeful intent"* "Group Blasts Video Game/ Haitian-Americans Say It Is Racist; Threaten Legal Action," *Newsday*, November 26, 2003, A27.

163 *"This racist game"* "Suit Threatened over 'Racist Game,'" *Calgary Herald*, November 30, 2003, A6.

164 *"We empathize with the concerns"* "Haiti Vows to Sue over Video Game; Game Encourages Users to 'Kill the Haitians,'" CNN, December 1, 2003.

164 *"It's disgraceful, it's vulgar"* "Fury over Sick New Vid Game," *Mirror*, December 11, 2003, 33.

165 *"As with literature, movies, music"* "Statement from Take-Two Interactive Software and Rockstar Games," cited in "Software Maker Removes Offensive Remarks about Haitians and Cubans from Video Game," www.heritagekonpa .com/archives/Haiti%20Press%20Release.htm, December 9, 2003.

165 *"I'm outraged against Rockstar"* "Haitians Protest Video Game," *Newsday*, December 16, 2003, A61.

165 "It was something" *"Grand Theft Auto:*The Inside Story," *Edge*, March 17, 2008.

18. Sex in *San Andreas*

170 *"On a good date"* Cited in www.muchgames.ca/guides/ps2/gtasa.txt, accessed August 9, 2011.

172 *"What are we doing here?"* Ibid.

172 *"We have put an enormous amount"* "Rockstar Announces *Grand Theft Auto: San Andreas*," *Business Wire*, March 1, 2004.

173 *"'[J]ennifer"* United State District Court Southren District of New York in Re Take-Two Interactive Securities Litigation, Consolidated Third Amended Class Action Complaint for Violations of Federal Securities Laws, Exhibit B-3, Filed 9/15/08.

173 *"Kolbe wasn't encouraging"* Ibid., 1.

175 *"We need to move VERY fast"* Ibid. 1.

175 *"As you know"* "Report of Special Litigation Committee of Nominal Defendant Take-Two Interactive, Inc.," United States District Court Southern District of New York, February 16, 2007, 40.

176 *"This game should be banned"* "Murder by PlayStation," *Daily Mail*, July 29, 2004.

178 *"Unfortunately, here is the Situation"* United State District Court Southern District of New York in Re Take-Two Interactive Securities Litigation, Consolidated Third Amended Class Action Complaint for Violations of Federal Securities Laws, Exibit B-5, Filed 9/15/08.

179 *"This is WAY"* United States District Court Southern District of New York in Re Take-Two Interactive Securities Litigation, Consolidated Third Amended Class Action Complaint for Violations of Federal Securities Laws, Exhibit B-10, Filed 9/15/08.

180 "That's not good" Ibid.

180 "Wow..." Ibid.

180 "This is shame" Ibid, Exhibit B-12.

180 "I know" Ibid.

181 *"I believe this is the right time"* "Take-Two Founder Resigns Amid Probe," Associated Press, March 17, 2004, http://accounting.smartpros.com/x42886.xml.

181 *"Hi, can we confirm"* United States District Court Southern District of New York in Re Take-Two Interactive Securities Litigation, Consolidated Third Amended Class Action Complaint for Violations of Federal Securities Laws, Exhibit B-13, Filed 9/15/08.

181 *"This stuff was so cool"* Ibid., Exhibit B-14.

182 *"If you and the crew feel"* Ibid., B-14.

19. Unlock the Darkness

188 *"The modding scene"* United States District Court Southern District of New York in Re Take-Two Interactive Securities Litigation, Consolidated Third Amended Class Action Complaint for Violations of Federal Securities Laws, 47.

190 *"a stunning milestone"* *"Grand Theft Auto: San Andreas,"* *MobyGames,* www
.mobygames.com/game/grand-theft-auto-san-andreas/mobyrank, accessed
July 28, 2011.

190 *"extraordinary—something that I believe"* Ibid.

190 *"a terrific unending"* Ibid.

190 *"just as disturbing"* "Pick a Number It's Sequel Season," *New York Times,*
November 11, 2004, www.nytimes.com/2004/11/11/technology/circuits/
11game.html?ex=1101182925&ei=1&en=97892a034956e34c.

191 *"even though there's a lead"* "If You Play 'San Andreas,' You'll Be a Black Male.
Does It Matter?" *Chicago Tribune,* November 1, 2004, www.chicagotribune.
com/features/chi-0411010009nov01,0,2316605,full.story.

191 *"underscores what some critics"* "The Color of Mayhem," *New York Times,* August
12, 2004, www.nytimes.com/2004/08/12/technology/circuits/12urba.html.

191 *"explore any additional content"* Report of Special Litigation Committee of
Nominal Defendant Take-Two Interactive, Inc., United States District Court
Southern District of New York, February 16, 2007, 42.

191 *"We will get the sex"* Ibid.

191 *"And may I say how happy"* Ibid.

191 *"Yes we will go"* Ibid.

192 *"sex is going to be released"* Ibid., 43.

193 "Grand Theft Auto *is a world governed"* "Can a Video Game Lead to
Murder?" *60 Minutes,* March 5, 2005.

193 *"Life is like a video game"* "Life Is a 'Video Game,'" *Tuscaloosa News,*
December 2, 2004.

195 *"I was enjoying this"* Jack Thompson, *Out of Harm's Way* (Tyndale, IL: Carol
Stream, 2005), 167.

195 *"Dad, I think it's great"* Ibid., 185.

197 "SEX . . . KISSING" *United States District Court Southern District of New York
in Re Take-Two Interactive Securities Litigation, Consolidated Third Amended Class
Action Complaint for Violations of Federal Securities Laws,* 45.

197 *"I never EVER thought"* Report of Special Litigation Committee of Nominal Defendant Take-Two Interactive, Inc., February 16, 2007, Exhibit F.

20. Hot Coffee

203 *"consistently meet or exceed"* See http://money.cnn.com/magazines/fortune/
fortune_archive/2005/08/22/8270037/index.htm.

205 *"They found it"* *United States District Court Southern District of New York in Re
Take-Two Interactive Securities Litigation, Consolidated Class Action Complaint for
Violations of Federal Securities Laws,* 25.

205 *"unlock this gem"* Report of Special Litigation Committee of Nominal Defendant Take-Two Interactive, Inc., United States District Court Southern District of New York, February 16, 2007, 44.

205 *"We don't have to do anything"* Report of Special Litigation Committee of
Nominal Defendant Take-two Interactive, Inc. United States District Court
Southern District of New York, February 16, 2007, 44.

205 *"[W]hen we originally"* Ibid.

205 *"is the entire sex animation"* United States District Court Southern District of New York in Re Take-Two Interactive Securities Litigation, Consolidated Second Amended Class Action Complaint for Violations of Federal Securities Laws, 25.

205 *"We locked it away"* Ibid., 4.

206 *"There is some sexualized content"* "Report of Special Litigation Committee of Nominal Defendant Take-Two Interactive, Inc.," United States District Court Southern District of New York, February 16, 2007, 45.

207 *"The integrity of the ESRB"* "Statement by ESRB President Patricia Vance regarding *Grand Theft Auto: San Andreas* Modification," ESRB, July 8, 2005.

207 *"Today, one of the most popular"* "ESRB Investigating San Andreas Minigame," *GameSpot*, July 8, 2005, www.gamespot.com/news/6128759.html.

211 *"Well, that's pretty damn clear"* "Rockstar Officially Denies Making Hot Coffee," *Kotaku*, July 13, 2005.

213 *"We are sure that . . . Rockstar Games"* United States District Court Southern District of New York in Re Take-Two Interactive Securities Litigation, Consolidated Third Amended Class Action Complaint for Violations of Federal Securities Laws, Exhibit F-122.

21. Adults Only

220 *"after a thorough investigation"* "ESRB Concludes Investigation into *Grand Theft Auto: San Andreas*; Revokes M (Mature) Rating," ESRB, July 20, 2005, www.esrb.org/about/news/7202005.jsp.

22. Busted!

221 *"Question"* See http://answers.yahoo.com/question/index?qid=20080517 185445AAA5cBY, accessed August 9, 2011.

222 *"Wait a minute"* "Motormouth: A *GTA* Q&A," *1up*, www.1up.com/features/sam-houser-speaks, accessed July 28, 2011.

223 *"It looks like Take-Two Interactive"* "Hidden Sex Scenes Spark Furor over Video Game," *Los Angeles Times*, July 21, 2005.

224 *"GTA is the ultimate urban thuggery"* "Warren Spector Questions *GTA* at Montreal Keynote," November 4, 2005.

224 *"The video game industry"* "Why the Video Game Industry Is Losing the Culture War," *GameDaily*, September 29, 2005, www.businessweek.com/innovate/content/sep2005/id20050929_066963.htm.

225 *"These guys are are out to get us"* Harold Goldberg, *All Your Base Are Belong to Us: How Fifty Years of Videogames Conquered Pop Culture* (New York: Three Rivers Press, 2011), 239.

226 *"Certainly it's frustrating"* "Gangs of New York," *New York Times*, October 16, 2005.

227 *"I don't want that game"* "*Grand Theft Auto*: The Inside Story," *Edge*, March 17, 2008.

228 *"These games are training our children"* "Controversy over New Video Game 'Bully,'" *WABC Eyewitness News*, October 31, 2006, http://abclocal.go.com/wabc/story?section=news/local&id=4711946.

23. Bullies

230 *"Are you crazy?"* "Rumor Control Update: Bush Bros. in Madden, x05 Lands in Amsterdam, Revolution Pics . . . Again," *GameSpot*, August 8, 2005.

230 *"Shoot the messenger' is the video game industry's strategy"* "Teen Charged with Harassing Antigame Activist," *GameSpot*, December 9, 2005.

235 *"These Grand Theft Auto games"* "Lawyer Pushes to Have Standing in Video Game Lawsuit," *Tuscaloosa News*, November 4, 2005.

235 *"Most of these communications"* "Judge Stands by Fayette Decision," *Tuscaloosa News*, November 22, 2005.

236 *"Dear Judge"* See http://forums.kombo.com/showthread.php?t=12737, accessed October 1, 2010.

236 *"I felt those people"* "Motormouth: A *GTA* Q&A," *1up*, www.1up.com/features/sam-houser-speaks, accessed July 28, 2011.

237 *"Why are they so concerned"* Harold Goldberg, *All Your Base Are Belong to Us: How Fifty Years of Videogames Conquered Pop Culture* (New York: Three Rivers Press, 2011), 240.

238 *"so far this year it has sliced"* "Worst CEO: Paul Eibeler of Take-Two," MarketWatch, December 8, 2005, www.marketwatch.com/story/correct-worst-ceo-of-the-year.

238 *In a feature story in* Fortune "Sex, Lies, and Videogames," *Fortune*, August 22, 2005.

241 *"When Jamie King (a Rockstar co-founder)"* "Employee Exodus at Rockstar Games," *GameDaily*, www.gamedaily.com/articles/features/employee-exodus-at-rockstar-games/69151/?biz=1.

245 *"Rockstar is a very robust organization"* "Terry Donovan Leaves Rockstar," *GameSpot*, January 12, 2007.

24. Flowers for Jack

246 *"Flowers"* See http://gta.wikia.com/Flowers, accessed August 9, 2011.

248 *"The publishers and developers who make controversial content"* "D.I.C.E.: Lowenstein Ends ESA Career with a Bang," *Gamasutra*, February 8, 2007.

255 *"The problem is poor working conditions"* See http://games.slashdot.org/story/06/07/07/2122206/Employee-Exodus-at-Rockstar-Games, accessed July 28, 2011.

25. New York City

258 *"Finale"* Tim Bogen and Rick Barba, *Grand Theft Auto IV*, Brady Games Signature Series Guide, 234.

259 *"If videogames are going to develop"* "Dan Houser's Very Extended Interview about Everything 'Grand Theft Auto IV' and Rockstar," *Variety*, April 19, 2008.

259 *"That's my dream"* Ibid.

260 *"On the one hand"* "Motormouth: A *GTA* Q&A," *1up*, www.1up.com/features/sam-houser-speaks, accessed July 28, 2011.

260 *"What epitomizes New York?"* "Dan Houser's Very Extended Interview about Everything 'Grand Theft Auto IV' and Rockstar," *Variety*, April 19, 2008.

264 *"Are we going to have"* "Grand Theft Auto IV Developer Announces Release Date, Says Whether There Will Be Another 'Hot Coffee,'" *MTV News*, January 24, 2008.

265 *"I'm not running"* "Grand Theft Auto: The Inside Story," *Edge*, March 17, 2008.

266 *"Niko is a real person"* Ibid.

266 *"The idea of having feelings"* "Motormouth: A *GTA* Q&A," *1up*, www.1up. com/features/sam-houser-speaks, accessed July 28, 2011.

267 *"I didn't feel like I'd left"* "The Making of *Grand Theft Auto IV*," *Edge*, March 18, 2008, www.next-gen.biz/features/making-grand-theft-auto-iv?page=2.

267 *"the series' best"* "GTA IV Review," *GameSpot*, April 28, 2008.

267 *"it completely changes"* MetaCritic, www.metacritic.com/publication/game-informer?sort_options=metascore&filter=games&num_items=30,   accessed July 28, 2011.

267 *"an instant classic"* "Grand Theft Auto IV," *GameSpy*, April 27, 2008.

268 *"embodies the future"* "Grand Theft Auto IV Embodies the Future of Entertainment," *Times*, April 26, 2008.

268 *"The real star of the game"* "Grand Theft Auto Takes on New York," *New York Times*, April 28, 2008.

268 *"It will finally allow us"* "Is Grand Theft Auto IV the Perfect New York City Stress Reliever? Yes," New York Magazine online, March 31, 2008, http://nymag.com/daily/entertainment/2008/03/is_grand_theft_auto_iv_the_perfect.html.

268 *"There was a sense that"* "Dan Houser Interview: Rockstar Games's Writer for *GTA 4* and *The Lost and Damned*," *Telegraph*, January 28, 2009.

269 *"a huge success"* "Oxford to Profit from *GTA IV*," Cherwell.org, May 2, 2008, www.cherwell.org/content/7385.

269 *"It's made our resolve"* "Grand Theft Auto: The Inside Story," *Edge*, March 17, 2008.

269 *"What have I got left"* "MCV Legends: Sam Houser," *MCV*, July 11, 2008.

Epilogue: Outlaws to the End

272 *"It feels at last"* "The Driving Force behind *Grand Theft Auto*," *Times*, November 13, 2009.

275 *"The last Grand Theft Auto"* "Wives of Rockstar San Diego Employees Have Collected Themselves," *Gamasutra Blogs*, January 7, 2010, www.gamasutra.com/blogs/RockstarSpouse/20100107/4032/Wives_of_Rockstar_San_Diego_employees_have_collected_themselves.php.

277 *"Until we've simulated the world"* "The Driving Force behind *Grand Theft Auto*," *Times*, November 13, 2009.

Index

ACLU, 14
Activision, 47, 48
Amiga 1000, 22
Andrews, Carl, 164
AOL Time Warner, 91
APB: All Points Bulletin, 277
Arista, 49
Aristide, Jean-Bertrand, 163
ASC Games, 50–51

B, Cliffy, 247
Baca, Joe, 105, 126
Baglow, Brian, 30, 33, 35, 36, 42–43, 51–52, 57, 69, 70–71, 269
Barrera, Jeronimo, 103, 265
Bede, Kim, 143–144
Benzies, Les, 180–182, 191, 206, 278
Best Buy, 94, 127, 219–220, 250
Blake, Jeremy, 57, 257
Blood Money, 23
Bloomberg, Michael, 164
BMG, 10, 15, 18–19, 26, 27–35, 37–45, 46–50
Bowie, David, 66
Brant, Peter, 47, 238
Brant, Ryan, 47–50, 53, 57, 78, 160, 180–181, 203–204, 228, 244
Breen, Mike, 64
Brownback, Sam, 67
Buckner, Donna, 147–158

Buckner, Joshua, 143–158
Buckner, Paul, 150
Buckner, Wayne, 147–158
Buckner, William, 143–158
Bully (Rockstar Games), 226–227, 251–252, 255
Bush, George H.W., 11
Bush, George W., 90–91, 225, 236

Campbell, Luther, 14
Campbell of Croy, Lord, 40–41
Capcom, 227–228
Carmack, John, 187
Carneal, Michael, 62, 91
Cartoon, Mr., 136, 166
Cashmere Games, 140, 160, 277
Chiat\Day, 28
Chicago Transit Authority, 268
Children Now, 105
Clinton, Bill, 91
Clinton, Hillary, 167, 216–220, 225, 231
Cohen, Florence, 224
Columbine (CO) shootings, 61–64, 90
Common Sense Media, 225, 256
"Commune," 51–54
Congressional Black Caucus, 168
Contemporary Pediatrics, 92
"Content and Teen-Rated Video Games" (Harvard University), 183–184

"Cop Killer" (Ice-T), 11–12, 14
Crackdown, 190, 227
Croft, Lara *(Tomb Raider),* 37, 66

Dailly, Mike, 25
Dale, Gary, 39, 42, 47, 227–228, 246
Defamation of Character, 233
Def Jam, 8–9
Deneau, Denise, 142–144, 156
Destructoid, 253
Diaz, Junot, 269
D.I.C.E. (2007), 247–250
Dickerson, Mary Lou, 94
Dixons, 177
DMA Design, 23–26, 27–35, 40, 48, 60–61,
    72–73, 79, 87, 242
Donovan, Terry
    game development and, 69, 70, 75–77,
        82, 175, 178–180, 181
    Hot Coffee, 206
    on Rockstar, 54, 57, 132
    Take-Two and, 110, 242–246
    U.S. move by, 49, 51–54
Doom, 17, 62, 63, 90, 91
Duncan, Theresa, 257

Eibeler, Paul, 78, 98, 107, 110, 160–161,
    208–210, 213, 220–221, 223–224,
    228, 245
Eighth Circuit U.S. Court of Appeals, 146
Electronic Arts, 47, 48, 53, 66, 78, 137–138,
    211, 247, 268
Electronic Entertainment Expo (E3),
    65–67, 93–94, 95, 201–202
Elite, 7–8
Entertainment Software Association,
    167–169, 204–205, 249–250
Entertainment Software Association
    Foundation, 234
Entertainment Software Ratings Board
    (ESRB)
    Hot Coffee, 205–206, 208, 216–221,
        223–224, 237–240, 273
    inception, 17
    Manhunt 2, 256
    process, 63, 183–185

Sam Houser on, 108
San Andreas, 174, 192, 195
U.S. Senate findings, 91, 92
Euphoria (Oxford University), 260, 270
Ewing, Kirk, 93, 95, 113
EyeToy (Sony), 176

Family and Youth Concern, 42
Family Entertainment Protection Act,
    225
Farley, Paul, 61
Fayette (AL) shootings, 193, 236–237
Federal Communications Commission, 13,
    194
Federal Trade Commission, 1–4, 91, 92,
    146, 218, 224, 237–240
Fentonmiller, Keith, 238
Fernandez, Marc, 61, 78–79, 107,
    113, 115–117, 133, 134–141,
    160, 277
First Amendment, arguments/legislation,
    13, 63, 126, 146, 168, 274
Florida Bar Association, 13, 275
Fonda, Peter, 118
Foreman, Gary, 33–34, 49–50, 51–54, 69,
    110, 121–122, 131–132, 182, 207, 213,
    241–246, 277
4mm Games, 277
Fuckstar, 70–71

Game Boy, 68
GameCube (Nintendo), 103
GameStop, 236
Garbut, Aaron, 2, 114, 122
Gardner, Tom, 257
Gathering of Developers (GOD), 68
Genesis (Sega), 16
Get Carter, 5–6
Gouranga!, 70, 98–99, 188
Grand Theft Auto: Liberty City Stories
    (Rockstar Games), 32, 82–88, 235,
    260
Grand Theft Auto: London 1969 (Rockstar
    Games), 59, 67
Grand Theft Auto: San Andreas (Rockstar
    Games)

Grand Theft Auto *(Continued)*
　Adults Only rating, 209, 216–221
　development, 32, 134–140, 159–162,
　　165–169, 170–175, 177–185
　releases, 190–200, 191–192, 199
　reviews, 190–191
　sales, 203
　See also Hot Coffee
Grand Theft Auto: Vice City (Rockstar
　Games)
　criticism/reviews, 121, 124–128, 128–130
　development, 32, 111–120, 113–123
　lawsuit, 252
　marketing, 121–123
　release, 120–123, 128–131
Grand Theft Auto: Vice City Stories
　(Rockstar Games), 255–256
Grand Theft Auto (BMG), 35–45, 48,
　50–54
Grand Theft Auto (franchise) (Rockstar
　Games)
　artificial intelligence, 260, 266, 270
　budget record, 264
　characters, 84–88, 97, 99, 114–115,
　　117–120, 136–137, 162, 166–169,
　　170–171, 174, 261, 262–263
　gameplay *vs.* graphics, 37–38, 44–45, 81
　high-definition, 260
　lighting, 114
　racial themes, 162–169, 191–192
　sales, 2, 45, 67, 95, 102–103, 128, 203,
　　273
　scriptwriting, 117, 166
　soundtracks/voice overs, 31, 34, 59, 115,
　　116–120, 123, 264–265
　3-D animation, 72–73, 80–88
　violent themes, 31, 34–35, 60, 69–70, 76,
　　82–88, 104, 107, 112, 114–115,
　　134–136, 166–169, 170–171, 222–223
　See also Rockstar Games; Take-Two
　　Interactive; *individual names of*
　　executives; individual names of games
Grand Theft Auto 2 (Rockstar Games), 52,
　59–60, 68–73, 74–77
Grand Theft Auto III (Rockstar Games)
　development, 80–88

implicated in shootings, 142–158
　release, 101–109
　sales, 102–103, 128
　Take-Two accounting investigation and,
　　109–110
　violent themes, 82–88, 104, 107
　(*See also* ratings; Thompson, Jack;
　　individual legislation)
Grand Theft Auto IV (Rockstar Games)
　development, 259–268, 272, 277
　release, 268–270
　sales, 2, 273
Gremlin Interactive, 40, 61
Gross, Jenefer, 206, 207
Grossman, Dave, 91
GTAforums.com, 189

Halo, 78, 103, 125
Hamel, Aaron, 142–144
Hanks, Colin, 101
Harris, Eric, 62–63, 90
Harrison, Phil, 18, 28, 81, 96, 103–104,
　175–177, 247–248
Harvard University, 183–184
Harvey, Simon, 177
Haze, 75
Henn, Heinz, 10
Heston, Charlton, 11–12, 14
Hetherington, Amanda, 151–153,
　155
Hickman, Marc, 143–144
Holkins, Jerry, 234
Hopper, Dennis, 118
Hornemann, Jurie, 241
Hot Coffee
　class-action lawsuits, 275
　FTC investigation, 3, 237–240
　mod makers, 186–190, 196–200,
　　204–205, 210–215
　naming of, 200
　ratings, 205–206, 208, 216–221,
　　223–224, 237–240, 273
　Rockstar public relations, 203–215,
　　216–221, 222–229
　Take-Two resignations, 239, 240–246
　wrapping, 183, 192

Houser, Dan
  biographical information, 6–7
  BMG joined by, 37
  game development, 32, 45, 77, 82, 85, 98,
    99, 105, 108–109, 112, 119–120, 260
  Hot Coffee public relations, 226
  Rockstar branding, 58
  Rockstar parties, 58, 68, 105–107,
    128–131, 190, 243–244, 257–258
  U.S. move by, 53
Houser, Sam
  biographical information, 6–10
  at BMG, 10, 15–19, 18–19, 46–50
  FTC testimony, 1–4
  game development, 45, 60, 61, 68–73,
    74–77, 82, 87–88, 90–100, 105–109,
    111–120, 120–123, 169, 170–175,
    177–185, 188, 226–227, 261
  Hot Coffee public relations, 203–204,
    206–215, 222–229, 226
  Jones and, 71–73
  marketing, 39–40
  Race 'n' Chase, 28–35
  reclusive image of, 202–203, 227
  Rockstar branding, 55–58
  Rockstar in-fighting, 131–133, 136–141
  Rockstar parties, 58, 68, 105–107,
    128–131, 190, 243–244, 257–258
  Take-Two accounting investigation, 110
  Take-Two management resignations,
    243–246
  U.S. move by, 51–54
  See also Rockstar Games; individual names
    of games
Houser, Walter, 6–10, 264
Hsu, Dan, 121

Ice-T, 11–12, 14
id Software, 91
Infogrames, 61, 72–73
Interactive Digital Software Association
  (IDSA), 17, 63, 92, 105, 125–128, 167

Jack (Destructoid), 253
Jameson, Jenna, 118–119
Jenkins, Henry, 102

Jones, Dave
  biographical information, 20–21
  game development, 21–26, 60, 61, 190,
    227, 277
  on gameplay vs. graphics, 37–38, 44–45, 81
  on Hot Coffee, 227
  marketing, 37, 39–40, 43
  Race 'n' Chase, 27–35
  Sam Houser and, 71–73
  on San Andreas, 190

Kaczynski, Barbara, 239
Khonsari, Navid, 82, 85, 107, 118, 119, 166,
  171
King, Jamie
  4mm Games, 277
  game development, 68, 69, 83, 85, 107,
    113, 117, 123, 130, 136, 159–162, 165,
    191, 195
  Hot Coffee, 228
  marketing, 38
  Race 'n' Chase, 28–35
  Rockstar branding, 56, 58, 67
  Rockstar in-fighting, 138
  Take-Two accounting investigation and,
    109, 110
  Take-Two resignation, 240–246, 254
  Take-Two role, 48–49
  U.S. move by, 51–54
King, Rodney, 12, 17, 135
Kingway Amateur Computer Club, 22
Klebold, Dylan, 62–63
Kohl, Herbert, 92, 105, 126
Kolbe, Jennifer, 173–174, 206, 243
Krahulik, Mike, 234

L.A. Noire (Rockstar Games, Team Bondi),
  276
Leblanc, Warren, 176
Lemmings, 23–24, 31
Lieberman, Joseph, 16–19, 63, 91, 126, 218,
  225, 231
Life during Wartime (Williams), 256
Limbaugh, Stephen, 126
Lincoln, Howard, 16, 25
Liotta, Ray, 117–118, 123

Little Computer People, 33
2 Live Crew, 14
Loonies, 60
Los Angeles, lawsuit against Take-Two, 226
Louisiana, proposed legislation, 254
Lowenstein, Doug
  at D.I.C.E., 249–250
  on ESRB, 92
  on game sales, 67
  GTA III, 97, 105
  Hot Coffee, 204–205, 208, 273
  Rockstar and, 167–169
  San Andreas, 191, 194
  on shootings, 63
  Thompson and, 145–146, 232, 235
  Vice City, 125–128
Lynch, Dustin, 145

MacLachlan, Kyle, 85
Madsen, Michael, 85
Majors, Lee, 118
Malvo, Lee Boyd, 124–125
Manhunt (Rockstar Games), 136–137, 138,
  167, 175–177
Manhunt 2 (Rockstar Games), 253, 256
Mario (Nintendo), 24, 30
Max Clifford Associates, 38–45
Max Payne (Rockstar), 103
Mazar, Debi, 85
McLean, Bethany, 239
McLuhan, Marshall, 3
Media Accountability Act, 92
Menace, 22
Microsoft, 80, 103, 201, 249, 263–264
Midnight Club: Los Angeles (Rockstar
  Games), 275
Miller, Scott, 242
Miyamoto, Shigeru, 24–25
Mizrahi, Elliot, 195
"Modest Video Game Proposal, A"
  (Thompson), 232–237
mod makers, 50, 186–190, 196–200,
  204–205, 210–215
Moffat, Geraldine, 5–6
Montone, John, 264
Moore, Devin, 193, 236–237

Mortal Kombat (Sega), 16, 17, 62, 63, 137
Muhammad, John, 124–125

National Education Association, 16
National Institute on Media and the
  Family, 105, 126–127, 209, 217,
  234–235
Nintendo
  Columbine-related lawsuits, 91
  Entertainment System, 16, 17
  GameCube, 103
  Jones and, 26
  Mario games, 24, 30
  Miyamoto and, 24–25
  Nintendo 64, 24, 68
  platform release schedule of, 80–81
  Revolution, 201
  Take-Two and, 48
  Wii, 248–249
Nottingham Trent University, 43
Nut Cases, 144–145

Olson, Cheryl, 273–274
Oriol, Estevan, 135, 136
Oxford University, 260, 270

Paducah (Ky), school shootings in, 62, 64,
  91, 126
Pakeerah, Stefan, 176–177
Parents Television Council, 220–221
Penn, Gary, 29, 32, 33, 37
PlayStation. *See* Sony
Pooh, PJ, 166
Pope, Jeremy
  Cashmere Games, 140, 160, 277
  game development, 78–79, 85–86,
    96–97, 98–99, 107, 115, 116, 131
  Rockstar in-fighting, 133, 138–141
Posy, Cody, 252
"Protect Children from Video Game Sex
  and Violence Act," 105, 126

Race 'n' Chase (DMA), 25–26, 27–35
ratings
  ESRB categories, 16
  M-rated games sold to minors, 127, 250

in non-U.S. countries, 41, 43, 50, 104, 178–180, 224, 256
process, 183–185
San Andreas development and, 173–175, 178–183
school shootings and, 63
See also Entertainment Software Ratings Board (ESRB); Lowenstein, Doug
Red Dead Redemption (Rockstar Games), 203, 275, 278
Rednecks, 60
Renderware, 81, 84
Reynolds, Burt, 119–120
Robina, Umberto, 162
Rockstar Games
  on allegations of violence, 146, 177
  branding, 51–54, 55–58, 67, 257
  employee lawsuits against, 275–276
  FTC investigation of, 1–4, 237–240
  Hot Coffee and public relations, 203–215, 216–221, 222–229
  in-fighting, 122–123, 131–133, 136–141, 227, 254–258
  legacy, 271
  on mod makers, 188
  office locations of, 52, 58, 238, 265
  parties of, 58, 68, 105–107, 128–131, 190, 243–244, 257–258
  Take-Two accounting investigation, 109–110
  Thompson/Take-Two settlement, 250–254
  See also ratings; Take-Two Interactive; *individual names of executives; individual names of games*
Rockstar Loft, 74–77
Rockstar North, 114, 122, 180–181, 261–268
Rockstar San Diego, 275–276
Rockstar Toronto, 226
Rockstar Vancouver, 226–227
Rockstar Vienna, 241
role-playing games, 171–172
Rompf, William, 243–244, 254–255, 276–277
Rubin, Jason, 107

Rubin, Rick, 8–9

Schwarzenegger, Arnold, 225
Scottish Motor Trade Association, 42
Second Hand, 166
Securities and Exchange Commission, 109–110, 180–181, 203–204
Sega, 16, 17, 26, 62, 63, 91, 137
Simmons, Russell, 8–9
Simpson, Don, 56, 95
Sims, The (Electronic Arts), 211, 247
Sinclair ZX Spectrum, 22
Slayer, 9
Smuggler's Run (Rockstar Games), 92–93
Sony
  advertising by, 70
  EyeToy, 176
  GTA III and, 99, 103–104
  Jones and, 26
  lawsuits, 91, 236, 252
  Manhunt and, 175–177
  PlayStation, 18, 28, 37, 50, 51, 70, 122–123
  PlayStation 2, 80–88, 189–190, 199
  PlayStation 3, 201–203, 249, 264
  PlayStation Portable, 203
  PSP, 232
  Take-Two and, 48
Spector, Warren, 225
Spitzer, Eliot, 239–240, 274
Starr, Freddie, 38
State of Emergency (Rockstar Games), 93–94, 96–97, 103
"Steal This Game" advertising campaign, 70
Steyer, James, 225, 256
Strickland, Arnold, 193
Super Mario Bros. (Nintendo), 30

Take That, 16
Take-Two Interactive
  accounting investigation of, 109–110, 180–181, 203–204
  BMG Interactive purchase, 46–50
  DMA Design purchase, 48, 72–73
  Electronic Arts hostile bid for, 268

Take-Two Interactive *(Continued)*
   ESRB and, 167–169
   Hot Coffee, 203–215, 220–221, 224, 226
   lobbying by, 161
   resignations, 239, 240–246, 254
   revenues, 130, 140
   Rockstar branding, 51–54, 57
   Thompson settlement, 250–254
   See also individual names of games
Tanktics, 71
Team Bondi, 276
Telling, Gillian, 133
Thompson, Jack, 124–128
   "A Modest Video Game Proposal,"
      232–237
   biographical information, 12–14
   FTC and, 3
   GTA IV and, 274–275
   Hot Coffee, 216–220, 228–229
   San Andreas and, 160–162, 192–196
   on shootings, 61–64, 89–92, 126,
      144–147
   Take-Two settlement, 250–254
   threats against, 230–232
Thompson, John Daniel Peace, 14, 89, 127,
   195–196, 250–251
"Thumbies," 248–249
Time Warner, 11–12, 14
Tomb Raider, 37, 66, 81
Twenty-First Century Media
   Accountability Act, 91
2K Games, 238
2 Live Crew, 14

United States District Court, Southern
   District of Florida, 253

U.S. Senate Commerce Committee, 67, 91
U.S. Supreme Court, 274

Vance, Patricia, 183–185, 195, 205–206,
   208, 218–221, 223–224, 273
Vaz, Keith, 177
Video and Computer Game Report
   (National Institute on Media and the
   Family), 105
Video Game Report Card, 126
Video Game Voters Network, 249–250
Vincent, Frank, 85

Wade, Corey, 120, 213
Wal-Mart, 4, 94, 156, 223, 236
Walsh, David, 126–127, 127, 217, 219–220,
   234–235
Warriors, The (Rockstar Games), 226, 227,
   251, 255
Waterduck, Barton, 197
Wii (Nintendo), 248–249
Wildenborg, Patrick, 186–190, 196–200,
   204–205, 210–215
Williams, Jeff, 106, 138, 256
Williams of Mostyn, Lord, 41
World Trade Organization, 94–95
wrapping, 183, 192
Wright, Will, 247

Xbox (Microsoft), 103, 249, 263–264

Yee, Leland, 209, 224
You Don't Know Jack, 37

Zelnick, Straus, 253, 274–275
Zuniga, Todd, 207–208, 213–214, 256